Contents

Preface

The X Window System™ is certainly one of the most important software developments in recent years. At a time when proprietary window systems are the norm for PCs, X™ provides an "open" window system that can support a variety of window managers, toolkits, and interface builders. Although X is not tied to any particular hardware or software system, at present, the UNIX®-based workstation community has benefited the most from X. When coupled with UNIX, X offers a powerful multiple-window, multitasking environment that supports a distributed client-server model.

In addition to its support for distributed client-server computing, one of X's most important characteristics is its "generic" support for window system operations. That is, X provides a broad and powerful graphical window system foundation with very few restrictions on the development of high-level applications that support X, including window managers and toolkits. Because X provides the mechanisms for implementing graphical user interfaces (GUIs) without imposing user-interface styles, the X (user) community is indirectly involved in, and partially responsible for, determining the future direction of X-based computing environments.

Each day, X Window System users, application programmers, and software developers on a variety of hardware platforms cast their "votes" for the look and feel of future X applications, simply by their choices in window managers, applications, and high-level toolkits—X users are active participants in the future of X. In many cases, one company's applications will operate under another company's window manager. It is this dynamic, ongoing involvement in the growth of X that makes X-based computing so exciting and enjoyable.

Sophisticated GUIs call for sophisticated programming environments. The X Window System is implemented in multiple software layers. At the lowest level, the X protocol provides hardware independence for clients and servers, or if you prefer, applications and workstations. In particular, an application running on one hardware platform can communicate with a server running on another hardware platform, as long as they both adhere to the X protocol.

At the next level, X provides Xlib, a C-based interface to the X Protocol. With Xlib, a programmer exercises a great amount of control over X applications, but must perform a host of chores that are handled automatically by higher level interfaces, X toolkits in particular. With large Xlib-based applications, a considerable portion of the software, and therefore a significant amount of the project's development time, may be devoted to relatively low-level programming that's required to support modern GUI objects such as cascading menus and pop-up dialog boxes.

One of the premises of this book is that these interface components should be implemented as pseudo-objects (in C). That is, Xlib programmers should look for common GUI components in their applications and develop self-contained modules that implement these objects. For example, Xlib programmers can develop high-level window modules that are reusable and have sufficient flexibility to support various extensions. In this case, a high-level Xlib window aggregate would encapsulate a **Window** data structure, secondary data structures, and (pointers to) functions that implement a window's behavior.

For projects that don't require the low-level capabilities of Xlib, Xt provides a high-level alternative that ensures a minimal look-and-feel standard across applications. In many cases Xt, in conjunction with a widget set, is preferable to Xlib because of its sophisticated support for application resources and high-level interface objects. A second premise of this book is that, even with Xt, it's important to factor applications into reusable modules. The proper breakdown of applications can be important for application maintenance, porting, and readability.

For some projects, a particular widget set simply doesn't provide all of the GUI components needed in the application. Generally speaking, in this situation it's better to develop additional widget classes that implement the required functionality than to patch together existing widgets within the application. Quite often, if you need a special-purpose GUI component for one application, you'll need it again in another application. Designing new widget classes that can service multiple applications is preferable to tweaking existing widgets to "be something that they aren't."

This book is organized *informally* into three parts. Primarily, this book focuses on X toolkit programming. In order to set the stage for Xt application and widget programming, part one addresses various aspects of Xlib programming. In particular, it advances the position that Xlib-based applications should be built from high-level Xlib modules. As illustrations of the latter, we discuss several sample modules that support (1) row- and column-oriented text windows, (2) callback functions, and (3) self-contained event loops. Because they are universally present in modern GUI-based software, we use various forms of dialog boxes to demonstrate these ideas. Of course, these principles apply to many other GUI components as well.

In part two we focus on Xt application programming. Part two follows logically from part one. That is, in part one we demonstrate how to design callback functions and self-contained event loops with the low-level interface to X, Xlib; then in part two we use Xt's built-in support for these same programming constructs. Part two first reviews basic Xt application programming, including the use of callback and action functions. Next, part two demonstrates how to develop a high-level Xt module that implements a *blocking*, dialog box. Part two concludes with a rather large application that demonstrates a variety of Xt programming facilities.

In part three we investigate Xt widget programming. In our opinion, it is important to address Xt application programming in part two, as both a background and a review of Xt, before delving into widget programming. In part three we develop six widget classes that are compatible with and extend the GUI capabilities of the Athena widget set.

This book is based on the Athena widget set primarily because the Athena widgets are available with the standard distribution of X. Most widget programmers develop widgets that extend the capabilities of an existing widget set. That is, widget programming, like other forms of object-oriented programming, involves deriving a new class from existing classes. To do so, widget programmers must peruse the source code for the superclasses. Because the source code for the Athena widgets is provided with standard X, the Athena widget set is an ideal starting point for building several public-domain widget classes.

In addition to focusing on the object-oriented aspects of Xt programming, one of our principal objectives is to provide a number of useful applications and widgets. For the most part, we employ real-world utilities to illustrate various aspects of Xlib and Xt application programming. In addition to the dialog boxes that we mentioned earlier, part one uses two utilities, *xclk* and *xdump*, to overview Xlib programming and to illustrate text processing modules, respectively. *xclk* is a simple digital clock utility that allows you to display the current time in any font. *xdump* is an assembler-style, hexadecimal dump utility that, like *more(1)*, displays each "page" of a file.

Part two concludes its discussion of Xt application programming with a six-module utility for file deletion and recovery. *wastebasket* is actually a pair of cooperating utilities, *delete* and *xwaste*. *delete* supports command-line file deletion, where the "deleted" files are moved to a wastebasket instead of being permanently deleted. *xwaste* is a GUI wastebasket utility that allows the user to browse through the wastebasket and either recover or permanently delete files. *xwaste* also supports file deletion to the wastebasket, like *delete*, except that it uses text entry boxes and command buttons as an alternative to the command line.

Part three discusses widget programming, including both simple and compound widget classes. As part of the widget programming coverage, part three describes six widget classes that have day-to-day utility for the Xt application programmer. These widgets include **XiStrSelect**, a string selection widget; **XiFileSelect**, a file selection box widget; **XiAlert**, a blocking, alert box widget; **XiButton**, a non-command, button widget; **XiChoice**, a multiple-choice item selection widget; and **XiSimpleText**, a one-line text entry box that hides the differences between Release 3 and Release 4 Athena text widgets.

All of the applications in this book have been tested with Release 3 and Release 4 of the standard X distribution. In addition, they have been tested with the public-domain X servers for both Releases 3 and 4, and on two different Sun Microsystems® CPU architectures.

The applications that we describe in this book require a considerable amount of source code. In general, we do not present all of the source code in each chapter when we describe an application. Instead, we focus on the most interesting aspects of each application. The complete source code for the applications is given in the appendixes.

With this approach, the chapters are not burdened with the task of presenting the complete application, yet the reader can turn to the appropriate appendix at any time for further investigation. For your convenience, the source code for this book is available for a small distribution fee on floppy diskette(s) or QIC-24 cartridge tape.

Many individuals have contributed to the development of the X Window System. The most prominent contributions have come from various collective efforts at MIT and at Digital Equipment Corporation. Many other programmers and organizations, however, have made *very* significant contributions as well, especially with respect to X clients.

In general, programmers are more aware of these contributions than are casual users. Many users will depend on clients such as *twm* without ever knowing their origins. On behalf of these users, it's important to take this opportunity to thank the many contributors of public-domain X software.

A number of individuals have contributed to the development of this book, including many individuals at John Wiley. I would like to thank the entire staff at John Wiley for their efforts toward the overall process. In particular, I would like to thank my primary editors, Diane Cerra, Terri Hudson, and Marcia Samuels.

Marcia Samuels managed the production of this book. In relative terms, an author's association with a production editor is short-lived. From the author's perspective, this association begins near the end of a book's production cycle. From the editor's perspective, the production phase is a complex process involving a number of individuals and deadlines. The author has one book to wrestle with; the production editor has several. With each book, an author gains a greater appreciation of the production process and the critical role of the production editor.

Terri Hudson orchestrated the development of this book. An author depends on the developmental editor for many things—for managing "routine" operations, as well as minor crises. If there is a "hazardous duty" position in publishing, this is it. On the soccer field, Terri Hudson would be a center halfback.

Diane Cerra is the senior editor for this book. Senior editors have many responsibilities in the publishing business; it's easy for authors to lose sight of this fact. Despite these responsibilities, Diane Cerra is a hands-on editor, constantly involved in the development and production of her books. This book is my second one with Ms. Cerra. Twice now, she has come to my rescue—expediting things—so that I could get what I needed, when I needed it, and thus stay on schedule. Diane Cerra is an author's editor.

JERRY D. SMITH

Signal Mountain, Tennessee
December 1990

The source code given in Appendixes A through U is available on diskette for a $30.00 distribution fee. A QIC-24 tape is also available for a $60.00 distribution fee. If you would like to order the source code, photocopy this page, fill in the order form, and send a check or money order for the proper amount (U.S. funds, drawn on a U.S. bank, please) to the address given below. You may want to call first, if you have special requirements.

Your order will be processed promptly and professionally.

This offer is being made solely by Iris Computing Laboratories. John Wiley & Sons, Inc., as publisher of this book, is not responsible for orders placed with Iris Computing Laboratories.

Mail to: **Phone:** 615 - 886 - 3429

Attn: Xt Source Offer
Iris Computing Laboratories
2439 Wood Sorrell Lane
Signal Mountain, Tennessee 37377

Name: ______________________________

Address: ______________________________

____

____

Diskette: 5.25" — 360K _____ 3.5" — 720K _____

(The 360K and 720K options are DOS format diskettes with UNIX format text files.)

Diskette: 3.5" — Sun *bar(1)* format _____

Tape: QIC-24 cartridge tape — *tar(1)* format _____

1

Introduction

This chapter addresses several rather general issues related to programming with the X Window System™ toolkits. The importance of a systematic approach to application and widget programming is a recurring theme that is introduced in this chapter and expanded upon in subsequent chapters. One premise of this book is that the X Window System is sufficiently complicated (sophisticated) to reward a layered approach to software development and to penalize the unstructured use of Xlib and the X toolkits.

1.1 Object-oriented Programming and the Toolkits

It seems unmistakable at this point that object-oriented (OO) programming (OOP) techniques are having a profound impact on the professional programming community. Many individuals believe that the contribution of OO programming rivals that of structured programming in the late 1970s and early 1980s. On the other hand, many programmers, especially system programmers, continue to prefer a language like C over a language such as C++, which provides syntactic support for OO programming. Wherever you stand on this issue, there is no denying that the principles of modular decomposition, functional abstraction, encapsulation, and so on are critically important in the development of large applications.

The X Window System is implemented with traditional programming techniques, and its standard programming interface, Xlib, is based on a traditional, not OO, language. Despite the traditional language orientation of the X Window System, its design is sufficiently flexible to encourage the development of various higher level interfaces, based on either traditional or object-oriented languages. In particular, LISP, C++, and Pascal interfaces are possible. From this view, the X Window System provides the computing community with an industry-standard, network-based, no-frills windowing platform. As object-oriented and user-interface technology matures and the industry develops and fine-tunes new technologies, the programming and user interfaces to the X Window System can be changed to reflect the latest industry trends.

The current trend is for application programmers to use a toolkit as a high-level interface to Xlib. Although the X Window System toolkits provide considerable programming power, they represent an immature technology with respect to their function as a higher level programming interface. With the current toolkits it is difficult to develop a real/commercial application without frequently resorting to the low-level interface, Xlib. From this perspective, many opportunities remain for research and development in the area of high-level interfaces to the X Window System. It will be up to the industry to decide whether these interfaces will employ object-oriented, traditional, or pseudo–object-oriented languages.

In this book we focus on the pseudo–object-oriented programming interface provided by X Window System toolkits, especially the standard release Xt Intrinsics, including the Athena widget set. Xt provides a C-based programming interface, built on top of the C-based, Xlib interface to the X Window System. Because it is based on C, Xt provides no compiler-level, syntactic support for object-oriented programming. On the other hand, Xt, in conjunction with a widget set, does encourage an object-oriented style of programming.

Widgets are central to the X toolkits, much as objects are central to an OO language such as C++. In this book we focus on a number of issues, such as portability, reusability, and so on, that arise in using an existing widget set, that is, application programming issues. We also address the development of widgets (widget sets and hierarchies), that is, the widget programming process.

1.2 The X Window System

The X Window System is a reasonably large software system that supports interactive computing among workstations. It provides device-independent support for low-level, network-based windowing operations.

In spite of these networking capabilities, it is, in general, more convenient to view the activities managed by the X Window System in terms of the communications that occur between applications and workstations. These activities may or may not occur over a (physical) network.

The software components that are collectively known as the X Window System can be viewed abstractly as layers of software built upon a base window system (see Figure 1.1). With this layered approach, only one software layer (the innermost layer) can interface directly with the base window system. The low-level programming interface that accompanies the X Window System can be viewed as a software layer that is in turn built upon the innermost layer, and so on.

We mention this low-to-high-level organization at this point for a reason. Specifically, the objective of this book is to accentuate the importance of a layered approach to software development for the X Window System. The development of quasi-independent modules of support software for the X Window System is important for both Xlib programmers and toolkit programmers, and for both application programmers and so-called widget programmers.

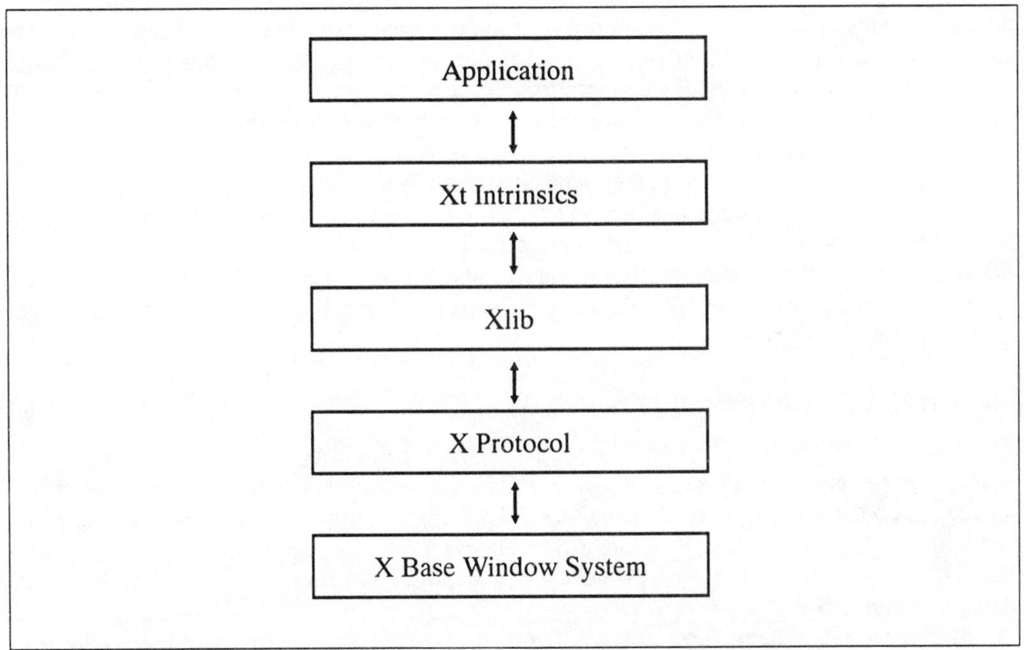

Figure 1.1 X Window System Software Layers

Although this book focuses primarily on object-oriented programming techniques for the X Window System toolkits (for example, the Xt Intrinsics and the Athena widget set) some attention is given to Xlib in introductory chapters. Discussion of Xlib is warranted because low-level Xlib programming can be helpful in explaining some of the capabilities built into the high-level toolkits (for example, callback functions). (In this book we often use the term "function" in a general way, including references to procedures that return a **void** value.) Moreover, many of the applications that are developed with a basic toolkit such as Xt rely quite heavily on Xlib for capabilities that are either missing from or inconvenient to handle with Xt. Lastly, the widget programmer must resort to Xlib quite often in developing new widgets.

1.3 Communication between Application and Workstation

At the lowest level an application communicates with a workstation via messages that follow a prescribed network protocol. Typically, an application produces messages that generate directives on the workstation, where the latter are scheduled for execution (for example, a line-drawing operation within a specific window). Because of the network orientation of the X Window System, it's possible for an application running on workstation *y* to display its output in a window on workstation *z*.

An application also designates the types/classes of workstation events in which it is interested, for example, a click of mouse button 1. When a relevant event occurs, the application is notified by the workstation, and typically, the application responds by sending additional messages to the workstation. From this perspective, the X Window System functions as a communications organizer and coordinator: (1) applications issue messages to one or more workstations, (2) workstations respond to messages and generate events, (3) applications respond selectively to certain events, generating more messages, and so on.

An application is often called a client, while a workstation is often referred to as a server, an X server. This terminology makes sense because the workstation serves the needs of the application, that is, provides a setting where client programs can display their work. For many individuals, the term *server* is more appropriate because *workstation* carries a stronger hardware connotation. Technically, it is more appropriate to equate *server* with the base window system software, accessible through X protocol messages, and not with the workstation hardware per se.

1.4 The User's Operating Environment

From a different perspective, the X Window System, or simply X, is designed to *support* multiple applications operating in a window-based environment that provides an interface to a traditional operating system, such as UNIX®. More importantly, the operating environment itself is just another X application. The strength and popularity of X derives from both what it provides and what it doesn't provide. It's often said that X implements *mechanism*, not *policy*.

In other words, X can carry out a full complement of fundamental window operations between one or more applications running on one or more workstations, where the look and feel of an application is dictated by external factors. The window manager, an application running on top of X, dictates much of the look and feel of other applications. Other aspects of the look and feel of a particular application are directly dependent on the toolkit, if any, that was used to develop the application. For example, the buttons within one application may look and operate differently from those within another application, regardless of the current window manager, depending on the choice of toolkit.

X's ability to accommodate heterogeneous applications is one of its greatest strengths. The X Window System provides the mechanism for carrying out operations that transcend current graphical user interface (GUI) trends. If the workstation industry decides to adopt a common, or even core, GUI across vendors, it will be straightforward to implement window managers that conform to that GUI design *as X applications*.

1.5 Functional Decomposition and Abstraction

With some windowing systems there is a tight coupling between the software components that implement basic windowing operations, such as queuing a mouse event, and those that make high-level interpretations of events, such as popping up a background menu when a mouse button is pressed. This tightly coupled approach is common with many PC windowing systems.

As we've mentioned, X takes a different approach. The basic premise behind X, and many other large software systems, is that a large system can be built from multiple, distinct, cooperating modules (in the generic sense). Modular decomposition and functional abstraction are, of course, distinct concepts; often, however, they operate hand in hand.

With X, one manifestation of its support for functional abstraction is the layering, or factoring, of fundamental windowing operations in terms of the X network protocol and

Xlib layers. The former is responsible for the low-level communications that occur between an application and a workstation (for example, a message/request to display a line of text in a window). The latter generates these messages from library function calls—for example, **XDrawImageString()**—that conform to the X network protocol and, hence, carry out the communications.

The motivation behind decomposing a large software system into semi-independent units involves much more than the desire to practice good software engineering. With X, one of the principal goals has been to produce an operating environment that can be implemented on various hardware architectures, ranging from high-end PCs to workstations and minis to mainframes.

In porting X to another hardware/software platform, the fundamental task is to interpret the X Window System protocol, that is, to carry out the tasks encoded in the messages that pass between a client and a server. Typically, a hardware/software system designed to serve this purpose also furnishes the programming community with a higher level interface to the system. With current X implementations, this interface is provided via a C subroutine library, namely Xlib.

Again, a major strength of the X Window System is that you, the programmer, can decide whether to work with the X protocol directly or to keep your distance and work exclusively with Xlib. And at a higher level, you can decide whether to develop your application with Xlib or with a toolkit.

1.6 X Window System Toolkits

The number of X toolkits and widget sets is too great to enumerate here. In this book, we focus primarily on the standard intrinsics and the widget set that accompany public-domain X, namely the Xt Intrinsics and the Athena widget set. In later chapters we provide several public-domain widgets that are compatible with the Athena widget set and serve to extend the GUI capabilities for application programmers who, for whatever reason, aren't using commercial widget sets. On occasion, we mention one commercial widget set, the OSF™/Motif™ widget set (OSF, 1990). Our demonstration programs, however, are based on the standard distribution and focus on issues that arise with all of the commercial toolkits.

From one point of view, a proliferation of toolkits and widgets sets provides the X community with much to choose from and fuels the acceptance of the X Window System. On the other hand, at least for the time being, many programmers and developers must be prepared to work with multiple toolkits. For those developers who are already maintaining multiple ports of a software product across different hardware architectures, providing a product with multiple user interfaces (Motif, OpenWindows™ [Sun Microsystems®, 1990], and so on), as implied by the choice of a particular toolkit, may be economically difficult, if not impossible. For our purposes, it's convenient and important to focus on a variety of programming issues that transcend a particular choice of toolkit(s).

1.7 Low-level versus High-level Approaches to Application Development

Some programmers prefer assembly language over a high-level language because they need (or appreciate) the greater degree of control afforded by assembly language programming. Compilers are designed to make a reasonably good 1:*n* translation of a high-level language statement to machine-level instructions. For a given application and task, however, an expert assembly language programmer can often write a better set of instructions.

The decision of whether to use Xlib or Xt is somewhat analogous to the assembler versus compiler issue. Once a programmer commits to using a toolkit, there still may be opportunities for improving efficiency by employing Xlib selectively. For a given application, a good Xlib programmer can choose an optimal mix of Xlib operations that may operate more efficiently than a toolkit function designed to perform (approximately) the same task.

Often, however, the real issue is not the efficiency of a set of instructions in a specific application, but the reusability of those instructions across numerous applications. This book is based on the assumption that, in most cases, reusability of compiled modules is much more important than the small gains in efficiency that can be achieved by hand-coding various windowing operations with Xlib that are supported by a toolkit such as Xt. (By *compiled module* we mean a family of C functions and common data structures collected in a file. Often, C programmers take advantage of C's file-level name scoping to encapsulate data and related operations. See Smith (1990) for an extensive treatment of this subject.) If the use of Xlib within an Xt-based application doesn't compromise reusability of the application or of any of the compiled modules that compose the application, then, at least with respect to reusability, there is no reason not to use Xlib along with a toolkit.

There are, of course, other reasons for using Xlib within a toolkit-based application that have nothing to do with efficiency considerations. Consider, for example, an application that allows an aerospace engineer to view changes in the shape of an aircraft wing that result from changes to certain critical parameters. In this case, the toolkit may provide all the GUI components necessary to build a mouse-based interface to the application, for example, buttons, gauges, and menus. On the other hand, a generic (interface) toolkit such as Xt does not (was not designed to) provide low-level functions for the graphics imaging required by the aircraft design software—that is the domain of Xlib.

A third and common use of Xlib is in building new widgets. (A widget is a collection of data structures encapsulated with a public functional interface that implement a high-level GUI component, such as a menu.) Extending a toolkit's tools, in this case, its set of widgets, can be useful in introducing additional uniformity in a class of applications.

Consider, for example, a software developer that produces several X products, say, a suite of typesetting packages for graphics workstations running UNIX. Suppose that the developer uses the standard Xt toolkit along with the commercial widget set *xyz* across all of its applications, in the interest of inter-application uniformity. Suppose, in addition, that each application requires a common GUI component not available with widget set *xyz*, say, an exclusive-selection choice box. The developer essentially has two choices: (1) let the development teams for each application *informally* implement the GUI component from other GUI components (widgets), as best they can; or (2) *formally* build a new widget that implements the GUI component, and then make this widget available to each development team.

Most programmers and developers would favor the second approach. Formally implementing the GUI component as a widget leads to applications with greater uniformity in both the user interface and the source code for each application. With respect to programming methodology, widgets enhance reusability, functional and data abstraction, and so on. A potential disadvantage of the second approach is that widget programming is inherently lower level than application programming. In some cases, it is more difficult to port widgets across toolkits than to port application code. Later in this book we'll address the creation of high-level objects via widget programming versus the traditional use of compiled modules in application programming.

So far we've discussed the merits and justifications for "peppering" a toolkit application with Xlib-based operations. One last Xlib versus toolkit issue that we mention is whether to use a toolkit at all. Suppose you intend to develop a small programmer's editor, either as a stand-alone product or as a module that can be incorporated into a variety of applications. Of course, your decision between using Xlib exclusively or employing a toolkit would depend on a number of issues, such as whether or not your past and future applications have been and will be toolkit-based (uniformity of the interface), and the extent to which you want the restrictions, dependencies, and advantages that accompany toolkit usage.

One of the advantages of a toolkit is the programming power that it provides. With a toolkit, a relatively small amount of source code can create a powerful interface complete with pull-down menus, buttons, and pop-up windows. However, each toolkit-based application is automatically endowed with capabilities that can be very useful in one application, but constitute nothing more than excess baggage in another. There are, for example, applications that simply can't take advantage of (don't require) a toolkit's extensive capabilities for processing X resources.

It can be overwhelming to compare the efficiency (mostly, space efficiency) of a simple editor created from a toolkit to that of a custom-made editor created exclusively with Xlib. The latter can be one-half the size of the former. In many cases, the use of shared libraries can reduce the discrepancy in the size of executables for applications created solely from Xlib and those that employ a toolkit. Again, the issues of uniformity across applications, reusability of existing source code modules, and so on must be considered.

Given the title of this book, it's obvious that we intend to champion the merits of toolkit-based programming. The consensus in the industry is that for many, if not most, applications a toolkit can insulate application programmers from many X-related issues that are too far removed from the concerns that should dominate the normal application development process.

For the record, although we regularly develop applications with the toolkits, we also develop applications for which we prefer the low-level characteristics of pure Xlib programming. For those who thoroughly enjoy and campaign for unadulterated Xlib programming, consider the following scenario.

A carpenter in a family-owned construction business in an earlier time, say, 1900, that took great pride in building houses from scratch might scoff at the idea of using prefabricated windows. Today, prefabricated windows are the norm in most houses. Operating in today's home construction environment, that same carpenter, in building the most carefully constructed home (or mansion), would likely use a selection of the best prefabricated windows, complemented with one or more custom-built windows where necessary.

The X toolkits provide very high-quality prefabricated windows: windows for text editing, scrolling the contents of a sibling window, selecting from a menu, and so on. The special circumstances that arise with certain applications, for example, the use of tailor-made digital and analog gauges/meters, offer many opportunities for Xlib and widget programming that complements a particular toolkit's prefabricated GUI components. In one sense, the measure of an X programmer, like a carpenter, is in his or her ability to produce an elegant combination of prefabricated and custom-built components.

2

Object-oriented Programming and the X Window System

In this chapter we discuss some of the strengths of object-oriented programming and then focus on the high-level support for encapsulation, functional abstraction, and so on that is available with X toolkits. To set the stage for our focus on the OO programming capabilities of Xt, it's convenient to make comparisons between C++ and Xt. Our investigation of C++ is quite minor; this chapter assumes no prior knowledge of C++. For the most part, in subsequent chapters we confine our discussion to the object-oriented issues of programming with X and Xt.

2.1 Principles of OO Programming

2.1.1 Encapsulation

A traditional language allows a programmer to package related data into one syntactic unit, using, for example, a C **struct** or a Pascal **record**. These program units are convenient for describing various types of program entities, for example, a window. Traditionally, programmers envisioned this type of program entity in terms of its program state at a given point in time, as represented by a composite data structure—the data structure *defined* the object, in our example, a window. Describing an object in terms of the operations that could take place against it was of secondary importance. Traditional languages reflect this view of programming.

Object-oriented languages such as C++ (Stroustrup, 1986; Lippman, 1989) and Smalltalk (Goldberg and Robson, 1983) provide formal mechanisms for packaging one or more data structures with the family of procedures that operate on those structures. This type of encapsulation encourages a programmer to think of a program entity in terms of both the data and the procedures that can take place against it. For example, a window is an object that (typically) occupies part of the display screen, as delineated by its border, and that can be moved from one location to another, placed beneath or on top of a sibling window, iconified, and so on.

Suppose you were to walk up to an enthusiastic X Window System programmer (or user), claim complete ignorance of modern GUI environments, and ask the question: "What is a window, and why would I want one on my computer screen?" The X enthusiast would likely make a few comments about a window being a rectangular area where information is either typed in or displayed, and then launch into a discussion of all the things you can *do* to a window: move it, resize it, hide it, overlap it, and so on. That is, the window is defined as much, if not more, by its dynamic as by its static characteristics.

Viewing an entity in terms of its dynamic *and* static attributes is the essence of object-oriented programming. Even before OO languages matured and became popular, many programmers recognized the power and importance of this type of encapsulation for software reusability. C, in particular, allows a programmer to use an object-oriented style of programming. More specifically, a programmer can use C's support for file-level name scope to package a collection of data and related functions. Using the **static** modifier, a programmer can make a variable public to each of the functions within a file (compiled module), but private elsewhere:

```
...
static int height, width;
...
int get_width() {...}
void set_width(int w) {...}
...
```

Smith (1990) discusses these techniques extensively.

Using this approach it is reasonably straightforward to develop modules that implement text editing windows, dialog boxes, and so on. Once this type of file is developed, it can be reused in various applications; for example, a dialog box module could be compiled and stored in a library. In a sense, this approach to programming facilitates or reinforces an object-oriented view of things like windows.

There are, however, disadvantages to using a traditional language to impose an object-oriented view on the data (and the programmer). One of the most significant problems in using C's file scope mechanism to build pseudo-objects is that it's inconvenient for handling a type of object that has both instance and class data.

Class data, that is, data that's common to multiple instances of a dialog box, can be handled by **static** variables within the compiled module, as just described. Instance data, data that's unique for each occurrence of a dialog box object, can't (easily) be handled with this mechanism. For example, if dialog box height and width were to exist as simple **static** variables, there would be no way to handle multiple dialog boxes of varying size.

Of course, the case of multiple instances of an object can be handled by setting up templates (**typedefs**) for composite data structures and designing the associated functions to operate on the dialog box that's passed as a pointer to each function:

```
...
typedef struct {
    int height, width;
    ...
} response_box;
...
int get_width(response_box *resp_box) {...}
...
```

With this technique, the programmer using the dialog box module must allocate a dialog box structure and an ID (a pointer) for each such window *within the application*:

```
...
response_box resp_box1, *resp_box_ptr1 = &resp_box1;
...
...
window_activate(resp_box_ptr1, ...);
...
```

In this case, programming with multiple windows becomes an exercise in juggling window IDs. By definition, the allocation and manipulation of pointers in an application constitutes a form of low-level programming.

In contrast, a language like C++ provides a formal syntactic mechanism for encapsulating an object and its operations. Thus, for our example, to create multiple dialog boxes the application programmer can simply allocate each window and send the appropriate messages:

```
...
response_box resp_box1;
...
resp_box1.activate(...);
...
```

When OO languages first began to gain acceptance, many traditionalists shunned the OO approach, for example, arguing that C programmers could do OO programming just like C++ programmers, but without having to learn a new language. Invariably, sample code segments such as the previous two were used to argue that the traditional approach was almost as concise as the OO approach. Conciseness isn't the most important consideration, however; the incremental gain in abstraction demonstrated in the second code segment can be very significant in large and complex applications.

2.1.2 Inheritance

Encapsulation is one of the most powerful programming techniques available; it is critically important in developing extensible and reusable software modules. As we've demonstrated, encapsulation can be promoted with either traditional or OO languages. Traditionalists who discounted the importance of OO and pseudo-OO programming techniques failed to recognize the significance of the second principal programming feature available with OO languages, namely, inheritance.

Objects rarely exist in isolation. Just like the traditional programmer who requires composite data structures to group together related variables, an OO programmer must be able to build complex objects from simpler objects and from simple variables. With traditional languages *composition* is the only mechanism available for building higher level data structures. From our earlier example, a dialog box is a collection, or composition, of variables, including **height** and **width**.

C's **struct** and **typedef** constructs are adequate for building simple composite structures. Consider an application, or set of applications, that require a more sophisticated arrangement of composite data structures. A system of windows would be one example. In this case, a base window structure could define variables that are common to all windows, for example, height and width. At the next higher level, another composite structure could provide variables for the class of windows that support the display and entry of text. And at an even higher level, another composite structure could be used to define a type of dialog box. And so on.

With C, it is certainly possible to handle this type of complex arrangement using simple composition; however, C's syntactic limitations make this approach cumbersome: ("window.text_window.response_box.<whatever>"). OO languages provide full syntactic support for class (data structure) *inheritance*, in addition to the traditional provisions for composition. As a consequence, OO programmers can more readily create interrelated, complex data structures, such as window hierarchies. Formal syntactic support for class inheritance encourages programmers to plan ahead in designing their data structures so that other applications can reuse existing modules.

Syntactic support for class inheritance provides secondary benefits as well. For example, C++ provides a mechanism for initializing (complex) objects at the same time their storage is allocated, such that initialization data is propagated upward through the instance hierarchy. With respect to our earlier example, width and height values would be propagated up to the base window object:

```
// width == 75, height == 25
response_box resp_box1(75, 25, <other initializers>...);
```

2.1.3 Dynamic Binding

The third principal feature of OO languages is *dynamic binding*. Dynamic binding works in conjunction with encapsulation and inheritance. Using our window example again, consider a hierarchy of windows that includes read-only browsers, dialog boxes, text editing windows, and so on. Each window (object) carries with it a full complement of operations. For a browser, these operations include displaying text in the window and paging through a file. For a text editing window, these operations include text browsing as well as text modification.

With dynamic binding a program can determine the type (class) of a window (object) at run-time, and allow the appropriate operations. Run-time binding is important in, for example, being able to pass objects of differing type to a high-level function, such as a command dispatcher. It's true that a C programmer can use *tags* in data structures, in conjunction with case structures, to achieve programmatic distinction between object types. This approach, however, carries several negative ramifications for software reusability. Moreover, the form of dynamic binding supported by C++ and Smalltalk supports/encourages programming methodologies that cannot realistically be achieved with a language like C. A full discussion of these topics is beyond the scope of this book; see Lippman (1989) or Smith (1990) for more extensive treatments of encapsulation, inheritance, and dynamic binding.

2.2 Object-oriented Programming with Xlib

The type of OO programming supported by C++ and Smalltalk is impossible with Xlib. This comment is not meant as a criticism of X or Xlib; Xlib is a *low-level* programming interface to the X Window System. We argued earlier that higher level programming interfaces to X can and will be provided as X-related technology matures and evolves.

X is a very sophisticated windowing system. Earlier we advanced the view that X programmers should build layers of successively higher level modules for use across X applications, as a means of enhancing source code readability and module reusability. For example, Xlib provides a function for creating windows named **XCreateSimpleWindow()**. It is a reasonably high-level function; its parameters include window width, height, parent, and so on. Thus, some of the characteristics of a window created with **XCreateSimpleWindow()** are set during window creation.

More importantly, a variety of other window attributes are not set by this function, but must be set with functions such as **XChangeWindowAttributes()**, **XSetNormalHints()**, **XSetStandardProperties()**, and others. In addition, some window attributes change over time. With X, each window has a fixed number of window attributes associated with it; attribute values can be queried with **XGetWindowAttributes()**. For many applications, it may be necessary to supplement these attributes, for example, to maintain window dimensions in pixel and row/column metrics, or for convenience, to make your own associations between each window and a graphics context, font, cursor, or whatever.

These secondary associations between data structures that may be convenient for one application, or required with other applications to ensure reusability, are the motivation for a layered approach to application development with Xlib. In particular, even with a low-level interface to X, it is quite possible to build high-level "objects," such as dialog boxes that support a closed set of operations. These modules can be compiled and stored in a library.

As we review X and introduce low-level X programs in subsequent chapters to discuss various Xt-like capabilities, we'll provide complete examples, based on our window and dialog box discussion from earlier in this chapter. For example, we'll discuss how to create high-level dialog boxes with buttons that support callback functions.

2.3 Object-oriented Programming with Xt

An X Window System toolkit is composed of the toolkit intrinsics and an accompanying widget set. In this book we focus on the standard X toolkit, Xt, specifically, the Xt Intrinsics and the Athena widget set. We will occasionally make comparisons with and discuss selected aspects of the commercial OSF/Motif widget set.

With respect to the X software layers, Xlib is the lowest level above the X network protocol, and the Xt Intrinsics are built on top of Xlib; see Figure 2.1. In essence, the Athena widget set forms a software layer above the Xt Intrinsics. For convenience, in this book "Xt" implies both the Xt Intrinsics and the Athena widget set, unless otherwise stated. An application constitutes a fourth software layer, when built upon the Xt Intrinsics and the Athena widget set. As mentioned, however, many Xt-based applications must also deal directly with Xlib, so these layers are not necessarily distinct.

We've already mentioned the importance of using software layers to promote reusability across X applications. Hence, in subsequent chapters we'll address various steps that a programmer can take to build a fifth software layer. In some cases, building a software layer between the toolkit and the application can help isolate the effects of toolkit revisions, and can facilitate the porting process from one toolkit to another.

Earlier we described an object as a collection of data, along with the operations that can be applied to that data. C++'s syntactic support for objects reinforces this view. That is, for a given object both (public) variable components (called member variables) and procedural components (called member functions) are referenced with the same syntax. For example, consider a hypothetical pop-up dialog box that asks for the user's account number:

```
...
resp_box1.prompt = "Please enter your 75-digit account number";
...
resp_box1.activate();
result = resp_box1.get_response();
...
```

In most cases, it would be more appropriate to prohibit outside access to a variable like **prompt**, using a function instead to set the user prompt, for example, **activate()**. The point here is that the syntax is the same for accessing both variable and function members of an object.

Because Xt relies on C for implementing its objects, or *widgets*, objects must be created, destroyed, and manipulated using functions—application programmers shouldn't modify widget instance variables directly. Hereafter, we use *object* and *widget* somewhat interchangeably, since by definition a widget is Xt's version of a (window) object.

For common operations against various widget classes, such as widget creation and deletion, the Xt Intrinsics provide the necessary (public) functions. But for those operations that are unique to a particular widget class, such as querying a choice box for the user's response, the widget programmer must provide the proper functions.

In most respects, the lack of syntactic support in C for objects is not a problem for the application programmer using Xt. Specifically, the principles of software engineering dictate that objects be manipulated via access functions, and not by direct modification of object instance variables. One of the principal functions of the Xt Intrinsics is to provide a

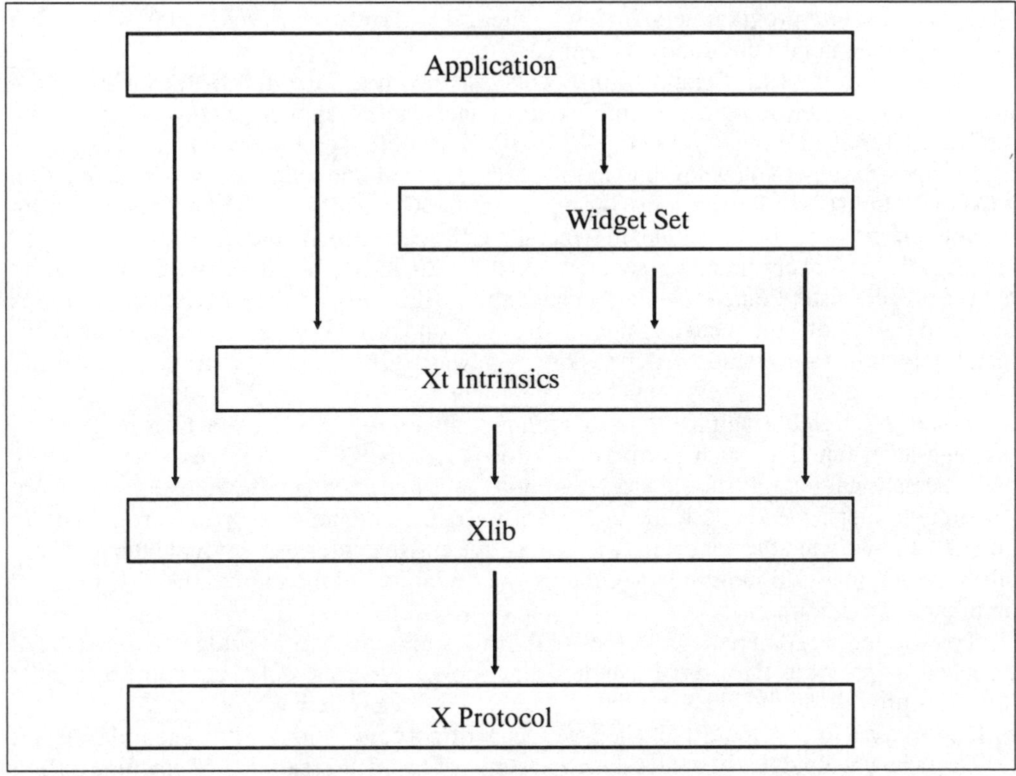

Figure 2.1 X Window System Software Layers

consistent procedural interface for common tasks that occur across object types (widget classes). Thus, the application programmer can use **XtCreateManagedWidget()** to create an instance of any widget from the Athena set, or from any other widget class.

2.4 Standard Protocols and the Xt Intrinsics

We've mentioned the idea of having a common function name for performing similar operations across different widget classes, and that the Xt Intrinsics support this consistency. In essence, this is the principle of *standard protocols*, as provided in most OO languages. It is impossible to overestimate the importance of standard protocols for software readability in real-world applications.

Regardless of whether you're using C to create a system of compiled modules for various types of windows, or using C++ to create a window hierarchy, it's important to use common names for functions that perform analogous operations across modules/classes. Suppose, for example, that a dialog box is activated with the function call "response_activate(resp_box1)" and an alert box is activated with the function call "popup_alert(alert_box1)", and this inconsistency exists throughout your software system. It's obvious that future programmers, including the original software developer(s), will have a difficult time remembering function names.

Xt promotes the use of standard protocols in two ways. First, the Xt Intrinsics follow this practice by providing a host of functions that can be applied to any widget class: **XtCreateManagedWidget()**, **XtMapWidget()**, **XtParent()**, plus many others. Regardless of the type of widget you want to map to the display, you know that the common function **XtMapWidget()** will do the job. Moreover, both Xlib and Xt following other naming conventions as well. For example, in general, verbs in function names like "get," "install," "manage," "set," occur immediately after "X. . ." with Xlib and "Xt. . ." with Xt. Beyond the use of a consistent function naming convention, Xlib and Xt follow certain conventions for the ordering of arguments/parameters in function calls. For example, function arguments for widget and window dimension are always given in the order: . . . <width>, <height>, ...

Where it's possible, application programmers should follow these practices in developing high-level functions such as **make_window()**, **create_GC()**. We don't want to imply that all creation functions should use a common verb such as "make" or "create," and so on. As programmers, we don't want to be restricted by dogmatic company programming policies, and we want the opportunity to be creative and to express our individualism. There are, however, many opportunities to enhance the readability of the source code that's passed on to other programmers.

For widget programmers, both the Xt Intrinsics and the Athena widget set have been designed to promote the use of standard protocols. First, as we've mentioned, the Xt Intrinsics provide public functions that can be used with any new widget that you develop, as long as you follow the established widget writing conventions. For example, if you develop a new widget that allocates dynamic storage during its creation or at any time during its use, you simply have to provide a destroy method that releases this storage, and properly register it within the widget class record. The Xt Intrinsics automatically provide the application programmer with a public interface to this method, namely, **XtDestroyWidget()**.

The Athena and Motif widget sets support standard protocols in the naming conventions used in the public interface to each widget. Consider the following: **XtDialogGetValueString()** from the Athena **Dialog** widget class, **XtFormDoLayout()** from the Athena **Form** widget class, and **XtPanedAllowResize()** and **XtPanedSetMinMax()** from the Athena **VPaned** widget class (for X11 Release 3). More importantly, Xt supports the seamless integration of other widget sets with the Athena widget set. Nye and O'Reilly (1990, Appendix D) discusses the naming conventions that have been suggested for widget programming. We'll address this issue in more detail in subsequent chapters on widget programming.

2.5 Xt Widgets versus C++ Objects

Although we have no particular interest in C++ in this book, we should take a brief look at the design differences between Xt widgets and C++ objects. Because we do not assume any knowledge of C++ here, we consider only the central issues in developing C++ classes. Also for this overview, class skeletons are adequate for both C++ classes and Xt widget classes. A more complete discussion of C++ class development is given in books such as

Stroustrup (1986), Lippman (1989), Smith (1990), and many others. A more complete discussion of widget programming is given in later chapters.

2.5.1 A C++ Class Hierarchy

Consider the following C++ class definition:

```
class window {
protected:
    int width, height;        // every window has these variables
    ...
    <other variables>...
    window(<parameter types>...);              // the class constructor
    ...
    void activate(<parameter types>...);  // method prototypes
    <other methods>...
public:
    <public methods>...                        // the class interface
};
```

If you're not familiar with C++, it's sufficient to note that **class** is an enhancement of **struct**. It can have **private**, **protected**, and **public** sections, and both variable and function members (methods). Members (variables and methods) of a **private** section can be accessed by members of that class only; access to **protected** members is limited to members of that class and *derived* classes (see below); and public members can be accessed by any outside agent.

window is an abstract base class. **window** is *abstract* because it is incomplete; it contains only those variables that are common to all windows. **window** is a *base* class because it is designed for use in deriving other classes (subclasses); it is the root class in a window class hierarchy.

With C++ it's easy to control access to variables and methods. As mentioned, members of the **protected** section of a class definition are accessible only by the methods of that class and its descendants. The **public** keyword is used to specify the class interface. Typically, only methods are made public; variable members of a class are accessible to the methods of that class and its descendants, or to outside agents via an access function/method. (We ignore the C++ **friend** construct).

Each class has a constructor (shown in the example) and a destructor (not shown). The constructor is invoked during storage allocation for an object and, typically, is designed to accept initialization information for the object:

```
response_box resp_box1(<width>, <height>, ...);
```

Destructors are invoked during storage reclamation.

Earlier we discussed inheritance, one of the three principal concepts supported by OO languages. Inheritance encourages what is often called *programming by difference*. Class hierarchies are designed such that the root class is a generic, foundation class and classes located near the extremities of the hierarchy are more specific, that is, more specialized. A class is derived from its superclass (base class) by adding variables and methods that *differentiate* it from its superclass(es).

Suppose we would like to derive a more specialized class from **window** that supports certain text processing operations. With C++, the derived class and base class names are specified as follows:

```
class text_window : public window {
protected:
    int cursor_x, cursor_y;         // text cursor coordinates
    ...
    <other variables>...
    <methods>...
public:
    int get_cursor_x(void);         // public method prototypes
    ...
    <other public methods>...
};
```

The new class is specified first, in this case, **text_window**. Here, the base class is specified after the keyword **public**. The class definition includes those variables and methods that differentiate a text window from a generic window. By convention, the new class inherits the variables and methods of its superclass(es) (except for those specified in a special section with the keyword **private**).

Finally, a more specific class can be derived, say, a class that supports a restricted form of text processing:

```
class response_box : public text_window {
protected:
    char *response;
    ...
public:
    char *get_response(void);           // public method prototypes
    ...
};
```

Here, our class definition implies that after a dialog box has been activated, a user has made a response, and the box has been deactivated, the user's response can be retrieved any number of times using the access method **get_response()**, which returns a pointer to the data referenced by the variable **response**.

2.5.2 An Xt Class Hierarchy

Xt's support for classes is provided by the library, not by the compiler. To create a new class a widget programmer must follow a number of conventions established by Xt. In particular, a widget is a composite data structure, built from collections of C **struct**s and pointers to **struct**s. **typedef**s are used to provide the application programmer with a high-level widget interface.

Each widget class is implemented in three files. A public header file describes the interface to the widget, primarily, the class name and the public functions. A private header file describes the central data structures that comprise that widget, data structures that are hidden from the application programmer. The procedural interface to the widget is defined in a separate file, along with the methods required by the Xt Intrinsics and the various support functions necessary to implement the widget's behavior.

Xt widgets implement GUI components—high-level windows. Thus, each widget must contain the various data structures and functions that are necessary to implement a widget's behavior: allocating and deallocating memory, making a window visible, reorganizing a window's contents, and so on. Because each widget requires many of the same data structures and operations as other widgets, Xt widgets are built from a widget hierarchy.

The information and functionality that are required by all widgets are implemented in a base, or root, class known as the *Core* widget class. Thus, every widget class has the (abstract) **Core** widget class as a superclass. By itself, a core widget is (in most cases) too incomplete to be instantiated. A button widget could, for example, be designed as a simple widget, derived from a core widget, as shown in Figure 2.2.

In many cases, a programmer may need to build a complex widget, that is, a widget that contains the functionality necessary to manage other widgets. Xt provides the **Composite** widget class as a building block for widgets that must perform simple management of a collection of widgets. Typically, a widget derived from a composite widget does little more than "provide housing" for other widgets in the collection. A simple button box would be an example of a composite widget. Buttons could be added to the button box with the latter serving as a container widget, using fixed/common rules for organizing and decorating the buttons. A composite widget hierarchy is shown in Figure 2.3.

For situations that require more sophisticated rules for the arrangement of child widgets, Xt provides the **Constraint** widget class. At its name implies, a constraint widget implements the functionality necessary for imposing specific geometric constraints, especially constraints on the relationships that exist among child widgets. Being able to inherit constraint functionality from a toolkit-supplied widget is important because (1) widgets that have **Constraint** as a superclass will exhibit similar behavior, and (2) the widget programmer's work is minimized. In some case, it may be necessary to supplement or refine the new widget's constraint rules. A constraint-based widget would have the class hierarchy shown in Figure 2.4.

The superclasses for the multiple-choice item selection box are members of a fundamental Xt widget class hierarchy as shown in Figure 2.5. The **Shell** widget class has subclasses (not shown) that define a variety of shells that interact with the window manager.

2.5.3 Widget Data Structures

In this section we briefly overview the internal data structures involved in widget design and the external interface provided for the application programmer. The widget programming chapters deal with these structures extensively. At present, we're only interested in demonstrating Xt's high-level interface to widgets, while alluding to the complexity of the low-level data structures.

Earlier we demonstrated how easy it is for the C++ application programmer to create an object, given the existence of the proper object class, for example

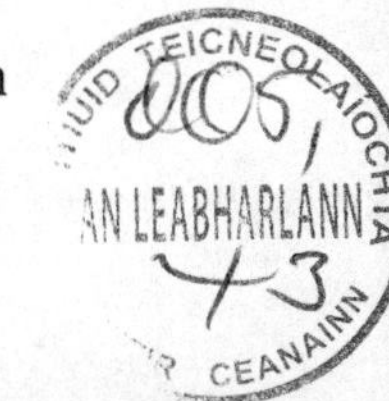

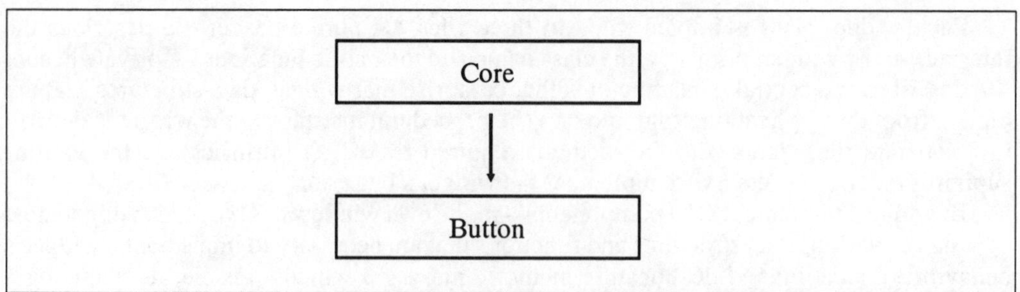

Figure 2.2 The Widget Hierarchy for a Simple Button Widget

```
response_box dialog_box(<initializers>...);
```

C++ allows variable definitions to occur (almost) anywhere in a program, unlike C, which requires that declarations and definitions occur at the beginning of a block of code.

Because Xt is implemented in C, the Xt application programmer must first establish an identifier and then instantiate it:

```
Widget dialogBox;     /* near the beginning of a block of code * /
...
dialogBox = XtCreateManagedWidget("dialogBox",
    dialogWidgetClass, topLevel, NULL, 0);
```

With C++, the number of initializers given in the constructor depends on the class definition. With Xt, widgets are created/instantiated with a common function

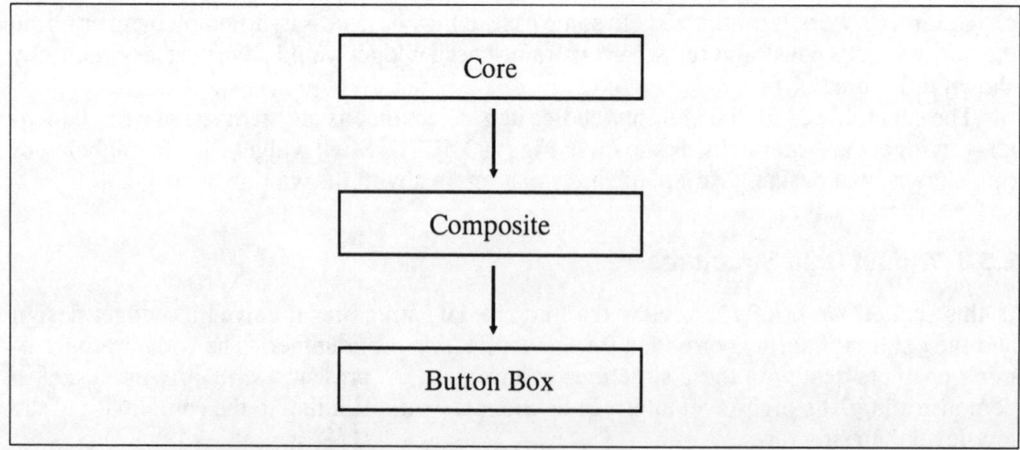

Figure 2.3 The Widget Hierarchy for a Composite Button Box Widget

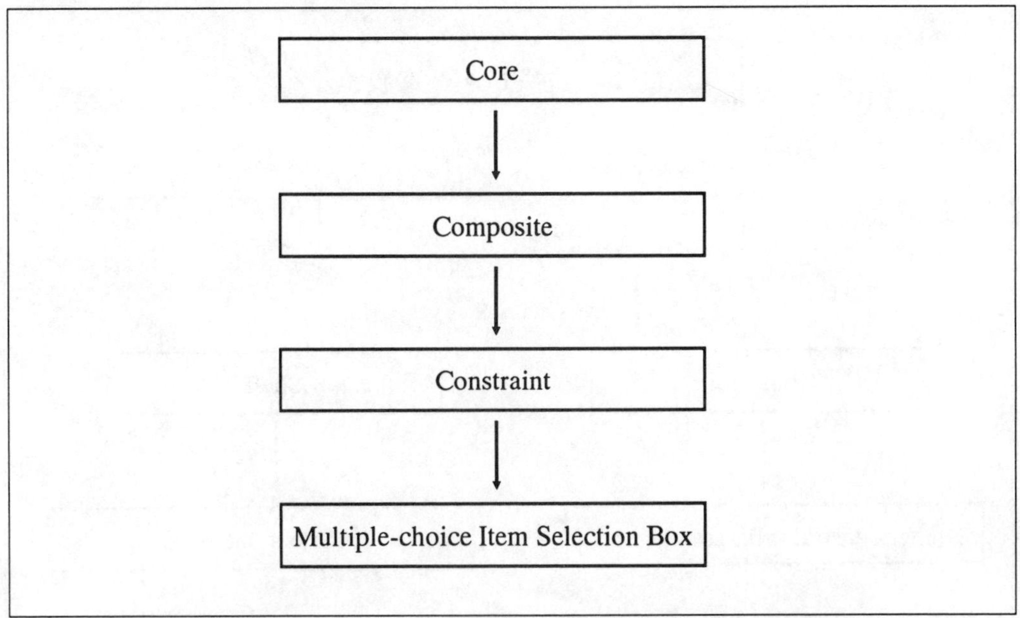

Figure 2.4 The Widget Hierarchy for a Constraint-based Widget

XtCreateManagedWidget(), that takes a fixed number of arguments regardless of the widget class. When certain arguments don't apply, the application programmer uses **NULL**s and 0s, as in the previous example.

Consider the code segment in the Xt example. To use a familiar expression, "There's a lot more going on here than meets the eye." First, there is absolutely no question that the widget interface is high-level—we've created a powerful dialog box with three lines of code. It's important to reiterate the point that widgets implement high-level windows that typically support many operations. Regardless of the implementation language, C or C++, it takes a lot of code to build a window hierarchy that supports window resizing, movement, automatic rearrangement of components, and so on. As we'll see in subsequent chapters, Xt does a tremendous job of hiding the details of the complex operations that take place, making it quite easy for an application programmer to implement a complex window interface to an application.

But what's actually happening? Consider a simple C variable. When you define an integer as a local variable:

```
int n;
...
n = 1;
```

the variable definition (**int n;**) leads to the allocation of integer storage with an undefined value. Thus, **n**'s value is meaningless until legitimate data is stored there.

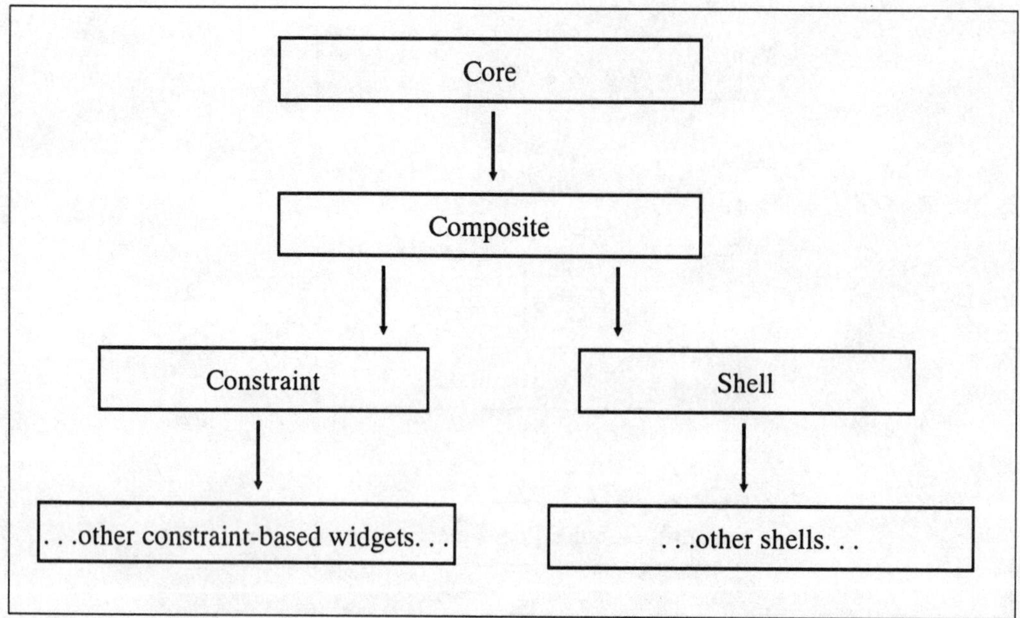

Figure 2.5 The Fundamental Xt Widgets

A similar situation exists with widgets, except that widgets are complex data structures. A "**Widget**" variable such as **dialogBox** is really just a pointer to the storage locations that constitute a widget instance. Behind the scenes, **Widget** is defined as:

```
typedef struct _WidgetRec *Widget;
```

Thus, Xt promotes a high-level view of widgets by using **typedef**s for public structures and their pointers. For the application programmer, the interface is quite simple and straightforward. The widget programmer, on the other hand, must work with several of the low-level data structures that are hidden by the high-level interface.

Each widget class can be dichotomized in two ways: (1) in terms of its public and private components, and (2) in terms of its class and instance components. We can demonstrate the high- versus low-level components by investigating the dialog widget from the Athena widget set.

First, consider the public versus private view of a widget. The public header file *Dialog.h* contains the following:

```
extern WidgetClass dialogWidgetClass;
```

That is, the "widget type" identifier that we used to create the **dialogBox** widget in our earlier example, specifically, **dialogWidgetClass** is an external (public) name of type **WidgetClass**, where the latter is defined (behind the scenes) as:

```
typedef struct _WidgetClassRec *WidgetClass;
```

Many of the low-level **typedefs** used to present the abstract view of widgets are contained in the header file *Intrinsics.h*.

Dialog.h is also responsible for the function declarations that define the public (procedural) interface. For the **Dialog** widget class, it contains function *declarations* for **XtDialogAddButton()** and **XtDialogGetValueString()**. An application programmer can use the former to add buttons to a dialog box; buttons are optional. An application can retrieve the user's response for a previously displayed dialog box using **XtDialogGetValueString()**. These functions are implemented (defined) in *Dialog.c*, which also defines (storage for) the widget class structure (the class record).

The data structures (data types) that define the organization of each widget instance are given in the private header file *DialogP.h*. This file is used by Xt during widget-related operations, but is of no interest to the application programmer—it does not have to be referenced by any of the application files. We can take a quick peek at this file to demonstrate the instance versus class breakdown of a widget, the second dichotomy that we mentioned earlier. (In our discussion of C++ we ignored the class components of an object's class definition.)

Next, consider the class and instance organization that's hidden by the high-level interface. *DialogP.h* contains several structure definitions. First, the class record for a dialog widget:

```
typedef struct {int empty;} DialogClassPart;

typedef struct _DialogClassRec {
    CoreClassPart       core_class;
    CompositeClassPart  composite_class;
    ConstraintClasspart constraint_class;
    FormClassPart       form_class;
    DialogClassPart     dialog_class;
} DialogClassRec;
```

Xt is designed to handle widgets that have both class and instance components, as discussed earlier. In the case of a dialog widget, however, the **dialog_class** widget component of the class structure is null/empty. To satisfy the requirements of Xt and the compiler, a **dialog_class** component structure is created with a dummy variable. For the convenience of the widget programmer, and to satisfy the requirements of the Xt Intrinsics, each widget class must set up public declarations for various structures, such as the class record:

```
extern DialogClassRec dialogClassRec;
```

Also, from the class structure definition we can see that this widget is a complex one, inheriting data and operations from the **Core**, **Composite**, **Constraint**, and **Form** widget classes. The details of Xt's "inheritance by composition" will be discussed in the widget programming chapters.

The instance record of a dialog widget contains several variables that are important in managing the operations of a dialog box, such as the dialog box label, the user's response, and so on:

```
typedef struct _DialogPart {
    ...
    ...
} DialogPart;
```

We can ignore those variables here because we're focusing on a widget's overall organization. Data structures are also set up to handle various constraints, but they are of no interest here.

Finally, we should mention that there are a couple of definitions in the public header file that are useful in certain circumstances; for the **Dialog** widget class these are:

```
typedef struct DialogClassRec *DialogWidgetClass;
typedef struct _DialogRec *DialogWidget;
```

The latter **typedef** creates a high-level data type for a pointer to a widget's instance record. For many widgets, it is useful in maintaining a distinction in the application between widgets of various types, and in passing arguments to various functions that make up a widget class's public interface. The Xt Intrinsics manipulate widgets, regardless of their "type," as generic widgets (widgets of type **Widget**). The methods that implement a particular widget class need access to the specific components of the widget; hence, a "typed" widget pointer is convenient for informing the compiler of a widget class's instance variables.

2.5.4 Comparing Widgets and Objects

With languages like C++ that provide full syntactic support for OO programming it is relatively easy to design new classes and class hierarchies—*in terms of setting up class definitions and so on*. The source code segments in the previous section demonstrate the ease with which new classes can be derived from existing classes.

On the other hand, the *logistics* of designing a class hierarchy can be quite involved. If you want a class hierarchy that truly is reusable across applications, you must be willing to invest a lot of time in designing the hierarchy. Typically, a class hierarchy goes through a process of iterative refinement *before* it is deemed safe for use across a variety of applications. The need for a substantial investment in the up-front design of a class or class hierarchy transcends OO languages and OO programming environments. In our experience, designing widget hierarchies with Xt is no more complicated or time-consuming than designing C++ class hierarchies, given a library of C++ classes of the magnitude of the Xt Intrinsics and an accompanying widget set.

In terms of their scope of support for object-orientation there is, however, an important difference between C++ and Xt. C++ is a true OO language; hence, you can use it to build classes for objects of virtually any type: GUI components (windows), a system of configuration objects for a software product, numeric classes such as rational and complex, or any other class that the developer requires. Consequently, you can develop libraries of modules and entire software systems that have uniform support for, and adherence to the principles of, object-oriented programming.

No matter how much we may like the OO-like capabilities of Xt, and the power that it provides application programmers, the uniform support for OO programming just isn't there. Suppose that you decide to design a wastebasket utility. Much of the GUI requirements of the application could be provide by widgets: menus, dialog boxes, and so on. Other components of the application could not be implemented as widgets. As far as Xt is concerned, widgets are window-related objects. The file processing component of a wastebasket application could not (realistically) be designed as a widget. It's true that we could design a wastebasket file widget that managed file operations, but the reusability of this type of widget is suspect. Reusability could be enhanced by including only generic file processing operations in the wastebasket file widget—display the names of the files from the wastebasket in a scrollable window, and so on. In this case, however, at best we have added another widget to our widget arsenal.

In particular, the wastebasket-specific file operations would still exist as application-specific operations, distinct from any widget. In general, the use of encapsulation and abstraction in an Xt application will always exist in two forms: (1) as provided by widgets for GUI components, and (2) as provided by compiled modules, for example, the wastebasket application's file module, containing private variables for managing the current (highlighted) file in the wastebasket browser, a function that redisplays the contents of the wastebasket, plus other interrelated variables and functions.

C++ provides the syntactic tools necessary to support encapsulation, inheritance, and dynamic binding. The compiler does not, however, force a programmer to practice OO program design, to develop standard protocols, or to follow any of the other tenets of OO programming. As a result, the style of programming exhibited by one C++ application, or library, may differ substantially from another.

The Xt Intrinsics support the first two facets of OO programming, but not the third. OO language purists would argue that OO programming with Xt is not OO programming at all—comparing widgets and objects is like comparing apples and oranges. For us, the distinction between encapsulation provided by a programming environment/library and encapsulation provided by a language definition (hence, compiler) isn't terribly important. The fact is that Xt provides a very significant percentage of the OO capabilities advocated by OO purists and recognized as critically important in developing complex applications. Xt, unlike C++, forces application programmers, and widget programmers especially, to prescribe to a certain programming style that has obvious benefits for complex applications.

2.6 Other High-level Tools

In Chapter 1 we put forth the view that X provides a good foundation from which the programming community can develop a variety of high-level interfaces. A C++ or Object Pascal interface could, for example, be designed for X. An OO language-derived interface could utilize the existing widget framework for using GUI components, or it could depart radically, being layered directly on top of Xlib.

The industry may, however, migrate in a different direction—toward higher level toolkits, such as 4GL interface builders. The Motif toolkit, for example, supplements the Xt Intrinsics, provides a substantial widget set, and unlike standard Xt, allows the programmer to build an application's interface either directly using the Intrinsics and widgets or indirectly using its User Interface Language (UIL) (OSF, 1990). Other interface development tools are beginning to appear, but it's still unclear what direction the industry will take with respect to high-level interfaces. It is clear that the X Window System provides a powerful foundation for future development tools.

3

Overview of Xlib Programming

X is an event-driven window system. Thus for even a basic application, a programmer must address a considerable number of window- and event-related details. In this chapter we develop a simple clock application, *xclk*, that displays the current time in a window. In spite of the simplicity of the application, *xclk* demonstrates a variety of Xlib programming operations that are common to most applications.

Because *xclk* is the first application in this book, we'll present the modules in fairly complete detail. In subsequent chapters, we'll highlight only selected aspects of a particular application. The complete source code for each application can be found in an appendix.

3.1 *xclk*: Displaying the Current Time—On Demand

xclock is a fairly sophisticated clock application that comes standard with the X Window System. It displays the time continuously in either analog or digital form. For some individuals, however, the day seems to pass more slowly if the current time is always on display. As an alternative, we'll develop a clock that displays the time only when requested. Figure 3.1 shows *xclk* in operation with the current time displayed.

We can design our application, *xclk*, to display a blank window under normal circumstances. By placing the mouse pointer in the clock window, the user can prod the application to display the current time. As soon as the pointer leaves the window, *xclk* should redisplay a blank window. Also, we want to design our clock so that it's easily terminated. Since enter- and leave-window events control whether or not the time is displayed, we can use a (mouse button) click operation to signal program termination.

Figure 3.1 An *xclk* Window

3.2 X Display-oriented Operations

X applications must perform a number of screen- and display-oriented operations during program start-up. Because these operations are common to and necessary with many X applications, it makes sense to isolate them in a separate compiled module. For our purposes, a simple module will be adequate.

Many Xlib functions require a pointer to the display as an argument. Other functions must have information about the display screen, expressed in either integer form or as a pointer to a **Screen** structure. In our case, we can set up a library module with several public variables that provide display and screen information for simple applications that display their output on the "default" server. Because our module addresses screen-oriented aspects of display operations as opposed to, say, keyboard or mouse operations, we'll name the module *screen.c*.

A public header file *screen.h* provides an interface to the screen module, that is, its public *declarations*:

```
/****  screen.h  ****  screen handling routines  ****/


#ifndef SCREENH
#define SCREENH 1


#include <X11/Xlib.h>
#include <X11/Xutil.h>
#include <X11/Xos.h>

#include <stdio.h>


/*
globals:
```

```
*/

extern Display *display;
extern Screen *screen_ptr;
extern int screen;
extern unsigned int display_width, display_height, display_depth;


/*
Functions:
*/

extern void init_display();
extern void load_font();


#endif
```

The first three variables provide information required by various Xlib functions; the latter two variables are included for convenience. As an alternative, you could add more protection by making these variables private to *screen.c* and using access functions to retrieve their values. For our purposes, because these variables are used so often as arguments to Xlib functions, and because they aren't likely to be modified accidentally, we're making them directly available.

Currently, there are two public functions. **init_display**() performs basic display initializations that are required with all X applications. This module also includes a function for loading a font, **load_font**(). Technically, of course, fonts are distinct from displays and screens. It's convenient, however, to include **load_font**() in this module, since initializing the display and loading a font often go hand in hand.

The implementation module, *screen.c*, defines storage for the public variables and implements the functions. It is a standard programming practice to have a module such as *screen.c depend* on its public header file for variable and function declarations:

```
#include "screen.h"
```

This practice ensures that the public interface and the actual implementation remain consistent over time. The actual variable definitions follow:

```
Display *display;
Screen *screen_ptr;
int screen;
unsigned int display_width, display_height, display_depth;
```

All display- and screen-oriented initializations are handled by a single function:

```
/*
init_display() initializes critical display and screen variables.
*/
```

```
void init_display(application_name)
char *application_name;
{
    char *display_name = NULL;

    if ((display = XOpenDisplay(display_name)) == NULL) {
        (void) fprintf(stderr,
            "%s: cannot connect to X server %s\n",
            application_name, XDisplayName(display_name));
            exit(-1);
    }
    screen_ptr = display->screens;
    screen = DefaultScreen(display);

    display_width = DisplayWidth(display, screen);
    display_height = DisplayHeight(display, screen);
    display_depth = DisplayPlanes(display, screen);
}   /* init_display */
```

The main purpose of this function is to connect the application to the X server. The Xlib function **XOpenDisplay()** performs this operation—the server is specified as an argument. For our purposes it is sufficient to use a null display name, forcing a connection to the server specified by the UNIX environment variable **DISPLAY**. If you are unfamiliar with these concepts, consult one of the books on X such as Nye (1988), Jones (1989), or Quercia and O'Reilly (1989).

XOpenDisplay() returns the address of the **Display** data structure that describes this connection. This address is required by many Xlib functions; therefore, it is stored in **display**. If the connection fails, the application terminates with an error message. If the connection succeeds, **screen_ptr** provides direct access to the array of screens and **screen** indexes the default screen. Although the latter is used more often than the former, it's convenient to define both.

Xlib provides a number of convenience macros such as **ScreenCount()**, **DefaultScreen()**, **DisplayWidth()**, and so on. In some situations a macro is inappropriate, so for many (but not all) of these macros, X also provides functions that perform the same operation. For those situations where a macro is inappropriate, it's difficult to remember whether or not a corresponding function exists. You can circumvent this inconsistency by defining your own variables, thereby avoiding a mixture of macro and function calls. We're not advocating this approach, but are simply explaining why we define certain variables for general use, **display_width** and **display_height**, in particular.

The second function that we define in *screen.c* is **load_font()**:

```
/*
load_font() loads the specified font, printing a message to
stderr in the event of an error.
*/

void load_font(font_info, application_name, font_name)
XFontStruct **font_info;
char *application_name;
```

```
char *font_name;
{
    if ((*font_info = XLoadQueryFont(display, font_name))
            == NULL) {
        (void) fprintf(stderr, "%s: cannot open %s font\n",
            application_name, font_name);
        exit(-1);
    }
}   /* load_font */
```

load_font() is a simple function that attempts to load the requested font. If the font can't be loaded, it issues an error message and terminates the application.

Both of these function are rather trivial, with respect to the magnitude of their operations. It would be easy to include their code in-line for each application. Most programmers, however, would prefer to isolate their operations and use them as abstract functions.

The purpose of this chapter is to overview some of the programming practices that we employ in subsequent chapters. With *screen.c* and *screen.h* we've illustrated a standard programming technique, namely, the encapsulation of data and related operations in a compiled module. Chapter 2 discussed our motivation for this approach. The object file *screen.o* can be used directly in the makefile for various applications, or included in a library that's referenced in the makefile. In any case, given the black-box capabilities of our *screen.c* module, we can now focus on the application-specific aspects of *xclk*.

3.3 *xclk*'s Data Structures and Program Initialization

xclk is a text-oriented application; it doesn't use line drawing or other sophisticated graphics capabilities. The central task is to provide a simple window in which the current time is displayed in text form, but only while the pointer is in the window. Because some X window managers don't provide a header (title) for an application, we'll design *xclk* so that the user can use a command line option to request that the application window include a simple title bar:

```
{user prompt} xclk [-h] &
```

If a header is requested, it will be displayed in the same window as the time. This approach is simpler than maintaining separate windows for the title and for the time.

A variety of X-related issues must be addressed, even for a simple clock application. For *xclk*, there are several categories of critical data structures that must be managed, in particular, windows, graphics contexts, and fonts. Because this application is quite simple, we can allocate the critical data structures as local variables in **main**(), using Xlib functions directly. In later chapters, we'll discuss the merits of designing, for example, high-level window structures complete with creation and access functions, encapsulated in a compiled module as demonstrated with *screen.c*.

Next, consider fonts. We want our application to support whatever font(s) the user prefers. Thus, in addition to the command-line option that requests a header, we should support options for header and clock fonts:

```
{user prompt} xclk [-h] [-hf<header_font>] [-cf<clock_font>] &
```

If either of the last two options is not specified, *xclk* uses a default font(s). Also, the *-h* option is redundant if the user also supplies the *-hf* option.

We've elected to place various **#include** and **#define** directives in a separate header file to avoid clutter in *xclk.c*. *xclk.h* includes the following:

```
/****   xclk.h   ****   constants for xclk.c   ****/


#include <stdio.h>
#include <string.h>
#include <ctype.h>
#include <X11/cursorfont.h>

#include "screen.h"


/*
xclk displays the time of day in the center of a
small window using a proportional font.
*/

#define BORDER_WIDTH     2

#define CLK_FONT         "ncenBI24"
#define HDR_FONT         "helvB14"

#define NORMAL           -1
#define REVERSE          -2

#define TRUE             1
#define FALSE            0


#define MAX_FONT_NAME    500

/*
Functions:
*/

void main(), cleanup_resources(), display_clock(),
    display_header(), update_clock(), set_up_GC(),
    set_up_size_hints(), process_font_options();
char *get_the_time();
```

Except for *screen.c*, *xclk* is implemented from a single source code module, *xclk.c*. Consequently, static function declarations/definitions aren't really necessary. In subsequent chapters where we build high-level modules it will be necessary to make a distinction between public and private functions.

Note that *xclk.h* doesn't need to include many of the X header files, since it includes *screen.h*, which performs this service indirectly. In addition to header inclusions and function declarations, *xclk* defines several constants that are useful throughout the application.

Next, consider **main()**:

```
/*
main() sets up the data structures, calls the display
routines, and then waits for the application to finish.
*/

void main(argc, argv)
int argc;
char *argv[];
{
    Window clk_win;
    XFontStruct *clk_font, *hdr_font;
    Cursor clk_cursor;
    GC gc, rgc;
    XSizeHints cw_size_hints;
    int has_hdr = FALSE, hdr_height = 0;     /* no header by default */
    int clk_width, clk_height;
    char hdr_font_name[MAX_FONT_NAME], clk_font_name[MAX_FONT_NAME];

    process_font_options(argc, argv, &has_hdr, hdr_font_name,
        clk_font_name);
    init_display(*argv);
    load_font(&hdr_font, *argv, hdr_font_name);
    load_font(&clk_font, *argv, clk_font_name);

    if (has_hdr) {
        hdr_height = hdr_font->max_bounds.ascent +
            hdr_font->max_bounds.descent;
        hdr_height += (hdr_height / 4);           /* add 25% */
    }
    set_up_size_hints(clk_font, &clk_width,
        &clk_height, hdr_height, &cw_size_hints);
    clk_win = XCreateSimpleWindow(display,
        RootWindow(display, screen), 0, 0,
        clk_width, clk_height, BORDER_WIDTH,
        BlackPixel(display, screen), WhitePixel(display, screen));
    XSetStandardProperties(display, clk_win, *argv, *argv,
        None, argv, argc, &cw_size_hints);
    XSelectInput(display, clk_win, ExposureMask | ButtonPressMask |
        EnterWindowMask | LeaveWindowMask);

    clk_cursor = XCreateFontCursor(display, XC_left_ptr);
    XDefineCursor(display, clk_win, clk_cursor);
    set_up_GC(&gc, clk_font, NORMAL);
    set_up_GC(&rgc, hdr_font, REVERSE);
    display_clock(clk_win, clk_font, hdr_font, gc, rgc,
        clk_width, clk_height, hdr_height);
    cleanup_resources(clk_win, clk_font, hdr_font, clk_cursor);
```

```
    exit(0);
}   /* main */
```

First, **main()** defines the central data structures as local variables, and then calls supporting functions that perform most services. For example, **process_font_options()** interprets the command-line options for header and clock fonts; and then, **init_display()** and **load_font()** are called to make the connection to the server and to load the appropriate fonts, respectively. The easiest way to accommodate the use of different fonts for displaying the time and the label is to set up separate graphics contexts (GCs) for each type of output; **set_up_GC()** performs this service. Once all of the data structures have been initialized properly, **main()** turns over control of the application to **display_clock()**. A separate routine, **cleanup_resources()**, is called to deallocate storage so that the application can exit gracefully.

3.4 Window-related Operations

As mentioned, in this application we've elected to define and manipulate the application's window directly with Xlib functions, as opposed to creating a higher level window data structure with support functions (as described in Chapter 2). Before creating the window, **main()** calls **set_up_size_hints()** to specify the window dimensions:

```
set_up_size_hints(clk_font, &clk_width,
    &clk_height, hdr_height, &cw_size_hints);
```

It returns the dimensions for the clock display area; subsequently, these values are passed to other functions.

Next, the clock window is created with **XCreateSimpleWindow()**:

```
clk_win = XCreateSimpleWindow(display,
    RootWindow(display, screen), 0, 0,
    clk_width, clk_height, BORDER_WIDTH,
    BlackPixel(display, screen), WhitePixel(display, screen));
```

Once the window is defined, **XSetStandardProperties()** can be called to set the basic properties required by the window manager:

```
XSetStandardProperties(display, clk_win, *argv, *argv,
    None, argv, argc, &cw_size_hints);
```

Also, **XSelectInput()** is called to designate events of interest to *xclk*:

```
XSelectInput(display, clk_win, ExposureMask | ButtonPressMask |
    EnterWindowMask | LeaveWindowMask);
```

The last window-related detail is to associate a (mouse) cursor with the window:

```
clk_cursor = XCreateFontCursor(display, XC_left_ptr);
XDefineCursor(display, clk_win, clk_cursor);
```

Although we could isolate these window-related operations in a separate function, doing so wouldn't change the fact that we're working purely at the Xlib level. For a simple application, there really isn't anything wrong with taking this approach. In the next chapter we'll discuss an alternate design.

3.5 Event Processing in *xclk*

X applications respond to selected events. With *xclk* we're interested in four types of events: exposures, button press events, the pointer entering the application window, and the pointer leaving the application window.

If an exposure occurs anywhere in the application window, we can simply redisplay the entire header. For such a small window where it's easy to regenerate the window contents, this approach is better than trying to distinguish which subset of the header area has been affected, if any, in order to perform selective updating. The function **display_header()** will perform this service.

As mentioned earlier, the rest of the window will remain blank until the user moves the pointer inside the application window. With this policy, *xclk* is simple to implement. Specifically, we don't have to update the clock continually based on a predetermined time slice. Moreover, we don't have to be concerned about exposures from overlapping windows in the area where the time is displayed, and so on. We'll use a procedure called **update_clock()** to display the current time. It will also be called on to clear the current time when the pointer leaves the window, that is, when a leave-window event is received.

Lastly, if a button press event occurs anywhere in the application window, it will be interpreted as a request to terminate *xclk*. The function **display_clock()** implements an event loop that executes until the user presses a button:

```
/*
display_clock() determines the time and displays it.
A button click terminates the event loop.
*/

void display_clock(clk_win, clk_font, hdr_font, gc, rgc,
    clk_width, clk_height, hdr_height)
Window clk_win;
XFontStruct *clk_font, *hdr_font;
GC gc, rgc;
int clk_width, clk_height, hdr_height;
{
    XEvent event;

    XMapRaised(display, clk_win);
    while (TRUE) {
        XNextEvent(display, &event);
        switch (event.type) {
            case Expose:
                display_header(clk_win, rgc, clk_width,
                    hdr_height, hdr_font);
                break;
            case EnterNotify:
```

```
                update_clock(clk_win, clk_font, gc, get_the_time(),
                    clk_width, clk_height, hdr_height);
                break;
            case LeaveNotify:
                update_clock(clk_win, clk_font, gc, NULL,
                    clk_width, clk_height, hdr_height);
                break;
            case ButtonPress:
                return;         /* terminate the program */
        }
    }
}   /* display_clock */
```

display_clock() functions as a clearinghouse for events that are of interest to *xclk*. It is called once, immediately after program initialization. Consequently, it first maps the window to the top of the display screen. Next, it executes the event loop, processing events as previously outlined. When **display_clock()** terminates, **main()** takes control and frees *xclk*'s data structures before terminating.

display_header() displays the title in reverse video using the font (GC) prescribed by **main()**:

```
/*
display_header() displays a reverse video header with a
"neutral" title centered in the header.  Some window managers
will add a title bar with the application name.
*/

void display_header(clk_win, rgc, clk_width, hdr_height, hdr_font)
Window clk_win;
GC rgc;
int clk_width, hdr_height;
XFontStruct *hdr_font;
{
    char *label = "time";

    if (hdr_height == 0)
        return;
    XSetFunction(display, rgc, GXset);
    XFillRectangle(display, clk_win, rgc,
        0, 0, clk_width, hdr_height);
    XSetFunction(display, rgc, GXcopy);
    XDrawImageString(display, clk_win, rgc,
        (clk_width - XTextWidth(hdr_font, label, strlen(label))) / 2,
        hdr_height - (hdr_height / 4),      /* 25% */
        label, strlen(label));
}   /* display_header */
```

If the height of the header area is 0, **display_header()** simply returns.

In the case of a leave-window event, the time-display function **update_clock()** is called with a null time value, a signal to clear the window:

```
/*
update_clock() displays the time in the center of the non-
header window area.  Proportional fonts are OK.
*/

void update_clock(clk_win, clk_font, gc, time,
    clk_width, clk_height, hdr_height)
Window clk_win;
XFontStruct *clk_font;
GC gc;
char *time;
int clk_width, clk_height, hdr_height;
{
    if (time == NULL)
        XClearArea(display, clk_win, 0, hdr_height, 0, 0, FALSE);
    else {
        int x_pos, y_pos;

        x_pos =
            (clk_width - XTextWidth(clk_font, time, strlen(time))) /
            2;
        y_pos = clk_height - clk_font->max_bounds.ascent;
        XDrawImageString(display, clk_win, gc,
            x_pos, y_pos, time, strlen(time));
    }
}   /* update_clock */
```

For an enter-window event, **update_clock()** is called with a time value returned by **get_the_time()**. (The latter function uses standard library functions to build a string representation of the current time; see Appendix B.)

As *xclk* demonstrates, the amount of source code required to implement the central task, in this case, displaying the current time, can be quite small in comparison to the amount of code required to implemented various GUI operations. This statement is, of course, debatable, depending on your perspective on GUI applications. That is, for some programmers the GUI-related operations *are* a central component of the application—they might even view the task of displaying the current time as secondary to managing the window!

In any case, we've focused on the GUI-related aspects of *xclk* as a review of basic Xlib application programming, and as a foundation for the somewhat more ambitious applications of subsequent chapters. We've omitted discussion of several of *xclk*'s routines, for example, **process_font_options()** and **get_the_time()**. As an exercise, you may want to investigate the remaining functions, or to modify *xclk* to fit your own needs. Complete source code is given in Appendix B.

4

Creating High-level Interfaces for Xlib Applications

In Chapter 3 we overviewed basic Xlib programming and introduced *screen.c*, a module that we will continue to use in our Xlib applications. In this chapter we discuss two additional general-purpose modules, one that's almost trivial and another that's more extensive in its support for high-level applications. All three modules will be used in the remaining Xlib applications that lead into our discussion of Xt.

4.1 The Importance of Higher Levels of Abstraction

Toolkits, and interface builders in various forms, are popular because they provide a powerful, high-level programming environment. In relative terms, a small amount of source code brings together a large contingent of library services. But there is another reason for the popularity of high-level programming environments. Indirectly, X toolkits, interface builders, and high-level, GUI-aware languages such as Actor (The Whitewater Group, 1990) impose a significant amount of structure on both the application and the programmer. As a by-product of this syntactic structure, applications often have a more consistent look and feel and, in almost all cases, the readability of their source code is improved.

C, in contrast, supports a broad array of programming styles and techniques. C is a very popular programming language largely because of its facility for low-level, pointer-based operations combined with its support for high-level data and control structures. Although this combination is ideal for many tasks, C's low-level capabilities are often abused, or at the very least, overused. In particular, C does very little to *encourage* programmers to develop high-level, abstract program modules.

In our opinion, C cannot be held accountable for the abuse of its low-level capabilities, as committed by some programmers. C provides a powerful mixture of programming tools; programmers, like carpenters, are responsible for choosing the proper tool(s) for the task at hand.

Beyond tools, however, there is the issue of materials. An accomplished carpenter views the walls of a house in terms of its corner posts, tees, and so on, not as a collection of 2x4s. Consider a complex, multilevel house with numerous walls juxtaposed at odd angles. We simply can't hold a hammer or nail accountable, if a carpenter can't envision how the walls, floors, and ceiling fit together, because he or she is overwhelmed by the number of nails and timbers that are involved in the overall construction project.

Programmers who develop software for modern GUI environments face a similar situation with respect to materials. It can be quite difficult to keep the application in perspective if it's designed as a collection of pointers and low-level data structures. Xt, for example, does a wonderful job of hiding the pointers and C **struct**s, allowing a programmer to create high-level widgets with a mimimum number of statements.

We've been discussing the data and control structures supported by C, but a similar situation exists with Xlib, which is our primary interest at this point. Like C, Xlib provides a variety of programming tools and materials. The level of abstraction supported by C and by Xlib is, of course, relative. The low-level structures of Xlib include, for example, **XCharStruct**, **XKeyboardState**, and so on. In some cases, an Xlib function requires the programmer to use these low-level structures directly. In most cases, however, Xlib provides relatively high-level data structures that are used more often than the low-level data structures. For example, it is more common for an Xlib programmer to *allocate* **XFontStruct** than **XCharStruct** records; the latter is a component of the former.

As we've mentioned, it is our opinion that in many cases the Xlib programmer must go even farther, creating additional high-level data structures and operators. In the previous chapter we built a window for *xclk* using **XCreateSimpleWindow()**, and then created distinct font structures and GCs. In this case the application provided the only "glue" that served to bind these structures together. As an alternative, we could have combined Xlib **Window**, **XFontStruct**, **GC**, and other structures to create a high-level, special-purpose window. It's true that if we design a specialized window, say, a text-oriented window structure, and then encapsulate this structure with a set of high-level operations, we've created a module that's useless in an application that's restricted to, say, performing line drawing operations in a window.

In general, however, when we strive for software reusability we're interested in reusability at the compiled module level. That is, it's quite common to use encapsulation to build special-purpose modules—if those modules have good prospects for reuse in other applications. Thus, if a developer intends to design one or more applications that make extensive use of pop-up dialog windows, text browsing windows, edit windows, and so on, it makes sense to design a special-purpose, text window module that can provide text processing capabilities across the applications.

In this chapter we develop a *simple* text processing module in order to illustrate this type of encapsulation. We must emphasize that the specific capabilities that we design into this module are mostly irrelevant. It is presumptious, if not impossible, to say that a particular approach to designing text windows, or whatever, is better than another one. Applications and classes of applications differ greatly; programmers must, of course, make design decisions that are best for their applications.

In this book, we are more interested in the motivations for developing high-level modules than in the utility of any particular module. Despite our interest in these general issues, we have chosen an example that will serve as a foundation for the next chapter where we'll develop a window-based dump utility and for Chapter 7 where we'll explore the use of callback functions with Xlib, as provided automatically with Xt.

4.2 Function Call Convenience and Consistency

In our text window-based applications we need to display characters and strings in a window. In this section we develop a simple two-function module that provides a small, but useful, front-end to the standard Xlib function **XDrawImageString()**. The main service provided by these two functions is to reduce the number of arguments to **XDrawImage-String()**, and to provide a more consistent argument syntax for both displaying a character and a string.

The header file contains two public declarations:

```
/****  display.h  ****  external declarations for display.c  ****/


#ifndef DISPLAYH
#define DISPLAYH    1


extern void display_string();
extern void display_char();


#endif
```

Two functions are declared for displaying characters, individually and in string form, hence, we've named this the "display" module: *display.h* and *display.c*. In this book we follow the common practice of using conditional compilation directives, **#ifndef**, **#define**, and **#endif**, to ensure that the compiler detects multiple attempts to include a header file.

The implementation file includes its own interface file to ensure consistency, plus the interface for the screen module:

```
/****  display.c  ****  X text display routines  ****/


#include "screen.h"
#include "display.h"

    ...
    ...
```

Xlib's standard function for displaying a string requires that the programmer provide the string's length as an argument:

```
XDrawImageString(display, drawable, gc,
    x-offset, y-offset, string, length);
```

This approach can improve the efficiency of an application in some circumstances, because **strlen()** performs an inherently slow operation. That is, if an application has prior knowledge of a string's length, it is wasteful to have a function like **XDrawImageString()** calculate the length automatically. Hence, the programmer is given the responsibility of providing/calculating the length.

In most cases we will not have prior knowledge of a string's length, so we want a function that performs the string-length calculation for us:

```
/*
display_string() displays a string in a window.
*/

void display_string(display, drawable, gc, x, y, str)
Display *display;
Drawable drawable;
GC gc;
int x, y;
char *str;
{
    XDrawImageString(display, drawable, gc, x, y, str, strlen(str));
}   /* display_string */
```

You may disagree with the motivation for defining this function, since it produces an extra function call in comparsion to calling **XDrawImageString()** directly. We've chosen to include this module partly because we feel that the extra overhead is worth the convenience of having the string-length operation handled automatically.

The other reason for defining *display.c* is to make it convenient to dislay a single character:

```
/*
display_char() displays a character in a window.
*/

void display_char(display, drawable, gc, x, y, ch)
Display *display;
Drawable drawable;
GC gc;
int x, y;
char ch;
{
    char str[2];

    str[0] = ch;
```

```
    str[1] = '\0';
    XDrawImageString(display, drawable, gc, x, y, str, 1);
}   /* display_string */
```

With **display_char()**, we avoid manually converting a character to string form.

4.3 A High-level Interface to Xlib's Windowing Functions

In this section we develop a high-level text window module. There is nothing special or universal about the capabilities of this particular module; in part, it is designed to serve our needs in subsequent chapters. In designing a similar type of module, you could make a number of different decisions.

4.3.1 *simplewin.h*: The Interface File

First, consider the interface file *simplewin.h*. It includes the headers for the *screen.c* and *display.c*:

```
/****     simplewin.h     ****/


#ifndef SIMPLEWINH
#define SIMPLEWINH  1


#include <X11/cursorfont.h>
#include "screen.h"
#include "display.h"
```

For convenience and readability, several macro constants are defined:

```
#define TRUE                1               /* logical constants */
#define FALSE               0
#define CANT_ALLOCATE_WIN   -99

#define EOS                 '\0'            /* special characters */
#define LF                  '\n'

#define REVERSE             0
#define NORMAL              1
```

Next, the template for our high-level window is defined:

```
typedef struct {
    Window xwin;          /* the associated X window */
    void *extension;      /* pointer to whatever, e.g, buttons */
    XFontStruct *font;
    XSizeHints *size_hints;
    int cursor_x;
    int cursor_y;
```

```
    int font_height, font_width;
    unsigned int width, height, trunc_height;
    int is_active;
} logical_window_frame;
```

Thus, a **logical_window_frame** is a collection of information that is useful in manipulating a simple text window. It brings together (the addresses of) several critical data structures that in combination define the logical window, in particular, the physical ID for the Xlib window, **xwin**, the structure that defines the font for this window, **font**, and the structure containing size information used during window creation, **size_hints**.

It's important to note that several items are defined redundantly. For example, once a window has been created, its dimensions can be determined by calling an Xlib function that returns window attribute information, as discussed in Chapter 2. In our opinion, allocating several additional bytes in a logical window structure for variables such as **width, height**, **font_width**, and **font_height**, is justified because it leads to more readable code. It is, for example, more convenient to refer to **font_height** than to "font->max_bounds.ascent + font->max_bounds.descent". Moreover, for some situations having these variables available minimizes the number of function calls that otherwise would be required to retrieve this type of information from Xlib structures.

Probably the most debatable aspect of our design is our decision to make four variables public:

```
/*
Globals:
*/

extern GC gc, rgc, hgc;
extern Cursor popup_cursor;
```

The truth is that more often than not we design modules such that all variable definitions are private, sometimes allowing read-only access to certain variables via an access function. For the purposes of this module, we feel that it is acceptable to make these variables public. Moreover, these variables are not critical to the logic of an application. They represent information that occasionally needs to be used in various Xlib function calls; hence, it is convenient to allow an application to reference these variables directly.

The last component of the interface file is the section that declares the public functions:

```
/*
Functions:
*/

extern void initialize_window_structures();
extern void cleanup_window_structures();
extern void make_window();
extern void cleanup_window();
extern void set_up_GC();
extern void make_popup_cursor();
extern void activate_window();
```

```
extern void deactivate_window();
extern void window_puts();
extern void window_puts_center();
extern int window_puts_by_char();
extern void window_puts_lf();
extern int window_putchar();
extern void window_clr_eol();
extern void window_display_header();
extern void window_reverse_row();
extern int window_go_xy();
extern int window_go_cr();
extern void window_clr_rest();
extern void window_cursor_bottom();
extern int r_pos();
extern int c_pos();
extern int last_row();
extern int last_col();
extern int get_keystroke();


#endif
```

You can see from several of the function names that our text-oriented, logical window module employs row-column metrics. Also, note that this module does *not* define a physical text cursor. The variables **cursor_x** and **cursor_y** are used to keep track of the position where the next character will be displayed. If a physical, viewable text cursor is needed, functions must be added to provide this service. (We don't need that capability for our example applications, so we're not including it. This book has a significant amount of source code, and we need to minimize the amount of source code where possible.)

4.3.2 *simplewin.c*: The Implementation File

The implementation file begins with the storage allocation for the four public variables:

```
/*
Globals:
*/

GC gc, rgc, hgc;                    /* used by all windows */
Cursor popup_cursor;
```

This module provides a high-level function that initializes these variables:

```
/*
initialize_window_structures() initializes data structures that
are shared by multiple windows -- module initialization.
*/

void initialize_window_structures(font)
XFontStruct *font;
```

```
{
    set_up_GC(&gc, font, NORMAL);
    set_up_GC(&rgc, font, REVERSE);
    set_up_GC(&hgc, font, NORMAL);
    XSetFunction(display, hgc, GXinvert);
    make_popup_cursor();
}   /* initialize_window_structures */
```

It uses **set_up_GC()**, which is also defined in this module, to initialize the GCs. This function isn't strictly text-window related, so you might prefer to move it to a library. It has the following definition:

```
/*
set_up_GC() creates a GC that can be used by a system of
similar windows.  In addition, it initializes the current
font for the GC.
*/

void set_up_GC(gc, font, mode)
GC *gc;
XFontStruct *font;
int mode;
{
    *gc = XCreateGC(display, RootWindow(display, screen), 0, NULL);
    XSetFont(display, *gc, font->fid);
    if (mode == REVERSE) {
        XSetForeground(display, *gc, WhitePixel(display, screen));
        XSetBackground(display, *gc, BlackPixel(display, screen));
    }
    else {
        XSetForeground(display, *gc, BlackPixel(display, screen));
        XSetBackground(display, *gc, WhitePixel(display, screen));
    }
}   /* set_up_GC */
```

It supports either a black-on-white or a white-on-black image, based on the third parameter, **mode**. Obviously, this function could be expanded to accommodate other colors.

The cursor for a text window is defined by **make_popup_cursor()**:

```
/*
make_popup_cursor() makes an arrow cursor.
*/

void make_popup_cursor()
{
    popup_cursor = XCreateFontCursor(display, XC_left_ptr);
}    /* make_popup_cursor */
```

simplewin.c also provides a function to free the storage for these special data structures:

```
/*
cleanup_window_structures() frees/deletes module-level
window data structures.
*/

void cleanup_window_structures()
{
    XFreeCursor(display, popup_cursor);
    XFreeGC(display, gc);
    XFreeGC(display, rgc);
    XFreeGC(display, hgc);
}   /* cleanup_window_structures */
```

The next function is **make_window**(); it is responsible for setting up each logical window:

```
/*
make_window() creates an unmapped window.  It sets certain
components of the size_hints structure for that window, as a
convenience to the calling module.  It stores the X window
id as a member of the logical window data structure, lwin.
The window font is set by store_window_font_info().
*/

void make_window(parent, lwin, x, y, width, height,
    border_width, size_hints, font)
Window parent;
logical_window_frame *lwin;
int x, y;                    /* row/column metrics */
unsigned int width, height;
unsigned int border_width;
XSizeHints *size_hints;
XFontStruct *font;
{
    lwin->font_height =
        font->max_bounds.ascent + font->max_bounds.descent;
    width *= font->max_bounds.width;   /* convert to pixels */
    height *= lwin->font_height;
    height += font->max_bounds.descent;    /* bottom padding */
    lwin->xwin = XCreateSimpleWindow(display, parent, x, y,
        width, height, border_width, BlackPixel(display, screen),
        WhitePixel(display, screen));

    size_hints->flags = PPosition | PSize | PMinSize | PMaxSize;
    size_hints->x = x;
    size_hints->y = y;
    size_hints->width = width;
    size_hints->height = height;
    lwin->size_hints = size_hints; /* keep a reference to this */
    lwin->font = font;             /* keep a reference to this */
```

```
    lwin->width = width;              /* convenience variables */
    lwin->height = height;
    lwin->font_width = font->max_bounds.width;
    lwin->trunc_height =              /* without the padding */
        (lwin->height / lwin->font_height) * lwin->font_height;

    lwin->cursor_x = 0;
    lwin->cursor_y = lwin->font_height;    /* a little extra at top */
    lwin->is_active = FALSE;
    lwin->extension = NULL;
    XDefineCursor(display, lwin->xwin, popup_cursor);
    XSelectInput(display, lwin->xwin, ExposureMask |
        KeyPressMask | KeyReleaseMask |
        ButtonPressMask | ButtonReleaseMask | OwnerGrabButtonMask |
        EnterWindowMask | LeaveWindowMask | StructureNotifyMask);
}   /* make_window */
```

Obviously, this function makes a number of assumptions about the windows associated with this module. In particular, it directs that window dimensions and position are program-specified and it designates which events the window will receive.

Other characteristics of a logical window are evident from **make_window()**. First, because the windows are text-oriented, the **width** and **height** *parameters* are specified in row-column metrics. In most cases, an application programmer would have a good idea how many rows and columns are needed in the window; it is probably less likely for the programmer to want to define a text window in terms of pixels.

On the other hand, many of the functions in this module need to manipulate the window in terms of pixels. Thus, **make_window()** converts and stores the values given for width and height arguments in pixel metrics.

There are two dimensions for window height. **height** is padded by several pixels, specifically, the height of the descenders for that font, so that the last row isn't too close to the bottom of the window. **trunc_height** is the window height excluding the extra spacing.

Note that there is a little extra space at the top of the window also—initially, the vertical coordinate is set to the font height. That is, you can think of the rows in a text window as being like lines on a page of (ruled) paper. In this case, the first (0th) "line" begins **font_height** pixels below the top of the window, and because of Xlib's reference mechanism for text display operations, the descenders will begin **font_height** pixels below the top of the window. Since **font_height** is "font->max_bounds.ascent + font->max_bounds.descent", there will be free space above the ascenders.

We've followed a common practice of incorporating an extension field in the logical window structure to accommodate "unforeseen" modifications to a logical window structure. We'll use this field in a subsequent module to extend a window; specifically, we'll add an array of buttons to the logical window structure.

In most cases, developing a high-level interface to some aspect of Xlib involves more that just tying together various low-level data structures to form a "super" data structure. In particular, there should be high-level operations that are applied to the corresponding high-level data structure. For example, the readability of an application can be enhanced if basic operations like mapping a window are expressed in terms of operations against the high-level data structure.

It's true that Xlib functions like **XMapRaised()** *are* high-level operations, in comparison to the lower level operations that are required to map a window and raise it to the top of the display/screen. With X, *low-* and *high-level* are relative terms. For a large application, activating a window should be an abstract operation.

With this in mind, **logical_window_frame** contains the field **is_active**, which is used to record whether or not the window is currently activated. A high-level function **activate_window()** is provided to activate a window of type **logical_window_frame** so that the user of this module doesn't have to perform window mappings with **Window** data structures and **XMapRaised()**. It's definition is:

```
/*
activate_window() maps the window to the top.  If there
is a message, it is dispalyed as a header.
*/

void activate_window(lwin, message)
logical_window_frame *lwin;
char *message;
{
    if (lwin->is_active)
        return;
    lwin->is_active = TRUE;
    XMapRaised(display, lwin->xwin);
    if (*message)
        window_display_header(lwin, message);
}     /* activate_window */
```

Most of the functions in this module take a pointer to a **logical_window_frame** as their first argument. Although we haven't done so here, it would be straightforward to design a more opaque (logical) window handle.

This function reveals other aspects of our logical window organization. Specifically, even though there is no dedicated field in **logical_window_frame** to record a header, or title, the public functions indirectly make provisions for a header. In most cases, the easiest way for the application programmer to provide a header is via an argument to the function that activates the window; this module implements this policy.

If a header is provided, **window_display_header()** is called to display it:

```
/*
window_display_header() can be used to display a left-justified
header on the top line of a window.
*/

void window_display_header(lwin, str)
logical_window_frame *lwin;
char *str;
{
    XSetFunction(display, rgc, GXset);
```

```
    XFillRectangle(display, lwin->xwin, rgc, 0, 0, lwin->width,
        lwin->font_height + lwin->font->max_bounds.descent);
    XSetFunction(display, rgc, GXcopy);
    display_string(display, lwin->xwin, rgc,
        lwin->font_width,
        lwin->font_height - lwin->font->max_bounds.descent, str);
}   /* window_display_header */
```

Note that **window_display_header()** uses a function from *display.c*.

There are several opportunities for incorporating additional flexibility into the *simplewin.c* module, for example, an argument could be added that specifies whether or not the header should be centered or left-justified.

We must provide a mechanism for removing a pop-up window; **deactivate_window()** is the complement of **activate_window()**:

```
/*
deactivate_window() unmaps the window and resets
the cursor coordinates.
*/

void deactivate_window(lwin)
logical_window_frame *lwin;
{
    if (!lwin->is_active)
        return;
    lwin->is_active = FALSE;
    XUnmapWindow(display, lwin->xwin);
    lwin->cursor_y = lwin->font_height;
    lwin->cursor_x = 0;
}   /* deactivate_window */
```

It unmaps the physical window from the screen and resets the cursor variables following the policy discussed earlier—the top "line" begins exactly **font_height** pixels below the top of the window.

There are quite a few additional functions that serve to distinguish the characteristics of a **logical_window_frame**. (An object is defined in terms of both its primary data structure(s) and the set of operations that it supports.) The function **window_puts()** can be used to display a string beginning at the current cursor position:

```
/*
window_puts() prints a string in a window w/o
interpreting each character.
*/

void window_puts(lwin, str, gc)
logical_window_frame *lwin;
char *str;
GC gc;      /* allow normal or reverse video */
{
```

```
    display_string(display, lwin->xwin, gc,
        lwin->cursor_x, lwin->cursor_y, str);
}   /* window_puts */
```

Note that we made the decision to have three public GCs in this module. The application programmer will be aware of this characteristic because of their declaration in the header file (and any additional supporting documentation that we provide). Hence, the user of the module (the application programmer) has a certain amount of control over the operation of **window_puts()** because the GCs are public and a GC must be specified with the third parameter.

You could easily modify this policy. For example, we could have the application programmer pass a message directing which GC to use in dipslaying the text, for example, **REVERSE** or **NORMAL**, or any other GC that we elect to accommodate. Another, typically inferior, alternative would be to provide multiple functions for displaying a string such that the display characteristics are encoded in the function name, for example, **window_puts_reverse()**. As it stands, the public GCs are somewhat vulnerable, but this makes it easy for the application programmer to substitute another GC.

simplewin.c contains many other text-display functions that can be used to display a string in the center of the window, to display a string that contains linefeed characters that should be interpreted, to clear the window from the cursor to the end of the row/line, and so on. Many of the functions hide the details of the lower level characteristics of a **logical_window_frame**. For example, **window_reverse_row()** performs the low-level adjustments/calculations that are necessary to reverse the video for an existing row of text:

```
/*
window_reverse_row() displays a row in reverse video.
*/

void window_reverse_row(lwin)
logical_window_frame *lwin;
{
    XSetFunction(display, rgc, GXset);
    XFillRectangle(display, lwin->xwin, rgc, 0,
        lwin->cursor_y - lwin->font->max_bounds.ascent, lwin->width,
        lwin->font_height + lwin->font->max_bounds.descent);
    XSetFunction(display, rgc, GXcopy);
}   /* window_reverse_row */
```

In most cases, the application is already quite complicated; having these types of high-level operations available as functional abstractions enhances the readability. See Appendix D for the definitions of the remaining text-display functions.

A number of the public functions perform their work beginning at the current cursor position, **window_puts()** is one example. Consequently, it is important to provide the application programmer with high-level functions for manipulating the cursor. Our high-level window is text-oriented in the sense that **make_window()**'s width and height parameters use row-column metrics and functions are provided for displaying rows of text (strings). To be consistent, we should provide a cursor manipulation function that accommodates row-column metrics:

```
/*
window_go_cr() sets the coordinates within a window
in rows and columns.
*/

int window_go_cr(lwin, col, row)
logical_window_frame *lwin;
int col, row;
{
    if (col < 0 || (col * lwin->font_width) >
                (lwin->width - lwin->font_width))
        return FALSE;
    if (row < 0 || ((row + 1) * lwin->font_height) >
            lwin->trunc_height)
        return FALSE;
    window_go_xy(lwin, col * lwin->font_width,
        (row + 1) * lwin->font_height);
    return TRUE;
}   /* window_go_cr */
```

window_go_cr()'s name and its parameter ordering is consistent with the Xlib policy of specifying horizontal coordinates (x, or c) before vertical coordinates (y, or r). It uses a lower level function **window_go_xy()** to do the actual work, after translating row-column values into pixel coordinates.

window_go_xy() is defined as a public function also:

```
/*
window_go_xy() sets the coordinates within a window in pixels.
*/

int window_go_xy(lwin, x, y)
logical_window_frame *lwin;
int x, y;
{
    if (x < 0 || x > lwin->width)
        return FALSE;
    if (y < 0 || y > lwin->height)
        return FALSE;
    lwin->cursor_x = x;
    lwin->cursor_y = y;
    return TRUE;
}   /* window_go_xy */
```

Whether or not this function should remain public after this module stabilizes is debatable. In large part, its public/private status depends on how the module will be used/extended for future applications. For now, it remains public. Note that **win-**

dow_go_xy() cannot be eliminated by having **window_go_cr()** perform cursor setting operations directly; it is used by a number of other functions in this module:

```
/*
window_cursor_bottom() takes the cursor to the bottom line of
the window in font-based metrics.
*/

void window_cursor_bottom(lwin)
logical_window_frame *lwin;
{
    window_go_xy(lwin, lwin->cursor_x, (int) lwin->trunc_height);
}   /* window_cursor_bottom */
```

There are too many cursor manipulation functions to examine here. See Appendix D for the definitions of convenience functions such as **r_pos()**, **c_pos()**, **last_row()**, and others.

Beyond the text-display and cursor manipulation functions, there are other high-level functions that enhance the convenience and efficiency of the *simplewin.c* module, for example:

```
/*
window_clr_rest() clears the remainder of a window, relative
to the cursor, that is, current row-column coordinates.
*/

void window_clr_rest(lwin)
logical_window_frame *lwin;
{
    XClearArea(display, lwin->xwin, lwin->cursor_x,
        lwin->cursor_y - lwin->font->max_bounds.ascent,
        lwin->width - lwin->cursor_x,
        lwin->font_height, FALSE);
    XClearArea(display, lwin->xwin, 0,
        lwin->cursor_y + lwin->font->max_bounds.descent,
        0, 0, FALSE);
}   /* window_clr_rest */
```

In particular, the application programmer should *not* have to display space characters in every row and column in order to clear the window (or a portion of the window).

We've made several compromises as far as the number of high-level functions available to the application programmer is concerned. For example, we have not provided a function to clear the entire window. To perform this operation, the programmer must first use **window_go_cr()** to move the cursor to the top-left corner of the window and then invoke **window_clr_rest()** to the remainder of the window.

Note that **window_clr_rest()** performs its work in two stages. First, it clears the remainder of the current row; then, it clears the portion of the window that lies below the current row. With this design **window_clr_rest()** can be used to clear every character that occurs logically "after" the cursor.

4.4 High-level Interfaces and Software Construction

In the beginning of this chapter we made a plea for the importance of higher levels of abstraction in applications. In particular, we advanced the opinion that modules such as *screen.c*, *display.c*, and *simplewin.c* can go a long way toward making complex applicatons manageable.

You may have opinions and ideas that call for a different type of text-processing window module. *simplewin.c* is adequate for a particular class of applications that require simple text input and output in a pop-up window—it has been designed to serve our needs for this book. There are a number of large applications that would require a more sophisticated and more complete arsenal of text-window functions.

We, for example, designed and then used a significantly larger version of *simplewin.c* to port an application originally designed for a text-oriented computer system to run in an X Window System environment. The modifications required in the original application were quite minimal and completely painless. Basically, a simple interface file was designed that translated window operations from the original source code into calls to the X-based, text-window module.

The need to port old-style character-based applications to modern GUI-based applications is *not* the real motivation for developing high-level interfaces to Xlib. Without high-level interfaces to Xlib, a programmer must continually resort to Xlib functions calls and data structures to piece together the functionality needed for the application. Even if this approach works with a particular application, there is no "natural order" that serves to enhance the readability of the current application. With this type of design, modifications to the application at a later date are accomplished by repeatedly hacking at small code segments here and there.

More importantly, there are ramifications for software reusability. At some point, a programmer will need to perform similar tasks in a new application. Without some mechanism for imposing high-level organization on the application(s), it may be impossible to separate the application-specific details of the old program from its more general components, which need to be carried forward in future application(s).

In other words, designing high-level modules for Xlib forces the programmer to *plan in advance* instead of "programming for the moment at hand." With a windowing system as sophisticated as X, and the demands of the typical GUI-based application, advanced planning is always a good idea.

In Chapters 6 and 7 we'll discuss additional high-level programming techniques that can be useful for Xlib programmers; in particular, self-contained event loops and callback functions. *simplewin.c* will simplify the design of pop-up dialog and alert boxes that we'll need in that chapter.

5

xdump: An X Window System Hex-dump Utility

This chapter demonstrates *simplewin.c* in a simple application. The text window module is used to build a hex-dump utility for displaying a file in a window.

5.1 *xdump*: An Assembler-style, Hex-dump Utility for X

The UNIX command *od(1)* is a versatile utility that performs various types of file dumps. If, however, you are only interested in a hex-dump of a file, a more condensed output format may be preferable. Our utility, *xdump*, takes a single file as a command line argument and dumps that file in a standard X window as shown in Figure 5.1.

The window has two status lines, one at the top and another at the bottom. The top status line shows the name of the current dump file. The bottom status line prompts the user for input. Specifically, a **<click-left>** operation advances to the next page and a **<click-right>** operation terminates the hex-dump.

The text for the file dump occupies the window between the top and bottom status line, exclusive. The dump output is divided into three sections. The left-most column in the window contains the starting address (file offset) for the text occupying that line in the window. The middle section of the window shows the hex values for each successive 16-byte segment in the file. The right-most section of the window shows the ASCII interpretation of the 16 bytes presented in the middle section of the window. If the ASCII interpretation is unprintable, a "." is displayed. Both the middle and right-hand sections are divided (visually) into two 8-byte fields using "-" as a separator.

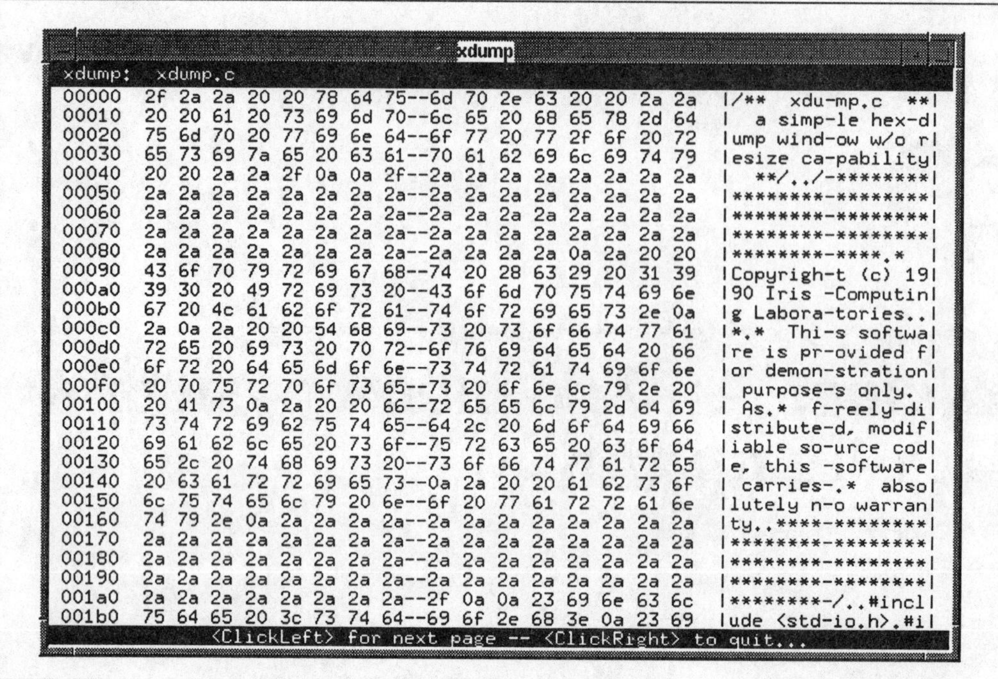

Figure 5.1 An *xdump* Window

5.2 *xdump.c*: The Implementation File

xdump is implemented from one source code file, *xdump.c*, plus the supplemental modules *screen.c*, *display,c*, and *simplewin.c*.

main() allocates storage for X-related structures and serves as a driver, calling initialization functions from various modules, plus **hex_dump()** from this file:

```
/*
main() tests for command line errors, sets up the
data structures, calls hex_dump(), and then waits for
the application to finish.
*/

void main(argc, argv)
int argc;
char *argv[];
{
    logical_window_frame lwindow, *lwin = &lwindow;
    XFontStruct *font;
    XSizeHints dw_size_hints;
    FILE *dump_file;
    char *app_name = "xdump";
```

```
    unsigned int font_height;

    if (argc != 2) {
        fprintf(stderr, "usage:  xdump <filename>\n");
        exit(-1);
    }
    if ((dump_file = fopen(argv[1], "rb")) == NULL) {
        fprintf(stderr, "Can't open input file %s\n", argv[1]);
        exit(-1);
    }
    init_display(app_name);
    load_font(&font, app_name, FONT_SIZE);
    initialize_window_structures(font);
    /* no support for resize */
    dw_size_hints.min_width = dw_size_hints.max_width =
        font->max_bounds.width * NUM_COLUMNS;
    font_height =
        font->max_bounds.ascent + font->max_bounds.descent;
    make_window(RootWindow(display, screen), lwin, 0, 0,
        NUM_COLUMNS, NUM_ROWS, BORDER_WIDTH, &dw_size_hints, font);
    XSetStandardProperties(display, lwin->xwin, app_name, app_name,
        None, argv, argc, &dw_size_hints);
    hex_dump(dump_file, lwin, argv[1]);
    cleanup_resources(lwin, font);
    exit(0);
}   /* main */
```

After checking the command line for the filename, **main()** opens the dump file in read-only mode. Next, functions from *screen.c* are used to initialize the screen/display and load the requested font. Currently, *xdump* is designed to use a specific font. You could, however, easily modify *xdump* to use any (fixed) font specified as a command line option.

Next, **initialize_window_structures()** is called to initialize critical window structures from the text window module, *simplewin.c*. Before the logical window is initialized, the size hints argument is initialized to prevent resizing, which doesn't make sense with this application. Ultimately, the logical window is created/initialized using the window ID **lwin**, defined at the top of **main()** as a local variable:

```
    logical_window_frame lwindow, *lwin = &lwindow;
```

When the application finishes, **cleanup_resources()** calls clean-up functions from the text window module and deallocates local X structures as well:

```
/*
cleanup_resources() performs an orderly clean-up.
*/

void cleanup_resources(lwin, font)
logical_window_frame *lwin;
XFontStruct *font;
{
```

```
    cleanup_window_structures();
    cleanup_window(lwin);
    XUnloadFont(display, font->fid);
    XCloseDisplay(display);
}   /* cleanup_resources */
```

Next, consider the event loop, which is implemented in **hex_dump()**:

```
/*
hex_dump() manages the initial exposure, events, etc.
*/

void hex_dump(dump_file, dump_win, filename)
FILE *dump_file;
logical_window_frame *dump_win;
char *filename;
{
    char header[NUM_COLUMNS + 1];
    char next_page[NUM_ROWS - 2][NUM_COLUMNS + 1];
    int eof = FALSE, stop = FALSE;
    XEvent event;

    strcpy(header, "xdump:  ");
    strncat(header, filename, NUM_COLUMNS - 9);
    eof = build_next_page(dump_file, next_page);
    activate_window(dump_win, "");
    while (!stop) {
        XNextEvent(display, &event);
        switch (event.type) {
            case Expose:
                window_go_cr(dump_win, 1, 0);
                window_display_header(dump_win, header);
                window_go_cr(dump_win, 0, 1);
                display_next_page(dump_win, next_page, eof);
                break;
            case ButtonPress:
                if (!eof && event.xbutton.button == Button1) {
                    eof = build_next_page(dump_file, next_page);
                    display_next_page(dump_win, next_page, eof);
                }
                if (event.xbutton.button == Button3)
                    stop = TRUE;
                break;
        }
    }
    deactivate_window(dump_win);
}   /* hex_dump */
```

hex_dump() first builds a title for the top status line. Note that there is no reason to pass the header to **activate_window()**; it should be displayed upon each window exposure.

Once the event loop begins, the application must respond to exposures and button-press events. For exposure events, the text window module provides the tools for handling the top status line—**window_display_header()** from *simplewin.c* can be used to update the window header dynamically. The bottom status line must be handled within the application; we've elected to update it during page-display operations.

A page of output is displayed upon each exposure and after each **<click-left>** operation. Note that paging is performed in two stages: (1) build the next page, then (2) display that page. The current page is stored in an internal buffer, **next_page**. The first page is built using **build_next_page()** before entering the event loop; subsequent pages are built in response to a **<click-left>** operation. The two-stage approach makes it easy to update the dump window upon exposures without having to reread the file.

Building each page is straightforward. Rather than reading successive 16-byte segments, we simply process the file as a byte stream. Hence, for each row of the new page, 16 bytes must be read from the file into an array, formatted for output, and then copied to the proper row in the new page. **build_next_page()** performs these operations:

```
/*
build_next_page() builds a page of formatted output.
*/

int build_next_page(dump_file, next_page)
FILE *dump_file;
char next_page[][NUM_COLUMNS + 1];
{
    static int count = 0, last = NUM_ROWS - 2;
    int ch, i, last_page = FALSE, row;
    char char_buffer[16];

    for (row = 0; !last_page && row < last; row++) {
        for (i = 0; i < 16; i++) {                 /* read file */
            if ((ch = getc(dump_file)) == EOF) {
                while (i < 16)
                    char_buffer[i++] = EOS;      /* pad buffer */
                last_page = TRUE;
                fclose(dump_file);
                break;
            }
            char_buffer[i] = (char) ch; /* just copy next byte */
        }
        strcpy(next_page[row], build_next_line(char_buffer, count));
        count++;
    }
    for ( ; last_page && row < last; row++)
        next_page[row][0] = EOS;
    return last_page;
}   /* build_next_page */
```

build_next_page() calls **build_next_line()** to format the next row of output. The formatting operations aren't very interesting so we won't discuss them here; see Appendix E.

Each page will have the same number of rows of output, except possibly the last page. For simplicity, if an end-of-file condition occurs in the "middle" of the last page, we simply fill the remainder of the current row with null characters and the remaining rows with null strings.

Once a page has been built, **display_next_page()** can display it as many times as necessary (once for each exposure):

```
/*
display_next_page() clears the window and dumps the next page
from the file.  In particular, it manages overall file read
operations and builds 16-byte buffers/chunks of raw data for
processing by build_next_line().  If the last chunk is less
that 16 bytes, it must be padded with 0s.
*/

int display_next_page(dump_win, next_page, last_page)
logical_window_frame *dump_win;
char next_page[][NUM_COLUMNS + 1];
int last_page;
{
    int last = NUM_ROWS - 2, row;

    window_go_cr(dump_win, 0, 1);
    window_clr_rest(dump_win);
    for (row = 0; row < last; row++) {
        window_go_cr(dump_win, 1, row + 1);
        window_puts(dump_win, next_page[row], gc);
    }
    window_cursor_bottom(dump_win);
    if (!last_page) {
        window_reverse_row(dump_win);
        window_puts_center(dump_win,
            " <ClickLeft> for next page -- <ClickRight> to quit...",
            rgc);
    }
    else {
        window_clr_eol(dump_win);
        window_reverse_row(dump_win);
        window_puts_center(dump_win,
            " <ClickRight> to finish...", rgc);
    }
    return last_page;
}   /* display_next_page */
```

display_next_page() doesn't evaluate the exposed region; it simply displays/redisplays the current page as requested by **hex_dump()**. As an exercise, you may want to add the statements necessary to update just that portion of the window affected by an exposure.

In retrospect, we believe that the readability of *xdump.c* is enhanced considerably by the use of functions and data structures from our higher-level modules. If we had used **XMapRaised()**, **XUnmapWindow()**, **XCreateSimpleWindow()**, **XDrawImageString()**, or performed cursor movement directly with Xlib functions, the surface-level complexity of the application would be considerably greater. More importantly, we have a set of modules that we can build upon in the next chapter.

The complete source code for *xdump.c* is given in Appendix E.

6

Self-contained Event Loops in a High-level Module

In this chapter we take the idea of high-level interfaces one step farther. In this case, we develop a more specialized module that incorporates a self-contained event loop. We demonstrate this idea in the first half of the chapter with a simple dialog box module, where the user's input is limited to button responses. Later, we extend the functionality of the dialog box by adding support for string input.

In both cases, the high-level, logical window (dialog box) requires data structures *and* functionality not provided by the text windows of *simplewin.c*. We add these capabilities by developing additional, higher-level modules that depend on *simplewin.c* for low-level functionality. In the OO world, this technique is called *programming by difference*, or *subclassing*. We are using a traditional language, C, to build/extend our window hierarchy.

6.1 Implementing a Simple Button-only Dialog Box

A high-level module such as *simplewin.c*, by definition, imposes certain restrictions on the application programmer. For example, a window of type **logical_window_frame** designates exactly which types of events that it will receive. We could have designed *simplewin.c* such that the list (mask) of relevant event types must be specified as an argument. Eventually, however, we must accept certain restrictions in any *specialized* module—if the design is wrong, restrictions become impositions.

The modules that we develop in this chapter have restrictions, by design. Our first dialog box's primary restriction is that it doesn't support keyboard input from the user. With the button-only form of input our dialog box is useful in a variety of situations that call for simple general-information messages and simple interrogations in a pop-up window.

Our dialog box module does support a certain amount of generalization, or adaptation. Specifically, the module user (application programmer) can control the number of buttons, the button names, and the button value. For the programmer's convenience, each button can have an application-specific integer value associated with it; this value is returned when its button is selected/pressed. This module, like many UNIX and C programs, makes certain assumptions about the range of values that can be used for button values (positive only); it uses values outside this range to signal special events. The interface file *dialog.h* describes these conditions.

6.1.1 Button Data Structures

Our dialog box module, *dialog.c*, is designed so that, in the application, a programmer can specify the buttons for the dialog box by defining a simple, null-terminated button array, for example:

```
static button buttons[] = {
     {"Button One", 1},
     {"Button Two", 2},
     {"Button Three", 3},
     {NULL, NULL},
};
```

For each button in the dialog box there are several pieces of information that must be maintained, including, for example, the x-y coordinates of the button within the dialog box window. We want these secondary button components to remain hidden from the application programmer; thus, we should use a two-stage, or nested, definition for the button components.

The interface file, *dialog.h*, defines the **button** structure as follows:

```
typedef struct {
     char *label;
     int value;
} button;
```

It provides the *application-oriented* view of buttons. **button** is used in conjunction with a second structure, **lbutton**, that brings together all button-related information:

```
typedef struct {
     Window bid;
     Window parent;
     char *label;
     int value;          /* value returned when a button selected */
     int x, y;           /* relative to parent */
     unsigned int width, height;
} lbutton;
```

Specifically, **lbutton** redundantly defines the information from **button**, plus other items of information such as the button ID (bid), the parent window for the button, in this case, the dialog box window, and so on.

The redundant definitions for each button label and button value may seem wasteful, but keep in mind that each button is defined within the application. Thus, it's a good idea to make a copy of the data from each **button** structure within the corresponding **lbutton** structure—the latter is defined privately. With this approach, the dialog box is protected from accidental changes made to the button data.

Note that, for our purposes, it is sufficient to define both button structures, along with various **#define** constants and the public function declarations in the interface file for the module, *dialog.h*. In a commercial setting you would probably prefer to separate this information into two header files; see Appendix F.

6.1.2 Allocating and Deallocating a Dialog Box

dialog.c, like *simplewin.c*, provides one function for initializing a dialog box's button structures and another for releasing them. **make_dialog_buttons()** attaches the list of buttons to an existing window of type **logical_window_frame**, as described in the following comment:

```
/*
make_dialog_buttons() attaches a set of buttons to an existing
window derived from logical_window_frame; see simplewin.[ch].
Buttons are specified with the "button" structure; see dialog.h.
Buttons are spaced evenly in the dialog box, and button labels
are centered in equal-sized buttons.  All button-related internal
structures are allocated from the heap and attached to the
"extension" pointer in logical_window_frame.
*/

int make_dialog_buttons(lwin, buttons)
logical_window_frame *lwin;
button *buttons;
{
    int btn_x, btn_y, i, len, num_btn, most_chars;
    unsigned btn_width, btn_height;
    lbutton *btn_win;

    for (most_chars = num_btn = 0; buttons[num_btn].label;
            num_btn++)
        if ((len = strlen(buttons[num_btn].label)) > most_chars)
            most_chars = len;
    btn_win = (lbutton *)
        malloc((unsigned) ((num_btn + 1) * sizeof(lbutton)));
    if (btn_win == NULL)
        return FALSE;
    lwin->extension = (lbutton *) btn_win; /* attach to window */
    btn_y = lwin->height - lwin->font_height -
        lwin->font->max_bounds.descent - (BUTTON_BORDER_WIDTH * 5);
    btn_height = lwin->font_height +
```

```
        lwin->font->max_bounds.descent;
    btn_width = lwin->font_width * most_chars;
    for (i = 0; i < num_btn; i++) {
        btn_x = (lwin->width / (num_btn * 2)) -
            (btn_width / 2) + (i * (lwin->width / num_btn));
        btn_win[i].bid = XCreateSimpleWindow(display, lwin->xwin,
            btn_x, btn_y, btn_width, btn_height,
            BUTTON_BORDER_WIDTH,
            BlackPixel(display, screen),
            WhitePixel(display, screen));
        XDefineCursor(display, btn_win[i].bid, popup_cursor);
        XSelectInput(display, btn_win[i].bid, ExposureMask |
            EnterWindowMask | LeaveWindowMask |
            ButtonReleaseMask | ButtonPressMask |
            OwnerGrabButtonMask);
        if (!allocate_and_center_button_text(&btn_win[i], &buttons[i],
                most_chars)) {
            free(btn_win);
            for ( ; --i >= 0; )
                free(btn_win[i].label);
            return FALSE;
        }
        btn_win[i].value = buttons[i].value;
        btn_win[i].parent = lwin->xwin;
        btn_win[i].x = btn_x;
        btn_win[i].y = btn_y;
        btn_win[i].width = btn_width;
        btn_win[i].height = btn_height;
    }   /* for */
    btn_win[i].bid = EOB;    /* logically terminate  */
                             /* the set of buttons   */
    XMapSubwindows(display, lwin->xwin);
    return TRUE;
}   /* make_dialog_buttons */
```

The first argument to **make_dialog_buttons()** is a logical window handle. After determining the number of buttons for the dialog box, **make_dialog_buttons()** allocates an array of buttons from the heap and attaches this array to the **extension** field of the logical window that implements the dialog box.

During the process of determining the number of buttons, **make_dialog_buttons()** also records the length of the longest button label. With this information, **make_dialog_buttons()** can then determine the x-y coordinates of each button. This information is in turn used to allocate windows for the buttons; the buttons are child windows of the dialog box window, **lwin**. In addition, the button (window) must be set up to receive the proper events, and a cursor must be defined for each button.

Lastly, each button's data must be collected for the logical button data structure, including the label text, and modified so that it can be centered within the button window. The latter operation is handled by the following function:

```
/*
allocate_and_center_button_text() creates private (safe)
copies of the client's button text strings.
*/

static int allocate_and_center_button_text(btn_win,
    btn_data, max_len)
lbutton *btn_win;
button *btn_data;
int max_len;
{
    int j, pad_len;

    j = strlen(btn_data->label);         /* center each button */
    pad_len = (max_len - j) / 2;
    btn_win->label = (char *) malloc((unsigned) (j + pad_len + 1));
    if (btn_win->label == NULL)
        return FALSE;
    for ( ; j > -1; j--)
        btn_win->label[j + pad_len] = btn_data->label[j];
    for (j = 0; j < pad_len; j++)
        btn_win->label[j] = ' ';
    return TRUE;
}   /* allocate_and_center_button_text */
```

As mentioned previously, private storage is allocated for each label; we don't want to depend on the continued existence of the array of **button** data structures in the application.

When the application no longer needs the dialog box, **cleanup_dialog_button_structures**() should be called to free the dynamic storage and the X-related structures used by the buttons:

```
/*
cleanup_dialog_button_structures() first frees the heap space
used for labels, and then frees the heap-based array.
*/

void cleanup_dialog_button_structures(lwin)
logical_window_frame *lwin;
{
    int i;
    lbutton *btn_win = (lbutton *) lwin->extension;

    if (btn_win == NULL)
        return;
    for (i = 0; btn_win[i].bid != EOB; i++)
        free(btn_win[i].label);
    free(lwin->extension);
    XDestroySubwindows(display, lwin->xwin);
}   /* cleanup_dialog_button_structures */
```

It's clear from our discussion so far that we've taken only one of several possible approaches to "merging" our logical text window and dialog box modules. In particular, we've designed them as parallel, cooperating modules. As an alternative, we could have encapsulated the logical text window within the dialog box, so that the application programmer would be unaware of the existence of the **lwin** entity. We have in fact used this type of nesting, or composition, in the previous chapters. One of our tasks, however, is to point out various alternatives to designing cooperating modules; consequently, we are deviating somewhat from our previous proposal for hierarchically organized modules. As an exercise, you may want to modify *dialog.c* such that the dialog box is a higher level structure, encapsulating the logical text window structure.

6.1.3 Adding a Self-contained Event Loop

With a few minor additions for completeness, we could close the *dialog.c* module at this point. In this chapter, however, our main objective is to point out that typically there are a variety of options for building even higher levels of functionality into a module. The ways in which you can design higher level modules varies greatly, depending on the intended applications.

For brevity, we can illustrate this idea by adding a self-contained event loop to *dialog.c*. For the application programmer, this design offers the advantage of more power—a larger percentage of the operational duties associated with the dialog box are off-loaded onto the module. Consequently, this approach reduces the possibility for errors in the application and minimizes the "reinvent the wheel" phenomenon that would otherwise exist in each application requiring a dialog box.

The event loop is implemented in **dialog_loop()**:

```
/*
dialog_loop() loops over the input and returns the
value associated with the activated button.
*/

int dialog_loop(lwin, header, message)
logical_window_frame *lwin;
char *header, *message;
{
    lbutton *btn_win = (lbutton *) lwin->extension;
    XEvent event;
    int i;

    if (btn_win == NULL)
        return FALSE;
    activate_window(lwin, "");
    while (TRUE) {
        XNextEvent(display, &event);
        switch (event.type) {
            case Expose:
                while (XCheckTypedWindowEvent(display, lwin->xwin,
                        Expose, &event))
                    ;
```

```
                if (event.xexpose.window == lwin->xwin) {
                    window_display_header(lwin, header);
                    window_go_cr(lwin, 1, 2);
                    window_puts(lwin, message, gc);
                    display_buttons(lwin, gc);
                }
                break;
            case EnterNotify:
                for (i = 0; btn_win[i].bid != EOB; i++)
                    if (event.xcrossing.window == btn_win[i].bid) {
                        highlight_button(&btn_win[i]);
                        break;
                    }
                break;
            case LeaveNotify:
                for (i = 0; btn_win[i].bid != EOB; i++)
                    if (event.xcrossing.window == btn_win[i].bid) {
                        unhighlight_button(&btn_win[i]);
                        break;
                    }
                break;
            case ButtonRelease:
                for (i = 0; btn_win[i].bid != EOB; i++) {
                    if (event.xbutton.window == btn_win[i].bid) {
                        unhighlight_button(&btn_win[i]);
                        deactivate_window(lwin);
                        return btn_win[i].value;
                    }
                }
                break;
        }
    }
}   /* dialog_loop */
```

Note that the exposure-handling section of the event loop must redisplay the dialog box header, the optional message, and the text for each button. The latter operation is handled by **display_buttons()**:

```
/*
display_buttons() is a public routine used by display_loop()
to display the buttons' text.  X displays the buttons' borders.
*/

void display_buttons(lwin, gc)
logical_window_frame *lwin;
GC gc;
{
    int i;
    lbutton *btn_win = (lbutton *) lwin->extension;

    if (btn_win == NULL)
```

```
        return;
    for (i = 0; btn_win[i].bid != EOB; i++)
        XDrawImageString(display, btn_win[i].bid, gc,
            0, lwin->font_height - 1, btn_win[i].label,
            strlen(btn_win[i].label));
}   /* display_buttons */
```

This function is public, because we want this module to remain fairly "open" for use by additional higher-level modules, as illustrated in the second half of this chapter.

Consider the other events monitored by the dialog box. If the user's mouse pointer enters a button, the dialog box should acknowledge this event by highlighting that button:

```
/*
highlight_buttons() is a public routine that draws a one
pixel wide rectangle on the inside of the window.
*/

void highlight_button(bw)
lbutton *bw;
{
    XDrawRectangle(display, bw->bid, hgc, 0, 0,
        bw->width - 1, bw->height - 1);
}   /* highlight_button */
```

We use a simple method for highlighting a button; specifically, the dialog box draws a thin rectangle inside the window border that forms the button outline. Highlighting and unhighlighting are really quite easy. Because we made the GCs public for the logical text window, we can use them here as well; in this case, we use **hgc**, a GC that is designed especially for highlighting operations. (If you are unclear regarding the design of complementary GCs for tasks such as highlighting and unhighlighting, see one of the X programmer references such as Nye [1988] or Jones [1989].)

When a leave-window (leave-button) event occurs, the dialog box must remove/reverse the highlighting:

```
/*
unhighlight_button() is a public routine that erases the
one pixel wide rectangle inside the button border.
*/

void unhighlight_button(bw)
lbutton *bw;
{
    XDrawRectangle(display, bw->bid, hgc, 0, 0,
        bw->width - 1, bw->height - 1);
}   /* unhighlight_button */
```

The final event of interest in **dialog_loop()** is a (mouse) button-release within a dialog box button. If this event occurs, we unhighlight the selected button, deactivate the dialog box, terminate the event loop, and return the value associated with the selected button.

6.1.4 The Dialog Box in Operation

Appendix F also includes a short test program for the dialog box module, which we won't present here. It produces the dialog box shown in Figure 6.1.

A short excerpt from the test program illustrates that a small amount of application code is sufficient for operating the dialog box:

```
...
static button buttons[] = {
    {"Button One", 1},
    {"Button Two", 2},
    {"Button Three", 3},
    {NULL, NULL},
};
logical_window_frame lwindow, *lwin = &lwindow;
...
...
button_result = dialog_loop(lwin,
    "This is the test window.",
    "Press a button.");
fprintf(stdout, "You pressed button: %d\n", button_result);
...
```

As discussed earlier, we could achieve additional power by encapsulating the text window within the dialog box. As it stands, the application must create the text window and the buttons, before using **dialog_loop()**.

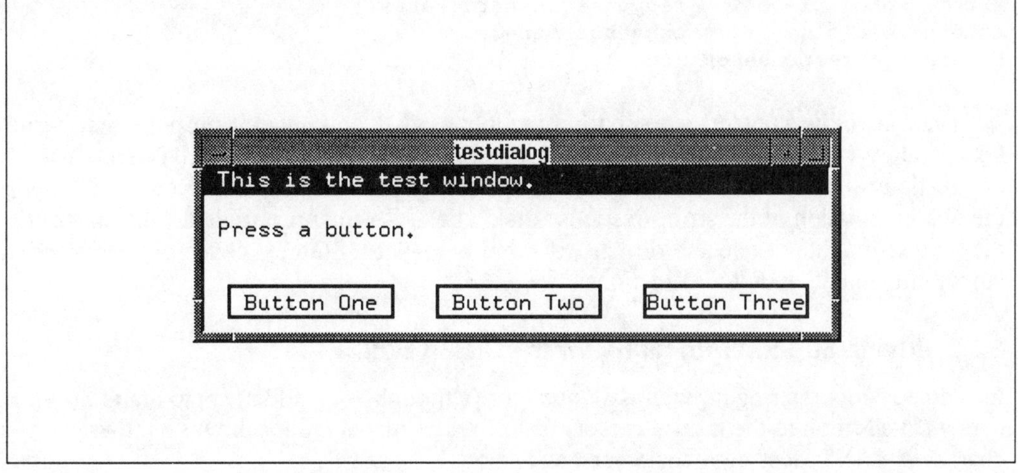

Figure 6.1 A Simple Button-oriented Dialog Box

6.2 Implementing a Dialog Box that Supports String Responses

As currently designed, **logical_window_frame** does not support string input. The *simplewin.c* module is sufficiently flexible that we can add those capabilities, as required, in other modules. We could build a read-write extension to *simplewin.c* that supports character- and string-oriented user responses. In all likelihood, we would want to add various forms of self-contained event loops to increase the power of the module, and add other capabilities as well. In fact, we have a module of this type that we've used in non-toolkit, commercial software products.

The type of generalized module that we've just described is too lengthy to meet the space requirements of this book, considering that object-oriented toolkit programming is our primary objective. If you're familiar with the X toolkits, you're aware by this point that these preliminary chapters serve a dual role, providing (1) an argument for the utility of high-level interfaces for Xlib programming, and (2) a taste or appreciation for the behind-the-scenes data structures and operations that the X toolkits employ in order to present a high-level interface to various GUI components.

In this section we illustrate the fundamentals of supporting string input in a text window in an application-specific manner—by superimposing string-input capabilities on the dialog box module. More general and more complete support for string input would be handled similarly.

6.2.1 *response.h*: The Interface File

The interface to this dialog box module, *response.h*, defines three public functions that parallel their counterparts from *dialog.h*:

```
/*
Functions:
*/

extern void initialize_responsebox_structures();
extern void cleanup_responsebox_structures();
extern int responsebox_loop();
```

There are quite a few private support functions as well. In a general-purpose, read-write, text window module many of the private functions would be made available for use by applications and higher level modules. In this case, however, they exist solely to support the implementation of the string-response dialog box. It is inappropriate for the user of the dialog box module to execute directly, or even be aware of the existence of, string input, cursor movement, and other functions.

6.2.2 Private Support Functions for the Dialog Box

In order to support string input, it is a good idea (although not mandatory) to maintain a text cursor (in addition to the mouse cursor) that provides visual feedback while the user types characters, backspaces over characters, and so on.

For this demonstration module we use a very simple technique for displaying and moving the text cursor. Specifically, we define two small pixmaps, one contains the text cursor image, the other records the image that the text cursor overlays. The first pixmap can be copied to the dialog box window as a prompt for the next character. The text cursor can then be "moved" by (1) redisplaying the "before" pixels as stored in the "save-point" pixmap, and (2) copying the text cursor pixmap to a new location in the dialog box window. We need two private pixmaps for this purpose:

```
/*
Globals:
*/

static Pixmap point, save_point;
```

We create each pixmap for the text cursor, or "point," with **make_point()**:

```
/*
make_point() makes a window point/cursor
that can be used for keyboard processing.
*/

static void make_point()
{
    if (display_depth == 1) {
        point = XCreateBitmapFromData(display,
            RootWindow(display, screen),
            point_bits, point_width, point_height);
        save_point = XCreateBitmapFromData(display,
            RootWindow(display, screen), savepoint_bits,
            savepoint_width, savepoint_height);
    }
    else {
        point = XCreatePixmapFromBitmapData(display,
            RootWindow(display, screen),
            point_bits, point_width, point_height,
            BlackPixel(display, screen), WhitePixel(display, screen),
            display_depth);
        save_point = XCreatePixmapFromBitmapData(display,
            RootWindow(display, screen), savepoint_bits,
            savepoint_width, savepoint_height,
            BlackPixel(display, screen), WhitePixel(display, screen),
            display_depth);
    }
}   /* make_point */
```

Two additional functions are required to display and "un-display" the text cursor during cursor movement operations:

```
static void window_no_point(lwin)
logical_window_frame *lwin;
{
    XCopyArea(display, save_point, lwin->xwin, gc, 0, 0,
```

```
        point_width, point_height, lwin->cursor_x - 2,
        lwin->cursor_y + 2);
}    /* window_no_point */


static void window_put_point(lwin)
logical_window_frame *lwin;
{
    XCopyArea(display, lwin->xwin, save_point, gc,
        lwin->cursor_x - 2, lwin->cursor_y + 2,
        point_width, point_height, 0, 0);
    XCopyArea(display, point, lwin->xwin, gc, 0, 0,
        point_width, point_height, lwin->cursor_x - 2,
        lwin->cursor_y + 2);
}    /* window_put_point */
```

Given these functions, we can define a high-level routine for displaying a string with a text cursor, for example, a dialog box prompt:

```
/*
window_puts_point() prints a string, followed by the point,
in a window w/o interpreting each character.
*/

static void window_puts_point(lwin, str, gc)
logical_window_frame *lwin;
char *str;
GC gc;          /* allow normal or reverse video */
{
    int text_width;

    window_puts(lwin, str, gc);
    text_width = XTextWidth(lwin->font, str, strlen(str));
    lwin->cursor_x += text_width;
    window_go_xy(lwin, lwin->cursor_x, lwin->cursor_y);
    window_put_point(lwin);
}   /* window_puts_point */
```

Note that we can *reuse* functions from *simplewin.c*; thus, we only need to add text cursor-related functionality at this point.

For the complementary string operation, namely, reading a user's (string) response to a prompt, we must design a function that collects the characters typed by the user and builds a string. The first consideration is that the user should be allowed to terminate the input sequence abnormally—characters are entered via the keyboard, so termination should be supported by the keyboard. We'll use the **<Esc>** key for this operation; you may want to generalize this module so that it supports an application-supplied, or even a user-supplied, "escape" key. Because the dialog box also supports buttons, the string-input function must be designed to respond to button events as well. It's clear that our function must implement its own (private) event loop.

Another issue that we must address is the set of legitimate characters. For this module, we'll adopt the policy that printable ASCII characters are acceptable, and also that input will be terminated immediately if an unprintable character is typed.

The final design consideration is maximum string length. It's best not to place any limit on string length—let the application programmer take care of this issue, including the storage allocation for the string. It is, however, important to make sure that the number of characters typed by the user doesn't exceed the application-specified maximum string length.

Consider the following implementation:

```
/*
window_gets_filter() reads a string from a window, up to some maximum
limit, as long as printable ASCII characters are entered.  If <Esc>
is pressed, it returns FALSE.
*/

static int window_gets_filter(lwin, str, limit, header, message)
logical_window_frame *lwin;
char *str;
int limit; /* the max. number of chars. that can be read. */
char *header;
char *message
{
    lbutton *btn_win = (lbutton *) lwin->extension;
    XEvent event;
    KeySym keysym;
    char ch, *temp, *start;
    int i, j, row, col;

    temp = start = str;
    for (i = 0, row = r_pos(lwin), col = c_pos(lwin), limit--;
            i < limit; ) {
        XNextEvent(display, &event);
        switch (event.type) {
            case Expose:
                while (XCheckTypedWindowEvent(display,
                        lwin->xwin, Expose, &event))
                    ;
                if (event.xexpose.window == lwin->xwin) {
                    *str = EOS;
                    window_display_header(lwin, header);
                    window_go_cr(lwin, 1, 2);
                    window_clr_eol(lwin);
                    window_puts(lwin, message, gc);
                    window_go_cr(lwin, col, row);
                    window_puts_point(lwin, str, gc);
                    display_buttons(lwin, gc);
                }
                break;
            case ButtonPress:
```

```
                break;
            case ButtonRelease:
                if (btn_win == NULL) {
                    *start = EOS;
                    return FALSE;
                }
                else {
                    *str = EOS;
                    for (j = 0; btn_win[j].bid != EOB; j++)
                        if (event.xbutton.window == btn_win[j].bid)
                            return btn_win[j].value;
                }
                break;
            case KeyPress:
                ch = (char) window_getche(lwin, &event, &keysym);
                if (keysym == XK_Escape) {
                    *start = EOS;       /* return a null string */
                    return FALSE;
                }
                else if (keysym == XK_BackSpace ||
                        keysym == XK_Delete) {
                    if (str > temp) {
                        str--;
                        i--;
                        backspace_char(lwin);
                    }
                }
                else if (keysym == XK_Return) {
                    *str = EOS;
                    return TRUE;
                }
                else if (keysym >= XK_space &&
                        keysym <= XK_asciitilde) {
                    *str = ch;
                    str++;
                    i++;
                }   /* end if-then-else */
                break;
            default:
                break;
        }   /* end switch */
    }   /* end for loop */
    if (i == limit)     /* reached limit, terminate string */
        *str = EOS;
    return TRUE;
}   /* window_gets_filter */
```

The percentage of the dialog box window that actually contains text will typically be quite small. Therefore, in the event of an exposure, the dialog box header, message, button labels, and the text entered prior to the exposure, are all redisplayed.

If either a button is selected or the **<Enter>** key is pressed, the string is terminated with a null character and the function returns **TRUE**. In the case of the former event, the button value is returned instead. If **<Esc>** is pressed, **window_gets_filter()** returns **FALSE**.

Low-level keyboard processing, including reading characters and backspacing, is handled by secondary functions. Their definitions are straightforward, and secondary to our interest here, so we refer you to Appendix F.

6.2.3 Public Dialog Box Functions for String- and Mouse-based Input

To create and activate a string-response version of the dialog box, the application programmer must invoke the three functions described in this section, in lieu of their counterparts from the button-only version.

The first function is **initialize_responsebox_structures()**:

```
/*
initialize_responsebox_structures() sets up the
data structures needed to support the response box
in a window.
*/

void initialize_responsebox_structures(font)
XFontStruct *font;
{
    initialize_window_structures(font);
    make_point();
}   /* initialize_responsebox_structures */
```

It handles data structure initialization for both the dialog box window and for the pixmaps that store text cursor-related data. The second function, **cleanup_responsebox_structures()**, frees these structures:

```
/*
cleanup_responsebox_structures() frees dynamic
data structures.
*/

void cleanup_responsebox_structures()
{
    cleanup_window_structures();
    XFreePixmap(display, point);
    XFreePixmap(display, save_point);
}   /* cleanup_responsebox_structures */
```

The most important function, **responsebox_loop()**, provides a high-level interface to the dialog box, merging button- and keyboard-related operations:

```
/*
responsebox_loop() processed key and button input.
```

```
It returns the value associated with the selected button.
*/

int responsebox_loop(lwin, header, message, response)
logical_window_frame *lwin;
char *header, *message, *response;
{
    lbutton *btn_win = (lbutton *) lwin->extension;
    XEvent event;
    int btn_result = FALSE, key_result = FALSE;
    int i, terminate = FALSE;

    activate_window(lwin, "");
    while (!terminate) {
        XNextEvent(display, &event);
        switch (event.type) {
            case Expose:
                while (XCheckTypedWindowEvent(display, lwin->xwin,
                        Expose, &event))
                    ;
                if (event.xexpose.window == lwin->xwin) {
                    window_display_header(lwin, header);
                    window_go_cr(lwin, 1, 2);
                    window_clr_eol(lwin);
                    window_puts_point(lwin, message, gc);
                    *response = EOS;
                    display_buttons(lwin, gc);
                }
                break;
            case KeyPress:
                XPutBackEvent(display, &event);
                key_result =
                    window_gets_filter(lwin, response, MAX_STR,
                        header, message);
                terminate = TRUE;
                break;
            case EnterNotify:
                if (btn_win == NULL)
                    break;
                for (i = 0; btn_win[i].bid != EOB; i++)
                    if (event.xcrossing.window == btn_win[i].bid) {
                        highlight_button(&btn_win[i]);
                        break;
                    }
                break;
            case LeaveNotify:
                if (btn_win == NULL)
                    break;
                for (i = 0; btn_win[i].bid != EOB; i++)
                    if (event.xcrossing.window == btn_win[i].bid) {
                        unhighlight_button(&btn_win[i]);
```

```
                        break;
                    }
                break;
            case ButtonRelease:
                if (btn_win == NULL)
                    break;
                for (i = 0; btn_win[i].bid != EOB; i++) {
                    if (event.xbutton.window == btn_win[i].bid) {
                        unhighlight_button(&btn_win[i]);
                        btn_result = btn_win[i].value;
                        terminate = TRUE;
                    }
                }
                break;
        }   /* switch */
    }   /* while */
    deactivate_window(lwin);
    if (btn_result)
        return btn_result;
    else
        return (!key_result) ? ESC_KEY : key_result;
}   /* responsebox_loop */
```

Overall, it is very similar to **dialog_loop()**. In terms of its return value, it makes a distinction between keyboard- and button-initiated deactivation of the dialog box. If the user pressed a button, it returns the associated value; if the user pressed **<Esc>**, it returns **ESC_KEY**; otherwise, it returns **TRUE**. You may prefer to make a distinction between a button value of 1 and the traditional use of 1 (or a non-zero value) to indicate that a function operated without error; however, for most applications this issue would not be significant.

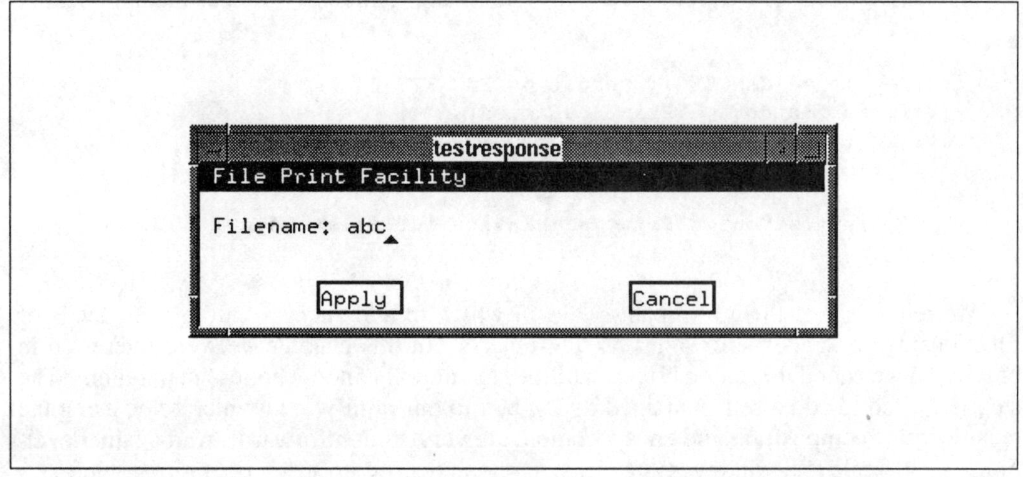

Figure 6.2 A Simple String-oriented Dialog Box

Note that this function manages high-level event processing for the dialog box; as part of this operation it branches to **window_gets_filter()**, if necessary, which uses a lower level event loop to build the user's string response.

6.2.4 The String-response Dialog Box in Operation

The appearance of this version of the dialog box is similar to that of the button-only dialog box, except for the text for the user's response; see Figure 6.2.

A test program is given in Appendix F that is not presented here. We can look at an excerpt from that program in order to illustrate a point about how the application programmer can use the return values. Specifically, if it is important to distinguish between termination of the dialog box by the **<Esc>** key and by a special "cancel" button, you can do so simply by adding the "cancel" button and testing for its value:

```
...
#define APPLY       1                   /* button responses */
#define CANCEL      2
...
...
    static button buttons[] = {         /* positive values only */
        {"Apply", APPLY},
        {"Cancel", CANCEL},
        {NULL, NULL},
    };
    ...
    result = responsebox_loop(lwin, "File Print Facility",
        "Filename: ", filename);
    ...
```

In this case, we want the application to support a "cancel" button, but we don't need to distinguish between the two return values—either value simply terminates the application:

```
    ...
    if (result == CANCEL || result == ESC_KEY)
        fprintf(stdout, "Print canceled.\n");
    else if (!strlen(filename))
        fprintf(stdout, "Invalid filename; print canceled.\n");
    else
        fprintf(stdout, "Print simulation for file: %s\n", filename);
    ...
```

We reiterate that there are many ways in which to add successively higher levels of functionality to windows, or other pseudo-objects. In this chapter we were interested in brevity, so we added the dialog box capabilities to our text window boxes "in parallel." The steps required to add a self-contained dialog box to our mini-window hierarchy, using the techniques of composition and encapsulation, are very straightforward. And again, developing a full-scale text window system that supports read-write string operations is left as a medium-scale exercise for the reader.

7

Callback Functions and Composition in a High-level Module

In this chapter we address two basic techniques of software construction that allow us to enhance the power and reusability of a module. Primarily, we're interested in the enhancements that these techniques can offer the simpler designs of previous chapters. Thus, we will continue to build on the dialog box example. It should be clear that the techniques of this and previous chapters can be applied to a broad class of programming tasks.

First, we demonstrate how to provide support for callback functions in Xlib pseudo-objects, for example, a dialog box from Chapter 6. In comparison to associating an integer value with a dialog box button, which must be interrogated directly by the application, callback functions impose an additional level of structure on the applications—they enhance functional abstraction.

This chapter concludes our formal discussion of Xlib programming. On occasion, however, we will use Xlib primitives in our investigation of Xt, especially when we address widget programming. Starting with Chapter 8, we'll be looking at Xt's support for high-level programming—its interface to Xlib. It's appropriate that we conclude our discussion of Xlib with another example of how composition can be used to reduce the complexity of interface to a module. Specifically, we build a higher level dialog box that completely encapsulates the lower-level text window and dialog box discussed in Chapters 4 through 7.

7.1 Adding Callback Function Support to a Dialog Box

With the dialog box design that we used in Chapter 6, the application can employ a dialog box, specifically, its buttons, to interrogate the user and make run-time decisions. With respect to application functionality, the dialog box introduced in this section provides exactly the same capabilities.

Why, then, should we introduce a more sophisticated (more complicated) design? Callback function support is important because, in most cases, and if properly used, it can reduce the surface complexity of the application. With the simpler dialog box design, which returns the integer associated with the selected button, the application programmer must interject decision-structure code to test the return values from the dialog box event loop, for example, a cluster of if-then-else code, a **switch-case** structure, or whatever. In addition, the programmer must link the decision-making code to the source code that implements the operations associated with each dialog box button.

With callback function support, the amount of decision making code is often reduced. Specifically, the application programmer can simply supply a function that implements or initiates the operations that are associated with each dialog box button. In most cases, a significant portion of the burden for decision-making is off-loaded from the application to the dialog box module. Once the module is developed, each programmer can simply *use* the module's built-in decision-making capabilities, instead of having to re-write and debug them for each application. In general, this approach leads to cleaner application designs.

There is another more important reason for supporting callback functions: uniformity across applications. Without support for callback functions, applications are likely to differ greatly in how they handle the user's response to a dialog box. This variability in the applications has significance for readability. As programmers move from one application to another, they must invest a significant amount of time studying each application's approach to handling user responses to a dialog box button.

Callback functions add a measure of consistency to each application—an additional degree of structure. In this case, the programmer can simply look for the question posed by a dialog box, and then study the action taken by the callback function that's associated with each button.

7.1.1 Callback Function Data Structures

Registering callback functions with buttons is an alternative to registering integers. Therefore, it is inappropriate to provide this support on top of our previous dialog box modules; Appendix G provides complete replacements for (alternatives to) the simpler dialog box modules given in Appendix F. In this and subsequent sections we discuss only those aspects of the button-only and string-response dialog boxes that differ from our previous design.

The header file *cbdialog.h* provides a **typedef** for a "pointer to a function/procedure returning **void**:"

```
typedef void (*ptr_void_proc)();
```

Some programmers prefer the use of a **typedef** such as this one because it enhances the abstraction, and readability, of the application, and in our case, the high-level module.

The **button** data structure must be changed to allow the user to register, or associate, the label-callback function pair with each button:

```
typedef struct {
    char *label;
    ptr_void_proc callback;
} button;
```

lbutton must be changed in a similar manner:

```
typedef struct {
    Window bid;
    Window parent;
    char *label;
    ptr_void_proc callback; /* (ptr. to) procedure to    */
                            /* execute upon selection    */
    int x, y;               /* relative to parent */
    unsigned int width, height;
} lbutton;
```

7.1.2 Callback Functions in Button-only Dialog Boxes

Actually, the changes required to implement callback function support are quite minor; see *cbdialog.c* in Appendix G for the complete source code. Having discussed the non-callback function versions extensively in Chapter 6, in this chapter we can limit our discussion to the relevant code segments. First, consider **make_dialog_buttons()**. It's identical to the Chapter 6 version of **make_dialog_buttons()**, except for the assignment statement that establishes the association between the application-supplied callback function and the logical button data structure:

```
    btn_win[i].callback = *buttons[i].callback;
```

Specifically, we must dereference the callback function component of the **button** data structure to get the stored value, which is the address of the application-supplied callback function.

Next, we must modify **dialog_loop()** so that the callback function is invoked:

```
    ...
    case ButtonRelease:
        for (i = 0; btn_win[i].bid != EOB; i++) {
            if (event.xbutton.window == btn_win[i].bid) {
                unhighlight_button(&btn_win[i]);
                deactivate_window(lwin);
                if (*btn_win[i].callback == NULL)
                    return FALSE;
                else {
                    (*btn_win[i].callback)();
                    return TRUE;
                }
```

```
            }
        }
        break;
    ...
```

Note that we must accommodate applications that don't need the callback function capabilities, and therefore have registered **NULL**-valued pointers. If this condition occurs, we simply return **FALSE**. Otherwise, **dialog_loop()** dereferences the callback function pointer and executes the function at that address:

```
(*btn_win[i].callback)();
```

7.1.3 Callback Functions in String-response Dialog Boxes

Again, support for callback functions can be accomplished with minor modifications to the string-response dialog box module from Chapter 6. This section outlines the required changes.

First, for convenience and readability the interface file *cbrespbox.h* defines several constants that are useful in communicating and interpreting the return value from **responsebox_loop()**:

```
#define NO_KEY_NO_BUTTON    -1
#define KEY_RESPONSE        -2
#define ESC_KEY             -3
```

(The header file provides an interpretation of these constants for the application programmer.)

In the implementation file, *cbrespbox.c*, changes are limited to two functions: Near the beginning of **responsebox_loop()** two local variables are initialized that assist in distinguishing among an **<Esc>**-key user response; a normal keyboard termination, for example, using **<Enter>**; and a button response. A third local variable, **callback**, is initialized as well; it's used in storing the callback function address, if any:

```
int btn_result = FALSE, key_result = FALSE;
ptr_void_proc callback = NULL;
```

In the event loop section where key-press events are processed, **key_result** records the **<Esc>**-key versus **<Enter>**-key distinction:

```
...
case KeyPress:
    XPutBackEvent(display, &event);
    key_result = window_gets_filter(lwin, response,
        MAX_STR, &callback, header, message);
    deactivate_window(lwin);
    key_result = (key_result) ? KEY_RESPONSE : ESC_KEY;
    terminate = TRUE;
    break;
...
```

Note that the callback function pointer variable must be passed to **window_gets_filter()**; see below.

Next, in the event loop section where button-release events are processed, we set the value for **callback**:

```
...
case ButtonRelease:
    if (btn_win == NULL)
        break;
    for (i = 0; btn_win[i].bid != EOB; i++) {
        if (event.xbutton.window == btn_win[i].bid) {
            unhighlight_button(&btn_win[i]);
            deactivate_window(lwin);
            callback = *btn_win[i].callback;
            terminate = btn_result = TRUE;
        }
    }
    break;
...
```

Lastly, if it exists, we execute the callback function, immediately before returning the value that encodes the type of action that occurred:

```
    ...
    if (callback != NULL)              /* execute the callback */
        (*callback)();
    return (btn_result) ? btn_result : key_result;
}   /* responsebox_loop */
```

The application can test the return value to decide how to proceed. Specifically, if

responsebox_loop() returns:	interpretation:
KEY_RESPONSE	normal response — the string has been null-terminated
ESC_KEY	user pressed **<Esc>** key
otherwise	user pressed a button w/o entering text

A return value of **KEY_RESPONSE** means that you can safely use the string response, although it may have a length of zero. That is, the user pressed either **<Enter>** or a button after text entry.

Note that, based on this scheme, the significance of a selected button *must* be detected from within the callback functions. Also, a button-associated callback function will be executed only if a button is selected. If the user first types text and then presses **<Enter>**, **responsebox_loop()** simply returns **KEY_RESPONSE** with a null-terminated string.

The function that builds the string response must be modified to return the address of the callback function, if the user presses a dialog box button:

```
int window_gets_filter(lwin, str, limit, callback, header, message)
logical_window_frame *lwin;
char *str;
int limit; /* the max. number of chars. that can be read. */
ptr_void_proc *callback;
char *header;
char *message;
{
    ...
    case ButtonRelease:
        if (btn_win == NULL) {
            *start = EOS;
            return FALSE;
        }
        else {
            *str = EOS;
            for (j = 0; btn_win[j].bid != EOB; j++)
                if (event.xbutton.window == btn_win[j].bid) {
                    *callback = *btn_win[j].callback;
                    return TRUE;
                }
        }
        break;
    ...
```

7.1.4 The String-response Dialog Box in Operation

The appearance of the dialog box is, of course, unchanged by the provision for callback functions; see Figure 7.1 for a sample dialog box based on the test application from Appendix G.

Suppose that we define the following buttons and host window:

```
    static button buttons[] = {
        {"South of France", cb_france},
        {"North Pole", cb_arctic},
        {"Early Retirement", cb_retire},
        {NULL, NULL},
    };
    logical_window_frame lwindow, *lwin = &lwindow;
```

In this example, the callback functions **cb_france()**, **cb_artic()**, and **cb_retire()** are registered with three buttons in the dialog box. Each callback function is given a definition in the application, for example:

```
/*
Mission Impossible callbacks.
*/
```

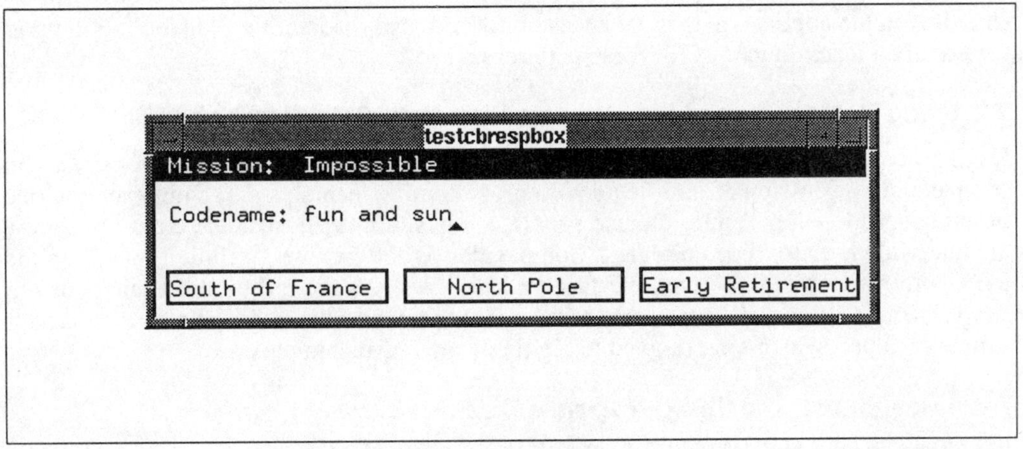

Figure 7.1 A Callback-based Dialog Box

```
void cb_france()
{
    if (strcmp(codename, "fun and sun") != 0) {
        fprintf(stdout,
            "Invalid codename -- mission canceled.\n");
        return;
    }
    fprintf(stdout,
    "As always, if you're discovered, we'll deny everything.\n");
}   /* cb_france */
```

If the user selects the button associated with **cb_france()**, the dialog box (specifically, **responsebox_loop()**) will *call back* to the application and execute this function.

In addition, the application can test the return value for keyboard- versus button-related conditions, if necessary:

```
    ...
    result = responsebox_loop(lwin, "Mission:  Impossible",
        "Codename: ", codename);
    if (result == ESC_KEY)
        fprintf(stdout, "Mission canceled.\n");
    else
        /* ignore other non-button-initiated activities */;
    ...
```

It's true that we haven't eliminated the need in some circumstances for decision structures in the application. In particular, we want the application to be able to take special steps for special circumstances. It should be clear, however, that this approach does reduce the amount of decision-making code in the application, *and* in addition, imposes a form of structure on the application that enhances uniformity and readability. The toolkits support the use of callback functions for these very reasons.

7.2 Using Composition to Encapsulate High-level Data Structures

Having investigated the mechanism of using and supporting callback functions, we can complete our discussion of high-level Xlib programming techniques by implementing one of our suggestions in Chapter 6—use simple composition to encapsulate the text window module with a dialog box module. Composition is the primary technique used by the toolkits to provide a high-level interface to Xlib—widgets are the toolkit analogs of our simple Xlib modules. Widgets are, of course, considerably more sophisticated that our simple modules, which are designed to highlight specific techniques.

7.2.1 Response: The String-response Data Structure

In order to create a higher level dialog box, we need a simple data structure that will insulate the application programmer from lower level data structures such as **logical_window_frame**. Also, we should make it convenient for the user to allocate and free each pseudo-object. Consider the following data type:

```
typedef struct {
    void *self;
    logical_window_frame lwindow;
} _Response, *Response;
```

_Response is a (private) data type used by the implementation file *response.c*. For the user of this module, we define **Response**, a pointer to a variable of type **_Response**. That is, **Response** is an opaque handle that gives the application programmer the *illusion* that he or she is defining an "object," instead of working with a pointer. In this version we've included a self-referential pointer in the structure that is used by the implementation module to assist in clean-up operations.

7.2.2 *response.c*: A Three-function Interface to the Dialog Box

Operationally, we need to provide a high-level interface to *cbrespbox.c*. Consider **response_create()**:

```
/*
response_create() creates and returns a pointer to a response box.
Multiple response boxes can be created; in this implementation,
they share the same font.
*/


Response response_create(row_width, row_height, border_width,
    buttons, app_name, font, argv, argc)
unsigned int row_width, row_height, border_width;
button *buttons;
char *app_name;
XFontStruct *font;
char *argv[];
```

```
int argc;
{
    static int common_structures_already_freed = FALSE;
    XSizeHints size_hints;
    Response response;

    response = (Response) malloc(sizeof(_Response));
    if (response == NULL) {
        fprintf(stderr, "%s: can't allocate response box.\n",
            app_name);
        return NULL;
    }
    if (!common_structures_already_created) {
        common_structures_already_created = TRUE;
        initialize_responsebox_structures(font);
    }
    size_hints.min_width = row_width * font->max_bounds.width;
    size_hints.min_height = row_height *
        (font->max_bounds.ascent + font->max_bounds.descent);
    make_window(RootWindow(display, screen), &response->lwindow, 0, 0,
        row_width, row_height, border_width, &size_hints, font);
    XSetStandardProperties(display, response->lwindow.xwin,
        app_name, app_name, None, argv, argc, &size_hints);
    if (!make_dialog_buttons(&response->lwindow, buttons)) {
        fprintf(stderr, "%s: can't create window buttons!\n",
            app_name);
        return NULL;
    }
    response->self = response;          /* self-reference pointer   */
    return (Response) response->self;   /* for free() operations    */
}   /* response_create */
```

This function takes care of the details that we had to account for in the previous dialog box applications, namely, allocating the text window for the dialog box, creating and attaching the buttons, and so on. The text window's address is stored in the **_Response** record, allocated from the heap with **malloc()**. Note that the text window's handle must be passed to both **make_window()** and **make_dialog_buttons()**.

Lastly, after the dialog box's principal structures have been initialized, it records the address of the dynamically allocated record; that is, it sets a pointer to itself. This address is then returned so that the application can initialize the dialog box handle (in order to distinguish among different dialog boxes).

Next, we must provide a function for invoking the dialog box:

```
/*
Operationally, response_loop() is the same as responsebox_loop()
from the lower level module; it is provided for consistency
of protocol.
*/

int response_loop(response, title, prompt, response_return_string)
```

```
Response response;
char *title, *prompt, *response_return_string;
{
    return responsebox_loop(&response->lwindow, title,
        prompt, response_return_string);
}   /* response_loop */
```

responsebox_loop() already provides the functionality that we need. It's important, however, to provide **response_loop()** as a "wrapper" around **responsebox_loop()**, in order to maintain consistency in our function names for this module—every function name in *response.c* begins with "response_...".

The third and last function is a high-level function that performs storage deallocation for the application:

```
/*
response_cleanup() frees response box structures.
*/

void response_cleanup(response)
Response response;
{
    static int common_structures_already_freed = FALSE;

    cleanup_dialog_button_structures(&response->lwindow);
    if (!common_structures_already_freed) {
        common_structures_already_freed = TRUE;
        cleanup_responsebox_structures();
    }
    cleanup_window(&response->lwindow);
    free(response->self);
}   /* response_cleanup */
```

It's important to note that the first argument to each function is a dialog box handle of type **Response**, except for **response_create()**, which returns a **Response** "object." Because we've used a **typedef** to create an opaque dialog box handle, the application programmer is unaware of the pointer manipulation. In this sense, the application programmer can view **Response** as a dialog box "class."

7.2.3 Using the Response Class in an Application

To create a dialog box of type **Response**, a programmer must first define the buttons—the button labels and their callback functions:

```
    static button respbox_btns[] = {
        {"Apply", print_response},
        {"Cancel", print_cancel},
        {NULL, NULL},
    };
```

Next, IDs are needed for each dialog box:

```
Response respbox1, respbox2;
```

The application must invoke **response_create()** for each dialog box using the proper ID:

```
respbox1 = response_create(53, 7, 1, respbox_btns,
    application_name, font, argv, argc);
respbox2 = response_create(53, 7, 1, respbox_btns,
    application_name, font, argv, argc);
```

Next, **response_loop()** activates the dialog box:

```
result1 = response_loop(respbox1, "Response Box 1",
    "What is your first name: ", first_name);
```

For a graceful termination, the application should free the storage used by each object:

```
response_cleanup(respbox1);
response_cleanup(respbox2);
```

It's important to point out that in most cases it would be inappropriate for the dialog box module to take on the responsibility of performing other initialization operations, for example, having it load fonts. Typically, it's best for the application to handle these more general operations so that resources can be shared.

Figure 7.2 illustrates both dialog boxes from this test program.

7.2.4 Xlib Modules versus Toolkits

We've accomplished our primary objective, illustrating how high-level interfaces to Xlib can be used to enhance readability, power, reusability, and so on. In addition, with our simple Xlib pseudo-objects, we've introduced several of the most important programming concepts employed by the toolkits, which we turn to next.

For example, consider our final module, *response.c*. It promotes pseudo-object classes, in this case, the **Response** class. This "class" is built on top of (depends on) other modules, as are toolkit widget classes. With the *response.c* module we can create, use, and destroy objects, somewhat as we would with widgets in a toolkit application. For example, compare the following two code segments:

```
Widget dialogBox;
...
dialogBox = XtCreateManagedWidget("dialogBox",
    dialogWidgetClass, topLevel, NULL, 0);

Response respbox;
...
respbox = response_create(53, 7, 1, respbox_btns,
    application_name, font, argv, argc);
```

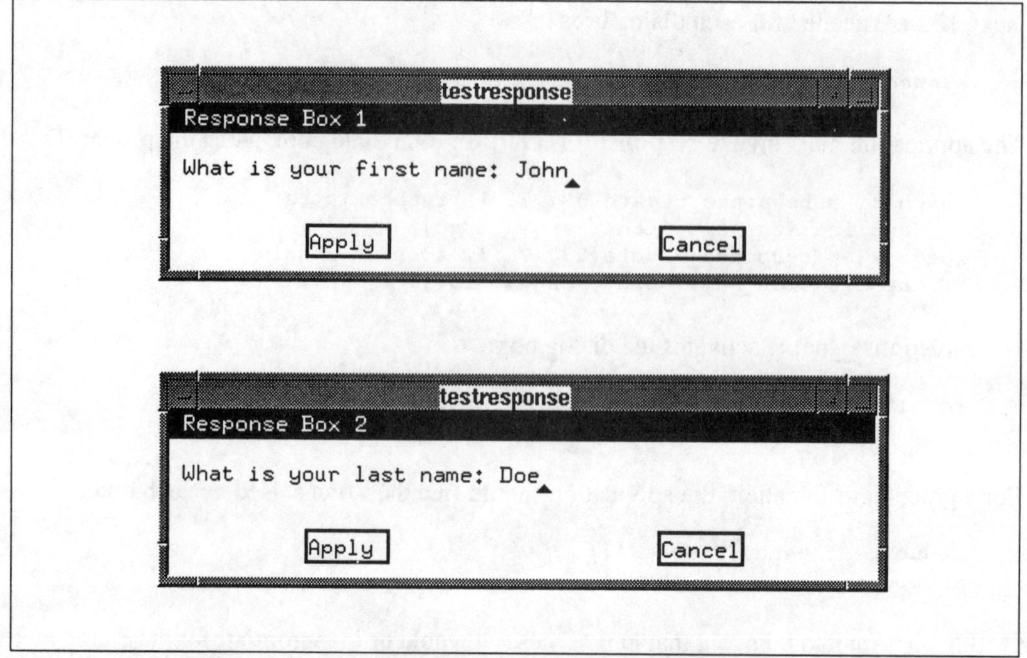

Figure 7.2 Response-based Dialog Boxes

Despite their similarities, these two examples belie the true difference between Xlib and Xt programming. For all the pseudo-classes that we create with Xlib, say, a window hierarchy of read-only and read-write text windows, dialog boxes, and so on, we must make design decisions regarding simple issues such as function and variable naming conventions, as well as more important issues that have downstream effects on reusability. An Xlib programmer confronts the same design decisions again and again. More importantly, the applications that use these modules will reflect the design inconsistencies that arise within one programmer's work, as well as other programmers' work.

A widget programmer, on the other hand, has the support of a carefully designed system of toolkit intrinsics, along with a foundation of widget classes. Although the widget programmer does have to design widget-specific functions that handle widget initialization and provide basic widget functionality, the programmer doesn't have to create interfaces for *common* operations, for example, **XtCreateManagedWidget()** and **XtDestroyWidget()**.

The toolkits provide much more than standard protocols for generic widget operations. The built-in support for resource processing and the facility for inheriting functionality from foundation classes minimize the programming effort required to design and implement a new widget class.

It's easy for the novice widget programmer to criticize various aspects of the widget class concept, especially with respect to the library-level support, as opposed to C++'s compiler-level support, for objects. The learning curve for widget programmers can be steep and painful. Seemingly unexplainable core dumps can be common. But, the widgets orchestrate a massive number of GUI operations. Despite their present immaturity, the toolkits provide the widget programmer with a powerful arsenal that would require a tremendous amount of programming to mimic with Xlib. More importantly, this arsenal is available to any programmer.

For the application programmer, the toolkits guarantee a minimal level of commonality and a high level of built-in functionality. Regardless of the application, or the developer, all Xt applications exhibit common programming landmarks.

8

Overview of Xt Application Programming

Xt is the most readily available, high-level programming interface to the X Window System. For convenience, we use the term *Xt* to refer to both the Xt Intrinsics and the (default) widget set, the Athena widgets. The X Consortium has established a standard for X programming environments that requires both Xlib and Xt.

Toolkit vendors can, of course, extend the Xt Intrinsics in a variety of ways. In addition, alternate widget sets are available. In this book we focus primarily on the standard Xt Intrinsics and the Athena widget set, because both of these are provided as part of the standard distribution and, hence, available to most programmers. In the first three chapters of our material on Xt we use the Athena widget set as a vehicle for discussion. Later, we extend our GUI capabilities by developing a set of widgets that complement the Athena widget set.

Xt is a general-purpose *GUI* toolkit for C programmers. It provides powerful programming capabilities with respect to the development of an application's user interface, or GUI components. It's important to note that Xt's support for object-oriented programming is restricted to the widget-related aspects of an application. The programmer must take responsibility for designing and factoring an application so that various programming components exhibit a high level of readability and are reusable in other applications.

As with Xlib, C source code modules can be used to build high-level pseudo-objects. When programmers first confront Xt, there is a tendency to use widgets directly; for example, using an Athena dialog widget to implement a pop-up dialog box that's used for a specific task in a specific application. In some situations, the direct use of widgets is appropriate; in others, it's best to design a high-level module that implements a pseudo-object (GUI component and its operations) that can be reused across applications. Of course, there are no absolute rules with respect to the best way to use widgets.

In this book we assume a minimal familiarity with Xt, focusing on the OO programming aspects of Xt. As mentioned earlier, the series on the X Window System from O'Reilly & Associates (in particular, Volumes 4 and 5) includes tutorial and reference information on various aspects of Xt such as resources, geometry management, special event handling, and so on, which are outside the focus of this book. Also, Young (1990) provides broad coverage of Xlib and Xt.

In this chapter we build on our discussion of high-level Xlib techniques from Chapters 6 and 7. In particular, our earlier material on self-contained event loops and callback functions provides some insight into the hidden operations provided by the Xt Intrinsics. For continuity, in the examples of the immediately following chapters we continue to use dialog boxes, which are common across all types of GUIs.

8.1 The Xt Application Framework

The Xt Intrinsics provide a framework for applications that extends beyond the encapsulation of data and operations for widgets. In particular, the Intrinsics provide functions for operations that are common across applications. Every X application must perform a host of operations that are related to the basic event-driven philosophy of X (and other GUI programming environments as well). For example, in our earlier Xlib examples one of the first orders of business was the initialization of certain data structures: display, screen, font, and other structures.

For our Xlib programs we developed modules that encapsulated the data structures and operations associated with, say, program start-up. That is, we imposed a higher level of organization on our Xlib applications than required by Xlib—because we wanted to ensure a minimal level of uniformity and reusability across our Xlib applications. In the later chapters on Xlib we introduced additional mechanisms, or conventions, for enhancing uniformity and reusability in the applications, such as self-contained event loops and callback functions.

The X toolkits are designed to provide application programmers with similar high-level programming facilities. Of course, with the toolkits, the high-level programming interface is more complete and more robust, with tools that extend to almost every aspect of GUI programming for X applications. In particular, Xt embraces the X resource concept in a manner that gives the programmer great latitude to fine-tune GUI components for a variety of applications.

A minimal Xt application must (1) create and initialize Xt-related data structures, (2) loop through the events that occur in the windows that comprise the user interface for that application, and (3) provide some mechanism for graceful termination. Strictly speaking the third provision is optional, as evidenced by several of the applications that accompany the standard distribution of X; however, we consider graceful termination a required provision.

Operations (1) and (2) can be handled directly with Xt Intrinsics. **XtInitialize()** performs basic initializations for the display and screen, as well as initializations for behind-the-scenes, Xt-related structures such those associated with the resource database. In addition, **XtInitialize()** is responsible for the operations associated with creation of a default application context and application shell.

The Xt Intrinsics are based on a "master plan" wherein the X windows that comprise an application are organized in a hierarchy (or hierarchies) of instantiated widgets—an Xt application creates high-level widgets (widget class instances) that allocate and manage the low-level windows that comprise the user interface for the application. **XtInitialize()** returns the (ID for the) application shell that serves as the parent of the widget hierarchy that comprises the user interface.

Once the widget hierarchy for an application is known, Xt can make decisions regarding basic dimensions, plus other geometry requests, and create and initialize the low-level windows for each widget, or GUI component. This process is initiated with **XtRealizeWidget()**. Typically, it's sufficient for the application to "realize" the top-level widget in a hierarchy of widget instances. **XtRealizeWidget()** automatically (that is, recursively) realizes each child (widget) of the parent widget. **XtRealizeWidget()** also consults various flags that determine whether or not it should initiate other operations, such as mapping a widget's window.

With Xlib, the programmer is responsible for providing event loops that specify the relevant events, and how to respond to those events, for each window of the application. With Xt, the widgets handle event processing automatically. The programmer can, of course, override default behaviors and supplement widget-related operations via callback functions and actions. In any case, **XtMainLoop()** functions as a top-level event dispatcher. (For more information on event dispatching and OO hierarchical dispatching operations see Smith [1990]).

Thus, a skeleton for a minimal Xt application would include:

```
...
Widget topLevel, quit;
...
topLevel = XtInitialize(...);
...
/*
create a button for a graceful exit:
*/
quit = XtCreateManagedWidget(..., topLevel, ....);
...
XtRealizeWidget(topLevel);
XtMainLoop();
...
```

8.2 Callback Functions in Xt Applications

In Chapter 7 we added support for callback functions to our dialog box example. Our provision for callback functions in Xlib-based modules, although simple, was quite useful—an application-defined function could be associated with any dialog box button. In many cases, this level of support for callback functions is adequate. There are situations, however, where the application programmer needs more control over the management of callback functions.

In providing support for callback functions in Xlib-based modules, such as our dialog box example in Chapter 7, it's sufficient to provide a single mechanism for registering the callback functions. Recall that we defined a **button** data structure with which the application programmer could provide a null-terminated list of button label and callback function (pointer) pairs. In our case, we established the convention that callback functions are defined in the application as **void** functions (functions returning **void**), and then registered with the dialog box through pointers to the callback functions.

With Xt, the support for callback functions is implemented in both the Intrinsics and the widget set(s). That is, the Intrinsics provide several "universal functions" for callback function management, and individual widgets are responsible for implementing callback function behavior.

This shared support for callback functions is achieved by establishing specific rules regarding the data types associated with callback functions, as well as rules regarding how widgets support callback functions. Consider the (return value) data type for callback functions and for their parameters. Xt defines the data type **XtCallbackProc** for specifying the return data type for callback functions. At present, it is a **typedef** for "pointer to a function returning **void**:"

```
typedef void (*XtCallbackProc)(...);
```

This data type is similar to **ptr_void_proc** in Chapter 7.

Xt callback functions should be defined with three parameters:

```
void AnyCallbackFunction(w, client_data, call_data)
Widget w;
caddr_t client_data, call_data;
{
    ...
}
```

The first parameter represents the widget that the callback function is registered with, that is, the widget that will invoke the callback function. The second and third parameters represent data that will be passed to the callback upon invocation by the widget.

Although the Intrinsics provide several functions for callback management, widgets are primarily responsible for establishing, or defining, the role that callback functions play—Xt is widget-oriented. For example, the Athena command widget processes/recognizes two types of callback functions: (1) those that are executed when the command widget is destroyed, and (2) those that are executed when the command widget is selected (notified). Of course, the support for callback functions differs from one widget class to another.

Resources provide the primary means of communication between a widget and an application. When a widget programmer designs a widget class, there must be a mechanism whereby the application programmer can specify various critical values that determine a widget instance's behavior and/or characteristics. For example, a text edit widget class should allow the application programmer to specify the number of rows and columns for the text window.

A widget class is designed such that resources can be used to associate callback functions with a widget (instance). All widget classes inherit the resource **XtNdestroy-Callback**, and its associated operations, so that an application can specify callback functions that are executed as part of a widget's destruction. A widget programmer can define as many different callback-related resources (and operations) as necessary to ensure that the widget class is sufficiently flexible and powerful. For example, the Athena scrollbar widget defines the callback resources **XtNjumpProc** and **XtNscrollProc**, among others.

A basic premise in Xt's support for callback functions is that the application programmer should be allowed to register multiple callback functions for a given "event," such as selecting a command button. (In our dialog box example we supported only one callback function per button.) Support for the registration of multiple callback functions for a particular resource is provided through the data type **XtCallbackList**, which is just a **typedef**:

```
typedef struct _XtCallbackRec *XtCallbackList;
```

where **_XtCallbackRec** is defined as:

```
typedef struct _XtCallbackRec {
    XtCallbackProc callback;
    caddr_t closure;                /* client_data */
} XtCallbackRec;
```

That is, for a given widget, a command button, the application programmer can provide a list of pairs where each pair contains a *pointer to* a callback function and a pointer to application-supplied data that should be passed as the second argument when the callback is executed. (This list should be null-terminated.)

Once the list of callback functions is defined, it can be registered using **XtSetArg()** and **XtSetValues()**:

```
void CBFunc1(), CBFunc2();
...
XtCallbackRec cb_list[] = {
    {(XtCallbackProc) CBFunc1, (caddr_t) NULL},
    {(XtCallbackProc) CBFunc2, (caddr_t) NULL},
    {(XtCallbackProc) NULL, (caddr_t) NULL}
};
...
Arg args[<num_args>];
int i;
...
XtSetArg(args[i], XtN<whatever>Callback, (XtArgVal) cb_list); i++;
...
XtSetValues(<some_widget>, args, i);
```

This code segment registers the callback list **cb_list** with the **XtN<whatever>Callback** resource for the widget **<some_widget>**. Or, you can use the convenience function **XtAddCallbacks()** in lieu of the latter two function calls:

```
XtAddCallbacks(<some_widget>, XtN<whatever>Callback, cb_list);
```

Or, you can register the callback functions with a widget one at a time using **XtAddCallback()**, as we'll illustrate in a subsequent example.

There are other conventions in Xt's support for callback functions. For example, **XtCallbackStatus** is an enumerated type that describes the range of values that can be returned by the predicate **XtHasCallbacks()**, which is used to query the callback list status of a callback resource. A number of other functions, such as **XtCallCallbacks()** and **XtRemoveCallbacks()** are provided as well.

8.3 *simplepopup*: An Xt Application Illustrating Callback Functions

As an example of a complete Xt application that illustrates one of the most common uses of callback functions, consider a simple pop-up window that can be activated (made visible) by pressing a command button. The main application window contains two buttons, one for quitting the application and another for activating the pop-up window, as illustrated in Figure 8.1.a. If we press/select the "Test Popup" button, a secondary window is activated, as illustrated in Figure 8.1.b.

There are several ways to program even this simple application. In this case, we want to avoid using the Athena **Dialog** widget to implement the pop-up window, in order to illustrate a straightforward use of callback functions. For the main window we use an Athena **Box** widget to house the "Quit" and "Test Popup" buttons, and for the secondary window we use an Athena **Form** widget to arrange a label, "Press a Button", above two buttons, "Button 1" and "Button 2".

We supply callback functions for each button, illustrating two different, but common, strategies. In the main window the callback functions implement the operations associated with quitting the application and popping up the secondary window, a different callback function for each button. In the secondary window a single callback function is shared by both buttons. For this simple demonstration, we use the callback functions to print short messages to the standard output file, usually the command window that initiated the application.

Since this is our first complete Xt application, we show the complete source code. As with our Xlib applications, in subsequent examples we focus on program segments, referring the reader to an appendix for the complete source code.

First, each Xt application program must contain the necessary header files that define miscellaneous X and Xt constants and data types:

```
#include <X11/Intrinsic.h>
#include <X11/StringDefs.h>
#include <X11/Shell.h>
```

Also, you must include the (public) header files for each widget class that you use:

```
#ifdef X11R3
#include <X11/Box.h>
#include <X11/Command.h>
#include <X11/Form.h>
```

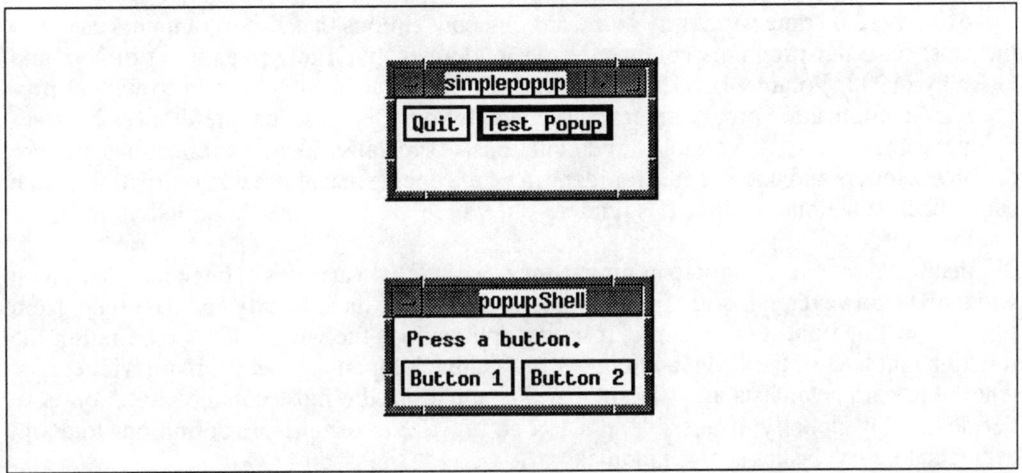

Figure 8.1 Implementing a Dialog Box with an Athena **Dialog** Widget

```
#include <X11/Label.h>
#else
#include <X11/Xaw/Box.h>
#include <X11/Xaw/Command.h>
#include <X11/Xaw/Form.h>
#include <X11/Xaw/Label.h>
#endif
```

In this book, all of our examples have been tested with X11 Release 3 and X11 Release 4. If you have the source code and want to compile one of the programs, no release-related, special steps are necessary for X11 Release 4. If you're using X11 Release 3, you need to define the macro **X11R3** either on the command line or in your makefile:

```
{user prompt} cc ... -DX11R3 ...
```

In either case, no changes are required to the source code.

The last class of header files is the application-specific, non-X-related headers, for this application:

```
#include <stdio.h>
```

In our programs we typically follow the practice of including up-front declarations for all functions in a module, as opposed to arranging functions in any special order so that the declarations can be avoided:

```
void main(), create_main_widgets(), create_popup_widgets();
void ActivatePopup(), DeactivatePopup(), Quit();
```

Also, there is some variability in the naming conventions that X programmers use. For the most part, our programs conform to the guidelines given in Appendix D of Nye and O'Reilly (1990, Volume 4). These conventions, however, mostly pertain to widget programming; application programmers continue to follow their personal preferences in establishing names for local variables and functions. Typically, in our applications we use lowercase letters and underscores for identifiers, except in special X-related situations, such as callback functions, widget IDs, and so on, where we use mixed-case letters in the X tradition.

In most cases, we attempt to minimize the use of global variables in our examples. With widget IDs, however, it is sometimes impractical to define them locally and pass them from function to function. For example, in many applications the widget ID is required in the function that creates the widget *and* in various callback functions that compare widget IDs, where the parameter lists are "fixed." In this situation, the most common solution is to define the IDs globally; if possible, it's a good practice to use private definitions to avoid accidental name clashes across modules.

For *simplepopup* we need the following widgets:

```
static Widget topLevel, buttonBoxMain, buttonPopup, buttonQuit;
static Widget popupShell, popupLabel, popupBox,
    popupButton1, popupButton2;
```

For this application, **main()** calls **XtInitialize()** to process command-line arguments, initialize the resource data base, and so on, and then delegates the creation and arrangement of widgets within windows to other functions:

```
void main(argc, argv)
int argc;
char *argv[];
{
    topLevel = XtInitialize(argv[0], "TestPopup", NULL, 0,
        &argc, argv);
    create_main_widgets();
    create_popup_widgets();
    XtRealizeWidget(topLevel);
    XtMainLoop();
}   /* main */
```

Once the widgets and their parent windows (actually shells) have been created, **XtRealizeWidget()** initiates the behind-the-scenes operations required to create and initialize the various low-level structures, in particular the (X) windows, for each widget.

Lastly, **XtMainLoop()** is called to begin the event processing; it is the main dispatcher. Each widget contains the logic necessary to process the events that it recognizes. In particular, the widget that implements the "Quit" command button recognizes button presses and executes any callback functions associated with button selection, in our case, the **Quit()** callback function.

create_main_widgets() sets up the primary application window:

```
/*
create_main_widgets() sets up the buttonbox, buttons,
and their callbacks.
*/

void create_main_widgets()
{
    Arg args[5];
    int i;

    buttonBoxMain = XtCreateManagedWidget("buttonBoxMain",
        boxWidgetClass, topLevel, NULL, 0);
    i = 0;
    XtSetArg(args[i], XtNlabel, (XtArgVal) "Quit"); i++;
    buttonQuit = XtCreateManagedWidget("buttonQuit",
        commandWidgetClass, buttonBoxMain, args, i);
    XtAddCallback(buttonQuit, XtNcallback, Quit, NULL);
    i = 0;
    XtSetArg(args[i], XtNlabel, (XtArgVal) "Test Popup"); i++;
    buttonPopup = XtCreateManagedWidget("buttonPopup",
        commandWidgetClass, buttonBoxMain, args, i);
    XtAddCallback(buttonPopup, XtNcallback, ActivatePopup, NULL);
}   /* create_main_widgets */
```

A box widget is created first, and then the command (button) widgets are "attached." Resources are used to set the necessary widget characteristics, for example, button labels. Also, **XtAddCallback()** is used to associate a callback function with each command widget. The final argument to **XtAddCallback()** is null, because, for this example, we don't need to pass any application-specific data when a command button is selected.

Again, there are several books that provide basic information on Xt application programming, as cited earlier in this chapter; that information is not duplicated here.

Application programmers differ in their preferences for when, where, and how they set resource values. Some programmers tend to use application resource files to specify things such as button labels. Others prefer to set resource values in the source code. In general, the best approach is determined by the specific application. Here, we assume that readers are familiar with and know the advantages and disadvantages of both approaches; therefore, in this setting we set resource values in the source code. This approach allows us to avoid introducing numerous resource files in the text, as well as in the appendixes. It is, of course, quite trivial to modify our examples to use resource files.

The next task is to create the secondary, pop-up window and its components:

```
/*
create_popup_widgets() sets up the pop-up shell, its buttons,
and their callbacks.
*/

void create_popup_widgets()
{
    Arg args[5];
```

```
    int i;

    popupShell = XtCreatePopupShell("popupShell",
        transientShellWidgetClass, topLevel, NULL, 0);
    popupBox = XtCreateManagedWidget("popupBox",
        formWidgetClass, popupShell, NULL, 0);
    i = 0;
    XtSetArg(args[i], XtNlabel, (XtArgVal) "Press a button."); i++;
    XtSetArg(args[i], XtNborderWidth, (XtArgVal) 0); i++;
    popupLabel = XtCreateManagedWidget("popupLabel",
        labelWidgetClass, popupBox, args, i);
    i = 0;
    XtSetArg(args[i], XtNlabel, (XtArgVal) "Button 1"); i++;
    XtSetArg(args[i], XtNfromVert, (XtArgVal) popupLabel); i++;
    popupButton1 = XtCreateManagedWidget("popupButton1",
        commandWidgetClass, popupBox, args, i);
    XtAddCallback(popupButton1, XtNcallback, DeactivatePopup,
        "application data for button 1");
    i = 0;
    XtSetArg(args[i], XtNlabel, (XtArgVal) "Button 2"); i++;
    XtSetArg(args[i], XtNfromVert, (XtArgVal) popupLabel); i++;
    XtSetArg(args[i], XtNfromHoriz, (XtArgVal) popupButton1); i++;
    popupButton2 = XtCreateManagedWidget("popupButton2",
        commandWidgetClass, popupBox, args, i);
    XtAddCallback(popupButton2, XtNcallback, DeactivatePopup,
        "application data for button 2");
}   /* create_popup_widgets */
```

With Xt, pop-up "windows" are housed in shells that have the capability to interact with the window manager. In most applications, **XtCreatePopupShell()** is used to create a pop-up window shell. Strictly speaking, the shell (widget) and its contents are collectively referred to as the pop-up window. In this book, it's convenient to use the term "window" in the general sense to refer to the window that the user sees on the screen, and in referring to the low-level (X) window that's created behind the scenes to house the widget. In many cases, we depend on context to distinguish these two uses.

A pop-up window as described here is a child of the top-level, or main application, window—with respect to the widget hierarchy. Behind the scenes, the low-level X window associated with the shell widget is a descendant of the root window. This window hierarchy is required in order to allow the pop-up window to appear outside the confines of the main application window. In general, these details are not important here, and only serve to obscure our interest in higher level issues, specifically, application programming with widgets.

In our example **topLevel** is the parent of **popupShell**. Specifically, even though a pop-up window is housed in a shell that can appear outside the confines of the main application window, the pop-up shell is created as an instance of **transient-ShellWidgetClass**, which must have a parent widget. Xt provides other functions for manipulating a pop-up shell, some of which are used in this example's callback functions.

Next, consider the internals of the pop-up window. In this example we use an Athena form widget, specifically, its resources, to organize the position of the label and buttons.

The form widget, **popupBox**, is a child of **popupShell**, and the parent of **popupLabel**, **popupButton1**, and **popupButton2**.

Also, note that we've illustrated the use of application-specific (client) data with callback functions. In this case, when the callbacks are registered with each command button using **XtAddCallback()**, a string is provided as client data. When a command button is selected, (the address of) its client data will be passed as the second argument to the callback function.

Let's consider the callback functions. First, **Quit()**, the callback function associated with the "Quit" button, gracefully terminates the application after printing a comment in the command window:

```
void Quit(w, client_data, call_data)
Widget w;
caddr_t client_data;
caddr_t call_data;
{
    printf("You pressed the Quit button.\n");
    exit(0);
}   /* Quit */
```

Quit() is defined with the three parameters that are required by Xt in all callback functions. In this example, these three parameters are unused; depending on your usage of *lint* and your personal preferences, you may prefer to place the *lint(1)* directive "/*ARGSUSED*/" on the line before the function. We omit them here.

When the user selects the "Test Popup" button, the application must pop up, or activate, the secondary window; this operation is implemented by associating a callback function with that button:

```
void ActivatePopup(w, client_data, call_data)
Widget w;
caddr_t client_data;
caddr_t call_data;
{
    XtPopup(popupShell, XtGrabNone);
}   /* ActivatePopup */
```

In this case, all that's required to map the window to the screen (display) is to call **XtPopup()** with the name of the shell (widget) that houses the composite widget, which in turn houses the label and buttons. The second argument to **XtPopup()** specifies the type of grab that should be imposed, if any. For our high-level uses of pop-up windows, grabs typically are either not necessary or not applicable. With pop-up shells, grabs are typically used to control the behavior of cascading pop-ups, as in a cascading menu system.

In this application we want to remove (unmap) the pop-up window when the user presses either "Button 1" or "Button 2". To do so, we simply register a callback function, common to both command widgets, that invokes **XtPopdown()** against the shell widget:

```
void DeactivatePopup(w, client_data, call_data)
Widget w;
```

```
caddr_t client_data;    /* the application data */
caddr_t call_data;
{
    XtPopdown(popupShell);
    if (w == popupButton1)
        printf(
            "You pressed button 1; its associated data is:\n%s\n",
            client_data);
    else
        printf(
            "You pressed button 2; its associated data is:\n%s\n",
            client_data);
}   /* DeactivatePopup */
```

In order to illustrate the use of client data with callback functions, in **create_popup_widgets()** we registered a string with each callback function. Thus, in **DeactivatePopup()** we examine the first argument to determine which button was selected, and then print a message and the client data, passed as the second argument, in the command window.

simplepopup provides a nontrivial, although simple, application that exhibits many of the features required in more complex Xt applications. In later chapters we provide applications and widgets that further illustrate the use of callback functions.

For consistency between chapters and appendixes, the source code for *simplepopup* is given in Appendix H.

8.4 Actions in Xt Applications

Callback functions allow an application to register operations that should be performed when a particular event occurs, such as a button press/selection. Occasionally, however, an application needs to register an operation with an "event" for which there is no callback resource. The Xt Intrinsics provides a translations-and-actions facility to handle these circumstances. Specifically, the application programmer can set up an action table that associates a "public" action identifier with an action function *in the application*:

```
static void Action1(), Action2();    /* declare the action functions */

static XtActionRec actionTable[] = {
    {"action1", Action1},
    {"action2", Action2}
};
...
[definitions for the action functions]
...
```

The application must also call **XtAddActions()** to register the list of actions—to register the associations between the public identifiers and the action functions.

Given these prescribed actions, either the user, via a resource file, *or* the application, via source code, can set up an association between an event and an action function, for example:

```
*translations:  <Btn1Down>:  action1()
```

This two-stage, or indirect, pairing of events and actions is necessary because resource files contain characters; hence, translations must be accepted in string form, whereas the translations tables used internally by the translation manager must be in a compiled format. In other words, there are in effect two types of translation tables: a string-oriented translation table provided by the user or the application before the application is executed, and an internalized translation table that accompanies each widget.

The translation manager compiles the translation tables specified in resource files and merges the translations with a widget's existing translations, but the application is responsible for parsing and merging translation tables that are provided in the source code.

Actions are important to the widget programmer as well. In particular, they allow a widget class to be designed with default associations between events and operations, for example, a user pressing mouse button 1 and a text edit widget moving the text cursor to the edit buffer position indicated by the mouse cursor. With this design, the user can then supply a resource file that overrides various default mappings.

Note that there are a number of differences between callback functions and actions with respect to issues such as widget class inheritance, parameters, and others that are outside the scope of this book; see one (preferably all) of the books cited at the beginning of this chapter. In our chapters on widget programming we'll use actions in implementing callback resources, that is, in providing for the execution of callback functions by the widget.

8.5 *simpleact*: An Xt Application Illustrating Actions

We can illustrate a straightforward use of actions by rewriting *simplepopup* to use actions in place of selected callback functions. Specifically, for the main application window, the callback functions **Quit()** and **ActivatePopup()** are registered with **buttonQuit** and buttonPopup, respectively, as before. But, for the pop-up window, we can use actions to implement the same behavior as provided by callback functions in our previous example.

First, we must provide an action table in the application, for example:

```
static XtActionsRec button_actions[] = {
    {"buttonaction", ButtonAction},
};
```

For our demonstration program, a table with one entry is adequate; typically, action tables have multiple entries. In this table we make an association between the string "buttonaction" and the function **ButtonAction()**. As mentioned, the string "buttonaction" serves as translation table-interface to the action function.

Given this association, a translation table can specify an event, or series of events, that should signal the execution of the action function. Although we could place the translation table in a resource file, for convenience, we'll hard-code it within the application in the form:

```
static char button_translations[] =
    "#override\n\
    <Btn1Down>,<Btn1Up>:    buttonaction()";
```

Specifically, if the user presses and releases mouse button 1, the action function **ButtonAction()** will be invoked.

The changes to *simplepopup* that are required to implement *simpleact* are handled in the function that creates the pop-up window widgets and in an action function. The pop-up window is created and initialized by **create_widgets_with_actions()**:

```
/*
create_widgets_with_actions() sets up the pop-up shell,
its buttons, and implements their actions.
*/

void create_widgets_with_actions()
{

    static char button_translations[] =
        "#override\n\
        <Btn1Down>,<Btn1Up>:    buttonaction()";
    static XtActionsRec button_actions[] = {
        {"buttonaction", ButtonAction},
    };
    XtTranslations button_trans_table;
    Arg args[5];
    int i;

    XtAddActions(button_actions, XtNumber(button_actions));
    button_trans_table =
        XtParseTranslationTable(button_translations);
    actionShell = XtCreatePopupShell("actionShell",
        transientShellWidgetClass, topLevel, NULL, 0);
    actionBox = XtCreateManagedWidget("actionBox",
        formWidgetClass, actionShell, NULL, 0);
    i = 0;
    XtSetArg(args[i], XtNlabel, (XtArgVal) "Press a button."); i++;
    XtSetArg(args[i], XtNborderWidth, (XtArgVal) 0); i++;
    actionLabel = XtCreateManagedWidget("actionLabel",
        labelWidgetClass, actionBox, args, i);
    i = 0;
    XtSetArg(args[i], XtNlabel, (XtArgVal) "Button 1"); i++;
    XtSetArg(args[i], XtNfromVert, (XtArgVal) actionLabel); i++;
    actionButton1 = XtCreateManagedWidget("actionButton1",
        commandWidgetClass, actionBox, args, i);
    XtOverrideTranslations(actionButton1, button_trans_table);
    i = 0;
    XtSetArg(args[i], XtNlabel, (XtArgVal) "Button 2"); i++;
    XtSetArg(args[i], XtNfromVert, (XtArgVal) actionLabel); i++;
    XtSetArg(args[i], XtNfromHoriz, (XtArgVal) actionButton1); i++;
    actionButton2 = XtCreateManagedWidget("actionButton2",
        commandWidgetClass, actionBox, args, i);
    XtOverrideTranslations(actionButton2, button_trans_table);
}   /* create_widgets_with_actions */
```

There are several statements that are critical to adding the support for actions. First, **XtAddActions()** is called to register the action function and its external identifier:

```
    XtAddActions(button_actions, XtNumber(button_actions));
```

Second, **XtParseTranslationTable()** is called to compile the external, string-oriented translation table into an internal form, specifically, an **XtTranslations** structure:

```
    button_trans_table =
        XtParseTranslationTable(button_translations);
```

Then, the new translations must be installed to override existing command widget translations:

```
    XtOverrideTranslations(actionButton1, button_trans_table);
    ...
    XtOverrideTranslations(actionButton2, button_trans_table);
```

Given these modifications to the behavior of an Athena **Command** widget, a button click operation on mouse button 1 will trigger **ButtonAction()**:

```
void ButtonAction(w, event)
Widget w;
XEvent *event;
{
    XtPopdown(actionShell);
    if (w == actionButton1) {
        printf("You pressed button 1.\n");
        printf("Button 1 resides in the window with id: %ld\n",
            (long) event->xbutton.window);
    }
    else {
        printf("Button 2 resides in the window with id: %ld\n",
            (long) event->xbutton.window);
        printf("You pressed button 2.\n");
    }
}   /* ButtonAction */
```

Within this function we can perform operations similar to those implemented in **DeactivatePopup()** from *simplepopup*. Specifically, we first remove the pop-up window and then print a message(s) in the user's command window. Note, however, that we *cannot* pass application-specific data to an action function, at least not data referenced by the application's source code, as in *simplepopup*.

Actions do support a primitive mechanism of passing data in string form, using two additional arguments/parameters. With this approach the third argument is a pointer to a string that represents a collection of data/arguments and the fourth argument is a count of the number of arguments, much like the **argv** and **argc** arguments passed to a C program during start-up. In a resource file's translation string, these arguments are passed within the parentheses of the external identifier representing the action function, but separated by spaces, not commas.

In general, actions should be used (1) to implement callback capabilities within widgets, as we'll discuss in our chapters on widget programming, and (2) to override or supplement widget behavior. They do not, and were not intended to, provide a true alternative to callback functions in an application. The use of actions in circumstances where the argument-passing capabilities of callback functions are more appropriate, can lead to the overuse of global variables.

The complete source code for *simpleact* is given in Appendix I. Its output is the same as for *simplepopup* in Figure 8.1.

9

Creating High-level Interfaces for Xt Applications

In the chapters on Xlib we illustrated how to create a blocking, pop-up dialog box as part of our broader interest in self-contained, high-level modules that employ callback functions and other techniques. Although Xt provides an extensive, high-level interface to X application programming, is it appropriate to create even higher level modules that insulate the programmer from the intricacies of Xt programming?

In our opinion, there are two broad situations where higher level interfaces are appropriate. First, even though the X toolkits provide a high-level interface to X, they are designed to supply general-purpose interface-building components. Hence, depending on the programming environment, you may still want to design higher level GUI components tailored to a specific application or even a class of applications.

Second, many applications are quite complex, with respect to both their user- and non-user-interface components. With a highly complex application(s), it may be inappropriate to "sprinkle" the application with calls to **XtPopup()**, **XtPopdown()**, **XtMapWidget()**, **XtParseTranslationTable()**, and others. Alternatively, in this situation it may be prudent to factor the application(s) so that higher level abstractions are implemented in self-contained modules.

Of course, different applications or programming environments call for different solutions. In general, the argument for developing higher level modules to handle (1) specialized and (2) complex applications is consistent with basic principles of software construction that encourage programmers to use encapsulation, data and functional abstraction, and so on to maximize readability, portability, and reusability of source code.

For commercial software developers with X-based applications, the presence of multiple, popular toolkits greatly increases the development costs (time) for their products. In many cases, it's possible to isolate toolkit-dependent source code in separate modules as one measure in minimizing the debugging problems and overall costs of porting across X environments.

In this chapter we address these issues with an example of a (small) high-level Xt module. For consistency with the previous chapters, we use a dialog box as the focal GUI component. The idea of designing high-level containment modules for lower level Xt data structures and operations is applicable in many other areas as well, especially very specialized uses of GUI components. For our purposes, however, it's better to focus on a common interface component.

9.1 Designing a Blocking Dialog Box

The pop-up window that we used in Chapter 8 to illustrate callbacks and actions is an example of a nonblocking pop-up. In an application with multiple windows of that type, it's possible to activate one pop-up window and then activate additional pop-ups before deactivating the first pop-up. That is, the first pop-up *does not block* user activity while it's active.

A typical pop-up window is composed of a shell widget that houses a composite widget, which in turn manages several subordinate widgets (such as label and command widgets). Each widget is, in effect, designed to recognize and respond to certain events that occur within its window. Thus, if two pop-up windows are active at the same time, they operate independently. This policy allows us to design applications such as a compiler tool where the user can have multiple secondary windows active at the same time, for setting compiler options, viewing compilation errors, setting *make(1)* options, or editing a source code file.

Occasionally, however, it's necessary for an application to display a pop-up window and block until there's a response from the user—that is, the logic of the application depends on the user's response. There are several approaches to creating a blocking dialog box. For this example, we want a simple implementation that performs consistently from one release of X to another without taking advantage of any "hidden" features of Xt.

There are two issues, or tasks, to consider in creating a blocking dialog box that returns the user's response. First, once the dialog box is activated, we must control the sequence of X events that take place (within the application), in order to capture the user's response. Second, we must control the behavior of the pop-up window with respect to the other windows (widgets) that comprise the application's user interface. That is, once the pop-up window has been activated, other windows (widgets) must be disabled. The first task can be accomplished with several small functions that initiate a secondary event loop and test for the user's response. The second task is easily accomplished with the proper argument to **XtPopup()**.

9.2 *respbox.c*: Overview of the Blocking Dialog Box Module

It's important to have a simple, straightforward interface for this type of pseudo-object—if the application programmer must indirectly understand the details of the blocking mechanism, then the dialog box module has failed to provide the proper level of abstraction. For our design, we'll provide five public functions to the dialog box; the following external declarations are taken from the public header file, *respbox.h*:

```
extern int response_create();
extern void response_cleanup();
extern int response_add_buttons();
extern void response_query();
extern int response_get_result();
```

For consistency, each public function name begins with "response". Operationally, in order to use this module, the application must create and add buttons to a response box in two stages using **response_create()** and **response_add_buttons()**. This approach is consistent with that of the Athena **Dialog** widget. Also, before terminating, the application should invoke **response_cleanup()** to free all dynamic data structures used by the module.

respbox.c provides two public functions for controlling the dialog box: **response_query()** activates the dialog box and **response_get_result()** gets the user's response. Typically, these functions occur back to back in the source code; it would be possible to combine them as one function, reducing the interface. For this implementation, however, we'll use two separate functions to emphasize the two separate tasks that are taking place. As an exercise, you may want to combine them. (We combine these operations in *alert.c* in Chapter 10.)

The implementation file, *respbox.c*, has several private components. First, there is one callback function that is invoked whenever a dialog box button is selected; it's primary function is to deactivate the dialog box and reset critical variables:

```
static void ResponseBox();
```

Next, a private variable is used to ensure that the user does not create multiple dialog boxes. This issue is discussed later.

```
static int response_created = FALSE;     /* explicit init as */
                                         /* reminder         */
```

Next, three private widgets (their IDs) are defined:

```
static Widget responseShell, responseLabel, responseBox;
```

These widgets are referenced by the callback function and by other functions in this module, where it's inappropriate to pass widgets as arguments.

Two private variables are used to control the blocking activity and record the user's response:

```
static int query_result;      /* holds the result of  */
                              /* a response box query */
static int query_wait;        /* controls the blocking        */
                              /* activity of a response box   */
```

Next, one private variable is used as a convenience variable within this module to record the parent of the dialog box:

```
static Widget box_parent;         /* for reference only; used */
                                  /* with XtDisplay(...),     */
                                  /* XtWindow(...), etc.      */
```

Lastly, three private variables are used in managing the button-related dynamic data structure:

```
static int num_buttons = 0;       /* button variables */
static int max_buttons = 0;
static Widget *buttons;
```

(For readability, we don't depend on compiler initializations of global variables.) With this overview of the data structures and functions, let's consider one approach to implementing the two primary tasks outlined in Section 9.1.

9.3 Implementing the Blocking Dialog Box

The application programmer should be allowed to specify the number of buttons for a dialog box—there shouldn't be any arbitrary maximum. In the current module, we'll implement this capability in two stages.

First, when the application creates the dialog box, it must specify the maximum number of buttons as an argument. This information can then be used by the dialog box module to allocate an array from dynamic storage. **response_create()** performs this task in addition to creating the widgets and initializing critical variables:

```
/*
response_create() creates a multi-button response box.
It returns FALSE in the event of an error.
*/

int response_create(parent, max_num_btns)
Widget parent;
int max_num_btns;
{
    Arg args[3];
    int i;

    if (response_created) {      /* currently, supports one box */
        fprintf(stderr, "Response box already exists!\n");
        return FALSE;
    }
    response_created = TRUE;
    box_parent = parent;
    max_buttons = max_num_btns;
    buttons = (Widget *)
        XtMalloc((unsigned) ((max_buttons) * sizeof(Widget *)));
    if (buttons == NULL) {
```

```
        fprintf(stderr, "Can't allocate memory for buttons!\n");
        return FALSE;
    }
    i = 0;
    XtSetArg(args[i], XtNallowShellResize, (XtArgVal) TRUE); i++;
    responseShell = XtCreatePopupShell("responseShell",
        transientShellWidgetClass, parent, args, i);
    responseBox = XtCreateManagedWidget("responseBox",
        formWidgetClass, responseShell, NULL, 0);
    i = 0;
    XtSetArg(args[i], XtNresize, (XtArgVal) TRUE); i++;
    XtSetArg(args[i], XtNborderWidth, (XtArgVal) 0); i++;
    responseLabel = XtCreateManagedWidget("responseLabel",
        labelWidgetClass, responseBox, args, i);
    return TRUE;
}   /* response_create */
```

Many of the operations are similar to those in our examples from Chapter 8. In this case, however, note that we don't allocate any command buttons, or a label. Also, if the dynamic storage for the buttons can't be allocated, **response_create()** returns **FALSE** and prints a diagnostic message.

Buttons are added by the application using a separate function:

```
/*
response_add_button() adds buttons to the response box. It
returns the number of the button added, or FALSE/0 if the
limit is reached.
*/

int response_add_button(name, label)
char *name;
char *label;
{
    Arg args[5];
    int i;

    if (num_buttons == max_buttons) {
        fprintf(stderr,
            "Maximum number of buttons already allocated!\n");
        return FALSE;
    }
    i = 0;
    XtSetArg(args[i], XtNlabel, (XtArgVal) label); i++;
    XtSetArg(args[i], XtNfromVert, (XtArgVal) responseLabel); i++;
    if (num_buttons) {
        XtSetArg(args[i], XtNfromHoriz,
            (XtArgVal) buttons[num_buttons - 1]); i++;
    }
    buttons[num_buttons] = XtCreateManagedWidget(name,
        commandWidgetClass, responseBox, args, i);
    XtAddCallback(buttons[num_buttons], XtNcallback, ResponseBox, NULL);
```

```
    return ++num_buttons;
}   /* response_add_button */
```

If the application attempts to add more buttons than requested during response box creation, **response_add_buttons()** returns **FALSE**, immediately after printing a warning message. Otherwise, the requested button is added to the dialog box in a left-to-right format. The application can specify both a name and a label for each button. The **name** argument is used to specify an external identifier in the resource database for that button instance. Unlike our earlier Xlib examples, there is no provision for specifying an application-specific button value. In this implementation, each button's value is simply its left-to-right position in the dialog box; the leftmost button is button 1.

Lastly, note that the callback function **ResponseBox()** is associated with each command button. It is a general-purpose callback function that's used to deactivate the dialog box when a button is selected. In addition, **ResponseBox()** must determine which button has been selected (record the user's response):

```
/*
ResponseBox() determines which option has been selected
in a dialog window and resets the 'wait' variable; it works
with response_query().
*/
/*ARGSUSED*/
static void ResponseBox(w, client_data, call_data)
Widget w;
caddr_t client_data;
caddr_t call_data;
{
    int i;

    XtPopdown(responseShell);
    for (i = 0; i < num_buttons; i++)
        if (w == buttons[i]) {
            query_result = i + 1;       /* non-zero-based */
            query_wait = FALSE;
            return;
        }
    query_result = FALSE;
    query_wait = FALSE;
}   /* ResponseBox */
```

The last two statements are included as a defensive measure against future tampering. At present, the function will return from within the loop, as soon as it finds the matching command button, records the button number in the private variable **query_result**, and resets a wait variable that's used to control event processing, as described next.

To implement the blocking action we need a mechanism for overriding the normal Xt event processing that's initiated by **XtMainLoop()**. Recall that once **XtMainLoop()** gains control of an application, the individual widgets that comprise the user interface, in effect, take over event processing while the mouse cursor is within their window. Thus, all we have to do is "grab" normal event processing with a secondary loop. **response_get_result()** implements this operation and returns the user's response:

```
/*
response_get_result() is a pop-up window function for waiting
on the user's selection to the yes-no response query.
*/

int response_get_result()
{
    XEvent event;

    query_wait = TRUE;              /* block until the user */
    while (query_wait) {            /* presses a button     */
        XtNextEvent(&event);
        XtDispatchEvent(&event);
    }
    return query_result;
}   /* response_get_result */
```

Unlike the primary loop initiated by **XtMainLoop()**, the secondary event loop is conditional; it's terminated as soon as **query_wait** is reset to **FALSE**.

Recall that **query_wait** is reset by **ResponseBox()**, the callback function that deactivates the dialog box. Thus, **response_get_result()** and **ResponseBox()** work together to (1) initiate the blocking action, (2) terminate the blocking action, and (3) return the user's response.

At this point, we've implemented the mechanics of a blocking dialog box, except for (1) the basic task of activating the dialog box, and (2) coordinating the blocking action of the secondary event loop with the normal event processing of other widgets in the application. **response_query()** performs these tasks:

```
/*
response_query() pops up a dialog window; it works with
ResponseBox().  The response box is positioned at the cursor.
*/

void response_query(message)
char *message;
{
    Arg args[3];
    int i;
    Window dummy_w;
    int root_x, root_y, dummy_xy;
    unsigned int dummy_keys;

    XQueryPointer(XtDisplay(box_parent),
        XtWindow(box_parent), &dummy_w, &dummy_w, &root_x,
        &root_y, &dummy_xy, &dummy_xy, &dummy_keys);
    i = 0;
    XtSetArg(args[i], XtNx, (XtArgVal) (root_x - 20)); i++;
```

```
    XtSetArg(args[i], XtNy, (XtArgVal) (root_y - 20)); i++;
    XtSetValues(responseShell, args, i);
    i = 0;
    XtSetArg(args[i], XtNlabel, (XtArgVal) message); i++;
    XtSetValues(responseLabel, args, i);
    XtPopup(responseShell, XtGrabExclusive);    /* block */
}   /* response_query */
```

Both of the previously mentioned tasks are accomplished in one function call to **XtPopup()**. This function call maps the dialog box and sets its behavior to be consistent with **query_result()**. That is, **query_result()** implements the *dialog box-specific behavior* necessary in order to wait for and record a user's response, while the second argument to **XtPopup()** requests that all events (for this application) be sent to this pop-up window. (If we were to specify **XtGrabNone** here, the dialog box would record the user's response properly, but there would be nothing to prevent the user from selecting some other command button in the application, say, the "Quit" button, while the dialog box was still active.)

In addition to coordinating the blocking behavior, **response_query()** (1) calculates the current position of the mouse cursor, (2) alters characteristics of the dialog box so that it appears at this location, and (3) sets the label, or message, that will be displayed in the dialog box. With this approach to setting the dialog box label, a different message can be displayed each time the dialog box is activated.

9.4 The Blocking Dialog Box in an Application

As a simple test and demonstration of *respbox.c*, we'll use a two-button primary application window, as shown in Figure 9.1.a. The second command button, "Test Buttons...", activates the dialog box, which simply asks whether the user wants to exit the program or cancel the dialog box; see Figure 9.1.b. The dialog box then blocks until the user makes a response. If the user chooses to exit the application, a second user response is solicited to confirm the exit; see Figure 9.1.c.

To program this application we must include the interface file for *respbox.c*:

```
#include "respbox.h"
```

Also, we'll set up two constants to represent button values:

```
#define EXIT_BTN    1           /* button values */
#define CANCEL_BTN  2
```

main() calls **create_main_buttons()** to create the command buttons for the primary application window, as in Chapter 8:

```
/*
main() manages a simple demonstration of a two-button,
blocking response box.
*/

void main(argc, argv)
```

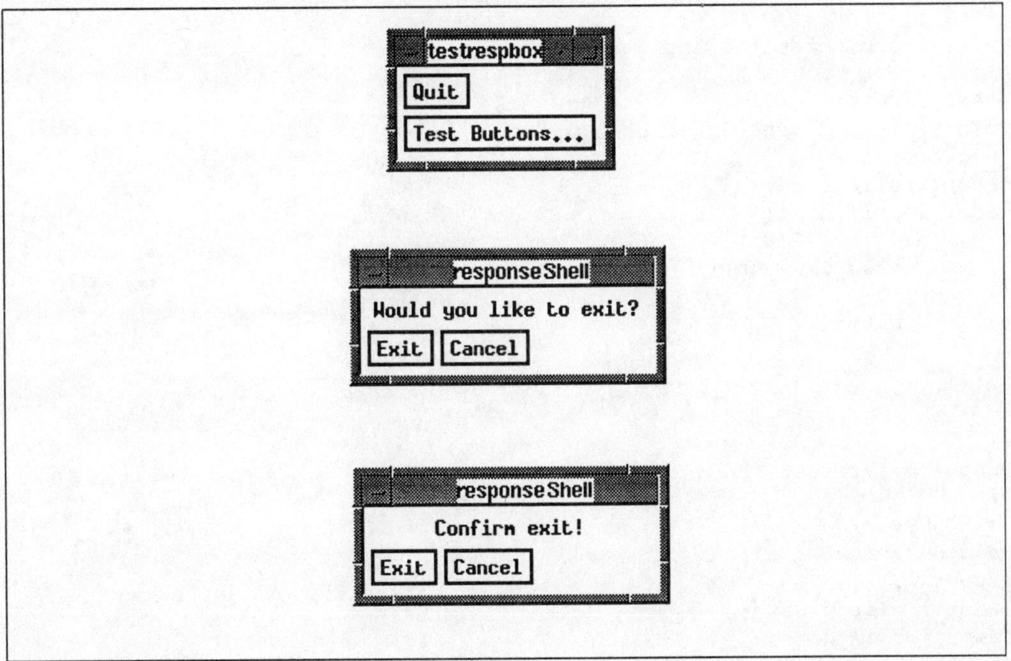

Figure 9.1 A Blocking Pop-up Dialog Box

```
int argc;
char *argv[];
{
    topLevel = XtInitialize(argv[0], "TestResponse", NULL, 0,
        &argc, argv);

    create_main_buttons(topLevel);
    response_create(topLevel, 2);           /* no error checks */
    response_add_button("exitButton", "Exit");
    response_add_button("cancelButton", "Cancel");

    XtRealizeWidget(topLevel);
    XtMainLoop();
}   /* main */
```

In addition, **main()** calls **response_create()** to specify the parent widget in the hierarchy (used during shell creation) and the number of buttons. Then, **response_add_button()** is used to install each command button.

Each command button in the primary window has a callback. **Quit()** terminates application gracefully by calling **response_cleanup()** to free the internal data structures used by the dialog box:

```
/*
Quit() terminates the application.
*/
/*ARGSUSED*/
void Quit(w, client_data, call_data)
Widget w;
caddr_t client_data;
caddr_t call_data;
{
    response_cleanup();
    exit(0);
}   /* Quit */
```

The second callback, **Question()**, exercises the blocking dialog box:

```
/*
Question() raises the question.
*/
/*ARGSUSED*/
void Question(w, client_data, call_data)
Widget w;
caddr_t client_data;
caddr_t call_data;
{
    response_query("Would you like to exit?");
    if (response_get_result() == EXIT_BTN) {
        response_query("Confirm exit!");
        if (response_get_result() == EXIT_BTN) {
            printf("Application terminated.\n");
            response_cleanup();
            exit(0);
        }
        else
            printf("Application NOT terminated.\n");
    }
    else
        printf("Application NOT terminated.\n");
}   /* Question */
```

Question() illustrates that even though *respbox.c* is limited to a single dialog box, it can be invoked as many times as necessary in an application. Now that the dialog box functions have been demonstrated in an application, you may want to refer to **ResponseBox()** and **response_get_result()** to note how the critical variables are used to coordinate (1) retrieval of the user's response to the dialog box, and (2) blocking of other user responses *within the application*. The complete source code for this chapter is given in Appendix J.

9.5 Handling Multiple, Simultaneous Dialog Boxes

Our primary objective in this chapter has been to demonstrate that a high-level module can be useful for the application programmer. Our secondary objective has been to demonstrate the mechanics of designing/implementing a blocking dialog box. In particular, we didn't want to complicate the second objective by adding the additional array processing necessary to support simultaneous, blocking dialog boxes. It should be clear from the current implementation of *respbox.c* that support for multiple dialog boxes is straightforward.

Another reason for not doing so here is that we want to use this chapter to motivate our interest in widget programming, which we address beginning with Chapter 11. From *respbox.c*, it's clear that support for multiple instantiations of a pseudo-object, such as a dialog box, can be handled by setting up a private composite variable (**struct**) for each instance. But this type of encapsulation is exactly what Xt is designed to support through its facilities for widget programming.

In our opinion, if designing a straightforward high-level module can increase the readability, reusability, and/or portability of an application, or class of applications, it's probably a good idea. But if various instance-management issues arise, this is typically a signal that the high-level application module should be redesigned as a widget class.

10

xwaste: An Xt Wastebasket Application

In Chapter 9 we developed a simple high-level module that implemented a blocking dialog box, *respbox.c*. It is representative of high-level modules that are fairly easily developed, yet provide considerable utility across applications. In this chapter we develop a larger application that combines multiple modules, where the individual modules have very little reusability across applications. That is, in developing the individual modules, most of the source code is related to designing the user interface for the current application.

Chapters 9 and 10 reflect two extreme design considerations that arise with many Xt applications. In many cases, given the costs of software development, a programmer wants to maximize the reusability of each module that's being developed. But, in some cases, an application has certain characteristics that require, or tend to encourage, the programmer to focus on the best design for *that* particular software product, all other (potential) applications notwithstanding.

Thus, our primary goal in this chapter is to develop an application where the design goals are different than those of a reusable (application) module, such as a blocking dialog box. At this point in the book it's appropriate to develop a more complete application, in comparison to those of previous chapters, which were designed to address specific issues. A larger application allows us to illustrate a more realistic collection of X and Xt components, such as pixmaps, GCs, fonts, and widgets.

A third objective is to provide the reader with an application that is quite useful on X-based UNIX systems. At the time of this writing, UNIX is enjoying a surge in popularity as part of the rapid increase in engineering workstations with modern GUI capabilities. Accompanying, and possibly because of, this growth in (new) UNIX users, there seems to be a renewed interest in prescriptions for the common *rm(1)* ailment, namely, accidentally deleted files ("rm * .bak").

Over the years there have been a number of public-domain programs that offer support for this malady—too many to list or give credit to their authors here. Many of these programs provide an alternative to *rm(1)* that renames a file instead of actually deleting it, so that the user can retrieve an accidentally deleted file(s). Others simply move "deleted" files to a special directory. Most of these programs provide some mechanism for automated removal of "deleted" files, for example, providing a *cron(8)* daemon that's executed once a day to cleanse the file system.

With the emergence of GUI-based UNIX systems there has been a number of file manager-type utilities with file deletion capabilities. The support for file "un-deletion" in these utilities has been quite varied. The less robust utilities maintain a "deleted" file in a temporary (primary storage-resident) trash bin, or wastebasket. The file deletion capabilities for many of these utilities are not used by long-time UNIX users/programmers, because these individuals do much of their work from the command line and often don't want file manager programs running in the background consuming precious resources.

Our *rm(1)* alternative attempts to strike a balance on several of these issues, in order to provide a file deletion utility that's useful for both programmers and ordinary users.

We begin by looking at several design considerations in order to give you an idea of the major tasks performed by each module. Next, we discuss the development of a command line-based file deletion utility, including the basic design of the wastebasket. After that, we focus on developing a medium-scale, GUI-based wastebasket utility. For the most part, with the latter application we use a top-down analysis of its design and its components.

10.1 *wastebasket*: Design Considerations

X provides modern GUI capabilities for UNIX environments. Even so, if you survey UNIX users who regularly operate under the X Window System, it's apparent that the old-style command window is still quite popular. Despite the increasing number of software products that provide a self-contained user environment, programmers (and others) still use the command line for perusing files and directories, launching applications, system administration, and other activities. In our view, one of the greatest features of X is its dual support for command-line operations and GUI-based applications.

With this in mind, we feel that it's important to provide support for (simple) file recovery that doesn't force the user to operate from the command line or from an icon-based trash bin—the user should be able to choose either approach, depending on the situation at hand. Our *rm(1)* alternative, *wastebasket*, is composed of a pair of cooperating programs named *delete* and *xwaste*. That is, *wastebasket* isn't a program, it's a generic name that we use for convenience in referring to the utilities and file structures that implement our file recovery application.

delete is a command-line utility that removes files, much like *rm(1)* with the interactive option ("rm -i *.bak"). *delete*'s X-based companion, *xwaste*, supports file deletion as well, plus wastebasket browsing, permanent file deletion (from the wastebasket), and file recovery. With this design, you can use *delete* from the command line, even without having *xwaste* running in the background. If you make a file deletion error, you can invoke *xwaste* to browse the wastebasket and recover the file. Or, you can maintain *xwaste* as a background process for mouse-based file deletion and recovery at any time.

Given this outline of *wastebasket*'s method of operation, let's consider several design issues. First, we'll design our file recovery application so that it stores all "deleted" files, regardless of their origin, in a common directory. Although this approach requires a little more work to implement, we've found it to be much tidier than alternatives that store renamed files in the same directory as the deleted file. Thus, the file structures and a class of file deletion operations required to implement the wastebasket utility are common to both *delete* and *xwaste*. Hence, we'll use a single module, *commondel.c* to house both the common data structures and common wastebasket operations, such as testing for an empty wastebasket.

Next, if we use a common wastebasket directory for deleted files arriving from other directories, we must be prepared for name clashes—it's quite likely that a programmer, for example, will have multiple files with the same name, organized by directories. In addition, the use of a common directory implies that we must retain information as to the original location (directory) of a deleted file, in order to carry out a file recovery operation.

In this implementation of *wastebasket* we address these issues by encoding the original directory and filename into the new filename. Specifically, we take advantage of the support for long filenames (on many UNIX systems) by building the new filename from a concatenation of the original directory pathname and filename. UNIX systems that severely restrict the length of filenames will require an alternate technique for recording the original directory path and filename. For example, a separate file could be used to store a record of this information, one file record for each deleted file. This alternative is left as an exercise.

Another major issue is the technique used to eliminate "overflow" of the wastebasket, that is, to prevent unlimited growth. As mentioned, we could use a *cron(8)* daemon to perform this type of operation at periodic intervals, for example, at 3:00 AM each day when (most) systems are relatively inactive. With this type of periodic removal of excess files, there are no inherent limits on the maximum size of the wastebasket. You may or may not prefer a system that imposes limits on wastebasket size. A related concern is whether or not to remove *all* files from the wastebasket, if the wastebasket is "dumped" periodically.

Obviously, there a variety of approaches to handling wastebasket overflow. For this implementation we use a simple approach whereby the wastebasket continually monitors its capacity. Once the wastebasket fills to capacity, with each addition to the wastebasket the oldest file is removed. *Oldest* is defined in terms of when a file is deleted (moved to the wastebasket), *not* by it's creation date. That is, deleted files are "placed" in the top of the wastebasket and, if the wastebasket is full, the file on the bottom of the wastebasket is removed (permanently deleted). Although *wastebasket* has a default capacity, the user can specify an alternate wastebasket size via an environment variable.

Next, consider the user interface. *delete* is a simple command-line utility that expands wildcard file specifications and prompts the user with each matching filename before performing the deletion. *xwaste* allows the user to browse through the wastebasket, recover or permanently delete files, and perform wastebasket file deletion as with *delete*. Figure 10.1 provides an illustration.

The wastebasket browser can be implemented as a scrollable window using an Athena **Viewport** widget. In order to carry out a browser-based operation, the user should be able to (1) click on a filename (select a file), and (2) execute a command (recovery or permanent

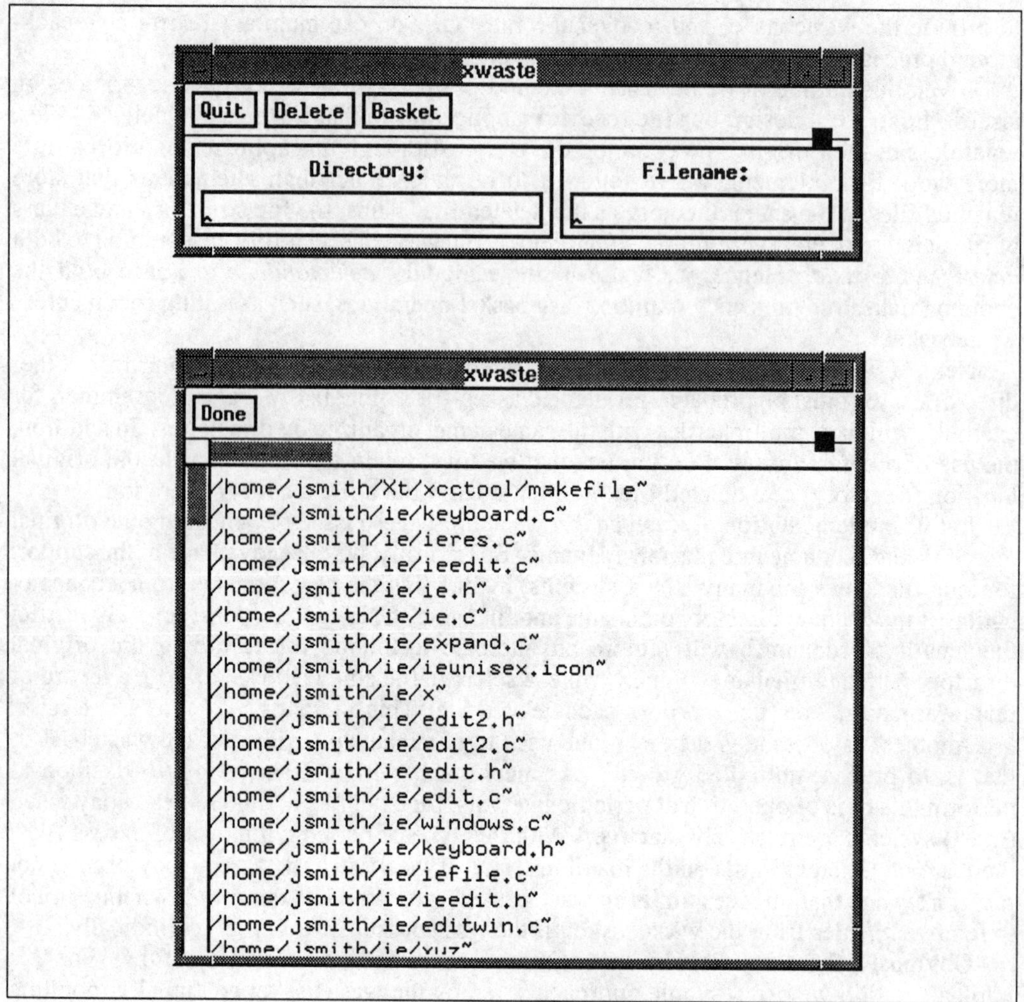

Figure 10.1 *xwaste*'s Main Panel and the Wastebasket Browser

deletion). Task (1) can be implemented by setting up a GC for highlighting the selected file, and by providing an action/translation table that recognizes a mouse click within the viewable portion of the browser window. Although we could provide command buttons for file recovery and permanent deletion, we'll use a simple menu system to support task (2). Since the Athena widget set (for X11 Release 3) doesn't provide a menu widget, we'll use a stack of command buttons to implement the menu.

In addition to the browser-based operations, *xwaste* should allow the user to delete files (add files to the wastebasket). For file specification entry, we'll use two Athena **Text** widgets, one for the directory path and one for the filename. The "Delete" command button expands the file specification given in the text entry fields, prompting the user for each file deletion with a pop-up dialog box.

Lastly, consider source code organization. We can factor our application into modules of related (GUI) operations. *delete*, the command-line utility, is GUI-independent and fairly limited in scope. Hence, we can implement it from one dedicated module, *delete.c*, plus the module of common routines and data structures, *commondel.c*.

For this implementation, we'll assemble *xwaste* from modules that give special consideration to the types of widgets needed for the interface. This approach enhances the possibility of porting *xwaste* to an alternate widget set, say, the OSF/Motif widget set. (A Motif version is *not* included in the appendixes due to space requirements, but is included on the source code diskette/tape.)

xwaste is built from the following modules:

- *xwaste.c* — coordinates overall operations
- *xwaste.bskt.c* — handles file recovery and pixmap operations
- *xwaste.menu.c* — implements a menu for the browser
- *alert.c* — a specific, alert box module
- *commondel.c* — common functions and data structures

Other aspects of *wastebasket*'s design are discussed on a module-by-module basis. With this overview, we first address the module shared by *delete* and *xwaste*.

10.2 *commondel.c*: Common Data Structures and Operations

As stated, we want to take into consideration any efforts to port this application to an alternate widget set, possibly, the Motif widget set. Having common, *non-GUI* operations in one module implies that this module will be immune to porting operations, and is a good idea even if no ports are anticipated.

Because this is a shared module, there are several public functions and data structures. The following function declarations are included in *commondel.h*:

```
extern int file_size(), load_buffer();
extern int get_home_directory();
extern int get_max_files();
extern int wastebasket_emtpy();
extern void encode_file_spec(), decode_file_spec();
```

The function of most of these routines is apparent from their names. We'll discuss several in this section; others we'll just use in context (see Appendix K for their definitions).

Although there are several shared variables, note that only one of these variables has a frequently changing value, namely, **current_num_files**:

```
extern char *temp_wastebasket_file;
extern char *wastebasket_file;
extern char *wastebasket_dir;
extern char home_directory[];
extern int  current_num_files, max_basket_entries;
```

Typically these variables, for example, **wastebasket_dir**, have the same value throughout the execution of the program, thus the possibility of run-time, logical errors due to inadvertent modification of global variables is minimized.

These variables are defined globally, and several are initialized, in *commondel.c*:

```
char *temp_wastebasket_file =
    "iriswastebasket/temp.wastebasket.record";
char *wastebasket_file = "iriswastebasket/wastebasket.record";
char *wastebasket_dir = "iriswastebasket";
char home_directory[MAX_PATH_LEN];

int max_basket_entries = MAX;
int current_num_files;
```

We've used the name "iriswastebasket" instead of "wastebasket" for our wastebasket directory to avoid conflicts with other wastebasket applications; you may want to substitute another name.

In our implementation, we store each deleted file in the wastebasket directory, along with a text file that lists the contents of the wastebasket—in a specific order. We can't work from, say, a system-call-based list of filenames because *wastebasket* deletes the oldest file with each new entry (if the wastebasket is filled to capacity). On several occasions the application must process this file; the easiest way to do so is to read it into a buffer and scan the buffer for each filename. The function **load_buffer()** reads a file into a buffer:

```
/*
load_buffer() loads a buffer with text from a file.
*/

int load_buffer(file_spec, buffer)
char *file_spec, *buffer;
{
    FILE *file_ptr;

    if ((file_ptr = fopen(file_spec, "r")) == NULL)
        return FALSE;
    while ((*buffer = fgetc(file_ptr)) != EOF)
        buffer++;
    *buffer = EOS;
    fclose(file_ptr);
    return TRUE;
}   /* load_buffer */
```

We mentioned that the user should be able to set the wastebasket size (its capacity). **get_max_files()** attempts to read the current value of **WASTEBASKET_SIZE**:

```
/*
get_max_files() examines the environment
for the value of $WASTEBASKET_SIZE.
*/
```

```
int get_max_files()
{
    int size;
    char *str_size;

    if ((str_size = (char *)getenv("WASTEBASKET_SIZE")) == NULL)
        return MAX;
    if ((size = atoi(str_size)) < 1)
        return MAX;
    return size;
}   /* get_max_files */
```

If it finds a positive value for this variable, it returns its value; otherwise, **get_max_files()** returns the default maximum capacity, as stored in **MAX**.

Next, consider the tasks of moving a deleted file to the wastebasket directory and, subsequently, recovering a file to its original directory. We could retain knowledge of a file's origin in the special wastebasket file mentioned earlier. In fact, the complete, original file specification *is* stored in this special file. But even if the directory path of each deleted file is stored in this special file, we can't just strip off the path and store the deleted file by its original name—files from different directories with the same name would conflict.

There are several ways to handle these conditions, but, for simplicity, we'll encode the *complete file specification* for a deleted file as part of its filename in the wastebasket directory, replacing forward slashes with a special character sequence, for example:

```
/home/jdoe/c/any.c  ——→  <spec>home<spec>jdoe<spec>c<spec>any.c
```

where *<spec>* is an arbitrary/special character sequence.

This approach isn't perfect. With SunOS™, for example, the maximum length for any component of a file specification is 256 characters. Hence, our encoding mechanism won't work for files where the original file specification length exceeds 256, including the character sequence substituted for each forward slash.

We offer several defenses for choosing this approach. First, in most cases, the length limitation isn't a problem—users simple don't create tremendously long file specifications. (Some applications do generate files with long names, but in many cases these aren't subject to normal deletion by the user where the need for recovery is likely.) Second, the effects of our encoding technique are limited to a small area of the application; hence, you can easily replace this technique with one of your own derivation and preference—many solutions would be system-dependent. Third, in this book we should maximize our focus on GUI, not file processing, issues. Fourth, this application is already quite long for inclusion in a book, so we need to conserve space wherever we can.

As an exercise you may want to consider the use of signatures, or some other technique, to generate keys for each file specification. These keys can be used as a filename and stored in the special wastebasket file. Specifically, each file record would include the original file specification and the signature-based filename for the wastebasket directory.

The simple method that we use for encoding file specifications is implemented in **encode_file_spec()**:

```
void encode_file_spec(after, before)
char *after, *before;
{
     char ch, *encode_ptr;

     while (ch = *before++)
          if (ch != '/')
               *after++ = ch;
          else {
               encode_ptr = ENCODE_STR;
               while (*after++ = *encode_ptr++)
                    ;
               after--;     /* don't want EOS */
          }
     *after = EOS;
}    /* encode_file_spec */
```

ENCODE_STR contains the special character sequence that substituted for each forward slash. UNIX is quite liberal in permitting special characters in filenames—except for those that it interprets in a special way. This policy makes it difficult to choose a replacement for the forward slash that will work with every UNIX version. We'll use "_SLASH_"; you could replace this sequence with whatever suits your needs.

The remaining common routines, including **decode_file_spec()**, are given in Appendix K.

10.3 *delete.c*: The Command-line Replacement for *rm(1)*

This module works with *commondel.c* to provide interactive command-line deletion of files. **main()** checks the command line, initializes two of the shared variables, and calls **delete_filenames()** with the array of filenames:

```
/*
main() allows the user to delete a set of files matching
a wildcard spec.
*/

void main(argc, argv)
int argc;
char *argv[];
{
     if (argc < 2) {
          fprintf(stderr, "Usage: delete <file specification>\n");
          exit(-1);
     }
     if (!get_home_directory(home_directory))
          exit(-1);
     max_basket_entries = get_max_files();
     delete_filenames(argc, argv);
     exit(0);
}    /* main */
```

delete_filenames() also does very little work, calling **build_file_spec()** to build a complete file specification for **delete_file()**:

```
/*
delete_filenames() applies delete_file() to
each filename from the command line expansion.
*/

void delete_filenames(argc, argv)
int argc;
char *argv[];
{
    char file_spec[MAX_CHARS];
    int continue_deletions = TRUE;

    while (--argc > 0 && continue_deletions) {
        build_file_spec(file_spec, *++argv);
        continue_deletions = delete_file(file_spec);
    }
}   /* delete_filenames */
```

Note that we can't simply perform the file deletions with each file specification passed in the array. Although a partial file specification is adequate for referencing a file (given the current working directory), we must build a complete file specification for storage in *wastebasket*'s special file—for use in file recovery at a later time.

build_file_spec() handles this task:

```
/*
build_file_spec() concatenates a path and a file specification.
*/

void build_file_spec(file_spec, partial_file_spec)
char *file_spec, *partial_file_spec;
{
    if (*partial_file_spec == '/')
        strcpy(file_spec, partial_file_spec);
    else {
        getwd(file_spec);
        strcat(file_spec, "/");
        strcat(file_spec, partial_file_spec);
    }
}   /* build_file_spec */
```

Once we have a complete file specification, we can call **delete_file()**, which handles interactive prompting and initiates file deletion, if requested:

```
/*
delete_file() is used to delete files using
an interactive prompt.
*/
```

```
int delete_file(file_spec)
char *file_spec;
{
    char answer, answer_str[MAX_STR];

    if (file_size(file_spec) == -1) {
        fprintf(stderr, "No matching file(s).\n");
        return TRUE;
    }
    do {
        printf("Delete file: %s\nyes, no, or quit [y|n|q]? ",
            file_spec);
        gets(answer_str);        /* substitute a robust gets() here */
        answer = answer_str[0];
        if (islower(answer))
            answer = toupper(answer);
    } while (!isupper(answer) ||
                !(answer == 'Y' || answer == 'N' || answer == 'Q'));
    if (answer == 'Y')
        add_to_basket(file_spec);
    return (answer == 'Q') ? FALSE : TRUE;
}   /* delete_file */
```

If the user gives an affirmative response, there are several steps that must be carried out. First, if the user is attempting to add to the wastebasket for the first time, none of the wastebasket file structures will exist. In this case, we must dynamically create the directory and the special wastebasket file.

Next, the file deletion scheme must accommodate an empty wastebasket. That is, the wastebasket (directory and special file) may physically exist, but in an empty state. (For example, the user could systematically delete every file in the wastebasket with the menu command for permanent file deletion.)

Beyond these special conditions, we must encode the filename for the target file and add it as the first/newest file in the wastebasket. To add a file to the wastebasket we must (1) move it from its original directory to the wastebasket directory, and (2) update the special wastebasket file. The latter step can be accomplished by creating a new wastebasket file, followed by a destructive rename operation.

add_to_basket() performs these operations:

```
/*
add_to_basket() puts the passed file spec. in the top of the
wastebasket, removing the oldest wastebasket contents, if
the wastebasket is overflowing.
*/

void add_to_basket(file_spec)
char *file_spec;
{
    FILE *waste_fd, *temp_waste_fd;
    char encoded_file_spec[MAX_CHARS];
```

```
char temp_file_spec[MAX_CHARS];
char temp_file_spec_2[MAX_CHARS];
int position, waste_exists = FALSE;
char *more_entries;

sprintf(temp_file_spec, "%s/%s", home_directory,
    wastebasket_dir);
if (file_size(temp_file_spec) == -1)
    mkdir(temp_file_spec, 0755);
sprintf(temp_file_spec, "%s/%s", home_directory,
    wastebasket_file);
if (file_size(temp_file_spec) != -1) {
    if ((waste_fd = fopen(temp_file_spec, "r")) != NULL)
        waste_exists = TRUE;
    else {
        fprintf(stderr, "Error opening wastebasket!\n");
        return;
    }
}
sprintf(temp_file_spec, "%s/%s.%d",
    home_directory, temp_wastebasket_file, getpid());
if ((temp_waste_fd = fopen(temp_file_spec, "w")) == NULL) {
    fprintf(stderr,
"Error opening temporary file during wastebasket operations!\n");
    return;
}

encode_file_spec(encoded_file_spec, file_spec);
strcat(encoded_file_spec, "\n");
/* write the file spec. as the first wastebasket entry */
fputs(encoded_file_spec, temp_waste_fd);

if (waste_exists) {
    more_entries = fgets(temp_file_spec, MAX_CHARS, waste_fd);
    for (position = 1; more_entries != NULL; position++) {
        if (position < max_basket_entries) {
            if (strcmp(encoded_file_spec, temp_file_spec) != 0)
                /* not a duplicate */
                fputs(temp_file_spec, temp_waste_fd);
        }
        else {
            temp_file_spec[strlen(temp_file_spec) - 1] = EOS;
            sprintf(temp_file_spec_2, "%s/%s/%s",
                home_directory, wastebasket_dir, temp_file_spec);
            unlink(temp_file_spec_2);
        }
        more_entries = fgets(temp_file_spec, MAX_CHARS, waste_fd);
    }
    fclose(waste_fd);
}
fclose(temp_waste_fd);
encoded_file_spec[strlen(encoded_file_spec) - 1] = EOS;
```

```
    sprintf(temp_file_spec, "%s/%s/%s",
        home_directory, wastebasket_dir, encoded_file_spec);
    rename(file_spec, temp_file_spec);
    sprintf(temp_file_spec_2, "%s/%s.%d",
        home_directory, temp_wastebasket_file, getpid());
    sprintf(temp_file_spec, "%s/%s",
        home_directory, wastebasket_file);
    rename(temp_file_spec_2, temp_file_spec);
}   /* add_to_basket */
```

Note that **add_to_basket()** must account for duplicates files. In this implementation, if the wastebasket already includes a file with the same directory path and filename, *wastebasket* retains only the most recent file. You can easily modify this policy; for example, instead of deleting the previous/older file, you could append an extension to the filename(s) to distinguish different generations of a file.

There are two rename operations. First, we must move the deleted file to the wastebasket directory. Second, we must replace the old wastebasket file with the updated file. Note that the temporary file that's used in building the updated wastebasket file uses the current process identification number in its filename to avoid potential name conflicts.

We reiterate that *delete* performs one task only: wastebasket file deletion. If the user wants to recover an accidentally deleted file, *xwaste* must be used. The remainder of the delete module is given in Appendix K.

10.4 *xwaste.c*: The Coordinating Module for *xwaste*

The modules *commondel.c* and *delete.c* are quite small, yet *delete* fully implements file deletion operations using a simple command-line user interface. *xwaste*, on the other hand, is a good example of the burden that a graphical user interface imposes on an application. Like many applications, most of *xwaste* is devoted to implementing and managing the command buttons, text entry areas, browser window, and menu system. In this book, it's the GUI-related part of the application that we're actually interested in, so we can't complain about its magnitude. More importantly, *xwaste* is large enough to provide a good cross-section of Xt and Xlib programming in one application.

So far, our Xt applications have been quite simple; primarily, we've used applications to overview Xt application programming, to illustrate callback functions and actions, and to test our high-level dialog box. A medium-scale application such as *xwaste* typically requires a broader array of Xt data structures. Moreover, since Xt is designed to support the most common GUI demands, programmers often have to craft part of the interface with Xlib. In our case, we use Xlib for many of the operations and data structures required to implement the wastebasket browser. For example, we use a pixmap to implement the browser's off-screen canvas.

The primary function of *xwaste.c* is to bring together the wastebasket components provided in four other modules: *alert.c*, *commondel.c*, *xwaste.bskt.c*, and *xwaste.menu.c*. In addition, *xwaste.c* defines the widgets for the main panel (primary application window) and a second top-level application window (browser window), and it provides the data structures and functions necessary to support application-specific resources and actions. In this section, we overview *xwaste*'s support for resources and actions, plus the overall organization of the application. Some of these issues will be addressed again as we discuss the other modules.

10.4.1 Application Resources

With many Xt applications it's necessary to support application-specific resources in addition to the standard resource support that's provided automatically with each widget. For example, we must provide browser-related resources so that the user can set the dimensions and font for the browser window.

Xt provides a straightforward technique for defining resources for an application. Specifically, Xt recognizes an application data structure that contains a variable for each resource used by the application. This structure is used by the resource database system to record the current value for each application-specific resource. For *xwaste*, the format of the resource data record is:

```
typedef struct {
    int browser_rows;
    int browser_columns;
    char *browser_font_name;
} ApplicationData, *ApplicationDataPtr;
```

These resources differ with each application; the data types for the variables in this structure are application-specific. Hence, there must be a mechanism for informing the resource database of the (byte) offset of the field associated with a particular resource. This template is used for calculating field offsets, among other things.

With X applications there is a standard convention for specifying resources. With Xlib-based applications, resources are defined at the application level. With Xt-based applications, resources can usually be set for the various widgets that compose the user interface. In addition, the application may define resources. In our case, we provide three application-level resources to be used with the wastebasket (browser) widget, which we create from the **Core** widget class.

In addition to the template **ApplicationData**, which describes the format for the data structure that stores the resource *values*, we must define the resource *names*. First, we must define resource name *constants* in the Xt tradition. Specifically, each resource has a name that begins with "XtN. . ." and a class that begins with "XtC. . .".

Resource names and classes are defined as macro constants and included as part of the application interface. The following names and classes are defined in *xwaste.h*:

```
#define XtNbrowserRows        "browserRows"
#define XtCBrowserRows        "BrowserRows"
#define XtNbrowserColumns     "browserColumns"
#define XtCBrowserColumns     "BrowserColumns"
#define XtNbrowserFont        "browserFont"
#define XtCBrowserFont        "BrowserFont"
```

The distinction between names and classes, resource naming conventions, and the resource manager's matching algorithm, are described in various X and Xt reference manuals, including Quercia and O'Reilly (1989).

Here, we're interested in how to make the resource manager aware of the application resources for *xwaste*. Given these resource names and classes, we must (1) define a resource data structure, (2) set up a table that associates each resource name/class with a particular field in the resource data structure, (3) initiate a request at run-time that sets each field in the resource data structure, and (4) check the values in each field to ensure that the user has supplied legitimate resource values. (We've omitted several details that are discussed later.)

We can define the resource data structure as a local variable in **main()**:

```
ApplicationData browser_data;
```

Consider task (2), pairing resource names with fields in the application data structure. Xt requires a table of type **XtResource**:

```
static XtResource resources[] = {
    {XtNbrowserRows, XtCBrowserRows, XtRInt, sizeof(int),
        XtOffset(ApplicationDataPtr, browser_rows), XtRImmediate,
        (caddr_t) DEFAULT_BROWSER_ROWS},
    {XtNbrowserColumns, XtCBrowserColumns, XtRInt, sizeof(int),
        XtOffset(ApplicationDataPtr, browser_columns), XtRImmediate,
        (caddr_t) DEFAULT_BROWSER_COLUMNS},
    {XtNbrowserFont, XtCBrowserFont, XtRString, sizeof(char *),
        XtOffset(ApplicationDataPtr, browser_font_name),
        XtRString, DEFAULT_BROWSER_FONT_NAME},
};
```

The fifth field for each resource entry pairs resources with application data structure fields. Specifically, **XtOffset()** takes a pointer to a structure and a field within that structure and calculates the byte offset.

Actually, this table does more than specify resource-to-data structure mappings. In a resource file, resource values are in string form, for example:

```
xwaste*browserRows:   30
xwaste*browserFont:   8x13
```

But the fields in the application data structure may be a different type, for example, **int**. Xt provides a resource conversion facility that converts the resource data to the proper type before storing it in the application data structure. Thus, in addition to the field offsets, this table provides conversion information, specifically, the target data type and the size for that data type (fields three and four).

There are several resource data *representation types*, for example, **XtRBoolean**, **XtRFloat**, **XtRPosition**, and others. In our case, two of the resource fields, **browser_rows** and **browser_columns**, require integers:

```
typedef struct {
    int browser_rows;
    int browser_columns;
    char *browser_font_name;
} ApplicationData, *ApplicationDataPtr;
```

Thus, the converter type for these fields is **XtRInt** and the field size is "sizeof(int)". In contrast, for the browser font field the representation type is **XtRString**, because we want the font name in string form, just as it's specified in the resource file. (In designing a widget class, we would make the application responsible for setting up the font, and passing in a pointer to its structure as a resource.)

Parenthetically, we've used "sizeof(char *)" in specifying the size of the font name field. X defines the data type **String** as a synonym for **char ***; you can substitute the former if you prefer. Generally, we use the special data types defined by X, such as **Dimension**, **Position**, and so on. We have nothing against C and the **typedef** concept. Some programmers, however, object to the use of "String" as a euphemism for character arrays. For most programmers, C's lack of (complete) support for strings isn't a problem; **gets()** is, perhaps, a grand exception. Whether C does or does not really support strings is a philosophical issue that is irrelevant here.

There's one other aspect of the resource database system that we haven't mentioned, namely, the provision for default values. Xt must accommodate default values, because the application cannot simply assume that the user will provide values for all, or any, of the resources. The last two fields in each resource table entry specify the data type and value, respectively, for the resource:

```
    ..., XtRImmediate, (caddr_t) DEFAULT_BROWSER_ROWS}, ...
```

For the browser rows resource, we've supplied the value **DEFAULT_BROWSER_ROWS**, which is defined as:

```
#define DEFAULT_BROWSER_ROWS          150
```

Specifically, the value is already in integer form; hence, the special representation type **XtRImmediate** is used to indicate that no further conversion is needed.

We've described the first two tasks in application resource processing; tasks (3) and (4) are described later when we discuss **main()** and **process_resources()**.

10.4.2 Adding Actions for the Wastebasket Browser

Next, we must provide actions for the wastebasket browser. As described earlier, *xwaste* allows the user to select any file displayed in the browser window, and then invoke the menu system for permanent file deletion or file recovery.

There are two other operations that can be implemented as actions. First, if the user attempts an operation out of context, we should provide some form of feedback, rather than simply doing nothing. For example, if the user invokes the menu without first selecting a file, *xwaste* can't know which file to delete or recover. Also, if the user attempts to type a carriage return or linefeed character within either of the one-line text windows, we should signal the user and ignore that character. We use a terminal beep for user feedback.

Second, there are several conditions/events that require the browser to be redisplayed; some originate within the application, others are external to the application. For example, if a file is deleted, the browser (and its off-sceeen pixmap) must be updated to remove that file from the list of filenames. Also, when the user first invokes the browser, its window must be filled with the pixmap of filenames.

The latter condition is really a special case of a more general event—an exposure. Exposures are handled automatically by each widget. However, the browser must be built from a core widget, so we must provide the operations that (1) update the browser pixmap when its list of filenames is out of date, and (2) map the pixmap to the browser window. Task (2) must be performed after every occurrence of task (1), and after an exposure.

The following action table pairs an external identifier with an action function that implements each of the actions that we've described:

```
static XtActionsRec actionsTable[] = {
    {"selectFile", (XtActionProc) SelectFile},
    {"menuUp", (XtActionProc) MenuUp},
    {"menuDown", (XtActionProc) MenuDown},
    {"beep", (XtActionProc) Beep},
    {"fillBasket", (XtActionProc) FillBasket},
};
```

In contrast to the simple applications in Chapter 8, with *xwaste* we'll make the associations between actions and events (translations) in a resource file. This approach gives the user some latitude in modifying the behavior of *xwaste*. (It also allows a naive user to disable the application inadvertently!)

The following resource file, *XWaste*, provides one example of translations:

```
!
! XWaste resource file
!
*directoryBox*width:          200
*filenameBox*width:           150

*menuShell*hSpace:            0
*menuShell*vSpace:            0
*menuShell*Command.width:     200
*menuShell*borderWidth:       1
*menuBox.Command.translations:  #replace\n\
    <Enter>:                     highlight()\n\
    <Leave>:                     reset()\n\
    <BtnDown>,<BtnUp>:          set() notify() unset()
*wasteBasket.translations:    #replace\n\
    <Btn1Down>,<Btn1Up>:        selectFile()\n\
    <Btn2Down>,<Btn2Up>:        menuDown()\n\
    <Btn3Down>,<Btn3Up>:        menuUp()\n\
    <Expose>:                    fillBasket()
*fileSpecForm*translations: #override\n\
    Ctrl<Key>J:                  beep()\n\
    Ctrl<Key>O:                  beep()\n\
    Ctrl<Key>M:                  beep()\n\
    <Key>Linefeed:               beep()\n\
    <Key>Return:                 beep()
!*iconic:                          yes
xwaste*browserFont:           8x13
```

XWaste includes resource settings for the browser actions as well as for other widgets in the application. In order to set these resources, the user documentation must include the names of the widgets. For example, the main panel text entry widgets for specifying a directory and a filename are housed within a form widget named **fileSpecForm**. With this approach, the user can take advantage of the resource manager's matching algorithm and provide one set of translations that applies to both text entry widgets. Here, specific linefeed-related, key-press events are overridden with the action function that's referred to externally as "beep()".

At present, we're interested in the translations for the wastebasket browser (widget). According to the current settings, the user can click-left to select a file, and then click-right to invoke a menu command. Or, the user can click-middle to remove the menu.

10.4.3 Other Data Structures

Now that we've described the resources and actions, and their private data structures, let's mention the other private variables before looking at **main()**. *xwaste.c* and *xwaste.bskt.c* are more closely connected than the other modules. The latter module implements pixmap-related operations for the browser window. The browser window is created from a viewport widget (outer) and a core widget (inner)—we've described the actions that provide its external behavior. It's common to define actions and resources in the coordinating module, as we've done in *xwaste.c*. Because of the close association between the browser (widget) and the actions and resources, we'll define the basic browser-related widgets in *xwaste.c* as well. The browser's off-screen pixmap is a low-level structure, therefore it will be created within *xwaste.bskt.c*.

The private widgets for the top-level windows are:

```
static Widget basketShell, topLevel, fileSpecForm,
    directoryBox, filenameBox, buttonBoxMain, vPort,
    vPane, vPaneBasket, wasteBasket, buttonBoxBasket,
    buttonQuit, buttonDelete, buttonBasket, buttonDoneBasket;
```

The widgets for the alert boxes and the menu system are defined in their respective modules.

Lastly, private data structures are defined in *xwaste.c* for the application icon and for the browser font, which is used by multiple modules:

```
static Pixmap icon_pixmap;        /* freed by Quit() */
static XFontStruct *font;         /* freed by Quit() */
```

10.4.4 Start-up Considerations

Next, consider **main()**, which provides an overview of *xwaste*'s start-up operations:

```
/*
main() determines the home directory and basket dimensions,
creates the main widgets, sets up the alert boxes, initializes
data structures, etc.
*/
```

```
void main(argc, argv)
int argc;
char *argv[];
{
    unsigned int basket_width, basket_height;
    Arg args[5];
    int i;
    ApplicationData browser_data;

    if (!get_home_directory(home_directory))
        exit(-1);
    if (argc > 1) {
        fprintf(stderr, "Usage: xwaste\n");
        exit(-1);
    }

    topLevel = XtInitialize(argv[0], "XWaste", NULL, 0,
        &argc, argv);
    process_resources(&browser_data, &font);
    i = 0;
    XtSetArg(args[i], XtNinput, (XtArgVal) TRUE); i++;
    XtSetValues(topLevel, args, i);

    create_main_panel_widgets();
    basket_create_offscreen_pixmap(topLevel, font,
        browser_data, &basket_width, &basket_height);
    create_basket_widgets(basket_width, basket_height);
    max_basket_entries = get_max_files();
    XtAddActions(actionsTable, XtNumber(actionsTable));

    menu_create(basketShell);
    alert_create_ync(topLevel);
    alert_create_continue(topLevel);
    set_alert_reset_proper_keyboard_focus(
        reset_proper_keyboard_focus);

    initialize_shell_structures();

    XtRealizeWidget(topLevel);
    XtRealizeWidget(basketShell);

    XtMainLoop();
}   /* main */
```

After initialization, **process_resources**() is called first to handle tasks (3) and (4) of the four-step process of implementing application resources:

```
/*
process_resources() reads dimensions for the browser (off-screen
pixmap of the wastebasket), checks their bounds, and exits with
warning message(s), if there are problems.
```

```
*/

void process_resources(browser_data, font)
ApplicationData *browser_data;
XFontStruct **font;
{
    XtGetApplicationResources(topLevel, browser_data, resources,
        XtNumber(resources), NULL, 0);
    if (browser_data->browser_rows < 1 ||
            browser_data->browser_rows > MAX_BROWSER_ROWS) {
        fprintf(stderr, "xwaste: Illegal row dimension: %d\n",
            browser_data->browser_rows);
        fprintf(stderr,
            "Number of rows must be in the interval: [1,%d]\n",
            MAX_BROWSER_ROWS);
        exit(-1);
    }
    if (browser_data->browser_columns < 1 ||
            browser_data->browser_columns > MAX_BROWSER_COLUMNS) {
        fprintf(stderr, "xwaste: Illegal column dimension: %d\n",
            browser_data->browser_columns);
        fprintf(stderr,
            "Number of columns must be in the interval: [1,%d]\n",
            MAX_BROWSER_COLUMNS);
        exit(-1);
    }
    if ((*font = XLoadQueryFont(XtDisplay(topLevel),
            browser_data->browser_font_name)) == NULL) {
        fprintf(stderr,
            "Couldn't load font: %s; using default browser font.\n",
            browser_data->browser_font_name);
        if ((*font = XLoadQueryFont(XtDisplay(topLevel),
                DEFAULT_BROWSER_FONT_NAME)) == NULL) {
            fprintf(stderr,
        "Couldn't load default browser font either, exiting...\n");
            exit(-1);
        }
    }
}   /* process_resources */
```

First, **process_resources()** calls **XtGetApplicationResources()** to fill in the application resource data structure, using information from resource list, as described earlier. Once these resource values have been set, they must be verified—a user could override the defaults with illegal values. With respect to the browser font, we simply use **XtLoad-QueryFont()** to verify the legitimacy of the font name. If the font requested by the user can't be loaded, we issue a message in the command window and load the default font instead. If the latter isn't available, we terminate the application.

If *xwaste* gets past this point, **main()** creates the widgets for the main panel, creates the pixmap, creates the browser window widgets, checks the wastebasket capacity, and sets up the actions, in that order. Once the widgets for the two top-level application windows have been created, the widgets for the menu system and the alert boxes are created. **initialize_shell_structures()** is a function designed to perform miscellaneous start-up operations; at present, it simply sets up the application icon.

10.4.5 Top-level Widget Hierarchies

Before entering the main application event loop, **XtRealizeWidget()** must be called to create the windows for each widget—once for the main panel widget hierarchy and once for the browser window widget hierarchy. *xwaste* provides our only example of dual, top-level application windows. Their widget hierarchies are discussed next.

The main panel is implemented with a vertical pane widget, **vPane**, and several subordinate widgets:

```
/*
create_main_panel_widgets() creates/initializes the widgets that
constitute the top-level, main panel.
*/

void create_main_panel_widgets()
{
    Arg args[5];
    int i;

    vPane = XtCreateManagedWidget("vPane",
#ifdef X11R3
        vPanedWidgetClass, topLevel, NULL, 0);
#else
        panedWidgetClass, topLevel, NULL, 0);
#endif
    buttonBoxMain = XtCreateManagedWidget("buttonBoxMain",
        boxWidgetClass, vPane, NULL, 0);
    fileSpecForm = XtCreateManagedWidget("fileSpecForm",
        formWidgetClass, vPane, NULL, 0);
    i = 0;
    XtSetArg(args[i], XtNlabel, (XtArgVal) "Directory:"); i++;
    XtSetArg(args[i], XtNvalue, (XtArgVal) ""); i++;
    directoryBox = XtCreateManagedWidget("directoryBox",
        dialogWidgetClass, fileSpecForm, args, i);
    i = 0;
    XtSetArg(args[i], XtNlabel, (XtArgVal) "Filename:"); i++;
    XtSetArg(args[i], XtNvalue, (XtArgVal) ""); i++;
    XtSetArg(args[i], XtNfromHoriz, (XtArgVal) directoryBox); i++;
    filenameBox = XtCreateManagedWidget("filenameBox",
        dialogWidgetClass, fileSpecForm, args, i);
    i = 0;
    XtSetArg(args[i], XtNlabel, (XtArgVal) "Quit"); i++;
    buttonQuit = XtCreateManagedWidget("buttonQuit",
        commandWidgetClass, buttonBoxMain, args, i);
    XtAddCallback(buttonQuit, XtNcallback, Quit, NULL);
    i = 0;
    XtSetArg(args[i], XtNlabel, (XtArgVal) "Delete"); i++;
```

```
    buttonDelete = XtCreateManagedWidget("buttonDelete",
        commandWidgetClass, buttonBoxMain, args, i);
    XtAddCallback(buttonDelete, XtNcallback, Delete, NULL);
    i = 0;
    XtSetArg(args[i], XtNlabel, (XtArgVal) "Basket"); i++;
    buttonBasket = XtCreateManagedWidget("buttonBasket",
        commandWidgetClass, buttonBoxMain, args, i);
    XtAddCallback(buttonBasket, XtNcallback, Basket, NULL);
}   /* create_main_panel_widgets */
```

You may want to refer to Figure 10.1.a in Section 10.1 at this point. For convenience (and sanity) we use the same names for widget IDs and for their external identifiers. The main panel's command buttons are collected in a box widget, **buttonBoxMain**. As mentioned earlier, a form widget is used to house the text entry widgets for the directory and filename, so that translations can be applied to each text entry box simultaneously.

Each command button, **buttonQuit**, **buttonDelete**, and **buttonBasket**, uses a callback function to initiate its operations. The "Quit" button terminates the application; "Delete" deletes (moves to the wastebasket) the file specified in the text entry boxes; and "Basket" invokes the wastebasket browser.

To some extent the application programmer can control the user's potential for modifying various aspects of *xwaste*'s appearance and behavior through the list of widget names given in the documentation. Of course, regardless of which widget names are publicly available, the user can still, say, change all command buttons to the color red.

The browser window is implemented in a vertical pane widget as well:

```
/*
create_basket_widgets() creates/initializes the widgets
in the pop-up wastebasket frame.
*/

void create_basket_widgets(basket_width, basket_height)
unsigned int basket_width, basket_height;
{
    Arg args[5];
    int i;

    i = 0;
    XtSetArg(args[i], XtNallowShellResize, (XtArgVal) TRUE); i++;
    XtSetArg(args[i], XtNmappedWhenManaged, (XtArgVal) FALSE); i++;
    basketShell = XtCreateApplicationShell("basketShell",
        topLevelShellWidgetClass, args, i);
    vPaneBasket = XtCreateManagedWidget("vPaneBasket",
#ifdef X11R3
        vPanedWidgetClass, basketShell, NULL, 0);
#else
        panedWidgetClass, basketShell, NULL, 0);
#endif
    buttonBoxBasket = XtCreateManagedWidget("buttonBoxBasket",
        boxWidgetClass, vPaneBasket, NULL, 0);
    i = 0;
```

```
    XtSetArg(args[i], XtNallowHoriz, (XtArgVal) TRUE); i++;
    XtSetArg(args[i], XtNallowVert, (XtArgVal) TRUE); i++;
    XtSetArg(args[i], XtNforceBars, (XtArgVal) TRUE); i++;
    XtSetArg(args[i], XtNwidth,
        (XtArgVal) DEFAULT_BASKET_WIDTH); i++;
    XtSetArg(args[i], XtNheight,
        (XtArgVal) DEFAULT_BASKET_HEIGHT); i++;
    vPort = XtCreateManagedWidget("vPort",
        viewportWidgetClass, vPaneBasket, args, i);
    i = 0;
    XtSetArg(args[i], XtNlabel, (XtArgVal) "Done"); i++;
    buttonDoneBasket = XtCreateManagedWidget("buttonDoneBasket",
        commandWidgetClass, buttonBoxBasket, args, i);
    XtAddCallback(buttonDoneBasket, XtNcallback, BasketDone, NULL);
    i = 0;
    XtSetArg(args[i], XtNwidth, (XtArgVal) basket_width); i++;
    XtSetArg(args[i], XtNheight, (XtArgVal) basket_height); i++;
    wasteBasket = XtCreateManagedWidget("wasteBasket", widgetClass,
        vPort, args, i);
    basket_set_reference_widget(wasteBasket);
}   /* create_basket_widgets */
```

In this case, however, the vertical pane **vPaneBasket** is a child of **basketShell**, a top-level shell widget. The latter is created with **XtCreateApplicationShell()**, whereas our earlier secondary (pop-up) windows were created with **XtCreatePopupShell()**.

As with the main panel, a box widget, **buttonBoxBasket**, is used to house the command buttons for this window. Currently, there is only one button, **buttonDoneBasket**. The "Done" button simply removes (unmaps) the browser window.

There are two other widgets of interest at this point. A viewport widget, **vPort**, is used to implement the scrollable browser window. For this implementation, we've chosen to attach both vertical and horizontal scrollbars (force their appearance). You may prefer an alternative arrangement.

A core widget, **wasteBasket**, is created as a child of the viewport. (We call the former the inner, or wastebasket, window.) The browser's pixmap will be displayed in the window associated with **wasteBasket**. (The off-screen pixmap and **wasteBasket** have the same dimensions, **basket_width** by **basket_height**.)

Before moving on to the callback and action functions, note that both top-level windows can be iconified. **initialize_shell_structures()** installs the icon that you supply in *xwaste.icon* as the common icon for these windows:

```
/*
initialize_shell_structures sets up miscellaneous structures
for the top-level widgets (currently, just the icon).
*/

void initialize_shell_structures()
{

#include "xwaste.icon"
```

```
    Arg args[3];

    icon_pixmap = XCreateBitmapFromData(XtDisplay(topLevel),
        RootWindowOfScreen(XtScreen(topLevel)), xwaste_bits,
        xwaste_width, xwaste_height);
    XtSetArg(args[0], XtNiconPixmap, (XtArgVal) icon_pixmap);
    XtSetValues(topLevel, args, 1);
    XtSetArg(args[0], XtNiconPixmap, (XtArgVal) icon_pixmap);
    XtSetValues(basketShell, args, 1);
}   /* initialize_shell_structures */
```

10.4.6 *xwaste*'s Action Functions

Recall from our earlier coverage of actions and translations that we need action functions for several application-defined events, as well as for exposures on the wastebasket widget. With one exception, in *xwaste.c* we simply call the functions in other modules that implement these operations. We'll describe three of the action functions here; see Appendix K for the others.

First, **Beep()** provides user feedback by calling an Xlib function directly:

```
/*ARGSUSED*/
static void Beep(w, event)          /* ring the terminal bell */
Widget w;
XEvent *event;
{
    XBell(XtDisplay(w), 80);
}   /* Beep */
```

If you prefer, you could modify the call to **XBell()** to accept a resource value for the bell's loudness.

Next, **SelectFile()** calls a function from *xwaste.bskt.c* to highlight the file selected by the user:

```
/*ARGSUSED*/
static void SelectFile(w, event)    /* highlight the filename */
Widget w;
XEvent *event;
{
    basket_select_file(event);
}   /* SelectFile */
```

The last action function that we mention is **FillBasket()**, which clears the current selection before displaying the wastebasket filenames:

```
/*ARGSUSED*/
static void FillBasket(w, event)
Widget w;
XEvent *event;
{
```

```
    basket_reset_current_file();
    basket_fill_with_filenames(NO_HIGHLIGHT);
}   /* FillBasket */
```

This action function is associated with exposure events using a translation in the resource file. (See the action table and resource file given in Section 10.4.2.)

10.4.7 *xwaste*'s Callback Functions

The callback functions are straightforward; we consider the two most interesting callbacks here. First, **Delete()** implements the operations of the "Delete" command button. Specifically, it builds a complete file specification from the text entry boxes and calls **expand_delete_filename()**:

```
/*
Delete() is the starting point for file deletions.
*/
/*ARGSUSED*/
void Delete(w, client_data, call_data)
Widget w;
caddr_t client_data;
caddr_t call_data;
{
    char *filename;

    XtSetSensitive(buttonDelete, FALSE);
    if ((filename = get_filename()) != NULL)
        expand_delete_filename(filename);
    XtSetSensitive(buttonDelete, TRUE);
}   /* Delete */
```

Many of the file deletion operations that occur here are similar to those described for *delete*; however, these applications do not use common functions. With *xwaste* it's important (whenever possible) to use an alert box to display messages, as opposed to printing simple text to the standard output and standard error fiies. For example, **expand_delete_filename()** includes the following messages:

```
/*
expand_delete_filename() expands wildcards and then applies
delete_file() to each filename in the expansion.
*/

void expand_delete_filename(filename)
char *filename;
{
    ...
    if (file_size(temp_file) == -1) {
        alert("Unknown error during creation of a temporary file!");
        return;
    }
```

```
    if ((filename_buffer =
            (char *) malloc((unsigned) (file_size(temp_file) + 1)))
                == NULL) {
        alert("Memory allocation error!");
        unlink(temp_file);
        return;
    }
    if (!load_buffer(temp_file, filename_buffer)) {
        alert("Unable to access a temporary file!");
        free(filename_buffer);
        unlink(temp_file);
        return;
    }
    ...
}   /* expand_delete_filename */
```

The operations that **expand_delete_filename()** has in common with its *delete.c* counterpart are not shown. There are slight variances, however, in the file deletion-related operations. For example, it must consider the directory specified in the text entry box:

```
/*
get_updated_directory() manages and returns
the "current" directory.
*/

char *get_updated_directory()
{
    static char previous_dir[MAX_PATH_LEN];
    char *current_dir;

#ifdef X11R3
    current_dir = XtDialogGetValueString(directoryBox);
#else
    current_dir = XawDialogGetValueString(directoryBox);
#endif
    if (strlen(current_dir) == 0) {
        if ((current_dir = (char *)
                getcwd(previous_dir, MAX_PATH_LEN)) == NULL) {
            fprintf(stderr,
                "Unable to determine current working directory!!\n");
            exit(-1);
        }
    }
    if (strcmp(current_dir, previous_dir))
        strcpy(previous_dir, current_dir);
    return previous_dir;    /*  now, same as current_dir */
}   /* get_updated_directory */
```

Also, it calls **delete_files()**, which uses an alert box as well:

```
/*
delete_file() is used to delete a file. An alert
box is used to make sure of the deletion.
*/

int delete_file(file_spec)
char *file_spec;
{
    char msg[MAX_FILE_SPEC + 25];
    int result;

    if (file_size(file_spec) == -1) {
        sprintf(msg, "No matching file(s):  %s", file_spec);
        alert(msg);
        return TRUE;
    }
    sprintf(msg, "Delete file:  %s", file_spec);
    result = alert_query(msg);
    if (result == ALERT_YES)
        basket_add_file(file_spec);
    return (result != ALERT_CANCEL) ? TRUE : FALSE;
}   /* delete_file */
```

Note that the alert box implementation has been modified so that **alert_query()** invokes the alert box and returns the user's response, as suggested in Chapter 9.

The second callback function that we mention is **Basket()**. It maps the browser window after using **XtTranslateCoords()** to set its position so that the browser appears directly below the main panel:

```
/*
Basket() is the starting point for
wastebasket recovery/browser operations.
*/
/*ARGSUSED*/
void Basket(w, client_data, call_data)
Widget w;
caddr_t client_data;
caddr_t call_data;
{
    Position x, y;
    Arg args[3];
    int i;
    Dimension height;

    if (wastebasket_empty()) {
        alert("The wastebasket is empty.");
        return;
    }
    XtSetArg(args[0], XtNheight, &height);
    XtGetValues(topLevel, args, 1);
    XtTranslateCoords(topLevel, (Position) 0,
```

```
        (Position) (height + POPUP_Y_OFFSET), &x, &y);
    i = 0;
    XtSetArg(args[i], XtNx, (XtArgVal) x); i++;
    XtSetArg(args[i], XtNy, (XtArgVal) y); i++;
    XtSetValues(basketShell, args, i);
    XtMapWidget(basketShell);
    basket_reset_current_file();/* no highlighted file at        */
                               /* start-up, or after exposure  */
    if (!basket_fill_with_filenames(NO_HIGHLIGHT))
        return;
    if (current_num_files > max_basket_entries) {
        alert_beep(8);
        alert("Please read the message in the console window!");
        fprintf(stderr,
"The wastebasket contains more entries than\n\
specified by the environment variable\n\
WASTEBASKET_SIZE (currently:  %d).\n\
If you make modifications, your wastebasket\n\
size will be reduced accordingly.\n", max_basket_entries);
    }
}   /* Basket */
```

There are several interesting details here. First, you may have noticed that in **basket_create_widgets()** we used an argument/resource to suppress the default automatic mapping of the top-level application window, specifically, for the **basketShell** widget:

```
    XtSetArg(args[i], XtNmappedWhenManaged, (XtArgVal) FALSE); i++;
```

Normally, the browser window should be hidden (preservation of real estate). The user can activate the browser as needed with the command button labelled "Basket". The browser window can be removed from the display screen by iconifying it, or by pressing the "Done" command button. A related point is that, since **basketShell** is not a pop-up shell, we don't use **XtPopup()** to activate it; instead, we use **XtMapWindow()**.

Next, this application enforces the policy that each time the browser is mapped, the wastebasket filename list is reset. That is, there will be no "selected file," even if one had been selected when the browser was removed from the screen. This policy forces the user to select a file before every menu operation (deletion or recovery). You can easily modify this action by (1) providing an access function in the module *xwaste.bskt.c* that returns the number of the current file, (2) removing the calls to **basket_reset_current_file()** in **FillBasket()** and **Basket()**, and (3) using the value for the current file in the calls to **basket_fill_with_filenames()**.

The final aspect of **Basket()** that we mention is the sequence of error messages that's generated if the current number of files exceeds the wastebasket's capacity. Under normal operation, this condition never occurs. If, however, the user (1) sets a wastebasket capacity (via the environment variable) to, say, 100, (2) uses either *delete* or *xwaste* until the wastebasket is either at or near this capacity, and (3) sets a smaller wastebasket capacity, the next deletion operation will cause the wastebasket to be truncated to this new capacity. (See the next section, or recall *delete*'s **add_to_basket()**.) In this case, the user should be warned that there may be a substantial reduction in the wastebasket's size. It's quite common to assume a higher level of sophistication for command line users, so we didn't include this warning with *delete*. You can easily add this feature to *delete*, or remove it from *xwaste*, in order to make the two programs consistent.

10.4.8 Miscellaneous Details—Keyboard Focus

The last function in *xwaste.c* that we mention is **reset_proper_keyboard_focus()**:

```
/*
reset_proper_keyboard_focus() allows the keyboard focus to be
reestablished after a transient shell is popped up and down.
Calling this routine is necessary with twm, but not with uwm.
*/

void reset_proper_keyboard_focus()
{
    XtSetKeyboardFocus(vPane, fileSpecForm);
}   /* reset_proper_keyboard_focus */
```

It resets the keyboard focus to the child (grandchildren) of **vPane**, namely, the text entry widgets. Due to certain characteristics of Xt and the Athena **Text** widgets that are outside the scope of this book, this operation is required under certain conditions (with some window managers). You may want to see one of the Xt reference books for a more complete discussion of this issue; however, it is best understood by studying the source code for Xt and the Athena widgets. Henceforth, we do not mention this function, but we do include it in the source code listings where appropriate.

10.5 *xwaste.bskt.c*: The Wastebasket Module

So far we've discussed the overall operation of *xwaste*, plus the data structures and operations related to resources and actions that are handled within *xwaste.c*. In particular, we've taken an abstract view of the wastebasket window, the alert boxes, and menu system. We've viewed the browser window as a scrollable viewport, supplemented by resources and actions, that displays a pixmap-based list of filenames from the wastebasket window. A menu system is available within the browser for permanent file deletion or file recovery. And, the user is prompted for information and informed of various conditions with a system of pop-up alert boxes.

We now discuss the details of what have been abstractions up to this point. This section discusses the low-level details related to implementing the pixmap-based list of filenames: including both display-oriented details, such as the GCs, pixmap, and font; and wastebasket-oriented details, such as highlighting the currently selected file, adding a file to the wastebasket, and updating the browser window. In this module we continue our abstract view of the remaining modules that implement the menu system and the alert boxes.

10.5.1 Wastebasket-related Data Structures

First, consider the private data structures that are required by *xwaste.bskt.c*:

```
static Pixmap wastebasket;  /* off-screen image for wastebasket     */
static GC wgc, cgc, hgc;    /* see basket_create_offscreen_pixmap() */

static Widget wbrw;       /* wastebasket reference widget--used    */
                          /* in an XtDisplay(wbrw)-type capacity   */

static int row_increment, current_file;
static unsigned int basket_width, basket_height;
```

A private, off-screen pixmap, **wastebasket**, is used as a canvas onto which a list of filenames is built for display. Once an off-screen list of filenames is built, we can copy it to the viewport widget, **wasteBasket** (uppercase "B"). In building the list of filenames for the wastebasket viewport, we must be able to display filenames in normal video, clear the pixmap, and highlight the currently selected file with reverse video. In this module we create a separate GC for each of these video tasks.

On several occasions, the off-screen pixmap must be copied to the wastebasket window (implemented in the widget **wasteBasket**). **wbrw** is a convenience variable that's defined for conciseness of expression in referencing the wastebasket widget **wasteBasket**. Recall that in *xwaste.c* the function **create_basket_widgets()** includes the statement:

```
basket_set_reference_widget(wasteBasket);
```

This function is defined in this module as:

```
/*
basket_set_reference_widget() communicates the reference widget
for the wastebasket.
*/

void basket_set_reference_widget(w)
Widget w;
{
    wbrw = w;
}   /* basket_set_reference_widget */
```

This approach makes it convenient to reference the wastebasket's window, for example, "XtWindow(wbrw)", without imposing unwieldy argument passing on the application programmer.

Lastly, there are four private variables that are used for low-level manipulation of the pixmap. Recall that during the initialization of *xwaste*, **main()** called **basket_create_offscreen_pixmap()** to create and initialize the hidden pixmap-related structures. Its definition is:

```
/*
basket_create_offscreen_pixmap() creates and sets the dimensions
of the basket pixmap (the virtual basket image).
*/

void basket_create_offscreen_pixmap(w, font,
```

```
        pixmap_data, width, height)
Widget w;
XFontStruct *font;
ApplicationData pixmap_data;
unsigned int *width, *height;
{
    XGCValues values;
    Display *display = XtDisplay(w);
    int screen = XDefaultScreen(display);
    unsigned int depth = XDisplayPlanes(display, screen);

    values.foreground = XBlackPixel(display, screen);
    values.background = XWhitePixel(display, screen);
    values.font = font->fid;
    wgc = XCreateGC(XtDisplay(w), RootWindowOfScreen(XtScreen(w)),
        GCForeground | GCBackground | GCFont, &values);
    cgc = XCreateGC(XtDisplay(w), RootWindowOfScreen(XtScreen(w)),
        GCForeground | GCBackground | GCFont, &values);
    XSetFunction(XtDisplay(w), cgc, GXclear);
    values.foreground = XWhitePixel(display, screen);
    values.background = XBlackPixel(display, screen);
    hgc = XCreateGC(XtDisplay(w), RootWindowOfScreen(XtScreen(w)),
        GCForeground | GCBackground | GCFont, &values);
    row_increment = font->max_bounds.ascent +
        font->max_bounds.descent + 2;
    *width = basket_width =
        pixmap_data.browser_columns * font->max_bounds.width;
    *height = basket_height =
        pixmap_data.browser_rows * row_increment;
    wastebasket = XCreatePixmap(XtDisplay(w),
        RootWindowOfScreen(XtScreen(w)), *width, *height, depth);
}   /* basket_create_offscreen_pixmap */
```

First, this function creates the GCs, using the font that's passed as an argument. The font will be either a user-specified font (a browser resource) or the application's default font ("fixed"). The regular wastebasket GC, **wgc**, and the GC that's used to clear the pixmap, **cgc**, are created with a black foreground and white background. For the latter GC, the Xlib function **XSetFunction()** is used to set the (bit-wise) logical operation. For highlighting, **hgc** is created as a white-on-black GC.

The convenience variable **row_increment** is set in this function to a pixel height that's slightly larger that the normal height of a character in the selected font. Two other pixmap-related, private variables, **basket_width** and **basket_height**, are initialized, along with two call-by-reference parameters that provide the calling function with information on the pixmap's dimensions. Note that the pixmap's width and height are a function of user-supplied resource values (browser dimensions and font).

Lastly, this function creates the off-screen pixmap, **wastebasket**, using the Xlib function **XCreatePixmap()**. Its dimensions are based on the previously calculated width and height. We use **XDisplayPlanes()** to determine the pixmap depth, so that the application will operate properly with monochrome as well as color workstations.

10.5.2 Managing Filenames in the Browser Window

In our discussion of *xwaste.c* we mentioned the following function:

```
/*
basket_reset_current_file() sets the "current file pointer"
to a null value.
*/

void basket_reset_current_file()
{
    current_file = NO_FILE;
}   /* basket_reset_current_file */
```

The action function **FillBasket()** and the callback function **Basket()** both invoke **basket_reset_current_file()** in order to prevent a previously selected/highlighted filename from being highlighted when the browser window is mapped. We mentioned earlier that it's possible to alter this policy by removing calls to this function, and by adding a function to the module that returns the currently selected file. (See the paragraphs following **Basket()** in Section 10.4.7.)

Next, consider the task of building the list of filenames on the off-screen pixmap. First, there is no way that we can display a list of filenames if the wastebasket file is missing. This condition must be checked and, if it occurs, reported in an alert box. We will *not* make a distinction between various types of errors. If **fopen()** returns NULL, we simply report that the wastebasket is empty. In particular, we don't want to make assumptions about the nature of the error, since a naive user could be led astray by a misdiagnosis. You may want to change this policy.

Given that there are filenames to display, we can't simply step through the pixmap writing each filename to a row of the pixmap, because the filename for a particular row may be shorter than the filename previously displayed at that position in the pixmap. Hence, if there are wastebasket files, the first step is to clear the pixmap. For efficiency, it's best to clear the entire pixmap, rather than attempting to clear a specific area.

Starting with a clean slate, the next step is to advance from the top of the pixmap toward its bottom, displaying each filename in successive rows, based on the value of **row_increment**. If there is a currently selected file, it must be highlighted as it's displayed.

Lastly, the pixmap must be copied to the wastebasket window. Although we could implement this step in a separate function, we'll consider updating the pixmap and updating the window as integral tasks.

With this overview, consider **basket_fill_with_filenames()**:

```
/*
basket_fill_with_filenames() fills the basket pixmap with the
names of the files stored in the wastebasket.
*/

int basket_fill_with_filenames(highlight_position)
int highlight_position;
{
```

```
    FILE *waste_fd;
    char file_spec[MAX_CHARS], temp_file_spec[MAX_CHARS];
    int len, offset;
    char *more_entries;

    sprintf(file_spec, "%s/%s", home_directory, wastebasket_file);
    if ((waste_fd = fopen(file_spec, "r")) == NULL) {
        alert("The wastebasket is empty.");
        return FALSE;
    }
    XFillRectangle(XtDisplay(wbrw), wastebasket, cgc, 0, 0,
        basket_width, basket_height);
    current_file = NO_FILE;
    more_entries = fgets(file_spec, MAX_CHARS, waste_fd);
    for (offset = row_increment, current_num_files = 0;
            more_entries != NULL && offset < basket_height;
            offset += row_increment, current_num_files++) {
        decode_file_spec(temp_file_spec, file_spec);
        len = strlen(temp_file_spec) - 1;    /* drop the <Return> */
        temp_file_spec[len] = EOS;
        XDrawImageString(XtDisplay(wbrw), wastebasket, wgc,
            0, offset, temp_file_spec, len);
        if (highlight_position != NO_HIGHLIGHT)
            if (highlight_position == current_num_files) {
                /* this is it */
                XDrawImageString(XtDisplay(wbrw), wastebasket,
                    hgc, 0, offset, temp_file_spec, len);
                current_file = current_num_files;
            }
        more_entries = fgets(file_spec, MAX_CHARS, waste_fd);
    }
    fclose(waste_fd);
    XCopyArea(XtDisplay(wbrw), wastebasket, XtWindow(wbrw),
        wgc, 0, 0, basket_width, basket_height, 0, 0);
    return TRUE;
}   /* basket_fill_with_filenames */
```

In our overview we ignored several details. First, the wastebasket filenames are encoded, as described in Section 10.2. Hence, for each filename that's retrieved from the wastebasket file, we must call **decode_file_spec()** to produce the filename that the user expects to see in the browser window. **XDrawImageString()** can then be used to copy the filename to the pixmap.

Next, recall that in **basket_create_offscreen_pixmap()** we created the pixmap with the same depth as the screen. This approach ensures that other functions, such as **XFillRectangle()**, will operate properly with the pixmap and the display screen. There are other approaches, but for this application our primary interest is conciseness and support for both monochrome and color workstations. One alternative would be to create a single-plane pixmap and use **DefaultDepthOfScreen()** to distinguish between monochrome and color environments. In this case, either **XCopyArea()** or **XCopyPlane()**, depending on the screen depth, would be used to copy the pixmap to the destination window.

Third, consider the process of determining the current file. Each time **basket_fill_with_filenames()** is invoked, it begins by resetting the current file. If the requested highlight position (row number) matches the count for the next file in the loop (zero-based), that filename is highlighted *and then becomes the current file*. This correspondence between the highlighted and current files remains until the user selects another file or the browser window (not the inner window) is redisplayed (remapped).

A final consideration, which is really a significant implementation issue, is the situation where there may be too many filenames for the pixmap. For several reasons, we do not attempt any form of dynamic determination of the maximum pixmap dimensions needed to display every filename in the wastebasket. (The core widget, **wasteBasket**, that's used as the inner window for the viewport is created with the same dimensions; see Section 10.4.5.) From one point of view, it's inappropriate to place an arbitrary limit on the size of the wastebasket, simply to control the size of the pixmap needed to represent the entire wastebasket. It's also quite difficult and inefficient to retrieve (rebuild repeatedly) selected portions of the wastebasket's list of filenames, in order to guarantee that every filename can be displayed on a fixed-size pixmap for a very large wastebasket.

We've adopted a compromise solution where the user controls his or her own destiny. That is, the user can choose a wastebasket size without any arbitrary limitations, and can also control the browser's inner window (and pixmap) sizes with resource settings. If, however, the user sets up a wastebasket system in which the wastebasket capacity exceeds the display limitations of the browser, the oldest files in the wastebasket simply aren't viewable. Specifically, the **for** loop in **basket_fill_with_filenames()** terminates if an end-of-file condition occurs for the wastebasket file, or if the next row increment produces a coordinate that's outside the drawable—whichever occurs first.

Next, consider the task of selecting, or highlighting, a file in the browser window. We use a conservative approach whereby the pixmap is rebuilt each time the user selects a(nother) file. Hence, the unique task that's required to highlight a selection is determining the location of the mouse cursor at the time of the select-file operation:

```
/*
basket_select_file() calculates the "row" offset for
a filename and then calls basket_fill_with_filenames() to
either clear the current highlighted file or highlight
another file, depending on the legitimacy of the position.
*/

void basket_select_file(event)
XEvent *event;
{
    int highlight_position;

    highlight_position = event->xbutton.y / row_increment;
    if (highlight_position > current_num_files)
        basket_fill_with_filenames(NO_HIGHLIGHT);
    else
        basket_fill_with_filenames(highlight_position);
}   /* basket_select_file */
```

basket_select_file() calculates the position of the mouse using the vertical coordinate data from the event structure, and, after dividing by the row increment, calls **basket_fill_with_filenames()** to redisplay the list of filenames. Note that if the user selects a position below the last filename in the list, we simply redisplay the wastebasket window. This approach provides the user with a method for deselecting a filename, although this capability isn't really needed.

10.5.3 Wastebasket File Operations

With this background in display and pixmap-based operations, consider the main panel's analog of *delete*, controlled by the "Delete" button, and the menu operations. Let's begin with file deletion from *xwaste*'s main panel (moving a file to the wastebasket). (In Section 10.3 we discussed the preliminary operations: the callback function for the "Delete" command button and building the file specification.)

In terms of operations against the wastebasket's file structures, we need a function that's identical to *delete.c*'s **add_to_basket()**. There are, however, two additional considerations related to the user interface. First, the command window error messages must be replaced by alert box error messages. Second, if the browser window is mapped, the list of filenames must be redisplayed.

Because of its similarity to **add_to_basket()**, we'll ignore the non-GUI-related statements in **basket_add_file()**:

```
/*
basket_add_file() puts the passed file spec. in the top of the
wastebasket, removing the oldest wastebasket contents, if the
wastebasket is overflowing.
*/

void basket_add_file(file_spec)
char *file_spec;
{
    ...
    /* local definitions and start-up operations */
    ...
        else {
            alert("Error opening wastebasket!");
            return;
        }
    }
    ...
    if ((temp_waste_fd = fopen(temp_file_spec, "w")) == NULL) {
        alert(
    "Error opening temporary file during wastebasket operations!");
        return;
    }
    ...
    /*
    encode filename, write it as the first entry, write out the other
    filenames, move the deleted file, and replace the wastebasket file
    */
```

```
    ...
    basket_fill_with_filenames(NO_HIGHLIGHT);
}   /* basket_add_file */
```

Again, we've used a conservative approach. We add the file to the wastebasket and then rebuild the pixmap and wastebasket window. If the browser window is mapped, the list of filenames will reflect the new entry in (the top of) the wastebasket.

The browser window supports two menu operations: (1) file restoration, and (2) permanent file deletion (purging a file from the wastebasket). In order to restore a file to its original directory, we must (1) find the entry in the wastebasket file corresponding to the currently selected file, (2) decode the filename, (3) *copy* the named file from the wastebasket to its original directory, and (4) update the pixmap. **basket_restore_file()** performs these tasks:

```
/*
basket_restore_file() copies a file in the wastebasket back to
its original directory--the wastebasket entry is NOT deleted.
*/

void basket_restore_file()
{
    FILE *waste_fd;
    char cmd_string[MAX_CHARS];
    char file_spec[MAX_CHARS];
    char decoded_file_spec[MAX_CHARS];
    int position;
    char *more_entries;

    if (current_file == NO_FILE) {
        alert("First, you must click left to select a filename.");
        return;
    }
    sprintf(file_spec, "%s/%s", home_directory, wastebasket_file);
    if ((waste_fd = fopen(file_spec, "r")) == NULL) {
            alert("The wastebasket is empty.");
            return;
    }
    if ((more_entries = fgets(file_spec, MAX_CHARS, waste_fd))
            == NULL) {
        alert("The wastebasket is empty.");
        fclose(waste_fd);
        return;
    }
    for (position = 0;
            more_entries != NULL && position < current_file;
            position++)
        more_entries = fgets(file_spec, MAX_CHARS, waste_fd);
    if (position == current_file) {
        file_spec[strlen(file_spec) - 1] = EOS;
        decode_file_spec(decoded_file_spec, file_spec);
```

```
        sprintf(cmd_string, "cp %s/%s/%s %s",
                home_directory, wastebasket_dir, file_spec,
                decoded_file_spec);
        system(cmd_string);
    }
    fclose(waste_fd);
    basket_fill_with_filenames(NO_HIGHLIGHT);
}   /* basket_restore_file */
```

In the current implementation, we do *not move* the deleted file, we simply place a *copy* of it in the original directory. Hence, there will be two files. If there is a subsequent file deletion, the older wastebasket entry will be purged. You can modify the command string ("mv . . .") to suit your personal preferences. You might consider a move operation to be more technically accurate, since it reverses the earlier deletion. When dealing with file deletions, however, there is always some potential for lost information, so we prefer the more conservative approach.

The second menu operation allows the user to purge a file from the wastebasket manually. If the wastebasket utilities are used regularly, any given file will be purged automatically—eventually. The command for permanent file deletion allows the user to purge references to, say, a file containing sensitive information. **basket_delete_file()** steps through the list of filenames, much like **basket_restore_file()**, except that it unlinks the current file:

```
/*
basket_delete_file() permanently deletes a file from
the wastebasket directory.
*/

void basket_delete_file()
{
    FILE *waste_fd, *temp_waste_fd;
    char temp_file_spec[MAX_CHARS];
    char file_spec[MAX_CHARS];
    int position;
    char *more_entries;

    if (current_file == NO_FILE) {
        alert("First, you must click left to select a filename.");
        return;
    }
    sprintf(file_spec, "%s/%s", home_directory, wastebasket_file);
    if ((waste_fd = fopen(file_spec, "r")) == NULL) {
            alert("The wastebasket is empty.");
            return;
    }
    sprintf(temp_file_spec, "%s/%s.%d", home_directory,
        temp_wastebasket_file, getpid());
    if ((temp_waste_fd = fopen(temp_file_spec, "w")) == NULL) {
        alert(
    "Error opening temporary file during wastebasket operations!");
```

```
        fclose(waste_fd);
        return;
    }
    if ((more_entries = fgets(file_spec, MAX_CHARS, waste_fd))
            == NULL) {
        alert("The wastebasket is empty.");
        fclose(waste_fd);
        fclose(temp_waste_fd);
        return;
    }

    for (position = 0; more_entries != NULL; position++) {
        if (position == current_file ||
                position >= max_basket_entries) {
            file_spec[strlen(file_spec) - 1] = EOS;
            sprintf(temp_file_spec, "%s/%s/%s",
                    home_directory, wastebasket_dir, file_spec);
            unlink(temp_file_spec);
        }
        else
            fputs(file_spec, temp_waste_fd);
        more_entries = fgets(file_spec, MAX_CHARS, waste_fd);
    }
    fclose(waste_fd);
    fclose(temp_waste_fd);
    sprintf(temp_file_spec, "%s/%s.%d",
            home_directory, temp_wastebasket_file, getpid());
    sprintf(file_spec, "%s/%s",
            home_directory, wastebasket_file);
    rename(temp_file_spec, file_spec);
    basket_fill_with_filenames(NO_HIGHLIGHT);
}   /* basket_delete_file */
```

Parenthetically, there are three or four locations (depending on your view) where we've repeated a section of code that could be replaced with a call to some common function. For example, much of the start-up code in the previously two functions is similar, although there are some differences. We've made no special efforts to reduce these redundancies because, in these cases, the savings would be minimal and doing so could complicate our ability to alter the error messages in the future. This argument applies to the similarities and redundancies in **add_to_basket()** and **basket_add_file()**.

10.6 *xwaste.menu.c*: A Simple Menu for *xwaste*

xwaste's browser window supports two wastebasket operations against the currently selected file: permanent file deletion and file recovery. In the previous section we addressed their implementation details; in this section we address their user interface.

The most straightforward way to implement these commands is with buttons. Currently, the browser window has one command button, "Done", which unmaps the browser. We could supplement it's button box with two additional command buttons and the callback functions to invoke **basket_restore_file()** and **basket_delete_file()**. If you prefer this organization, it's quite easy to drop this module (and the related translations and actions) from the application, adding the buttons and callbacks in *xwaste.c*.

For this implementation we use a simple menu system, mostly because we want to *illustrate a menu system* with Xt, but partially due to our general preference for menus. With respect to the user interface, it's easier (on average) to add new features to a menu-based system of commands than to a panel of command buttons. Invariably, there is a point of saturation where the number of buttons becomes unwieldy—the button panel "takes over the user interface." In some cases this situation is acceptable, even preferred, for example, a calculator application.

With menus, a debate arises over whether a button-activated menu or a background menu is most appropriate. With the former approach, the command button provides the user with an on-screen reminder of the menu's existence. Some individuals believe that the latter approach requires a somewhat more sophisticated user, since the menu's existence is not readily apparent. In some cases, however, using background menus can reduce the amount of real estate used by the application, yielding a less cluttered screen or providing more space for viewing other applications. Within an application, if background menus are used effectively, for example, cascading menus, they can provide intuitive operation and a less-cluttered appearance.

One negative aspect of a menu-based command system is the lack of support for menus in the X11 Release 3 Athena widget set. Although the X11 Release 4 Athena widget set does provide a simple menu widget, we want *xwaste* to be compatible with both Release 3 and Release 4. For the type of simple menu that needed with our wastebasket browser, we'll coerce two command buttons into a vertical arrangement that masquerades as a menu.

Parenthetically, if you want real, professional-looking menus, you must use one of the commercial widget sets, or write you own menu system with Xlib. It's straightforward to develop an Xlib module that supports cascading, or pull-right, menus. In fact, we have an Xlib-based, pull-right menu module that recursively descends the menu system. (A recursive design simplifies the application programming interface.) The major negative aspect of Xlib-based modules (pseudo-objects) is the difficulty in providing a high level of resource support. In one of our widget programming chapters we'll extend a multiple-choice selection box so that it supports a simple, non-cascading menu.

For our two-command, menu module we need four widget identifiers:

```
static Widget menuShell, menuBox, menuButtonRestore,
    menuButtonDelete;
```

No other private variables are required.

To create the menu system, we'll set up a button box in a pop-up shell with two command buttons:

```
/*
menu_create() allocates the widgets for the basket menu
and sets up the callback functions.
*/

void menu_create(parent)
Widget parent;
```

```
{
    Arg args[3];
    int i;

    i = 0;
    XtSetArg(args[i], XtNallowShellResize, (XtArgVal) TRUE); i++;
    menuShell = XtCreatePopupShell("menuShell",
        transientShellWidgetClass, parent, args, i);
    menuBox = XtCreateManagedWidget("menuBox",
        boxWidgetClass, menuShell, NULL, 0);
    i = 0;
    XtSetArg(args[i], XtNlabel,
        (XtArgVal) "Restore to Original Directory"); i++;
    menuButtonRestore = XtCreateManagedWidget("menuButtonRestore",
        commandWidgetClass, menuBox, args, i);
    i = 0;
    XtSetArg(args[i], XtNlabel,
        (XtArgVal) "Permanently Delete/Remove"); i++;
    menuButtonDelete = XtCreateManagedWidget("menuButtonDelete",
        commandWidgetClass, menuBox, args, i);
    XtAddCallback(menuButtonDelete, XtNcallback, MenuDelete, NULL);
    XtAddCallback(menuButtonRestore, XtNcallback, MenuRestore, NULL);
}   /* menu_create */
```

By default, a box widget arranges its children in rows. As long as the lengths of the labels for the command buttons are fairly uniform, we'll get a vertical menu. Also, note that each command button has a callback function. (If the menu items' labels differ greatly in length, a form widget can be used to force a vertical organization.)

Recall that in *xwaste.c* we provided two actions for mapping and unmapping the menu:

```
static XtActionsRec actionsTable[] = {
    ...
    {"menuUp", (XtActionProc) MenuUp},
    {"menuDown", (XtActionProc) MenuDown},
    ...
};
```

MenuUp() and **MenuDown()** are action functions provided in *xwaste.c*; they call **menu_up()** and **menu_down()**, respectively, from *xwaste.menu.c*.

Also, two translations were provided for associating events with these actions:

```
*wasteBasket.translations:  #replace\n\
    ...
    <Btn2Down>,<Btn2Up>:     menuDown()\n\
    <Btn3Down>,<Btn3Up>:     menuUp()\n\
    ...
```

With this design, clicking on the third mouse button invokes an action function, which in turn invokes the menu, and if the user makes a menu selection, a callback function initiates a request to subordinate functions that carry out the actual file purge or restoration. If the user decides not to perform a menu operation, a second action function removes the menu.

Consider **menu_up()**:

```
/*
menu_up() places and pops up the menu.
*/
/*ARGSUSED*/
void menu_up(w, event)
Widget w;
XButtonEvent *event;
{
    Arg args[3];
    int i;

    i = 0;
    XtSetArg(args[i], XtNx, (XtArgVal) (event->x_root - 20)); i++;
    XtSetArg(args[i], XtNy, (XtArgVal) (event->y_root - 20)); i++;
    XtSetValues(menuShell, args, i);
    XtPopup(menuShell, XtGrabNone);
}   /* menu_up */
```

It simply raises the menu in the vicinity of the mouse cursor. **menu_down()** is equally straightforward; it calls **XtPopdown()** (see Appendix K).

The callback functions are straightforward as well, as evidenced by **MenuRestore()**:

```
/*
MenuRestore() restores a file to its original directory.
*/
/*ARGSUSED*/
void MenuRestore(w, client_data, call_data)
Widget w;
caddr_t client_data;
caddr_t call_data;
{
    basket_restore_file();
    XtPopdown(menuShell);
    reset_proper_keyboard_focus();
}   /* MenuRestore */
```

If you use an X11 Release 4 server exclusively, consider using the Athena **SimpleMenu** widget class to replace the button box- and command button-based menu system.

10.7 *alert.c*: One- and Three-button Generic Alert Boxes

For completeness, in this section we briefly mention the alert box module that's used by *xwaste*. Our discussion is brief because we developed a similar module in Chapter 9. There, we discussed the limitation(s) of that dialog box module, primarily, its support for only one dialog box. We also suggested that multiple, high-level dialog boxes can be implemented more efficiently with a widget class.

There are situations, however, where the application programmer needs a high-level GUI object in several variations and, for whatever reason, prefers to avoid widget programming. Currently, we need multiple alert boxes for *xwaste*, and since we address application programming before widget programming in this book, we'll use this opportunity to illustrate a *limited* form of support for multiple dialog boxes.

For *xwaste*, and possibly other applications, we need a yes-no-cancel alert box for confirming file deletions (to the wastebasket). In addition, there are several situations where errors and general information must be reported. In this case, a single "Continue" button alert box is more appropriate. It's possible to handle these dual tasks with one alert box by manipulating the appearance of buttons in the box. But again, this approach requires a considerable programming investment—and it is inferior to the widget programming approach to multiple dialog boxes.

For *xwaste* we simply define two alert boxes. Overall, the module is very similar to the dialog box module from Chapter 9. Specifically, the blocking action, as implemented with a secondary event loop, and the method of returning the user's response are identical. With this in mind, we'll highlight several aspects of the alert boxes, referring you to Appendix K for the complete source code.

alert.c includes private variables for the alert box shell, label, and button widgets:

```
static Widget alertShellYesNoCancel, alertShellContinue,
    alertLabelYesNoCancel, alertLabelContinue,
    alertYesNoCancel, alertContinue,
    alertButtonYes, alertButtonNo,
    alertButtonCancel, alertButtonContinue;
```

There are private "query" variables for managing the user's response and the blocking action:

```
static int query_result;          /* holds the result of  */
                                  /* an alert box query   */
static int query_wait;            /* controls the blocking   */
                                  /* activity of an alert box */
```

We don't need two sets of these variables because each dialog box *blocks* until the user responds.

Although it isn't necessary, it is convenient to use separate callback functions to unmap each alert box. **AlertYesNoCancel()** unmaps the three-button and return the user's response:

```
/*
AlertYesNoCancel() determines which option has been selected
in a dialog window and resets the 'wait' variable; it works
with alert_query().
*/
/*ARGSUSED*/
void AlertYesNoCancel(w, client_data, call_data)
Widget w;
caddr_t client_data;
```

```
caddr_t call_data;
{
    XtPopdown(alertShellYesNoCancel);
    alert_reset_proper_keyboard_focus();
    if (w == alertButtonYes)
        query_result = ALERT_YES;
    else if (w == alertButtonNo)
        query_result = ALERT_NO;
    else if (w == alertButtonCancel)
        query_result = ALERT_CANCEL;
    query_wait = FALSE;
}   /* AlertYesNoCancel */
```

AlertContinue() is similar, but doesn't modify **query_result**:

```
/*
AlertContinue() terminates the pop-up message window
invoked by alert().
*/
/*ARGSUSED*/
void AlertContinue(w, client_data, call_data)
Widget w;
caddr_t client_data;
caddr_t call_data;
{
    XtPopdown(alertShellContinue);
    alert_reset_proper_keyboard_focus();
    query_wait = FALSE;
}   /* AlertContinue */
```

For the yes-no-cancel alert box that returns the user's response, the functions that invoke the alert box and retrieve the user's response have been combined such that the application calls only one function:

```
/*
alert_query() pops up a dialog window;
it works with AlertYesNoCancel().
*/

int alert_query(message)
char *message;
{
    Arg args[3];
    int i;
    Window dummy_w;
    int root_x, root_y, dummy_xy;
    unsigned int dummy_keys;

    XQueryPointer(XtDisplay(ync_parent),
        XtWindow(ync_parent), &dummy_w, &dummy_w, &root_x,
        &root_y, &dummy_xy, &dummy_xy, &dummy_keys);
```

```
    i = 0;
    XtSetArg(args[i], XtNx, (XtArgVal) (root_x - 20)); i++;
    XtSetArg(args[i], XtNy, (XtArgVal) (root_y - 20)); i++;
    XtSetValues(alertShellYesNoCancel, args, i);
    i = 0;
    XtSetArg(args[i], XtNlabel, (XtArgVal) message); i++;
    XtSetValues(alertLabelYesNoCancel, args, i);
    XtPopup(alertShellYesNoCancel, XtGrabExclusive);
    return get_alert_result();
}   /* alert_query */
```

(See the definition of **delete_file()** in Section 10.4.7.)

In most other respects, this module is very similar to *respbox.c*, thus, we refer you to Appendix K.

10.8 *wastebasket*: A Retrospective

Throughout the chapter we've highlighted a number of implementation decisions that could be handled differently. In our opinion, the most significant of these decisions would be the method chosen for encoding (decoding) filenames. We don't like any approach that leaves miscellaneous "clutter" scattered throughout various directories—filesystem litter. With the approach used here, in which every deleted file is stored in a common wastebasket directory, it *is* possible to guarantee that *wastebasket* can accommodate any legal filename. You can explore this option, if you feel that it's warranted for your version of UNIX.

You may want to consider an alternative to maintaining both an off-screen pixmap and an inner window for the browser's viewport widget. Although maintaining both drawables is somewhat costly, in general, we prefer this approach because the viewable window is not tampered with until the complete image is ready to be displayed.

The text entry boxes, the menu system, and the alert box modules are adequate. There are alternatives, however, several of which we mentioned in our earlier discussions. No matter how hard you try, you simply can't make a professional-looking menu from a stack of command buttons (the silk purse/sow's ear phenomenon). We feel, however, that it is important to illustrate this type of menu system, since many programmers use the standard distribution of X, including the Athena widget set. If you use the older version of X, consider designing your own menu widget class, or use one of the public-domain menu widgets (or the extended, multiple-choice item widget that we'll develop later).

The alert box module isn't very reusable—it was designed just for this application. Even though this book assumes a considerable knowledge of X, we felt that it was important to cover Xt application programming, and provide a significant example, before addressing Xt widget programming. From this perspective, the alert box module is short and it serves a purpose. Once we develop a simple alert box widget, you can incorporate it into *alert.c*. *xwaste* is designed so that you can make this change completely within *alert.c*—no changes are required in any other modules.

Lastly, you may prefer an alternative to the use of dual text entry boxes (widgets) for the file specification. With this approach, it's convenient and intuitive to provide a filename only (in the filename box), and let *xwaste* use the current working directory for the pathname. One alternative would be to use a file selection box, similar to that provided with the OSF/Motif widget set. In a subsequent chapter, we'll provide an Athena widget set-compatible file selection box that you can use in place of the text entry boxes.

11

Overview of Xt Widget Programming

This chapter begins with some comments on the development of widget hierarchies and widget programming in general. To some extent these comments reflect our own biases and should be recognized as such. Subsequently, we discuss the widget concept in terms of data structures, fundamental widget operations, inheritance, resource support, and other issues. This chapter also includes an overview of compound widgets. Regardless of your position on compound widgets, this book would be incomplete if we failed to address them in this and the following chapters.

In the chapters that follow this overview, we develop a variety of widget classes that address specific issues raised in this chapter. We've chosen a semiheterogeneous set of classes that provides a reasonable demonstration of simple and compound, and abstract and concrete widgets. We hope that these widget classes have practical utility in your applications, and that you can use them in designing other widget classes.

11.1 The Importance of Xlib Programming

With Xlib, there are very few restrictions that hinder an application programmer's ability to build high-level modules of reusable GUI components. You can, in fact, design a system of modules that supports most of the GUI requirements for an entire family of applications. Moreover, you can implement whatever look and feel that you believe is best for your applications.

One of the most important advantages of Xlib-based software development is the immunity that your Xlib modules provide from the quirks that come with the newly emerging X toolkits. Suppose you need blocking, pop-up dialog boxes or cascading menus for your next application, and your current toolkit doesn't provide them. Or, you need a high-level drawing canvas in your application, which you are porting to two different hardware platforms. On one hardware platform, users are accustomed to the look and feel provided by one toolkit; on the other, most applications are based on a different toolkit, consequently, a different look and feel. Even worse, one toolkit provides a canvas-like widget and the other doesn't. With Xlib these issues simply don't arise.

11.2 The Disadvantages of Xlib Programming

But, given the freedom of Xlib programming and the industry's immaturity with respect to toolkits, is it realistic to develop a major software product with an Xlib-based interface? In our opinion, it's impossible to give an unqualified answer to this question, different projects require different considerations. In Chapter 1, however, we compared the decision between Xlib and a toolkit to the decision between assembly and a high-level language. To answer the question indirectly, we could note that very few new software projects rely extensively on assembly language programming. It's just too difficult to maintain large amounts of assembly-level source code.

It has been our experience that Xlib-based applications require periodic attention. In general, new releases of X are very compatible with older releases. With a software product as large as X, however, there are inevitable, occasional implementation differences that can affect Xlib-based applications.

Release-specific differences are very possible in the X servers. For the X Window System standard release tape, X servers are contributed by programming teams from various sites. In addition, there are a number of commercial X servers for both X11 Release 3 and Release 4. Public-domain and commercial widget sets provide convenient reliability checks for testing the X servers. That is, when new servers are developed, it's standard procedure to test them with Xt-based applications. Hence, toolkit-based applications tend to be highly reliable across releases and servers. Although a particular server may have been tested extensively with Xlib applications, the *probability* of release- and server-specific differences is greater for Xlib-based applications.

In our experience with X, we've encountered only very minimal release-specific inconsistencies in our toolkit-based applications. We attribute this consistency to the availability of toolkit-based applications during server development and to the high-level interface that Xt provides. In contrast, our Xlib code has required more attention. For example, with one small- to medium-sized application (approximately 15,000 lines of source code), we had one function that behaved unexpectedly on one of the Release 4 servers (until we modified the software to avoid the server-related problems).

11.3 The Importance of Widget Programming

There is little question that the toolkits provide better *long-term* prospects for developers, as well as for most other programming environments. With maturity and feedback from the user community, the toolkits will stabilize, become more complete, and be available on virtually all hardware platforms. Moreover, widespread acceptance, or dominance, will guarantee a minimal level of commonality across applications and developers; this commonality is almost impossible with Xlib-based application development. With this maturity, Xlib will remain an important tool for programmers who must craft special-purpose GUI components, including widgets.

In earlier chapters we addressed various techniques for promoting a higher level of abstraction in Xlib modules, and to some extent, in Xt application modules. In most cases, these programmer-applied techniques can enhance the reusability and portability of applications. Beginning with this chapter, however, we focus more closely on Xt's built-in support for data and procedural abstraction—widgets. Widgets provide the toolkit programmer with a mechanism for supplementing, or extending, the capabilities of a *particular* widget set.

Xt represents a particular approach to high-level X programming—a particular type of toolkit philosophy. Xt provides the programming community with a library of intrinsics that support *the widget concept.* In particular, Xt establishes standards for the data structures (widget classes) that GUI components are built from and, through the Xt Intrinsics, provides broad support for operations that are common to all types of widgets. With this foundation and Xt's openness for extension, the user and programming communities can establish de facto standards for widget sets.

11.4 Enhancing Existing Widget Classes

A widget programmer designs and develops widgets, or more precisely, widget classes. With the emergence and maturity of commercial widget sets, widget programmers will play an increasingly important role in designing special-purpose widgets. In fact, there are a number of application areas that may require complete, special-purpose widget sets, for example, engineering (dials and gauges) and financial (charts and graphs). Thus, in our view, most widget programmers will (1) enhance the existing, common widget sets by developing *miscellaneous* widgets, or (2) develop *homogeneous* collections of specialized widgets. In either case, they will be designing widget classes that coexist with an existing library of intrinsics and with a common widget set that provides a foundation for their widget class development.

In building upon existing widget sets, it's important to recognize the importance of *abstract* widget classes. That is, in addition to the existing foundation classes, namely, **Core**, **Composite**, **Constraint**, and **Shell**, it's important for developers to look for commonalities in their widget classes. These commonalities can be incorporated into incomplete, or intermediate, widget classes that can be used to build *concrete* widget classes, that is, widget classes that can be used in an application. Object-oriented programmers have long recognized the importance of deep class hierarchies (Johnson, 1989), and the principle of *programming by difference* (Johnson and Foote, 1988), which is the practice of using existing classes to derive new a class that more correctly meets your current (and future) needs.

11.5 Generic Widget Classes

In our opinion, widget programmers have been less sensitive than OO programmers to the importance of well-designed class hierarchies and less inclined to take advantage of programming by difference. In what respects? Consider commercial widget sets. The currently available widget sets provide a variety of concrete widgets that are useful in many applications, for example, file selection, dialog, and text entry widgets. In general, however, the focus is on providing an *assortment* of widget classes for application programming. And unfortunately, different widget sets provide different widget classes. The lack of commonality in the concrete classes (across widget sets), along with the absence of abstract classes, makes it difficult for developers to port applications between different "GUI systems."

In our opinion, the commercial widget set developers, and those of us who develop special-purpose widget classes, should strive to "see" the fundamental GUI operations that exist in all GUI environments—from the widget, not the application, programmer's perspective. For example, a file selection widget that's designed for displaying filenames should be a specialization of a generic string selection widget—and the latter should be designed as either an abstract widget, or as a concrete widget that's supports specializations other than the file selection widget.

It's true that commercial widget sets do provide widget classes with generic behavior; for example, drawing surface/canvas widgets, form and bulletin board widgets, and others. But in most cases, they are designed with the application programmer in mind.

You could argue that the provision of generic widget classes invites specializations that don't fully subscribe to a particular widget set's look and feel. In our opinion, this risk is necessary in order to enhance the reusability of a widget set—for the widget programmer.

Obviously, given our decision in this book to provide a number of usable examples with complete source code in the appendices, we can't build a deep hierarchy of widget classes in the remaining chapters. We do provide one widget class that's designed mostly as an abstract class (a string selection widget) from which we later build a concrete class (file selection widget). In addition, we design both simple and compound widget classes. (In this book we use the terminology *simple widget class* to refer to any non-compound widget class.) Compound widgets provide many opportunities for discussion, several of which we address in detail.

11.6 Compound Widgets

Reusability is important for widget programmers. The development of a new widget class can be a lengthy and tedious process. Yet, among certain widget programmers there seems to be an unwritten rule against the development of *compound widgets*, that is, widget classes that are built from other (simple/concrete) widget classes. (The Athena text widget, for example, is a *simple widget*, even though its implementation file is quite large.) We should point out that the Athena widget set does include one compound widget, namely, the dialog box widget.

Compound widgets should not be confused with composite widgets. A composite widget, such as an Athena **Box** widget, serves in a widget management capacity *in an application*. For example, an application programmer can use a box widget to house a collection of command buttons. In contrast, a compound widget class is developed *by a widget programmer* from other widget classes for instantiating a stand-alone widget whose behavior is a collection of the behaviors of its component widgets.

In other words, a composite widget is a general-purpose container (like an ordinary bucket) that serves little purpose without its contents, whereas a compound widget is a specially designed complex object (like a computer) that is *defined by* its components. As mentioned, the Athena widget set provides one compound widget, the dialog widget; it is composed of a label, a text entry box, and command buttons.

It's true that compound widgets present certain problems with respect to the Xt philosophy of user- and application-level control of widgets. The Xt Intrinsics, the Xt widget sets, and Xt applications depend on the resource database facilities for allowing users to modify the behavior and characteristics of an application's GUI components. If a widget programmer assembles a widget (class) from other widgets, the encapsulated widgets are, in some sense, hidden from the application programmer and from the user. It is still possible to control a number of characteristics of the windows for the encapsulated widgets, provided that the widget programmer hasn't taken steps to override user and application-based resource settings.

In some cases there may be resource ambiguities, problems with resizing requests, and so on, but these minor problems reflect the immaturity of early versions of Xt. In practice, that is, *in programming shops where widget programmers are designing special-purpose widgets to meet specific needs*, compound widgets provide a viable means of building new GUI components as specializations and compositions of those provided by a more general widget set.

Indeed, if an X toolkit is to become a high-level programming standard for X software development, it must support fundamental programming techniques. A widget is the Xt analog of an object—at the very least, a high-level data structure that supports encapsulation and the like. It's clear that Xt should support, and that programmers will want to develop, aggregates of *the* fundamental data structure (widget).

We can illustrate several issues related to compound widgets by taking an advance look at an Xt application that's built from two compound widgets. Consider the application in Figure 11.1. *xconvert* is a simple (integer) base-conversion application built from two widgets that we'll discuss in subsequent chapters. The upper portion of *xconvert* includes an **XiSimpleText** widget, which supports a one-line text entry box preceded by a label. The middle portion of *xconvert* includes an **XiChoice** widget, which supports multiple-choice button/item selection. The lower portion of *xconvert* includes a button box with three command buttons, as in several of our previous applications.

In this application we're using the **XiSimpleText** widget to provide a text entry area (for integers) and the **XiChoice** widget to allow the user to select a numeric base. To use

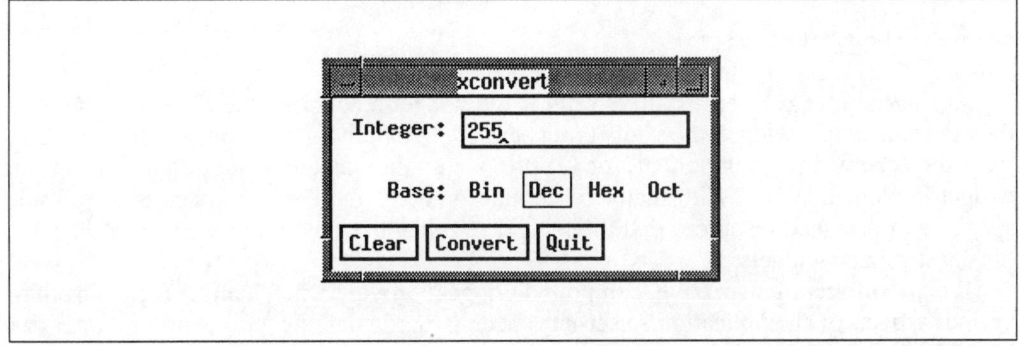

Figure 11.1 *xconvert*, a Hexadecimal Conversion Utility

xconvert, the user first types in an integer, and then selects a base by clicking on the appropriate selection. Once the new base has been selected, the "Convert" button converts the integer to the newly selected base; the integer is "converted from" the previously selected base.

We'll discuss *xconvert* and these widgets in more detail in later chapters. In this overview, we're simply introducing compound widgets as one mechanism for building widgets from an existing widget(s). Compound widgets support reusability through *specialization* and *composition*, standard programming techniques that have syntactic support in OO languages such as C++.

The **XiSimpleText** widget encapsulates an Athena **Label** widget and an Athena **Text** widget. (With C, it's always possible to circumvent encapsulation, but we don't consider those violations here.) An **XiSimpleText** widget also imposes certain policies, for example, the text entry area doesn't accept linefeed and carriage return characters. To some extent, the label and text entry widgets are hidden. For example, the external identifiers for the label and text entry widgets (widget names) are specified within the implementation file for the **XiSimpleText** widget (in the initialization code).

Thus, the external names for the encapsulated widgets must be made available, for example, in the **XiSimpleText** widget's documentation, before users can set their resources (by name). But this situation is really no different than that presented by applications built from simple widgets—from the user's perspective, applications encapsulate widgets. In both cases the user must have the external names in order to make *specific* resource settings. For example, with an **XiSimpleText** widget the external identifier for the Athena text widget is "text". Thus, the user can make a specific request for a one-pixel border around the text entry box by using the following resource setting (for *xconvert*):

```
xconvert*text*borderWidth:  1
```

There are, of course, other ways of achieving the same result. (Although this resource specification contains wildcards, there is no other widget named "text", thus, it is adequate.)

For many applications, users set resources using wildcards and classes. In general, wildcard and class specifications apply to encapsulated widgets as well. For example, a user could *request* a border width of 5 for all windows within *xconvert* with the following resource setting:

```
xconvert*borderWidth:  5
```

Again, the user can set resources only if the widget recognizes them. Specifically, in the case of a simple widget, the widget must either (1) inherit those resources, for example, from the **core** widget (component), or (2) provide explicit resource support as part of the widget implementation. With many compound widgets, the best approach is to provide specifically designed resources that the widget can then translate into resource settings for the encapsulated widgets.

From a different perspective, compound widgets provide a mechanism for controlling various aspects of an application's user interface. In particular, the widget programmer can prohibit the user from making certain resource settings. Consider *xconvert* again. The **XiSimpleText** and **XiChoice** widgets explicitly set the border width for their labels to 0, overriding any attempts by the user to put a border around the label. In addition, *xconvert* (the application) overrides the user's attempt to place a border around either the items or the multiple-choice item box. Thus, although "xconvert*borderWidth: 5" requests a border width of 5 pixels for all windows, only the text entry box and the command buttons honor this request.

The question of who should have ultimate control over a GUI component's appearance and behavior certainly is debatable. It's clear, however, that no GUI system allows the user to reconfigure *everything*; otherwise, its look and feel would be transient. In our opinion, the widget programmer has the right, and in some cases the obligation, to limit the degree of configurability of a widget. For the **XiSimpleText** widget, the widget programmer has an *obligation* to enforce the distinction between the text entry box and its label, considering the likelihood of naive users. (The Athena **Dialog** widget also prohibits the user from configuring it with a border around its label.)

An **XiChoice** widget places certain limits on the application as well. Specifically, the label cannot have a border, in this case, because an encompassing box/outline is used to highlight an item. Should the widget programmer who designs the **XiChoice** widget class also prevent the user from putting a border around each item (its window), or around the entire multiple-choice selection box (its window)?

Although we believe a widget programmer has the right to impose restrictions, we tend to follow the practice of leaving the less clear-cut decisions up to the application programmer, who can then either enforce a policy or in turn leave the decision up to the user. With an **XiChoice** widget, leaving these decisions up to the application programmer increases the utility of the widget. For example, in one application, an **XiChoice** widget can be configured to have a radio-button appearance, in another, a menu-like appearance.

xconvert prohibits borders around the multiple-choice box for numeric base, in order to prevent confusion over which area supports text entry (and to maintain an uncluttered appearance)—the application programmer made a unilateral decision. Also, for this application each item's label is a single word. If, on the other hand, an application requires (multiple-choice) items with multiple-word labels ("Enable Self-destruct Mode"), the programmer may want to impose a border on each item to prevent confusion.

We mentioned that there can be ambiguities with respect to resources. For example, an **XiChoice** widget contains (non-command) buttons and a label. Buttons and labels are GUI components, thus, the user may want to modify their resources. How does a widget programmer permit the user (or the application programmer) to configure a compound widget such that one encapsulated widget has a border and another doesn't (either by default, by the user's choice, or by force)?

Usually, there are a number of possibilities. With only two encapsulated widgets, if the widget programmer wants to enforce a specific resource setting for one widget but not the other, the simplest technique may be to hard-code the resource setting during the compound widget's initialization phase. In other cases, depending on the number of encapsulated widgets and the extent to which they support resources with common names, it may be preferable to provide a dedicated resource for the compound widget that is mapped to the encapsulated widget. For example, an **XiChoice** widget supports a resource with the name "itemBorderWidth".

The point is that we can't brand compound widgets are "bad," simply because they introduce certain complexities. In general, if we can assemble a widget from other widgets, and if it's use is straightforward for the user and the application programmer, then we have (1) carried forth the look and feel of familiar widgets in our new widgets, and (2) reused an existing body of source code. Clearly, the importance of reusability of widget classes (through inheritance and composition) should be considered in designing future widget sets.

11.7 Overview of Widget Data Structures and Operations

In the abstract sense, a widget is a user interface object that binds together a window(s) and the operations that it supports. At a lower level, a widget is a collection of data, functions, and pointers to data and functions that implements a widget's behavior. This collection includes instance-specific data, class-specific data, data that's inherited from superclasses, class-specific methods, widget interface functions, and inherited methods. In addition, each widget "inherits" the support of the Xt Intrinsics.

For a given application, there may be multiple widget instances from a particular class, for example, instances of the **Command** widget class. Each widget instance includes unique data, for example, the callback list for a particular command button. It's clear, however, that the widget concept must support widget classes where instances share common information; see Figure 11.2. For example, a blocking dialog box could be designed such that the variable(s) controlling the blocking action are stored in a common data area—shared by all members of this class. For some widget classes, shared data may be necessary for cooperation or coordination among widgets; for others, a common data area simply conserves storage that otherwise would have to be declared for each widget instance.

This dichotomy between unique and shared instance data does not extend to functions; all instances of a particular widget class share the same methods, general-purpose functions, and widget interface functions. *Methods* are widget functions that implement that class's primitive widget operations—operations that are recognized by the Xt Intrinsics. For example, every widget class must provide a destroy method (or indicate that one is not needed). This method is invoked when an application calls **XtDestroyWidget()** to destroy an instance of that widget class.

Xt is based on the premise that (1) a finite, even limited, number of different types of widgets is adequate for building the user interface for most applications, (2) exceptions can

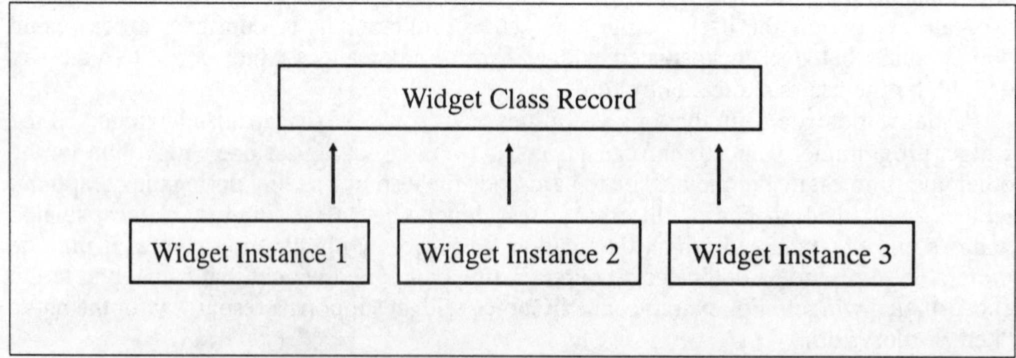

Figure 11.2 Sharing Class Data with Widgets

be handled via extension—by allowing the programmer to create special-purpose widgets, and (3) different widget types have a number of data structures and operations in common. Thus, in addition to provisions for the sharing of data among instances of a particular class, there must be provisions for sharing data and functions across widget classes.

Data that's shared among widget classes is essentially hidden from the widget programmer. It exists on the intrinsics-side of an application; thus, the widget programmer doesn't have to be concerned with unrelated widget classes during the development of a new class. The Intrinsics, of course, provide the best example of shared functionality.

Beyond the behind-the-scenes sharing of data and functionality, all widgets have certain common requirements. For example, every widget has a window in which to display its external behavior. Windows, in turn, have borders, (often) support resizing, must eventually be destroyed, and so on.

Xt uses a primitive form of inheritance as the primary mechanism for specifying common data and operations. When a widget programmer creates a new widget class, the fundamental data structures and functions that are required to manage a widget instance are inherited from superclasses. The **Core** widget class is the most fundamental superclass, the root class, in a widget class hierarchy. (The **Core** widget class is actually an abstraction, built from more primitive classes, but these lower level classes are hidden from the widget programmer.) If, for example, a widget class must support simple containment of other widgets, it should inherit from the **Composite** widget class as well. Chapter 2 includes an overview of the fundamental widget classes—those supported by every Xt Intrinsics implementation.

Note that an application programmer can build a specialized widget by adding features to a widget *instance*. For example, in Chapter 10 we built the wastebasket browser's inner window by adding features to an instance of the **Core** widget class. Most notably, we added actions; loosely speaking, we added/attached an off-screen pixmap, special GCs, and so on. In some situations, it's appropriate to prototype a new widget class by building upon an existing widget class at the application programming level. Once the details of the embellished widget are worked out, a widget programmer can implement a widget class that approximates the functionality of the prototype widget.

11.8 Widget Data Structures

Xt provides for unique and shared widget data, plus class-specific and generic widget operations, by factoring the information that constitutes each widget into several structures. These structures are in turn factored into three separate files: *<class>.h* contains public identifiers, *<class>P.h* contains private (P) type definitions, macros, and so on, and *<class>.c* is the implementation file that defines the class-specific data and the functions. In order to instantiate a widget, you must include (among other things) the public header for that class:

```
#include <class>.h
```

Consider the breakdown for the **Core** widget class, which every widget class must inherit. By itself, a core widget is almost too primitive to be instantiated. (There are exceptions; we used a core widget to build the inner window for *xwaste*'s browser.) The

Core widget class serves as a good example for our discussion because it's relatively simple. In the next chapter, we'll consider the class organization for a string selection widget that's derived from a core widget.

In order to create an instance of a core widget, the application programmer first establishes a widget ID (handle) and then associates it with a particular widget instance. Consider the following statements from *xwaste*:

```
static Widget ..., wasteBasket, ...        /* from xwaste.c */
...
wasteBasket = XtCreateManagedWidget("wasteBasket", widgetClass,
    vPort, args, i);
...
```

The second argument to **XtCreateManagedWidget()** is, of course, the class (name) of the widget instance. For a dialog widget the class is **dialogWidgetClass**, for a label widget the class is **labelwidgetclass**, for a core widget the class is **widgetClass**. (**coreWidgetClass** is acceptable with X11 Release 4.)

This identifier is defined in *Core.h* as:

```
externalref WidgetClass widgetclass;
```

(Or, if you prefer: "extern WidgetClass widgetclass;".) The data type **WidgetClass** is defined in *Intrinsics.h* as:

```
typedef struct _WidgetClassRec *WidgetClass;
```

It is simply a pointer to a structure of type **_WidgetClassRec**, which is defined in *CoreP.h* as:

```
typedef struct _WidgetClassRec {
    CoreClassPart core_class;
} WidgetClassRec;
```

This structure contains one field, **core_class**. The entire structure is the template for a **Core** class record.

Widget classes that are derived from the **Core** widget class contain multiple components, one for each inherited class. Recall our overview in Section 2.5.3 of the **Dialog** widget's class record:

```
typedef struct _DialogClassRec {
    CoreClassPart        core_class;
    CompositeClassPart   composite_class;
    ConstraintClasspart  constraint_class;
    FormClassPart        form_class;
    DialogClassPart      dialog_class;
} DialogClassRec;
```

A dialog widget's class record contains five components. It inherits functionality from **Core**, **Composite**, **Constraint**, and **Form**, in addition to its own contribution to the class record. We discuss class inheritance subsequently; here, we're focusing on the more general issue of class versus instance records, and so on. For now, the best interpretation of the **Core** class record is simply: The **Core** widget class "inherits itself."

Note the naming conventions. A class record (type) is named "<class>ClassRec", for example, "DialogClassRec". As we've already witnessed, there appear to be exceptions in the names chosen for certain components of the **Core** widget class. From the names used within **DialogClassRec**, that is, "<class>ClassPart" (including "CoreClassPart"), you might expect the name "CoreClassRec", instead, it is "WidgetClassRec". One explanation for these exceptions is the desire to convey the idea of a generic widget type: **Widget**, **widgetClass**, **WidgetClass**, **WidgetClassRec**. The Intrinsics operate on widgets of all types, and "Widget. . ." conveys this idea.

Continuing with our discussion of a **Core** class record, **CoreClassPart**, the data type of **core_class**, is defined in *CoreP.h* as well:

```
typedef struct _CoreClassPart {
    WidgetClass          superclass;
    String               class_name;
    Cardinal             widget_size;
    XtProc               class_initialize;
    XtWidgetClassProc    class_part_initialize;
    Boolean              class_inited;
    XtInitProc           initialize;
    XtArgsProc           initialize_hook;
    XtRealizeProc        realize;
    XtActionList         actions;
    Cardinal             num_actions;
    XtResourceList       resources;
    Cardinal             num_resources;
    XrmClass             xrm_class;
    Boolean              compress_motion;
    Boolean              compress_exposure;
    Boolean              compress_enterleave;
    Boolean              visible_interest;
    XtWidgetProc         destroy;
    XtWidgetProc         resize;
    XtExposeProc         expose;
    XtSetValuesFunc      set_values;
    XtArgsFunc           set_values_hook;
    XtAlmostProc         set_values_almost;
    XtArgsProc           get_values_hook;
    XtWidgetProc         accept_focus;
    XtVersionType        version;
    struct _XtOffsetRec *callback_private;
    String               tm_table;
    XtGeometryHandler    query_geometry;
    XtStringProc         display_accelerator;
    caddr_t              extension;
} CoreClassPart;
```

Even though we're still dealing with the class component only, you can get a feeling for the encapsulation that's required to produce what the application (and widget) programmer knows as a widget. The first field of each class record is a pointer to the superclass that it's derived from. Also, there are a number of fields that are clearly related to widget characteristics that are important at the class level, such as the Boolean variables that record whether or not certain types of events will be compressed.

In addition to the "data" fields, there are several entries that represent functions. Although their data types represent high-level function declarations, it's clear (due to the nature of C) that each field stores a pointer to a function. For example, **XtWidgetProc** is defined as a pointer to a void function (procedure):

```
typedef void (*XtWidgetProc)();
```

Several widget methods are declared with this type, including **destroy()**, **resize()**, and **expose()**. For each widget class, the widget programmer must provide the methods that are referenced in this record—methods that are used with each widget instance. Each method must be either (1) defined in the class implementation file, (2) inherited from a superclass, or (3) specified as NULL (if it isn't needed).

How is the class record used? As mentioned in Section 11.7, all widgets of a particular class share the same class record. Also, the *structure* of various parts of this record are the same for every widget class. Specifically, every class record starts with the **core_class** component. The order of any remaining components depends on the class and on certain conventions established by Xt. Thus, the Intrinsics "know" the organization (layout) of a particular widget's class record. If, for example, the application programmer calls **XtDestroyWidget()** to destroy a widget, the Intrinsics consult the proper field of the widget class record, which points to the destroy method. The Intrinsics invoke this method, which is responsible for carrying out a graceful clean-up—freeing GCs, pixmaps, or anything else allocated by that widget.

Each widget has instance-specific data, for example, the border width of its window. This information is managed by the instance record. *CoreP.h* includes the following type definition:

```
typedef struct _WidgetRec {
    CorePart core;
} WidgetRec;
```

As with the class record, a core widget's instance record has only one field; classes derived from **Core** have a field for each class in the derivation path.

Note the naming conventions. **WidgetClassRec** is the class record template; **WidgetRec** is the instance record template. Also, the field names for the class and instance records are **core_class** and **core**, respectively. In general, the convention is to drop "class" ("Class") in forming the instance record analog.

CoreP.h defines the type/layout for the **core** component of the instance record:

```
typedef struct _CorePart {
    Widget               self;
    WidgetClass          widget_class;
    Widget               parent;
    XrmName              xrm_name;
    Boolean              being_destroyed;
    XtCallbackList       destroy_callbacks;
    caddr_t              constraints;
    Position             x, y;
    Dinemsion            width, height;
    Dimension            border_width;
    ...                  ...
    String               name;
    ...                  ...
    Boolean              visible;
    Boolean              mapped_when_managed;
} CorePart;
```

The first field is a self-referencing field. (We used a similar field in one of our Xlib dialog box implementations; recall the definition of **_Response** in Section 7.2.1.) The second field establishes a connection to the widget's class record. The third field is used by the Intrinsics in maintaining the widget tree(s) that defines the application's interface. (This tree is a hierarchy of widget instances, not widget classes). For example, when an application calls **XtRealizeWidget()**, Xt must navigate this widget tree creating windows (and performing other duties) for each widget.

Other fields store commonly needed information, for example, window characteristics; keeping this information with the application reduces the number of server requests.

11.9 Widget Class and Instance Initialization

The entity that we view abstractly as a widget is actually a system of structures within structures within structures (plus functions) aligned by their class-versus-instance affiliation. It would be easy to jump to the conclusion that the class and instance records should somehow be combined to produce a *complete* widget record.

In reality, class and instance records must be distinct, since there is only one class record (shared by each instance of that widget class). As noted earlier, the **widget_class** variable within the **core** variable/component of every instance record establishes a connection between each widget and its class record.

Each time an application calls **XtCreateManagedWidget()** (or **XtCreateWidget()**) an instance record must be allocated to store the "essence" of that particular widget; this record is created from dynamic storage, based on the value of **widget_size** in the **core_class** component of the widget's class record (see the example in the next paragraph). **XtCreateManagedWidget()** returns a pointer to this storage, which the application views as a widget ID (type **Widget**). With this scenario, it's clear that the class record must exist before widget instances can be created.

The compiler handles the task of creating the class record for a widget. Specifically, storage for the widget class record is defined (with file-level scope) and initialized within its implementation file. The following record is defined and initialized near the beginning of *Core.c*:

```
WidgetClassRec widgetClassRec = {
{
    (WidgetClass) &windowObjClassRec,     /* superclass */
    "Core",                               /* class name */
    sizeof(WidgetRec),                    /* instance record size */
    ...
    FALSE,                                /* class initialized? */
    ...
}
};
```

Then, the external identifier that's used by an application is defined and pointed at the previously defined class record:

```
WidgetClass widgetClass = &widgetClassRec;
```

In comparison, *Dialog.c* defines the following:

```
DialogClassRec dialogClassRec = {
{
    (WidgetClass) &formClassRec,          /* superclass */
    "Dialog",                             /* class name */
    sizeof(DialogRec),                    /* instance record size */
    ...
    FALSE,                                /* class initialized? */
    ...
}
    ...
};

WidgetClass dialogWidgetClass = (WidgetClass) &dialogClassRec;
```

From these statements, you can see the interplay of class and instance record definitions, occurring at program start-up and during widget initialization, respectively. Specifically, since the class record is initialized during program start-up, **XtCreateManagedWidget()** has all the information it needs for run-time allocation of an instance record.

From the abstract view of the application programmer, the second argument to **XtCreateManagedWidget()** identifies the *type* of the widget that's being created:

```
    wasteBasket = XtCreateManagedWidget("wasteBasket", widgetClass,
        vPort, args, i);
```

But, for the Xt Intrinsics, this argument is a pointer to a data structure that's used to create and manipulate each widget instance. For example, during widget creation it consults the third field of the class record for the instance record's space requirements.

Once an instance record has been allocated, the second field of the instance record:

```
typedef struct _CorePart {
    Widget              self;
    WidgetClass         widget_class;    /* point at class record */
    Widget              parent;
    ...                 ...
    String              name;
    ...
} CorePart;
```

is initialized to point to the class record. For the **wasteBasket** widget, the initialization would be loosely equivalent to:

```
wasteBasket->core.widget_class = widgetClass;
```

Likewise, the third argument to **XtCreateManagedWidget()** is used to initialize the third field in the instance record, something like:

```
wasteBasket->core.parent = vPort;
```

Using the link to the class record that's provided by the **widget_class** field, the Intrinsics can retrieve shared data on demand. For example, in order to retrieve a widget's resource data (from the resource database that's built during program start-up), the resource manager uses the resource name field in the instance record, plus the class name from the class record (the resource class). The resource data values are used by the resource manager to set resource-dependent fields in the instance record.

Lastly, you may have noticed that the **class_inited** field is *initialized* to **FALSE** *during initialization*:

```
WidgetClassRec widgetClassRec = {
{
    ...
    FALSE,                                  /* class initialized? */
    ...
}
};
```

Although this may seem like a contradiction, it really isn't. Even though many of the class record's fields are given explicit values during storage allocation (the compiler also resolves the pointers to the class methods), there are additional start-up operations that must be performed for each widget class that's incorporated into an application. These operations should be performed only once; Xt sets this field to indicate that they have been completed.

In this section we've focused on selected fields in the class and instance records, those that were important in describing the rationale behind the widget concept. The reference and programming manuals for Xt (for example, Nye and O'Reilly [1990]) provide descriptions for *each* field in these structures. In the chapters that follow, many of these fields will be addressed by example.

11.10 Inheritance

In deriving a new class from existing widget classes, there are essentially two ways to proceed: (1) inheritance and (2) composition. Xt's inheritance technique requires the widget programmer to assemble widget class and instance records as aggregates of the unique class and instance components of all widget classes between the root of the class hierarchy and the current point of derivation.

For example, the fundamental widget classes are arranged in the hierarchy given in Figure 11.3. Therefore, in creating a new class, say, **Carton**, that inherits the capabilities provided by the **Constraint** widget class, you would include the class components for **Constraint** and all of its superclasses, plus the class component for the derived class, **CartonClassPart**:

```
typedef struct _CartonClassRec {
    CoreClassPart       core_class;
    CompositeClassPart  composite_class;
    ConstraintClassPart constraint_class;
    CartonClassPart     carton_class;
} CartonClassRec;
```

Likewise, the instance record for **Carton** would be composed of the **core**, **composite**, **constraint**, and **carton** instance components.

The second approach to deriving (in the generic sense) a new class from existing classes is by developing compound widgets—composition of data structures where the structures are widgets. In our earlier discussion of compound widgets we made the point that compound widgets present certain design problems. As a consequence, many widget programmers either don't use or design them, or they approach them with trepidation. Despite their limitations, compound widgets represent the application of a basic programming technique, composition, to Xt's central high-level data structure, the widget.

Parenthetically, it's easy to confuse (1) Xt's approach to widget class inheritance, which involves the (manual) assembly of a composite, or aggregate, of superclass/instance components, with (2) the principle of composition as supported by traditional and OO languages. Xt requires the widget programmer to use structure composition in *specifying* the inheritance hierarchy. Using these structures, Xt then mimics the form of inheritance supported in OO languages. This approach to inheritance supports class derivation by specialization. For example, **Carton** is a specialization of **Constraint** that includes additional "carton-like" constraints.

With an OO language there is syntactic (compiler) support for this type of class inheritance, as described in the C++ example in Section 2.5.1. As a result, it's quite straightforward to create deep object class hierarchies where each subclass is a specialization of its superclass. When there's syntactic support for inheritance, the compiler does a lot of the work that's required in specifying which variables and methods are inherited by

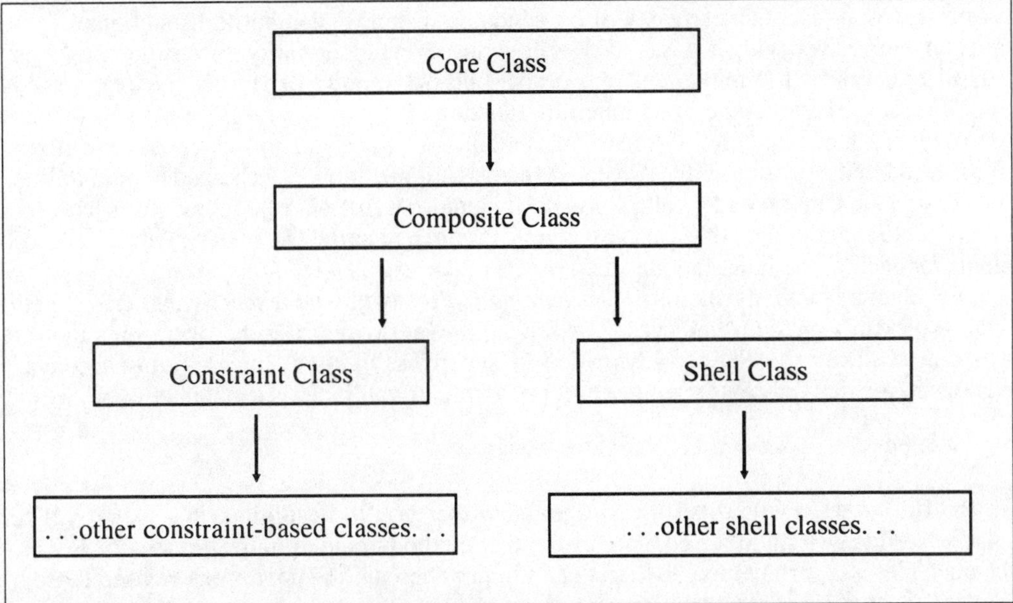

Figure 11.3 The Fundamental Xt Widget Classes

which classes; thus, for the programmer, class definitions can be relatively simple in many cases.

For example, with C++ the **public** keyword followed the class name for a superclass, **window**, is sufficient for indicating that a derived class, **text_window**, should inherit the variables and methods of its superclass, and those of its superclass's superclasses:

```
class text_window : public window {
    ...
    // variables and methods added by text_window
    ...
};
```

Thus, it's important to keep inheritance and composition in perspective, especially with Xt. Although the widget programmer uses composition as part of the derivation process, the composition of structures in the Xt inheritance scheme is distinct from the composition of widgets from other widgets.

There are a number of inheritance-related details that the widget programmer must take care of *manually*. We've mentioned the requirement that the widget programmer specify the class and instance components for each superclass in deriving the new widget class.

With Xt there are two fundamental considerations in class derivation, data and methods. Even though setting up the class and instance records for a new widget class accounts for many of the data-related considerations, doing so provides no *guarantee* that the methods associated with each superclass will be adequate in terms of inherited functionality. In general, the derived widget class (1) inherits some of its functionality from superclasses, (2) supplies methods that implement the derived class's unique behavior, and (3) possibly modifies or overrides some of its inherited functionality.

With Xt, there two types of (inherited) methods: chained and non-chained. **Initialize()**, the method that performs widget (instance record) initialization, is a chained method. When you design the **Carton** widget class, you must include an **Initialize()** method that sets values in the **carton** component of a carton widget's instance record. The instance record components for each of the inherited classes must be initialized as well.

For chained methods, the Intrinsics *automatically* invoke the respective inherited methods—you can't prevent this action. You can, however, override the operations that are performed during the chained invocation of superclass methods by providing secondary actions in the derived class's method. For example, if you include a statement such as

```
current_widget->core.width = 300;
```

in the **Initialize()** method for the widget class that you're designing, this value will replace/override any value stored there by another method in the initialization chain. For any chained method, if the derived widget class requires no unique operations beyond those of the superclasses' methods, you can simply set that field in the class record to **NULL**—the inherited methods do their work automatically.

Expose() is an example of a non-chained method—you *must* specify how exposures are to be handled. If the immediate superclass's **Expose()** method is adequate, you can inherit it simply by placing the special symbol **XtInheritExpose** in the appropriate position in the derived widget's class record:

```
CartonClassRec cartonClassRec = {
{
    (WidgetClass) &constraintClassRec,       /* superclass */
    "Carton",                                /* class name */
    ...
    XtInheritExpose,                         /* expose method */
    ...
}
    ...
};
```

(Each of the fundamental widget classes provides **XtInherit...** symbols for their respective non-chained methods.)

If, on the other hand, the derived widget class requires considerably different exposure-handling, you should provide an expose method, say, **Expose()**, and reference this function during class record initialization:

```
CartonClassRec cartonClassRec = {
{
    (WidgetClass) &constraintClassRec,       /* superclass */
    "Carton",                                /* class name */
```

```
    ...
    Expose,                                   /* expose method */
    ...
}
};
...
...
static void Expose(w)
Widget w;
{
    ...
}
...
```

A third alternative is to provide an expose method for the derived class that references the superclass's expose method. This approach is appropriate when the derived class needs to supplement or override (a portion of) the operations of the superclass's method.

11.11 Single versus Multiple Inheritance

Xt supports single inheritance by chaining together the class record of each widget class that contributes to the derived widget class. For example, the Athena **Dialog** widget class inherits from four classes:

```
typedef struct _DialogClassRec {
    CoreClassPart       core_class;
    CompositeClassPart  composite_class;
    ConstraintClasspart constraint_class;
    FormClassPart       form_class;
    DialogClassPart     dialog_class;
} DialogClassRec;
```

This record structure reflects the inheritance hierarchy of the fundamental widget classes (see Chapter 2) and the Athena widget classes. Specifically, the Athena **Form** widget class is a subclass of the **Constraint** widget class and the Athena **Dialog** widget class is a subclass of the Athena **Form** widget class.

The superclass field in the **core_class** component of each class record points to the class record of the superclass:

```
DialogClassRec dialogClassRec = {
{
    (WidgetClass) &formClassRec,          /* superclass */
    "Dialog",                             /* class name */
    ...
}
    ...
};
```

In this case, **Dialog** inherits from **Form**; thus, its superclass field points to **Form**'s class record, **formClassRec**. The chaining of class records extends from the derived class back to the **Core** widget class, which references the (otherwise hidden) **windowObj** class record:

```
WidgetClassRec widgetClassRec = {
{
    (WidgetClass) &windowObjClassRec,    /* superclass */
    "Core",                              /* class name */
    ...
}
};
```

This implementation of single inheritance with C provides much of the functionality that's available with OO languages that support single inheritance only. As we've mentioned, Xt's support for OO programming applies to widget programming only.

Many OO languages support multiple inheritance; that is, a derived class can have more than one (immediate) superclass. Typically, multiple inheritance is used to derive a class from two or more classes where the parent classes (base classes in C++ terminology) belong to distinct class hierarchies. For example, a class representing microcomputers and a class representing UNIX-based computers could be subclassed to produce a class representing UNIX-based microcomputers.

In this case, the microcomputer class might belong to a hardware-oriented class hierarchy that represents all computers, whereas the UNIX-based computer class might belong to a operating system-oriented computer class hierarchy. In justifying this particular derivation, we would argue that a UNIX-based microcomputer "is a" microcomputer and it "is a" UNIX-based computer. (The *is-a* relationship is often used as one of the criteria in establishing the merit of a derivation.)

There is a moderate amount of disagreement in the OO programming community over the relative importance of multiple inheritance. Multiple inheritance is often overused, or abused. When languages support multiple inheritance it's tempting to use this feature for quick-and-dirty class building. In fact, you might argue that our UNIX-based microcomputer class is a concoction of classes motivated by the desire to reuse (inappropriately) an existing inventory of classes.

The alternative, of course, is composition. In general, it would be inappropriate to inherit from the class **chocolate** and the class **ice_cream_bar**, in order to derive the class **chocolate_ice_cream_bar**. A chocolate ice cream bar "is an" ice cream bar, but it "is not a" chocolate. Using composition, however, you could derive **chocolate_ice_cream_bar** from **ice_cream_bar**, adding **chocolate** as a component (instance variable).

Another point is that with Xt, all widgets classes are derived from the same root, namely, the **Core** widget class. Suppose that you would like to build a *pop-up*, alert box widget class. Building an **alert** class *without* the pop-up functionality is straightforward—you could use the same inheritance path as the **Dialog** widget class, substituting **alert_class** for **dialog_class**:

```
typedef struct _AlertClassRec {
    CoreClassPart       core_class;
    CompositeClassPart  composite_class;
```

```
    ConstraintClasspart constraint_class;
    FormClassPart       form_class;
    AlertClassPart      alert_class;
} AlertClassRec;
```

Adding the pop-up functionality is more difficult. Logically, you can't inherit from the **TransientShell** widget class, because a pop-up alert box "is not a" transient shell. Physically, you can't do this, due to the chaining technique that's used in widget class inheritance. Specifically, **TransientShell** is part of an inheritance path that extends from the **Composite** widget class:

Core —> Composite —> Shell —> WMShell —> VendorShell —> TransientShell

Inheriting from both the **TransientShell** and **Form** widget classes would be a cockeyed form of multiple inheritance.

One way out of this predicament is to argue that an alert box shouldn't be *confined* to a pop-up shell of any particular type—don't restrict its potential usage. With this argument, the alert box widget class would be assembled with everything but the shell. Then, each application would have to provide a pop-up shell to house each alert box widget. We use this approach in Chapter 13.

This chapter addressed a number of widget programming issues, focusing primarily on basic concepts and rationale while omitting many of the details of widget class development. In the chapters that follow we investigate widget programming more closely.

12

XiStrSelect: Designing Simple Widgets

This is the first of several chapters that address widget programming in detail by presenting a complete, working widget class that supplements the Athena widget set. We've chosen the Athena widget set as a foundation because it is almost universally available to X programmers. The widget programming principles that apply to the Athena widgets are valid with other widget sets as well.

There are several objectives in this chapter. First, we must address a number of first-time issues, such as the use of public and private header files to promote encapsulation and abstraction, the initialization of a class record, and the organization and contents of the implementation file. Our second objective is to illustrate the development of a *simple*, simple widget class, one that builds on the foundation provided by the **Core** widget class. Subsequent chapters will focus on widgets with a richer class hierarchy (for example, a class that inherits functionality from **Core**, **Composite**, **Constraint**, and others).

Because we're developing our first widget class in this chapter, another objective is to implement a widget whose operations are somewhat familiar. This approach will allow us to focus on the mechanics of widget development without becoming distracted by the widget's functionality. With this in mind, we'll develop a string selection widget that allows the application programmer to present a series (list) of strings in a window. (Motif [OSF, 1990] provides a similar, although higher level, widget.) The user can select a string and then apply an operation to the selected string. Many of the operations required to select a string are quite similar to those of the enhanced core widget that we used as the inner window in *xwaste*'s browser.

Another objective is to fulfill our promise in Chapter 11 to provide an example of an abstract widget class, from which more specialized widgets can be developed. For example, in a subsequent chapter we use the string selection widget to "derive" a file selection widget. Although an application programmer could create a string selection widget, this class is primarily designed as a superclass for more specialized widget classes.

12.1 Widget Naming Conventions

For the most part we adhere to the accepted naming conventions for widget-related components; these conventions are summarized in Nye and O'Reilly (1990, Appendix D). Thus, our widgets should be usable without modification in many programming environments. It's generally accepted that each widget set should use a prefix with its widget component names, in order to minimize the possibility of name clashes in a heterogeneous programming environment. Following these naming conventions, the Motif widget set (OSF, 1990) appends either "Xm" or "xm" to the beginning of the names of various widget components. We use the prefixes "Xi" and "xi" for our mini widget set.

For our widget class files, we use filenames that are reasonably short, yet provide adequate mnemonics and are compatible with systems that restrict the length of filenames. For the string selection widget class, we'll use the filenames *StrSelect.c* for the implementation file, *StrSelect.h* for the public header file, and *StrSelectP.h* for the private header file. You can modify these names, according to your personal preferences.

We do not make assumptions about your preferences for directories and so on. You may want to organize these widget classes in a common directory, following the style used with the Motif widget set. In this case, your **#include** directives would have the form

```
#include <Xi/StrSelect.h>
```

assuming that this directory is included in the list of automatically searched directories.

Several of the naming conventions for widget components are exhibited in the following: a widget class name, **XiStrSelect**; a widget class pointer, **xiStrSelectWidgetClass**; a public function, **XiStrSelectGetSelection()**; a resource name, **XiNdelimiters**; and others. The best way to become accustomed to the recognized naming conventions is to look at a commercial widget set such as Motif, refer to the Xt programming manual cited earlier, and consult the widget source code that follows. Note that the Athena widget set was developed before these conventions were established.

We deviate slightly from the convention in our choice of macro names for controlling preprocessor inclusion of files. Specifically, we use mixed case, where others have suggested uppercase characters:

```
#ifndef _XiStrSelect_h
#define _XiStrSelect_h  1
```

This type of minor variation is easily modified, depending on your personal preferences.

12.2 XiStrSelect: Overview

Although this widget class is primarily designed as a foundation for more specialized widget classes, it is possible to create a string selection widget. The demonstration program presented at the end of this chapter includes two pop-up string selection boxes, one of which appears in Figure 12.1.

The basic idea behind the string selection widget is that the user should be able to select an item from a list of items (in a window) by clicking a mouse button. The user can then apply an operation to the selected item, or dismiss the string selection box, by selecting a command button. Items are represented in the application in a row, or list, form—the string-oriented representation of items is transparent to the user.

In this chapter we're viewing a string selection widget from the application- and widget-programming perspective—when the application retrieves a selected item, the function returns a null-terminated string. Hence, we refer to the widget as a string selection box, as opposed to an item selection box. When this widget class is used to build a higher level widget class, or used directly by an application, the widget will have a simple list- or row-oriented arrangement of text as the principal component in a file selection box.

The **XiSrtSelect** widget class provides a framework for these operations, where the application programmer (minimally) creates the widget, specifies the list as a resource, and uses public functions to interact with the widget. For example, the application can use **XiStrSelectGetSelection()** to retrieve the currently selected item/string, **XiStrSelect-SetString()** to set the reference string, and **XiStrSelectRedisplay()** to redisplay a new list.

Resources allow the user (or the application programmer) to control the list of items, the size of the pixmap (box) that the list is displayed in, the font, and so on.

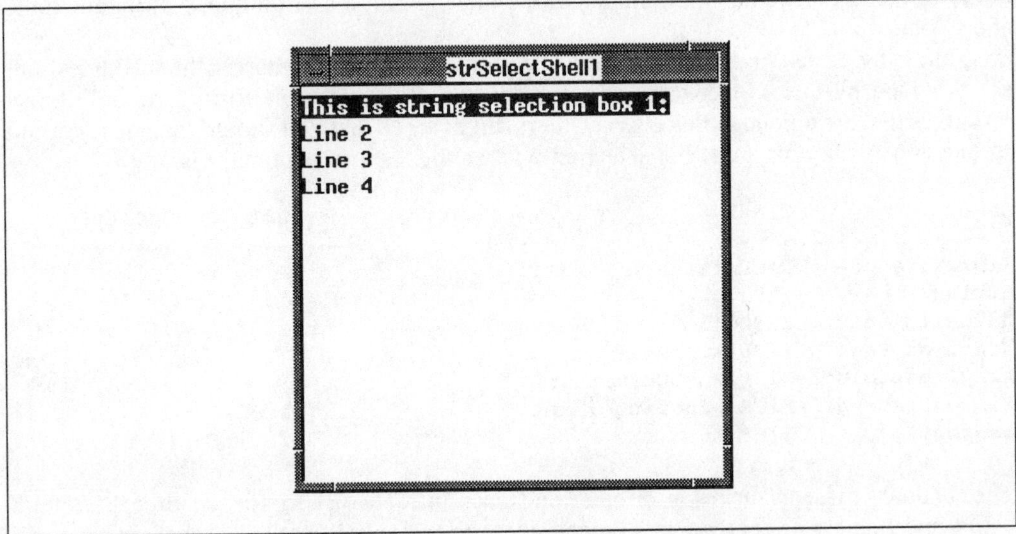

Figure 12.1 A String Selection Widget Housed within a Pop-up Shell

12.3 *StrSelect.h*: The Public Interface

The public header file begins with the normal preprocessor directives that prevent a header file from being included multiple times:

```
#ifndef _XiStrSelect_h
#define _XiStrSelect_h  1
```

These directives are followed by comment information that we omit here. There is an informal convention that dictates that the widget programmer should include rudimentary documentation in the source file to assist other programmers who need a quick synopsis of the widget class.

Although it's reasonable to assume that anyone interested in these comments would have access to both header files and the implementation file, the convention has been to place these extended comments in the public header file, for example:

```
/*********************************************************************
This widget implements a string selection box.  The basic idea is
that a string/buffer can be displayed in a window (a simple
pixmap-based widget) with client-specified line/row delimiters.
One possible usage for this widget would be the display of
filenames in a window.
...
...
*********************************************************************/
```

These comments should provide the widget programmer with an application-programmer perspective of this widget class. That is, the comment area should include a basic summary of the widget's functionality, highlights of the most important, or unique, public functions, and so on.

Following these comments the public header file should summarize the resources that are provided by this widget class. In our opinion, it's acceptable to include only those resources that are unique to this class. Others might argue that you should include inherited resources as well. For the string selection widget, the resource summary is:

```
Name             Class            Data Type        Default          Modify?
----             -----            ---------        -------          -------
XiNreference-    XiCReference-    String           "Nothing to      OK
String           String                            display!"
XiNdelimiters    XiCDelimiters    String           "\n\r\t"         OK
XiNpixmapRows    XiCPixmapRows    int              50
XiNpixmapColumnsXiCPixmapColumnsint                100
XiNrowSpacing    XiCRowSpacing    int              2 (pixels)
XiNfont          XiCFont          XFontStruct *    XtDefaultFont
```

The summary presents the resource name and class, the data type for the resource, its default value, and whether or not the widget recognizes run-time modifications to that resource. (If not, the resource is used only during start-up/configuration operations.)

By convention, these comments are followed by the **#include** directives that are required for this widget class:

```
#ifdef X11R3
#include <X11/Simple.h>
#else
#include <X11/Xaw/Simple.h>
#endif
```

X11 Release 3 and Release 4 differ with respect to the location of the Athena widget public header files. We've included compiler directives to account for these differences; by default, our source code assumes that you're using Release 4. If you are using Release 3, you must define the (compiler) constant **X11R3** (somewhere) before compiling this file—for example, as an option to *cc(1)*:

```
{user prompt} cc ... -DX11R3 ...
```

Parenthetically, note that the widget's public header file includes the superclass's public header file, whereas the widget's private header file includes the superclass's private header file.

At this point we should explain the **Simple** widget class. A simple widget is essentially a core widget, plus support for a user-defined cursor and border sensitivity. It is included with both X11 Release 3 and Release 4. Although this class is not included in the public description of the Athena widget set (and it's not a fundamental widget class), *for the purposes of widget development*, it's convenient to treat it as a member of the Athena set.

In general, widgets are designed such that if you include the header for a particular class, you don't have to include headers for its superclass(es). In this case, the **Simple** widget class inherits from **Core**; thus, its header files' directives include **Core**'s header files. Because the string selection widget is a specialization of a simple widget, we simply include **Simple**'s public header file.

Next, the public header file must define the resource identifiers for this widget. In general, adding resource support for widgets is very similar to adding resource support for applications. You may want to refer to our discussion of resource handling in *xwaste.c* (see Section 10.4.1). For *xwaste*, we set up application resource names and classes that began with "XtN..." and "XtC...". Here, we use "XiN..." and "XiC..." as prefixes to distinguish resource names in a heterogeneous environment, and for consistency in our naming conventions. (Motif uses "XmN..." and "XmC...".) The resources for the **XiSrtSelect** class are:

```
#define XiNreferenceString   "referenceString"   /* OK to modify */
#define XiNdelimiters        "delimiters"        /* OK to modify */
#define XiNfont              "font"
#define XiNpixmapRows        "pixmapRows"
#define XiNpixmapColumns     "pixmapColumns"
#define XiNrowSpacing        "rowSpacing"
#define XiCReferenceString   "ReferenceString"
#define XiCDelimiters        "Delimiters"
#define XiCFont              "Font"
```

```
#define XiCPixmapRows        "PixmapRows"
#define XiCPixmapColumns     "PixmapColumns"
#define XiCRowSpacing        "RowSpacing"
```

The list of resources provides an outline of the capabilities and overall operation of the string selection widget. In particular, the "strings" displayed in the string selection box are actually components (lines) of a larger string, where components are delimited by arbitrary characters (for example, newlines). **XiNreferenceString** is the resource that's used to specify a multi-item list in string form where items are separated by *any* character in the set represented by the resource **XiNdelimiters**. Also, the application can control the cursor shape and the font, can vary the row spacing between each item, and can specify the number of rows and columns for the pixmap.

Note that you may want to substitute a higher level name component for the inner window than "Pixmap," for example, "Canvas" or "Browser". You should consider the fact that higher level names sometimes carry connotations that prevent them from being applied consistently across widgets. "Canvas" implies a drawing surface to many users, and "Browser" typically implies a scrollable window. If pixmaps are used for a variety of purposes in a widget set, it may be more important to use a more generic name such as "Pixmap," even though its meaning is somewhat vague, in order to maintain consistency across the widget set.

Following Xt convention, the public header file also defines the data types for (pointers to) the class and instance records:

```
typedef struct _XiStrSelectClassRec *XiStrSelectWidgetClass;
typedef struct _XiStrSelectRec *XiStrSelectWidget;
```

This practice borders on breaking widget encapsulation rules; however, it is used with the Athena widgets and with other widget sets. For this particular widget class, the implementation would still compile properly if these statements were moved to the private header file. For some classes, the public definitions are necessary in coercing widget components to the proper type—this depends on the arguments to the public functions, that is, the "openness" of the widget class.

The widget class identifier (pointer) must be public as well. It's used in calls to **XtCreateWidget()**, **XtIsSubclass()**, and others:

```
extern WidgetClass xiStrSelectWidgetClass;
```

The last component of the public header file is the list of function declarations that define the public interface. Typically, these declarations include the function parameters as comments:

```
extern void XiStrSelectPopup();
/*  XiStrSelectWidget str_select_widget;
*/
```

In this case, the **XiSrtSelect** widget class defines a convenience function that can be used to activate a string selection box, if the application has created it as a child of a pop-up shell.

XiStrSelectPopup() takes one argument, the ID of the string selection widget. Thus, the application can create multiple string selection widgets and activate them by specifying their ID.

Following the declarations for the public functions, we must provide a compiler directive that marks the end of the conditional inclusion of source code:

```
#endif /* _XiStrSelect_h  */
```

12.4 *StrSelectP.h*: The Private Widget Data Structures

As with *StrSelect.h*, we use compiler directives to prevent multiple inclusions of this file and to reference the proper Athena widget directory:

```
#ifndef _XiStrSelectP_h
#define _XiStrSelectP_h


#include "StrSelect.h"
#ifdef X11R3
#include <X11/SimpleP.h>
#else
#include <X11/Xaw/SimpleP.h>
#endif
```

The widget implementation file uses several constants that we define as macros (for convenience):

```
#define STR_NOTHING                    "Nothing to display!"

#define STR_DEFAULT_WIDTH              300
#define STR_DEFAULT_HEIGHT             150

#define STR_DEFAULT_PIXMAP_ROWS        50
...
#define STR_NO_HIGHLIGHT               -1  /* ignore mouse, just   */
                                           /* redisplay strings    */
#define STR_NO_STR                     -2  /* no currently selected str */

#define STR_DELIMITERS   "\n\r\t"          /* used with strtok() */
```

The constants begin with "STR_" to minimize the possibility of name conflicts with other modules. Every book has page-width limitations, hence, we're using a rather short prefix here. You can easily substitute a more descriptive/unique prefix.

Next, we must define the string selection component of the class record. **XiSrtSelect** has no class data, thus, we simply provide a placeholder field in the structure:

```
typedef struct _XiStrSelectClassPart {       /* class definition */
    int dummy;
} XiStrSelectClassPart;
```

Next, we define the class hierarchy (the inheritance path) in the class record for a string selection widget:

```
typedef struct _XiStrSelectClassRec {
    CoreClassPart core_class;
    SimpleClassPart simple_class;
    XiStrSelectClassPart str_select_class;
} XiStrSelectClassRec;
```

Again, following Xt widget encapsulation and naming conventions, we provide a public declaration for the class record:

```
extern XiStrSelectClassRec xiStrSelectClassRec;
```

Note that this *declaration* corresponds to *the* class record *definition* that appears in the implementation file, as described in Chapter 11. Each widget class must provide this public declaration so that subclasses can reference the superclass record. (If the organization of declarations and definitions seems confusing, the source code and discussion in Section 12.5.4 will help clarify the interplay between public and private declarations and the class record definition in the implementation file.)

Next, the private header file defines the fields (layout) of the instance record:

```
typedef struct _XiStrSelectPart {        /* instance definition */
    char *str;                           /* the string/buffer */
    char *buffer;                        /* internal copy of str,      */
                                         /* strtok() modifies arg.     */
    char *delimiters;                    /* what separates each line */
    char *selection;                     /* holds current selection */
    XFontStruct *font;
    int pixmap_rows, pixmap_columns;     /* row/column metrics */
    int pixmap_width, pixmap_height;     /* pixel metrics */
    int row_spacing;                     /* space between rows */
    int row_increment;                   /* height of a row */
    Pixmap pixmap;
    GC gc;                               /* regular text display GC */
    GC cgc;                              /* clear text GC */
    GC hgc;                              /* highlight text GC */
    int current_str;
    int current_num_strs;
} XiStrSelectPart;
```

These variables are discussed in the next section. As mentioned, we want our first widget to have similarities to something that we've done previously, so that we can focus on the mechanics of widget programming. You can see from these variable names that the internal operations of the string selection widget are quite similar to those of the browser's inner window for *xwaste*.

Given the previous structure, we can define the template for an instance record, which **XtCreateWidget()** allocates dynamically:

```
typedef struct _XiStrSelectRec {
    CorePart core;
    SimplePart simple;
    XiStrSelectPart str_select;
} XiStrSelectRec;

#endif  /* _XiStrSelectP_h */
```

12.5 *StrSelect.c*: The Implementation File

Recall from Chapter 11 that the implementation file (1) defines the class record, (2) defines the class methods, and (3) defines the public functions, in addition to handling secondary tasks and data structures related to translations and resources.

12.5.1 Declarations

First, we must include the appropriate header files, including *StrSelectP.h*:

```
#include <stdio.h>

#include <X11/Xlib.h>
#include <X11/Xos.h>
#include <X11/IntrinsicP.h>
#include <X11/StringDefs.h>
#include <X11/Shell.h>

#ifdef X11R3
#include <X11/Simple.h>
#else
#include <X11/Xaw/XawInit.h>
#include <X11/Xaw/Simple.h>
#endif

#include "StrSelectP.h"
```

The latter file includes *StrSelect.h*. Note that for Release 4 it's important to include *XawInit.h* so that you can reference the Release 4 class initialization function in the class record (see the subsequent discussion of this *extremely important* function).

This file defines four class methods; they should *not* be available publically:

```
static void Initialize();
static void Destroy();
static Boolean SetValues();
static void Redisplay();
```

In addition, a number of private functions are defined that support the class methods and public functions:

```
static void create_offscreen_pixmap();
static void fill_pixmap_and_redisplay();
static void fill_pixmap();
static void redisplay_pixmap();
static void select_str();
```

12.5.2 Actions and Translations

A string selection widget implements the string selection operation with an action function:

```
static void SelectStr();

static char pixmap_translations[] =
    "<Btn1Down>:  select()";

static XtActionsRec pixmap_actions[] = {
    {"select", (XtActionProc) SelectStr},
};
```

We've included a default translation here. The user can modify this translation for any application that uses this class. For example, the following resource setting replaces the current translation for all string selection boxes in the application *xanyapp*:

```
xanyapp*StrSelect*translations: #replace\n\
    <Btn2Down>:        select()
```

12.5.3 Resources

Next, as with our earlier application *xwaste*, we must define the resources:

```
#define res_offset(field) XtOffset(XiStrSelectWidget, field)

static XtResource resources[] = {
    {XiNreferenceString, XiCReferenceString, XtRString,
        sizeof(char *), res_offset(str_select.str),
        XtRString, STR_NOTHING},
    {XiNdelimiters, XiCDelimiters, XtRString, sizeof(char *),
        res_offset(str_select.delimiters),
        XtRString, STR_DELIMITERS},
    {XiNfont, XiCFont, XtRFontStruct, sizeof(XFontStruct *),
        res_offset(str_select.font),
        XtRString, "XtDefaultFont"},
    {XiNpixmapRows, XiCPixmapRows, XtRInt, sizeof(int),
        res_offset(str_select.pixmap_rows),
        XtRImmediate, (caddr_t) STR_DEFAULT_PIXMAP_ROWS},
    {XiNpixmapColumns, XiCPixmapColumns, XtRInt, sizeof(int),
        res_offset(str_select.pixmap_columns),
        XtRImmediate, (caddr_t) STR_DEFAULT_PIXMAP_COLUMNS},
    {XiNrowSpacing, XiCRowSpacing, XtRInt, sizeof(int),
        res_offset(str_select.row_spacing),
        XtRImmediate, (caddr_t) STR_DEFAULT_ROW_SPACING},
```

```
};
```

A string selection box is a significant GUI component; it should make provisions for font and cursor specification. For the cursor in particular, it's inappropriate to depend on the default X policy whereby a window inherits the cursor of its parent. Since **XiSrtSelect** inherits from **Simple**, it doesn't have to provide a cursor resource. Specifically, the resource manager will set the cursor field in the **simple** component of the instance record.

Assuming that the application hasn't hard-coded the cursor resource, there are several ways to set the cursor from a resource file. If, for example, an application named *xanyapp* employs a string selection widget named "strSelectBox1", the following resource setting will set the cursor to a sailboat shape:

```
xanyapp*strSelectBox1*cursor:   sailboat
```

If that application has multiple string selection widgets, the following resource (class) setting will set the cursor to a dot shape for every string selection widget:

```
xanyapp*StrSelect*cursor:   dot
```

There can be many different ways to achieve the same effect, depending on the complexity of the widget tree(s) in the application. There will be other examples at the end of this chapter and in subsequent chapters.

Because **XiSrtSelect** inherits from **Core** and **Simple** only, and neither of these provide a font resource, **XiSrtSelect** must support the font directly. There are a number of ways to handle resources such as fonts and cursors. For example, we could have the widget load the font, saving the application programmer from this chore. The accepted practice, however, is to have the application load the font and pass a pointer to the font structure as a resource. This approach gives the *application programmer* complete flexibility in sharing font structures. That is, the application could load two different fonts to be used by ten widgets from six widget classes. We use the latter approach in our widgets. Hence, the string selection widget stores a pointer to the font structure as an instance variable, namely, **str_select.font**. (Font loading operations are handled automatically when resources are set from a resource file.)

Several other widget parameters are handled as resources as well. For example, the list of items that's displayed in the string selection box is passed as a string using the resource **XiNreferenceString**; a pointer to this string is stored in **str_select.str**. Parenthetically, we could have represented the list of items as an array of strings—you may prefer this approach. In this implementation, we simply concatenate each item with an arbitrary delimiter(s) into one giant string, for example, "Item1\nItem2\nItem3".

The set of delimiters (in string form) that's used to break the reference string into displayable items (lines)—for example, "\n\r"—is specified via the resource **XiNdelimiters** and stored in the instance variable **str_select.delimiters**. Similarly, an **XiStrSelect** widget stores pixmap-related resources in the instance record.

12.5.4 The Class Record

As described in Chapter 11, *StrSelect.c* defines the class record that's shared by string selection widgets:

```
XiStrSelectClassRec XistrSelectClassRec = {
    { /* core_class variables */
        (WidgetClass) &simpleClassRec,    /* ancestor */
        "StrSelect",                      /* class name */
        sizeof(XiStrSelectRec),           /* widget size */
#ifdef X11R3
        NULL,                             /* class initialize */
#else
        XawInitializeWidgetSet,           /* class initialize */
#endif
        NULL,                             /* class part init. */
        FALSE,                            /* class inited */
        Initialize,                       /* initialize */
        NULL,                             /* initialize hook */
        XtInheritRealize,                 /* realize */
        pixmap_actions,                   /* actions */
        XtNumber(pixmap_actions),         /* number of actions */
        resources,                        /* resources */
        XtNumber(resources),              /* number of resources */
        NULLQUARK,                        /* xrm class */
        TRUE,                             /* compress motions */
        TRUE,                             /* compress exposures */
        TRUE,                             /* compress enter/leave */
        FALSE,                            /* visibility interest */
        Destroy,                          /* destroy */
        NULL,                             /* resize */
        Redisplay,                        /* expose */
        SetValues,                        /* set values */
        NULL,                             /* set values hook */
        XtInheritSetValuesAlmost,         /* set values almost */
        NULL,                             /* get values hook */
        NULL,                             /* accept focus */
        XtVersion,                        /* version */
        NULL,                             /* callback private */
        pixmap_translations,              /* translation table */
        XtInheritQueryGeometry,           /* query geometry */
        XtInheritDisplayAccelerator,      /* display accelerator */
        NULL,                             /* extension */
    },
    { /* simple_class variables */
        XtInheritChangeSensitive,
    },
    { /* str_select_class variables */
        0,
    },
}; /* XistrSelectClassRec */
```

One of the reasons that **XiSrtSelect** inherits from **Simple** instead of from **Core** is so that we can emphasize the organization of (the components that comprise) the class record, while we're still dealing with a relatively simple widget. The **Simple** widget class provides two enhancements to the **Core** widget class, namely, a cursor for the pixmap and widget sensitivity.

The **simple** component of the simple widget's instance record includes two fields for storing this information:

```
typedef struct {
    Cursor  cursor;
    Pixmap  insensitive_border;
} SimplePart;
```

As mentioned earlier, if an application hard-codes the cursor resource, or if a user provides a resource setting, the resource manager will set this field as requested; otherwise, the string selection widget's window will inherit the cursor of its parent. (**Simple**'s default cursor is no cursor at all.)

Border sensitivity is provided by a method. This function is used by all simple widgets, thus, the **simple_class** component of the class record has the form:

```
typedef struct {
    Boolean (*change_sensitive)();
} SimpleClassPart;
```

Consequently, the class record for an **XiStrSelect** widget has three components, namely,

```
typedef struct _XiStrSelectClassRec {
    CoreClassPart core_class;
    SimpleClassPart simple_class;
    XiStrSelectClassPart str_select_class;
} XiStrSelectClassRec;
```

each of which must be accounted for in the definition/initialization of **XistrSelectClassRec**.

Note that (the pointer to) the Boolean function for managing border sensitivity can be inherited for most subclasses, including **XiSrtSelect**; thus, the second component in **XistrSelectClassRec (simple_class)** is initialized with the macro/keyword that signals inheritance of this functionality:

```
XiStrSelectClassRec XistrSelectClassRec = {
    ...
    { /* simple_class variables */
        XtInheritChangeSensitive,
    },
    ...
}; /* XistrSelectClassRec */
```

Next, consider the **str_select_class** component of the class record, which has the form:

```
typedef struct _XiStrSelectClassPart {
    int dummy;
} XiStrSelectClassPart;
```

Since a string selection widget has no class data, this field is simply set to a null value, in this case, 0:

```
XiStrSelectClassRec XistrSelectClassRec = {
    ...
    { /* str_select_class variables */
        0,
    },
}; /* XistrSelectClassRec */
```

Next, consider the **core_class** component, where there are a number of critical initializations. We won't mention every field, becaue we addressed many of them in Chapter 11.

First, the superclass field is initialized with the address of the **Simple**'s class record:

```
XiStrSelectClassRec XistrSelectClassRec = {
    { /* core_class variables */
        (WidgetClass) &simpleClassRec,  /* ancestor */
        ...
    },
    ...
}; /* XistrSelectClassRec */
```

This record is defined in the implementation file *Simple.c*; thus, this storage is linked into the executable file that's built from the Athena widget library, and others.

It should be clear from this reference to **simpleClassRec** why each widget class must provide a public declaration for its class record in its private header file, for example:

```
                                                 /* taken from:  */
extern WidgetClassRec widgetClassRec;            /* CoreP.h      */
extern SimpleClassRec simpleClassRec;            /* SimpleP.h    */
extern DialogClassRec dialogClassRec;            /* DialogP.h    */
extern XiStrSelectClassRec xiStrSelectClassRec; /* StrSelectP.h */
```

Specifically, derived widget classes must have access to their superclass's class record; hence, each widget class must be compiled with a public class record in anticipation of being subclassed. With respect to the proper file, the widget programmer needs to reference this field, but the application programmer doesn't; hence, it's placed in the private header file. (Recall from Section 12.4 that *StrSelectP.h* includes *SimpleP.h*.)

Parenthetically, the high-level encapsulation of data structures that's provided by widgets works well in practice. Most (application) programmers have no reason to abuse the miscellaneous public declarations of otherwise hidden data structures, such as **xiStrSelectClassRec**. As a widget programmer you must know the name of the superclass's class record. In addition, with most derived widget classes, you will have to study the superclass's methods in order to determine how to override (or supplement) its behavior.

Next, note the value in the **class_name** field, in this case, "StrSelect". By convention, the "Xi" prefix is omitted. With this approach it's possible to build applications (and widget sets) where a user can supply a class-level resource, say, for "Label", and have this resource setting apply to all instances of *any* label widget class (across compatible widget sets).

The next field that we mention is the pointer to the class initialization method. For the widget classes that you develop under X11 Release 3, you can simply omit this method, specifying NULL. With Release 4, however, you should reference the Athena widget initialization function, **XawInitializeWidgetSet()**. *This initialization is important*. Failing to initialize this field properly "can be hazardous to your health, specifically, your sanity."

There are a number of methods that we simply inherit. For example, there is nothing specific to **XiSrtSelect** that requires special processing during widget realization, hence, we inherit this functionality from **Simple** (which inherits it from **Core**). You can find detailed information on the "inner workings" of these methods in the Xt programming and reference manuals; for our purposes, it's more important to focus on each widget class's unique functionality.

XiSrtSelect defines four methods that implement the unique aspect of a string selection widget's behavior. These methods must be *declared* prior to the definition and initialization of the class record. The following declarations were mentioned in Section 12.5.1:

```
static void Initialize();
static void Destroy();
static Boolean SetValues();
static void Redisplay();
```

Each method should be defined privately to emphasize that the application should not reference them. Note, however, that the Intrinsics must have access to these methods—**XtDestroyWidget()** calls a widget's destroy method. Access to these class methods is provided by the function pointers in the class record:

```
XiStrSelectClassRec XistrSelectClassRec = {
    { /* core_class variables */
        ...
        Initialize,                             /* initialize */
        ...
        Destroy,                                /* destroy */
        ...
        Redisplay,                              /* expose */
        SetValues,                              /* set values */
        ...
    },
    ...
}; /* XistrSelectClassRec */
```

After our discussion of the class record, we address each of these methods in detail.

In Sections 12.5.2 and 12.5.3 we addressed **XiSrtSelect**'s actions and translations and its resources. Although these data structures are defined as private variables, they must be made available to the Intrinsics as well:

```
XiStrSelectClassRec XistrSelectClassRec = {
    { /* core_class variables */
        ...
        pixmap_actions,                 /* actions */
        XtNumber(pixmap_actions),       /* number of actions */
        resources,                      /* resources */
        XtNumber(resources),            /* number of resources */
        ...
        pixmap_translations,            /* translation table */
        ...
    },
    ...
}; /* XistrSelectClassRec */
```

We should mention the four indicator variable for event compression and visibility interest:

```
XiStrSelectClassRec XistrSelectClassRec = {
    { /* core_class variables */
        ...
        TRUE,                           /* compress motions */
        TRUE,                           /* compress exposures */
        TRUE,                           /* compress enter/leave */
        FALSE,                          /* visibility interest */
        ...
    },
    ...
}; /* XistrSelectClassRec */
```

It's impossible to make blanket statements about event compression; however, in most cases, compression is justified. By filtering out unnecessary events, or combining events, it's possible to improve overall performance. Occasionally, a series of events will build up in the queue such that intervening events are of no interest. For example, if you move the mouse (pointing device) frantically, you may or may not be interested in the intervening **MotionNotify** events, depending on the widget. If the widget implements a string selection box, the most recent cursor/pointer coordinate is the only one of interest (in selecting the current item). If, on the other hand, you're implementing a drawing canvas widget, each **MotionNotify** event (or a sampling of the motion history) is important.

If exposures are compressed, **Expose** events are combined such that the resulting event contains the union of all exposed areas. In some situations, this type of event compression would allow the widget to redisplay the exposed area in one step. For a string selection widget we can't make assumptions about the type of font, so we simply compress all exposures and then redisplay the entire window.

In most situations, **VisibilityNotify** events are irrelevant, thus, the visibility field is initialized to FALSE. A string selection box depends on **Expose** events for an indication that the widget's window should be updated.

Defining the class record establishes a (static) relationship among the class records/components for a particular widget. In addition, however, the implementation file must define the class pointer that an application references in order to create a widget. Hence, immediately after the class record definition, we include the following:

```
WidgetClass xiStrSelectWidgetClass =
    (WidgetClass) &XistrSelectClassRec;
```

Here, we set the class pointer to the address of the previously defined class record for a string selection widget. Recall from Section 12.1 that the public header file declares this pointer as a public, opaque type:

```
extern WidgetClass xiStrSelectWidgetClass;
```

12.5.5 The XiStrSelect Methods

The first method is **Initialize**(); it's called during widget creation to set instance variables, plus the window size. In addition, it should check resource settings to ensure that the user hasn't specified any illegal values. When Xt dynamically allocates a widget, it passes two instance records (actually their pointers) to the widget's initialize method:

```
/*
Initialize() initializes each instance of a string selection box.
A string selection box implements a pixmap in a SimpleWidget.
*/
/*ARGSUSED*/
static void Initialize(request, new)
XiStrSelectWidget request, new;
{
    if (new->str_select.pixmap_rows < STR_MIN_ROWS)
        new->str_select.pixmap_rows = STR_DEFAULT_PIXMAP_ROWS;
    if (new->str_select.pixmap_columns < STR_MIN_COLUMNS)
        new->str_select.pixmap_columns = STR_DEFAULT_PIXMAP_COLUMNS;
    if (!new->str_select.str)
        new->str_select.str = STR_NOTHING;
    if (!new->str_select.delimiters)
        new->str_select.delimiters = STR_DELIMITERS;
    if (!strlen(new->str_select.delimiters))
        new->str_select.delimiters = STR_DELIMITERS;

    create_offscreen_pixmap(new);

    new->str_select.selection = NULL;
    new->str_select.buffer = NULL;
    new->core.width = new->str_select.pixmap_width;
    new->core.height = new->str_select.pixmap_height;

    fill_pixmap(new, STR_NO_HIGHLIGHT);
}   /* Initialize */
```

request contains the instance variable settings that were performed by the resource manager; **new** reflects any changes that have been made to superclass components by the respective chained initialize methods. **request** is a temporary widget instance record that may be useful in determining at which stages instance record fields were set. **new** is the permanent instance record, thus, changes should be made to it.

Initialize() is responsible for setting instance variables that aren't available to the resource manager (via the resource data structure), and for checking the values of variables set by the resource manager. **Initialize()** first checks basic resource-related instance variables, and modifies their values if they are out of range. In the current implementation we are checking only the lower-bound pixmap dimensions. Logistically, it may be difficult to establish upper bounds for the pixmap dimensions. In particular, you would be imposing arbitrary restrictions on the user (or application programmer).

As a rule, it's impossible to be too cautious in checking the resource-related fields of the instance record. In this implementation **Initialize()** checks to make sure that the reference string and delimiter string pointers have values:

```
if (!new->str_select.str)
    new->str_select.str = STR_NOTHING;
if (!new->str_select.delimiters)
    new->str_select.delimiters = STR_DELIMITERS;
```

If one of these is null, it's pointed at the default string, which displays a message to that effect in the string selection box. Note that there is nothing to prevent an application from starting up with an empty reference string.

On the other hand, the set of delimiters (in string form) can't be empty; if it is, it's initialized to the default value:

```
if (!strlen(new->str_select.delimiters))
    new->str_select.delimiters = STR_DELIMITERS;
```

Typically, a widget has non–resource-related instance variables—variables that record the current widget state. For example, a string selection widget has a variable named **str_select.selection** that maintains a record of the currently selected item. Depending on the operations that take place in the widget, these variables may need to be initialized during widget creation. In this implementation, the current (item) selection is pointed at "nothing" during widget initialization:

```
new->str_select.selection = NULL;
```

At run-time when the user selects an item, a (null-terminated) copy is held in dynamically allocated storage; **str_select.selection** references this storage.

A secondary function, **create_offscreen_pixmap()**, performs the pixmap-related initializations. As with the browser pixmap for *xwaste*, we use three GCs to handle normal text, reverse text, and text clearing operations. The GCs, pixmap, and other pixmap-related variables are used by several functions that manipulate and update the string selection box. In this situation, maintaining this information in instance variables is preferable to passing it around from function to function. The pixmap-related instance variables are:

```
typedef struct _XiStrSelectPart {          /* instance definition */
```

```
    ...
    XFontStruct *font;
    int pixmap_rows, pixmap_columns;     /* row/column metrics */
    int pixmap_width, pixmap_height;     /* pixel metrics */
    int row_spacing;                     /* space between rows */
    int row_increment;                   /* height of a row */
    Pixmap pixmap;
    GC gc;                               /* regular text display GC */
    GC cgc;                              /* clear text GC */
    GC hgc;                              /* highlight text GC */
    ...
} XiStrSelectPart;
```

Because of the inconsistencies in parameter types among certain Xlib and Xt functions and Xlib data structures, especially with respect to unsigned and signed integers, we use **int** for all dimension related variables in the instance record.

create_offscreen_pixmap()'s definition is similar to that of **basket_create_offscreen_pixmap()** from *xwaste*:

```
/*
create_offscreen_pixmap() creates and sets the dimensions of the
string selection box pixmap.  Other comments in source file...
*/

static void create_offscreen_pixmap(w)
XiStrSelectWidget w;
{
    XGCValues values;
    Display *display = XtDisplay(w);
    int screen = XDefaultScreen(display);
    int depth = XDisplayPlanes(display, screen);

    values.foreground = XBlackPixel(display, screen);
    values.background = XWhitePixel(display, screen);
    values.font = w->str_select.font->fid;
    w->str_select.gc = XCreateGC(XtDisplay(w),
        RootWindowOfScreen(XtScreen(w)),
        GCForeground | GCBackground | GCFont, &values);
    w->str_select.cgc = XCreateGC(XtDisplay(w),
        RootWindowOfScreen(XtScreen(w)),
        GCForeground | GCBackground | GCFont, &values);
    XSetFunction(XtDisplay(w), w->str_select.cgc, GXclear);
    values.foreground = XWhitePixel(display, screen);
    values.background = XBlackPixel(display, screen);
    w->str_select.hgc = XCreateGC(XtDisplay(w),
        RootWindowOfScreen(XtScreen(w)),
        GCForeground | GCBackground | GCFont, &values);
    w->str_select.row_increment =
        w->str_select.font->max_bounds.ascent +
        w->str_select.font->max_bounds.descent +
        w->str_select.row_spacing;
```

```
    w->str_select.pixmap_width = w->str_select.pixmap_columns *
        w->str_select.font->max_bounds.width;
    w->str_select.pixmap_height = w->str_select.pixmap_rows *
        w->str_select.row_increment;
    w->str_select.pixmap = XCreatePixmap(XtDisplay(w),
        RootWindowOfScreen(XtScreen(w)), w->str_select.pixmap_width,
        w->str_select.pixmap_height, depth);
}   /* create_offscreen_pixmap */
```

For simplicity, the string selection box is designed to operate in monochrome mode on the default screen. This information is required because we're using **XCreateGC()** instead of **XtGetGC()** (see the next paragraph). After creating each GC with the proper attributes, including the pixmap font, **create_offscreen_pixmap()** calculates the row height and the pixmap dimensions, based on the resource settings that we mentioned earlier. Recall from our earlier discussion that **str_select.row_spacing** (**XiNrowSpacing**) allows the user to vary the amount of spacing between each row/item. The sum of the font height and the row spacing is stored in the instance variable **str_select.row_increment** for use by the support functions that rebuild the pixmap after each exposure.

As mentioned, we use the Xlib function **XCreateGC()** instead of the Xt function **XtGetGC()**. The latter function employs a caching mechanism whereby GCs are created in a read-only mode and shared among the applications's widgets. **XtGetGC()** offers one other (minor) advantage, namely, you don't have to provide a drawable as an argument. (**XCreateGC()** uses the drawable argument to determine the screen and its depth.) In this case, however, we're creating a pixmap for this widget, therefore we must determine the screen anyway. (Pixmaps are created relative to a particular screen.)

In this situation there are two reasons for using **XCreateGC()**. First, string selection widgets can't share GCs, due to font considerations. Specifically, the GCs are used with the pixmap for displaying the contents of the string selection box. Because (1) a string selection widget displays text on the pixmap, (2) the font for the text is a widget resource, and (3) string selection widgets in the same application can be configured with different fonts, we must set the font for the GCs. Hence, different string selection widgets *require* different GCs.

A secondary motivation for using **XCreateGC()** is that you may want to modify the string selection widget class with respect to other GC-related attributes. Additional enhancements to **XiSrtSelect** would lead us too far away from our primary interest, widget programming.

Next, consider the modifications to **width** and **height** in the **core** component of the instance record. After **create_offscreen_pixmap()** has been called to create the pixmap and the GCs, the window dimensions must be initialized:

```
    new->core.width = new->str_select.pixmap_width;
    new->core.height = new->str_select.pixmap_height;
```

Typically, a widget's initialize method sets these variables, because there can be no guarantee that an application, or a user, will do it (correctly). For a string selection widget, it doesn't make sense to depend on application- or user-specified window dimensions, because there are higher level resources, namely, **XiNpixmapRows** and **XiNpixmap-Columns**, that directly affect the window.

Lastly, after the primary structures are created and initialized, **Initialize()** calls a support function, **fill_pixmap()**, to build the item list for the pixmap.

Next, consider the destroy method. As with most dynamic data structures in C, if an application doesn't destroy its widgets, the storage for each widget (instance) will be deallocated during program termination. In general, however, the widget programmer can't anticipate whether or not an application will create and destroy widgets periodically as part of its normal execution; hence, each widget class should provide a destroy method that cleans up dynamic data structures when the application calls **XtDestroyWidget()**. For **XiSrtSelect**, the destroy method must free the GCs, pixmap, and the dynamic storage that's used to hold a private copy of the reference string (**str_select.buffer**) and the current selection (**str_select.selection**):

```
/*
Destroy() cleans up dynamic data structures.
*/

static void Destroy(w)
XiStrSelectWidget w;
{
    if (w->str_select.buffer != NULL)
        XtFree(w->str_select.buffer);
    if (w->str_select.selection != NULL)
        XtFree(w->str_select.selection);
    if (w->str_select.gc != NULL)
        XFreeGC(XtDisplay(w), w->str_select.gc);
    if (w->str_select.cgc != NULL)
        XFreeGC(XtDisplay(w), w->str_select.cgc);
    if (w->str_select.hgc != NULL)
        XFreeGC(XtDisplay(w), w->str_select.hgc);
    if (w->str_select.pixmap != NULL)
        XFreePixmap(XtDisplay(w), w->str_select.pixmap);
}   /* Destroy */
```

Destroy() frees data structures for the **str_select** component of the instance record only. After **Destroy()** finishes, the inherited destroy methods are invoked in reverse order—that is, subclass to superclass order.

The next method is the set-values method, which handles modifications to resource-related instance variables:

```
/*
SetValues() handles modifications to resource-related
instance variables.  Since all pixmap-related processing is
based on 'pixmap_width' and 'pixmap_height', and these fields
are modified only during widget creation, it really isn't
necessary to check for modified row and column metrics.
*/
/*ARGSUSED*/
```

```
static Boolean SetValues(current, request, new)
Widget current, request, new;
{
    XiStrSelectWidget sw = (XiStrSelectWidget) new;
    XiStrSelectWidget old_sw = (XiStrSelectWidget) current;

    if (!sw->str_select.str)
        sw->str_select.str = STR_NOTHING;
    if (!sw->str_select.delimiters)
        sw->str_select.delimiters = STR_DELIMITERS;
    if (!strlen(sw->str_select.delimiters))
        sw->str_select.delimiters = STR_DELIMITERS;
    if (strcmp(sw->str_select.str, old_sw->str_select.str))
        fill_pixmap(sw, STR_NO_HIGHLIGHT);
    if (strcmp(sw->str_select.delimiters,
            old_sw->str_select.delimiters))
        fill_pixmap(sw, STR_NO_HIGHLIGHT);
    return FALSE;
}   /* SetValues */
```

This method is called by Xt when an application calls **XtSetValues()** to modify a resource. Xt passes three copies of the instance record to **SetValues()**. The name **current** is somewhat of a misnomer. **current** and **request** differ with respect to the values of resource-related instance variables before and after the call to **XtSetValues()**, respectively. For many widget classes it's important to have access to both states in order to make decisions about errors, how the changes affect the widget overall, and so on. Any corrections should be made in **new**, the permanent instance record.

A string selection widget processes changes to two resources, the reference and delimiter strings. In this case, it's important to make sure that there are no null pointers, because **strcmp()** is used to compare the old and new reference and delimiter strings. Also, the current implementation enforces the policy that the set of delimiters shouldn't be empty. If either of these strings has changed, the pixmap must be rebuilt.

The expose method, **Redisplay()**, is the last method that's defined in *StrSelect.c*:

```
/*
Redisplay() calls redisplay_pixmap() to update the pixmap
window upon an exposure.  Note that the pixmap is not updated–
just the pixmap window.
*/
/*ARGSUSED*/
static void Redisplay(w, event)
Widget w;
XEvent *event;
{
    redisplay_pixmap(w);
}   /* Redisplay */
```

It simply calls a support function that copies the pixmap to the widget's window. These low-level functions are discussed in a later section.

12.5.6 The Action Functions

In the current implementation, there is one action function, **SelectStr()**:

```
/*
SelectStr() simply calls the private function select_str().
*/

static void SelectStr(w, event)
Widget w;
XEvent *event;
{
    select_str(w, event);
}   /* SelectStr */
```

At present, its only task is to call a secondary function, **select_str()**, that highlights the entry in the string selection box that's (vertically) nearest to the mouse cursor.

12.5.7 The Public Interface

XiSrtSelect provides a number of public functions that an application can call to pop up the selection box, get the current selection, modify the reference string, and so on. In order to get a feel for how an application can use a string selection box, this section mentions several of the public functions.

Although it's not very likely, a string selection box could be instantiated as a child of a pop-up shell. In this case, it's convenient to have a public function that will pop up the string selection box—that is, the application can focus on the string selection box, not the shell. **XiStrSelectPopup()** uses the parent field of the **core** component of the instance record to check the parent's widget class:

```
/*
XiStrSelectPopup() invokes (pops up) the string selection box.
This convenience is useful ONLY if the string selection box's
parent is a pop-up shell.
*/

void XiStrSelectPopup(ssw)
XiStrSelectWidget ssw;
{
    if (XtIsSubclass(ssw->core.parent, (WidgetClass) shellWidgetClass))
        XtPopup(ssw->core.parent, XtGrabNone);
}   /* XiStrSelectPopup */
```

In this implementation, we *assume* that the string selection box should be *nonblocking*. If the application wants the pop-up window to block, it can call **XtPopup()** directly, instead of using this function.

Our naming convention for public functions follows the recommendations that we mentioned earlier in this chapter. Although the Release 4 Athena widgets continue to use class names without an "Xaw" prefix, their public functions do follow the recommended convention.

The principal public function is **XiStrSelectGetSelection()**:

```
/*
XiStrSelectGetSelection() retrieves the value stored in the private
field 'selection'; this is the currently selected string.
*/

char *XiStrSelectGetSelection(ssw)
XiStrSelectWidget ssw;
{
    return ssw->str_select.selection;
}   /* XiStrSelectGetSelection */
```

It returns a pointer to the currently selected string. An Xt application is supposed to respect the "widget concept;" it should not perform evil acts against innocent widgets. Accidents do happen, however, especially with C. In this case, the application could inadvertently modify the data at the location returned by **XiStrSelectGetSelection()**. For this reason, **str_select.selection** always points to a separately stored string that's independent of the primary reference string. Even though there's no way to protect the current selection from a destructive modification, it's a good idea to protect the reference string from corruption. These low-level issues are discussed in a subsequent section.

XiStrSelect provides a convenience function for establishing a new reference string:

```
/*
XiStrSelectSetString() establishes a pointer to the string
(buffer) that the widget displays.  It assumes that a zero-
length string is OK.
*/

void XiStrSelectSetString(ssw, str)
XiStrSelectWidget ssw;
char *str;
{
    if (!str)           /* check for null pointer */
        fprintf(stderr,
        "string selection box: the reference string is null!\n");
    ssw->str_select.str = str;
    fill_pixmap(ssw, STR_NO_HIGHLIGHT);
}   /* XiStrSelectSetString */
```

This function simply updates **str_select.str** to point to the new reference string—*the one that's provided by the application*. This string is never used directly by the pixmap-related functions. Each time **fill_pixmap()** is called to build a new pixmap, it first builds its own private copy of the reference string. This approach provides some protection against application errors.

Note that we've used **fprintf()** to display run-time error messages. This practice reflects our personal biases, developed over several years from past experiences with software systems in various stages of development ("bugginess"). In this case, our inclination is to avoid a system's own error handler while developing software under that system. In practice, at some point we would replace **fprintf()** with either the low-level error handler, **XtWarning()**, or the higher level **XtWarningMsg()**.

Typically, a string selection widget will be used by an application (or another widget class) to create a higher level GUI component. In this situation, the application may have to force the string selection box to be redisplayed. **XiStrSelectRedisplay()** provides this capability:

```
/*
XiStrSelectRedisplay() allows an application to force a
redisplay of the pixmap.
*/

void XiStrSelectRedisplay(ssw)
XiStrSelectWidget ssw;
{
    redisplay_pixmap(ssw);
}   /* XiStrSelectRedisplay */
```

From the high-level functions that we've discussed so far, it's evident that pixmap operations are factored into (1) redisplaying the pixmap, which is a copy operation from the off-screen pixmap to the widget's window, and (2) rebuilding the pixmap. **XiStrSelect-Redisplay()** and the expose method, **Redisplay()**, perform the former operation.

In addition to simply redisplaying the current pixmap, an application may need to clear the string selection widget. This process involves (1) resetting certain pixmap-related variables in the instance record, (2) clearing the pixmap, and (3) clearing the (visible) window. **XiStrSelectReset()** performs this service:

```
/*
XiStrSelectReset() allows an application to force the
clearing of the pixmap and related variables.
*/

void XiStrSelectReset(ssw)
XiStrSelectWidget ssw;
{
    ssw->str_select.current_str = STR_NO_STR;
    ssw->str_select.str = NULL;
    if (ssw->str_select.selection != NULL) {
        XtFree(ssw->str_select.selection);
        ssw->str_select.selection = NULL;
    }
    if (ssw->str_select.buffer != NULL)
        XtFree(ssw->str_select.buffer);
    XFillRectangle(XtDisplay(ssw), ssw->str_select.pixmap,
        ssw->str_select.cgc, 0, 0, ssw->core.width, ssw->core.height);
    if (XtIsRealized(ssw))
        XClearWindow(XtDisplay(ssw), XtWindow(ssw));
```

```
}    /* XiStrSelectReset */
```

This function includes several low-level operations. In particular, it must free the private copies of the current selection and the reference string (**str_select.buffer**). Also, it uses Xlib functions to clear the pixmap and the widget's window. Note that, as a general rule, it's a good idea to use the predicate **XtIsRealized()** to make sure that a window exists before referencing it.

12.5.8 Manipulating the Off-screen Pixmap

This section discusses the low-level pixmap operations. They are quite similar to those used in *xwaste.bskt.c* to build and display the browser's pixmap. If you're primarily interested in the mechanics of widget programming, you may prefer to skip this section.

First, we define a convenience function for building and redisplaying the pixmap:

```
/*
fill_pixmap_and_redisplay() builds the pixmap and refreshes
the window.
*/

static void fill_pixmap_and_redisplay(w, highlight_position)
XiStrSelectWidget w;
int highlight_position;
{
    fill_pixmap(w, highlight_position);
    redisplay_pixmap(w);
}   /* fill_pixmap_and_redisplay */
```

fill_pixmap_and_redisplay() is used by **select_str()** to highlight the current selection:

```
/*
select_str() calculates the "row" offset for a string/item and then
calls fill_pixmap_and_redisplay() to either clear the current
highlighted string or highlight another string, depending on the
legitimacy of the position.  The vertical button position is
"adjusted" by 1/2 the height of a row.  NOTE: This function
indirectly sets/modifies the current selection.
*/

static void select_str(w, event)
XiStrSelectWidget w;
XEvent *event;
{
    int highlight_position;

    highlight_position =
        (event->xbutton.y - (w->str_select.row_increment / 2)) /
            w->str_select.row_increment;
    if (highlight_position > w->str_select.current_num_strs)
        fill_pixmap_and_redisplay(w, STR_NO_HIGHLIGHT);
```

```
    else
        fill_pixmap_and_redisplay(w, highlight_position);
}   /* select_str */
```

The redisplay operation involves copying the off-screen pixmap to the string selection box's window; it is carried out by **redisplay_pixmap()**:

```
/*
redisplay_pixmap() copies the pixmap to the window.
*/

static void redisplay_pixmap(w)
XiStrSelectWidget w;
{
    if (!XtIsRealized(w))
        return;
    XCopyArea(XtDisplay(w), w->str_select.pixmap,
        XtWindow(w),
        w->str_select.gc, 0, 0, w->str_select.pixmap_width,
        w->str_select.pixmap_height, 0, 0);
}   /* redisplay_pixmap */
```

It uses the standard technique of testing the screen depth before copying the pixmap. If the screen isn't monochrome, it "expands" the source rectangle across planes in the destination.

The last function is **fill_pixmap()**; it's used to (re)build the off-screen image for the selection box and manage the private storage that's used for the reference string and the current selection:

```
/*
fill_pixmap() tests for errors and then displays the string
on the pixmap.  NOTE: This function sets the current selection.
*/

static void fill_pixmap(w, highlight_position)
XiStrSelectWidget w;
int highlight_position;
{
    int len, offset;
    char *next;

    if (!w->str_select.str)
        return;
    if (!strlen(w->str_select.str)) {
        fprintf(stderr,          /** !!! remove? **/
        "string selection box: reference string is empty!\n");
        return;
    }
    w->str_select.current_str = STR_NO_STR;
    if (w->str_select.selection != NULL) {
        XtFree(w->str_select.selection);
```

```
        w->str_select.selection = NULL;
    }
    if (w->str_select.buffer != NULL)
        XtFree(w->str_select.buffer);
    /*
    copy the user's string -- strtok() modifies its string argument
    */
    if ((len = strlen(w->str_select.str)) > -1) {
        w->str_select.buffer = XtMalloc((unsigned) (len + 1));
        strcpy(w->str_select.buffer, w->str_select.str);
    }
    else
        w->str_select.buffer = "";
    /*
    clear pixmap before it filling with a new string:
    */
    XFillRectangle(XtDisplay(w), w->str_select.pixmap,
        w->str_select.cgc, 0, 0, w->core.width, w->core.height);
    next = (char *)
        strtok(w->str_select.buffer, w->str_select.delimiters);
    for (offset = w->str_select.row_increment,
            w->str_select.current_num_strs = 0;
            next != NULL && offset < w->str_select.pixmap_height;
            offset += w->str_select.row_increment,
            w->str_select.current_num_strs++) {
        len = strlen(next);
        XDrawImageString(XtDisplay(w), w->str_select.pixmap,
            w->str_select.gc, 0, offset, next, len);
        if (highlight_position != STR_NO_HIGHLIGHT)
            if (highlight_position ==
                    w->str_select.current_num_strs) {
                /* this is it */
                XDrawImageString(XtDisplay(w), w->str_select.pixmap,
                    w->str_select.hgc, 0, offset, next, len);
                w->str_select.current_str =
                    w->str_select.current_num_strs;
                w->str_select.selection =
                    XtMalloc((unsigned) (len + 1));
                strcpy(w->str_select.selection, next);
            }
        next = (char *) strtok(NULL, w->str_select.delimiters);
    }
}   /* fill_pixmap */
```

Before building the pixmap, this function first destroys any existing storage for these variables. The private copy of the reference string is built first. Inside the **for** loop, if **highlight_position** carries a message to highlight the *n*th row, this text is copied to a private storage location as well. Note that it's important to clear the pixmap before copying text to it, because there may be extraneous text from the previous image.

12.6 A String Selection Box Demonstration

teststrsel.c exercises the string selection widget class. It creates two string selection widgets in pop-up shells, in order to test for (1) conflicts among multiple widgets, (2) proper exposure handling, (3) proper widget-level font support, and (4) proper operation of both techniques of setting a reference string. Figure 12.2 shows the second selection box with the current selection highlighted. (Figure 12.1 demonstrates the first selection box.)

This program is rather lengthy, because it creates several top-level command buttons in a button box for mapping and unmapping the string selection boxes; also, it makes quite a few tests. In this section, we discuss a subset of the source code that illustrates one of the selection boxes, along with assorted statements related to the other selection box. Appendix M provides complete source code for the string selection widget class and this test program.

We should also mention that several of the widget test programs use one or more miscellaneous functions, for example, **load_font()**. Appendix L lists these functions; on our computer system, they are stored in a library that is referenced as necessary in the make files.

The test program begins by including several Xlib/Xt header files, including header files for the string selection widget and the library of miscellaneous functions:

```
/****  teststrsel.c  ****  tests the string selection box widget ****/

#include <stdio.h>
#include <X11/Intrinsic.h>
#include <X11/StringDefs.h>
#include <X11/Shell.h>
#include <X11/cursorfont.h>
```

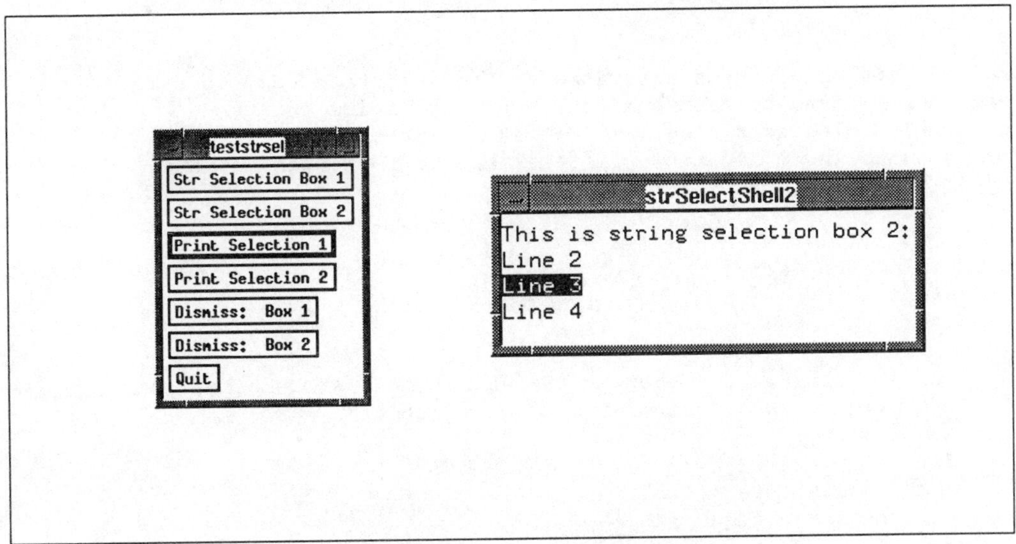

Figure 12.2 *teststrsel's* Main Panel and the Second String Selection Box

```
#ifdef X11R3
#include <X11/Box.h>
#include <X11/Command.h>
#else
#include <X11/Xaw/Box.h>
#include <X11/Xaw/Command.h>
#endif

#include <Ximisc.h>
#include "StrSelect.h"
```

Next, there are several private widget IDs and a font structure:

```
static Widget strSelectShell1, strSelectShell2,
    testSelectBox1, testSelectBox2,
    doneButton1, doneButton2;
```

Each selection box has its own reference string:

```
static char *test_str1 = "This is string selection box 1:\n\
Line 2\nLine 3\nLine 4";
static char *test_str2 = "This is string selection box 2:\n\
Line 2\nLine 3\nLine 4";
```

One of the selection boxes uses the default font and the other uses the font loaded in **main()** using the library function **load_font()**:

```
static XFontStruct *font;

/*
main() sets up a button-activated string selection box.  A simple
callback is used to test the retrieval facilities for the
currently selected string.  NOTE:  It's important to test for
proper handling of multiple widgets, and to test both methods for
specifying a reference string.
*/

void main(argc, argv)
int argc;
char **argv;
{
    Widget topLevel, testBox, strSelectButton1, strSelectButton2,
        printButton1, printButton2, quitButton;
    Arg args[5];
    int i;
    char *delimiters = "\n";
    Cursor pixmap_cursor;

    topLevel = XtInitialize(argv[0], "TestStrSel",
```

```
        NULL, 0, &argc, argv);
    font = load_font(topLevel, "teststrsel", "8x13");
    i = 0;
    XtSetArg(args[i], XtNallowShellResize, (XtArgVal) TRUE); i++;
    strSelectShell1 = XtCreatePopupShell("strSelectShell1",
        transientShellWidgetClass, topLevel, args, i);
    i = 0;
    XtSetArg(args[i], XtNallowShellResize, (XtArgVal) TRUE); i++;
    strSelectShell2 = XtCreatePopupShell("strSelectShell2",
        transientShellWidgetClass, topLevel, args, i);
    i = 0;
    XtSetArg(args[i], XiNdelimiters, (XtArgVal) delimiters); i++;
    XtSetArg(args[i], XiNreferenceString, (XtArgVal) test_str1); i++;
    XtSetArg(args[i], XiNpixmapRows, (XtArgVal) 15); i++;
    XtSetArg(args[i], XiNpixmapColumns, (XtArgVal) 35); i++;
    testSelectBox1 = XtCreateManagedWidget("testSelectBox1",
        xiStrSelectWidgetClass, strSelectShell1, args, i);
    i = 0;
    XtSetArg(args[i], XiNfont, (XtArgVal) font); i++;
    XtSetArg(args[i], XiNpixmapRows, (XtArgVal) 5); i++;
    XtSetArg(args[i], XiNpixmapColumns, (XtArgVal) 31); i++;
/*  pixmap_cursor = XCreateFontCursor(XtDisplay(topLevel), XC_right_ptr);
    XtSetArg(args[i], XtNcursor, (XtArgVal) pixmap_cursor); i++;*/
    testSelectBox2 = XtCreateManagedWidget("testSelectBox2",
        xiStrSelectWidgetClass, strSelectShell2, args, i);
    XiStrSelectSetString(testSelectBox2, test_str2);
    /*
    set up command buttons to pop-up, dismiss, and print selection...
    */
    XtRealizeWidget(topLevel);
    XtMainLoop();
}   /* main */
```

Note that in the first selection box, we use **XtSetArg()** to specify the reference string and in the second selection box we specify the reference string with the public function **XiStrSelectSetString()**. Also, the default font is used for the first selection box, whereas an "8x13" font is supplied for the second selection box. Lastly, the source code for creating the second selection box includes a test for the **XtNcursor** resource. Using a specification similar to those in Section 12.5.3, you can also set the cursor for one or both selection boxes from a resource file.

The callback functions that pop up the selection box shells and print the current selections are similar to those that we've written in previous chapters; see Appendix M.

13

XiAlert: Designing Compound Widgets

This chapter introduces compound widgets as a mechanism for building an interface/front-end to other widgets, for building special-purpose widget classes, and for prototyping simple widgets. As a straightforward example of a compound widget, we develop the **XiAlert** widget class.

XiAlert is modeled after the Athena **Dialog** widget class, but without the text entry box. Specifically, it combines a label and buttons, plus the blocking behavior that we demonstrated in earlier chapters to implement a blocking, pop-up alert widget. In contrast to a normal dialog widget, it supports user responses through button selection only.

With **XiStrSelect**, we addressed each widget-related file in detail. Beginning with **XiAlert**, we focus on selected aspects of the header and implementation files. The complete source code for each widget class is given in the respective appendices, for **XiAlert**, Appendix N.

13.1 Simple versus Compound Widgets

In Chapter 12 we focused on the development of a simple widget class, that is, a widget class that inherits data structures and functionality from other widget classes, but that does *not* encapsulate other widget instances. Even though a simple widget class inherits from other classes, in relative terms this type of class development is the widget programming equivalent of "programming from scratch."

In developing complex GUI components via simple widgets, the programmer must have a fairly extensive knowledge of the data structures and functionality that's inherited from other classes. In relative terms, **XiStrSelect** is a very modest simple widget class. In particular, it doesn't require any form of sophisticated, special-purpose geometry management, input, or output. In developing sophisticated simple widgets, however, you must be prepared to supplement the widget class with additional methods that implement class-specific constraints, geometry management, and so on. Moreover, in *some* situations the widget programmer must delve inside one or more of the superclasses as part of coordinating the inherited and unique behavior of the resulting widget.

In this chapter we address compound widgets, that is, widget classes that assemble a unique widget from other widgets (widget instances). It's common to think of a compound widget as providing an *interface* to other widgets. Alternatively, an application programmer could assemble widgets on demand, in order to produce a custom GUI component that's required for the application. If, however, the widget assembly operation is carried out at the widget programming level, this functionality can be reused with greater consistency in the applications.

Consider an organization where programmers in different software development teams develop applications in parallel. Typically, these applications have certain commonalities, as in a collection of business applications for accounting, inventory, and so on. Software reusability can be important in this situation not only because it maximizes the use of existing code and minimizes maintenance costs, but also because it guarantees a moderate degree of uniformity across applications. With respect to the user interface, reusable high-level GUI components lead to a consistent look and feel within and across applications.

Widgets, both simple and compound, are important for software reusability in an X programming environment. In general, simple widgets provide a greater degree of control over the behavior of lower level widget components than do compound widgets. In particular, the widget programmer can provide methods that account for every possibility that arises during window resizing events on low-level components, during partial exposures, and so on. Although possible in some cases, it can be more difficult with compound widgets to control the behavior and interaction of low-level (encapsulated) widgets. In many cases, however, the compound widget approach provides a viable, perfectly adequate, means of building a high-level GUI component.

In our opinion, there are three circumstances where compound widgets can be quite useful. First, as mentioned, compound widgets can be used to provide a *controlled* interface to other widgets. In particular, a simple widget can be "wrapped" in a compound widget in order to enforce certain policies, for example, whether or not a label can have a border (encompassing box), as discussed in Chapter 11. Second, compound widgets provide a mechanism for building custom GUI components that will be used in a specialized, restricted environment, such as building a widget set used for in-house engineering applications.

Third, compound widgets can be used for prototyping. That is, in developing a special-purpose widget set, you can start out by assembling GUI components as compound widgets. These widgets can be refined through an iterative process wherein GUI objects are demonstrated to users and application programmers and modified. Ultimately, if necessary, a compound widget can be reimplemented as a simple widget.

We've attempted to motivate our development of compound widgets by addressing some of the common criticisms in advance. Our up-front overview, qualification, and defense of compound widgets emphasizes that we do *not* champion compound widgets as a preferred, or primary, approach to widget class development. In this book we're interested in discussing a variety of widget programming issues, including how to design and use compound widgets. With this in mind, the remaining chapters use compound widgets as a vehicle for addressing a number of widget programming issues that arise with both simple and compound widgets.

13.2 XiAlert: Overview

An alert widget implements a pop-up, blocking message window that supports buttons. It can be used to query the user with yes-no-cancel type messages, or for displaying simple warning and informatory messages that require a one-button, "Continue" type response. Unlike our earlier alert box implementation, an application can create any number of alert boxes.

An alert widget is shell-less; the client must provide the enclosing shell. A convenience function, **XiAlertPopup()**, is provided for popping up the alert box. This function returns the button values associated with the selected button. **XiAlertPopup()**'s arguments include the widget ID, the message that should be displayed, and either **XiBEEP** or **XiNOBEEP**. The duration of the beep is controlled by a resource, **XiNbeepDuration**. A separate convenience function, **XiAlertBeep()**, is available for sounding the terminal bell an arbitrary number of times, independent of **XiNbeepDuration**.

An application can add buttons to an alert box with **XiAlertAddButton()**. A button label, a button value (integer), a callback function, and callback data can be associated with each button.

Figure 13.1 shows a typical alert box.

13.3 *Alert.h*: The Public Interface

The **XiAlert** widget class provides three resources:

```
#define XiNmessage        "message"          /* OK to modify */
#define XiNbeepDuration   "beepDuration"     /* OK to modify */
#define XiNfont           "font"
#define XiCMessage        "Message"
#define XiCBeepDuration   "BeepDuration"
#define XiCFont           "Font"
```

Consider **XiNmessage**. Normally an application calls **XiAlertPopup()** to display a message:

```
    result = XiAlertPopup(alertBox, "Abandon changed text?", XiBEEP);
```

The third argument indicates that the terminal bell should be sounded, as many times as indicated by the resource **XiNbeepDuration**.

In some applications it may be necessary to display the same (lengthy) message throughout the application. For this type for situation, **XiAlert** provides another convenience function, **XiAlertMap()**, that simply maps the alert box, displaying the message associated with **XiNmessage**:

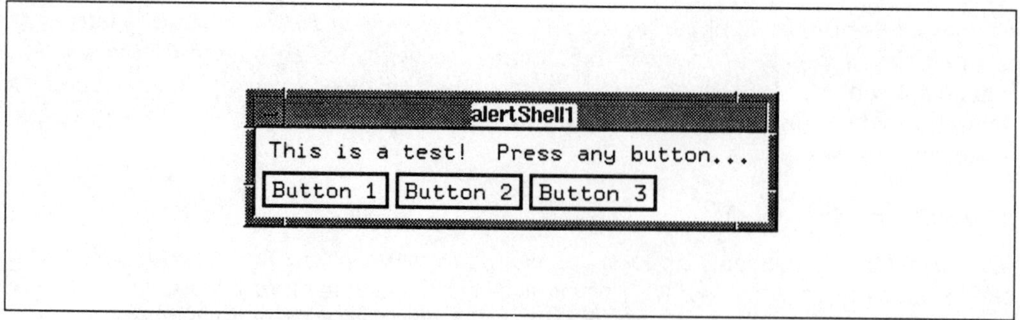

Figure 13.1 A Blocking Pop-up Alert Box

```
    result = XiAlertMap(alertBox);
```

XtSetValues() can be used to set or change the message as necessary.

With **XiAlertMap()** there is no function argument for the terminal bell; the bell is sounded automatically. An application can, however, turn off the bell by setting **XibeepDuration** to 0.

With most applications, the user should be given control of the terminal bell. Assuming that the application doesn't require strict control of the bell, the user has the option of suppressing it for a particular alert box, or across all alert boxes in the application, using either a resource name or class specification. Note that for critical situations, an application can record the current value of the beep duration, modify it, sound the bell, and then restore the duration.

Next, consider the two message constants that are used with **XiAlertPopup()** for beep versus no-beep behavior. The constants are defined as macros in the public header file:

```
#define XiNOBEEP     0
#define XiBEEP       1
```

With a large widget set, it might be preferable to move them to a common header file that's shared by the entire widget library.

Next, following the Xt convention, the public header file defines opaque type definitions for the instance and class records:

```
typedef struct _XiAlertClassRec *XiAlertWidgetClass;
typedef struct _XiAlertRec *XiAlertWidget;
```

Next, the widget class pointer must be made public:

```
extern WidgetClass xiAlertWidgetClass;
```

Lastly, the public functions are declared. One of the public functions that we haven't mentioned is **XiAlertAddButton()**:

```
extern void XiAlertAddButton();
/*  XiAlertWidget alert_widget;
    char *button_name;
    int button_value;
    void (*callback_proc)();
    caddr_t callback_arg;
*/
```

Buttons and their callback functions do not have resources. An application adds buttons, button values, button callbacks, and button data with this function. The remaining public functions are discussed in subsequent sections.

13.4 *AlertP.h*: The Private Widget Data Structures

XiAlert is a subclass of the Athena **form** widget class; hence, *AlertP.h* must include *FormP.h*:

```
#include "Alert.h"
#ifdef X11R3
#include <X11/FormP.h>
#else
#include <X11/Xaw/FormP.h>
#endif
```

Several constants are defined for use in the implementation file:

```
#define ALERT_MAX_BUTTONS            5
#define ALERT_STD_BEEP_DURATION      1
#define ALERT_MAX_BEEP_DURATION      25
#define ALERT_DEFAULT_WIDTH          400
#define ALERT_DEFAULT_HEIGHT         175

#define ALERT_DEFAULT_MSG          "A message goes here!"
```

In our Xlib dialog boxes we dynamically allocated the storage for each button; that is, there was no physical limit on the number of buttons. For the alert box class, however, we're setting an arbitrary limit. The use of arbitrary limits, or magic numbers, is often condemned, but in this type of situation there is some justification for arbitrary limits.

First, unlike with many aggregate data structures, the number of buttons is fairly predictable—no one is likely to require, say, 20 buttons in an alert box. Second, with dynamic data structures of this type there is always the possibility of an application inadvertently defining too many buttons in a loop; thus, there should be some type of test on a maximum allowable number of buttons—hence, an arbitrary limit.

If you prefer not to have arbitrary limits, the modifications to support an unlimited number of buttons are quite trivial (see the examples in the earlier Xlib chapters).

The next definition is the structure that represents an alert box's contribution to the complete class record:

```
typedef struct _XiAlertClassPart {      /* class definition */
```

```
    int dummy;
} XiAlertClassPart;
```

In this implementation there is no shared data. Recalling our earlier alert box implementation, you could argue that the variable **query_wait** should be allocated in the class record. Specifically, because an alert box blocks until the user responds, there would be no contention among alert boxes with respect to this variable.

For this widget class, however, this (blocking) control variable is the only possible shared variable. If it were part of the class record, several of **XiAlert**'s functions would require (the **alert_class** component of) the class record as a parameter. This requirement is unjustified, given the minimal overhead associated with storing this variable in each widget instance record.

Next, the layout of the class record (the inheritance path) is defined:

```
typedef struct _XiAlertClassRec {
    CoreClassPart core_class;
    CompositeClassPart composite_class;
    ConstraintClassPart constraint_class;
    FormClassPart form_class;
    XiAlertClassPart alert_class;
} XiAlertClassRec;
```

XiStrSelect inherited from the **Core** and **Simple** widget classes. **XiAlert** inherits functionality from **Composite**, **Constraint**, and **Form** as well as **Core**. An alert box manages multiple widgets with constraints. Specifically, the message widget is positioned across the top of the alert box and the command buttons are located below the message in a horizontal layout. The **Form** widget class provides the functionality for enforcing these types of constraints; hence, **XiAlert** is designed as an immediate subclass of **Form**.

Following the type definition of the class record, the class record is made public. As mentioned in Chapter 12, by convention (the address of) the class record must be available for other classes that are derived from the this class:

```
extern XiAlertClassRec xiAlertClassRec;
```

As with our earlier Xlib dialog boxes, an application programmer can associate a value with each button. Unlike our Xlib dialog boxes, alert box buttons are implemented as **Command** widgets. In order to manage this button-level data, we define an aggregate instance record component that holds the button's widget ID and the button value:

```
typedef struct _XiAlertButtonPart {
    Widget wid;
    int value;
} XiAlertButtonPart;
```

Each instance record includes an array of these records:

```
typedef struct _XiAlertPart {           /* instance definition */
```

```
    char *msg;
    int std_beep_duration;
    XFontStruct *font;
    Widget msgW;
    XiAlertButtonPart buttonW[ALERT_MAX_BUTTONS];
    int num_buttons;
    int query_result;
    int query_wait;
} XiAlertPart;
```

The instance record includes a field, **num_buttons**, for keeping track of the current number of buttons.

In contrast to a string selection box, an alert box doesn't perform any ongoing operations against the string variable that's passed by the application. A simple **char** pointer, **msg**, is adequate for manipulating the message that's displayed in the alert box.

The second resource-related variable is **std_beep_duration**—this variable does *not* represent the default value for the number of beeps. If no resource specification is provided, **std_beep_duration** is initialized to a default value. But, the application, and in some situations the user, can modify its value to reflect the significance of the alert message. For example, if the user were about to destroy a very significant amount of data, the application could temporarily set this variable to a large value. We chose not to use the name **current_beep_duration**, because there is a convenience function for ringing the terminal bell an arbitrary number of times that does not consult this variable.

The third resource is **XiNfont**. The instance record stores a pointer to the application-supplied font structure in **font**. This variable is used during the initialization of encapsulated widgets (see the next section). **XiAlert** does not recognize dynamic changes to this variable.

Two components in the instance record distinguish **XiAlert** as a compound widget—namely,

```
    Widget msgW;
```

and the widget ID field in each element of **buttonW**:

```
    XiAlertButtonPart buttonW[ALERT_MAX_BUTTONS];
```

First, the initialize method creates an internal/encapsulated widget in the instance record for managing the message. In addition, internal command widgets are used to implement each button.

Next, we must define the instance record, which includes components for each inherited class:

```
typedef struct _XiAlertRec {
    CorePart core;
    CompositePart composite;
    ConstraintPart constraint;
    FormPart form;
    XiAlertPart alert;
```

```
} XiAlertRec;
```

Each of these components includes fields that are important in enforcing constraints on a collection of widgets.

Typically, a class that's derived from the **Constraint** widget class must supply the behavior that's unique to the derived class. Depending on the characteristics of the derived widget class, additional variables may be required for managing constraint information. Thus, Xt and the **Constraint** widget class is designed to accommodate a special constraints record. Each subclass of **Constraint** contributes a component to this record:

```
typedef struct {
    int dummy;
} XiAlertConstraintsPart;
```

XiAlert does not require any special constraint-related fields. As we'll see in the next section, all (supplemental) constraints management is handled by way of existing variables.

Form is the superclass of **XiAlert** and the immediate subclass of **Constraint**; hence, its constraints component must be included in the constraints record:

```
typedef struct _XiAlertConstraintsRec {
    FormConstraintsPart form;
    XiAlertConstraintsPart alert;
} XiAlertConstraintsRec, *XiAlertConstraints;
```

In the next section, we address the specific details of constraints management for an alert box.

13.5 *Alert.c*: The Implementation File

Alert.c must (1) define the class record, (2) define the class methods, (3) define the public functions, and (4) make provisions for access to resource-related instance variables.

13.5.1 Resources

The mapping of resources to instance record variables is straightforward:

```
static XtResource resources[] = {
    {XiNmessage, XiCMessage, XtRString, sizeof(char *),
        XtOffset(XiAlertWidget, alert.msg), XtRString, ""},
    {XiNbeepDuration, XiCBeepDuration, XtRInt, sizeof(int),
        XtOffset(XiAlertWidget, alert.std_beep_duration),
        XtRImmediate, (caddr_t) ALERT_STD_BEEP_DURATION},
    {XiNfont, XiCFont, XtRFontStruct, sizeof(XFontStruct *),
        XtOffset(XiAlertWidget, alert.font),
        XtRString, "XtDefaultFont"},
};
```

In this case, the use of **XtR...** types for resource conversion is similar to that of *xwaste* and **XiStrSelect**.

13.5.2 The Class Record

XiAlert's class record is larger than **XiStrSelect**'s; it includes initialization information for each of the four class components:

```
XiAlertClassRec XialertClassRec = {
    { /* core_class variables */
        (WidgetClass) &formClassRec,        /* ancestor */
        "Alert",                            /* class name */
        sizeof(XiAlertRec),                 /* widget size */
#ifdef X11R3
        NULL,                               /* class initialize */
#else
        XawInitializeWidgetSet,             /* class initialize */
#endif
        NULL,                               /* class part init. */
        FALSE,                              /* class inited */
        Initialize,                         /* initialize */
        NULL,                               /* initialize hook */
        XtInheritRealize,                   /* realize */
        NULL,                               /* actions */
        0,                                  /* number of actions */
        resources,                          /* resources */
        XtNumber(resources),                /* number of resources */
        NULLQUARK,                          /* xrm class */
        TRUE,                               /* compress motions */
        TRUE,                               /* compress exposures */
        TRUE,                               /* compress enter/leave */
        FALSE,                              /* visibility interest */
        Destroy,                            /* destroy */
        XtInheritResize,                    /* resize */
        XtInheritExpose,                    /* expose */
        SetValues,                          /* set values */
        NULL,                               /* set values hook */
        XtInheritSetValuesAlmost,           /* set values almost */
        NULL,                               /* get values hook */
        NULL,                               /* accept focus */
        XtVersion,                          /* version */
        NULL,                               /* callback private */
        NULL,                               /* translation table */
        XtInheritQueryGeometry,             /* query geometry */
        XtInheritDisplayAccelerator,        /* display accelerator */
        NULL,                               /* extension */
    },
    { /* composite_class variables */
        XtInheritGeometryManager,           /* geometry manager */
        XtInheritChangeManaged,             /* change managed */
        XtInheritInsertChild,               /* insert child */
        XtInheritDeleteChild,               /* delete child */
        NULL,                               /* extension */
    },
    { /* constraint_class fields */
```

```
        NULL,                          /* subresources */
        0,                             /* number of subresources */
        sizeof(XiAlertConstraintsRec), /* record size */
        ConstraintInitialize,          /* initialize */
        NULL,                          /* destroy */
        NULL,                          /* set values */
        NULL,                          /* extension */
    },
    { /* form_class fields */
#ifdef X11R3
        0,
#else
        XtInheritLayout,
#endif
    },
    { /* alert_class variables */
        0,
    },
}; /* XialertClassRec */

WidgetClass xiAlertWidgetClass = (WidgetClass) &XialertClassRec;
```

Following Xt's design, the class pointer, **xiAlertWidgetClass**, points to this record.

XiAlert is a subclass of **Form**, therefore, the superclass field points to **Form**'s class record, which is defined in *Form.c*. As recommended by current naming conventions, we're using "Alert" as the class name (string) in the class-name field of the **core_class** component. *With respect to resource classes*, if you want to make a distinction among similar alert widget classes, you should do so here.

Again, when you design a new widget, don't forget the initialization function, **XawInitializeWidgetSet**(), for Release 4 widgets. Typically, if you use **NULL** in the class-initialization field with Release 4, you'll experience "core" records of another type (only indirectly related to the **Core** widget class).

XiStrSelect provided its own expose method, because its display operations were unique. (There is no way that **Core** and/or **Simple** could anticipate the need to display rows of strings in a window!) **XiAlert**, on the other hand, encapsulates widgets that have their own expose methods, thus, no expose method is required.

Note that, because **XiAlert** provides an interface to other widgets and has no special actions or translations the respective fields have either 0 or **NULL**.

Consider the **composite_class** component. A **Composite** class record supplements **Core**'s functionality with four methods for managing multiple widgets:

```
typedef struct _CompositeClassPart {
    XtGeometryHandler geometry_manager;
    XtWidgetProc change_managed;
    XtWidgetProc insert_child;
    XtWidgetProc delete_child;
    caddr_t extension;
} CompositeClassPart;
```

The insert-child method, for example, manages the position determination and insertion operations that are required in order to insert a child widget within a composite parent widget. These methods are discussed in the Xt documentation.

For **XiAlert** (and many other widget classes), these methods are simply inherited:

```
XiAlertClassRec XialertClassRec = {
    ...
    { /* composite_class variables */
        XtInheritGeometryManager,           /* geometry manager */
        XtInheritChangeManaged,             /* change managed */
        XtInheritInsertChild,               /* insert child */
        XtInheritDeleteChild,               /* delete child */
        NULL,                               /* extension */
    },
    ...
}; /* XialertClassRec */
```

(Note that, for each fundamental class, the keyword macros that signal method inheritance [**XtInherit. . .**] are provided in the Xt documentation. Young [1990] discusses the **Composite** widget class with respect to a simple widget class that's derived from **Composite**, whereas we're focusing on a compound widget that inherits composite widget functionality. In this book we use the terminology *simple widget class* to refer to any non-compound widget class.)

Constraint is next in the inheritance path. **Composite** provides basic geometry management through its geometry-manager and change-managed methods. In many cases, a simple widget class that's derived from **Composite** will have to supplement, or redefine, the functionality that's available from **Composite**.

The Athena **Box** widget class, for example, which is derived from **Composite**, provides it own geometry management methods. Basically, these methods coordinate parent-child geometry-management requests and perform layout operations when a widget is managed. (Recall that **XtRealizeWidget()** initiates change-managed operations on each widget in the application's widget [instance] hierarchy.)

If you've used the **Box** widget class in an application, you know that it's capabilities are rather limited—essentially, it stacks its children in a column, as long as they have similar widths. **Constraint** sets the stage for considerably more sophisticated geometry management, including geometry-related resource support in derived classes. Much of the generic functionality for enforcing widget constraints is handled behind the scenes by the Intrinsics. **Constraint**'s primary contribution is to serve as a starting point for widget class derivations. These derivations add unique constraints—constraints that define a class's look and feel.

XiAlert must initialize the **constraint_class** component properly. **Constraint**'s class record includes the following:

```
typedef struct _ConstraintClassPart {
    XtResourceList resources;
    Cardinal num_resources;
    Cardinal constraint_size;
    XtInitProc initialize;
    XtWidgetProc destroy;
```

```
    XtSetValuesFunc set_values;
    caddr_t extension;
} ConstraintClassPart;
```

With some widget classes, it's necessary to provide methods (and resources) that manage parent-child constraints. In general, these methods are similar to the widget's primary methods. A constraint-destroy method, for example, (represented in the fourth field of **ConstraintClassPart**) may be necessary if the widget allows children to be destroyed (as part of normal execution, as opposed to when the entire widget is destroyed). A constraint-set-values method takes care of geometry management that's required by dynamic changes to constraint-related resources.

With **XiAlert** these fields are initialized as follows:

```
XiAlertClassRec XialertClassRec = {
    ...
    { /* constraint_class fields */
        NULL,                             /* subresources */
        0,                                /* number of subresources */
        sizeof(XiAlertConstraintsRec),    /* record size */
        ConstraintInitialize,             /* initialize */
        NULL,                             /* destroy */
        NULL,                             /* set values */
        NULL,                             /* extension */
    },
    ...
}; /* XialertClassRec */
```

Specifically, there are no constraint-related resources and there is no support for dynamic destruction of child widgets. We must, however, specify the size of the constraints record and provide a constraints-initialize method. This method is described subsequently.

For a simple alert box implementation, **Form**'s layout constraints and geometry management resources are perfectly adequate, hence, we simply inherit this functionality:

```
XiAlertClassRec XialertClassRec = {
    ...
    { /* form_class fields */
#ifdef X11R3
        0,
#else
        XtInheritLayout,
#endif
    },
    ...
}; /* XialertClassRec */
```

For X11 Release 3, the **form_class** component contributes nothing to the class record, therefore the placeholder constant is 0; for X11 Release 4, we simply inherit the default layout method. (With Release 4, the layout/reconfiguration function is specified here—as a class method—so that a widget programmer has the option of replacing it in a derived class.)

Lastly, the **alert_class** component is initialized to 0:

```
XiAlertClassRec XialertClassRec = {
    ...
    { /* alert_class variables */
        0,
    },
}; /* XialertClassRec */
```

13.5.3 The XiAlert Methods

XiAlert defines four methods:

```
static void Initialize();
static void ConstraintInitialize();
static Boolean SetValues();
static void Destroy();
```

First, **Initialize()** sets the window size variables in the **core** component of the instance record:

```
/*
Initialize() creates the label widget for the alert box
message; it has a zero-width border.  Other variables are
initialized as well.
*/
/*ARGSUSED*/
static void Initialize(request, new)
XiAlertWidget request, new;
{
    Arg args[5];
    int i;

    if (new->core.width == 0)
        new->core.width = ALERT_DEFAULT_WIDTH;
    if (new->core.height == 0)
        new->core.height = ALERT_DEFAULT_HEIGHT;
    if (new->alert.std_beep_duration < 0 ||
            new->alert.std_beep_duration > ALERT_MAX_BEEP_DURATION)
        new->alert.std_beep_duration = ALERT_STD_BEEP_DURATION;
    i = 0;
    XtSetArg(args[i], XtNlabel,
        (XtArgVal) ALERT_DEFAULT_MSG); i++;
    XtSetArg(args[i], XtNborderWidth, (XtArgVal) 0); i++;
    XtSetArg(args[i], XtNresizable, (XtArgVal) TRUE); i++;
    XtSetArg(args[i], XtNfont, (XtArgVal) new->alert.font); i++;
    new->alert.msgW = XtCreateManagedWidget("message",
        labelWidgetClass, new, args, i);
    new->alert.num_buttons = 0;
```

```
}    /* Initialize */
```

In addition, **Initialize**() checks **std_beep_duration** to ensure that **XiNbeepDuration** has been used properly. Lastly, **Initialize**() creates an encapsulated widget for displaying the message in the alert box.

In this implementation, an Athena **Label** widget hosts the message. Note that because **Initialize**() sets the border width to 0, an application, or user, cannot change this value. On the other hand, if a user specifies a font for the alert box, it (a pointer to its structure) is passed on to the label widget by way of **alert.font**.

Lastly, the label widget's **XtNresizable** resource must be set to **TRUE**. If this resource setting were omitted, the label widget's size would be fixed, based on the first message to be displayed. Subsequently, longer messages would be truncated on the right and shorter messages would not fill the label widget. (Also, because the application must provide the shell, the application must set the **XtNallowShellResize** resource to **TRUE** as well.)

The alert box buttons are implemented with Athena **Command** widgets. An application adds buttons subsequent to alert box creation using the public function **XiAlert-AddButton**(), as described in Section 13.5.4.

As mentioned, a secondary initialize method is required to enforce an alert box's unique constraints. **ConstraintInitialize**() carries out these tasks:

```
/*
ConstraintInitialize() sets up the form widget that
houses the alert message and buttons.
*/
/*ARGSUSED*/
static void ConstraintInitialize(request, new)
Widget request, new;
{
    XiAlertWidget aw = (XiAlertWidget) new->core.parent;
    Widget *child, *children = aw->composite.children;
    XiAlertConstraints constraint =
        (XiAlertConstraints) new->core.constraints;

    if (!XtIsSubclass(new, commandWidgetClass))
        return;
    constraint->form.left = constraint->form.right = XtChainLeft;
    constraint->form.vert_base = aw->alert.msgW;
    if (aw->composite.num_children > 1) {
        for (child = children + aw->composite.num_children - 1;
                child > children; child--) {
            if (XtIsManaged(*child) &&
                    XtIsSubclass(*child, commandWidgetClass)) {
                constraint->form.horiz_base = *child;
                break;
            }
        }
    }
}    /* ConstraintInitialize */
```

ConstraintInitialize() first coerces the **new** widget to a widget **aw** of type **XiAlertWidget**, in order to access the proper fields. Child widgets, on the other hand, are referenced as generic widgets, because it isn't necessary to access their internal fields. The constraints record for each widget is stored in the **core** component of the instance record. Thus, it must be coerced to **XiAlertConstraints** to set the constraints (see Section 13.4). The constraints record's structure is:

```
typedef struct _XiAlertConstraintsRec {
    FormConstraintsPart form;
    XiAlertConstraintsPart alert;
} XiAlertConstraintsRec, *XiAlertConstraints;
```

We should point out at this point that Xt widget programming typically requires some knowledge of the widgets from which the derived widget is inheriting functionality. Having to look inside the parent widget may at first seem like a violation of the rules of encapsulation. The benefits of encapsulation, however, are intended *primarily* for the application programmer. In this respect, Xt is no different from an OO language such as C++. With C++, a derived class inherits variables and methods from its parent (the base class). In many cases, there is no way that the class developer can extend/specialize one class from another without being aware of (and referencing) the fields and methods in the parent class(es).

With **XiAlert**, it's necessary to enforce certain constraints against each child of the alert box. The **Composite** widget class provides the instance variables that are necessary for managing multiple children. Child widgets are maintained in a simple array within the **composite** component of the instance record; **composite.num_children** specifies the total number of child widgets—there is no breakdown by type. For an alert box, typically, there would be a label widget and one or more command button widgets.

In order to "traverse" the array of widgets, we've defined two pointers to a variable of type **Widget**:

```
    Widget *child, *children = aw->composite.children;
```

child points at the current child during list traversal and **children** points at the list of children. Note that Xt defines a special type for a list of widgets, specifically, **WidgetList**:

```
typedef Widget *WidgetList;
```

Using this **typedef** we could have written

```
    WidgetList children = aw->composite.children;
```

in order to reference the array. In many situations an opaque type is useful; at present, however, it hides the true data type, which we want to highlight. That is, you must already know that **WidgetList** is a pointer to a **Widget**, in order to accept and understand the array manipulation that occurs in the method.

Next, consider the body of the function/method. The constraints method is called for each child that's added to an alert widget. An alert box is composed of a label and command buttons. The label is added first, when the application calls **XtCreateWidget()** and we don't need to enforce any constraints against it. Thus, **ConstraintInitialize()** simply returns if the current child is not a command button:

```
if (!XtIsSubclass(new, commandWidgetClass))
    return;
```

Next, according to the current alert widget design, for each command button an alert box enforces the constraint that widgets are chained from left to right with a fixed amount of spacing between buttons:

```
constraint->form.left = constraint->form.right = XtChainLeft;
```

The application programmer can create a form widget and add children using the **XtNfromHoriz** and **XtNfromVert** resources. The widget programmer, on the other hand, must have a minimal understanding of the implementation of Athena **Form** widget class, in order to derive other classes from it. Obviously, we don't have the space in this book to describe each of the Athena widget classes in detail. Therefore we'll mention only those aspects of the superclasses that are important for our discussion. You are encouraged to study the source code for the Athena widgets for a more complete understanding of the details.

Here, we must set **form.left** and **form.right** to **XtChainLeft** because these variables are examined as part of the layout operation that's applied to each child of a **Form**-derived widget. During the layout of child widgets, the vertical position within the form is calculated relative to other (child) widgets. For an alert widget, each command button should be placed below the label widget, hence, **form.vert_base** is initialized with the ID of the label widget:

```
constraint->form.vert_base = aw->alert.msgW;
```

Lastly, we must indicate the horizontal constraint for the button that's currently being added. Specifically, the new command button should be placed (horizontally) adjacent to the previously added command button.

In general, child widgets are added to the alert box's **composite** component's **children** field using normal 0-to-*n* positioning, thus, the most recently added command widget is the last managed widget in the list. This organization means that we *could* set the horizontal constraint with something like the following:

```
if (aw->composite.num_children > 1) {
    child = children + aw->composite.num_children - 1;
    constraint->form.horiz_base = *child;
}
```

Some widget classes, however, provide their own insert-child and delete-child methods that (re-)organize these children. Moreover, an application can add a child widget (using **XtCreateWidget()**) at any time. The list of children for a composite widget, contains *all* the child widgets, whatever their type. It's really impossible to deal with this situation adequately, but the approach that's used in **ConstraintInitialize()** is better than just assuming that the last child in the list is a command widget. We should acknowledge that our loop-based approach is patterned after the one used with the Athena **Dialog** widget class.

With so much pointer-based processing of the instance record, it's easy to lose sight of which widgets are involved in the constraint relationships. Each time **ConstraintInitialize()** is called, there are two widgets involved in each horizontal and vertical relationship. Specifically, the constraint record, **constraint**, is a component of **new**:

```
XiAlertConstraints constraint =
    (XiAlertConstraints) new->core.constraints;
```

which is the command button that's currently being added to the alert box. Thus,

```
constraint->form.vert_base = aw->alert.msgW;
```

stores the label widget's ID in the **vert_base** field of the new command button. Likewise,

```
constraint->form.horiz_base = *child;
```

establishes a relationship between the new command button and the previously added command button.

ConstraintInitialize() is the only secondary method that's necessary with **XiAlert**. By studying **ConstaintInitialize()**, the primary methods in this and our other widgets classes, and the Athena widget source code for the relevant widget classes, you can develop a feel for how to provide unique constraints for each new widget class.

The next method is **SetValues()**:

```
/*
SetValues() updates the stored message or the beep duration.
*/
/*ARGSUSED*/
static Boolean SetValues(current, request, new)
Widget current, request, new;
{
    XiAlertWidget aw = (XiAlertWidget) new;
    XiAlertWidget old_aw = (XiAlertWidget) current;
    Arg args[2];
    int i;

    if (aw->alert.msg != NULL) {
        i = 0;
        XtSetArg(args[i], XtNlabel, (XtArgVal) aw->alert.msg); i++;
        XtSetValues(aw->alert.msgW, args, i);
    }
    if (aw->alert.std_beep_duration < 0 ||
            aw->alert.std_beep_duration > ALERT_MAX_BEEP_DURATION)
        aw->alert.std_beep_duration = ALERT_STD_BEEP_DURATION;
    return FALSE;
}   /* SetValues */
```

There are two resources that **XiAlert** must monitor for dynamic changes, specifically, **XiNbeepDuration** and **XiNmessage**. If the **XiNmessage** resource value changes, **SetValues()** simply passes this information on to the message widget using the **XtNlabel** resource. If a new duration is specified for the terminal bell, it's checked for negative or huge values. As mentioned in our earlier discussion of resources, a user can turn off the bell by setting this resource value to 0, provided that the application hasn't overridden the user's settings.

The last method is **Destroy()**:

```
/*
Destroy() frees encapsulated widgets.
*/

static void Destroy(aw)
XiAlertWidget aw;
{
    int i;

    XtDestroyWidget(aw->alert.msgW);
    for (i = 0; i < aw->alert.num_buttons; i++)
        XtDestroyWidget(aw->alert.buttonW[i].wid);
}   /* Destroy */
```

Although it's fairly common for widget programmers to omit clean-up operations, you really shouldn't depend on the Intrinsics' implicit rules for freeing dynamic data structures. In this case, the label widget should be released, along with the command widgets that implement the alert box buttons.

13.5.4 The Public Interface

The first function that an application uses is **XiAlertAddButton()**:

```
/*
XiAlertAddButton() adds buttons to an alert box, one at a time.
A value is associated with each button; this value is returned
by XiAlertPopup(), the function that invokes the alert box.  A
callback function may be registered with the button as well.
A hidden/internal callback function is used to pop down the
alert box after a button selection; see internal_callback_proc().
*/

void XiAlertAddButton(aw, button_name, button_value,
    callback_proc, client_data)
XiAlertWidget aw;
char *button_name;
int button_value;
void (*callback_proc)();     /* or, XtCallbackProc callback_proc; */
caddr_t client_data;
{
```

```
    Arg args[7];
    int i;

    if (aw->alert.num_buttons >= ALERT_MAX_BUTTONS) {
        fprintf(stderr,
            "alert box: too many buttons for the alert box\n");
        fprintf(stderr,
            "alert box: the maximum number of buttons is: %d.\n",
            ALERT_MAX_BUTTONS);
        return;
    }
    i = 0;
    XtSetArg(args[i], XtNlabel, (XtArgVal) button_name); i++;
    XtSetArg(args[i], XtNfont, (XtArgVal) aw->alert.font); i++;
    aw->alert.buttonW[aw->alert.num_buttons].wid =
        XtCreateManagedWidget(button_name, commandWidgetClass,
            aw, args, i);
    aw->alert.buttonW[aw->alert.num_buttons].value = button_value;
    XtAddCallback(aw->alert.buttonW[aw->alert.num_buttons].wid,
        XtNcallback, internal_callback_proc, button_value);
    if (callback_proc != NULL)
        XtAddCallback(aw->alert.buttonW[aw->alert.num_buttons].wid,
            XtNcallback, callback_proc, client_data);
    aw->alert.num_buttons++;
}   /* XiAlertAddButton */
```

It adds buttons, one at a time, with provisions for a button label, value, callback function, and callback data.

There must be a mechanism for removing an alert box, once the user selects a command button. Because each command button can have multiple callback functions associated with it, **XiAlertAddButton()** adds an internal callback function, **internal_callback_proc()**, as the first callback on each command button's callback list:

```
    XtAddCallback(aw->alert.buttonW[aw->alert.num_buttons].wid,
        XtNcallback, internal_callback_proc, button_value);
```

This *internal* callback is responsible for popping down the alert box. The application-supplied callback function, if any, is added as the second callback function on each list.

An application must provide a shell for each alert box. **XiAlert** provides a convenience function that allows an application to pop up the alert box, display a message, and either beep or not beep the user:

```
/*
XiAlertPopup() pops up a message window.  It is the working
interface to the alert box that's used by the application.
*/

int XiAlertPopup(aw, msg, ring_bell)
XiAlertWidget aw;
char *msg;
```

```
Boolean ring_bell;
{
    Arg args[3];
    int i;

    query_set_pos(aw);
    if (ring_bell)
        XiAlertBeep(aw, aw->alert.std_beep_duration);
    i = 0;
    XtSetArg(args[i], XiNmessage, (XtArgVal) msg); i++;
    XtSetValues(aw, args, i);
    XtPopup(aw->core.parent, XtGrabExclusive);
    return get_query_result(aw);
}   /* XiAlertPopup */
```

query_set_pos() is a library function (from the miscellaneous library [Appendix L] that we described at the end of Chapter 12) that tests the cursor position and sets the pop-up shell to map at this location on the screen. **XiAlertBeep()** is a public function that the application programmer can call directly to ring the terminal bell an arbitrary number of times. Here, it's used from within **XiAlertPopup()** to sound the bell as many times as indicated by **XiNbeepDuration**.

It's definition is simply:

```
/*
XiAlertBeep() is provided for consistency to allow independent
beeps by the application programmer.
*/

void XiAlertBeep(w, num_beeps)
Widget w;
int num_beeps;
{
    alert_beep(w, num_beeps);
}   /* XiAlertBeep */
```

That is, it calls a lower level function that calls **XBell()**.

In Section 13.3 we mentioned **XiAlertMap()**, an alternative to **XiAlertPopup()** that uses the current values of **XiNbeepDuration** and **XiNmessage**. With **XiAlertMap()** the application programmer must specify just one argument to invoke the alert box:

```
/*
XiAlertMap() is like XiAlertPopup(), except it uses the message
previously set with XtSetValues().  You can turn off the (automatic)
beep by setting the beep-duration resource to 0.
*/

int XiAlertMap(aw)
XiAlertWidget aw;
{
    query_set_pos(aw);
```

```
    XiAlertBeep(aw, aw->alert.std_beep_duration);
    XtPopup(aw->core.parent, XtGrabExclusive);
    return get_query_result(aw);
}   /* XiAlertMap */
```

13.5.5 Support Functions

When the user selects a command button, the alert box must be popped down. As we mentioned, the easiest way to accomplish this is to install an internal callback function as the first entry in each command button's callback list:

```
/*
internal_callback_proc() is installed as the first callback
function for each button; see XiAlertAddButton().  Primarily,
it handles removal of the alert box.
*/
/*ARGSUSED*/
static void internal_callback_proc(w, button_value, call_data)
Widget w;    /* the button */
int button_value;
caddr_t call_data;
{
    XiAlertWidget aw = (XiAlertWidget) w->core.parent;

    aw->alert.query_result = button_value;
    aw->alert.query_wait = FALSE;
    XtPopdown(aw->core.parent);
    alert_reset_proper_keyboard_focus();
}   /* internal_callback_proc */
```

(See the earlier discussion describing **XiAlertAddButton**().)

This function is responsible for more than popping down the alert box. First, it must set the variable that controls the blocking behavior that's implemented with the secondary event loop. Second, because callback functions do not return values, this function must set the variable that **XiAlertPopup**(), or **XiAlertMap**(), returns as the user's response. The button value is stored with the callback when each command button is added with **XiAlertAddButton**():

```
    ...
    XtAddCallback(aw->alert.buttonW[aw->alert.num_buttons].wid,
        XtNcallback, internal_callback_proc, button_value);
    ...
```

This client data is passed as the second argument to **internal_callback_proc**(). Because this function is a private callback, it can interpret the second parameter as an **int**.

Many of the remaining support functions are similar to their counterparts in Chapters 9 and 10; they are given in Appendix N.

13.6 An Alert Box Demonstration

Figure 13.2 demonstrates two pop-up alert boxes that are created by the demonstration program *testalert*. This test program simply exercises the alert box and demonstrates how to set up a shell, create an alert box, and employ the public functions.

testalert defines two alert box IDs and a font structure that are used throughout the program:

```
static Widget testAlert1, testAlert2;
static XFontStruct *font;
```

To exercise **XiAlert** fully, we need two alert boxes, one that uses the default font and one that's allocated by the application as an alternative. In addition, each alert box must have multiple command buttons with different button values and callback functions. Although simple, **main()** is somewhat lengthy, in order to test each possibility. The complete function is:

```
void main(argc, argv)
int argc;
char **argv;
{
    Widget topLevel, testBox, alertShell1, alertShell2,
        testButton1, testButton2, quitButton;
    Arg args[7];
    int i;

    topLevel = XtInitialize(argv[0], "TestAlert",
        NULL, 0, &argc, argv);
    font = load_font(topLevel, "testalert", "8x13");
    i = 0;
    XtSetArg(args[i], XtNallowShellResize, (XtArgVal) TRUE); i++;
    alertShell1 = XtCreatePopupShell("alertShell1",
        transientShellWidgetClass, topLevel, args, i);
    i = 0;
    XtSetArg(args[i], XtNfont,          /* test this one with   */
        (XtArgVal) font); i++;          /* an alternate font    */
    testAlert1 = XtCreateManagedWidget("testAlert1",
        xiAlertWidgetClass, alertShell1, args, i);
    i = 0;
    XtSetArg(args[i], XtNallowShellResize, (XtArgVal) TRUE); i++;
    alertShell2 = XtCreatePopupShell("alertShell2",
        transientShellWidgetClass, topLevel, args, i);
    testAlert2 = XtCreateManagedWidget("testAlert2",
        xiAlertWidgetClass, alertShell2, NULL, 0);

    testBox = XtCreateManagedWidget("box", boxWidgetClass,
        topLevel, NULL, 0);
    i = 0;
    XtSetArg(args[i], XtNlabel, (XtArgVal) "Button Set 1..."); i++;
    testButton1 = XtCreateManagedWidget("testButton1",
```

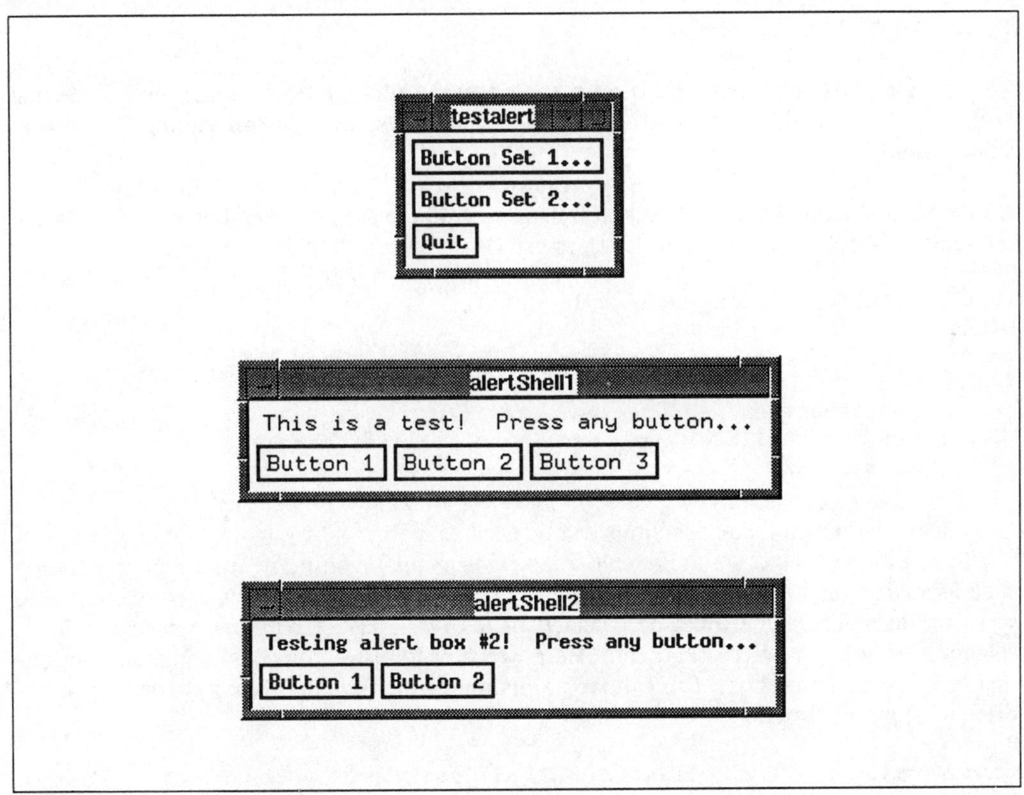

Figure 13.2 *teststrsel*'s Main Panel and Alert Boxes

```
        commandWidgetClass, testBox, args, i);
    i = 0;
    XtSetArg(args[i], XtNlabel, (XtArgVal) "Button Set 2..."); i++;
    testButton2 = XtCreateManagedWidget("testButton2",
        commandWidgetClass, testBox, args, i);
    i = 0;
    XtSetArg(args[i], XtNlabel, (XtArgVal) "Quit"); i++;
    quitButton = XtCreateManagedWidget("quitButton",
        commandWidgetClass, testBox, args, i);
    XtAddCallback(testButton1, XtNcallback, TestAlertBox1, NULL);
    XtAddCallback(testButton2, XtNcallback, TestAlertBox2, NULL);
    XtAddCallback(quitButton, XtNcallback, Quit, NULL);
    XiAlertAddButton(testAlert1, "Button 1", 3, AlertCB, "three");
    XiAlertAddButton(testAlert1, "Button 2", 6, AlertCB, "six");
    XiAlertAddButton(testAlert1, "Button 3", 9, AlertCB, "nine");
    XiAlertAddButton(testAlert2, "Button 1", 2, AlertCB, "two");
    XiAlertAddButton(testAlert2, "Button 2", 4, AlertCB, "four");
    XtRealizeWidget(topLevel);
    XtMainLoop();
```

```
}   /* main */
```

The first alert box sets the **XtNfont** resource to test the alternate font capabilities. Note that both alert box shells set the **XtNallowShellResize** resource before calling **XtCreate-PopupShell()**.

After creating the top-level command buttons that invoke the alert boxes, **XiAlertAddButton()** is called several times to install the alert box buttons. For simplicity, the same callback function, **AlertCB()**, is used with each button:

```
void AlertCB(w, client_data, call_data)
Widget w;
caddr_t client_data, call_data;
{
    printf("A button was pressed...\n");
    printf("Its callback data was: %s\n", client_data);
}   /* AlertCB */
```

Of course, distinct callback functions can be used as well.

To test an alert box, we must have a mechanism for invoking it. In a real application such as *xwaste*, an alert box would be used to communicate with the user, for example, to warn the user that a file must be selected in the wastebasket window before making a selection from the wastebasket menu. Here, we simply install top-level command buttons that invokes each alert box. The callback function for the first alert box illustrates the most often used public function:

```
void TestAlertBox1(w, client_data, call_data)
Widget w;
caddr_t client_data, call_data;
{
    int result;

    result = XiAlertPopup(testAlert1,
        "This is a test!  Press any button...", XiBEEP);
    /*
    Normally, you would do something useful with the value attached
    to the pressed button; for now, just print the value.
    */
    printf("You chose the button with value: %d\n", result);
}   /* TestAlertBox1 */
```

In this case, the message that's supplied to **XiAlertPopup()** is displayed in the alternate font (see Figure 13.2) and the bell is sounded.

For the second alert box, the callback function **TestAlertBox2()** (1) sets the message beforehand, (2) hard-codes the beep duration within the application, and (3) uses **XiAlertMap()** to invoke the alert box:

```
void TestAlertBox2(w, client_data, call_data)
Widget w;
caddr_t client_data, call_data;
```

```
{
    Arg args[3];
    int i, result;

    i = 0;
    XtSetArg(args[i], XiNmessage,
        (XtArgVal) "Testing alert box #2!  Press any button..."); i++;
    XtSetArg(args[i], XiNbeepDuration, (XtArgVal) 4); i++;
    XtSetValues(testAlert2, args, i);
    result = XiAlertMap(testAlert2);
    /*
    Normally, you would do something useful with the value attached
    to the pressed button; for now, just print the value.
    */
    printf("You chose the button with value: %d\n", result);
}   /* TestAlertBox2 */
```

If, for example, you provide

```
testalert*beepDuration: 10
```

in your *.Xdefaults* file, the terminal bell will be sounded ten times when the first alert box is popped up, but only four times with the second alert box.

For the record, we personally don't like beeping applications. There are times, however, when it's critically important to get the user's attention and suspend the application until the user responds. A beeping, alert box will usually do the job. For these critical situations, it's usually a good idea to (1) hard-code the beep duration as we did with the second alert box, or (2) call **XiAlertBeep()** immediately before invoking the alert box. The latter function does *not* depend on the resource **XiNbeepDuration**; thus, you can be assured that the warning will be accompanied by the proper sound effects (provided that the terminal bell operates properly).

13.7 XiAlert in an Application

We believe that it was important to present a reasonably large Xt application before delving into widget programming. In Chapter 10 we implemented *xwaste* as a system of modules where *alert.c* took care of alert box operations. At that time, we did not have the encapsulation capabilities provided by widgets; hence, we used two distinct alert box implementations. In retrospect, the contrasting approaches to alert box implementation emphasize the true usefulness of widgets in particular and OO programming in general.

At this point you should consider modifying *xwaste*'s *alert.c* such that **XiAlert** widgets replace the tailor-made alert boxes. Given the modular design of *xwaste*, this exercise is quite simple. Note that if you keep *alert.c*'s public interface intact, no changes are required in the other modules. Appendix O provides one possible **XiAlert**-based implementation of *alert.c*.

14

XiFileSelect: Building a High-level Interface Widget

The Motif widget set (OSF, 1990) includes a widget named **XmFileSelectionBox** that presents a list of filenames in a window for all files matching a particular filter, or mask. In this chapter we use **XiStrSelect**, along with several of the Athena widgets, to build a widget that is similar in operation to **XmFileSelectionBox**. Unlike **XmFileSelectionBox**, our file selection box does not allow the user to edit the text of the selected filename (in a special edit box).

XiFileSelect provides another example of a compound widget. With **XiAlert** we had to coordinate the constraints provided by the Athena **Form** widget class with those that were unique to an alert box. With **XiFileSelect**, on the other hand, we demonstrate a higher level approach to building a widget from existing widgets, where the encapsulated (internal) widgets are used "as is." This type of widget assembly is particularly useful during widget class prototyping for a set of applications. This chapter also provides our first example of building an *Xi* widget that encapsulates another *Xi* widget.

14.1 Widget Class Reusability

The concept of reusability is fundamental to the principles of OO programming. If a programmer builds two classes *A* and *B*, and the nature of these two classes is such that it makes sense, logically, to incorporate both *A* and *B* into a new class *C*, then the programmer should be able to do so using standard (OO) programming techniques. In particular, a new class *C* might be designed wherein *A* and *B* participate as instance variables. Goldstein (1989) discusses this type of composition in an object-oriented context.

Likewise, a widget programmer should be able to develop a file selection box by putting together existing widgets, in our case, *Xaw* and *Xi* widgets. Indeed, if a widget programmer were forced to write 80 to 90 percent of every new widget class "from scratch," the programming community would have to reconsider the viability of the widget set and the Intrinsics in question. With modern high-level interfaces such as Xt, the benefits of reusability must extend to the widget programmer as well as the application programmer.

14.2 XiFileSelect: Overview

There are a number of different designs that you could consider in developing a file selection box. In this chapter we develop a modest file selection box that allows the user to enter a filter such as "*.c" in a text entry box and display every file that matches the mask. Then, the user can select an entry with the mouse and apply an application-defined operation to that file. Figure 14.1 illustrates a file selection box created by the first demonstration program from Appendix P.

XiFileSelect is implemented as a vertical pane widget. The primary components of the pane are the text entry area for the file filter, the scrollable display area, and the command buttons. The scrollable file display is implemented with an **XiStrSelect** widget.

A file selection box is shell-less. Consequently, an application can create a file selection box that exist alone in a pop-up window, or as a companion to other widgets in a top-level (or pop-up) window. If an **XiFileSelect** widget is created as a child of a pop-up shell, it automatically provides a "Dismiss" button. If its parent is not a pop-up shell, it assumes that there may be companion widgets, hence, a "Dismiss" button is inappropriate. In the latter case, it is the application's responsibility to put the file selection box where it won't be overlaid by another widget. Also, because of Xt's automatic geometry negotiation, row/column dimensions should be considered as requests.

XiFileSelect provides several public functions. For example, an application can use **XiFileSelectGetSelection**() to retrieve the currently selected filename. Also, an application can attach a callback function to the "Apply" button with **XiFileSelectAddApplyProc**().

14.3 *FileSelect.h*: The Public Interface

XiFileSelect defines several resources that control various characteristics of the encapsulated widgets:

```
#define XiNfilter           "filter"
#define XiNfilterWidth      "filterWidth"
#define XiNrows             "rows"
#define XiNcolumns          "columns"
#define XiNpixmapRows       "pixmapRows"
#define XiNpixmapColumns    "pixmapColumns"
#define XiNrowSpacing       "rowSpacing"
#define XiNpixmapCursor     "pixmapCursor"
#define XiNpixmapFont       "pixmapFont"
#define XiCFilter           "Filter"
#define XiCFilterWidth      "FilterWidth"
#define XiCRows             "Rows"
#define XiCColumns          "Columns"
#define XiCPixmapRows       "PixmapRows"
```

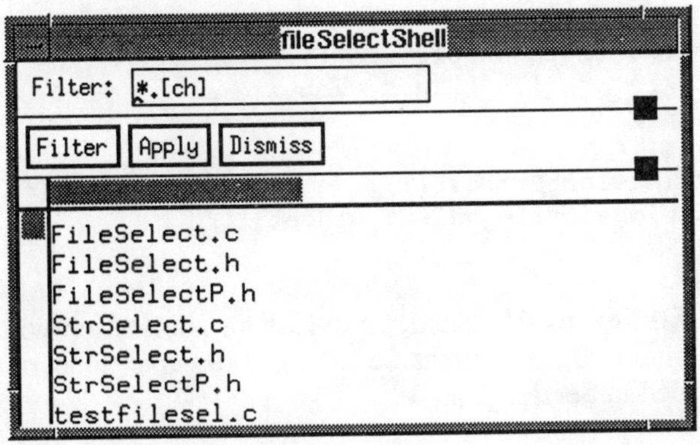

Figure 14.1 A File Selection Box in a Pop-up Shell

```
#define XiCPixmapColumns      "PixmapColumns"
#define XiCRowSpacing         "RowSpacing"
#define XiCPixmapCursor       "PixmapCursor"
#define XiCPixmapFont         "PixmapFont"
```

Most of these are self-explanatory, given our earlier applications and widgets. **XiNfilterWidth** allows an application (or user) to control the width of the text entry box for the file selection mask. It uses pixel metrics. **XiNfilter** provides a mechanism for setting the file selection mask during program start-up. The user can modify the current mask at any time and display the matching files by pressing the "Filter" button. **XiNpixmapFont** allows the user to specify a font for the file selection area. Otherwise, the fonts depend on the resource name and class settings in any relevant resource files, such as the *.Xdefaults* file.

The public structure definitions and the public declaration of the class pointer follow next:

```
typedef struct _XiFileSelectClassRec *XiFileSelectWidgetClass;
typedef struct _XiFileSelectRec *XiFileSelectWidget;

extern WidgetClass xiFileSelectWidgetClass;
```

Lastly, *FileSelect.h* defines four public functions:

```
extern void XiFileSelectPopup();
/*  XiFileSelectWidget file_select_widget;
*/

extern char *XiFileSelectGetSelection();
/*  XiFileSelectWidget file_select_widget;
```

```
*/

extern void XiFileSelectAddApplyProc();
/*  XiFileSelectWidget file_select_widget;
*/

extern void XiFileSelectRefresh();
/*  XiFileSelectWidget file_select_widget;
*/
```

The last function, **XiFileSelectRefresh()**, provides an application with a mechanism for redisplaying the contents of (the filename area of) the file selection box. The public functions are described in Section 14.5.3.

14.4 *FileSelecP.h*: The Private Widget Data Structures

Several convenience constants are defined that provide an overview of the various file selection box characteristics:

```
#define FILE_DEFAULT_FILTER            "*"

#define FILE_DEFAULT_WIDTH             300
#define FILE_DEFAULT_HEIGHT            150
#define FILE_DEFAULT_FILTER_WIDTH      150

#define FILE_DEFAULT_ROWS              10
#define FILE_DEFAULT_COLUMNS           30
#define FILE_DEFAULT_PIXMAP_ROWS       50
#define FILE_DEFAULT_PIXMAP_COLUMNS    100
#define FILE_DEFAULT_ROW_SPACING       2

#define FILE_MIN_FILTER_WIDTH          20
#define FILE_MIN_ROWS                  1
#define FILE_MIN_COLUMNS               10

#define FILE_MAX_FILTER                100
#define FILE_MAX_FILE_SPEC             1280     /* 1024 + 255 + 1 */

#define FILE_DELIMITERS          "\n\r\t "      /* used with strtok() */
#define EOS                      '\0'

#define FILE_NO_HIGHLIGHT        -1  /* ignore mouse, just    */
                                     /* redisplay files       */
#define FILE_NO_FILE             -2  /* no currently selected file */
```

We don't attempt to include conditional compiler directives to handle the multitude of arbitrary restrictions on directory path and filename length that exist across UNIX platforms. As a placeholder, we've chosen a rather large maximum file specification length. This value is used in routines that manipulate the filenames displayed in the file selection box and the current selection.

Next, there are definitions for the class-related structures. First, the file selection component of the class record is empty:

```
typedef struct _XiFileSelectClassPart {      /* class definition */
    int dummy;
} XiFileSelectClassPart;
```

XiFileSelect inherits from **Core**, **Composite**, **Constraint**, plus **VPaned/Paned**:

```
typedef struct _XiFileSelectClassRec {
    CoreClassPart core_class;
    CompositeClassPart composite_class;
    ConstraintClassPart constraint_class;
#ifdef X11R3
    VPanedClassPart vpaned_class;
#else
    PanedClassPart vpaned_class;
#endif
    XiFileSelectClassPart file_select_class;
} XiFileSelectClassRec;
```

The latter class provides the high-level geometry management for the vertical arrangement of the file filter, the filename area, and the command button area.

Hereafter, we ignore the name difference between a Release 3 and a Release 4 vertical paned widget. In our discussion we simply refer to **Paned** widgets, although, like the Athena widget source code, we reserve the right to use a "v" in local variable names.

The file selection box contributes quite a few variables to the instance record:

```
typedef struct _XiFileSelectPart {      /* instance definition */
    char *filenames;                    /* the list of files */
    char *filter;                       /* text entry area */
    char *default_filter;               /* start-up filter */
    XFontStruct *font;
    Dimension filter_width;             /* ftr. window size--pixels */
    int rows, columns;                  /* for the viewport */
    int row_spacing;                    /* space between rows */
    int pixmap_rows, pixmap_columns;    /* row/column metrics */
    Cursor pixmap_cursor;
    Widget viewportW, strSelectW;
    Widget filterBoxW, labelW, filterW;
    Widget buttonBoxW, dismissButtonW,
        filterButtonW, applyButtonW;
} XiFileSelectPart;
```

For the most part, the variable names are self-explanatory; many variables have counterparts in the **XiStrSelect** widget from Chapter 12.

The complete class record is:

```
typedef struct _XiFileSelectRec {
```

```
    CorePart core;
    CompositePart composite;
    ConstraintPart constraint;
#ifdef X11R3
    VPanedPart vpaned;
#else
    PanedPart vpaned;
#endif
    XiFileSelectPart file_select;
} XiFileSelectRec;
```

Note that **XiFileSelect** *inherits* functionality from four classes: **Core, Composite, Constraint**, and **Paned**, but not from **XiStrSelect**. That is, a string selection widget, like a command widget, is a *component* of a file selection widget—its functionality is nested, not inherited.

The distinction is important. A file selection box "is *not* a" string selection box—it is much more. That is, a file selection box is not a specialization of a string selection box. The latter could be *specialized* to produce a particular type of string selection box, say, with additional, specific constraints that modify its functionality/behavior. In this case, the derived widget class would get its string-selection functionality by inheritance. In contrast, a file selection box "is a" **Paned** widget.

In this implementation we do not attempt to enforce any specific constraints on the overall widget, hence, there is no need for (additional) constraint-related variables:

```
typedef struct {
    int dummy;
} XiFileSelectConstraintsPart;
```

Although **XiAlert**'s constraints record was empty as well, **XiAlert** did impose several constraints on the layout of an alert box. Likewise, as an exercise you might consider adding unique constraints to a file selection box.

14.5 *FileSelect.c*: The Implementation File

XiFileSelect uses several nested widgets; the public header files for the encapsulated widgets must be included, as well as **XiFileSelect**'s private header file:

```
#ifdef X11R3
#include <X11/AsciiText.h>
#include <X11/Box.h>
#include <X11/Command.h>
#include <X11/Viewport.h>
#else
#include <X11/Xaw/XawInit.h>
#include <X11/Xaw/AsciiText.h>
#include <X11/Xaw/Box.h>
#include <X11/Xaw/Command.h>
#include <X11/Xaw/Viewport.h>
#endif
```

```
#include "StrSelect.h"
#include "FileSelecP.h"
```

14.5.1 Resources

One of the first considerations is cursor support. Recall that **XiStrSelect** is a simple widget; hence, it provides cursor support by inheriting this functionality from the **Simple** widget class—there is no need for a dedicated cursor resource. **XiFileSelect**, on the other hand, is a composite (and a compound) widget; hence, a different technique must be used. For this implementation, **XiFileSelect** provides a cursor resource, **XiNpixmapCursor**, that's applied to the string selection box only.

Alternatively, you could provide multiple cursor resources for the various internal widgets, but this really isn't necessary. The user can set the cursor for the internal widgets, such as the command buttons, in the normal manner from a resource file. For example, placing

```
xanyapp*Command*cursor:  dot
```

in the *.Xdefaults* file specifies a dot cursor for all command buttons in *xanyapp*.

Strictly speaking, **XiNpixmapCursor** is redundant; that is, the pixmap is part of a string selection box that already has a cursor resource. For example, you could request a dot cursor for the file selection area with the following resource specification:

```
xanyapp*StrSelect*cursor:  dot
```

We made the decision to provide **XiNpixmapCursor** because we don't consider **XiStrSelect** to be a high-level widget class. A command button, in contrast, is a common widget; almost all Athena widget set-based applications have widgets that are instances of **Command**. Therefore, we can expect the user to be familiar with using the "Command" resource class to control an application's command buttons.

By providing a resource such as **XiNpixmapCursor** for all widgets in a widget set where a pixmap/canvas is used for browsing operations, you introduce a measure of consistency and commonality that the user can depend on. In our opinion, we should not expect users to be aware that the file selection area is implemented with a string selection box.

In Chapter 12 we introduced **XiStrSelect** as an abstract class, a class that widget programmers can subclass to derive more specialized classes, or can be nested within higher level widget classes, as we're doing here with **XiFileSelect**. **XiFileSelect**, on the other hand, is a concrete class, a high-level that can be described in the user documentation. With the latter, there should be special resources for widget components whose classes aren't apparent to the user.

By default, **XiFileSelect** provides no cursor at all. If neither the user nor the application specify a cursor, the string selection box (window) will adopt the cursor of its parent window. We've used the same technique that's used with the **Simple** widget class for establishing a null default cursor. Specifically, a private cursor variable is initialized with **None**:

```
static Cursor default_pixmap_cursor = None;
```

Next, the resource table uses this cursor as the default:

```
    {XiNpixmapCursor, XiCPixmapCursor, XtRCursor, sizeof(Cursor),
        res_offset(file_select.pixmap_cursor),
        XtRCursor, (caddr_t) &default_pixmap_cursor},
```

There are several specialized resources for a file selection box. For example, **XiNpixmapFont** can be used to specify a font for the file selection area, again, without having to know the resource class. The complete resource table is:

```
#define res_offset(field) XtOffset(XiFileSelectWidget, field)

static XtResource resources[] = {
    {XiNfilter, XiCFilter, XtRString, sizeof(char *),
        res_offset(file_select.default_filter),
        XtRString, FILE_DEFAULT_FILTER},
    {XiNfilterWidth, XiCFilterWidth, XtRDimension, sizeof(Dimension),
        res_offset(file_select.filter_width),
        XtRImmediate, (caddr_t) FILE_DEFAULT_FILTER_WIDTH},
    {XiNrows, XiCRows, XtRInt, sizeof(int),
        res_offset(file_select.rows),
        XtRImmediate, (caddr_t) FILE_DEFAULT_ROWS},
    {XiNcolumns, XiCColumns, XtRInt, sizeof(int),
        res_offset(file_select.columns),
        XtRImmediate, (caddr_t) FILE_DEFAULT_COLUMNS},
    {XiNpixmapRows, XiCPixmapRows, XtRInt, sizeof(int),
        res_offset(file_select.pixmap_rows),
        XtRImmediate, (caddr_t) FILE_DEFAULT_PIXMAP_ROWS},
    {XiNpixmapColumns, XiCPixmapColumns, XtRInt, sizeof(int),
        res_offset(file_select.pixmap_columns),
        XtRImmediate, (caddr_t) FILE_DEFAULT_PIXMAP_COLUMNS},
    {XiNrowSpacing, XiCRowSpacing, XtRInt, sizeof(int),
        res_offset(file_select.row_spacing),
        XtRImmediate, (caddr_t) FILE_DEFAULT_ROW_SPACING},
    {XiNpixmapCursor, XiCPixmapCursor, XtRCursor, sizeof(Cursor),
        res_offset(file_select.pixmap_cursor),
        XtRCursor, (caddr_t) &default_pixmap_cursor},
    {XiNpixmapFont, XiCPixmapFont, XtRFontStruct,
        sizeof(XFontStruct *), res_offset(file_select.font),
        XtRString, "XtDefaultFont"},
};
```

There is another consideration related to the consistency of resource names and classes. You might argue that it's fine to have resources with special names, such as **XiNfilter**, **XiNrows**, **XiNpixmapRows**, when these resources are related to unique characteristics of a particular widget. But, for more common resources such as fonts and cursors, there should be consistency across widget classes. In our opinion, introducing specialized font resources, if they're properly documented, doesn't hinder the user.

If you have a different opinion, in this case you could derive a subclass from **XiStrSelect** with a higher level class name, solely as a mechanism for distinguishing the file selection area of the file selection box from those components that are implemented from common widget classes such as **Command**. For example, in a large widget set there could be several widget classes with box-like display areas. In order to introduce consistency in resource specifications, you could "surround" each such class with a widget class where the class name field of the class record is "DisplayBox". This approach would allow resource settings such as:

```
xanyapp*DisplayBox*cursor:  sailboat
```

Even with this approach the user must be given specific information regarding these naming conventions, specifically, their availability. It may be just as reasonable to have the user specify a special resource name:

```
xanyapp*pixmapCursor:  dot
```

14.5.2 The Class Record

As mentioned in the overview, **XiFileSelect** provides a simple encapsulation of several Athena widgets and **XiStrSelect**, along with specific resources and translations. It imposes no special constraints on the encapsulated widgets, hence, most of the implementation code is devoted to widget initialization and to the public interface.

XiFileSelect's complete class record is:

```
XiFileSelectClassRec XifileSelectClassRec = {
    { /* core_class variables */
#ifdef X11R3
        (WidgetClass) &vPanedClassRec,    /* ancestor */
#else
        (WidgetClass) &panedClassRec,     /* ancestor */
#endif
        "FileSelect",                     /* class name */
        sizeof(XiFileSelectRec),          /* widget size */
#ifdef X11R3
        NULL,                             /* class initialize */
#else
        XawInitializeWidgetSet,           /* class initialize */
#endif
        NULL,                             /* class part init. */
        FALSE,                            /* class inited */
        Initialize,                       /* initialize */
        NULL,                             /* initialize hook */
        XtInheritRealize,                 /* realize */
        NULL,                             /* actions */
        0,                                /* number of actions */
        resources,                        /* resources */
        XtNumber(resources),              /* number of resources */
        NULLQUARK,                        /* xrm class */
```

```
        TRUE,                           /* compress motions */
        TRUE,                           /* compress exposures */
        TRUE,                           /* compress enter/leave */
        FALSE,                          /* visibility interest */
        Destroy,                        /* destroy */
        XtInheritResize,                /* resize */
        XtInheritExpose,                /* expose */
        SetValues,                      /* set values */
        NULL,                           /* set values hook */
        XtInheritSetValuesAlmost,       /* set values almost */
        NULL,                           /* get values hook */
        NULL,                           /* accept focus */
        XtVersion,                      /* version */
        NULL,                           /* callback private */
        NULL,                           /* translation table */
        XtInheritQueryGeometry,         /* query geometry */
        XtInheritDisplayAccelerator,    /* display accelerator */
        NULL,                           /* extension */
    },
    { /* composite_class variables */
        XtInheritGeometryManager,       /* geometry manager */
        XtInheritChangeManaged,         /* change managed */
        XtInheritInsertChild,           /* insert child */
        XtInheritDeleteChild,           /* delete child */
        NULL,                           /* extension */
    },
    { /* constraint_class fields */
        NULL,                           /* subresources */
        0,                              /* number of subresources */
        sizeof(XiFileSelectConstraintsRec),    /* record size */
        NULL,                           /* initialize */
        NULL,                           /* destroy */
        NULL,                           /* set values */
        NULL,                           /* extension */
    },
    { /* vpaned_class variables */
#ifdef X11R3
        XtInheritSetMinMax,
        XtInheritRefigureMode,
#else
        0,
#endif
    },
    { /* file_select_class variables */
        0,
    },
}; /* XifileSelectClassRec */

WidgetClass xiFileSelectWidgetClass =
    (WidgetClass) &XifileSelectClassRec;
```

Having discussed class records in detail in earlier chapters, we'll focus on the distinguishing features of **XiFileSelect**'s class record. First, **XiFileSelect** is a subclass of the **Paned** widget class; hence, we must code the proper Release 3 or Release 4 class pointer in the superclass field. Next, the resource class name is "FileSelect".

In particular, note that there are no action or translation tables specified in the class record. Unlike **XiStrSelect**, which provides class-level actions and translations, **XiFileSelect** imposes actions and translations on the encapsulated widgets, as described in the next section.

Next, the **composite_class** component simply inherits the default method. **XiFileSelect** adds no constraints beyond those provided by the **Paned** widget class, thus, the **constraint_class** component is coded with 0s and NULLs, except for the constraints record. Next, note that Release 3 and Release 4 differ with respect to the class record contribution for the **Paned** widget class. Lastly, **XiFileSelect** contributes no variables to the class record.

14.5.3 The XiFileSelect Methods

Initialize() has the rather large task of setting up the nested widgets. For this particular operation one giant method is at least as readable as a small method with numerous secondary functions. In this section we'll present the method section by section; you can refer to Appendix P if you'd like an uninterrupted display of the source code, including the preliminary and intermediate comments.

The first task is to set up local definitions for the actions and translations that **Initialize()** applies to the text entry widget, plus other local variables:

```
static void Initialize(request, new)
XiFileSelectWidget request, new;
{
    static char filter_translations[] =          /* filter trans */
        "#override\n\
        Ctrl<Key>J:         beep()\n\
        Ctrl<Key>M:         beep()\n\
        Ctrl<Key>O:         beep()\n\
        <Key>Linefeed:      beep()\n\
        <Key>Return:   beep()";
    static XtActionsRec filter_actions[] = {
        {"beep", (XtActionProc) Beep},
    };
    XtTranslations filter_trans_table;

    Arg args[15];
    int i, col_width, row_height;
    ...
```

Since the file filter box is a one-line text entry box, **XiFileSelect** overrides carriage returns, linefeeds, and so on. An action function provides user feedback by ringing the terminal bell.

Initialize() begins by checking the user- and/or application-supplied resources:

```
    ...
    if (new->file_select.rows < FILE_MIN_ROWS)
```

```
        new->file_select.rows = FILE_DEFAULT_ROWS;
    if (new->file_select.columns < FILE_MIN_COLUMNS)
        new->file_select.columns = FILE_DEFAULT_COLUMNS;
    if (new->file_select.pixmap_rows < FILE_MIN_ROWS)
        new->file_select.pixmap_rows = FILE_DEFAULT_PIXMAP_ROWS;
    if (new->file_select.pixmap_columns < FILE_MIN_COLUMNS)
        new->file_select.pixmap_columns = FILE_DEFAULT_PIXMAP_COLUMNS;
    if (!strlen(new->file_select.default_filter))
        new->file_select.default_filter = FILE_DEFAULT_FILTER;
    ...
```

The file selection area should dominate the file selection box. That is, the dimensions of the **XiStrSelect** widget are more important in sizing the file selection widget than, say, those of the file filter box. The overall dimensions are based on the font width and height and the number of rows and columns. First, a secondary function retrieves the font dimensions, and the height is incremented by the value given for **XiNrowSpacing**:

```
...
get_font_width_height(new, &col_width, &row_height);
row_height += new->file_select.row_spacing;
...
```

Next, we set the width and height fields in the **core** component:

```
...
new->core.width = (new->file_select.columns + 2) * col_width;
new->core.height = (new->file_select.rows + 2) * row_height;
...
```

A **Paned** widget's geometry management is both complex and simplistic. There is no (normal) support for width. That is, the geometry management scheme simply adopts the value of **<widget>->core.width**. One straightforward way around these problems is to approximate the width and height by setting the fields directly in **core**. These values are modified during geometry negotiations, but the file selection area dominates the widget; therefore, the final dimensions will be fairly close to the user's request. As an exercise, if you would like the row and column requests to be honored exactly, you can provide special geometry management and constraints enforcement, which we did with **XiAlert**.

Next, **Initialize()** compiles the actions and translations for the filter box:

```
...
XtAddActions(filter_actions, XtNumber(filter_actions));
filter_trans_table =
    XtParseTranslationTable(filter_translations);
...
```

Following these preliminary operations, **Initialize()** must create each of the internal widgets. The remainder of **Initialize()** resembles an Xt application; for example, it uses **XtSetArg()** to set the resources of the internal widgets. Alternatively, the resource-related fields in the instance record could be set directly, for example, **allow_resize**, but this approach is unnecessary. With **XiFileSelect()** we're demonstrating a "manager" widget; hence, **Initialize()** uses a strictly high-level approach to widget configuration.

Recall from Figure 14.1 that there are three panes. The top pane includes the filter label and text entry area, and the bottom pane includes the file selection area. The middle pane includes the buttons that govern the operation of the file selection box—they are placed between the filter area and the file selection area. For the application in Figure 14.1, note that the "Quit" button is part of the application, not the file selection box; the bounding box for the vertical pane does not include the "Quit" button.

First, a box widget is created to organize the filter label and the text entry area:

```
...
new->file_select.filterBoxW = XtCreateManagedWidget("filterBox",
    boxWidgetClass, new, NULL, 0);
...
```

In order to avoid confusion between the label and the text entry area, the label is hard-coded with no border:

```
...
i = 0;
XtSetArg(args[i], XtNborderWidth, (XtArgVal) 0); i++;
XtSetArg(args[i], XtNlabel, (XtArgVal) "Filter:"); i++;
new->file_select.labelW = XtCreateManagedWidget("filterLabel",
    labelWidgetClass, new->file_select.filterBoxW, args, i);
...
```

Next, **Initialize()** must create the text entry area. The requirements are quite different for the Release 3 and Release 4 **Text** widget classes. Specifically, with Release 3 the text entry space must be allocated beforehand and initialized with the default filter text. With Release 4, a text widget handles memory allocation internally, therefore **filter** is simply initialized to the address of the default filter:

```
    ...
    i = 0;
#ifdef X11R3
    new->file_select.filter = XtMalloc(FILE_MAX_FILTER + 1);
    strncpy(new->file_select.filter, new->file_select.default_filter,
        FILE_MAX_FILTER);
    if (strlen(new->file_select.default_filter) >= FILE_MAX_FILTER)
        new->file_select.filter[FILE_MAX_FILTER] = EOS;
    XtSetArg(args[i], XtNtextOptions,
        (XtArgVal) (resizeWidth | resizeHeight)); i++;
    XtSetArg(args[i], XtNeditType, (XtArgVal) XttextEdit); i++;
#else
    new->file_select.filter = new->file_select.default_filter;
    XtSetArg(args[i], XtNresize, (XtArgVal) XawtextResizeBoth); i++;
    XtSetArg(args[i], XtNeditType, (XtArgVal) XawtextEdit); i++;
#endif
```

```
...
```

Note that several of the resources, including resizing requests, are handled differently as well.

Next, several other resources are set before creating the text entry widget:

```
    ...
    XtSetArg(args[i], XtNstring,
        (XtArgVal) new->file_select.filter); i++;
    XtSetArg(args[i], XtNborderWidth, (XtArgVal) 1); i++;
    XtSetArg(args[i], XtNlength, (XtArgVal) FILE_MAX_FILTER); i++;
    XtSetArg(args[i], XtNwidth,
        (XtArgVal) new->file_select.filter_width); i++;
    XtSetArg(args[i], XtNresizable, TRUE); i++;
    new->file_select.filterW = XtCreateManagedWidget("filterText",
#ifdef X11R3
        asciiStringWidgetClass,
#else
        asciiTextWidgetClass,
#endif
        new->file_select.filterBoxW, args, i);
    XtOverrideTranslations(new->file_select.filterW,
        filter_trans_table);
    ...
```

Note that after the file filter component is initialized, **XtOverrideTranslations()** is called to install the actions and translations that accompany a one-line text entry box.

Next, **Initialize()** creates the button box for the middle pane:

```
...
new->file_select.buttonBoxW =
    XtCreateManagedWidget("fileButtonBox",
        boxWidgetClass, new, NULL, 0);
...
```

The third pane houses the viewport that houses the string selection box:

```
...
i = 0;
XtSetArg(args[i], XtNallowHoriz, (XtArgVal) TRUE); i++;
XtSetArg(args[i], XtNallowVert, (XtArgVal) TRUE); i++;
XtSetArg(args[i], XtNforceBars, (XtArgVal) TRUE); i++;
XtSetArg(args[i], XtNheight,
    (XtArgVal) new->file_select.rows * row_height); i++;
XtSetArg(args[i], XtNwidth,
    (XtArgVal) new->file_select.columns * col_width); i++;
new->file_select.viewportW = XtCreateManagedWidget("fileViewport",
    viewportWidgetClass, new, args, i);
...
```

For symmetry, **Initialize()** forces the viewport to have both vertical and horizontal scrollbars. Also, the **XtNheight** and **XtNwidth** resources should be set so that the viewport doesn't expand to include the entire pixmap.

Next, the file selection box's pixmap resources are applied to the string selection widget:

```
...
i = 0;
XtSetArg(args[i], XiNdelimiters, (XtArgVal) FILE_DELIMITERS); i++;
XtSetArg(args[i], XiNfont,
    (XtArgVal) new->file_select.font); i++;
XtSetArg(args[i], XiNpixmapColumns,
    (XtArgVal) new->file_select.pixmap_columns); i++;
XtSetArg(args[i], XiNpixmapRows,
    (XtArgVal) new->file_select.pixmap_rows); i++;
if (new->file_select.pixmap_cursor != None) {
    XtSetArg(args[i], XtNcursor,
        (XtArgVal) new->file_select.pixmap_cursor); i++;
}
new->file_select.strSelectW = XtCreateManagedWidget("fileListBox",
    xiStrSelectWidgetClass, new->file_select.viewportW, args, i);
set_filename_reference_buffer(new);
...
```

set_filename_reference_buffer() is a secondary function that sets up the string (buffer) of filenames that match the filter; it is described in Section 14.5.7.

At this point the overall layout has been established and **Initialize()** creates the command buttons:

```
...
i = 0;
XtSetArg(args[i], XtNlabel, (XtArgVal) "Filter"); i++;
new->file_select.filterButtonW =
    XtCreateManagedWidget("fileButtonFilter",
        commandWidgetClass, new->file_select.buttonBoxW, args, i);
XtAddCallback(new->file_select.filterButtonW, XtNcallback,
    FileSelectBoxFilter, NULL);

i = 0;
XtSetArg(args[i], XtNlabel, (XtArgVal) "Apply"); i++;
new->file_select.applyButtonW =
    XtCreateManagedWidget("fileButtonApply",
        commandWidgetClass, new->file_select.buttonBoxW, args, i);
/*
Note:  The client should use XiFileSelectAddApplyProc() to
add the callback for the previous button.
*/

if (XtIsSubclass(XtParent(new), shellWidgetClass)) {
    i = 0;
    XtSetArg(args[i], XtNlabel, (XtArgVal) "Dismiss"); i++;
```

```
        new->file_select.dismissButtonW =
            XtCreateManagedWidget("fileButtonDismiss",
                commandWidgetClass, new->file_select.buttonBoxW,
                args, i);
        XtAddCallback(new->file_select.dismissButtonW, XtNcallback,
            FileSelectBoxDismiss, NULL);
    }
}   /* Initialize */
```

The "Filter" and "Apply" buttons are created unconditionally. The "Dismiss" button, however, should be created only if the parent of the file selection box is a shell. Each button has an internal callback function that initiates the appropriate operations.

In this implementation, the "Apply" button accompanies every file selection box. You may prefer to make its presence conditional as well. As it stands, an application is expected to supply a callback function that initiates an application-specific operation against the currently selected file.

Destroy() is the second method. It frees each of the internal widgets and the buffer that contains the filenames:

```
/*
Destroy() cleans up dynamic data structures.
*/

static void Destroy(w)
XiFileSelectWidget w;
{
    XtDestroyWidget(w->file_select.labelW);
    XtDestroyWidget(w->file_select.filterW);
    XtDestroyWidget(w->file_select.filterBoxW);
    XtDestroyWidget(w->file_select.viewportW);
    XtDestroyWidget(w->file_select.strSelectW);
    XtDestroyWidget(w->file_select.applyButtonW);
    XtDestroyWidget(w->file_select.dismissButtonW);
    XtDestroyWidget(w->file_select.filterButtonW);
    XtDestroyWidget(w->file_select.buttonBoxW);
    if (w->file_select.filenames != NULL)
        free(w->file_select.filenames);
}   /* Destroy */
```

SetValues() is the final method. At present, **XiFileSelect** does not monitor changes to resource-related fields; hence, **SetValues()** does nothing:

```
/*
SetValues() handles modifications to resource-related instance
variables.  Typically, these don't need to be checked--most
resources are used during widget initialization only; others
simply assume the new values.
*/

static Boolean SetValues(current, request, new)
```

```
Widget current, request, new;
{
    /*
    at present, nothing to update...
    */
    return FALSE;
}   /* SetValues */
```

You may prefer to omit this method, placing **NULL** in the class record for the set-values method. We've included an empty method here, in order to provide a comment in the vicinity where a programmer would normally expect this method, and to emphasize the "manager" orientation of **XiFileSelect**.

14.5.4 The Action Functions

Currently, **XiFileSelect** has only one action function. **Beep()** provides feedback if the user attempts to enter a carriage return or linefeed character in the filter's text entry box:

```
/*
Beep() is a general-purpose function; one use is to beep the
users if they try to enter a character that results in a line
feed operation; see Initialize().
*/

static void Beep(w, event)
Widget w;
XEvent *event;
{
    XBell(XtDisplay(w), 50);
}   /* Beep */
```

14.5.5 The Public Interface

As with the other *Xi* widgets, there is a convenience function that allows an application to map the file selection box:

```
/*
XiFileSelectPopup() invokes (pops up) the file selection box.  This
convenience function is useful ONLY if the file selection box's
parent is a pop-up shell.
*/

void XiFileSelectPopup(fsw)
XiFileSelectWidget fsw;
{
    /*
    shell -> file selection box -> ...
    */
    if (XtIsSubclass(XtParent(fsw), shellWidgetClass))
        XtPopup(fsw->core.parent, XtGrabNone);
}   /* XiFileSelectPopup */
```

The second public function, **XiFileSelectGetSelection()**, retrieves the currently selected filename:

```
/*
XiFileSelectGetSelection() retrieves the value stored in the
private field 'selection'; this is the currently selected
file.  Unlike XiStrSelectGetSelection(), this (higher level)
function doesn't allow the return value to be null.
*/

char *XiFileSelectGetSelection(fsw)
XiFileSelectWidget fsw;
{
    char *select;

    if ((select = XiStrSelectGetSelection(fsw->file_select.strSelectW))
            != NULL)
        return select;
    else
        return "";
}   /* XiFileSelectGetSelection */
```

Note that we've made an arbitrary decision in this implementation to return (a pointer to) a zero-length string if there is no currently selected file.

Next, **XiFileSelectApplyProc()** associates a callback function with the internal "Apply" button.

```
/*
XiFileSelectAddApplyProc() allows the user to register a function
(procedure) to be executed when the apply button is pressed.  Note
that no data is returned; an application should retrieve the
current selection with XiFileSelectGetSelection().
*/

void XiFileSelectAddApplyProc(fsw, callback_proc)
XiFileSelectWidget fsw;
void (*callback_proc)();
{
    if (callback_proc != NULL)
        XtAddCallback(fsw->file_select.applyButtonW, XtNcallback,
            callback_proc, NULL);
}   /* XiFileSelectAddApplyProc */
```

Using **XiFileSelectAddApplyProc()** a delete-files application, for example, could supply a function that unlinks the currently selected file.

Alternatively, a file selection widget could allow the application to specify the label for the "Apply" button. As currently implemented, the fixed button labels guarantee consistency across applications and file selection boxes. In this case, the semantics of "Apply" must be provided by the application.

XiFileSelectRefresh() is the last public function. It provides the application with a mechanism for refreshing the file selection area:

```
/*
XiFileSelectRefresh() allows the application programmer to update
the file selection box window manually.  This function does NOT
check for changes to the filter.
*/

void XiFileSelectRefresh(fsw)
XiFileSelectWidget fsw;
{
    set_filename_reference_buffer(fsw);
    XiStrSelectRedisplay(fsw->file_select.strSelectW);
}   /* XiFileSelectRefresh */
```

If, for example, the application supplies an "Apply" function that indirectly modifies the set of files that match the filter, it will have to refresh (update) the file selection area.

14.5.6 Private Callback Functions

XiFileSelect uses two internal callback functions to initiate button-related operations for the "Dismiss" and "Filter" buttons. First, **FileSelectBoxDismiss()** unmaps the file selection box, if its parent is a shell:

```
static void FileSelectBoxDismiss(w, client_data, call_data)
Widget w;
caddr_t client_data, call_data;
{
    /*
    shell -> file selection box -> button box -> button
    */
    XiFileSelectWidget fsw =
        (XiFileSelectWidget) XtParent(w->core.parent);
    if (XtIsSubclass(XtParent(fsw), shellWidgetClass))
        XtPopdown(XtParent(fsw));
}   /* FileSelectBoxDismiss */
```

Next, **FileSelectBoxFilter()** updates the file selection area when the user presses the "Filter" button:

```
static void FileSelectBoxFilter(w, client_data, call_data)
Widget w;
caddr_t client_data, call_data;
{
    /*
    shell -> file selection box -> button box -> button
    */
    XiFileSelectWidget fsw =
        (XiFileSelectWidget) XtParent(w->core.parent);
```

```
#ifdef X11R3
#else
    Arg args[1];
    char *filter_text;

    XtSetArg(args[0], XtNstring, &filter_text);
    XtGetValues(fsw->file_select.filterW, args, 1);
    fsw->file_select.filter = filter_text;
#endif
    set_filename_reference_buffer(fsw);
    XiStrSelectRedisplay(fsw->file_select.strSelectW);
}   /* FileSelectBoxFilter */
```

Because Release 4 manages text buffer operations internally, **FileSelectBoxFilter()** must use a resource to retrieve the current filter. Release 3, on the other hand, performs editing operations destructively on the buffer that **Initialize()** allocates externally; hence, **file_select.filter** always points to the current edit buffer.

14.5.7 Low-level, System-dependent Functions

There are several low-level functions that perform the file operations necessary to build a list of filenames that match the filter. In this section we discuss one of these secondary functions, **set_filename_reference_buffer()**; it is referenced three times in the functions presented in the previous sections, specifically, in **Initialize()**, **XiFileSelectRefresh()**, and **FileSelectBoxFilter()**. This function provides an interface between the widget and the file system. We also briefly mention **expand_file_spec()**, which **set_filename_reference_buffer()** calls to build the buffer of filenames.

Obviously, a file selection widget must perform file operations. Unfortunately, different UNIX systems have very different file systems, plus subtle differences in the high-level commands such as *ls(1)* that interface with the file system. We've made no attempt to accommodate different UNIX systems with conditional compilation directives—there are too many possibilities. You may have to modify **set_filename_reference_buffer()** and **expand_file_spec()**. These functions have been tested on Sun workstations running SunOS™ 4.0.*x*.

This implementation of **XiFileSelect** uses *echo(1)* with a standard Bourne shell to expand the file filter. The output from *echo(1)* is temporarily stored in a (local) file. These operations are performed by **expand_file_spec()**, which returns a pointer to a dynamically allocated string that's passed to the string selection widget. The file processing and memory allocation are managed local to **expand_file_spec()**, with two exceptions. First, when the widget is destroyed, it should free the dynamic storage that holds the filenames displayed in the file selection box:

```
static void Destroy(w)
XiFileSelectWidget w;
{
    ...
    if (w->file_select.filenames != NULL)
```

```
        free(w->file_select.filenames);
}   /* Destroy */
```

Second, with a Bourne shell, if there are no matching files, *echo(1)* returns the file filter itself. Hence, **set_filename_reference_buffer()** must manipulate the filename buffer; it must check the buffer to determine if it's equal to the filter, and if so, reset the contents of the file selection area. If there's something there other than the filter, **set_filename_reference_buffer()** must call **XiStrSelectSetString()** to display the new contents of the file selection box.

The complete function is:

```
/*
set_filename_reference_buffer() expands the file specification
given by the filter, and then updates the StrSelect widget's
reference string.
*/

static void set_filename_reference_buffer(w)
XiFileSelectWidget w;
{
    char *filename_buffer, *filter;
    int match;

    if (!*w->file_select.filter) {
        fprintf(stderr,                         /** !!! remove? **/
            "file selection box: no value for filter!\n");
        XiStrSelectReset(w->file_select.strSelectW);
        return;
    }

    filename_buffer = expand_file_spec(w->file_select.filter);

    if (filename_buffer == NULL) {
        fprintf(stderr,
        "file selection box: error attempting to expand filter!\n");
        XiStrSelectReset(w->file_select.strSelectW);
        return;
    }

    if (w->file_select.filenames != NULL)
        free(w->file_select.filenames);
    w->file_select.filenames = filename_buffer;

    /*
    Check to see if the expansion is nothing more than the filter,
    and if so, make sure that there is no matching file.  Note
    that the expanded filename will have a linefeed appended.
    */
    if (strlen(w->file_select.filter) + 1 ==
            strlen(filename_buffer)) {
```

```
        match = TRUE;
        filter = w->file_select.filter;
        while (*filename_buffer && *filter)
            if (*filename_buffer++ != *filter++)
                match = FALSE;
        if (match && file_size(w->file_select.filter) == -1) {
            fprintf(stderr,                  /** !!! remove? **/
                "file selection box: no match for filter!\n");
            free(w->file_select.filenames);
            w->file_select.filenames = NULL;
            XiStrSelectReset(w->file_select.strSelectW);
        }
        else
            XiStrSelectSetString(w->file_select.strSelectW,
                w->file_select.filenames);
    }
    else
        XiStrSelectSetString(w->file_select.strSelectW,
            w->file_select.filenames);
}   /* set_filename_reference_buffer */
```

Note that **set_filename_reference_buffer**() enforces a particular policy regarding a no-match condition. Specifically, if the user enters a mask, presses "Filter", and there is no match, **set_filename_reference_buffer**() uses **XiStrSelectReset**() to clear the text from the file selection area. If this step were not performed, the filter and the displayed text would be in an inconsistent state.

The remaining low-level functions are given in Appendix P.

14.6 A File Selection Box Demonstration

Figure 14.2 presents a simple demonstration of a file selection box. The demonstration program, *testfilesel2*, is outlined in this section.

main() set up the top-level window:

```
/*
main() sets up a button-activated file selection box inside a
box widget in the main window.  A simple callback is used to
test the retrieval facilities for the currently selected file.
*/

void main(argc, argv)
int argc;
char **argv;
{
    Widget topLevel, testBox, quitButton;
    Arg args[5];
    int i;
    Cursor pixmap_cursor;

    topLevel = XtInitialize(argv[0], "TestFileSel2",
        NULL, 0, &argc, argv);
```

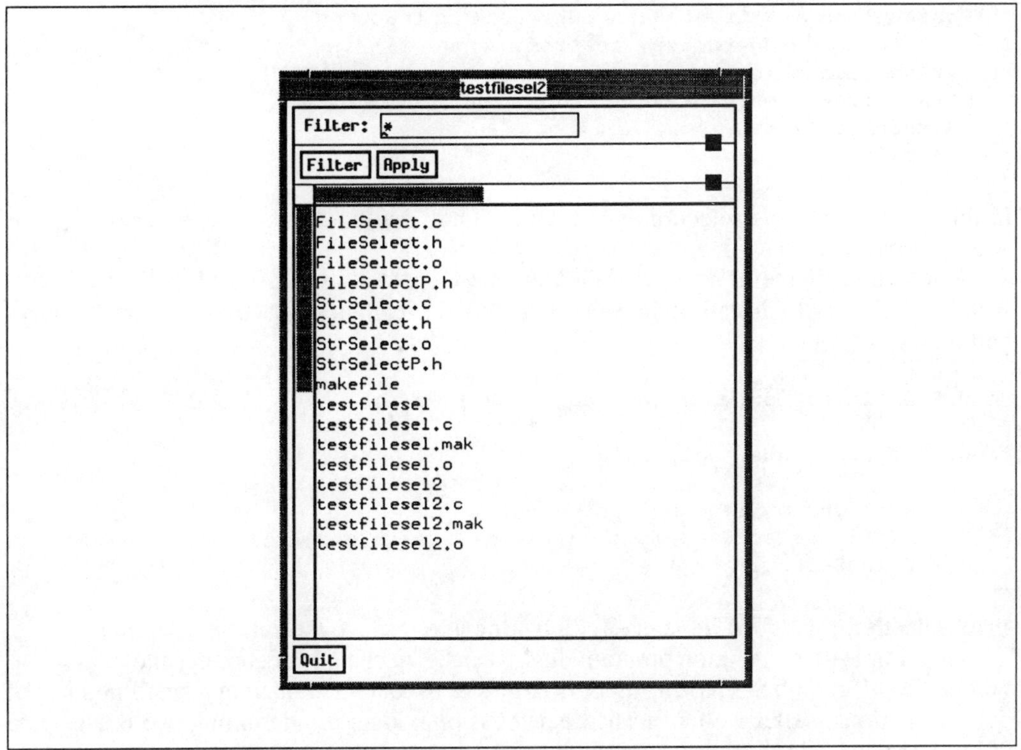

Figure 14.2 A File Selection Box within a Vertical Pane

```
    font = load_font(topLevel, "testfilesel2", "8x13");
    testBox = XtCreateManagedWidget("testBox", formWidgetClass,
        topLevel, NULL, 0);
    i = 0;
    XtSetArg(args[i], XiNrows,              /* just testing */
        (XtArgVal) 20); i++;
    XtSetArg(args[i], XiNcolumns,           /* just testing */
        (XtArgVal) 40); i++;
/*  pixmap_cursor = XCreateFontCursor(XtDisplay(topLevel), XC_dot);
    XtSetArg(args[i], XiNpixmapCursor, (XtArgVal) pixmap_cursor); i++;*/
    XtSetArg(args[i], XiNrowSpacing,        /* just testing */
        (XtArgVal) 5); i++;
    XtSetArg(args[i], XiNpixmapFont,        /* just testing */
        (XtArgVal) font); i++;
    testFileSelectBox = XtCreateManagedWidget("testFileSelectBox",
        xiFileSelectWidgetClass, testBox, args, i);
    XiFileSelectAddApplyProc(testFileSelectBox, PrintSelection);
    i = 0;
    XtSetArg(args[i], XtNlabel, (XtArgVal) "Quit"); i++;
    XtSetArg(args[i], XtNfromVert, (XtArgVal) testFileSelectBox); i++;
```

```
    quitButton = XtCreateManagedWidget("quitButton",
        commandWidgetClass, testBox, args, i);
    XtAddCallback(quitButton, XtNcallback, Quit, NULL);
    XtRealizeWidget(topLevel);
    XtMainLoop();
}   /* main */
```

In this program the file selection box and the "Quit" button are created as children of an Athena **Form** widget.

After the file selection widget has been created, **main()** calls **XiFileSelect-AddApplyProc()** to install **PrintSelection()** as the callback function for the "Apply" button:

```
void PrintSelection(w, client_data, call_data)
Widget w;
caddr_t client_data, call_data;
{
    printf("The current selection is: %s\n",
        XiFileSelectGetSelection(testFileSelectBox));
}   /* PrintSelection */
```

PrintSelection() calls **XiFileSelectGetSelection()** to retrieve the current selection.

This simple demonstration program illustrates the mechanics of creating and interacting with a file selection box. **XiFileSelect** is largely self-contained, having a small number of public functions. After we've finished our focus on widget programming, we'll use some of our widgets in simple applications.

14.7 XiFileSelect versus OSF/Motif's XmFileSelectionBox

If you've looked at the OSF/Motif widget, **XmFileSelectionBox**, it's clear that it is more powerful than **XiFileSelect**. For many situations, however, **XiFileSelect** is reasonably adequate. You can easily modify and extend **XiFileSelect** to support the additional features of **XmFileSelectionBox**. If you are unfamiliar with Motif, we'll highlight the major differences here.

First, **XmFileSelectionBox** has another text entry box where the current selection is displayed. When you select a filename, it's displayed in the file selection text edit area where you can further modify it before notifying the application of your selection with the "OK" button. ("OK" is equivalent to **XiFileSelect**'s "Apply" button.)

A second difference is that **XmFileSelectionBox** allows an application to modify the filter and redisplay the matching files, using either **XtSetValues()** or a public function. **XmFileSelectionBox** supports several other resources as well.

The last difference that we mention is the behavior of the **<Enter>** key. If you press a carriage return in the filter text entry area, the mask is reevaluated and the list of filenames is redisplayed.

15

XiButton: Low-level, Non-command Buttons

So far, we've used the default callback facilities of **Command** widgets and others, but we have not illustrated how to build a widget with a callback list(s). In this chapter we design a simple widget that supports the **XiNselectCallback** resource.

XiButton is *not* a replacement for the **Command** widget class. Although there is some possibility for behavior modification, **Command** widgets are designed primarily to support the execution of quasi-independent application operations, that is, application "commands." **XiButton**, on the other hand, is designed to support applications that allow the user to set options. For example, a programmer's calculator normally supports four decimal bases: binary, decimal, hexadecimal, and octal. Each base could be represented by a button, so that the programmer could switch numeric bases by clicking on the appropriate button.

The simplest possible use of a button would be to represent an application parameter where the user can toggle between two values, representing an "on" or "off" state for that parameter. More often, however, applications require buttons in groups with group labels, for example, the numeric base option of a programmer's calculator. In this case, a higher level widget is required. In Chapter 16 we'll design a button-oriented selection box that supports horizontal and vertical arrangements of related buttons. First, however, we must develop **XiButton**.

15.1 XiButton: Overview

By default, **Command** widgets highlight their borders while the cursor is within the command button, and temporarily highlight the entire button when the user selects the command button. In contrast, a button widget that's used to set options should exhibit a somewhat different behavior; **XiButton** displays a rectangular outline inside the button window while that option is selected. Although a button widget could be created for stand-alone use, **XiButton** is designed to serve as a foundation widget for building higher level widgets, such as choice boxes and simple menus.

An **XiButton** widget supports a selection callback list. A button also allows an integer value to be associated with it. This feature is provided so that the client program can associate an application-specific value with each button in, say, a choice box, and then determine which button is currently selected by manipulating button values. Note that the client is responsible for imposing this logic on a *set* of buttons; a button widget can only get and set button values. A public function, **XiButtonGetValue()** returns the integer value associated with a button. A value can be provided or modified dynamically with the resource **XiNvalue** or by calling the function **XiButtonSetValue()**.

A button widget can be selected and deselected. By default this action behaves as a toggle when the user clicks the first mouse button; however, a higher level widget can override the default behavior. Two public functions, **XiButtonSelect()** and **XiButton-Deselect()**, can be used for programmatic selection and deselection, respectively. A selected button is "highlighted" with a one-pixel wide rectangle inside the button's border. When a button is selected, its callback list, if any, is traversed—after all other selection operations are complete. A third function, **XiButtonSelectNoCB()**, can be use to select a button programmatically without executing any associated callbacks.

An **XiButton** widget's label can be modified dynamically; however, the pixmap and window are not resized in this case. If the new label is longer the former label, there may be clipping in the Button window. Note that by default the width of a button is based on the number of characters in the label. Thus, by default a collection of buttons will having varying width.

The client can override this behavior with the XiNlength resource, which specifies the number of *characters* to use in determining a button's length/width. For example, when adding several buttons to a higher level widget, or application, you can determine the maximum number of characters in the longest label, and then use this value for the XiNlength resource for each button, in order to produce buttons of uniform width. This resource is used only during the creation of buttons; you cannot "expand" a button dynamically.

In earlier chapters we provided reasonably complete discussions of each widget class's public, private, and implementation files. In this chapter especially, and to some extent in the next chapter, we take the liberty of focusing on the more interesting and most unique characteristics of each widget class. The remaining sections overview selected features of an **XiButton** widget.

15.2 *Button.h*: The Public Interface

In the overview of **XiButton** we mentioned several resources; the complete set of resource name and class identifiers is:

```
#define XiNlabel                    "label"        /* OK to modify */
#define XiNlength                   "length"
#define XiNvalue                    "value"        /* OK to modify */
```

```
#define XiNselectCallback            "selectCallback"/* OK to modify */
#define XiNwidth                     "width"
#define XiNheight                    "height"
#define XiNborderWidth               "borderWidth"
#define XiNfont                      "font"
#define XiCLabel                     "Label"
#define XiCLength                    "Length"
#define XiCValue                     "Value"
#define XiCSelectCallback            "SelectCallback"
#define XiCCallback                  "Callback"
#define XiCWidth                     "Width"
#define XiCHeight                    "Height"
#define XiCBorderWidth               "BorderWidth"
#define XiCFont                      "Font"
```

Note that three of these resources, namely, **XiNwidth**, **XiNheight**, and **XiNborderWidth**, apply to inherited resources. That is, *Button.h* is simply supplying "**XiN**" equivalents of the "**XtN**" resource name and class identifiers.

Normally, a widget set should adopt a policy regarding whether or not to provide "**XtN**" resource names and classes equivalents for inherited resources. Providing alternate names makes the inheritance path transparent for application programmers and adds a measure of consistency to the widget set. On the other hand, the documentation has the burden of explaining that these redundant names refer to inherited resources and are not replacements or modifications of resources in the respective inherited widget class.

For the *Xi* widgets we normally limit name and class identifiers to resources that are *unique* to that class. For tutorial purposes, however, because **XiButton** is quite small, we've added resources identifiers for three inherited resources to illustrate the alternate approach. The demonstration program in Appendix Q has (commented out) statements that set the respective **core** fields in the instance record.

We've emphasized this point by specifying alternate identifiers for only three of the inherited resources. If a widget set adopts this approach, for consistency it should specify resource identifiers for *all* inherited resources, including destroy callback lists, translations, and others. For this reason, we normally just define resource identifiers for each class's unique resources.

15.3 *ButtonP.h*: The Private Widget Data Structures

The **XiButton** widget class is a subclass of **Simple**:

```
typedef struct _XiButtonClassRec {
    CoreClassPart core_class;
    SimpleClassPart simple_class;
    XiButtonClassPart button_class;
} XiButtonClassRec;
```

Its class record component is empty:

```
typedef struct _XiButtonClassPart {       /* class definition */
    int dummy;
```

```
} XiButtonClassPart;
```

Its instance record component includes variables for representing the button label in an arbitrary font, associating an integer value with each button, and registering one or more callback functions:

```
typedef struct _XiButtonPart {              /* instance definition */
    char *label;                        /* resource-supplied label */
    char *private_label;                /* private copy of label */
    XFontStruct *font;
    Pixmap pixmap;
    GC gc;                              /* for text and rectangle */
    GC cgc;                             /* clears the rectangle */
    Dimension width, height;            /* does not include padding */
    Boolean selected;                   /* is button currently selected? */
    int value;                          /* optional */
    int length;                         /* length in chars. of button text */
    XtCallbackList cb_list;             /* see select_button() */
} XiButtonPart;
```

Each button builds its label from a private copy of the label text on a pixmap that's copied to the button window after each **Expose** event. **XiButton** uses two GCs: one for displaying the label text and the highlighting rectangle and one for clearing the pixmap. **XiButton** supports an Intrinsics-compatible callback list, as described in Section 8.2.

15.4 *Button.c*: The Implementation File

15.4.1 Actions and Translations

XiButton, like **XiStrSelect** and unlike **XiFileSelect**, provides top-level default actions and translations (at present, just one). The action function **SelectButton()** implements the behavior for a button selection operation:

```
static void SelectButton();

static char button_translations[] =
    "<Btn1Down>:  select()";

static XtActionsRec button_actions[] = {
    {"select", (XtActionProc) SelectButton},
};
```

With most widgets, selections are normally performed with the first mouse button, and the second and higher mouse buttons are used for other tasks, such as invoking a background menu. Button widgets, however, are quite simple and it's unlikely that the user would expect there to be any special operations associated with the other mouse buttons, thus, **XiButton** could add (selection) translations for the other mouse buttons as well. Moreover, the user (or the application) can always override the default translations.

Note that we haven't defined a "deselect" action. With **XiButton**, button selection and deselection are implemented as a toggle. That is, if the button is currently selected, selecting it again will deselect it. We could use one action function to select the button and another action function to deselect it. It's equally straightforward to perform both operations from a single action function.

15.4.2 Resources

XiButton defines five resource-related entry points in the instance record:

```
#define res_offset(field) XtOffset(XiButtonWidget, field)

static XtResource resources[] = {
    {XiNlabel, XiCLabel, XtRString, sizeof(char *),
        res_offset(button.label),
        XtRString, BTN_NOTHING},
    {XiNlength, XiCLength, XtRInt, sizeof(int),
        res_offset(button.length),
        XtRImmediate, (caddr_t) BTN_DEFAULT_LENGTH},
    {XiNvalue, XiCValue, XtRInt, sizeof(int),
        res_offset(button.value),
        XtRImmediate, (caddr_t) BTN_DEFAULT_VALUE},
    {XiNfont, XiCFont, XtRFontStruct, sizeof(XFontStruct *),
        res_offset(button.font),
        XtRString, "XtDefaultFont"},
    {XiNselectCallback, XiCSelectCallback, XtRCallback,
        sizeof(caddr_t), res_offset(button.cb_list),
        XtRCallback, (caddr_t) NULL},
};
```

By default, buttons have a zero-length character label and a minimum button width/length. Unless otherwise directed, buttons display their label using Xt's default font. As with **XiStrSelect** and the other widgets, an application can load one font and pass the address of its font structure to each button widget.

XiButton defines a callback list. The resource type converter is **XtRCallback**. By default, the selection callback list is null; applications can use **XtAddCallback()** (or **XtAddCallbacks()**) to add callback functions for buttons, just as with Athena command buttons.

Overall, the Intrinsics manage callback lists behind the scenes. **XiButton** simply has to indicate *when* a button should call back to these functions; that is, it must define the behavior that initiates callback operations. With **XiButton**, the action "select" initiates callback operations; specifically, a low-level function, **select_button()**, calls **XtCallCallbacks()**, among other things, with **XiNselectCallback** as an argument (see Section 15.4.7).

15.4.3 The Class Record

XiButton is a subclass of **Simple**, thus, its class record is similar to that of **XiStrSelect**:

```
XiButtonClassRec XibuttonClassRec = {
```

```
    { /* core_class variables */
        (WidgetClass) &simpleClassRec,   /* ancestor */
        "Button",                        /* class name */
        sizeof(XiButtonRec),             /* widget size */
#ifdef X11R3
        NULL,                            /* class initialize */
#else
        XawInitializeWidgetSet,          /* class initialize */
#endif
        NULL,                            /* class part init. */
        FALSE,                           /* class inited */
        Initialize,                      /* initialize */
        NULL,                            /* initialize hook */
        XtInheritRealize,                /* realize */
        button_actions,                  /* actions */
        XtNumber(button_actions),        /* number of actions */
        resources,                       /* resources */
        XtNumber(resources),             /* number of resources */
        NULLQUARK,                       /* xrm class */
        TRUE,                            /* compress motions */
        TRUE,                            /* compress exposures */
        TRUE,                            /* compress enter/leave */
        FALSE,                           /* visibility interest */
        Destroy,                         /* destroy */
        NULL,                            /* resize */
        Redisplay,                       /* expose */
        SetValues,                       /* set values */
        NULL,                            /* set values hook */
        XtInheritSetValuesAlmost,        /* set values almost */
        NULL,                            /* get values hook */
        NULL,                            /* accept focus */
        XtVersion,                       /* version */
        NULL,                            /* callback private */
        button_translations,             /* translation table */
        XtInheritQueryGeometry,          /* query geometry */
        XtInheritDisplayAccelerator,     /* display accelerator */
        NULL,                            /* extension */
    },
    { /* simple_class variables */
        XtInheritChangeSensitive,
    },
    { /* button_class variables */
        0,
    },
}; /* XibuttonClassRec */

WidgetClass xiButtonWidgetClass = (WidgetClass) &XibuttonClassRec;
```

In this case, the class resource name is "Button", the class pointer is **xiButtonWidgetClass**, and four methods are defined within the implementation file: **Initialize**(), **Destroy**(), **Redisplay**(), and **SetValues**().

15.4.4 The XiButton Methods

The first method is **Initialize()**. Most widget initialization operations are performed by secondary functions:

```
/*
Initialize() initializes each instance of a button.
A button implements a pixmap in a Simple widget.
*/
/*ARGSUSED*/
static void Initialize(request, new)
XiButtonWidget request, new;
{
    if (!new->button.label)
        new->button.label = BTN_NOTHING;
    create_button_pixmap(new);
    new->button.selected = FALSE;
    fill_pixmap(new);
}   /* Initialize */
```

When each button is created, **Initialize()** must create a pixmap for the off-screen image of a button, check resource-related instance variables, and then fill the pixmap with the text for the button label.

The second method, **Destroy()**, frees pixmap-related GCs, the pixmap, and the storage for the private copy of the button label:

```
/*
Destroy() cleans up dynamic data structures.
*/

static void Destroy(w)
XiButtonWidget w;
{
    if (w->button.private_label != NULL)
        XtFree(w->button.private_label);
    if (w->button.gc != NULL)
        XFreeGC(XtDisplay(w), w->button.gc);
    if (w->button.cgc != NULL)
        XFreeGC(XtDisplay(w), w->button.cgc);
    if (w->button.pixmap != NULL)
        XFreePixmap(XtDisplay(w), w->button.pixmap);
}   /* Destroy */
```

The third method, **SetValues()**, is responsible for checking the validity of dynamic modifications to resource-related instance variables:

```
/*
SetValues() handles dynamic modifications to resource-related
instance variables, where necessary.  Most resources are used
only during widget creation.  The 'value' field can be set by
```

```
a resource either during creation or dynamically; however, its
value doesn't need to be checked here.  If a button's 'label'
field is changed dynamically via a resource setting, it's
necessary to free and then reallocate space for the label.
This implementation does NOT dynamically resize the pixmap, if
the label text changes.
*/
/*ARGSUSED*/
static Boolean SetValues(current, request, new)
Widget current, request, new;
{
    XiButtonWidget bw = (XiButtonWidget) new;
    XiButtonWidget old_bw = (XiButtonWidget) current;

    if (!bw->button.label)
        bw->button.label = BTN_NOTHING;
    if (strcmp(bw->button.label, old_bw->button.label)) {
        if (old_bw->button.private_label != NULL)
            XtFree(old_bw->button.private_label);
        /*
        does NOT resize pixmap:
        */
        allocate_and_center_button_text(bw, strlen(bw->button.label));
        fill_pixmap(bw);
    }
    return TRUE;
}   /* SetValues */
```

As indicated in the comments, this implementation of **XiButton** allows the label to change dynamically, but does not destroy and recreate a new pixmap, in order to take into consideration any change in the size of the button window. With this implementation, if a new, longer label is associated with a button, the label will be clipped on the right. It's straightforward to add the resize capability if you feel that the overhead is warranted. In most applications, however, buttons are laid out in advance and their labels do not change.

The expose method, **Redisplay()**, repaints the button window:

```
/*
Redisplay() calls redisplay_pixmap() to update the pixmap
window upon an exposure.
*/
/*ARGSUSED*/
static void Redisplay(w, event)
Widget w;
XEvent *event;
{
    redisplay_pixmap(w);
}   /* Redisplay */
```

This method simply calls **redisplay_pixmap()**, which copies the off-screen pixmap to the button window.

15.4.5 The Action Functions

SelectButton() is the only action function. It implements a button's toggle behavior by calling either **deselect_button()** or **select_button()**, depending on the value of the indicator variable **button.selected**:

```
static void SelectButton(w, event)
XiButtonWidget w;
XEvent *event;
{
    if (w->button.selected)
        deselect_button(w);
    else
        select_button(w, BTN_WITH_CB);
}   /* SelectButton */
```

select_button() is invoked with the message **BTN_WITH_CB**, indicating that the callback list should be traversed.

15.4.6 The Public Interface

There are several public functions. The first two functions manipulate the optional button-related data. As mentioned in our Xlib discussion, in some cases the complexity of an application can be reduced if an application can store simple data with each button. For example, a calculator application could store 2, 8, 10, and 16 with the buttons that represent binary, octal, decimal, and hexadecimal operation, respectively. Of course, with anything other than simple integer values, an application must use callback functions to organize and access button-related data.

The first public function, **XiButtonGetValue()**, retrieves a button's integer value, which is stored in **value**:

```
/*
XiButtonGetValue() returns the button's value.
This is an optional field.
*/

int XiButtonGetValue(w)
XiButtonWidget w;
{
    return w->button.value;
}   /* XiButtonGetValue */
```

This field can be initialized at widget creation (or thereafter) with the resource **XiNvalue**. In most situations, however, it would be simpler to modify this value dynamically with the convenience function **XiButtonSetValue()**:

```
/*
XiButtonSetValue() sets the button's value.
This is an optional field.
*/
```

```
void XiButtonSetValue(w, value)
XiButtonWidget w;
int value;
{
    w->button.value = value;
}   /* XiButtonSetValue */
```

As with our earlier use of buttons in Xlib dialog boxes, an application *should* use an arbitrary enumeration of (positive) integer values, if possible. If an application requires the full range of negative integers, positive integers, and 0, it's difficult to distinguish whether or not an integer has been associated with a particular button. During widget creation, if no value is provided by the resource **XiNvalue**, **button.value** is initialized to BTN_DEFAULT_VALUE, which has the value XiBUTTON_NOVALUE. The latter is a public identifier that an application can compare to the value returned by **XiButtonGetValue()**.

An application can determine whether or not a particular button is currently selected with the predicate **XiButtonIsSelected()**:

```
/*
XiButtonIsSelected() determines whether or not
the button is currently selected.
*/

int XiButtonIsSelected(w)
XiButtonWidget w;
{
    return (int) w->button.selected;
}   /* XiButtonIsSelected */
```

Based on its interaction with the user, an application may elect to select a button manually; **XiButtonSelect()** handles this task:

```
/*
XiButtonSelect() programmatically selects a button.
*/

void XiButtonSelect(w)
XiButtonWidget w;
{
    if (!w->button.selected)
        select_button(w, BTN_WITH_CB);
}   /* XiButtonSelect */
```

Alternatively, an application can select a button without executing the functions on its callback list:

```
/*
XiButtonSelectNoCB() programmatically selects a button,
but doesn't attempt to execute any associated callbacks.
```

```
*/

void XiButtonSelectNoCB(w)
XiButtonWidget w;
{
    if (!w->button.selected)
        select_button(w, BTN_WITHOUT_CB);
}   /* XiButtonSelect */
```

The last public function is **XiButtonDeselect()**:

```
/*
XiButtonDeselect() programmatically deselects a button.
*/

void XiButtonDeselect(w)
XiButtonWidget w;
{
    if (w->button.selected)
        deselect_button(w);
}   /* XiButtonDeselect */
```

15.4.7 Secondary Functions

In this section we mention several of the low-level functions; the complete source code for **XiButton** is given in Appendix Q.

The first function, **create_button_pixmap()**, sets up the GCs and the pixmap for each button widget:

```
/*
create_button_pixmap() creates the GCs, allocates the button's
text, and builds the button's pixmap.
*/

static int create_button_pixmap(w)
XiButtonWidget w;
{
    XGCValues values;
    Display *display = XtDisplay(w);
    int num_btn_chars, screen = XDefaultScreen(display);
    int depth = XDisplayPlanes(display, screen);

    values.foreground = XBlackPixel(display, screen);
    values.background = XWhitePixel(display, screen);
    values.font = w->button.font->fid;
    w->button.gc = XCreateGC(XtDisplay(w),
        RootWindowOfScreen(XtScreen(w)),
        GCForeground | GCBackground | GCFont, &values);
    w->button.cgc = XCreateGC(XtDisplay(w),
        RootWindowOfScreen(XtScreen(w)),
        GCForeground | GCBackground | GCFont, &values);
```

```
    XSetFunction(XtDisplay(w), w->button.cgc, GXclear);

    num_btn_chars = (w->button.length == BTN_DEFAULT_LENGTH) ?
        strlen(w->button.label) : w->button.length;
    if (!allocate_and_center_button_text(w, num_btn_chars))
        fprintf(stderr,
        "button: unable to allocate space for the button's text!\n");

    if (w->core.width == 0) {
        if (*w->button.private_label)
            w->core.width = strlen(w->button.private_label) *
                w->button.font->max_bounds.width;
        else
            w->core.width = BTN_DEFAULT_WIDTH;
    }
    if (w->core.height == 0) {
        if (*w->button.private_label)
            w->core.height = w->button.font->max_bounds.ascent +
                w->button.font->max_bounds.descent;
        else
            w->core.height = BTN_DEFAULT_HEIGHT;
    }
    w->core.width = w->button.width =
        w->core.width + (2 * BTN_INTERNAL_HORIZ_PAD);
    w->core.height = w->button.height =
        w->core.height + (2 * BTN_INTERNAL_VERT_PAD);
    w->button.pixmap = XCreatePixmap(XtDisplay(w),
        RootWindowOfScreen(XtScreen(w)),
        w->button.width, w->button.height, depth);
}   /* create_button_pixmap */
```

After setting up the GCs, **create_button_pixmap()** checks the **XiNlength**-related field to determine if there is a request for a specific button length/width. If not, the button's (text) width is based on the length of the button label. **allocate_and_center_button_text()** is called to set up the button labels (see Appendix Q).

Next, if there has not been a button width specification with a **Core** resource (using **XtNwidth** or **XiNwidth**), the widget's width is set directly, based on the length of the private label and the font. A similar technique is used to set the button's height in **core.height**. Subsequently, these values are incremented by a padding factor that ensures that there will be enough space surrounding the label for the button outline that's used to highlight a button while it is selected.

Once the button's width and height have been determined, these values are stored in **button.width** and **button.height**. The latter fields are used to build and manipulate the off-screen pixmap, because there is no support for resizing the pixmap.

Next, consider the function that implements selection behavior:

```
/*
select_button() draws a one pixel wide rectangle
on the inside of the pixmap, and then, if requested,
calls functions on the client-specified callback list.
```

```
*/

static void select_button(w, call_CB)
XiButtonWidget w;
int call_CB;
{
    w->button.selected = TRUE;
    XDrawRectangle(XtDisplay(w), w->button.pixmap, w->button.gc,
        1, 1, w->button.width - 3, w->button.height - 3);
    redisplay_pixmap(w);
    if (call_CB == BTN_WITH_CB)
        XtCallCallbacks(w, XiNselectCallback,
            (caddr_t) &w->button.value);
}   /* select_button */
```

select_button() sets the **button.selected** field in the instance record, highlights the button by drawing an outline rectangle on the pixmap, redisplays the pixmap, and if requested executes the functions on the button's **XiNselectCallback** callback list.

The companion function, **deselect_button()**, resets **selected**, erases the outline rectangle, and redisplays the pixmap; it is given in Appendix Q, along with **redisplay_pixmap()**, and others.

Appendix Q also includes a test program that we do not mention here because of its simplicity. In the next chapter, we use **XiButton** to implement a multiple-choice selection box that supports exclusive and nonexclusive button selection behavior using either a horizontal, vertical, or menu arrangement for the buttons.

16

XiChoice: A Button-oriented Selection Box

With each of the *Xi* widgets in earlier chapters we've raised a different widget programming issue: designing simple widgets, designing compound widgets, inheriting from the **Simple** widget class and from constraint-based widget classes such as **Form**, imposing start-up constraints with a constraint-initialize method, and designing high-level manager widgets such as **XiFileSelect**.

In this the final widget programming chapter we develop a widget class that has (implementation) similarities with several of the previous *Xi* widget classes. **XiChoice**, like **XiAlert**, is a subclass of **Form**. Like **XiFileSelect**, **XiChoice** provides a number of resources that are used to control an encapsulated *Xi* widget, in this case, **XiButton**. **XiChoice** is our most powerful and most configurable widget. **XiChoice** implements a multiple-choice, button-oriented, item selection box. **XiChoice** widgets can be configured to have horizontal or vertical (button) arrangement, to have their labels on the left of or above the buttons, to support exclusive or nonexclusive item selection, and to have standard or menu-style behavior.

16.1 XiChoice: Overview

Figure 16.1 provides a simple demonstration of an **XiChoice** widget. Also, in our preliminary discussion of compound widgets in Section 11.6, we discussed an application, *xconvert*, which employs a choice box; see Figure 11.1.

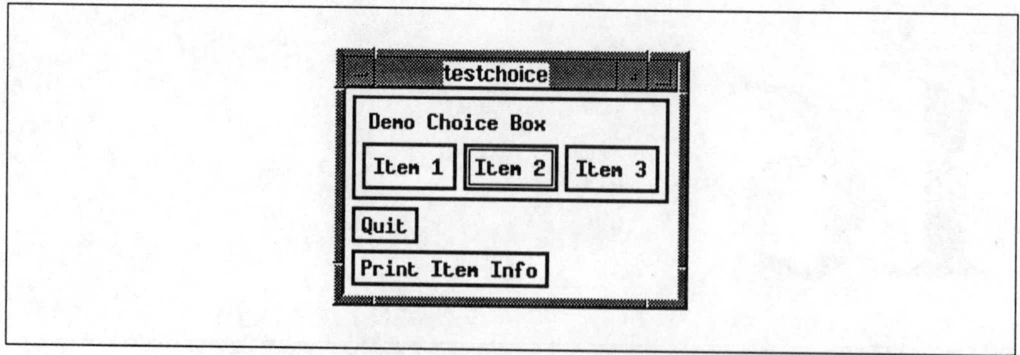

Figure 16.1 A Multiple-choice Item Selection Box in a Pop-up Shell

A choice, or option, widget collects **XiButton** widgets within a box. An application can use choice widgets to allow the user to configure application options. In a programmer's calculator a choice widget could be used to select the appropriate numeric base.

An application controls the behavior of a choice widget and enforces certain policies through resources. For example, if **XiNexclusive** is TRUE, only one item can be selected at a time. Another resource, **XiNmenuForm** provides simple, pop-up menu operation (see Figure 16.2). For exclusive-mode choice boxes that are *not* in menu form, a default item can be specified using the resource **XiNdefaultItem**.

By default, the label (if any) appears in the top of the choice box; this can be altered with the resource **XiNlabelOnLeft**. Items, by default, are arranged from left to right below the label/title; this can be altered with the resource **XiNvertical**.

Normally, the choice box inherits its cursor from its parent; however, you can specify a different cursor for the buttons (items) using the resource **XiNitemCursor**.

An application adds buttons to a choice box after the choice widget is created using either **XiChoiceAddItem()**, for adding items one at a time, or **XiChoiceAddItems()**, for adding items by way of an array specification.

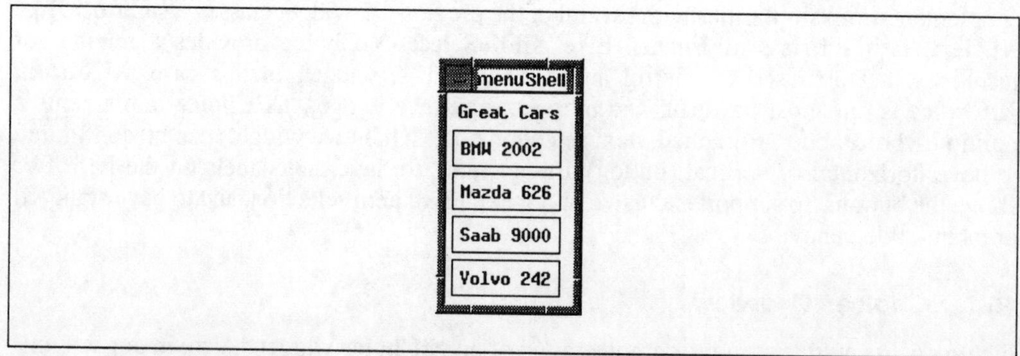

Figure 16.2 A Vertically Arranged, Menu-style Item Selection Box in a Pop-up Shell

16.2 *Choice.h*: The Public Interface

As mentioned, an **XiChoice** widget provides a number of configuration options through the resource database. The resource identifiers are:

```
#define XiNlabel                        "label"
#define XiNexclusive                    "exclusive"
#define XiNdefaultItem                  "defaultItem"
#define XiNlabelOnLeft                  "labelOnLeft"
#define XiNvertical                     "vertical"
#define XiNmenuForm                     "menuForm"
#define XiNitemBorderWidth              "itemBorderWidth"
#define XiNitemCursor                   "itemCursor"
#define XiCLabel                        "Label"
#define XiCExclusive                    "Exclusive"
#define XiCDefaultItem                  "DefaultItem"
#define XiCLabelOnLeft                  "LabelOnLeft"
#define XiCVertical                     "Vertical"
#define XiCMenuForm                     "MenuForm"
#define XiCItemBorderWidth              "ItemBorderWidth"
#define XiCItemCursor                   "ItemCursor"
```

In the overview we discussed several of **XiChoice**'s resources that control a choice widget's behavior and overall layout.

For choice boxes, the buttons' border width can be set using normal resource matching rules or using the dedicated resource **XiNitemBorderWidth**. (As mentioned in Section 16.4.3, **XiNitemBorderWidth** may be preferable, if the label is configured to the left side of the buttons.) For example, the program *testchoice* (Appendix R) can request a border width of one pixel for its choice widget, as shown in Figure 16.3, with the following resource specification:

```
testchoice*Choice*BorderWidth:  1
```

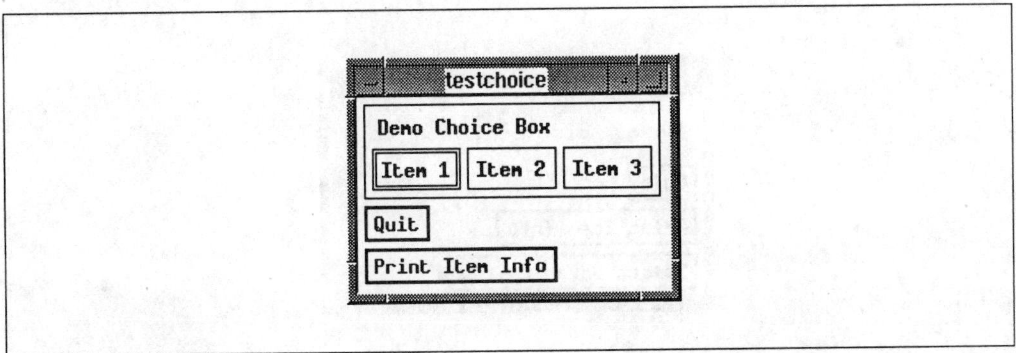

Figure 16.3 An Item Selection Box with a Border Width of One Pixel

Assuming there are no overriding resource setting elsewhere, the one-pixel wide border will apply to the choice box and to the buttons. There are, of course, other resource settings that would achieve the same result for this program. Note that border width is an inherited resource.

In many applications a choice widget's border width would be the same as for other widgets. The border width of each item, on the other hand, should be determined by the function that the choice widget serves, and by the names of the items. For example, if each item has a one-word label, it may be appropriate to set up the label on the left of the items and use a border width of 0 for each item. Figure 16.4 illustrates this particular layout. With this configuration, the choice box has a very uncluttered appearance. (In this example the choice box's border width is zero as well.)

If an application has multiple choice widgets, and if it's necessary to provide a different appearance for each choice widget, the application can either hard-code the widget designs or provide the user with external widget identifiers/names. In any case, the arrangement of multiple-item selection boxes is an application programming issue, not a widget programming issue.

XiChoice can be configured as either a choice box or a menu. With a choice box arrangement, an application specifies integer values for each item, as well as callback information. With a menu arrangement, there are no item values, just labels and callback information. **XiChoice** provides a public data type for both of these choice widget arrangements.

An application sets up a standard choice widget by defining an array of data of type **XiChoiceItem**. For example, **item_list** provides item information for a two-item choice widget:

```
static XiChoiceItem item_list[] = {
    {"Bin", 2, ChoiceCB, "Binary Data"},
    {"Dec", 10, ChoiceCB, "Decimal Data"},
    {NULL, NULL, NULL, NULL},
};
```

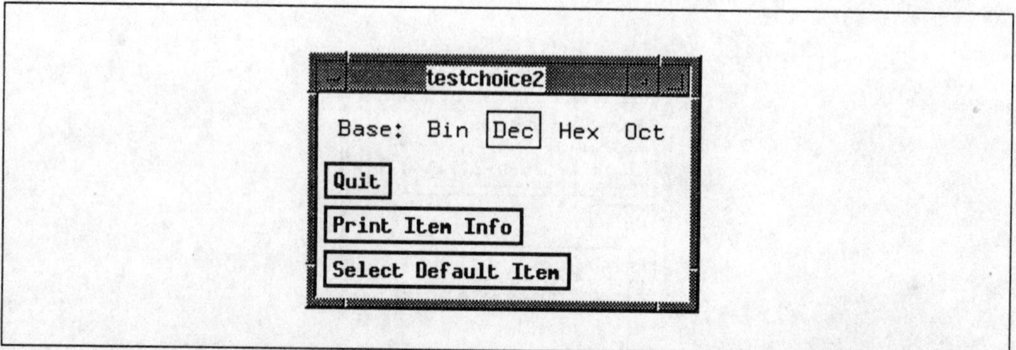

Figure 16.4 An Item Selection Box with the Label on the Left and Zero-width Borders

Subsequently, its widget could be created by the following statements:

```
example = XtCreateManagedWidget("example",
    xiChoiceWidgetClass, exampleParent, args, i);
XiChoiceAddItems(example, item_list);
```

The type definition in *Choice.h* for this structure is:

```
typedef struct {
    char *label;
    int value;
    void (*callback_proc)();            /* or, ...              */
/*  XtCallbackProc callback_proc; **** client's view?   */
    caddr_t client_data;
} XiChoiceItem;
```

Most application programmers define callback functions as **void** functions. Depending on your frame of reference, you could declare the third component using either the traditional syntax or the Xt **typedef** for a pointer to a callback function, **XtCallbackProc**.

Alternatively, to define a menu-style choice widget, an application uses **XiChoiceMenuItem** to specify the item information:

```
static XiChoiceMenuItem item_list[] = {
    {"Menu Label 1", MenuCB, "Menu Data 1"},
    {"Menu Label 2", MenuCB, "Menu Data 2"},
    {NULL, NULL, NULL},
};
```

Subsequently, a menu-style widget could be created just as with a standard choice box widget. The application, however, must request the menu arrangement with the **XiNmenuForm** resource:

```
XtSetArg(args[i], XiNmenuForm, (XtArgVal) TRUE); i++;
example = XtCreateManagedWidget("example",
    xiChoiceWidgetClass, exampleParent, args, i);
XiChoiceAddItems(example, item_list);
```

The type definition in *Choice.h* for the menu structure is:

```
typedef struct {
    char *label;
    void (*callback_proc)();            /* or, ...              */
/*  XtCallbackProc callback_proc; **** client's view?   */
    caddr_t client_data;
} XiChoiceMenuItem;
```

The value of the instance variable associated with **XiNmenuForm** is used to coerce the second argument to **XiChoiceAddItems()** (in this case, **item_list**) to the proper data type.

There are a number of public functions in addition to **XiChoiceAddItems()**; several of these functions are discussed in Section 16.4.4.

16.3 *ChoiceP.h*: The Private Widget Data Structures

As with **XiAlert**, the **XiChoice** widget class is a subclass of **Form**:

```
typedef struct _XiChoiceClassRec {
    CoreClassPart core_class;
    CompositeClassPart composite_class;
    ConstraintClassPart constraint_class;
    FormClassPart form_class;
    XiChoiceClassPart choice_class;
} XiChoiceClassRec;
```

Its class record component is empty:

```
typedef struct _XiChoiceClassPart {      /* class definition */
    int dummy;
} XiChoiceClassPart;
```

Its instance record component includes a composite field for each item (the button widget plus the item's value); this type structure is:

```
typedef struct _XiChoiceItemPart {
    XiButtonWidget wid;
    int value;
} XiChoiceItemPart;
```

In comparison to the other *Xi* widgets, a choice widget contributes several high-level, "management" variables to the instance record:

```
typedef struct _XiChoicePart {              /* instance definition */
    char *label;
    XFontStruct *font;               /* used during dimension calc.s */
    Cursor item_cursor;              /* used for buttons */
    Dimension width, height;         /* dimensions of the frame */
    int btn_border_width;            /* negative used to set default */
    Widget labelW;
    XiChoiceItemPart itemW[CHOICE_MAX_ITEMS];
    int num_items;
    int default_item;
    int items_selected[CHOICE_MAX_ITEMS];/* public list; see      */
                                         /* XiChoiceGetItems()    */
    Boolean exclusive;               /* allow exclusive choices only? */
    Boolean label_on_left;           /* label place on left or on top */
    Boolean vertical;                /* vertical or horiz. orientation? */
    int max_item_len;                /* used for uniform length items */
    Boolean menu_form;               /* impose menu policy? */
} XiChoicePart;
```

With respect to the basic operation of a choice widget, it's not necessary to maintain an array of the currently selected items—each button widget maintains a record of whether or not it is selected, and this condition can be queried with **XiButtonIsSelected()**. In particular, the array **items_selected** is used by a public function, **XiChoiceGetItems()**, that returns (a pointer to) a zero-terminated list of the currently selected items. This list is rebuilt each time an application calls **XiChoiceGetItems()**.

Like **XiAlert**, **XiChoice** imposes certain constraints on the layout of a choice widget. Although **XiChoice**'s layout policy is more sophisticated than **XiAlert**'s, its constraints are based largely on resources and there is no need for instance-level constraint variables:

```
typedef struct {
    int dummy;
} XiChoiceConstraintsPart;
```

Because we're inheriting from **Form**, a subclass of **Constraint**, the constraints record is:

```
typedef struct _XiChoiceConstraintsRec {
    FormConstraintsPart form;
    XiChoiceConstraintsPart choice;
} XiChoiceConstraintsRec, *XiChoiceConstraints;
```

16.4 *Choice.c*: The Implementation File

XiChoice is a compound widget that enforces certain characteristics and policies for a label widget and a collection of button widgets. **XiChoice** has no actions and translation beyond those provided by the internal label and button widgets.

16.4.1 Resources

By default, **XiChoice** widgets adopt the cursor of their parent windows. Although it's unnecessary to accommodate a special cursor for the background window, except through cursor adoption, it's a good idea to provide a cursor resource for the buttons/items.

As with **XiFileSelect**, we initialize a default item cursor to **None**:

```
static Cursor default_item_cursor = None;
```

Then, in the resource table this cursor is used as the default:

```
#define res_offset(field) XtOffset(XiChoiceWidget, field)

static XtResource resources[] = {
    {XiNlabel, XiCLabel, XtRString,
        sizeof(char *), res_offset(choice.label),
        XtRString, CHOICE_DEFAULT_LABEL},
    {XiNexclusive, XiCExclusive, XtRBoolean, sizeof(Boolean),
        res_offset(choice.exclusive),
        XtRImmediate, (caddr_t) FALSE},
    {XiNitemBorderWidth, XiCItemBorderWidth, XtRInt,
        sizeof(int), res_offset(choice.btn_border_width),
```

```
        XtRImmediate, (caddr_t) CHOICE_DEFAULT_BTN_BORDER_WIDTH},
    {XiNdefaultItem, XiCDefaultItem, XtRInt, sizeof(int),
        res_offset(choice.default_item),
        XtRImmediate, (caddr_t) CHOICE_DEFAULT_ITEM},
    {XiNlabelOnLeft, XiCLabelOnLeft, XtRBoolean, sizeof(Boolean),
        res_offset(choice.label_on_left),
        XtRImmediate, (caddr_t) FALSE},
    {XiNvertical, XiCVertical, XtRBoolean, sizeof(Boolean),
        res_offset(choice.vertical),
        XtRImmediate, (caddr_t) FALSE},
    {XiNmenuForm, XiCMenuForm, XtRBoolean, sizeof(Boolean),
        res_offset(choice.menu_form),
        XtRImmediate, (caddr_t) FALSE},
    {XiNitemCursor, XiCItemCursor, XtRCursor, sizeof(Cursor),
        res_offset(choice.item_cursor),
        XtRCursor, (caddr_t) &default_item_cursor},
    {XiNfont, XiCFont, XtRFontStruct, sizeof(XFontStruct *),
        res_offset(choice.font),
        XtRString, "XtDefaultFont"},
};
```

If the user prefers a special cursor for choice widget buttons, the default can be overridden with a setting from a resource file:

```
testchoice*itemCursor:  dot
```

Next, consider the resources that control a choice widget's layout and behavior. By default, a choice widget does not enforce **XiNexclusive** selection behavior—the user can select multiple items/options. If, however, an application requests exclusive operation, the value of **XiNdefaultItem** is used during widget creation to select the default item.

Normally, the label appears across the top as in Figure 16.1, but the application can set the **XiNlabelOnLeft** resource to override the default. Although applications are unlikely to do so, it's legal to set **XiNlabelOnLeft** along with either **XiNvertical** or **XiNmenuForm**. In the current implementation, if an application sets the **XiNmenuForm** resource, the item layout is always vertical.

16.4.2 The Class Record

The class record for **XiChoice** is similar to that of **XiAlert**:

```
XiChoiceClassRec XichoiceClassRec = {
    { /* core_class variables */
        (WidgetClass) &formClassRec,    /* ancestor */
        "Choice",                       /* class name */
        sizeof(XiChoiceRec),            /* widget size */
#ifdef X11R3
        NULL,                           /* class initialize */
#else
        XawInitializeWidgetSet,         /* class initialize */
#endif
```

```
        NULL,                               /* class part init. */
        FALSE,                              /* class inited */
        Initialize,                         /* initialize */
        NULL,                               /* initialize hook */
        XtInheritRealize,                   /* realize */
        NULL,                               /* actions */
        0,                                  /* number of actions */
        resources,                          /* resources */
        XtNumber(resources),                /* number of resources */
        NULLQUARK,                          /* xrm class */
        TRUE,                               /* compress motions */
        TRUE,                               /* compress exposures */
        TRUE,                               /* compress enter/leave */
        FALSE,                              /* visibility interest */
        Destroy,                            /* destroy */
        XtInheritResize,                    /* resize */
        XtInheritExpose,                    /* expose */
        NULL,                               /* set values */
        NULL,                               /* set values hook */
        XtInheritSetValuesAlmost,           /* set values almost */
        NULL,                               /* get values hook */
        NULL,                               /* accept focus */
        XtVersion,                          /* version */
        NULL,                               /* callback private */
        NULL,                               /* translation table */
        XtInheritQueryGeometry,             /* query geometry */
        XtInheritDisplayAccelerator,        /* display accelerator */
        NULL,                               /* extension */
    },
    { /* composite_class variables */
        XtInheritGeometryManager,           /* geometry manager */
        XtInheritChangeManaged,             /* change managed */
        XtInheritInsertChild,               /* insert child */
        XtInheritDeleteChild,               /* delete child */
        NULL,                               /* extension */
    },
    { /* constraint_class fields */
        NULL,                               /* subresources */
        0,                                  /* number of subresources */
        sizeof(XiChoiceConstraintsRec),     /* record size */
        ConstraintInitialize,               /* initialize */
        NULL,                               /* destroy */
        NULL,                               /* set values */
        NULL,                               /* extension */
    },
    { /* form_class fields */
#ifdef X11R3
        0,
#else
        XtInheritLayout,
#endif
    },
```

```
    { /* choice_class variables */
        0,
    },
}; /* XichoiceClassRec */

WidgetClass xiChoiceWidgetClass = (WidgetClass) &XichoiceClassRec;
```

XiChoice derives much of its functionality from **Form**, the immediate superclass, but provides a constraint-initialize method for implementing the label and button arrangement requested through the resources. Note that no special actions and translations are required beyond those provided by **XiButton**.

16.4.3 The XiChoice Methods

Initialize() (1) checks the basic dimensions in the **core** component of the instance record, (2) creates the label widget, and (3) sets the proper resource-related variables that indicate either menu or exclusive selection behavior:

```
/*
Initialize() initializes each instance of a choice box.
*/
/*ARGSUSED*/
static void Initialize(request, new)
XiChoiceWidget request, new;
{
    Arg args[5];
    int i;

    if (new->core.width == 0)
        new->core.width = CHOICE_DEFAULT_WIDTH;
    if (new->core.height == 0)
        new->core.height = CHOICE_DEFAULT_HEIGHT;

    if (*new->choice.label) {
        i = 0;
        XtSetArg(args[i], XtNlabel,
            (XtArgVal) new->choice.label); i++;
        XtSetArg(args[i], XtNborderWidth, (XtArgVal) 0); i++;
        XtSetArg(args[i], XtNresizable, (XtArgVal) TRUE); i++;
        XtSetArg(args[i], XtNfont, (XtArgVal) new->choice.font); i++;
        new->choice.labelW = XtCreateManagedWidget("label",
            labelWidgetClass, new, args, i);
    }
    else
        new->choice.labelW = NULL;
    new->choice.num_items = 0;
    new->choice.items_selected[0] = 0;

    if (new->choice.menu_form) {            /* force these values */
        new->choice.vertical = TRUE;
        new->choice.exclusive = TRUE;
```

```
        new->choice.default_item = FALSE;
        new->choice.max_item_len = CHOICE_IGNORE_ITEM_LEN;
        XtAddEventHandler(new, ButtonPressMask, FALSE, remove_menu,
            NULL);
    }
    else if (new->choice.exclusive) {
        if (new->choice.default_item < 1)
            new->choice.default_item = CHOICE_DEFAULT_ITEM;
    }
}   /* Initialize */
```

Note that if an application does not specify a choice widget label, none will be created. Also, because items are added with **XiChoiceAddItems()**, **choice.num_items** is initialized to 0. As a precaution, the list of currently selected items is initialized as a "null list" by placing a 0 in array position 0.

If an application has requested a menu arrangement of widgets (see Figure 16.2), it's necessary to provide a mechanism for removing a menu *without* making a menu selection. Menu removal *could* be accommodated by adding a "Remove Menu" item, but this approach is inadequate for obvious reasons. In the current implementation, we'll use a very simple approach for menu removal: if the user clicks a pointer button anywhere in the menu area outside of an item, the menu is removed. Specifically, when the menu pops up, the cursor will be placed in the top of the menu—in the label area. Thus, if the user simply clicks the pointer button, the menu will disappear—the user does not have to move the pointer.

The most straightforward way to implement this form of menu removal is by adding an event handler to the choice widget. When programmers are first becoming acquainted with Xt, they sometimes have a tendency to use event handlers instead of callback functions. In general, callback functions should be preferred over event handlers—we haven't used an event handler in any of our examples.

In this particular situation, however, an event handler provides a perfect mechanism for intercepting and supplementing pointer operations.

In the following code segment **XtAddEventHandler()** sets up an event handler, **remove_menu()**, for the choice widget that's triggered when a pointer button is pressed inside the widget:

```
if (new->choice.menu_form) {
    ...
    XtAddEventHandler(new, ButtonPressMask, FALSE, remove_menu,
        NULL);
}
```

If the pointer is within a button widget, the **XiButton** actions, translations, and callback functions are active as well.

The next major consideration is the layout constraints. A number of interactions can occur, based on the resources **XiNlabel**, **XiNlabelOnLeft**, and **XiNvertical**. First, the choice box label can be present or absent. If present, it may be on the left or across the top. If the label is present and on the left, the first button/item should be positioned horizontally to the right of the label. If the label is across the top, the first item must be below the label, regardless of the layout, vertical or horizontal.

XiChoice's layout constraints (options) are implemented with **ConstraintInitialize()**:

```
/*
ConstraintInitialize() organizes the form widget that
houses the choice label and items.  Note that the label
is optional; its presence or absence must be considered
when traversing the list of children.
*/
/*ARGSUSED*/
static void ConstraintInitialize(request, new)
Widget request, new;
{
    XiChoiceWidget cw = (XiChoiceWidget) new->core.parent;
    Widget *child, *children = cw->composite.children;
    XiChoiceConstraints constraint =
        (XiChoiceConstraints) new->core.constraints;
    int label;

    if (cw->choice.label_on_left &&
            XtIsSubclass(new, labelWidgetClass) &&
            cw->choice.btn_border_width !=
                CHOICE_DEFAULT_BTN_BORDER_WIDTH)
        constraint->form.dy +=
            constraint->form.dy + cw->choice.btn_border_width - 1;
    if (!XtIsSubclass(new, xiButtonWidgetClass))
        return;
    if (cw->choice.vertical)
        constraint->form.top = constraint->form.bottom = XtChainTop;
    else
        constraint->form.left = constraint->form.right = XtChainLeft;
    if (!cw->choice.label_on_left &&
            (!cw->choice.vertical || cw->choice.menu_form))
        constraint->form.vert_base = cw->choice.labelW;
    if (cw->choice.label_on_left && cw->choice.vertical)
        constraint->form.horiz_base = cw->choice.labelW;
    if (cw->composite.num_children == 0)
        return;
    label = (cw->choice.labelW != NULL && !cw->choice.label_on_left) ?
        1 : 0;
    if (cw->composite.num_children == 1 && label == 1)
        return;
    for (child = children + cw->composite.num_children - 1;
            child >= (children + label); child--) {
        if (XtIsManaged(*child)) {
            if (cw->choice.menu_form)
                constraint->form.vert_base = *child;
            else if (cw->choice.vertical &&
                    XtIsSubclass(*child, xiButtonWidgetClass))
                constraint->form.vert_base = *child;
```

```
            else
                constraint->form.horiz_base = *child;
            break;
        }
    }
}   /* ConstraintInitialize */
```

Consider the first conditional code segment, which controls text alignment of the widget label and the button labels:

```
    if (cw->choice.label_on_left &&
            XtIsSubclass(new, labelWidgetClass) &&
            cw->choice.btn_border_width !=
                CHOICE_DEFAULT_BTN_BORDER_WIDTH)
        constraint->form.dy +=
            constraint->form.dy + cw->choice.btn_border_width - 1;
```

With an **XiChoice** widget, the buttons' border width can be set in the usual manner from a resource file:

```
testchoice2*Choice*BorderWidth:  4
```

If the label is on the left, however, the label will be horizontally aligned with the *top* of the buttons (see Figure 16.5). Specifically, the border width of each internal widget is part of the calculation that a **Form** widget uses in determining the vertical positioning of each child. For obvious reasons, **XiChoice** enforces a border width of 0 for the label widget. If the buttons have a border width of 4, their labels will be four pixels lower than they would be with a border width of 0. Depending on the user's taste, and the characteristics of the application, this may or may not be the preferred layout.

If, however, the user prefers a precise horizontal alignment of the text for a choice widget's label and each button's label, or if the application wants to enforce this layout, the **XiNitemBorderWidth** resource should be used instead of the more general resource

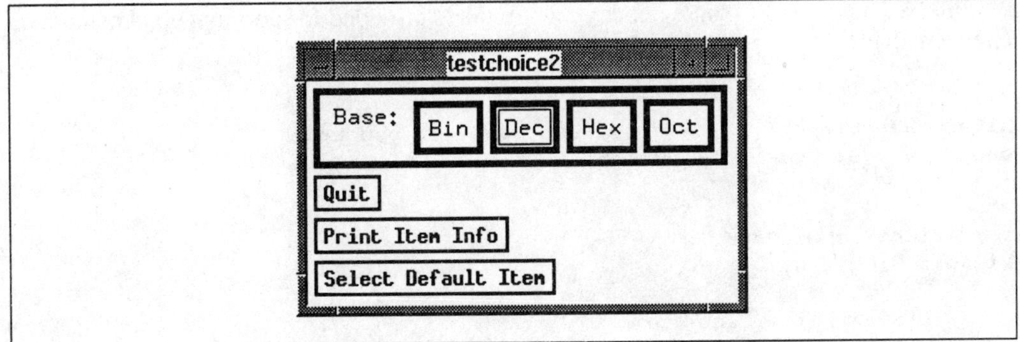

Figure 16.5 An Item Selection Box with a Border Width of Four Pixels

specification. Setting this resource provides **ConstraintInitialize()** with *up-front* knowledge of the border width before widget management takes place. In this case, the previous code segment will make the proper adjustments for the offset that's introduced by the border width of the buttons. Of course, if **XiNlabelOnLeft** is FALSE (the default), both approaches for setting button border width will produce the same result.

The remaining conditional statements are straightforward and similar to those that we used with **XiAlert**. They simply check for each combination of horizontal, vertical, or menu arrangement, label presence or absence, and label position.

Destroy() is the last method defined in *Choice.c*:

```
/*
Destroy() cleans up data structures, if any, and removes the
event handler.
*/

static void Destroy(w)
XiChoiceWidget w;
{
    int i;

    XtDestroyWidget(w->choice.labelW);
    for (i = 0; i < w->choice.num_items; i++)
        XtDestroyWidget(w->choice.itemW[i].wid);
    XtRemoveEventHandler(w, ButtonPressMask, FALSE, remove_menu,
        NULL);
}   /* Destroy */
```

It destroys the internal label widget and then iterates over the array of items, destroying each button widget. Note that each button widget is responsible for freeing its private label text. Lastly, **Destroy()** removes the choice widget's event handler.

16.4.4 The Public Interface

XiChoice provides more public functions than we can mention here. In this section we discuss the most interesting functions (see Appendix R for the remainder).

First we mention the convenience function that's provided for popping up a menu-style choice widget:

```
/*
XiChoiceMenuPopup() uses query_set_pos() to pop up a
choice widget under the cursor.
*/

void XiChoiceMenuPopup(w)
XiChoiceWidget w;
{
    if (!w->choice.menu_form)
        return;
    query_set_pos(w);
    XtPopup(w->core.parent, XtGrabNone);
```

```
}   /* XiChoiceMenuPopup */
```

Using the miscellaneous library function **query_set_pos()** (Appendix L), the menu is positioned beneath the pointer. As an alternative, you might consider designing this widget so that the menu is mapped precisely over (or just south of) the command button that triggers the menu. In order to implement this behavior, however, the widget must have the identity of the widget that invoked the menu. Of course, the disadvantage of this alternative approach is that it restricts the general usefulness of the widget. As currently designed, if a menu-style choice widget is invoked by a command button, it will be mapped over the command button anyway (provided that the user doesn't move the pointer very quickly).

Next, consider **XiChoiceAddItems()**. As described in Section 16.2, **XiChoiceAddItems()** is a high-level function for specifying items and their callback functions with an array, *after* a choice widget has been created:

```
...
static XiChoiceMenuItem item_list[] = {
    {"Menu Label 1", MenuCB, "Menu Data 1"},
    {"Menu Label 2", MenuCB, "Menu Data 2"},
    {NULL, NULL, NULL},
};
    ...
    example = XtCreateManagedWidget("example",
        xiChoiceWidgetClass, exampleParent, args, i);
    XiChoiceAddItems(example, item_list);
    ...
```

Because a choice widget can have either a standard or a menu-style arrangement, **XiChoiceAddItems()**'s second parameter must be coerced to the proper data type, based on **XiNmenuForm**:

```
void XiChoiceAddItems(cw, item_addr)
XiChoiceWidget cw;
caddr_t item_addr;
{
    int i, len, more_items = FALSE;

    if (item_addr == NULL) {
        fprintf(stderr, "choice box: item list is null!\n");
        return;
    }
    if (cw->choice.menu_form) {
        XiChoiceMenuItem *item = (XiChoiceMenuItem *) item_addr;
        cw->choice.max_item_len = 0;
        for (i = 0; item[i].label && i < CHOICE_MAX_ITEMS; i++)
            if ((len = strlen(item[i].label)) > cw->choice.max_item_len)
                cw->choice.max_item_len = len;
        for (i = 0; item[i].label && i < CHOICE_MAX_ITEMS; i++)
            XiChoiceAddItem(cw, item[i].label, FALSE,
                item[i].callback_proc, item[i].client_data);
```

```
        if (item[i].label != NULL)
            more_items = TRUE;
    }
    else {
        XiChoiceItem *item = (XiChoiceItem *) item_addr;
        for (i = 0; item[i].label && i < CHOICE_MAX_ITEMS; i++)
            XiChoiceAddItem(cw, item[i].label, item[i].value,
                item[i].callback_proc, item[i].client_data);
        if (item[i].label != NULL)
            more_items = TRUE;
    }
    if (i == CHOICE_MAX_ITEMS && more_items) {
        fprintf(stderr,
            "choice box: too many items for the choice box!\n");
        fprintf(stderr,
            "choice box: the maximum number of items is: %d.\n",
            CHOICE_MAX_ITEMS);
    }
}   /* XiChoiceAddItems */
```

XiChoiceAddItems() calls a lower level function, **XiChoiceAddItem()**, to add each item to the choice widget. If **XiNmenuForm** is TRUE, **choice.max_item_len** is set to the character length of the longest item's label.

Although (in most cases) the higher level function should be used by the application, **XiChoiceAddItem()** has been declared as a public function as well (see *Choice.h*):

```
/*
XiChoiceAddItem() is used to add items to a choice box after
the box has been created.  Buttons/items are added in left-
to-right order.  This form of item entry probably shouldn't be
publicly accessible; use XiChoiceAddItems() below.
*/

void XiChoiceAddItem(cw, item_name, item_value,
    callback_proc, client_data)
XiChoiceWidget cw;
char *item_name;
int item_value;
void (*callback_proc)();     /* or, XtCallbackProc callback_proc; */
caddr_t client_data;
{
    Arg args[10];
    int i;

    if (cw->choice.num_items >= CHOICE_MAX_ITEMS) {
        fprintf(stderr,
            "choice box: too many items for the choice box!\n");
        fprintf(stderr,
            "choice box: the maximum number of items is: %d.\n",
            CHOICE_MAX_ITEMS);
        return;
```

```
    }
    i = 0;
    XtSetArg(args[i], XiNlabel, (XtArgVal) item_name); i++;
    /*
    item 1 ==> itemW[0]:
    */
    XtSetArg(args[i], XiNvalue,
        (XtArgVal) (cw->choice.num_items + 1)); i++;
    if (cw->choice.btn_border_width !=
            CHOICE_DEFAULT_BTN_BORDER_WIDTH) {
        XtSetArg(args[i], XiNborderWidth,
            (XtArgVal) cw->choice.btn_border_width); i++;
    }
    if (cw->choice.item_cursor != None) {
        XtSetArg(args[i], XtNcursor,
            (XtArgVal) cw->choice.item_cursor); i++;
    }
    XtSetArg(args[i], XiNfont, (XtArgVal) cw->choice.font); i++;
    if (cw->choice.menu_form &&
            cw->choice.max_item_len != CHOICE_IGNORE_ITEM_LEN) {
        XtSetArg(args[i], XiNlength,
            (XtArgVal) cw->choice.max_item_len); i++;
    }
    cw->choice.itemW[cw->choice.num_items].wid = (XiButtonWidget)
        XtCreateManagedWidget(item_name, xiButtonWidgetClass,
            cw, args, i);
    XtAddCallback(cw->choice.itemW[cw->choice.num_items].wid,
        XiNselectCallback, internal_callback_proc, NULL);
    if (cw->choice.menu_form) {
        if (callback_proc != NULL)
            XtAddCallback(cw->choice.itemW[cw->choice.num_items].wid,
                XiNselectCallback, callback_proc, client_data);
    }
    cw->choice.itemW[cw->choice.num_items].value = item_value;
    cw->choice.num_items++;
    if (cw->choice.exclusive &&
            (cw->choice.num_items == cw->choice.default_item))
        XiButtonSelect(cw->choice.itemW[cw->choice.num_items - 1].wid);
}   /* XiChoiceAddItem */
```

XiChoiceAddItem() simply checks/sets the various button-related resources and calls **XtCreateManagedWidget()** for each button in the item list. Note that an internal callback function is added to each button; this callback function is described in Section 16.4.5.

XiChoiceAddItem() also checks **choice.max_item_len** to determine if it has been set; if so, this value is used with **XiButton**'s **XiNlength** resource:

```
    if (cw->choice.menu_form &&
            cw->choice.max_item_len != CHOICE_IGNORE_ITEM_LEN) {
        XtSetArg(args[i], XiNlength,
            (XtArgVal) cw->choice.max_item_len); i++;
    }
```

In our discussion of the resources, we mentioned that the border width of the items can be set with a dedicated resource, **XiNitemBorderWidth**, which corresponds to the instance variable **choice.btn_border_width**. We've used an illegal (negative) value as the default initialization (see the earlier resource table). Hence, if **choice.btn_border_width** is equal to **CHOICE_DEFAULT_BTN_BORDER_WIDTH**, **XiChoiceAddItem()** should *not* set the button's border width—the resource manager's setting is used instead. This approach ensures that an "unset" dedicated border width resource does not override a setting such as:

```
testchoice*Button*borderWidth:  1
```

Next, consider the task of determining which items are currently selected. For this task, it is unacceptable to make an application *poll* every item in a choice widget by calling **XiChoiceItemIsSelected()** in a loop:

```
/*
XiChoiceItemIsSelected() allows programmatic testing of
of an item's status.
*/

int XiChoiceItemIsSelected(w, item)
XiChoiceWidget w;
int item;
{
    if (item < 1 || item > w->choice.num_items)
        return FALSE;
    return XiButtonIsSelected(w->choice.itemW[item - 1].wid);
}   /* XiChoiceItemIsSelected */
```

Specifically, in addition to providing **XiChoiceItemIsSelected()** for testing selection status on an item by item basis, **XiChoiceGetItems()** builds a list of the currently selected items, in a zero-terminated array and then returns its address:

```
/*
XiChoiceGetItems() returns (a pointer to) a zero-terminated list
of the currently selected items.  Item numbers are NOT zero-
based, that is: item 1 ==> itemW[0].  The list is an array of
integers.
*/

int *XiChoiceGetItems(w)
XiChoiceWidget w;
{
    int i, j;

    for (i = j = 0; i < w->choice.num_items; i++)
        if (XiButtonIsSelected(w->choice.itemW[i].wid))
            w->choice.items_selected[j++] = i + 1;
    w->choice.items_selected[j] = 0;
    return w->choice.items_selected;
```

```
}   /* XiChoiceGetItems */
```

If, however, a choice widget is configured to enforce exclusive selection (**XiNexclusive**), it is more convenient to call **XiChoiceGetSelectedItem()** to determine which item (if any) is selected:

```
/*
XiChoiceGetSelectedItem() returns the currently
selected item for an exclusive choice box.
Note:  item 1 ==> itemW[0].
*/

int XiChoiceGetSelectedItem(w)
XiChoiceWidget w;
{
    int i;

    if (!w->choice.exclusive)
        return FALSE;
    for (i = 0; i < w->choice.num_items; i++)
        if (XiButtonIsSelected(w->choice.itemW[i].wid))
            return i + 1;
    return FALSE;
}   /* XiChoiceGetSelectedItem */
```

In the current implementation, exclusive selection implies that no more than one item can be selected simultaneously. This definition is more general than one that enforces the requirement that exactly one item must be selected at all times. The more strict requirement can be enforced from within the application.

XiChoice interprets the **XiNdefaultItem** resource when **XiNexclusive** is set to TRUE. For many applications, **XiChoiceSelectedItemIsDefault()** is useful in determining if a default option is in effect:

```
/*
XiChoiceSelectedItemIsDefault() tests whether or not
the selected item is the default item.
*/

int XiChoiceSelectedItemIsDefault(w)
XiChoiceWidget w;
{
    if (!w->choice.exclusive)
        return FALSE;
    if (XiChoiceGetNumItems(w) != 1)
        return FALSE;
    return (XiChoiceGetSelectedItem(w) == w->choice.default_item);
}   /* XiChoiceSelectedItemIsDefault */
```

XiChoice provides a number of other functions for selecting and deselecting items manually, for testing button values, and so on (see Appendix R).

16.4.5 Secondary Functions

XiChoice uses an internal callback function to enforce the exclusive selection policy, if it applies:

```
/*
internal_callback_proc() is installed as a private callback
function for each (internal) button; see XiChoiceAddItem().
The "exclusive" policy is enforced here -- if other items are
already selected, they must be deselected.
*/
/*ARGSUSED*/
static void internal_callback_proc(w, client_data, call_data)
Widget w;
caddr_t client_data;
caddr_t call_data;
{
    XiButtonWidget bw = (XiButtonWidget) w;
    XiChoiceWidget cw = (XiChoiceWidget) bw->core.parent;
    int i;

    if (!cw->choice.exclusive)
        return;
    for (i = 0; i < cw->choice.num_items; i++)
        if (cw->choice.itemW[i].wid != bw)
            XiButtonDeselect(cw->choice.itemW[i].wid);
    if (!cw->choice.menu_form)
        return;
    XtPopdown(cw->core.parent);
    XiButtonDeselect(bw);
}   /* internal_callback_proc */
```

This function will be called immediately after an item is selected. If the choice widget is configured as a standard choice box with exclusive selection, the previously selected item (if any) must be deselected. In addition, if the choice widget is configured as a simple menu, the newly selected item must be deselected and the choice widget must be unmapped.

We've already mentioned the second support function, namely, **remove_menu()**:

```
/*
For choice boxes in menu form, remove_menu() pops down the menu
if the user clicks the left mouse button in anywhere inside the
widget other than on a button.
*/
/*ARGSUSED*/
static void remove_menu(w, client_data, event)
XiChoiceWidget w;
caddr_t client_data;
```

```
XEvent *event;
{
    if (event->xbutton.button == Button1)
        XtPopdown(w->core.parent);
}   /* remove_menu */
```

The event handler is registered by **Initialize()** during the widget creation process:

```
    if (new->choice.menu_form) {
        ...
        XtAddEventHandler(new, ButtonPressMask, FALSE, remove_menu,
            NULL);
    }
```

With **XiChoice** the final argument to **XtAddEventHandler()** is NULL, because there is no need for client data, which is passed as the second argument to **remove_menu()**.

The demonstration programs, *testchoice* and *testchoice2*, that we've used for illustrations throughout this chapter are included in Appendix R. In the next chapter we discuss *xconvert*, a base conversion utility that includes an **XiChoice** widget for specifying a integer base.

17

Using the *Xi* Widget Set in Applications

In this chapter we illustrate the widgets from Chapters 12 through 16 in two small applications, *xdelete* and *xconvert*. *xconvert* uses one additional widget, **XiSimpleText**, which is defined in Appendix U.

17.1 *xdelete*: File Deletions from a File Selection Box

Users sometimes need to delete files from one or more directories when the target files don't correspond to any particular wildcard file sequence. That is, it's more convenient to delete files using a "pick and choose" strategy. In this situation, a file selection box provides a good mechanism for selecting and deleting files one at a time. With this approach, in which users first select a file from the file selection box and then request its deletion, naive (and experienced) users are less likely to delete files by accident. Moreover, a file filter can be used to trim the set of filenames displayed in the file selection box.

xdelete is a small application that implements a file selection box in the top-level application window, along with a "Quit" button. Figure 17.1 demonstrates *xdelete*'s top-level application window. *xdelete* also uses an alert box in a pop-up shell to display an error message. For example, if a user clicks on the "Apply" button without first selecting a filename, an alert is issued that explains the error.

xdelete is rather small, therefore **main()** creates each of the widgets directly:

```
/*
main() sets up a button-activated file selection box inside a
box widget in the main window.  A simple callback is used to
```

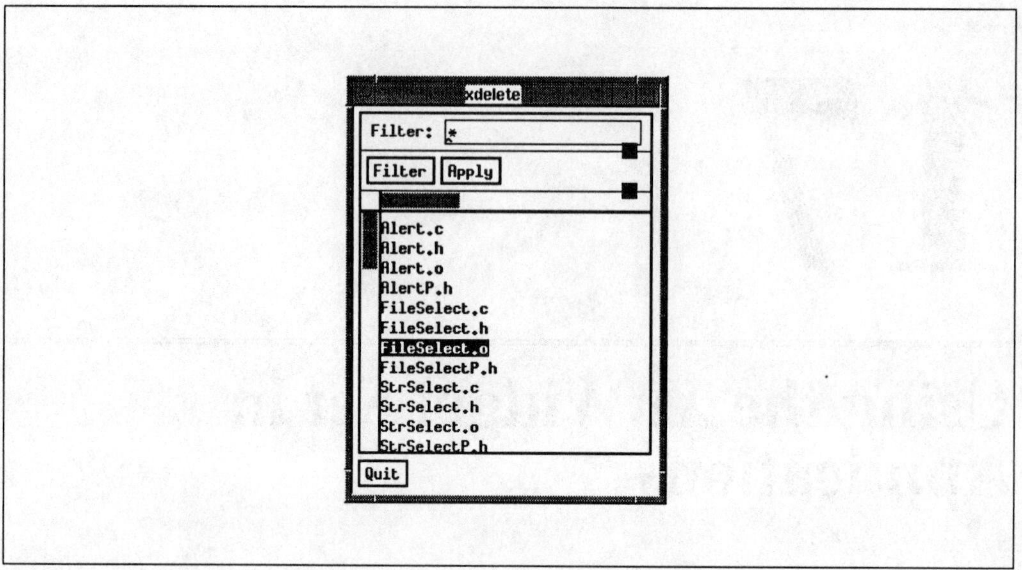

Figure 17.1 *xdelete*'s Top-level Window

```
perform the file deletion.
*/

void main(argc, argv)
int argc;
char **argv;
{
    Widget topLevel, alertShell, deleteBox, quitButton;
    Arg args[3];
    int i;

    topLevel = XtInitialize(argv[0], "XDelete",
        NULL, 0, &argc, argv);
    i = 0;
    XtSetArg(args[i], XtNallowShellResize, (XtArgVal) TRUE); i++;
    alertShell = XtCreatePopupShell("alertShell",
        transientShellWidgetClass, topLevel, args, i);
    i = 0;
    alertBox = XtCreateManagedWidget("alertBox",
        xiAlertWidgetClass, alertShell, args, i);
    XiAlertAddButton(alertBox, "Continue", 0, NULL, NULL);
    deleteBox = XtCreateManagedWidget("deleteBox", formWidgetClass,
        topLevel, NULL, 0);
    i = 0;
    XtSetArg(args[i], XiNrows, (XtArgVal) 20); i++;
    XtSetArg(args[i], XiNcolumns, (XtArgVal) 30); i++;
    deleteFileBox = XtCreateManagedWidget("deleteFileBox",
```

```
        xiFileSelectWidgetClass, deleteBox, args, i);
    XiFileSelectAddApplyProc(deleteFileBox, RemoveFile);
    i = 0;
    XtSetArg(args[i], XtNlabel, (XtArgVal) "Quit"); i++;
    XtSetArg(args[i], XtNfromVert, (XtArgVal) deleteFileBox); i++;
    quitButton = XtCreateManagedWidget("quitButton",
        commandWidgetClass, deleteBox, args, i);
    XtAddCallback(quitButton, XtNcallback, Quit, NULL);
    XtRealizeWidget(topLevel);
    XtMainLoop();
}   /* main */
```

alertBox and **deleteFileBox** are the principal widgets; they must be shared by **main()** and by the callback function **RemoveFile()**, thus they are defined as private widget IDs.

main() first creates the top-level application window, then its two children, **alertShell** and **deleteBox**. Next, **main()** creates **alertBox** as a child of **alertShell**, plus **deleteFileBox** and **quitButton** as children of **deleteBox**.

The public function **XiAlertAddButton()** adds a "Continue" button to the alert box, and **XiFileSelectAddApplyProc()** adds the **RemoveFile()** callback function to the file selection box. *xdelete* uses the alert box to display a simple message; hence, no callback function is registered with the "Continue" button.

RemoveFile() is activated when the user presses the "Apply" button in the file selection box:

```
/*
RemoveFile() unlinks the file specified by the current selection.
*/

void RemoveFile(w, client_data, call_data)
Widget w;
caddr_t client_data, call_data;
{
    char *filename = XiFileSelectGetSelection(deleteFileBox);

    if (!*filename) {
        XiAlertPopup(alertBox,
            "You must select a file first.",
            XiNOBEEP);
        return;
    }
    unlink(filename);
    XiFileSelectRefresh(deleteFileBox);
}   /* RemoveFile */
```

RemoveFile() uses three public functions: **XiAlertPopup()**, **XiFileSelectGetSelection()**, and **XiFileSelectRefresh()**. Note that the latter function must be called to refresh the file selection box, because the off-screen pixmap for the file selection box must be updated and the name of the deleted file should be removed from the window. **XiFileSelectRefresh()** is a high-level function—from the application's point of view, it makes sense that the file selection box must be updated after calling **unlink()**, because **unlink()** has no knowledge of the file selection box.

In this implementation of *xdelete* we used **unlink(2)** to remove files. As an alternative, you could develop a variation on *delete* from Chapter 10, say, *deleteq*, that does its work quietly (without prompts). The latter could be invoked by way of **system(3)**, so that accidental deletions could be undone with *xwaste*. Of course, this alternative implementation establishes a dependency between two applications, a dependency that we felt was unwarranted in the book.

The complete source code for *xdelete* is given in Appendix S.

17.2 *xconvert*: A Hexadecimal Conversion Utility

System programmers often need to convert integers from one base to another. A programmer's calculator typically provides this service as a central component of its data entry and display operations. In this section we discuss *xconvert*, a simple utility that performs base conversions, but no calculations.

We've mentioned *xconvert* on several occasions in earlier chapters; Figure 17.2 illustrates *xconvert* in operation. In this example, the user enters 255 as a decimal integer (Figure 17.2.a) and then converts it to its hexadecimal representation by selecting the new base and pressing "Convert" (Figure 17.2.b).

xconvert uses one Athena **Text** widget for text entry and display. It provides a "Clear" button so that the user can clear the display quickly without having to backspace over digits.

The "Convert" button performs the integer base conversion. Specifically, *xconvert* maintains a record of the currently selected base and the previously selected base. When the user presses "Convert", *xconvert* interprets the integer in the display based on the previously selected base, converting it to an integer representation in the currently selected base. Therefore, if a user enters an integer in the display without first selecting the proper (convert-from) base, this oversight can be corrected simply by selecting the convert-from base and then selecting the convert-to base before pressing "Convert". In particular, the user never has to reenter the integer because of failing to select the proper base first, a common annoyance with hand-held calculators.

xconvert uses the Athena widget set, plus **XiAlert**, **XiChoice**, and **XiSimpleText**. The latter widget implements a one-line text entry widget; it is a simple interface to the Athena **Text** widget class. Because **XiSimpleText** is a very simple widget class, it doesn't merit discussion in a separate chapter as did our other widgets. Its definition is given in Appendix U.

xconvert.c defines four convenience constants:

```
#define BIN 2
#define OCT 8
#define DEC 10
#define HEX 16
```

These constants are used to set up the choice widget, and throughout the program:

```
static XiChoiceItem item_list[] = { /* alphabetical ordering */
    {"Bin", BIN, UpdateBase, NULL},
```

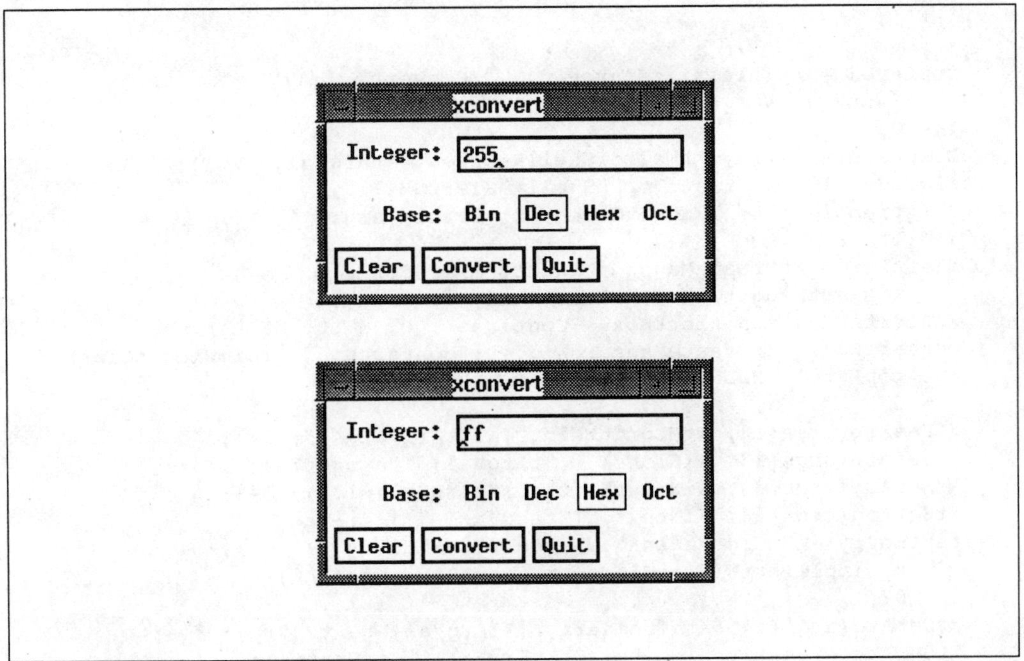

Figure 17.2 *xconvert*, a Hexadecimal Conversion Utility

```
    {"Dec", DEC, UpdateBase, NULL},
    {"Hex", HEX, UpdateBase, NULL},
    {"Oct", OCT, UpdateBase, NULL},
    {NULL, NULL, NULL, NULL},
};
```

Two private variables hold the current and previous numeric bases:

```
static int old_base = DEC, base = DEC;
```

Like *xdelete*, *xconvert* is rather small, therefore **main()** defines the widgets directly:

```
/*
main() builds the converter within a form widget.
*/

void main(argc, argv)
int argc;
char **argv;
{
    Widget topLevel, alertShell, convertBox, clearBtn, convertBtn,
        quitBtn;
    Arg args[10];
```

```
int i;

topLevel = XtInitialize(argv[0], "XConvert",
    NULL, 0, &argc, argv);
i = 0;
XtSetArg(args[i], XtNallowShellResize, (XtArgVal) TRUE); i++;
alertShell = XtCreatePopupShell("alertShell",
    transientShellWidgetClass, topLevel, args, i);
i = 0;
alertBox = XtCreateManagedWidget("alertBox",
    xiAlertWidgetClass, alertShell, args, i);
XiAlertAddButton(alertBox, "Continue", 0, NULL, NULL);
convertBox = XtCreateManagedWidget("convertBox", formWidgetClass,
    topLevel, NULL, 0);
i = 0;
XtSetArg(args[i], XtNborderWidth, (XtArgVal) 0); i++;
XtSetArg(args[i], XiNlabel, (XtArgVal) "Integer:"); i++;
XtSetArg(args[i], XiNtextWidth, (XtArgVal) 130); i++;
XtSetArg(args[i], XiNtext, (XtArgVal) ""); i++;
textEntry = XtCreateManagedWidget("textEntry",
    xiSimpleTextWidgetClass, convertBox, args, i);
i = 0;
XtSetArg(args[i], XtNfromVert, (XtArgVal) textEntry); i++;
XtSetArg(args[i], XiNlabel, (XtArgVal) "    Base:"); i++;
XtSetArg(args[i], XiNborderWidth, (XtArgVal) 0); i++;
XtSetArg(args[i], XiNitemBorderWidth, (XtArgVal) 0); i++;
XtSetArg(args[i], XiNexclusive, (XtArgVal) TRUE); i++;
XtSetArg(args[i], XiNdefaultItem, (XtArgVal) 2); i++;   /* DEC */
XtSetArg(args[i], XiNlabelOnLeft, (XtArgVal) TRUE); i++;
baseSelection = XtCreateManagedWidget("baseSelection",
    xiChoiceWidgetClass, convertBox, args, i);
XiChoiceAddItems(baseSelection, item_list);
i = 0;
XtSetArg(args[i], XtNfromVert, (XtArgVal) baseSelection); i++;
XtSetArg(args[i], XtNlabel, (XtArgVal) "Clear"); i++;
clearBtn = XtCreateManagedWidget("clearBtn",
    commandWidgetClass, convertBox, args, i);
XtAddCallback(clearBtn, XtNcallback, Clear, NULL);
i = 0;
XtSetArg(args[i], XtNfromVert, (XtArgVal) baseSelection); i++;
XtSetArg(args[i], XtNfromHoriz, (XtArgVal) clearBtn); i++;
XtSetArg(args[i], XtNlabel, (XtArgVal) "Convert"); i++;
convertBtn = XtCreateManagedWidget("convertBtn",
    commandWidgetClass, convertBox, args, i);
XtAddCallback(convertBtn, XtNcallback, Convert, NULL);
i = 0;
XtSetArg(args[i], XtNfromVert, (XtArgVal) baseSelection); i++;
XtSetArg(args[i], XtNfromHoriz, (XtArgVal) convertBtn); i++;
XtSetArg(args[i], XtNlabel, (XtArgVal) "Quit"); i++;
quitBtn = XtCreateManagedWidget("quitBtn",
    commandWidgetClass, convertBox, args, i);
XtAddCallback(quitBtn, XtNcallback, Quit, NULL);
```

```
    XtRealizeWidget(topLevel);
    XtMainLoop();
}   /* main */
```

main() defines a pop-up shell that houses the alert box, an **XiAlert** widget that's used to display a message, an **XiChoice** widget for selecting numeric bases, an **XiSimpleText** widget for the display and text entry area, plus Athena widgets that organize the top-level application window, including a button box for command buttons.

Most of **main()** is self-explanatory. We should, however, consider the statements associated with creating the text entry area and the choice box. **XiSimpleText** is a convenience widget. It allows an application programmer to set up a simple data entry area without having to consider the numerous differences between the Athena **Text** widget classes for Release 3 and Release 4. In particular, the different methods for establishing the text buffer are transparent when you use **XiSimpleText**. Essentially, an application defines a label, a width (in pixels) for the text entry box, and the initial text for the display:

```
i = 0;
XtSetArg(args[i], XtNborderWidth, (XtArgVal) 0); i++;
XtSetArg(args[i], XiNlabel, (XtArgVal) "Integer:"); i++;
XtSetArg(args[i], XiNtextWidth, (XtArgVal) 130); i++;
XtSetArg(args[i], XiNtext, (XtArgVal) ""); i++;
textEntry = XtCreateManagedWidget("textEntry",
    xiSimpleTextWidgetClass, convertBox, args, i);
```

XiSimpleText also supports a font resource, **XiNFont**, but in this application we're using the default font.

Parenthetically, **XiSimpleText** uses an arbitrary maximum size for the text buffer (256 characters). Alternatively, you could modify **XiSimpleText** such that it provides a resource for this parameter.

The second code segment from **main()** that we mention sets up the choice widget:

```
i = 0;
XtSetArg(args[i], XtNfromVert, (XtArgVal) textEntry); i++;
XtSetArg(args[i], XiNlabel, (XtArgVal) "    Base:"); i++;
XtSetArg(args[i], XiNborderWidth, (XtArgVal) 0); i++;
XtSetArg(args[i], XiNitemBorderWidth, (XtArgVal) 0); i++;
XtSetArg(args[i], XiNexclusive, (XtArgVal) TRUE); i++;
XtSetArg(args[i], XiNdefaultItem, (XtArgVal) 2); i++;   /* DEC */
XtSetArg(args[i], XiNlabelOnLeft, (XtArgVal) TRUE); i++;
baseSelection = XtCreateManagedWidget("baseSelection",
```

Note that we've requested a zero-width border for the choice box and its buttons; for applications where the options are quite simple, this approach provides a clean, uncluttered appearance. Also, *xconvert* enforces the exclusive selection policy. Except for a few integers, specifically, 0 through 9, an integer cannot be displayed in multiple bases simultaneously.

XiSimpleText also hides other Release 3 and Release 4 differences, for example, those associated with retrieving and updating the text buffer from within the application. **Clear()**, for example, calls **XiSimpleTextSetString()** to set the text buffer to a null string:

```
/*
Clear() clears out the display.
*/

void Clear(w, client_data, call_data)
Widget w;
caddr_t client_data, call_data;
{
   XiSimpleTextSetString(textEntry, "");
}  /* Clear */
```

Much of the work in *xconvert* takes place in the callback function **Convert()** that's associated with the "Convert" button:

```
/*
Convert() interprets the value in the display based on the
value of old_base, replacing the displayed value with the
converted value.
*/

void Convert(w, client_data, call_data)
Widget w;
caddr_t client_data, call_data;
{
   static char output[MAX_STR];
   char *text;
   int number, result;

   text = XiSimpleTextGetString(textEntry);
   if (!strlen(text))
      return;
   if (old_base == HEX)
      result = sscanf(text, "%x", &number);
   else if (old_base == OCT)
      result = sscanf(text, "%o", &number);
   else if (old_base == BIN)
      number = bin_str_to_integer(text, &result);
   else
      result = sscanf(text, "%d", &number);
   if (result == 0) {
      XiAlertPopup(alertBox,
         "Invalid data for the specified numeric base.",
         XiNOBEEP);
      return;
   }
   if (base == HEX)
      sprintf(output, "%x", number);
```

```
    else if (base == OCT)
        sprintf(output, "%o", number);
    else if (base == BIN)
        sprintf(output, "%s", integer_to_bin_str(number));
    else
        sprintf(output, "%d", number);
    XiSimpleTextSetString(textEntry, output);
}   /* Convert */
```

First, **XiSimpleTextGetString()** retrieves the string form of the integer in the display. Next, **Convert()** uses **sscanf()** and **sprintf()** to perform non-binary conversions. A support function, **bin_str_to_integer()**, performs conversions between a "binary string" and its integer representation; **integer_to_bin_str()** performs the complementary conversion. If the conversion is successful, **XiSimpleTextSetString()** updates the display.

Lastly, **UpdateBase()** is a callback function that's registered with each item in the choice widget:

```
void UpdateBase(w, client_data, call_data)
Widget w;
caddr_t client_data, call_data;
{
    old_base = base;
    base = XiChoiceGetValue(baseSelection,
        XiChoiceGetSelectedItem(baseSelection));
}   /* UpdateBase */
```

UpdateBase() simply updates the private variables that maintain a record of the current and previous integer base selections.

The complete source code for *xconvert* is given in Appendix T.

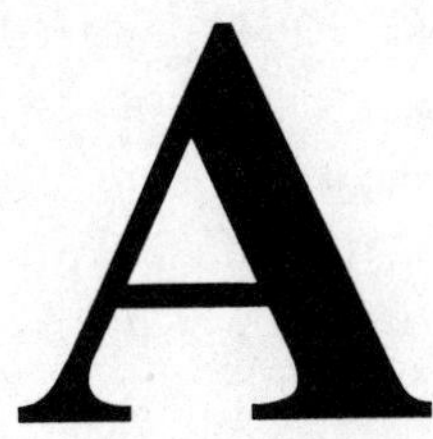

The Display Screen Module

```
/****  screen.h  ****  screen handling routines  ****/

/******************************************************************
*  Copyright (c) 1990 Iris Computing Laboratories.
*
*  This software is provided for demonstration purposes only.  As
*  freely-distributed, modifiable source code, this software carries
*  absolutely no warranty.
******************************************************************/


#ifndef SCREENH
#define SCREENH 1


#include <X11/Xlib.h>
#include <X11/Xutil.h>
#include <X11/Xos.h>

#include <stdio.h>


/*
globals:
*/

extern Display *display;
extern Screen *screen_ptr;
extern int screen;
extern unsigned int display_width, display_height, display_depth;
```

```
/*
Functions:
*/

extern void init_display();
extern void load_font();


#endif



/****  screen.c  ****  screen handling routines  ****/


#include "screen.h"


/*
globals:
*/

Display *display;
Screen *screen_ptr;
int screen;
unsigned int display_width, display_height, display_depth;


void init_display(application_name)
char *application_name;
{
    char *display_name = NULL;

    if ((display = XOpenDisplay(display_name)) == NULL) {
        (void) fprintf(stderr,
            "%s: cannot connect to X server %s\n",
            application_name, XDisplayName(display_name));
            exit(-1);
    }
    screen_ptr = display->screens;
    screen = DefaultScreen(display);

    display_width = DisplayWidth(display, screen);
    display_height = DisplayHeight(display, screen);
    display_depth = DisplayPlanes(display, screen);
}   /* init_display */


/*
load_font() loads the specified font, printing a message to
stderr in the event of an error.
*/

void load_font(font_info, application_name, font_name)
XFontStruct **font_info;
```

```
char *application_name;
char *font_name;
{
    if ((*font_info = XLoadQueryFont(display, font_name))
            == NULL) {
        (void) fprintf(stderr, "%s: cannot open %s font\n",
            application_name, font_name);
        exit(-1);
    }
}   /* load_font */
```

B

xclk: An X Window System Clock Application

```
/****  xclk.h  ****  constants for xclk.c  ****/


#include <stdio.h>
#include <string.h>
#include <ctype.h>
#include <X11/cursorfont.h>

#include "screen.h"


/*
xclk displays the time of day in the center of a
small window using a proportional font.
*/

#define BORDER_WIDTH      2

#define CLK_FONT          "ncenBI24"
#define HDR_FONT          "helvB14"

#define NORMAL            -1
#define REVERSE           -2

#define TRUE              1
#define FALSE             0
```

```
#define MAX_FONT_NAME   500

/*
Functions:
*/

void main(), cleanup_resources(), display_clock(),
    display_header(), update_clock(), set_up_GC(),
    set_up_size_hints(), process_font_options();
char *get_the_time();



/****  xclk.c  ****/

/*******************************************************************
*  Copyright (c) 1990 Iris Computing Laboratories.
*
*  This software is provided for demonstration purposes only.  As
*  freely-distributed, modifiable source code, this software carries
*  absolutely no warranty.
*******************************************************************/

/*
xclk displays the time in a small window, but only when
"prodded" to do so.  When the pointer enters the window,
the time is displayed; when the pointer exits the window,
the time is cleared.  A optional header is available for
use with uwm.
*/

#include "xclk.h"



/*
main() sets up the data structures, calls the display
routines, and then waits for the application to finish.
*/

void main(argc, argv)
int argc;
char *argv[];
{
    Window clk_win;
    XFontStruct *clk_font, *hdr_font;
    Cursor clk_cursor;
    GC gc, rgc;
    XSizeHints cw_size_hints;
    int has_hdr = FALSE, hdr_height = 0;    /* no header by default */
    int clk_width, clk_height;
    char hdr_font_name[MAX_FONT_NAME], clk_font_name[MAX_FONT_NAME];

    process_font_options(argc, argv, &has_hdr, hdr_font_name,
        clk_font_name);
    init_display(*argv);
    load_font(&hdr_font, *argv, hdr_font_name);
```

```
    load_font(&clk_font, *argv, clk_font_name);

    if (has_hdr) {
        hdr_height = hdr_font->max_bounds.ascent +
            hdr_font->max_bounds.descent;
        hdr_height += (hdr_height / 4);          /* add 25% */
    }
    set_up_size_hints(clk_font, &clk_width,
        &clk_height, hdr_height, &cw_size_hints);
    clk_win = XCreateSimpleWindow(display,
        RootWindow(display, screen), 0, 0,
        clk_width, clk_height, BORDER_WIDTH,
        BlackPixel(display, screen), WhitePixel(display, screen));
    XSetStandardProperties(display, clk_win, *argv, *argv,
        None, argv, argc, &cw_size_hints);
    XSelectInput(display, clk_win, ExposureMask | ButtonPressMask |
        EnterWindowMask | LeaveWindowMask);

    clk_cursor = XCreateFontCursor(display, XC_left_ptr);
    XDefineCursor(display, clk_win, clk_cursor);
    set_up_GC(&gc, clk_font, NORMAL);
    set_up_GC(&rgc, hdr_font, REVERSE);
    display_clock(clk_win, clk_font, hdr_font, gc, rgc,
        clk_width, clk_height, hdr_height);
    cleanup_resources(clk_win, clk_font, hdr_font, clk_cursor);
    exit(0);
}   /* main */


/*
process_font_options() parses the command line and
initializes font-related variables.
*/

void process_font_options(argc, argv, has_hdr, hdr_font_name,
    clk_font_name)
int argc;
char *argv[];
int *has_hdr;
char *hdr_font_name, *clk_font_name;
{
    int syntax_error = FALSE;
    char *app_name = argv[0];

    if (argc > 4) {
        fprintf(stderr,
        "usage: %s [-h] [-hf<header_font>] [-cf<clock_font>]\n",
            app_name);
        exit(-1);
    }
    strcpy(hdr_font_name, HDR_FONT);          /* the defaults */
    strcpy(clk_font_name, CLK_FONT);
    while (--argc > 0) {
        argv++;
        if (strlen(*argv) == 1)
            syntax_error = TRUE;
        if (strlen(*argv) == 2 && strcmp(*argv, "-h"))
```

```
            syntax_error = TRUE;
        if (strlen(*argv) > 2 &&
                (strncmp(*argv, "-hf", 3) &&
                    strncmp(*argv, "-cf", 3)))
            syntax_error = TRUE;

        if (strcmp(*argv, "-h") == 0)
            *has_hdr = TRUE;
        else if (strncmp(*argv, "-hf", 3) == 0) {
            strncpy(hdr_font_name, &(*argv)[3], MAX_FONT_NAME);
            *has_hdr = TRUE;
        }
        else if (strncmp(*argv, "-cf", 3) == 0)
            strncpy(clk_font_name, &(*argv)[3], MAX_FONT_NAME);
        else
            /* do nothing */;
    }
    if (syntax_error) {
        fprintf(stderr,
        "usage: %s [-h] [-hf<header_font>] [-cf<clock_font>]\n",
            app_name);
        exit(-1);
    }
}   /* process_font_options */


/*
display_clock() determines the time and displays it.
A button click terminates the event loop.
*/

void display_clock(clk_win, clk_font, hdr_font, gc, rgc,
    clk_width, clk_height, hdr_height)
Window clk_win;
XFontStruct *clk_font, *hdr_font;
GC gc, rgc;
int clk_width, clk_height, hdr_height;
{
    XEvent event;

    XMapRaised(display, clk_win);
    while (TRUE) {
        XNextEvent(display, &event);
        switch (event.type) {
            case Expose:
                display_header(clk_win, rgc, clk_width,
                    hdr_height, hdr_font);
                break;
            case EnterNotify:
                update_clock(clk_win, clk_font, gc, get_the_time(),
                    clk_width, clk_height, hdr_height);
                break;
            case LeaveNotify:
                update_clock(clk_win, clk_font, gc, NULL,
                    clk_width, clk_height, hdr_height);
                break;
            case ButtonPress:
```

```
                return;          /* terminate the program */
            }
        }
}   /* display_clock */


/*
display_header() displays a reverse video header with a
"neutral" title centered in the header.  Some window managers
will add a title bar with the application name.
*/

void display_header(clk_win, rgc, clk_width, hdr_height, hdr_font)
Window clk_win;
GC rgc;
int clk_width, hdr_height;
XFontStruct *hdr_font;
{
    char *label = "time";

    if (hdr_height == 0)
        return;
    XSetFunction(display, rgc, GXset);
    XFillRectangle(display, clk_win, rgc,
        0, 0, clk_width, hdr_height);
    XSetFunction(display, rgc, GXcopy);
    XDrawImageString(display, clk_win, rgc,
        (clk_width - XTextWidth(hdr_font, label, strlen(label))) / 2,
        hdr_height - (hdr_height / 4),      /* 25% */
        label, strlen(label));
}   /* display_header */


/*
update_clock() displays the time in the center of the non-
header window area.  Proportional fonts are OK.
*/

void update_clock(clk_win, clk_font, gc, time,
    clk_width, clk_height, hdr_height)
Window clk_win;
XFontStruct *clk_font;
GC gc;
char *time;
int clk_width, clk_height, hdr_height;
{
    if (time == NULL)
        XClearArea(display, clk_win, 0, hdr_height, 0, 0, FALSE);
    else {
        int x_pos, y_pos;

        x_pos =
            (clk_width - XTextWidth(clk_font, time, strlen(time))) /
            2;
        y_pos = clk_height - clk_font->max_bounds.ascent;
        XDrawImageString(display, clk_win, gc,
            x_pos, y_pos, time, strlen(time));
```

```
    }
}   /* update_clock */


/*
get_the_time() performs the time calculations,
and returns the result, stored in a local buffer.
*/

char *get_the_time()
{
    long tyme = time(0);
    struct tm *local_time = localtime(&tyme);
    int hour;
    static char char_time[20];

    hour = (int) local_time->tm_hour;
    if (hour == 0)
        hour = 12;
    else if (hour > 12)
        hour -= 12;
    sprintf(char_time, "%02d:%02d", hour, local_time->tm_min);
    return char_time;
}   /* get_the_time */


/*
set_up_GC() creates a GC that can be used by a system of
similar windows.  In addition, it initializes the current
font for the GC.
*/

void set_up_GC(gc, font, mode)
GC *gc;
XFontStruct *font;
int mode;
{
    *gc = XCreateGC(display, RootWindow(display, screen), 0, NULL);
    XSetFont(display, *gc, font->fid);
    if (mode == REVERSE) {
        XSetForeground(display, *gc, WhitePixel(display, screen));
        XSetBackground(display, *gc, BlackPixel(display, screen));
    }
    else {
        XSetForeground(display, *gc, BlackPixel(display, screen));
        XSetBackground(display, *gc, WhitePixel(display, screen));
    }
}   /* set_up_GC */


/*
cleanup_resources() performs an orderly clean-up
form the fonts, display, etc.
*/

void cleanup_resources(clk_win, clk_font, hdr_font, clk_cursor)
Window clk_win;
```

```
XFontStruct *clk_font, *hdr_font;
Cursor clk_cursor;
{
    XFreeCursor(display, clk_cursor);
    XDestroyWindow(display, clk_win);
    XUnloadFont(display, clk_font->fid);
    XUnloadFont(display, hdr_font->fid);
    XCloseDisplay(display);
}   /* cleanup_resources */


/*
set_up_size_hints() fills in the window dimensions.
xclk does not support resizing.
*/

void set_up_size_hints(clk_font, clk_width, clk_height,
    hdr_height, size_hints)
XFontStruct *clk_font;
int *clk_width;
int *clk_height;
int hdr_height;
XSizeHints *size_hints;
{
    char *time = get_the_time();

    size_hints->flags = PPosition | PSize | PMinSize | PMaxSize;
    size_hints->x = 0;
    size_hints->y = 0;
    *clk_width = XTextWidth(clk_font, time, strlen(time)) * 2;
    *clk_height = clk_font->max_bounds.ascent +
        clk_font->max_bounds.descent;
    *clk_height *= 2;
    *clk_height += hdr_height;
    size_hints->width = size_hints->min_width =
        size_hints->max_width = *clk_width;
    size_hints->height = size_hints->min_height =
        size_hints->max_height = *clk_height;
}   /* set_up_size_hints */
```

The Character and String Display Module

```
/****  display.h  ****  external declarations for display.c  ****/

/*******************************************************************
*  Copyright (c) 1990 Iris Computing Laboratories.
*
*  This software is provided for demonstration purposes only.  As
*  freely-distributed, modifiable source code, this software carries
*  absolutely no warranty.
*******************************************************************/


#ifndef DISPLAYH
#define DISPLAYH    1


extern void display_string();
extern void display_char();


#endif



/****  display.c  ****  X text display routines  ****/


#include "screen.h"
#include "display.h"
```

```
#define BLANK


/*
display_string() displays a string in a window.
*/

void display_string(display, drawable, gc, x, y, str)
Display *display;
Drawable drawable;
GC gc;
int x, y;
char *str;
{
    XDrawImageString(display, drawable, gc, x, y, str, strlen(str));
}   /* display_string */


/*
display_char() displays a character in a window.
*/

void display_char(display, drawable, gc, x, y, ch)
Display *display;
Drawable drawable;
GC gc;
int x, y;
char ch;
{
    char str[2];

    str[0] = ch;
    str[1] = '\0';
    XDrawImageString(display, drawable, gc, x, y, str, 1);
}   /* display_string */
```

The Text-oriented Window Module

```
/****    simplewin.h    ****/

/*******************************************************************
*  Copyright (c) 1990 Iris Computing Laboratories.
*
*  This software is provided for demonstration purposes only.  As
*  freely-distributed, modifiable source code, this software carries
*  absolutely no warranty.
*******************************************************************/


#ifndef SIMPLEWINH
#define SIMPLEWINH  1


#include <X11/cursorfont.h>
#include "screen.h"
#include "display.h"


#define TRUE                1           /* logical constants */
#define FALSE               0
#define CANT_ALLOCATE_WIN   -99

#define EOS                 '\0'        /* special characters */
#define LF                  '\n'

#define REVERSE             0
```

```
#define NORMAL              1


typedef struct {
    Window xwin;         /* the associated X window */
    void *extension;     /* pointer to whatever, e.g, buttons */
    XFontStruct *font;
    XSizeHints *size_hints;
    int cursor_x;
    int cursor_y;
    int font_height, font_width;
    unsigned int width, height, trunc_height;
    int is_active;
} logical_window_frame;


/*
Globals:
*/

extern GC gc, rgc, hgc;
extern Cursor popup_cursor;



/*
Functions:
*/

extern void initialize_window_structures();
extern void cleanup_window_structures();
extern void make_window();
extern void cleanup_window();
extern void set_up_GC();
extern void make_popup_cursor();
extern void activate_window();
extern void deactivate_window();
extern void window_puts();
extern void window_puts_center();
extern int window_puts_by_char();
extern void window_puts_lf();
extern int window_putchar();
extern void window_clr_eol();
extern void window_display_header();
extern void window_reverse_row();
extern int window_go_xy();
extern int window_go_cr();
extern void window_clr_rest();
extern void window_cursor_bottom();
extern int r_pos();
extern int c_pos();
extern int last_row();
extern int last_col();
extern int get_keystroke();
```

```
#endif


/****    simplewin.c    ****/


#include "simplewin.h"


/*
Globals:
*/

GC gc, rgc, hgc;                    /* used by all windows */
Cursor popup_cursor;



/*
initialize_window_structures() initializes data structures that
are shared by multiple windows -- module initialization.
*/

void initialize_window_structures(font)
XFontStruct *font;
{
    set_up_GC(&gc, font, NORMAL);
    set_up_GC(&rgc, font, REVERSE);
    set_up_GC(&hgc, font, NORMAL);
    XSetFunction(display, hgc, GXinvert);
    make_popup_cursor();
}   /* initialize_window_structures */


/*
cleanup_window_structures() frees/deletes module-level
window data structures.
*/

void cleanup_window_structures()
{
    XFreeCursor(display, popup_cursor);
    XFreeGC(display, gc);
    XFreeGC(display, rgc);
    XFreeGC(display, hgc);
}   /* cleanup_window_structures */


/*
make_window() creates an unmapped window.  It sets certain
components of the size_hints structure for that window, as a
convenience to the calling module.  It stores the X window
id as a member of the logical window data structure, lwin.
The window font is set by store_window_font_info().
*/
```

```
void make_window(parent, lwin, x, y, width, height,
    border_width, size_hints, font)
Window parent;
logical_window_frame *lwin;
int x, y;                       /* row/column metrics */
unsigned int width, height;
unsigned int border_width;
XSizeHints *size_hints;
XFontStruct *font;
{
    lwin->font_height =
        font->max_bounds.ascent + font->max_bounds.descent;
    width *= font->max_bounds.width;   /* convert to pixels */
    height *= lwin->font_height;
    height += font->max_bounds.descent;    /* bottom padding */
    lwin->xwin = XCreateSimpleWindow(display, parent, x, y,
        width, height, border_width, BlackPixel(display, screen),
        WhitePixel(display, screen));

    size_hints->flags = PPosition | PSize | PMinSize | PMaxSize;
    size_hints->x = x;
    size_hints->y = y;
    size_hints->width = width;
    size_hints->height = height;
    lwin->size_hints = size_hints; /* keep a reference to this */
    lwin->font = font;             /* keep a reference to this */

    lwin->width = width;           /* convenience variables */
    lwin->height = height;
    lwin->font_width = font->max_bounds.width;
    lwin->trunc_height =           /* without the padding */
        (lwin->height / lwin->font_height) * lwin->font_height;

    lwin->cursor_x = 0;
    lwin->cursor_y = lwin->font_height;   /* a little extra at top */
    lwin->is_active = FALSE;
    lwin->extension = NULL;
    XDefineCursor(display, lwin->xwin, popup_cursor);
    XSelectInput(display, lwin->xwin, ExposureMask |
        KeyPressMask | KeyReleaseMask |
        ButtonPressMask | ButtonReleaseMask | OwnerGrabButtonMask |
        EnterWindowMask | LeaveWindowMask | StructureNotifyMask);
}   /* make_window */


/*
cleanup_window() performs window-specific clean-up operations.
At present, the only structure is the window itself.
*/

void cleanup_window(lwin)
logical_window_frame *lwin;
{
    XDestroyWindow(display, lwin->xwin);
}  /* cleanup_window */
```

```
/*
set_up_GC() creates a GC that can be used by a system of
similar windows.  In addition, it initializes the current
font for the GC.
*/

void set_up_GC(gc, font, mode)
GC *gc;
XFontStruct *font;
int mode;
{
    *gc = XCreateGC(display, RootWindow(display, screen), 0, NULL);
    XSetFont(display, *gc, font->fid);
    if (mode == REVERSE) {
        XSetForeground(display, *gc, WhitePixel(display, screen));
        XSetBackground(display, *gc, BlackPixel(display, screen));
    }
    else {
        XSetForeground(display, *gc, BlackPixel(display, screen));
        XSetBackground(display, *gc, WhitePixel(display, screen));
    }
}   /* set_up_GC */


/*
make_popup_cursor() makes an arrow cursor.
*/

void make_popup_cursor()
{
    popup_cursor = XCreateFontCursor(display, XC_left_ptr);
}    /* make_popup_cursor */


/*
activate_window() maps the window to the top.  If there
is a message, it is dispalyed as a header.
*/

void activate_window(lwin, message)
logical_window_frame *lwin;
char *message;
{
    if (lwin->is_active)
        return;
    lwin->is_active = TRUE;
    XMapRaised(display, lwin->xwin);
    if (*message)
        window_display_header(lwin, message);
}    /* activate_window */


/*
deactivate_window() unmaps the window and resets
the cursor coordinates.
*/
```

```
void deactivate_window(lwin)
logical_window_frame *lwin;
{
    if (!lwin->is_active)
        return;
    lwin->is_active = FALSE;
    XUnmapWindow(display, lwin->xwin);
    lwin->cursor_y = lwin->font_height;
    lwin->cursor_x = 0;
}   /* deactivate_window */


/*
window_puts() prints a string in a window w/o
interpreting each character.
*/

void window_puts(lwin, str, gc)
logical_window_frame *lwin;
char *str;
GC gc;        /* allow normal or reverse video */
{
    display_string(display, lwin->xwin, gc,
        lwin->cursor_x, lwin->cursor_y, str);
}   /* window_puts */


/*
window_puts_center() centers a string in a window w/o
interpreting each character.
*/

void window_puts_center(lwin, str, gc)
logical_window_frame *lwin;
char *str;
GC gc;        /* allow normal or reverse video */
{
    int pad = (last_col(lwin) - strlen(str)) / 2;

    if (pad < 0)
        pad = 0;
    display_string(display, lwin->xwin, gc,
        lwin->cursor_x + (pad * lwin->font_width),
        lwin->cursor_y, str);
}   /* window_puts_center */


/*
window_puts_by_char() draws a string on a window by making
repeated calls to window_putchar().
*/

int window_puts_by_char(lwin, str)
logical_window_frame *lwin;
char *str;
{
```

```
    for ( ; *str; str++)
        window_putchar(lwin, *str);
    return TRUE;
}    /* window_puts_by_char */


/*
window_puts_lf() prints a string in a window on a
line-by-line basis, based on linefeed characters.
*/

void window_puts_lf(lwin, str, gc)
logical_window_frame *lwin;
register char *str;
GC gc;
{
    char *sub_string;

    sub_string = "";     /* null str ==> first loop not entered */
    while (*str) {
        sub_string = str;
        while (*str && *str != LF)
            str++;
        if (*str == LF) {
            *str = EOS;
            display_string(display, lwin->xwin, gc,
                lwin->cursor_x, lwin->cursor_y,
                sub_string);
            lwin->cursor_y += lwin->font_height;
            *str++ = LF;
        }
    }
    display_string(display, lwin->xwin, gc,
        lwin->cursor_x, lwin->cursor_y,
        sub_string);
}    /* window_puts_lf */


/*
window_putchar() prints a character in a window.
*/

int window_putchar(lwin, ch)
logical_window_frame *lwin;
char ch;
{
    if (ch == LF) {
        lwin->cursor_y += lwin->font_height;
        lwin->cursor_x = 0;
    }
    else {
        display_char(display, lwin->xwin, gc,
            lwin->cursor_x, lwin->cursor_y, ch);
        lwin->cursor_x += lwin->font_width;
    }
    return TRUE;
}    /* window_putchar */
```

```
/*
window_clr_eol() clears/overwrites the current line of a
window from the current position to the end of the line.
*/

void window_clr_eol(lwin)
logical_window_frame *lwin;
{
    XClearArea(display, lwin->xwin, lwin->cursor_x,
        lwin->cursor_y - lwin->font->max_bounds.ascent,
        lwin->width - lwin->cursor_x,
        lwin->font_height, FALSE);
}   /* window_clr_eol */


/*
window_display_header() can be used to display a left-justified
header on the top line of a window.
*/

void window_display_header(lwin, str)
logical_window_frame *lwin;
char *str;
{
    XSetFunction(display, rgc, GXset);
    XFillRectangle(display, lwin->xwin, rgc, 0, 0, lwin->width,
        lwin->font_height + lwin->font->max_bounds.descent);
    XSetFunction(display, rgc, GXcopy);
    display_string(display, lwin->xwin, rgc,
        lwin->font_width,
        lwin->font_height - lwin->font->max_bounds.descent, str);
}   /* window_display_header */


/*
window_reverse_row() displays a row in reverse video.
*/

void window_reverse_row(lwin)
logical_window_frame *lwin;
{
    XSetFunction(display, rgc, GXset);
    XFillRectangle(display, lwin->xwin, rgc, 0,
        lwin->cursor_y - lwin->font->max_bounds.ascent, lwin->width,
        lwin->font_height + lwin->font->max_bounds.descent);
    XSetFunction(display, rgc, GXcopy);
}   /* window_reverse_row */


/*
window_go_xy() sets the coordinates within a window in pixels.
*/

int window_go_xy(lwin, x, y)
logical_window_frame *lwin;
```

```
int x, y;
{
    if (x < 0 || x > lwin->width)
        return FALSE;
    if (y < 0 || y > lwin->height)
        return FALSE;
    lwin->cursor_x = x;
    lwin->cursor_y = y;
    return TRUE;
}   /* window_go_xy */


/*
window_go_cr() sets the coordinates within a window
in rows and columns.
*/

int window_go_cr(lwin, col, row)
logical_window_frame *lwin;
int col, row;
{
    if (col < 0 || (col * lwin->font_width) >
                (lwin->width - lwin->font_width))
        return FALSE;
    if (row < 0 || ((row + 1) * lwin->font_height) >
            lwin->trunc_height)
        return FALSE;
    window_go_xy(lwin, col * lwin->font_width,
        (row + 1) * lwin->font_height);
    return TRUE;
}    /* window_go_cr */


/*
window_clr_rest() clears the remainder of a window, relative
to the cursor, that is, current row-column coordinates.
*/

void window_clr_rest(lwin)
logical_window_frame *lwin;
{
    XClearArea(display, lwin->xwin, lwin->cursor_x,
        lwin->cursor_y - lwin->font->max_bounds.ascent,
        lwin->width - lwin->cursor_x,
        lwin->font_height, FALSE);
    XClearArea(display, lwin->xwin, 0,
        lwin->cursor_y + lwin->font->max_bounds.descent,
        0, 0, FALSE);
}   /* window_clr_rest */


/*
window_cursor_bottom() takes the cursor to the bottom line of
the window in font-based metrics.
*/

void window_cursor_bottom(lwin)
```

```
logical_window_frame *lwin;
{
    window_go_xy(lwin, lwin->cursor_x, (int) lwin->trunc_height);
}   /* window_cursor_bottom */


/*
r_pos() returns the current row (y-coordinate) within
a given window.
*/

int r_pos(lwin)
logical_window_frame *lwin;
{
    return (lwin->cursor_y / lwin->font_height) - 1;
}   /* r_pos */


/*
c_pos() returns the current column (x-coordinate) within
a given window.
*/

int c_pos(lwin)
logical_window_frame *lwin;
{
    return (lwin->cursor_x / lwin->font_width);
}   /* c_pos */


/*
last_row() returns the number of the last row in the
window, zero-based.
*/

int last_row(lwin)
logical_window_frame *lwin;
{
    return (lwin->trunc_height / lwin->font_height) - 1;
}    /* last_row */


/*
last_col() returns the number of the last column in the
window, zero-based.
*/

int last_col(lwin)
logical_window_frame *lwin;
{
    return (lwin->width / lwin->font_width) - 1;
}    /* last_col */


/*
get_keystroke() reads and returns a keystroke.
*/
```

```
int get_keystroke(event, keysym)
XEvent *event;
KeySym *keysym;      /* return the keysym */
{
    char text[20];
    int len;

    len = XLookupString(event, text, 20, keysym, 0);
    if (len == 1)
        return text[0];
    else
        return FALSE;
}   /* get_keystroke */
```

xdump: An X Window System Hex-dump Utility

```
/**  xdump.c  **  a simple hex-dump window w/o resize capability  **/

/*******************************************************************
*  Copyright (c) 1990 Iris Computing Laboratories.
*
*  This software is provided for demonstration purposes only.  As
*  freely-distributed, modifiable source code, this software carries
*  absolutely no warranty.
*******************************************************************/

#include <stdio.h>
#include <string.h>
#include <ctype.h>

#include "simplewin.h"


#define BORDER_WIDTH    2
#define NUM_ROWS        30
#define NUM_COLUMNS     78
#define FONT_SIZE       "8x13"



/*
Functions:
*/
```

```
void main(), hex_dump(), cleanup_resources();
int display_next_page(), build_next_page();
char *build_next_line();


/*
main() tests for command line errors, sets up the
data structures, calls hex_dump(), and then waits for
the application to finish.
*/

void main(argc, argv)
int argc;
char *argv[];
{
    logical_window_frame lwindow, *lwin = &lwindow;
    XFontStruct *font;
    XSizeHints dw_size_hints;
    FILE *dump_file;
    char *app_name = "xdump";

    if (argc != 2) {
        fprintf(stderr, "usage:  xdump <filename>\n");
        exit(-1);
    }
    if ((dump_file = fopen(argv[1], "rb")) == NULL) {
        fprintf(stderr, "Can't open input file %s\n", argv[1]);
        exit(-1);
    }
    init_display(app_name);
    load_font(&font, app_name, FONT_SIZE);
    initialize_window_structures(font);
    /* no support for resize */
    dw_size_hints.min_width = dw_size_hints.max_width =
        font->max_bounds.width * NUM_COLUMNS;
    make_window(RootWindow(display, screen), lwin, 0, 0,
        NUM_COLUMNS, NUM_ROWS, BORDER_WIDTH, &dw_size_hints, font);
    XSetStandardProperties(display, lwin->xwin, app_name, app_name,
        None, argv, argc, &dw_size_hints);
    hex_dump(dump_file, lwin, argv[1]);
    cleanup_resources(lwin, font);
    exit(0);
}   /* main */


/*
cleanup_resources() performs an orderly clean-up.
*/

void cleanup_resources(lwin, font)
logical_window_frame *lwin;
XFontStruct *font;
{
    cleanup_window_structures();
    cleanup_window(lwin);
```

```
    XUnloadFont(display, font->fid);
    XCloseDisplay(display);
}   /* cleanup_resources */


/*
hex_dump() manages the initial exposure, events, etc.
*/

void hex_dump(dump_file, dump_win, filename)
FILE *dump_file;
logical_window_frame *dump_win;
char *filename;
{
    char header[NUM_COLUMNS + 1];
    char next_page[NUM_ROWS - 2][NUM_COLUMNS + 1];
    int eof = FALSE, stop = FALSE;
    XEvent event;

    strcpy(header, "xdump:  ");
    strncat(header, filename, NUM_COLUMNS - 9);
    eof = build_next_page(dump_file, next_page);
    activate_window(dump_win, "");
    while (!stop) {
        XNextEvent(display, &event);
        switch (event.type) {
            case Expose:
                window_go_cr(dump_win, 1, 0);
                window_display_header(dump_win, header);
                window_go_cr(dump_win, 0, 1);
                display_next_page(dump_win, next_page, eof);
                break;
            case ButtonPress:
                if (!eof && event.xbutton.button == Button1) {
                    eof = build_next_page(dump_file, next_page);
                    display_next_page(dump_win, next_page, eof);
                }
                if (event.xbutton.button == Button3)
                    stop = TRUE;
                break;
        }
    }
    deactivate_window(dump_win);
}   /* hex_dump */


/*
display_next_page() clears the window and dumps the next page
from the file.  In particular, it manages overall file read
operations and builds 16-byte buffers/chunks of raw data for
processing by build_next_line().  If the last chunk is less
that 16 bytes, it must be padded with 0s.
*/

int display_next_page(dump_win, next_page, last_page)
logical_window_frame *dump_win;
char next_page[][NUM_COLUMNS + 1];
```

```
int last_page;
{
    int last = NUM_ROWS - 2, row;

    window_go_cr(dump_win, 0, 1);
    window_clr_rest(dump_win);
    for (row = 0; row < last; row++) {
        window_go_cr(dump_win, 1, row + 1);
        window_puts(dump_win, next_page[row], gc);
    }
    window_cursor_bottom(dump_win);
    if (!last_page) {
        window_reverse_row(dump_win);
        window_puts_center(dump_win,
            " <ClickLeft> for next page -- <ClickRight> to quit...",
            rgc);
    }
    else {
        window_clr_eol(dump_win);
        window_reverse_row(dump_win);
        window_puts_center(dump_win,
            " <ClickRight> to finish...", rgc);
    }
    return last_page;
}   /* display_next_page */


/*
build_next_page() builds a page of formatted output.
*/

int build_next_page(dump_file, next_page)
FILE *dump_file;
char next_page[][NUM_COLUMNS + 1];
{
    static int count = 0, last = NUM_ROWS - 2;
    int ch, i, last_page = FALSE, row;
    char char_buffer[16];

    for (row = 0; !last_page && row < last; row++) {
        for (i = 0; i < 16; i++) {              /* read file */
            if ((ch = getc(dump_file)) == EOF) {
                while (i < 16)
                    char_buffer[i++] = EOS;     /* pad buffer */
                last_page = TRUE;
                fclose(dump_file);
                break;
            }
            char_buffer[i] = (char) ch; /* just copy next byte */
        }
        strcpy(next_page[row], build_next_line(char_buffer, count));
        count++;
    }
    for ( ; last_page && row < last; row++)
        next_page[row][0] = EOS;
    return last_page;
}   /* build_next_page */
```

```
/*
build_next_line() builds the next line of hex-dumped output,
returning a pointer to the output line.  The output has
an assembler dump format.
*/

char *build_next_line(char_buffer, count)
char *char_buffer;
int count;
{
    static char dump_buffer[NUM_COLUMNS + 1];
    int i, j;

    sprintf(dump_buffer, "%05x ", count * 16);  /* change to + */
    for (i = 0, j = 6; i < 8; i++, j += 3)
        sprintf(&dump_buffer[j], " %02x", char_buffer[i]);
    sprintf(&dump_buffer[j], "--%02x", char_buffer[i++]);
    for (j += 4; i < 16; i++, j += 3)
        sprintf(&dump_buffer[j], " %02x", char_buffer[i]);
    sprintf(&dump_buffer[j], "  |");
    for (i = 0, j += 3; i < 8; i++, j++)
        sprintf(&dump_buffer[j], "%c",
            isprint(char_buffer[i]) ? char_buffer[i] : '.');
    sprintf(&dump_buffer[j], "-");
    for (j++; i < 16; i++, j++)
        sprintf(&dump_buffer[j], "%c",
            isprint(char_buffer[i]) ? char_buffer[i] : '.');
    sprintf(&dump_buffer[j], "|");
    dump_buffer[NUM_COLUMNS] = EOS;
    return dump_buffer;
}   /* build_next_line */
```

The Button-oriented Dialog Box Module

```
/****  dialog.h  ****  declarations for a simple dialog box  ****/

/*******************************************************************
*  Copyright (c) 1990 Iris Computing Laboratories.
*
*  This software is provided for demonstration purposes only.  As
*  freely-distributed, modifiable source code, this software carries
*  absolutely no warranty.
*******************************************************************/


#ifndef DIALOGH
#define DIALOGH 1


#include "simplewin.h"


#define BUTTON_BORDER_WIDTH      2
#define EOB                      -1


/*
The client can allocate an array of "buttons" to specify
the buttons for a dialog box.  The array should be NULL-
terminated.  If the button with the label value stored in
"label" is selected, the value of "value" is returned.
"value" MUST BE POSITIVE.
```

```
*/

typedef struct {
    char *label;
    int value;
} button;


typedef struct {
    Window bid;
    Window parent;
    char *label;
    int value;        /* value returned when a button selected */
    int x, y;         /* relative to parent */
    unsigned int width, height;
} lbutton;


/*
Functions:
*/

extern int make_dialog_buttons();
extern int dialog_loop();
extern void cleanup_dialog_structures();
extern void display_buttons();
extern void highlight_button();
extern void unhighlight_button();


#endif



/****  dialog.c  ****  a simple dialog box ****/

/*
The dialog box is built on top of the simplewin system, given
in simplewin.[ch].  This implementation provides a dialog box
header and optional secondary message, but supports
button-activated responses only.
*/

#include <stdio.h>
#include <string.h>
#include "dialog.h"


/*
Private functions:
*/

static int allocate_and_center_button_text();


/*
make_dialog_buttons() attaches a set of buttons to an existing
```

```
window derived from logical_window_frame; see simplewin.[ch].
Buttons are specified with the "button" structure; see dialog.h.
Buttons are spaced evenly in the dialog box, and button labels
are centered in equal-sized buttons.  All button-related internal
structures are allocated from the heap and attached to the
"extension" pointer in logical_window_frame.
*/

int make_dialog_buttons(lwin, buttons)
logical_window_frame *lwin;
button *buttons;
{
    int btn_x, btn_y, i, len, num_btn, most_chars;
    unsigned btn_width, btn_height;
    lbutton *btn_win;

    for (most_chars = num_btn = 0; buttons[num_btn].label;
            num_btn++)
        if ((len = strlen(buttons[num_btn].label)) > most_chars)
            most_chars = len;
    btn_win = (lbutton *)
        malloc((unsigned) ((num_btn + 1) * sizeof(lbutton)));
    if (btn_win == NULL)
        return FALSE;
    lwin->extension = (lbutton *) btn_win; /* attach to window */
    btn_y = lwin->height - lwin->font_height -
        lwin->font->max_bounds.descent - (BUTTON_BORDER_WIDTH * 5);
    btn_height = lwin->font_height +
        lwin->font->max_bounds.descent;
    btn_width = lwin->font_width * most_chars;
    for (i = 0; i < num_btn; i++) {
        btn_x = (lwin->width / (num_btn * 2)) -
            (btn_width / 2) + (i * (lwin->width / num_btn));
        btn_win[i].bid = XCreateSimpleWindow(display, lwin->xwin,
            btn_x, btn_y, btn_width, btn_height,
            BUTTON_BORDER_WIDTH,
            BlackPixel(display, screen),
            WhitePixel(display, screen));
        XDefineCursor(display, btn_win[i].bid, popup_cursor);
        XSelectInput(display, btn_win[i].bid, ExposureMask |
            EnterWindowMask | LeaveWindowMask |
            ButtonReleaseMask | ButtonPressMask |
            OwnerGrabButtonMask);
        if (!allocate_and_center_button_text(&btn_win[i], &buttons[i],
                most_chars)) {
            free(btn_win);
            for ( ; --i >=0; )
                free(btn_win[i].label);
            return FALSE;
        }
        btn_win[i].value = buttons[i].value;
        btn_win[i].parent = lwin->xwin;
        btn_win[i].x = btn_x;
        btn_win[i].y = btn_y;
        btn_win[i].width = btn_width;
        btn_win[i].height = btn_height;
    }   /* for */
```

```
    btn_win[i].bid = EOB;   /* logically terminate  */
                            /* the set of buttons   */
    XMapSubwindows(display, lwin->xwin);
    return TRUE;
}   /* make_dialog_buttons */


/*
allocate_and_center_button_text() creates private (safe)
copies of the client's button text strings.
*/

static int allocate_and_center_button_text(btn_win,
    btn_data, max_len)
lbutton *btn_win;
button *btn_data;
int max_len;
{
    int j, pad_len;

    j = strlen(btn_data->label);        /* center each button */
    pad_len = (max_len - j) / 2;
    btn_win->label = (char *) malloc((unsigned) (j + pad_len + 1));
    if (btn_win->label == NULL)
        return FALSE;
    for ( ; j > -1; j--)
        btn_win->label[j + pad_len] = btn_data->label[j];
    for (j = 0; j < pad_len; j++)
        btn_win->label[j] = ' ';
    return TRUE;
}   /* allocate_and_center_button_text */


/*
dialog_loop() loops over the input and returns the
value associated with the activated button.
*/

int dialog_loop(lwin, header, message)
logical_window_frame *lwin;
char *header, *message;
{
    lbutton *btn_win = (lbutton *) lwin->extension;
    XEvent event;
    int i;

    if (btn_win == NULL)
        return FALSE;
    activate_window(lwin, "");
    while (TRUE) {
        XNextEvent(display, &event);
        switch (event.type) {
            case Expose:
                while (XCheckTypedWindowEvent(display, lwin->xwin,
                        Expose, &event))
                    ;
                if (event.xexpose.window == lwin->xwin) {
```

```
                    window_display_header(lwin, header);
                    window_go_cr(lwin, 1, 2);
                    window_puts(lwin, message, gc);
                    display_buttons(lwin, gc);
                }
                break;
            case EnterNotify:
                for (i = 0; btn_win[i].bid != EOB; i++)
                    if (event.xcrossing.window == btn_win[i].bid) {
                        highlight_button(&btn_win[i]);
                        break;
                    }
                break;
            case LeaveNotify:
                for (i = 0; btn_win[i].bid != EOB; i++)
                    if (event.xcrossing.window == btn_win[i].bid) {
                        unhighlight_button(&btn_win[i]);
                        break;
                    }
                break;
            case ButtonRelease:
                for (i = 0; btn_win[i].bid != EOB; i++) {
                    if (event.xbutton.window == btn_win[i].bid) {
                        unhighlight_button(&btn_win[i]);
                        deactivate_window(lwin);
                        return btn_win[i].value;
                    }
                }
                break;
        }
    }
}   /* dialog_loop */


/*
cleanup_dialog_button_structures() first frees the heap space
used for labels, and then frees the heap-based array.
*/

void cleanup_dialog_button_structures(lwin)
logical_window_frame *lwin;
{
    int i;
    lbutton *btn_win = (lbutton *) lwin->extension;

    if (btn_win == NULL)
        return;
    for (i = 0; btn_win[i].bid != EOB; i++)
        free(btn_win[i].label);
    free(lwin->extension);
    XDestroySubwindows(display, lwin->xwin);
}   /* cleanup_dialog_button_structures */


/*
display_buttons() is a public routine used by display_loop()
to display the buttons' text.  X displays the buttons' borders.
```

```
*/

void display_buttons(lwin, gc)
logical_window_frame *lwin;
GC gc;
{
    int i;
    lbutton *btn_win = (lbutton *) lwin->extension;

    if (btn_win == NULL)
        return;
    for (i = 0; btn_win[i].bid != EOB; i++)
        XDrawImageString(display, btn_win[i].bid, gc,
            0, lwin->font_height - 1, btn_win[i].label,
            strlen(btn_win[i].label));
}   /* display_buttons */


/*
highlight_buttons() is a public routine that draws a one
pixel wide rectangle on the inside of the window.
*/

void highlight_button(bw)
lbutton *bw;
{
    XDrawRectangle(display, bw->bid, hgc, 0, 0,
        bw->width - 1, bw->height - 1);
}   /* highlight_button */


/*
unhighlight_button() is a public routine that erases the
one pixel wide rectangle inside the button border.
*/

void unhighlight_button(bw)
lbutton *bw;
{
    XDrawRectangle(display, bw->bid, hgc, 0, 0,
        bw->width - 1, bw->height - 1);
}   /* unhighlight_button */


/****  testdialog.c  ****  tests a simple dialog box  ****/


#include <stdio.h>
#include <string.h>

#include "simplewin.h"
#include "dialog.h"


/*
Functions:
```

```
*/

void main(), cleanup_resources();


/*
main() initializes the display, creates the dialog box
and tests the returned value.
*/

void main(argc, argv)
int argc;
char *argv[];
{
    static button buttons[] = {
        {"Button One", 1},
        {"Button Two", 2},
        {"Button Three", 3},
        {NULL, NULL},
    };
    logical_window_frame lwindow, *lwin = &lwindow;
    XSizeHints test_size_hints;
    XFontStruct *font;
    char *application_name = "testdialog";
    int button_result;

    init_display(application_name);
    load_font(&font, application_name, "8x13");
    initialize_window_structures(font);
    test_size_hints.min_width = 47 * font->max_bounds.width;
    test_size_hints.min_height =
        7 * (font->max_bounds.ascent + font->max_bounds.descent);
    make_window(RootWindow(display, screen), lwin, 0, 0,
        47, 7, 1, &test_size_hints, font);
    XSetStandardProperties(display, lwin->xwin, application_name,
        application_name, None, argv, argc, &test_size_hints);
    if (!make_dialog_buttons(lwin, buttons)) {
        fprintf(stderr, "%s: can't create window buttons!\n",
            application_name);
        exit(-1);
    }
    button_result = dialog_loop(lwin,
        "This is the test window.",
        "Press a button.");
    fprintf(stdout, "You pressed button: %d\n", button_result);
    cleanup_resources(lwin, font);
    exit(0);
}   /* main */


/*
cleanup_resources() performs an orderly clean-up.
*/

void cleanup_resources(lwin, font)
logical_window_frame *lwin;
XFontStruct *font;
```

```
{
    cleanup_dialog_button_structures(lwin);
    cleanup_window_structures();
    cleanup_window(lwin);
    XUnloadFont(display, font->fid);
    XCloseDisplay(display);
}   /* cleanup_resources */



/****  response.h  ****  declarations for response.c  ****/

/*********************************************************************
*  Copyright (c) 1990 Iris Computing Laboratories.
*
*  This software is provided for demonstration purposes only.  As
*  freely-distributed, modifiable source code, this software carries
*  absolutely no warranty.
*********************************************************************/


#ifndef RESPONSEH
#define RESPONSEH   1


#include <X11/cursorfont.h>
#include "simplewin.h"


#define TRUE                    1           /* logical constants */
#define FALSE                   0

#define EOS                     '\0'        /* special characters */
#define LF                      '\n'
#define TAB                     '\t'
#define BKSP                    '\b'
#define BLANK                   ' '
#define ESC                     27


#define MAX_STR                 80
#define ESC_KEY                 -1


/*
Functions:
*/

extern void initialize_responsebox_structures();
extern void cleanup_responsebox_structures();
extern int responsebox_loop();


/*
responsebox_loop() returns:
    ESC_KEY         -- user pressed <Esc>
    TRUE            -- user pressed <Return>
```

```
    <pos. value>  -- user pressed a button
*/

#endif



/****  response.c  ****  a simple char. input response box  ****/

/*
The response box is built on top of the simplewin and dialog
modules.  It provides routines to read a string response from
the user, in addition to the button support provided by the
dialog module.  See simplewin.[ch] and dialog.[ch].
*/

#include <X11/keysym.h>
#include "dialog.h"
#include "response.h"

#include "point.bit"
#include "savepoint.bit"



/*
Globals:
*/

static Pixmap point, save_point;


/*
Private functions:
*/

static void make_point();
static void backspace_char();
static void echo_char();
static void window_no_point();
static void window_put_point();
static void window_puts_point();
static int window_gets_filter();
static int window_getche_event_loop();
static int window_getche();
static void window_display_char_with_point();



/*
initialize_responsebox_structures() sets up the
data structures needed to support the response box
in a window.
*/

void initialize_responsebox_structures(font)
XFontStruct *font;
```

```
{
    initialize_window_structures(font);
    make_point();
}   /* initialize_responsebox_structures */


/*
cleanup_responsebox_structures() frees dynamic
data structures.
*/

void cleanup_responsebox_structures()
{
    cleanup_window_structures();
    XFreePixmap(display, point);
    XFreePixmap(display, save_point);
}   /* cleanup_responsebox_structures */


/*
responsebox_loop() processed key and button input.
It returns the value associated with the selected button.
*/

int responsebox_loop(lwin, header, message, response)
logical_window_frame *lwin;
char *header, *message, *response;
{
    lbutton *btn_win = (lbutton *) lwin->extension;
    XEvent event;
    int btn_result = FALSE, key_result = FALSE;
    int i, terminate = FALSE;

    activate_window(lwin, "");
    while (!terminate) {
        XNextEvent(display, &event);
        switch (event.type) {
            case Expose:
                while (XCheckTypedWindowEvent(display, lwin->xwin,
                        Expose, &event))
                    ;
                if (event.xexpose.window == lwin->xwin) {
                    window_display_header(lwin, header);
                    window_go_cr(lwin, 1, 2);
                    window_clr_eol(lwin);
                    window_puts_point(lwin, message, gc);
                    *response = EOS;
                    display_buttons(lwin, gc);
                }
                break;
            case KeyPress:
                XPutBackEvent(display, &event);
                key_result =
                    window_gets_filter(lwin, response, MAX_STR,
                        header, message);
                terminate = TRUE;
                break;
```

```
            case EnterNotify:
                if (btn_win == NULL)
                    break;
                for (i = 0; btn_win[i].bid != EOB; i++)
                    if (event.xcrossing.window == btn_win[i].bid) {
                        highlight_button(&btn_win[i]);
                        break;
                    }
                break;
            case LeaveNotify:
                if (btn_win == NULL)
                    break;
                for (i = 0; btn_win[i].bid != EOB; i++)
                    if (event.xcrossing.window == btn_win[i].bid) {
                        unhighlight_button(&btn_win[i]);
                        break;
                    }
                break;
            case ButtonRelease:
                if (btn_win == NULL)
                    break;
                for (i = 0; btn_win[i].bid != EOB; i++) {
                    if (event.xbutton.window == btn_win[i].bid) {
                        unhighlight_button(&btn_win[i]);
                        btn_result = btn_win[i].value;
                        terminate = TRUE;
                    }
                }
                break;
        }   /* switch */
    }   /* while */
    deactivate_window(lwin);
    if (btn_result)
        return btn_result;
    else
        return (!key_result) ? ESC_KEY : key_result;
}   /* responsebox_loop */


/*
make_point() makes a window point/cursor
that can be used for keyboard processing.
*/

static void make_point()
{
    if (display_depth == 1) {
        point = XCreateBitmapFromData(display,
            RootWindow(display, screen),
            point_bits, point_width, point_height);
        save_point = XCreateBitmapFromData(display,
            RootWindow(display, screen), savepoint_bits,
            savepoint_width, savepoint_height);
    }
    else {
        point = XCreatePixmapFromBitmapData(display,
            RootWindow(display, screen),
```

```
            point_bits, point_width, point_height,
            BlackPixel(display, screen), WhitePixel(display, screen),
            display_depth);
        save_point = XCreatePixmapFromBitmapData(display,
            RootWindow(display, screen), savepoint_bits,
            savepoint_width, savepoint_height,
            BlackPixel(display, screen), WhitePixel(display, screen),
            display_depth);
    }
}    /* make_point */


/*
The following two functions are used to display and "un-display"
the software-maintained cursor.
*/

static void window_no_point(lwin)
logical_window_frame *lwin;
{
    XCopyArea(display, save_point, lwin->xwin, gc, 0, 0,
        point_width, point_height, lwin->cursor_x - 2,
        lwin->cursor_y + 2);
}    /* window_no_point */


static void window_put_point(lwin)
logical_window_frame *lwin;
{
    XCopyArea(display, lwin->xwin, save_point, gc,
        lwin->cursor_x - 2, lwin->cursor_y + 2,
        point_width, point_height, 0, 0);
    XCopyArea(display, point, lwin->xwin, gc, 0, 0,
        point_width, point_height, lwin->cursor_x - 2,
        lwin->cursor_y + 2);
}    /* window_put_point */


/*
window_puts_point() prints a string, followed by the point,
in a window w/o interpreting each character.
*/

static void window_puts_point(lwin, str, gc)
logical_window_frame *lwin;
char *str;
GC gc;          /* allow normal or reverse video */
{
    int text_width;

    window_puts(lwin, str, gc);
    text_width = XTextWidth(lwin->font, str, strlen(str));
    lwin->cursor_x += text_width;
    window_go_xy(lwin, lwin->cursor_x, lwin->cursor_y);
    window_put_point(lwin);
}   /* window_puts_point */
```

```
/*
window_gets_filter() reads a string from a window, up to some maximum
limit, as long as printable ASCII characters are entered.  If <Esc>
is pressed, it returns FALSE.
*/

static int window_gets_filter(lwin, str, limit, header, message)
logical_window_frame *lwin;
char *str;
int limit; /* the max. number of chars. that can be read. */
char *header;
char *message;
{
    lbutton *btn_win = (lbutton *) lwin->extension;
    XEvent event;
    KeySym keysym;
    char ch, *temp, *start;
    int i, j, row, col;

    temp = start = str;
    for (i = 0, row = r_pos(lwin), col = c_pos(lwin), limit--;
            i < limit; ) {
        XNextEvent(display, &event);
        switch (event.type) {
            case Expose:
                while (XCheckTypedWindowEvent(display,
                        lwin->xwin, Expose, &event))
                    ;
                if (event.xexpose.window == lwin->xwin) {
                    *str = EOS;
                    window_display_header(lwin, header);
                    window_go_cr(lwin, 1, 2);
                    window_clr_eol(lwin);
                    window_puts(lwin, message, gc);
                    window_go_cr(lwin, col, row);
                    window_puts_point(lwin, start, gc);
                    display_buttons(lwin, gc);
                }
                break;
            case ButtonPress:
                break;
            case ButtonRelease:
                if (btn_win == NULL) {
                    *start = EOS;
                    return FALSE;
                }
                else {
                    *str = EOS;
                    for (j = 0; btn_win[j].bid != EOB; j++)
                        if (event.xbutton.window == btn_win[j].bid)
                            return btn_win[j].value;
                }
                break;
            case KeyPress:
                ch = (char) window_getche(lwin, &event, &keysym);
                if (keysym == XK_Escape) {
```

```
                    *start = EOS;           /* return a null string */
                    return FALSE;
                }
                else if (keysym == XK_BackSpace ||
                        keysym == XK_Delete) {
                    if (str > temp) {
                        str--;
                        i--;
                        backspace_char(lwin);
                    }
                }
                else if (keysym == XK_Return) {
                    *str = EOS;
                    return TRUE;
                }
                else if (keysym >= XK_space &&
                        keysym <= XK_asciitilde) {
                    *str = ch;
                    str++;
                    i++;
                }   /* end if-then-else */
                break;
            default:
                break;
        }   /* end switch */
    }   /* end for loop */
    if (i == limit)         /* reached limit, terminate string */
        *str = EOS;
    return TRUE;
}   /* window_gets_filter */


/*
backspace_char() attempts to remove the previously entered
character from the "buffer."
*/

static void backspace_char(lwin)
logical_window_frame *lwin;
{
    window_no_point(lwin);
    lwin->cursor_x -= lwin->font_width;
    if (lwin->cursor_x < 0)
        lwin->cursor_x = 0;
    display_char(display, lwin->xwin, gc,
        lwin->cursor_x, lwin->cursor_y, BLANK);
    window_put_point(lwin);
}   /* backspace_char */


/*
window_getche() reads a character from a window, with echo.
*/

static int window_getche(lwin, event, keysym)
logical_window_frame *lwin;
XEvent *event;
```

```
KeySym *keysym;
{
    int key, return_key;

    window_go_xy(lwin, lwin->cursor_x, lwin->cursor_y);
    key = get_keystroke(event, keysym);
    if (*keysym == XK_Escape)
        return_key = ESC;
    else if (*keysym == XK_Return)
        return_key = LF;
    else if (*keysym == XK_BackSpace || *keysym == XK_Delete)
        return_key = BKSP;
    else if (*keysym == XK_Tab)
        return_key = TAB;
    else if (*keysym >= XK_space && *keysym <= XK_asciitilde) {
        echo_char(lwin, (char) key);
        return_key = key;
    }
    else
        return_key = FALSE;
    if (lwin->cursor_y < 0)
        lwin->cursor_y = 0;
    if (lwin->cursor_y > lwin->height)
        lwin->cursor_y -= lwin->font_height;
    window_go_xy(lwin, lwin->cursor_x, lwin->cursor_y);
    return return_key;
}   /* window_getche */


/*
window_getche_event_loop() reads a character from a window, with echo
in an event loop.
*/

static int window_getche_event_loop(lwin)
logical_window_frame *lwin;
{
    XEvent event;
    KeySym keysym;
    int key, kontinue = TRUE;

    while (kontinue) {
        XNextEvent(display, &event);
        switch (event.type) {
            case KeyPress:
                key = window_getche(lwin, &event, &keysym);
                kontinue = FALSE;
                break;
            default:
                break;
        }
    }   /* end event loop */
    return key;
}   /* window_getche_event_loop */


/*
```

```
echo_char() echos a character to the screen.
*/

static void echo_char(lwin, ch)
logical_window_frame *lwin;
char ch;
{
    if (lwin->cursor_x < lwin->width)
        window_display_char_with_point(lwin, ch);
}   /* echo_char */


/*
window_display_char_with_point() implements the display of a software-
based keyboard cursor to accompany each displayed character.
*/

static void window_display_char_with_point(lwin, ch)
logical_window_frame *lwin;
char ch;
{
    window_no_point(lwin);
    display_char(display, lwin->xwin, gc,
        lwin->cursor_x, lwin->cursor_y, ch);
    lwin->cursor_x += lwin->font_width;
    window_put_point(lwin);
}    /* window_display_char_with_point */



/****  testresponse.c  ****  tests the response box  ****/


#include <stdio.h>
#include <string.h>

#include "dialog.h"
#include "response.h"


#define APPLY   1               /* button responses */
#define CANCEL  2



/*
Functions:
*/

void main(), cleanup_resources();


/*
main() initializes the display, creates the response box
(window), and acts on the returned value;
```

```
*/

void main(argc, argv)
int argc;
char *argv[];
{
    static button buttons[] = {     /* positive values only */
        {"Apply", APPLY},
        {"Cancel", CANCEL},
        {NULL, NULL},
    };
    logical_window_frame lwindow, *lwin = &lwindow;
    XSizeHints test_size_hints;
    XFontStruct *font;
    char *application_name = "testresponse";
    char filename[MAX_STR];
    int result;

    init_display(application_name);
    load_font(&font, application_name, "8x13");
    initialize_responsebox_structures(font);
    test_size_hints.min_width = 47 * font->max_bounds.width;
    test_size_hints.min_height =
        7 * (font->max_bounds.ascent + font->max_bounds.descent);
    make_window(RootWindow(display, screen), lwin, 0, 0,
        47, 7, 1, &test_size_hints, font);
    XSetStandardProperties(display, lwin->xwin, application_name,
        application_name, None, argv, argc, &test_size_hints);
    if (!make_dialog_buttons(lwin, buttons)) {
        fprintf(stderr, "%s: can't create window buttons!\n",
            application_name);
        exit(-1);
    }
    result = responsebox_loop(lwin, "File Print Facility",
        "Filename: ", filename);
    if (result == CANCEL || result == ESC_KEY)
        fprintf(stdout, "Print canceled.\n");
    else if (!strlen(filename))
        fprintf(stdout, "Invalid filename; print canceled.\n");
    else
        fprintf(stdout, "Print simulation for file: %s\n", filename);
    cleanup_resources(lwin, font);
    exit(0);
}   /* main */


/*
cleanup_resources() performs an orderly clean-up.
*/

void cleanup_resources(lwin, font)
logical_window_frame *lwin;
XFontStruct *font;
{
    cleanup_dialog_button_structures(lwin);
    cleanup_responsebox_structures();
    cleanup_window(lwin);
```

```
    XUnloadFont(display, font->fid);
    XCloseDisplay(display);
}   /* cleanup_resources */


#define savepoint_width 9
#define savepoint_height 5
static char savepoint_bits[] = {
   0x00, 0x00, 0x00, 0x00, 0x00, 0x00, 0x00, 0x00, 0x00, 0x00};


#define point_width 9
#define point_height 5
static char point_bits[] = {
   0x10, 0x00, 0x38, 0x00, 0x7c, 0x00, 0xfe, 0x00, 0xff, 0x01};
```

G

Dialog Boxes with Support for Callback Functions

```
/****  cbdialog.h  ****  declarations for a simple dialog box  ****/

/******************************************************************
*  Copyright (c) 1990 Iris Computing Laboratories.
*
*  This software is provided for demonstration purposes only.  As
*  freely-distributed, modifiable source code, this software carries
*  absolutely no warranty.
******************************************************************/


#ifndef CBDIALOGH
#define CBDIALOGH   1


#include "simplewin.h"


#define BUTTON_BORDER_WIDTH     2
#define EOB                     -1


/*
The client can allocate an array of "buttons" to specify
the buttons for a dialog box.  The array should be NULL-
terminated.  If the button with the callback procedure
stored in "callback" is selected, the callback procedure
is executed.
```

```
*/

typedef void (*ptr_void_proc)();

typedef struct {
    char *label;
    ptr_void_proc callback;
} button;


typedef struct {
    Window bid;
    Window parent;
    char *label;
    ptr_void_proc callback; /* (ptr. to) procedure to   */
                            /* execute upon selection   */
    int x, y;               /* relative to parent */
    unsigned int width, height;
} lbutton;


extern int make_dialog_buttons();
extern int dialog_loop();
extern void display_buttons();
extern void highlight_button();
extern void unhighlight_button();
extern void cleanup_dialog_structures();


#endif



/****  cbdialog.c  ****  a simple dialog box ****/

/*
The dialog box is built on top of the simplewin system, given
in simplewin.[ch].  This implementation provides a dialog box
header and optional secondary message, but supports button-
activated responses only.  If a callback is associated with
the selected button, it will be executed and TRUE will be
returned; otherwise FALSE is returned.
*/

#include <stdio.h>
#include <string.h>
#include "cbdialog.h"


/*
Private functions:
*/

static int allocate_and_center_button_text();
```

```
/*
make_dialog_buttons() attaches a set of buttons to an existing
window derived from logical_window_frame; see simplewin.[ch].
Buttons are specified with the "button" structure; see dialog.h.
Buttons are spaced evenly in the dialog box, and button labels
are centered in equal-sized buttons.  All button-related internal
structures are allocated from the heap and attached to the
"extension" pointer in logical_window_frame.
*/

int make_dialog_buttons(lwin, buttons)
logical_window_frame *lwin;
button *buttons;
{
    int btn_x, btn_y, i, len, num_btn, most_chars;
    unsigned btn_width, btn_height;
    lbutton *btn_win;

    for (most_chars = num_btn = 0; buttons[num_btn].label;
            num_btn++)
        if ((len = strlen(buttons[num_btn].label)) > most_chars)
            most_chars = len;
    btn_win = (lbutton *)
        malloc((unsigned) ((num_btn + 1) * sizeof(lbutton)));
    if (btn_win == NULL)
        return FALSE;
    lwin->extension = (lbutton *) btn_win; /* attach to window */
    btn_y = lwin->height - lwin->font_height -
        lwin->font->max_bounds.descent - (BUTTON_BORDER_WIDTH * 5);
    btn_height = lwin->font_height +
        lwin->font->max_bounds.descent;
    btn_width = lwin->font_width * most_chars;
    for (i = 0; i < num_btn; i++) {
        btn_x = (lwin->width / (num_btn * 2)) -
            (btn_width / 2) + (i * (lwin->width / num_btn));
        btn_win[i].bid = XCreateSimpleWindow(display, lwin->xwin,
            btn_x, btn_y, btn_width, btn_height,
            BUTTON_BORDER_WIDTH,
            BlackPixel(display, screen),
            WhitePixel(display, screen));
        XDefineCursor(display, btn_win[i].bid, popup_cursor);
        XSelectInput(display, btn_win[i].bid, ExposureMask |
            EnterWindowMask | LeaveWindowMask |
            ButtonReleaseMask | ButtonPressMask |
            OwnerGrabButtonMask);
        if (!allocate_and_center_button_text(&btn_win[i],
                &buttons[i], most_chars)) {
            free(btn_win);
            for ( ; --i >=0; )
                free(btn_win[i].label);
            return FALSE;
        }
        btn_win[i].callback = *buttons[i].callback;
        btn_win[i].parent = lwin->xwin;
        btn_win[i].x = btn_x;
        btn_win[i].y = btn_y;
        btn_win[i].width = btn_width;
```

```
        btn_win[i].height = btn_height;
    }   /* for */
    btn_win[i].bid = EOB;    /* logically terminate  */
                             /* the set of buttons   */
    XMapSubwindows(display, lwin->xwin);
    return TRUE;
}   /* make_dialog_buttons */


/*
allocate_and_center_button_text() creates private (safe)
copies of the client's button text strings.
*/

static int allocate_and_center_button_text(btn_win,
    btn_data, max_len)
lbutton *btn_win;
button *btn_data;
int max_len;
{
    int j, pad_len;

    j = strlen(btn_data->label);        /* center each button */
    pad_len = (max_len - j) / 2;
    btn_win->label = (char *) malloc((unsigned) (j + pad_len + 1));
    if (btn_win->label == NULL)
        return FALSE;
    for ( ; j > -1; j--)
        btn_win->label[j + pad_len] = btn_data->label[j];
    for (j = 0; j < pad_len; j++)
        btn_win->label[j] = ' ';
    return TRUE;
}   /* allocate_and_center_button_text */


/*
dialog_loop() loops over the input; it attempts to execute
the callback associated with the activated button.
*/

int dialog_loop(lwin, header, message)
logical_window_frame *lwin;
char *header, *message;
{
    lbutton *btn_win = (lbutton *) lwin->extension;
    XEvent event;
    int i;

    if (btn_win == NULL)
        return FALSE;
    activate_window(lwin, "");
    while (TRUE) {
        XNextEvent(display, &event);
        switch (event.type) {
            case Expose:
                while (XCheckTypedWindowEvent(display, lwin->xwin,
                        Expose, &event))
```

```
                ;
            if (event.xexpose.window == lwin->xwin) {
                window_display_header(lwin, header);
                window_go_cr(lwin, 1, 2);
                window_puts(lwin, message, gc);
                display_buttons(lwin, gc);
            }
            break;
        case EnterNotify:
            for (i = 0; btn_win[i].bid != EOB; i++)
                if (event.xcrossing.window == btn_win[i].bid) {
                    highlight_button(&btn_win[i]);
                    break;
                }
            break;
        case LeaveNotify:
            for (i = 0; btn_win[i].bid != EOB; i++)
                if (event.xcrossing.window == btn_win[i].bid) {
                    unhighlight_button(&btn_win[i]);
                    break;
                }
            break;
        case ButtonRelease:
            for (i = 0; btn_win[i].bid != EOB; i++) {
                if (event.xbutton.window == btn_win[i].bid) {
                    unhighlight_button(&btn_win[i]);
                    deactivate_window(lwin);
                    if (*btn_win[i].callback == NULL)
                        return FALSE;
                    else {
                        (*btn_win[i].callback)();
                        return TRUE;
                    }
                }
            }
            break;
        }
    }
}   /* dialog_loop */


/*
cleanup_dialog_button_structures() first frees the heap space
used for labels, and then frees the heap-based array.
*/

void cleanup_dialog_button_structures(lwin)
logical_window_frame *lwin;
{
    int i;
    lbutton *btn_win = (lbutton *) lwin->extension;

    if (btn_win == NULL)
        return;
    for (i = 0; btn_win[i].bid != EOB; i++)
        free(btn_win[i].label);
    free(lwin->extension);
```

```
    XDestroySubwindows(display, lwin->xwin);
}   /* cleanup_dialog_button_structures */


/*
display_buttons() is a private routine used by display_loop()
to display the buttons' text.  X displays the buttons' borders.
*/

void display_buttons(lwin, gc)
logical_window_frame *lwin;
GC gc;
{
    int i;
    lbutton *btn_win = (lbutton *) lwin->extension;

    if (btn_win == NULL)
        return;
    for (i = 0; btn_win[i].bid != EOB; i++)
        XDrawImageString(display, btn_win[i].bid, gc,
            0, lwin->font_height - 1, btn_win[i].label,
            strlen(btn_win[i].label));
}   /* display_buttons */


/*
highlight_buttons() is a private routine that draws a one
pixel wide rectangle on the inside of the window.
*/

void highlight_button(bw)
lbutton *bw;
{
    XDrawRectangle(display, bw->bid, hgc, 0, 0,
        bw->width - 1, bw->height - 1);
}   /* highlight_button */


/*
unhighlight_button() is a private routine that erases the
one pixel wide rectangle inside the button border.
*/

void unhighlight_button(bw)
lbutton *bw;
{
    XDrawRectangle(display, bw->bid, hgc, 0, 0,
        bw->width - 1, bw->height - 1);
}   /* unhighlight_button */


/****  cbrespbox.h  **** declarations for cbrespbox.c  ****/

/*********************************************************************
*  Copyright (c) 1990 Iris Computing Laboratories.
*
```

```
*  This software is provided for demonstration purposes only.  As
*  freely-distributed, modifiable source code, this software carries
*  absolutely no warranty.
*********************************************************************/


#ifndef CBRESPBOXH
#define CBRESPBOXH  1


/*
The response box is built on top of the simplewin.[ch] and
cbdialog.[ch] modules.  It provides routines to read a
string response from the user, in addition to the button
support provided by the cbdialog.[ch] module.
See simplewin.[ch] and cbdialog.[ch].

The user can distinguish among responses as follows:
    responsebox_loop() returns:     meaning
    -------------------------       -------
    KEY_RESPONSE                    normal response -- the string
                                    has been null-terminated
    ESC_KEY                         user pressed <ESC> key
    otherwise                       user pressed a button w/o
                                    entering text

A return value of KEY_RESPONSE means that you can safely use
the string response, although it may have a length of zero.
The user pressed either <Enter> or a button after text entry.

NOTE:  The significance of a selected button MUST be detected
via the callback functions.

NOTE:  A button-associated callback function will be executed
ONLY if a button is selected; typing text and pressing <Enter>
simply returns KEY_RESPONSE with a null-terminated string.
*/


#include <X11/cursorfont.h>
#include "simplewin.h"


#define TRUE                    1           /* logical constants */
#define FALSE                   0

#define EOS                     '\0'        /* special characters */
#define LF                      '\n'
#define TAB                     '\t'
#define BKSP                    '\b'
#define BLANK                   ' '
#define ESC                     27


#define MAX_STR                 80
#define NO_KEY_NO_BUTTON        -1
#define KEY_RESPONSE            -2
```

```
#define ESC_KEY          -3

/*
Functions:
*/

extern void initialize_responsebox_structures();
extern void cleanup_responsebox_structures();
extern int responsebox_loop();
extern void window_puts_point();
extern int window_gets_filter();
extern int window_getche_event_loop();

#endif


/****  cbrespbox.c  **** callback response box routines  ****/

/*
See cbrespbox.h for an explanation of this module.
*/

#include <X11/keysym.h>
#include "cbdialog.h"
#include "cbrespbox.h"

#include "point.bit"
#include "savepoint.bit"


/*
Private globals:
*/

static Pixmap point, save_point;


/*
Private functions:
*/

static void make_point();
static void backspace_char();
static void echo_char();
static void window_no_point();
static void window_put_point();
static int window_getche();
static void window_display_char_with_point();


/*
initialize_responsebox_structures() sets up the data
structures, including those from the simplewin module.
*/
```

```
void initialize_responsebox_structures(font)
XFontStruct *font;
{
    initialize_window_structures(font);
    make_point();
}   /* initialize_responsebox_structures */


/*
cleanup_responsebox_structures() free all window-related
data structures.  cleanup_dialog_button_structures() frees
button-related storage.
*/

void cleanup_responsebox_structures()
{
    cleanup_window_structures();
    XFreePixmap(display, point);
    XFreePixmap(display, save_point);
}   /* cleanup_responsebox_structures */


/*
responsebox_loop() implements the blocking responsebox.
If callback procedures are provided for the buttons,
a callback will be executed for the appropriate button.
*/

int responsebox_loop(lwin, header, message, response)
logical_window_frame *lwin;
char *header, *message, *response;
{
    lbutton *btn_win = (lbutton *) lwin->extension;
    XEvent event;
    int btn_result = FALSE, key_result = FALSE;
    int i, terminate = FALSE;
    ptr_void_proc callback = NULL;

    activate_window(lwin, "");
    while (!terminate) {
        XNextEvent(display, &event);
        switch (event.type) {
            case Expose:
                while (XCheckTypedWindowEvent(display, lwin->xwin,
                        Expose, &event))
                    ;
                if (event.xexpose.window == lwin->xwin) {
                    window_display_header(lwin, header);
                    window_go_cr(lwin, 1, 2);
                    window_clr_eol(lwin);
                    window_puts_point(lwin, message, gc);
                    *response = EOS;
                    display_buttons(lwin, gc);
                }
                break;
            case KeyPress:
```

```
                XPutBackEvent(display, &event);
                key_result = window_gets_filter(lwin, response,
                    MAX_STR, &callback, header, message);
                deactivate_window(lwin);
                key_result = (key_result) ? KEY_RESPONSE : ESC_KEY;
                terminate = TRUE;
                break;
            case EnterNotify:
                if (btn_win == NULL)
                    break;
                for (i = 0; btn_win[i].bid != EOB; i++)
                    if (event.xcrossing.window == btn_win[i].bid) {
                        highlight_button(&btn_win[i]);
                        break;
                    }
                break;
            case LeaveNotify:
                if (btn_win == NULL)
                    break;
                for (i = 0; btn_win[i].bid != EOB; i++)
                    if (event.xcrossing.window == btn_win[i].bid) {
                        unhighlight_button(&btn_win[i]);
                        break;
                    }
                break;
            case ButtonRelease:
                if (btn_win == NULL)
                    break;
                for (i = 0; btn_win[i].bid != EOB; i++) {
                    if (event.xbutton.window == btn_win[i].bid) {
                        unhighlight_button(&btn_win[i]);
                        deactivate_window(lwin);
                        callback = *btn_win[i].callback;
                        terminate = btn_result = TRUE;
                    }
                }
                break;
        }   /* switch */
    }   /* while */
    if (callback != NULL)           /* execute the callback */
        (*callback)();
    return (btn_result) ? btn_result : key_result;
}   /* responsebox_loop */


/*
make_point() makes a window point/cursor
that can be used for keyboard processing.
*/

static void make_point()
{
    if (display_depth == 1) {
        point = XCreateBitmapFromData(display,
            RootWindow(display, screen),
            point_bits, point_width, point_height);
        save_point = XCreateBitmapFromData(display,
```

```
            RootWindow(display, screen), savepoint_bits,
            savepoint_width, savepoint_height);
    }
    else {
        point = XCreatePixmapFromBitmapData(display,
            RootWindow(display, screen),
            point_bits, point_width, point_height,
            BlackPixel(display, screen), WhitePixel(display, screen),
            display_depth);
        save_point = XCreatePixmapFromBitmapData(display,
            RootWindow(display, screen), savepoint_bits,
            savepoint_width, savepoint_height,
            BlackPixel(display, screen), WhitePixel(display, screen),
            display_depth);
    }
}    /* make_point */


/*
The following two functions are used to display and
"un-display" the software-maintained cursor.
*/

static void window_no_point(lwin)
logical_window_frame *lwin;
{
    XCopyArea(display, save_point, lwin->xwin, gc, 0, 0,
        point_width, point_height, lwin->cursor_x - 2,
        lwin->cursor_y + 2);
}    /* window_no_point */


static void window_put_point(lwin)
logical_window_frame *lwin;
{
    XCopyArea(display, lwin->xwin, save_point, gc,
        lwin->cursor_x - 2, lwin->cursor_y + 2,
        point_width, point_height, 0, 0);
    XCopyArea(display, point, lwin->xwin, gc, 0, 0,
        point_width, point_height, lwin->cursor_x - 2,
        lwin->cursor_y + 2);
}    /* window_put_point */


/*
window_puts_point() prints a string, followed by the point,
in a window w/o interpreting each character.
*/

void window_puts_point(lwin, str, gc)
logical_window_frame *lwin;
char *str;
GC gc;          /* allow normal or reverse video */
{
    int text_width;

    window_puts(lwin, str, gc);
```

```
    text_width = XTextWidth(lwin->font, str, strlen(str));
    lwin->cursor_x += text_width;
    window_go_xy(lwin, lwin->cursor_x, lwin->cursor_y);
    window_put_point(lwin);
}   /* window_puts_point */


/*
window_gets_filter() reads a string from a window, up to
some maximum limit, as long as printable ASCII characters
are entered.  If <Esc> is pressed, it returns FALSE.  It
supports button activity as well.
*/

int window_gets_filter(lwin, str, limit, callback, header, message)
logical_window_frame *lwin;
char *str;
int limit; /* the max. number of chars. that can be read. */
ptr_void_proc *callback;
char *header;
char *message;
{
    lbutton *btn_win = (lbutton *) lwin->extension;
    XEvent event;
    KeySym keysym;
    char ch, *temp, *start;
    int i, j, row, col;

    temp = start = str;
    limit--;            /* did caller remember the EOS? */
    for (i = 0, row = r_pos(lwin), col = c_pos(lwin);
            i < limit; ) {
        XNextEvent(display, &event);
        switch (event.type) {
            case Expose:
                while (XCheckTypedWindowEvent(display,
                        lwin->xwin, Expose, &event))
                    ;
                if (event.xexpose.window == lwin->xwin) {
                    *str = EOS;
                    window_display_header(lwin, header);
                    window_go_cr(lwin, 1, 2);
                    window_clr_eol(lwin);
                    window_puts(lwin, message, gc);
                    window_go_cr(lwin, col, row);
                    window_puts_point(lwin, start, gc);
                    display_buttons(lwin, gc);
                }
                break;
            case ButtonPress:
                break;
            case ButtonRelease:
                if (btn_win == NULL) {
                    *start = EOS;
                    return FALSE;
                }
                else {
```

```
                *str = EOS;
                for (j = 0; btn_win[j].bid != EOB; j++)
                    if (event.xbutton.window == btn_win[j].bid) {
                        *callback = *btn_win[j].callback;
                        return TRUE;
                    }
            }
            break;
        case KeyPress:
            ch = (char) window_getche(lwin, &event, &keysym);
            if (keysym == XK_Escape) {
                *start = EOS;       /* return a null string */
                return FALSE;
            }
            else if (keysym == XK_BackSpace ||
                    keysym == XK_Delete) {
                if (str > temp) {
                    str--;
                    i--;
                    backspace_char(lwin);
                }
            }
            else if (keysym == XK_Return) {
                *str = EOS;
                return TRUE;
            }
            else if (keysym >= XK_space &&
                    keysym <= XK_asciitilde) {
                *str = ch;
                str++;
                i++;
            }   /* end if-then-else */
            break;
        case EnterNotify:
            if (btn_win == NULL)
                break;
            for (i = 0; btn_win[i].bid != EOB; i++)
                if (event.xcrossing.window == btn_win[i].bid) {
                    highlight_button(&btn_win[i]);
                    break;
                }
            break;
        case LeaveNotify:
            if (btn_win == NULL)
                break;
            for (i = 0; btn_win[i].bid != EOB; i++)
                if (event.xcrossing.window == btn_win[i].bid) {
                    unhighlight_button(&btn_win[i]);
                    break;
                }
            break;
        default:
            break;
    }   /* end switch */
}   /* end for loop */
if (i == limit)     /* reached limit, terminate string */
    *str = EOS;
```

```
    return TRUE;
}   /* window_gets_filter */


/*
backspace_char() attempts to remove the previously entered
character from the "buffer."
*/

static void backspace_char(lwin)
logical_window_frame *lwin;
{
    window_no_point(lwin);
    lwin->cursor_x -= lwin->font_width;
    if (lwin->cursor_x < 0)
        lwin->cursor_x = 0;
    display_char(display, lwin->xwin, gc,
        lwin->cursor_x, lwin->cursor_y, BLANK);
    window_put_point(lwin);
}   /* backspace_char */


/*
window_getche() reads a character from a window, with echo.
*/

static int window_getche(lwin, event, keysym)
logical_window_frame *lwin;
XEvent *event;
KeySym *keysym;
{
    int key, return_key;

    window_go_xy(lwin, lwin->cursor_x, lwin->cursor_y);
    key = get_keystroke(event, keysym);
    if (*keysym == XK_Escape)
        return_key = ESC;
    else if (*keysym == XK_Return)
        return_key = LF;
    else if (*keysym == XK_BackSpace || *keysym == XK_Delete)
        return_key = BKSP;
    else if (*keysym == XK_Tab)
        return_key = TAB;
    else if (*keysym >= XK_space && *keysym <= XK_asciitilde) {
        echo_char(lwin, (char) key);
        return_key = key;
    }
    else
        return_key = FALSE;
    if (lwin->cursor_y < 0)
        lwin->cursor_y = 0;
    if (lwin->cursor_y > lwin->height)
        lwin->cursor_y -= lwin->font_height;
    window_go_xy(lwin, lwin->cursor_x, lwin->cursor_y);
    return return_key;
}   /* window_getche */
```

```
/*
window_getche_event_loop() reads a character from a
window (with echo) in an event loop.
*/

int window_getche_event_loop(lwin)
logical_window_frame *lwin;
{
    XEvent event;
    KeySym keysym;
    int key, kontinue = TRUE;

    while (kontinue) {
        XNextEvent(display, &event);
        switch (event.type) {
            case KeyPress:
                key = window_getche(lwin, &event, &keysym);
                kontinue = FALSE;
                break;
            default:
                break;
        }
    }   /* end event loop */
    return key;
}   /* window_getche_event_loop */


/*
echo_char() echos a character to the screen.
*/

static void echo_char(lwin, ch)
logical_window_frame *lwin;
char ch;
{
    if (lwin->cursor_x < lwin->width)
        window_display_char_with_point(lwin, ch);
}   /* echo_char */


/*
window_display_char_with_point() displays a software-
based keyboard cursor with each displayed character.
*/

static void window_display_char_with_point(lwin, ch)
logical_window_frame *lwin;
char ch;
{
    window_no_point(lwin);
    display_char(display, lwin->xwin, gc,
        lwin->cursor_x, lwin->cursor_y, ch);
    lwin->cursor_x += lwin->font_width;
    window_put_point(lwin);
}    /* window_display_char_with_point */
```

```
/****  testrespbox.c  ****  tests the callback response box  ****/


#include <stdio.h>
#include <string.h>

#include "cbdialog.h"
#include "cbrespbox.h"


/*
Functions:
*/

void main(), cleanup_resources();
void cb_france(), cb_arctic(), cb_retire();


/*
Private globals:
*/

static char codename[MAX_STR];  /* secret! */


/*
main() exercises the response box.
*/

void main(argc, argv)
int argc;
char *argv[];
{
    static button buttons[] = {
        {"South of France", cb_france},
        {"North Pole", cb_arctic},
        {"Early Retirement", cb_retire},
        {NULL, NULL},
    };
    logical_window_frame lwindow, *lwin = &lwindow;
    XSizeHints test_size_hints;
    XFontStruct *font;
    char *application_name = "testcbrespbox";
    int result;

    init_display(application_name);
    load_font(&font, application_name, "8x13");
    initialize_responsebox_structures(font);
    test_size_hints.min_width = 53 * font->max_bounds.width;
    test_size_hints.min_height =
        7 * (font->max_bounds.ascent + font->max_bounds.descent);
    make_window(RootWindow(display, screen), lwin, 0, 0,
        53, 7, 1, &test_size_hints, font);
    XSetStandardProperties(display, lwin->xwin, application_name,
        application_name, None, argv, argc, &test_size_hints);
```

```
    if (!make_dialog_buttons(lwin, buttons)) {
        fprintf(stderr, "%s: can't create window buttons!\n",
            application_name);
        exit(-1);
    }
    result = responsebox_loop(lwin, "Mission:  Impossible",
        "Codename: ", codename);
    if (result == ESC_KEY)
        fprintf(stdout, "Mission canceled.\n");
    else
        /* ignore other non-button-initiated activities */;
    cleanup_resources(lwin, font);
    exit(0);
}   /* main */


/*
cleanup_resources() performs an orderly clean-up.
*/

void cleanup_resources(lwin, font)
logical_window_frame *lwin;
XFontStruct *font;
{
    cleanup_dialog_button_structures(lwin);
    cleanup_responsebox_structures();
    cleanup_window(lwin);
    XUnloadFont(display, font->fid);
    XCloseDisplay(display);
}   /* cleanup_resources */


/*
Mission Impossible callbacks.
*/

void cb_france()
{
    if (strcmp(codename, "fun and sun") != 0) {
        fprintf(stdout,
            "Invalid codename -- mission canceled.\n");
        return;
    }
    fprintf(stdout,
    "As always, if you're discovered, we'll deny everything.\n");
}   /* cb_france */


void cb_arctic()
{
    if (strcmp(codename, "frozen tundra") != 0) {
        fprintf(stdout,
            "Invalid codename -- mission canceled.\n");
        return;
    }
    fprintf(stdout,
    "As always, if you're discovered, we'll deny everything.\n");
```

```
}   /* cb_arctic */


void cb_retire()
{
    fprintf(stdout, "A secret agent can never retire...\n");
}   /* cb_retire */



/****    response.h    ****    declarations for response.c     ****/

/*********************************************************************
*  Copyright (c) 1990 Iris Computing Laboratories.
*
*  This software is provided for demonstration purposes only.  As
*  freely-distributed, modifiable source code, this software carries
*  absolutely no warranty.
*********************************************************************/


#ifndef RESPONSE_H
#define RESPONSE_H  1

#include <stdio.h>
#include <string.h>

#include "screen.h"
#include "display.h"
#include "cbdialog.h"
#include "cbrespbox.h"


typedef struct {
    void *self;
    logical_window_frame lwindow;
} _Response, *Response;


/*
Functions:
*/

extern Response response_create();
extern int response_loop();
extern void response_cleanup();


#endif



/****  response.c  ****  interface for a high-level response box ****/
```

```
/*
This module provide a three-function inteface to response boxes.
Operationally, it provides a high-level interface to cbrespbox.[ch].
Also, it supports the creation of multiple response boxes.
*/


#include "response.h"


/*
response_create() creates and returns a pointer to a response box.
Multiple response boxes can be created; in this implementation,
they share the same font.
*/

Response response_create(row_width, row_height, border_width,
    buttons, app_name, font, argv, argc)
unsigned int row_width, row_height, border_width;
button *buttons;
char *app_name;
XFontStruct *font;
char *argv[];
int argc;
{
    static int common_structures_already_created = FALSE;
    XSizeHints size_hints;
    Response response;

    response = (Response) malloc(sizeof(_Response));
    if (response == NULL) {
        fprintf(stderr, "%s: can't allocate response box.\n",
            app_name);
        return NULL;
    }
    if (!common_structures_already_created) {
        common_structures_already_created = TRUE;
        initialize_responsebox_structures(font);
    }
    size_hints.min_width = row_width * font->max_bounds.width;
    size_hints.min_height = row_height *
        (font->max_bounds.ascent + font->max_bounds.descent);
    make_window(RootWindow(display, screen), &response->lwindow, 0, 0,
        row_width, row_height, border_width, &size_hints, font);
    XSetStandardProperties(display, response->lwindow.xwin,
        app_name, app_name, None, argv, argc, &size_hints);
    if (!make_dialog_buttons(&response->lwindow, buttons)) {
        fprintf(stderr, "%s: can't create window buttons!\n",
            app_name);
        return NULL;
    }
    response->self = response;          /* self-reference pointer   */
    return (Response) response->self;   /* for free() operations    */
}   /* response_create */


/*
```

```
Operationally, response_loop() is the same as responsebox_loop()
from the lower level module; it is provided for consistency
of protocol.
*/

int response_loop(response, title, prompt, response_return_string)
Response response;
char *title, *prompt, *response_return_string;
{
    return responsebox_loop(&response->lwindow, title,
        prompt, response_return_string);
}   /* response_loop */


/*
response_cleanup() frees response box structures.
*/

void response_cleanup(response)
Response response;
{
    static int common_structures_already_freed = FALSE;

    cleanup_dialog_button_structures(&response->lwindow);
    if (!common_structures_already_freed) {
        common_structures_already_freed = TRUE;
        cleanup_responsebox_structures();
    }
    cleanup_window(&response->lwindow);
    free(response->self);
}   /* response_cleanup */


/****  testresponse.c  ****  tests the high-level response box  ****/


#include "response.h"


/*
Functions:
*/

void main();
void print_response(), print_cancel();


/*
Private globals:
*/

static char *str_response;
static int cancel = FALSE;


/*
```

```
main() exercises the response boxes.
*/

void main(argc, argv)
int argc;
char *argv[];
{
    static button respbox_btns[] = {
        {"Apply", print_response},
        {"Cancel", print_cancel},
        {NULL, NULL},
    };
    Response respbox1, respbox2;
    XFontStruct *font;
    char *application_name = "testresponse";
    int result1, result2;
    char first_name[MAX_STR], last_name[MAX_STR];

    init_display(application_name);
    load_font(&font, application_name, "8x13");
    respbox1 = response_create(53, 7, 1, respbox_btns,
        application_name, font, argv, argc);
    respbox2 = response_create(53, 7, 1, respbox_btns,
        application_name, font, argv, argc);
    str_response = first_name;      /* used by print_response() */
    result1 = response_loop(respbox1, "Response Box 1",
        "What is your first name: ", first_name);
    if (!(cancel || result1 == ESC_KEY)) {
        str_response = last_name;   /* used by print_response() */
        result2 = response_loop(respbox2, "Response Box 2",
            "What is your last name: ", last_name);
        if (!(cancel || result2 == ESC_KEY)) {
            if (result1 == KEY_RESPONSE && result2 == KEY_RESPONSE)
                printf("Goodbye, %s %s.\n", first_name, last_name);
        }
        else
            printf("Response box terminated.\n");
    }
    else
        printf("Response box terminated.\n");
    response_cleanup(respbox1);
    response_cleanup(respbox2);
    XUnloadFont(display, font->fid);
    XCloseDisplay(display);
    exit(0);
}   /* main */


void print_response()
{
    printf("You typed: %s.\n", str_response);
}   /* print_response */


void print_cancel()
{
    printf("Response box cancelled.\n");
```

```
    cancel = TRUE;
}   /* print_cancel */
```

Callback Functions in Xt Applications

```
/****  simplepopup.c  ****/


#include <X11/Intrinsic.h>
#include <X11/StringDefs.h>
#include <X11/Shell.h>

#ifdef X11R3
#include <X11/Box.h>
#include <X11/Command.h>
#include <X11/Form.h>
#include <X11/Label.h>
#else
#include <X11/Xaw/Box.h>
#include <X11/Xaw/Command.h>
#include <X11/Xaw/Form.h>
#include <X11/Xaw/Label.h>
#endif

#include <stdio.h>



/*
Functions:
*/

void main(), create_main_widgets(), create_popup_widgets();
```

```
void ActivatePopup(), DeactivatePopup(), Quit();


/*
Private Widgets:
*/

static Widget topLevel, buttonBoxMain, buttonPopup, buttonQuit;
static Widget popupShell, popupLabel, popupBox,
    popupButton1, popupButton2;


/*
main() delegates everything.
*/

void main(argc, argv)
int argc;
char *argv[];
{
    topLevel = XtInitialize(argv[0], "TestPopup", NULL, 0,
        &argc, argv);
    create_main_widgets();
    create_popup_widgets();
    XtRealizeWidget(topLevel);
    XtMainLoop();
}   /* main */


/*
create_main_widgets() sets up the buttonbox, buttons,
and their callbacks.
*/

void create_main_widgets()
{
    Arg args[5];
    int i;

    buttonBoxMain = XtCreateManagedWidget("buttonBoxMain",
        boxWidgetClass, topLevel, NULL, 0);
    i = 0;
    XtSetArg(args[i], XtNlabel, (XtArgVal) "Quit"); i++;
    buttonQuit = XtCreateManagedWidget("buttonQuit",
        commandWidgetClass, buttonBoxMain, args, i);
    XtAddCallback(buttonQuit, XtNcallback, Quit, NULL);
    i = 0;
    XtSetArg(args[i], XtNlabel, (XtArgVal) "Test Popup"); i++;
    buttonPopup = XtCreateManagedWidget("buttonPopup",
        commandWidgetClass, buttonBoxMain, args, i);
    XtAddCallback(buttonPopup, XtNcallback, ActivatePopup, NULL);
}   /* create_main_widgets */


/*
create_popup_widgets() sets up the pop-up shell, its buttons,
and their callbacks.
```

```
*/

void create_popup_widgets()
{
    Arg args[5];
    int i;

    popupShell= XtCreatePopupShell("popupShell",
        transientShellWidgetClass, topLevel, NULL, 0);
    popupBox = XtCreateManagedWidget("popupBox",
        formWidgetClass, popupShell, NULL, 0);
    i = 0;
    XtSetArg(args[i], XtNlabel, (XtArgVal) "Press a button."); i++;
    XtSetArg(args[i], XtNborderWidth, (XtArgVal) 0); i++;
    popupLabel = XtCreateManagedWidget("popupLabel",
        labelWidgetClass, popupBox, args, i);
    i = 0;
    XtSetArg(args[i], XtNlabel, (XtArgVal) "Button 1"); i++;
    XtSetArg(args[i], XtNfromVert, (XtArgVal) popupLabel); i++;
    popupButton1 = XtCreateManagedWidget("popupButton1",
        commandWidgetClass, popupBox, args, i);
    XtAddCallback(popupButton1, XtNcallback, DeactivatePopup,
        "application data for button 1");
    i = 0;
    XtSetArg(args[i], XtNlabel, (XtArgVal) "Button 2"); i++;
    XtSetArg(args[i], XtNfromVert, (XtArgVal) popupLabel); i++;
    XtSetArg(args[i], XtNfromHoriz, (XtArgVal) popupButton1); i++;
    popupButton2 = XtCreateManagedWidget("popupButton2",
        commandWidgetClass, popupBox, args, i);
    XtAddCallback(popupButton2, XtNcallback, DeactivatePopup,
        "application data for button 2");
}   /* create_popup_widgets */


/*
Callbacks:
*/

/*ARGSUSED*/
void Quit(w, client_data, call_data)
Widget w;
caddr_t client_data;
caddr_t call_data;
{
    printf("You pressed the Quit button.\n");
    exit(0);
}   /* Quit */


/*ARGSUSED*/
void ActivatePopup(w, client_data, call_data)
Widget w;
caddr_t client_data;
caddr_t call_data;
{
    XtPopup(popupShell, XtGrabNone);
}   /* ActivatePopup */
```

```
/*ARGSUSED*/
void DeactivatePopup(w, client_data, call_data)
Widget w;
caddr_t client_data;     /* the application data */
caddr_t call_data;
{
    XtPopdown(popupShell);
    if (w == popupButton1)
        printf(
            "You pressed button 1; its associated data is:\n%s\n",
            client_data);
    else
        printf(
            "You pressed button 2; its associated data is:\n%s\n",
            client_data);
}   /* DeactivatePopup */
```

I

Action Functions in Xt Applications

```
/****  simpleact.c  ****/


#include <X11/Intrinsic.h>
#include <X11/StringDefs.h>
#include <X11/Shell.h>

#ifdef X11R3
#include <X11/Box.h>
#include <X11/Command.h>
#include <X11/Form.h>
#include <X11/Label.h>
#else
#include <X11/Xaw/Box.h>
#include <X11/Xaw/Command.h>
#include <X11/Xaw/Form.h>
#include <X11/Xaw/Label.h>
#endif

#include <stdio.h>



/*
Functions:
*/

void main(), create_main_widgets(), create_widgets_with_actions();
```

```
void ActivatePopup(), ButtonAction(), Quit();


/*
Private Widgets:
*/

static Widget topLevel, buttonBoxMain, buttonPopup, buttonQuit;
static Widget actionShell, actionLabel, actionBox,
    actionButton1, actionButton2;


/*
main() delegates everything.
*/

void main(argc, argv)
int argc;
char *argv[];
{
    topLevel = XtInitialize(argv[0], "TestPopup", NULL, 0,
        &argc, argv);
    create_main_widgets();
    create_widgets_with_actions();
    XtRealizeWidget(topLevel);
    XtMainLoop();
}   /* main */


/*
create_main_widgets() sets up the buttonbox, buttons,
and their callbacks.
*/

void create_main_widgets()
{
    Arg args[5];
    int i;

    buttonBoxMain = XtCreateManagedWidget("buttonBoxMain",
        boxWidgetClass, topLevel, NULL, 0);
    i = 0;
    XtSetArg(args[i], XtNlabel, (XtArgVal) "Quit"); i++;
    buttonQuit = XtCreateManagedWidget("buttonQuit",
        commandWidgetClass, buttonBoxMain, args, i);
    XtAddCallback(buttonQuit, XtNcallback, Quit, NULL);
    i = 0;
    XtSetArg(args[i], XtNlabel, (XtArgVal) "Test Popup"); i++;
    buttonPopup = XtCreateManagedWidget("buttonPopup",
        commandWidgetClass, buttonBoxMain, args, i);
    XtAddCallback(buttonPopup, XtNcallback, ActivatePopup, NULL);
}   /* create_main_widgets */


/*
create_widgets_with_actions() sets up the pop-up shell,
its buttons, and implements their actions.
```

```
*/

void create_widgets_with_actions()
{

    static char button_translations[] =
        "#override\n\
        <Btn1Down>,<Btn1Up>:    buttonaction()";
    static XtActionsRec button_actions[] = {
        {"buttonaction", ButtonAction},
    };
    XtTranslations button_trans_table;
    Arg args[5];
    int i;

    XtAddActions(button_actions, XtNumber(button_actions));
    button_trans_table =
        XtParseTranslationTable(button_translations);
    actionShell= XtCreatePopupShell("actionShell",
        transientShellWidgetClass, topLevel, NULL, 0);
    actionBox = XtCreateManagedWidget("actionBox",
        formWidgetClass, actionShell, NULL, 0);
    i = 0;
    XtSetArg(args[i], XtNlabel, (XtArgVal) "Press a button."); i++;
    XtSetArg(args[i], XtNborderWidth, (XtArgVal) 0); i++;
    actionLabel = XtCreateManagedWidget("actionLabel",
        labelWidgetClass, actionBox, args, i);
    i = 0;
    XtSetArg(args[i], XtNlabel, (XtArgVal) "Button 1"); i++;
    XtSetArg(args[i], XtNfromVert, (XtArgVal) actionLabel); i++;
    actionButton1 = XtCreateManagedWidget("actionButton1",
        commandWidgetClass, actionBox, args, i);
    XtOverrideTranslations(actionButton1, button_trans_table);
    i = 0;
    XtSetArg(args[i], XtNlabel, (XtArgVal) "Button 2"); i++;
    XtSetArg(args[i], XtNfromVert, (XtArgVal) actionLabel); i++;
    XtSetArg(args[i], XtNfromHoriz, (XtArgVal) actionButton1); i++;
    actionButton2 = XtCreateManagedWidget("actionButton2",
        commandWidgetClass, actionBox, args, i);
    XtOverrideTranslations(actionButton2, button_trans_table);
}   /* create_widgets_with_actions */


/*
Callbacks:
*/

/*ARGSUSED*/
void Quit(w, client_data, call_data)
Widget w;
caddr_t client_data;
caddr_t call_data;
{
    printf("You pressed the Quit button.\n");
    exit(0);
}   /* Quit */
```

```
/*ARGSUSED*/
void ActivatePopup(w, client_data, call_data)
Widget w;
caddr_t client_data;
caddr_t call_data;
{
    XtPopup(actionShell, XtGrabNone);
}   /* ActivatePopup */


/*
Action functions:
*/

void ButtonAction(w, event)
Widget w;
XEvent *event;
{
    XtPopdown(actionShell);
    if (w == actionButton1) {
        printf("You pressed button 1.\n");
        printf("Button 1 resides in the window with id: %ld\n",
            (long) event->xbutton.window);
    }
    else {
        printf("Button 2 resides in the window with id: %ld\n",
            (long) event->xbutton.window);
        printf("You pressed button 2.\n");
    }
}   /* ButtonAction */
```

J

The High-level Xt Module for Dialog Boxes

```
/****     respbox.h     ****/

/****     external declarations for response.c     ****/

/*******************************************************************
*  Copyright (c) 1990 Iris Computing Laboratories.
*
*  This software is provided for demonstration purposes only.  As
*  freely-distributed, modifiable source code, this software carries
*  absolutely no warranty.
*******************************************************************/


#ifndef RESPBOX_H
#define RESPBOX_H   1

#include <X11/Intrinsic.h>
#include <X11/StringDefs.h>
#include <X11/Shell.h>

#ifdef X11R3
#include <X11/Box.h>
#include <X11/Command.h>
#include <X11/Form.h>
#include <X11/Label.h>
#else
#include <X11/Xaw/Box.h>
#include <X11/Xaw/Command.h>
```

```
#include <X11/Xaw/Form.h>
#include <X11/Xaw/Label.h>
#endif

#include <stdio.h>



/*
Functions:
*/

extern int response_create();
extern void response_cleanup();
extern int response_add_buttons();
extern void response_query();
extern int response_get_result();


#endif



/****  respbox.c  ****  a simple, variable-button response box  ****/

/*
Design:
    - create response box with response_create()
    - add buttons with response_add_buttons()
    - clean up structures with response_cleanup()
    - query user with response_query()
    - the value returned from response_get_result is the number of
      the selected button -- the first button is button 1
    - currently designed for one response box only
*/


#include "respbox.h"


/*
Private functions:
*/

static void ResponseBox();


/*
Private globals:
*/

static int response_created = FALSE;     /* explicit init as */
                                         /* reminder         */
static Widget responseShell, responseLabel, responseBox;

static int query_result;         /* holds the result of  */
```

```
                                /* a response box query */
static int query_wait;          /* controls the blocking        */
                                /* activity of a response box   */

static Widget box_parent;       /* for reference only; used */
                                /* with XtDisplay(...),     */
                                /* XtWindow(...), etc.      */

static int num_buttons = 0;     /* button variables */
static int max_buttons = 0;
static Widget *buttons;


/*
response_create() creates a multi-button response box.
It returns FALSE in the event of an error.
*/

int response_create(parent, max_num_btns)
Widget parent;
int max_num_btns;
{
    Arg args[3];
    int i;

    if (response_created) {     /* currently, supports one box */
        fprintf(stderr, "Response box already exists!\n");
        return FALSE;
    }
    response_created = TRUE;
    box_parent = parent;
    max_buttons = max_num_btns;
    buttons = (Widget *)
        XtMalloc((unsigned) ((max_buttons + 1) * sizeof(Widget *)));
    if (buttons == NULL) {
        fprintf(stderr, "Can't allocate memory for buttons!\n");
        return FALSE;
    }
    i = 0;
    XtSetArg(args[i], XtNallowShellResize, (XtArgVal) TRUE); i++;
    responseShell = XtCreatePopupShell("responseShell",
        transientShellWidgetClass, parent, args, i);
    responseBox = XtCreateManagedWidget("responseBox",
        formWidgetClass, responseShell, NULL, 0);
    i = 0;
    XtSetArg(args[i], XtNresize, (XtArgVal) TRUE); i++;
    XtSetArg(args[i], XtNborderWidth, (XtArgVal) 0); i++;
    responseLabel = XtCreateManagedWidget("responseLabel",
        labelWidgetClass, responseBox, args, i);
    return TRUE;
}   /* response_create */


/*
response_add_button() adds buttons to the response box. It
returns the number of the button added, or FALSE/0 if the
```

```
limit is reached.
*/

int response_add_button(name, label)
char *name;
char *label;
{
    Arg args[5];
    int i;

    if (num_buttons == max_buttons) {
        fprintf(stderr,
            "Maximum number of buttons already allocated!\n");
        return FALSE;
    }
    i = 0;
    XtSetArg(args[i], XtNlabel, (XtArgVal) label); i++;
    XtSetArg(args[i], XtNfromVert, (XtArgVal) responseLabel); i++;
    if (num_buttons) {
        XtSetArg(args[i], XtNfromHoriz,
            (XtArgVal) buttons[num_buttons - 1]); i++;
    }
    buttons[num_buttons] = XtCreateManagedWidget(name,
        commandWidgetClass, responseBox, args, i);
    XtAddCallback(buttons[num_buttons], XtNcallback, ResponseBox, NULL);
    return ++num_buttons;
}   /* response_add_button */


/*
response_cleanup() frees dynamic data structures.
*/

void response_cleanup()
{
    if (buttons != NULL)
        XtFree(buttons);
}   /* response_cleanup */


/*
ResponseBox() determines which option has been selected
in a dialog window and resets the 'wait' variable; it works
with response_query().
*/
/*ARGSUSED*/
static void ResponseBox(w, client_data, call_data)
Widget w;
caddr_t client_data;
caddr_t call_data;
{
    int i;

    XtPopdown(responseShell);
    for (i = 0; i < num_buttons; i++)
        if (w == buttons[i]) {
            query_result = i + 1;       /* non-zero-based */
```

```
            query_wait = FALSE;
            return;
        }
    query_result = FALSE;
    query_wait = FALSE;
}   /* ResponseBox */


/*
response_get_result() is a pop-up window function for waiting
on the user's selection to the yes-no response query.
*/

int response_get_result()
{
    XEvent event;

    query_wait = TRUE;                  /* block until the user */
    while (query_wait) {                /* presses a button     */
        XtNextEvent(&event);
        XtDispatchEvent(&event);
    }
    return query_result;
}   /* response_get_result */


/*
response_query() pops up a dialog window; it works with
ResponseBox().  The response box is positioned at the cursor.
*/

void response_query(message)
char *message;
{
    Arg args[3];
    int i;
    Window dummy_w;
    int root_x, root_y, dummy_xy;
    unsigned int dummy_keys;

    XQueryPointer(XtDisplay(box_parent),
        XtWindow(box_parent), &dummy_w, &dummy_w, &root_x,
        &root_y, &dummy_xy, &dummy_xy, &dummy_keys);
    i = 0;
    XtSetArg(args[i], XtNx, (XtArgVal) (root_x - 20)); i++;
    XtSetArg(args[i], XtNy, (XtArgVal) (root_y - 20)); i++;
    XtSetValues(responseShell, args, i);
    i = 0;
    XtSetArg(args[i], XtNlabel, (XtArgVal) message); i++;
    XtSetValues(responseLabel, args, i);
    XtPopup(responseShell, XtGrabExclusive);     /* block */
}   /* response_query */



/**  testrespbox.c  **  tests the variable-button response box  **/
```

```
#include "respbox.h"


#define EXIT_BTN    1          /* button values */
#define CANCEL_BTN  2


/*
Functions:
*/

void main(), create_main_buttons();
void Quit(), Question();


/*
Private Widgets:
*/

static Widget topLevel, buttonBox, buttonQuestion, buttonQuit;


/*
main() manages a simple demonstration of a two-button,
blocking response box.
*/

void main(argc, argv)
int argc;
char *argv[];
{
    topLevel = XtInitialize(argv[0], "TestResponse", NULL, 0,
        &argc, argv);

    create_main_buttons(topLevel);
    response_create(topLevel, 2);          /* no error checks */
    response_add_button("exitButton", "Exit");
    response_add_button("cancelButton", "Cancel");

    XtRealizeWidget(topLevel);
    XtMainLoop();
}   /* main */


/*
create_main_buttons() sets up the buttonbox, its buttons,
and their callbacks.
*/

void create_main_buttons(parent)
Widget parent;
{
    Arg args[3];
    int i;
```

```
    buttonBox = XtCreateManagedWidget("buttonBox",
        boxWidgetClass, parent, NULL, 0);
    i = 0;
    XtSetArg(args[i], XtNlabel, (XtArgVal) "Quit"); i++;
    buttonQuit = XtCreateManagedWidget("buttonQuit",
        commandWidgetClass, buttonBox, args, i);
    XtAddCallback(buttonQuit, XtNcallback, Quit, NULL);
    i = 0;
    XtSetArg(args[i], XtNlabel, (XtArgVal) "Test Buttons..."); i++;
    buttonQuestion = XtCreateManagedWidget("buttonQuestion",
        commandWidgetClass, buttonBox, args, i);
    XtAddCallback(buttonQuestion, XtNcallback, Question, NULL);
}   /* create_main_buttons */


/*
Quit() terminates the application.
*/
/*ARGSUSED*/
void Quit(w, client_data, call_data)
Widget w;
caddr_t client_data;
caddr_t call_data;
{
    response_cleanup();
    exit(0);
}   /* Quit */


/*
Ouestion() raises the question.
*/
/*ARGSUSED*/
void Question(w, client_data, call_data)
Widget w;
caddr_t client_data;
caddr_t call_data;
{
    response_query("Would you like to exit?");
    if (response_get_result() == EXIT_BTN) {
        response_query("Confirm exit!");
        if (response_get_result() == EXIT_BTN) {
            printf("Application terminated.\n");
            response_cleanup();
            exit(0);
        }
        else
            printf("Application NOT terminated.\n");
    }
    else
        printf("Application NOT terminated.\n");
}   /* Question */
```

wastebasket: A General-purpose Wastebasket Utility

```
/****    commondel.h    ****/


/*********************************************************/
/* commondel.c contains common routines and data         */
/* structures for the wastebasket deletion operations.   */
/*********************************************************/


#ifndef COMMONDEL_H
#define COMMONDEL_H 1

#include <memory.h>
#include <string.h>
#include <ctype.h>
#include <stdio.h>
#include <sys/types.h>
#include <sys/stat.h> /* stat() is used to verify file existence */


#define MAX               20       /* the DEFAULT maximum number    */
                                   /* of wastebasket entries        */

#define MAX_FILENAME_LEN           256
#define MAX_PATH_LEN               1024
#define MAX_FILE_SPEC              (MAX_PATH_LEN + MAX_FILENAME_LEN)
#define MAX_CHARS                  (MAX_FILE_SPEC * 2)
```

```
#define PARSE_TOKENS     " \t\n"/* used to parse filename lists */

#define EOS              '\0'

#define ENCODE_STR       "_SLASH_"   /* used during file spec.    */
                                     /* encode/decode operations */

#define TRUE             1
#define FALSE            0


/*
Function declarations:
*/

extern int file_size(), load_buffer();
extern int get_home_directory();
extern int get_max_files();
extern int wastebasket_emtpy();
extern void encode_file_spec(), decode_file_spec();


/*
Window-related globals:
*/

extern char *temp_wastebasket_file;
extern char *wastebasket_file;
extern char *wastebasket_dir;
extern char home_directory[];
extern int  current_num_files, max_basket_entries;


#endif



/****     commondel.c     ****/


/****************************************************/
/* This module contains common routines and data    */
/* structures for the wastebasket programs.         */
/****************************************************/


#include "commondel.h"


/*
Window-related globals used in delete.c and xwaste.c:
*/

char *temp_wastebasket_file =
    "iriswastebasket/temp.wastebasket.record";
char *wastebasket_file = "iriswastebasket/wastebasket.record";
```

```
char *wastebasket_dir = "iriswastebasket";
char home_directory[MAX_PATH_LEN];

int max_basket_entries = MAX;
int current_num_files;


/*
load_buffer() loads a buffer with text from a file.
*/

int load_buffer(file_spec, buffer)
char *file_spec, *buffer;
{
    FILE *file_ptr;

    if ((file_ptr = fopen(file_spec, "r")) == NULL)
        return FALSE;
    while ((*buffer = fgetc(file_ptr)) != EOF)
        buffer++;
    *buffer = EOS;
    fclose(file_ptr);
    return TRUE;
}   /* load_buffer */


/*
get_home_directory() examines the environment for
the value of HOME.
*/

int get_home_directory(directory)
char *directory;
{
    char *home;

    if ((home = (char *)getenv("HOME")) == NULL) {
        fprintf(stderr,
            "Unable to determine your home directory!!\n");
        return FALSE;
    }
    strcpy(directory, home);
    return TRUE;
}   /* get_home_directory */


/*
get_max_files() examines the environment
for the value of $WASTEBASKET_SIZE.
*/

int get_max_files()
{
    int size;
    char *str_size;

    if ((str_size = (char *)getenv("WASTEBASKET_SIZE")) == NULL)
```

```
        return MAX;
    if ((size = atoi(str_size)) < 1)
        return MAX;
    return size;
}   /* get_max_files */


/*
file_size() checks for the existence of a file using stat(),
returning -1 for a nonexistent file and the file size otherwise.
*/

int file_size(file_spec)
char *file_spec;
{
    struct stat statbuf;

    if (stat(file_spec, &statbuf) < 0)
        return -1;
    else
        return (int)statbuf.st_size;
}   /* file_size */


/*
The following two procedures are used to encode and decode
file specifications for storage in the wastebasket.
*/

void encode_file_spec(after, before)
char *after, *before;
{
    char ch, *encode_ptr;

    while (ch = *before++)
        if (ch != '/')
            *after++ = ch;
        else {
            encode_ptr = ENCODE_STR;
            while (*after++ = *encode_ptr++)
                ;
            after--;    /* don't want EOS */
        }
    *after = EOS;
}   /* encode_file_spec */


void decode_file_spec(after, before)
char *after, *before;
{
    int match;
    char *encode_ptr, *encode_str = ENCODE_STR, *next;

    while (*before) {
        if (*before == *encode_str) {
            match = TRUE;
            next = before;
```

```
            encode_ptr = encode_str;
            while (*next && *encode_ptr)
                if (*next++ != *encode_ptr++) {
                    match = FALSE;
                    break;
                }
            if (!match)
                *after++ = *before++;
            else {
                *after++ = '/';
                before = next;
            }
        }
        else
            *after++ = *before++;
    }
    *after = EOS;
}   /* decode_file_spec */


/*
wastebasket_empty() is a convenience function for determining
whether or not the wastebasket exists.
*/

int wastebasket_empty()
{
    char temp_file_spec[MAX_CHARS];

    sprintf(temp_file_spec, "%s/%s", home_directory,
        wastebasket_dir);
    if (file_size(temp_file_spec) == -1)
        return TRUE;
    sprintf(temp_file_spec, "%s/%s", home_directory,
        wastebasket_file);
    if (file_size(temp_file_spec) == -1)
        return TRUE;
    return FALSE;
}   /* wastebasket_empty */



/****    delete.h    ****/


/*
DELETE implements one-half of a two-stage file deletion
system.  See the complementary module xwaste.c.
*/


#ifndef DELETEH
#define DELETEH 1

#include <sys/param.h>
```

```
#define MAX_STR     100


extern void main();
extern void delete_filenames();
extern int delete_file();
extern void add_to_basket();
extern void build_file_spec();


#endif



/****    delete.c    ****/


/**********************************************************************
*  Copyright (c) 1990 Iris Computing Laboratories.
*
*  This software is provided for demonstration purposes only.  As
*  freely-distributed, modifiable source code, this software carries
*  absolutely no warranty.
**********************************************************************/


/*********************************************************/
/* DELETE implement a two-stage file deletion system.    */
/* See the complementary module waste.c.                 */
/*********************************************************/


#include "commondel.h"
#include "delete.h"


/*
main() allows the user to delete a set of files matching
a wildcard spec.
*/

void main(argc, argv)
int argc;
char *argv[];
{
    if (argc < 2) {
        fprintf(stderr, "Usage: delete <file specification>\n");
        exit(-1);
    }
    if (!get_home_directory(home_directory))
        exit(-1);
    max_basket_entries = get_max_files();
    delete_filenames(argc, argv);
    exit(0);
}   /* main */
```

```
/*
delete_filenames() applies delete_file() to
each filename from the command line expansion.
*/

void delete_filenames(argc, argv)
int argc;
char *argv[];
{
    char file_spec[MAX_CHARS];
    int continue_deletions = TRUE;

    while (--argc > 0 && continue_deletions) {
        build_file_spec(file_spec, *++argv);
        continue_deletions = delete_file(file_spec);
    }
}   /* delete_filenames */


/*
delete_file() is used to delete files using
an interactive prompt.
*/

int delete_file(file_spec)
char *file_spec;
{
    char answer, answer_str[MAX_STR];

    if (file_size(file_spec) == -1) {
        fprintf(stderr, "No matching file(s).\n");
        return TRUE;
    }
    do {
        printf("Delete file: %s\nyes, no, or quit [y|n|q]? ",
            file_spec);
        gets(answer_str);
        answer = answer_str[0];
        if (islower(answer))
            answer = toupper(answer);
    } while (!isupper(answer) ||
            !(answer == 'Y' || answer == 'N' || answer == 'Q'));
    if (answer == 'Y')
        add_to_basket(file_spec);
    return (answer == 'Q') ? FALSE : TRUE;
}   /* delete_file */


/*
add_to_basket() puts the passed file spec. in the top of the
wastebasket, removing the oldest wastebasket contents, if
the wastebasket is overflowing.
*/

void add_to_basket(file_spec)
char *file_spec;
{
```

```
FILE *waste_fd, *temp_waste_fd;
char encoded_file_spec[MAX_CHARS];
char temp_file_spec[MAX_CHARS];
char temp_file_spec_2[MAX_CHARS];
int position, waste_exists = FALSE;
char *more_entries;

sprintf(temp_file_spec, "%s/%s", home_directory,
    wastebasket_dir);
if (file_size(temp_file_spec) == -1)
    mkdir(temp_file_spec, 0755);
sprintf(temp_file_spec, "%s/%s", home_directory,
    wastebasket_file);
if (file_size(temp_file_spec) != -1) {
    if ((waste_fd = fopen(temp_file_spec, "r")) != NULL)
        waste_exists = TRUE;
    else {
        fprintf(stderr, "Error opening wastebasket!\n");
        return;
    }
}
sprintf(temp_file_spec, "%s/%s.%d",
    home_directory, temp_wastebasket_file, getpid());
if ((temp_waste_fd = fopen(temp_file_spec, "w")) == NULL) {
    fprintf(stderr,
"Error opening temporary file during wastebasket operations!\n");
    return;
}

encode_file_spec(encoded_file_spec, file_spec);
strcat(encoded_file_spec, "\n");
/* write the file spec. as the first wastebasket entry */
fputs(encoded_file_spec, temp_waste_fd);

if (waste_exists) {
    more_entries = fgets(temp_file_spec, MAX_CHARS, waste_fd);
    for (position = 1; more_entries != NULL; position++) {
        if (position < max_basket_entries) {
            if (strcmp(encoded_file_spec, temp_file_spec) != 0)
                /* not a duplicate */
                fputs(temp_file_spec, temp_waste_fd);
        }
        else {
            temp_file_spec[strlen(temp_file_spec) - 1] = EOS;
            sprintf(temp_file_spec_2, "%s/%s/%s",
                home_directory, wastebasket_dir, temp_file_spec);
            unlink(temp_file_spec_2);
        }
        more_entries = fgets(temp_file_spec, MAX_CHARS, waste_fd);
    }
    fclose(waste_fd);
}
fclose(temp_waste_fd);
encoded_file_spec[strlen(encoded_file_spec) - 1] = EOS;
sprintf(temp_file_spec, "%s/%s/%s",
    home_directory, wastebasket_dir, encoded_file_spec);
rename(file_spec, temp_file_spec);
```

```
    sprintf(temp_file_spec_2, "%s/%s.%d",
        home_directory, temp_wastebasket_file, getpid());
    sprintf(temp_file_spec, "%s/%s",
        home_directory, wastebasket_file);
    rename(temp_file_spec_2, temp_file_spec);
}   /* add_to_basket */


/*
build_file_spec() concatenates a path and a file specification.
*/

void build_file_spec(file_spec, partial_file_spec)
char *file_spec, *partial_file_spec;
{
    if (*partial_file_spec == '/')
        strcpy(file_spec, partial_file_spec);
    else {
        getwd(file_spec);
        strcat(file_spec, "/");
        strcat(file_spec, partial_file_spec);
    }
}   /* build_file_spec */


/****    xwaste.h    ****/

/****    external declarations for xwaste.c    ****/


/*******************************************************/
/* XWASTE implement a two-stage file deletion system. */
/*******************************************************/

#ifndef XWASTE_H
#define XWASTE_H    1

#include <X11/Intrinsic.h>
#include <X11/StringDefs.h>
#include <X11/Shell.h>

#ifdef X11R3
#include <X11/Box.h>
#include <X11/Command.h>
#include <X11/Dialog.h>
#include <X11/Form.h>
#include <X11/VPaned.h>
#include <X11/Viewport.h>
#else
#include <X11/Xaw/Box.h>
#include <X11/Xaw/Command.h>
#include <X11/Xaw/Dialog.h>
#include <X11/Xaw/Form.h>
#include <X11/Xaw/Paned.h>
#include <X11/Xaw/Viewport.h>
#endif
```

```
#include <stdio.h>


#include "alert.h"
#include "commondel.h"
#include "xwaste.menu.h"
#include "xwaste.bskt.h"


#define MAX_STR                  80
#define DEFAULT_BASKET_WIDTH     400          /* pixels */
#define DEFAULT_BASKET_HEIGHT    300          /* pixels */
#define POPUP_Y_OFFSET           25           /* pixels */


/*
Application resources:
*/

typedef struct {
    int browser_rows;
    int browser_columns;
    char *browser_font_name;
} ApplicationData, *ApplicationDataPtr;


#define XtNbrowserRows        "browserRows"
#define XtCBrowserRows        "BrowserRows"
#define XtNbrowserColumns     "browserColumns"
#define XtCBrowserColumns     "BrowserColumns"
#define XtNbrowserFont        "browserFont"
#define XtCBrowserFont        "BrowserFont"


/*
Function declarations:
*/

extern void main(), process_resources(),
    reset_proper_keyboard_focus();
extern void create_main_panel_widgets(), create_basket_widgets();
extern void initialize_shell_structures();
extern void SelectFile(), MenuUp(), MenuDown(), Beep(), FillBasket();
extern void Quit(), Delete(), Basket(), BasketDone();
extern char *get_filename(), *get_updated_directory();
extern void expand_delete_filename();
extern int delete_file();


#endif



/****    xwaste.c    ****/
```

```
/*****************************************************************
*  Copyright (c) 1990 Iris Computing Laboratories.
*
*  This software is provided for demonstration purposes only.  As
*  freely-distributed, modifiable source code, this software carries
*  absolutely no warranty.
*****************************************************************/


/*****************************************************/
/* XWASTE implement a two-stage file deletion system.   */
/* See the complementary module delete.c.               */
/*****************************************************/


#include "xwaste.h"


/*
Private globals:
*/

static XtResource resources[] = {
    {XtNbrowserRows, XtCBrowserRows, XtRInt, sizeof(int),
        XtOffset(ApplicationDataPtr, browser_rows), XtRImmediate,
        (caddr_t) DEFAULT_BROWSER_ROWS},
    {XtNbrowserColumns, XtCBrowserColumns, XtRInt, sizeof(int),
        XtOffset(ApplicationDataPtr, browser_columns), XtRImmediate,
        (caddr_t) DEFAULT_BROWSER_COLUMNS},
    {XtNbrowserFont, XtCBrowserFont, XtRString, sizeof(char *),
        XtOffset(ApplicationDataPtr, browser_font_name),
        XtRString, DEFAULT_BROWSER_FONT_NAME},
};


static XtActionsRec actionsTable[] = {
    {"selectFile", (XtActionProc) SelectFile},
    {"menuUp", (XtActionProc) MenuUp},
    {"menuDown", (XtActionProc) MenuDown},
    {"beep", (XtActionProc) Beep},
    {"fillBasket", (XtActionProc) FillBasket},
};


static Widget basketShell, topLevel, fileSpecForm,
    directoryBox, filenameBox, buttonBoxMain, vPort,
    vPane, vPaneBasket, wasteBasket, buttonBoxBasket,
    buttonQuit, buttonDelete, buttonBasket, buttonDoneBasket;


static Pixmap icon_pixmap;          /* freed by Quit() */
static XFontStruct *font;           /* freed by Quit() */


/*
main() determines the home directory and basket dimensions,
```

```
creates the main widgets, sets up the alert boxes, initializes
data structures, etc.
*/

void main(argc, argv)
int argc;
char *argv[];
{
    unsigned int basket_width, basket_height;
    Arg args[5];
    int i;
    ApplicationData browser_data;

    if (!get_home_directory(home_directory))
        exit(-1);
    if (argc > 1) {
        fprintf(stderr, "Usage: xwaste\n");
        exit(-1);
    }

    topLevel = XtInitialize(argv[0], "XWaste", NULL, 0,
        &argc, argv);
    process_resources(&browser_data, &font);
    i = 0;
    XtSetArg(args[i], XtNinput, (XtArgVal) TRUE); i++;
    XtSetValues(topLevel, args, i);

    create_main_panel_widgets();
    basket_create_offscreen_pixmap(topLevel, font,
        browser_data, &basket_width, &basket_height);
    create_basket_widgets(basket_width, basket_height);
    max_basket_entries = get_max_files();
    XtAddActions(actionsTable, XtNumber(actionsTable));

    menu_create(basketShell);
    alert_create_ync(topLevel);
    alert_create_continue(topLevel);
    set_alert_reset_proper_keyboard_focus(
        reset_proper_keyboard_focus);

    initialize_shell_structures();

    XtRealizeWidget(topLevel);
    XtRealizeWidget(basketShell);

    XtMainLoop();
}   /* main */


/*
process_resources() reads dimensions for the browser (off-screen
pixmap of the wastebasket), checks their bounds, and exits with
warning message(s), if there are problems.
*/

void process_resources(browser_data, font)
ApplicationData *browser_data;
```

```
XFontStruct **font;
{
    XtGetApplicationResources(topLevel, browser_data, resources,
        XtNumber(resources), NULL, 0);
    if (browser_data->browser_rows < 1 ||
            browser_data->browser_rows > MAX_BROWSER_ROWS) {
        fprintf(stderr, "xwaste: Illegal row dimension: %d\n",
            browser_data->browser_rows);
        fprintf(stderr,
            "Number of rows must be in the interval: [1,%d]\n",
            MAX_BROWSER_ROWS);
        exit(-1);
    }
    if (browser_data->browser_columns < 1 ||
            browser_data->browser_columns > MAX_BROWSER_COLUMNS) {
        fprintf(stderr, "xwaste: Illegal column dimension: %d\n",
            browser_data->browser_columns);
        fprintf(stderr,
            "Number of columns must be in the interval: [1,%d]\n",
            MAX_BROWSER_COLUMNS);
        exit(-1);
    }
    if ((*font = XLoadQueryFont(XtDisplay(topLevel),
            browser_data->browser_font_name)) == NULL) {
        fprintf(stderr,
            "Couldn't load font: %s; using default browser font.\n",
            browser_data->browser_font_name);
        if ((*font = XLoadQueryFont(XtDisplay(topLevel),
                DEFAULT_BROWSER_FONT_NAME)) == NULL) {
            fprintf(stderr,
        "Couldn't load default browser font either, exiting...\n");
            exit(-1);
        }
    }
}   /* process_resources */


/*
create_main_panel_widgets() creates/initializes the widgets that
constitute the top-level, main panel.
*/

void create_main_panel_widgets()
{
    Arg args[5];
    int i;

    vPane = XtCreateManagedWidget("vPane",
#ifdef X11R3
        vPanedWidgetClass, topLevel, NULL, 0);
#else
        panedWidgetClass, topLevel, NULL, 0);
#endif
    buttonBoxMain = XtCreateManagedWidget("buttonBoxMain",
        boxWidgetClass, vPane, NULL, 0);
    fileSpecForm = XtCreateManagedWidget("fileSpecForm",
        formWidgetClass, vPane, NULL, 0);
```

```
    i = 0;
    XtSetArg(args[i], XtNlabel, (XtArgVal) "Directory:"); i++;
    XtSetArg(args[i], XtNvalue, (XtArgVal) ""); i++;
    directoryBox = XtCreateManagedWidget("directoryBox",
        dialogWidgetClass, fileSpecForm, args, i);
    i = 0;
    XtSetArg(args[i], XtNlabel, (XtArgVal) "Filename:"); i++;
    XtSetArg(args[i], XtNvalue, (XtArgVal) ""); i++;
    XtSetArg(args[i], XtNfromHoriz, (XtArgVal) directoryBox); i++;
    filenameBox = XtCreateManagedWidget("filenameBox",
        dialogWidgetClass, fileSpecForm, args, i);
    i = 0;
    XtSetArg(args[i], XtNlabel, (XtArgVal) "Quit"); i++;
    buttonQuit = XtCreateManagedWidget("buttonQuit",
        commandWidgetClass, buttonBoxMain, args, i);
    XtAddCallback(buttonQuit, XtNcallback, Quit, NULL);
    i = 0;
    XtSetArg(args[i], XtNlabel, (XtArgVal) "Delete"); i++;
    buttonDelete = XtCreateManagedWidget("buttonDelete",
        commandWidgetClass, buttonBoxMain, args, i);
    XtAddCallback(buttonDelete, XtNcallback, Delete, NULL);
    i = 0;
    XtSetArg(args[i], XtNlabel, (XtArgVal) "Basket"); i++;
    buttonBasket = XtCreateManagedWidget("buttonBasket",
        commandWidgetClass, buttonBoxMain, args, i);
    XtAddCallback(buttonBasket, XtNcallback, Basket, NULL);
}   /* create_main_panel_widgets */


/*
create_basket_widgets() creates/initializes the widgets
in the pop-up wastebasket frame.
*/

void create_basket_widgets(basket_width, basket_height)
unsigned int basket_width, basket_height;
{
    Arg args[5];
    int i;

    i = 0;
    XtSetArg(args[i], XtNallowShellResize, (XtArgVal) TRUE); i++;
    XtSetArg(args[i], XtNmappedWhenManaged, (XtArgVal) FALSE); i++;
    basketShell = XtCreateApplicationShell("basketShell",
        topLevelShellWidgetClass, args, i);
    vPaneBasket = XtCreateManagedWidget("vPaneBasket",
#ifdef X11R3
        vPanedWidgetClass, basketShell, NULL, 0);
#else
        panedWidgetClass, basketShell, NULL, 0);
#endif
    buttonBoxBasket = XtCreateManagedWidget("buttonBoxBasket",
        boxWidgetClass, vPaneBasket, NULL, 0);
    i = 0;
    XtSetArg(args[i], XtNallowHoriz, (XtArgVal) TRUE); i++;
    XtSetArg(args[i], XtNallowVert, (XtArgVal) TRUE); i++;
    XtSetArg(args[i], XtNforceBars, (XtArgVal) TRUE); i++;
```

```
    XtSetArg(args[i], XtNwidth,
        (XtArgVal) DEFAULT_BASKET_WIDTH); i++;
    XtSetArg(args[i], XtNheight,
        (XtArgVal) DEFAULT_BASKET_HEIGHT); i++;
    vPort = XtCreateManagedWidget("vPort",
        viewportWidgetClass, vPaneBasket, args, i);
    i = 0;
    XtSetArg(args[i], XtNlabel, (XtArgVal) "Done"); i++;
    buttonDoneBasket = XtCreateManagedWidget("buttonDoneBasket",
        commandWidgetClass, buttonBoxBasket, args, i);
    XtAddCallback(buttonDoneBasket, XtNcallback, BasketDone, NULL);
    i = 0;
    XtSetArg(args[i], XtNwidth, (XtArgVal) basket_width); i++;
    XtSetArg(args[i], XtNheight, (XtArgVal) basket_height); i++;
    wasteBasket = XtCreateManagedWidget("wasteBasket", widgetClass,
        vPort, args, i);
    basket_set_reference_widget(wasteBasket);
}   /* create_basket_widgets */


/*
initialize_shell_structures sets up miscellaneous structures
for the top-level widgets (currently, just the icon).
*/

void initialize_shell_structures()
{

#include "xwaste.icon"

    Arg args[3];

    icon_pixmap = XCreateBitmapFromData(XtDisplay(topLevel),
        RootWindowOfScreen(XtScreen(topLevel)), xwaste_bits,
        xwaste_width, xwaste_height);
    XtSetArg(args[0], XtNiconPixmap, (XtArgVal) icon_pixmap);
    XtSetValues(topLevel, args, 1);
    XtSetArg(args[0], XtNiconPixmap, (XtArgVal) icon_pixmap);
    XtSetValues(basketShell, args, 1);
}   /* initialize_shell_structures */


/*
Action procedures for the wastebasket menu -- each must be
associated with a translation table entry.
*/

/*ARGSUSED*/
static void SelectFile(w, event)     /* highlight the filename */
Widget w;
XEvent *event;
{
    basket_select_file(event);
}   /* SelectFile */


static void MenuUp(w, event)         /* position/pop-up the menu */
```

```
Widget w;
XEvent *event;
{
    menu_up(w, event);
}   /* MenuUp */


static void MenuDown(w, event)      /* remove the menu */
Widget w;
XEvent *event;
{
    menu_down(w, event);
}   /* MenuUp */


/*ARGSUSED*/
static void Beep(w, event)          /* ring the terminal bell */
Widget w;
XEvent *event;
{
    XBell(XtDisplay(w), 80);
}   /* Beep */


/*ARGSUSED*/
static void FillBasket(w, event)
Widget w;
XEvent *event;
{
    basket_reset_current_file();
    basket_fill_with_filenames(NO_HIGHLIGHT);
}   /* FillBasket */


/*
Callback procedures:
*/

/*
Quit() terminates the application.
*/
/*ARGSUSED*/
void Quit(w, client_data, call_data)
Widget w;
caddr_t client_data;
caddr_t call_data;
{
    XFreePixmap(XtDisplay(w), icon_pixmap);
    XFreeFont(XtDisplay(w), font);
    exit(0);
}   /* Quit */


/*
Delete() is the starting point for file deletions.
*/
/*ARGSUSED*/
```

```
void Delete(w, client_data, call_data)
Widget w;
caddr_t client_data;
caddr_t call_data;
{
    char *filename;

    XtSetSensitive(buttonDelete, FALSE);
    if ((filename = get_filename()) != NULL)
        expand_delete_filename(filename);
    XtSetSensitive(buttonDelete, TRUE);
}   /* Delete */


/*
Basket() is the starting point for
wastebasket recovery/browser operations.
*/
/*ARGSUSED*/
void Basket(w, client_data, call_data)
Widget w;
caddr_t client_data;
caddr_t call_data;
{
    Position x, y;
    Arg args[3];
    int i;
    Dimension height;

    if (wastebasket_empty()) {
        alert("The wastebasket is empty.");
        return;
    }
    XtSetArg(args[0], XtNheight, &height);
    XtGetValues(topLevel, args, 1);
    XtTranslateCoords(topLevel, (Position) 0,
        (Position) (height + POPUP_Y_OFFSET), &x, &y);
    i = 0;
    XtSetArg(args[i], XtNx, (XtArgVal) x); i++;
    XtSetArg(args[i], XtNy, (XtArgVal) y); i++;
    XtSetValues(basketShell, args, i);
    XtMapWidget(basketShell);
    basket_reset_current_file();/* no highlighted file at       */
                               /* start-up, or after exposure  */
    if (!basket_fill_with_filenames(NO_HIGHLIGHT))
        return;
    if (current_num_files > max_basket_entries) {
        alert_beep(8);
        alert("Please read the message in the console window!");
        fprintf(stderr,
"The wastebasket contains more entries than\n\
specified by the environment variable\n\
WASTEBASKET_SIZE (currently:  %d).\n\
If you make modifications, your wastebasket\n\
size will be reduced accordingly.\n", max_basket_entries);
    }
}   /* Basket */
```

```
/*
BasketDone() removes the "basket" window.
*/
/*ARGSUSED*/
void BasketDone(w, client_data, call_data)
Widget w;
caddr_t client_data;
caddr_t call_data;
{
    XtUnmapWidget(basketShell);
}   /* BasketDone */


/*
General-purpose routines:
*/

/*
get_filename() gets a filename.
*/

char *get_filename()
{
    char *filename;

#ifdef X11R3
    filename = XtDialogGetValueString(filenameBox);
#else
    filename = XawDialogGetValueString(filenameBox);
#endif
    if (!strlen(filename)) {
        alert("Please select a file.");
        return NULL;        /* return if no selection */
    }
    else
        return filename;
}   /* get_filename */


/*
get_updated_directory() manages and returns
the "current" directory.
*/

char *get_updated_directory()
{
    static char previous_dir[MAX_PATH_LEN];
    char *current_dir;

#ifdef X11R3
    current_dir = XtDialogGetValueString(directoryBox);
#else
    current_dir = XawDialogGetValueString(directoryBox);
#endif
    if (strlen(current_dir) == 0) {
```

```
        if ((current_dir = (char *)
                getcwd(previous_dir, MAX_PATH_LEN)) == NULL) {
            fprintf(stderr,
                "Unable to determine current working directory!!\n");
            exit(-1);
        }
    }
    if (strcmp(current_dir, previous_dir))
        strcpy(previous_dir, current_dir);
    return previous_dir;     /*  now, same as current_dir */
}   /* get_updated_directory */


/*
expand_delete_filename() expands wildcards and then applies
delete_file() to each filename in the expansion.
*/

void expand_delete_filename(filename)
char *filename;
{
    char cmd_string[MAX_PATH_LEN + MAX_STR];
    char file_spec[MAX_PATH_LEN + MAX_STR];
    char *filename_buffer, *next;
    char temp_file[MAX_PATH_LEN + MAX_STR];
    int continue_deletions = TRUE;

    sprintf(temp_file, "%s.%d",
        "iris.wastebasket.delete.temp.filenames", getpid());
    unlink(temp_file);         /* if it exists */
    sprintf(file_spec, "%s/%s", get_updated_directory(), filename);
    sprintf(cmd_string, "echo %s > %s", file_spec, temp_file);
    system(cmd_string);
    if (file_size(temp_file) == -1) {
        alert("Unknown error during creation of a temporary file!");
        return;
    }
    if ((filename_buffer =
            (char *) malloc((unsigned) (file_size(temp_file) + 1)))
                == NULL) {
        alert("Memory allocation error!");
        unlink(temp_file);
        return;
    }
    if (!load_buffer(temp_file, filename_buffer)) {
        alert("Unable to access a temporary file!");
        free(filename_buffer);
        unlink(temp_file);
        return;
    }
    next = strtok(filename_buffer, PARSE_TOKENS);
    while (next != NULL && continue_deletions) {
        continue_deletions = delete_file(next);
        next = strtok(NULL, PARSE_TOKENS);
    }
    unlink(temp_file);
    free(filename_buffer);
```

```
}   /* expand_delete_filename */


/*
delete_file() is used to delete a file. An alert
box is used to make sure of the deletion.
*/

int delete_file(file_spec)
char *file_spec;
{
    char msg[MAX_FILE_SPEC + 25];
    int result;

    if (file_size(file_spec) == -1) {
        sprintf(msg, "No matching file(s):  %s", file_spec);
        alert(msg);
        return TRUE;
    }
    sprintf(msg, "Delete file:  %s", file_spec);
    result = alert_query(msg);
    if (result == ALERT_YES)
        basket_add_file(file_spec);
    return (result != ALERT_CANCEL) ? TRUE : FALSE;
}   /* delete_file */


/*
reset_proper_keyboard_focus() allows the keyboard focus to be
reestablished after after a transient shell is popped up and down.
Calling this routine is necessary with twm, but not with uwm.
*/

void reset_proper_keyboard_focus()
{
    XtSetKeyboardFocus(vPane, fileSpecForm);
}   /* reset_proper_keyboard_focus */



/****    xwaste.bskt.h    ****/

/****    external declarations for xwaste.bskt.c   ****/


#ifndef XWASTE_BSKT_H
#define XWASTE_BSKT_H   1

#include <X11/Intrinsic.h>

#include <stdio.h>

#include "alert.h"
#include "commondel.h"
#include "xwaste.h"
```

```
#define NO_HIGHLIGHT    -1  /* ignore mouse, just redisplay files */
#define NO_FILE         -2  /* no currently selected file */


#define DEFAULT_BROWSER_FONT_NAME   "fixed"
#define DEFAULT_BROWSER_ROWS        150
#define DEFAULT_BROWSER_COLUMNS     250
#define MAX_BROWSER_ROWS            250
#define MAX_BROWSER_COLUMNS         350


/*
Function declarations:
*/

extern void basket_create_offscreen_pixmap(),
    basket_set_reference_widget(), basket_select_file(),
    basket_delete_file(), basket_restore_file(),
    basket_add_file(), basket_reset_current_file();
extern int basket_fill_with_filenames();


#endif



/****    xwaste.bskt.c    ****/

/**** basket-related routines for xwaste.c    ****/


#include "xwaste.bskt.h"


/*
Private globals:
*/

static Pixmap wastebasket;  /* off-screen image for wastebasket */
static GC wgc, cgc, hgc;    /* see basket_create_offscreen_pixmap() */

static Widget wbrw;       /* wastebasket reference widget--used   */
                          /* in an XtDisplay(wbrw)-type capacity  */

static int row_increment, current_file;
static unsigned int basket_width, basket_height;


/*
basket_create_offscreen_pixmap() creates and sets the dimensions
of the basket pixmap (the virtual basket image).
*/

void basket_create_offscreen_pixmap(w, font,
        pixmap_data, width, height)
Widget w;
```

```
XFontStruct *font;
ApplicationData pixmap_data;
unsigned int *width, *height;
{
    XGCValues values;
    Display *display = XtDisplay(w);
    int screen = XDefaultScreen(display);
    unsigned int depth = XDisplayPlanes(display, screen);

    values.foreground = XBlackPixel(display, screen);
    values.background = XWhitePixel(display, screen);
    values.font = font->fid;
    wgc = XCreateGC(XtDisplay(w), RootWindowOfScreen(XtScreen(w)),
        GCForeground | GCBackground | GCFont, &values);
    cgc = XCreateGC(XtDisplay(w), RootWindowOfScreen(XtScreen(w)),
        GCForeground | GCBackground | GCFont, &values);
    XSetFunction(XtDisplay(w), cgc, GXclear);
    values.foreground = XWhitePixel(display, screen);
    values.background = XBlackPixel(display, screen);
    hgc = XCreateGC(XtDisplay(w), RootWindowOfScreen(XtScreen(w)),
        GCForeground | GCBackground | GCFont, &values);
    row_increment = font->max_bounds.ascent +
        font->max_bounds.descent + 2;
    *width = basket_width =
        pixmap_data.browser_columns * font->max_bounds.width;
    *height = basket_height =
        pixmap_data.browser_rows * row_increment;
    wastebasket = XCreatePixmap(XtDisplay(w),
        RootWindowOfScreen(XtScreen(w)), *width, *height, depth);
}   /* basket_create_offscreen_pixmap */


/*
basket_set_reference_widget() communicates the reference widget
for the wastebasket.
*/

void basket_set_reference_widget(w)
Widget w;
{
    wbrw = w;
}   /* basket_set_reference_widget */


/*
basket_reset_current_file() sets the "current file pointer"
to a null value.
*/

void basket_reset_current_file()
{
    current_file = NO_FILE;
}   /* basket_reset_current_file */


/*
basket_fill_with_filenames() fills the basket pixmap with the
```

```
names of the files stored in the wastebasket.
*/

int basket_fill_with_filenames(highlight_position)
int highlight_position;
{
    FILE *waste_fd;
    char file_spec[MAX_CHARS], temp_file_spec[MAX_CHARS];
    int len, offset;
    char *more_entries;

    sprintf(file_spec, "%s/%s", home_directory, wastebasket_file);
    if ((waste_fd = fopen(file_spec, "r")) == NULL) {
        alert("The wastebasket is empty.");
        return FALSE;
    }
    XFillRectangle(XtDisplay(wbrw), wastebasket, cgc, 0, 0,
        basket_width, basket_height);
    current_file = NO_FILE;
    more_entries = fgets(file_spec, MAX_CHARS, waste_fd);
    for (offset = row_increment, current_num_files = 0;
            more_entries != NULL && offset < basket_height;
            offset += row_increment, current_num_files++) {
        decode_file_spec(temp_file_spec, file_spec);
        len = strlen(temp_file_spec) - 1;    /* drop the <Return> */
        temp_file_spec[len] = EOS;
        XDrawImageString(XtDisplay(wbrw), wastebasket, wgc,
            0, offset, temp_file_spec, len);
        if (highlight_position != NO_HIGHLIGHT)
            if (highlight_position == current_num_files) {
                /* this is it */
                XDrawImageString(XtDisplay(wbrw), wastebasket,
                    hgc, 0, offset, temp_file_spec, len);
                current_file = current_num_files;
            }
        more_entries = fgets(file_spec, MAX_CHARS, waste_fd);
    }
    fclose(waste_fd);
    XCopyArea(XtDisplay(wbrw), wastebasket, XtWindow(wbrw),
        wgc, 0, 0, basket_width, basket_height, 0, 0);
    return TRUE;
}   /* basket_fill_with_filenames */


/*
basket_select_file() calculates the "row" offset for
a filename and then calls basket_fill_with_filenames() to
either clear the current highlighted file or highlight
another file, depending on the legitimacy of the position.
*/

void basket_select_file(event)
XEvent *event;
{
    int highlight_position;

    highlight_position = event->xbutton.y / row_increment;
```

```
    if (highlight_position > current_num_files)
        basket_fill_with_filenames(NO_HIGHLIGHT);
    else
        basket_fill_with_filenames(highlight_position);
}   /* basket_select_file */


/*
basket_restore_file() copies a file in the wastebasket back to
its original directory--the wastebasket entry is NOT deleted.
*/

void basket_restore_file()
{
    FILE *waste_fd;
    char cmd_string[MAX_CHARS];
    char file_spec[MAX_CHARS];
    char decoded_file_spec[MAX_CHARS];
    int position;
    char *more_entries;

    if (current_file == NO_FILE) {
        alert("First, you must click left to select a filename.");
        return;
    }
    sprintf(file_spec, "%s/%s", home_directory, wastebasket_file);
    if ((waste_fd = fopen(file_spec, "r")) == NULL) {
            alert("The wastebasket is empty.");
            return;
    }
    if ((more_entries = fgets(file_spec, MAX_CHARS, waste_fd))
            == NULL) {
        alert("The wastebasket is empty.");
        fclose(waste_fd);
        return;
    }
    for (position = 0;
            more_entries != NULL && position < current_file;
            position++)
        more_entries = fgets(file_spec, MAX_CHARS, waste_fd);
    if (position == current_file) {
        file_spec[strlen(file_spec) - 1] = EOS;
        decode_file_spec(decoded_file_spec, file_spec);
        sprintf(cmd_string, "cp %s/%s/%s %s",
                home_directory, wastebasket_dir, file_spec,
                decoded_file_spec);
        system(cmd_string);
    }
    fclose(waste_fd);
    basket_fill_with_filenames(NO_HIGHLIGHT);
}   /* basket_restore_file */


/*
basket_delete_file() permanently deletes a file from
the wastebasket directory.
*/
```

```
void basket_delete_file()
{
    FILE *waste_fd, *temp_waste_fd;
    char temp_file_spec[MAX_CHARS];
    char file_spec[MAX_CHARS];
    int position;
    char *more_entries;

    if (current_file == NO_FILE) {
        alert("First, you must click left to select a filename.");
        return;
    }
    sprintf(file_spec, "%s/%s", home_directory, wastebasket_file);
    if ((waste_fd = fopen(file_spec, "r")) == NULL) {
            alert("The wastebasket is empty.");
            return;
    }
    sprintf(temp_file_spec, "%s/%s.%d", home_directory,
        temp_wastebasket_file, getpid());
    if ((temp_waste_fd = fopen(temp_file_spec, "w")) == NULL) {
        alert(
    "Error opening temporary file during wastebasket operations!");
        fclose(waste_fd);
        return;
    }
    if ((more_entries = fgets(file_spec, MAX_CHARS, waste_fd))
            == NULL) {
        alert("The wastebasket is empty.");
        fclose(waste_fd);
        fclose(temp_waste_fd);
        return;
    }

    for (position = 0; more_entries != NULL; position++) {
        if (position == current_file ||
                position >= max_basket_entries) {
            file_spec[strlen(file_spec) - 1] = EOS;
            sprintf(temp_file_spec, "%s/%s/%s",
                    home_directory, wastebasket_dir, file_spec);
            unlink(temp_file_spec);
        }
        else
            fputs(file_spec, temp_waste_fd);
        more_entries = fgets(file_spec, MAX_CHARS, waste_fd);
    }
    fclose(waste_fd);
    fclose(temp_waste_fd);
    sprintf(temp_file_spec, "%s/%s.%d",
            home_directory, temp_wastebasket_file, getpid());
    sprintf(file_spec, "%s/%s",
            home_directory, wastebasket_file);
    rename(temp_file_spec, file_spec);
    basket_fill_with_filenames(NO_HIGHLIGHT);
}   /* basket_delete_file */
```

```
/*
basket_add_file() puts the passed file spec. in the top of the
wastebasket, removing the oldest wastebasket contents, if the
wastebasket is overflowing.
*/

void basket_add_file(file_spec)
char *file_spec;
{
    FILE *waste_fd, *temp_waste_fd;
    char encoded_file_spec[MAX_CHARS];
    char temp_file_spec[MAX_CHARS];
    char temp_file_spec_2[MAX_CHARS];
    int position, waste_exists = FALSE;
    char *more_entries;

    sprintf(temp_file_spec, "%s/%s", home_directory,
        wastebasket_dir);
    if (file_size(temp_file_spec) == -1)
        mkdir(temp_file_spec, 0755); /* you may want to change this */
    sprintf(temp_file_spec, "%s/%s", home_directory,
        wastebasket_file);
    if (file_size(temp_file_spec) != -1) {
        if ((waste_fd = fopen(temp_file_spec, "r")) != NULL)
            waste_exists = TRUE;
        else {
            alert("Error opening wastebasket!");
            return;
        }
    }
    sprintf(temp_file_spec, "%s/%s.%d",
        home_directory, temp_wastebasket_file, getpid());
    if ((temp_waste_fd = fopen(temp_file_spec, "w")) == NULL) {
        alert(
    "Error opening temporary file during wastebasket operations!");
        return;
    }

    encode_file_spec(encoded_file_spec, file_spec);
    strcat(encoded_file_spec, "\n");
    /* write the file spec. as the first wastebasket entry */
    fputs(encoded_file_spec, temp_waste_fd);

    if (waste_exists) {
        more_entries = fgets(temp_file_spec, MAX_CHARS, waste_fd);
        for (position = 1; more_entries != NULL; position++) {
            if (position < max_basket_entries) {
                if (strcmp(encoded_file_spec, temp_file_spec) != 0)
                    /* not a duplicate */
                    fputs(temp_file_spec, temp_waste_fd);
            }
            else {
                temp_file_spec[strlen(temp_file_spec) - 1] = EOS;
                sprintf(temp_file_spec_2, "%s/%s/%s",
                    home_directory, wastebasket_dir, temp_file_spec);
                unlink(temp_file_spec_2);
            }
```

```
            more_entries = fgets(temp_file_spec, MAX_CHARS, waste_fd);
        }
        fclose(waste_fd);
    }
    fclose(temp_waste_fd);
    encoded_file_spec[strlen(encoded_file_spec) - 1] = EOS;
    sprintf(temp_file_spec, "%s/%s/%s",
        home_directory, wastebasket_dir, encoded_file_spec);
    rename(file_spec, temp_file_spec);
    sprintf(temp_file_spec_2, "%s/%s.%d",
        home_directory, temp_wastebasket_file, getpid());
    sprintf(temp_file_spec, "%s/%s",
        home_directory, wastebasket_file);
    rename(temp_file_spec_2, temp_file_spec);
    basket_fill_with_filenames(NO_HIGHLIGHT);
}   /* basket_add_file */



/****  xwaste.menu.h  ****/

/****  external declarations for xwaste.menu.c  ****/


#ifndef XWASTE_MENU_H
#define XWASTE_MENU_H   1

#include <X11/Intrinsic.h>
#include <X11/StringDefs.h>
#include <X11/Shell.h>

#ifdef X11R3
#include <X11/Box.h>
#include <X11/Command.h>
#else
#include <X11/Xaw/Box.h>
#include <X11/Xaw/Command.h>
#endif

#include <stdio.h>

#include "xwaste.bskt.h"



#define MENU_CANCEL         -1
#define MENU_DELETE         -2
#define MENU_RESTORE        -3


/*
Function declarations:
*/

extern void MenuDelete(), MenuRestore();
extern void menu_create(), menu_up(), menu_down();
```

```
#endif


/****    xwaste.menu.c    ****/

/****     menu-related routines for xwaste.c    ****/


#include "xwaste.menu.h"


/*
Private globals:
*/


static Widget menuShell, menuBox, menuButtonRestore,
    menuButtonDelete;


/*
menu_create() allocates the widgets for the basket menu
and sets up the callback functions.
*/

void menu_create(parent)
Widget parent;
{
    Arg args[3];
    int i;

    i = 0;
    XtSetArg(args[i], XtNallowShellResize, (XtArgVal) TRUE); i++;
    menuShell = XtCreatePopupShell("menuShell",
        transientShellWidgetClass, parent, args, i);
    menuBox = XtCreateManagedWidget("menuBox",
        boxWidgetClass, menuShell, NULL, 0);
    i = 0;
    XtSetArg(args[i], XtNlabel,
        (XtArgVal) "Restore to Original Directory"); i++;
    menuButtonRestore = XtCreateManagedWidget("menuButtonRestore",
        commandWidgetClass, menuBox, args, i);
    i = 0;
    XtSetArg(args[i], XtNlabel,
        (XtArgVal) "Permanently Delete/Remove"); i++;
    menuButtonDelete = XtCreateManagedWidget("menuButtonDelete",
        commandWidgetClass, menuBox, args, i);
    XtAddCallback(menuButtonDelete, XtNcallback, MenuDelete, NULL);
    XtAddCallback(menuButtonRestore, XtNcallback, MenuRestore, NULL);
}   /* menu_create */


/*
menu_up() places and pops up the menu.
*/
```

```
/*ARGSUSED*/
void menu_up(w, event)
Widget w;
XButtonEvent *event;
{
    Arg args[3];
    int i;

    i = 0;
    XtSetArg(args[i], XtNx, (XtArgVal) (event->x_root - 20)); i++;
    XtSetArg(args[i], XtNy, (XtArgVal) (event->y_root - 20)); i++;
    XtSetValues(menuShell, args, i);
    XtPopup(menuShell, XtGrabNone);
}   /* menu_up */


/*
menu_down() removes the menu.
*/
/*ARGSUSED*/
void menu_down(w, event)
Widget w;
XButtonEvent *event;
{
    XtPopdown(menuShell);
    reset_proper_keyboard_focus();
}   /* menu_down */


/*
MenuDelete() permanently deletes a file.
*/
/*ARGSUSED*/
void MenuDelete(w, client_data, call_data)
Widget w;
caddr_t client_data;
caddr_t call_data;
{
    basket_delete_file();
    XtPopdown(menuShell);
    reset_proper_keyboard_focus();
}   /* MenuDelete */


/*
MenuRestore() restores a file to its original directory.
*/
/*ARGSUSED*/
void MenuRestore(w, client_data, call_data)
Widget w;
caddr_t client_data;
caddr_t call_data;
{
    basket_restore_file();
    XtPopdown(menuShell);
    reset_proper_keyboard_focus();
}   /* MenuRestore */
```

```
/****    alert.h    ****/

/****    external declarations for alert.c    ****/


#ifndef ALERT_H
#define ALERT_H 1

#include <X11/Intrinsic.h>
#include <X11/StringDefs.h>
#include <X11/Shell.h>
#include <X11/cursorfont.h>

#ifdef X11R3
#include <X11/Box.h>
#include <X11/Command.h>
#include <X11/Form.h>
#include <X11/Label.h>
#else
#include <X11/Xaw/Box.h>
#include <X11/Xaw/Command.h>
#include <X11/Xaw/Form.h>
#include <X11/Xaw/Label.h>
#endif

#include <stdio.h>


#define ALERT_YES       -1
#define ALERT_NO        -2
#define ALERT_CANCEL    -3



/*
Function declarations:
*/

extern void alert_create_ync(), alert_create_continue();
extern void AlertYesNoCancel(), AlertContinue();
extern void alert(), alert_beep();
extern void set_alert_reset_proper_keyboard_focus();
extern int alert_query();


#endif



/****    alert.c    ****    simple alert box implementation    ****/


#include "alert.h"
```

```
/*
Private functions:
*/

static int get_alert_result();
static void alert_reset_proper_keyboard_focus();


/*
Private globals:
*/

static Widget alertShellYesNoCancel, alertShellContinue,
    alertLabelYesNoCancel, alertLabelContinue,
    alertYesNoCancel, alertContinue,
    alertButtonYes, alertButtonNo,
    alertButtonCancel, alertButtonContinue;


static int query_result;          /* holds the result of  */
                                  /* an alert box query   */
static int query_wait;            /* controls the blocking     */
                                  /* activity of an alert box */

static Widget ync_parent, continue_parent;

/*
This is a pointer to a function to execute if the keyboard focus
needs resetting after pop-up operations.  See the functions
set_alert_reset_proper_keyboard_focus() and
alert_reset_proper_keyboard_focus() in this module.
*/

static void (*reset_keyboard_focus_proc)();



/*
alert_create_ync() creates a yes-no-cancel, three-button alert box.
*/

void alert_create_ync(parent)
Widget parent;
{
    Arg args[3];
    int i;

    ync_parent = parent;
    i = 0;
    XtSetArg(args[i], XtNallowShellResize, (XtArgVal) TRUE); i++;
    alertShellYesNoCancel = XtCreatePopupShell("alertShellYesNoCancel",
        transientShellWidgetClass, parent, args, i);
    alertYesNoCancel = XtCreateManagedWidget("alertYesNoCancel",
        formWidgetClass, alertShellYesNoCancel, NULL, 0);
    i = 0;
    XtSetArg(args[i], XtNresize, (XtArgVal) TRUE); i++;
```

```
    XtSetArg(args[i], XtNresizable, (XtArgVal) TRUE); i++;
    XtSetArg(args[i], XtNborderWidth, (XtArgVal) 0); i++;
    alertLabelYesNoCancel =
        XtCreateManagedWidget("alertLabelYesNoCancel",
            labelWidgetClass, alertYesNoCancel, args, i);
    i = 0;
    XtSetArg(args[i], XtNlabel, (XtArgVal) "Yes"); i++;
    XtSetArg(args[i], XtNfromVert,
        (XtArgVal) alertLabelYesNoCancel); i++;
    alertButtonYes = XtCreateManagedWidget("alertButtonYes",
        commandWidgetClass, alertYesNoCancel, args, i);
    i = 0;
    XtSetArg(args[i], XtNlabel, (XtArgVal) "No"); i++;
    XtSetArg(args[i], XtNfromVert,
        (XtArgVal) alertLabelYesNoCancel); i++;
    XtSetArg(args[i], XtNfromHoriz, (XtArgVal) alertButtonYes); i++;
    alertButtonNo = XtCreateManagedWidget("alertButtonNo",
        commandWidgetClass, alertYesNoCancel, args, i);
    i = 0;
    XtSetArg(args[i], XtNlabel, (XtArgVal) "Cancel"); i++;
    XtSetArg(args[i], XtNfromVert,
        (XtArgVal) alertLabelYesNoCancel); i++;
    XtSetArg(args[i], XtNfromHoriz, (XtArgVal) alertButtonNo); i++;
    alertButtonCancel = XtCreateManagedWidget("alertButtonCancel",
        commandWidgetClass, alertYesNoCancel, args, i);
    XtAddCallback(alertButtonYes, XtNcallback,
        AlertYesNoCancel, NULL);
    XtAddCallback(alertButtonNo, XtNcallback,
        AlertYesNoCancel, NULL);
    XtAddCallback(alertButtonCancel, XtNcallback,
        AlertYesNoCancel, NULL);
}   /* alert_create_ync */


/*
alert_create_continue() creates a one-button alert box.
*/

void alert_create_continue(parent)
Widget parent;
{
    Arg args[3];
    int i;

    continue_parent = parent;
    i = 0;
    XtSetArg(args[i], XtNallowShellResize, (XtArgVal) TRUE); i++;
    alertShellContinue = XtCreatePopupShell("alertShellContinue",
        transientShellWidgetClass, parent, args, i);
    alertContinue = XtCreateManagedWidget("alertContinue",
        formWidgetClass, alertShellContinue, NULL, 0);
    i = 0;
    XtSetArg(args[i], XtNresize, (XtArgVal) TRUE); i++;
    XtSetArg(args[i], XtNresizable, (XtArgVal) TRUE); i++;
    XtSetArg(args[i], XtNborderWidth, (XtArgVal) 0); i++;
    alertLabelContinue = XtCreateManagedWidget("alertLabelContinue",
        labelWidgetClass, alertContinue, args, i);
```

```
    i = 0;
    XtSetArg(args[i], XtNlabel, (XtArgVal) "Continue"); i++;
    XtSetArg(args[i], XtNfromVert,
        (XtArgVal) alertLabelContinue); i++;
    alertButtonContinue =
        XtCreateManagedWidget("alertButtonContinue",
            commandWidgetClass, alertContinue, args, i);
    XtAddCallback(alertButtonContinue, XtNcallback,
        AlertContinue, NULL);
}   /* alert_create_continue */


/*
AlertYesNoCancel() determines which option has been selected
in a dialog window and resets the 'wait' variable; it works
with alert_query().
*/
/*ARGSUSED*/
void AlertYesNoCancel(w, client_data, call_data)
Widget w;
caddr_t client_data;
caddr_t call_data;
{
    XtPopdown(alertShellYesNoCancel);
    alert_reset_proper_keyboard_focus();
    if (w == alertButtonYes)
        query_result = ALERT_YES;
    else if (w == alertButtonNo)
        query_result = ALERT_NO;
    else if (w == alertButtonCancel)
        query_result = ALERT_CANCEL;
    query_wait = FALSE;
}   /* AlertYesNoCancel */


/*
AlertContinue() terminates the pop-up message window
invoked by alert().
*/
/*ARGSUSED*/
void AlertContinue(w, client_data, call_data)
Widget w;
caddr_t client_data;
caddr_t call_data;
{
    XtPopdown(alertShellContinue);
    alert_reset_proper_keyboard_focus();
    query_wait = FALSE;
}   /* AlertContinue */


/*
set_alert_reset_proper_keyboard_focus() establishes a pointer to
the client's procedure that handles keyboard focus operations.
See the procedure alert_reset_proper_keyboard_focus().
*/
```

```
void set_alert_reset_proper_keyboard_focus(rkfp)
void (*rkfp)();
{
    reset_keyboard_focus_proc = rkfp;
}   /* set_alert_reset_proper_keyboard_focus */


/*
alert() pops up a message window; it works with AlertContinue().
*/

void alert(message)
char *message;
{
    Arg args[3];
    int i;
    Window dummy_w;
    int root_x, root_y, dummy_xy;
    unsigned int dummy_keys;

    XQueryPointer(XtDisplay(continue_parent),
        XtWindow(continue_parent), &dummy_w, &dummy_w, &root_x,
        &root_y, &dummy_xy, &dummy_xy, &dummy_keys);
    i = 0;
    XtSetArg(args[i], XtNx, (XtArgVal) (root_x - 20)); i++;
    XtSetArg(args[i], XtNy, (XtArgVal) (root_y - 20)); i++;
    XtSetValues(alertShellContinue, args, i);
    i = 0;
    XtSetArg(args[i], XtNlabel, (XtArgVal) message); i++;
    XtSetValues(alertLabelContinue, args, i);
    XtPopup(alertShellContinue, XtGrabExclusive);
}   /* alert */


/*
alert_query() pops up a dialog window;
it works with AlertYesNoCancel().
*/

int alert_query(message)
char *message;
{
    Arg args[3];
    int i;
    Window dummy_w;
    int root_x, root_y, dummy_xy;
    unsigned int dummy_keys;

    XQueryPointer(XtDisplay(ync_parent),
        XtWindow(ync_parent), &dummy_w, &dummy_w, &root_x,
        &root_y, &dummy_xy, &dummy_xy, &dummy_keys);
    i = 0;
    XtSetArg(args[i], XtNx, (XtArgVal) (root_x - 20)); i++;
    XtSetArg(args[i], XtNy, (XtArgVal) (root_y - 20)); i++;
    XtSetValues(alertShellYesNoCancel, args, i);
    i = 0;
    XtSetArg(args[i], XtNlabel, (XtArgVal) message); i++;
```

```
    XtSetValues(alertLabelYesNoCancel, args, i);
    XtPopup(alertShellYesNoCancel, XtGrabExclusive);
    return get_alert_result();
}   /* alert_query */


/*
alert_beep() rings the system bell n times.
*/

void alert_beep(num_beeps)
int num_beeps;
{
    while (num_beeps-- > 0)
        XBell(XtDisplay(continue_parent), 80);
}   /* alert_beep */


/*
get_alert_result() is a pop-up window function for waiting on the
user's selection to the yes-no-cancel alert query.
*/

static int get_alert_result()
{
    XEvent event;

    query_wait = TRUE;              /* block until the user */
    while (query_wait) {            /* presses a button     */
        XtNextEvent(&event);
        XtDispatchEvent(&event);
    }
    return query_result;
}   /* get_alert_result */


/*
alert_reset_proper_keyboard_focus() allows the keyboard focus to be
reestablished after after a transient shell is popped up and down.
Calling this routine is necessary with twm, but not with uwm.
*/

static void alert_reset_proper_keyboard_focus()
{
    if (reset_keyboard_focus_proc == NULL)
        return;
    reset_keyboard_focus_proc();
}   /* alert_reset_proper_keyboard_focus */



#define xwaste_width 40
#define xwaste_height 40
static char xwaste_bits[] = {
   0x00, 0x00, 0x00, 0x00, 0x00, 0x00, 0x00, 0x1c, 0xf8, 0x03, 0x00, 0x04,
   0x22, 0x44, 0x04, 0x00, 0x0a, 0x49, 0x22, 0x08, 0x00, 0x91, 0x84, 0x11,
   0x12, 0x80, 0x64, 0x12, 0x09, 0x09, 0x40, 0x42, 0x48, 0x86, 0x04, 0x20,
```

```
   0x89, 0x24, 0x44, 0x02, 0xfe, 0xff, 0xff, 0xff, 0x7f, 0xfe, 0xff, 0xff,
   0xff, 0x7f, 0x0c, 0x00, 0x00, 0x00, 0x30, 0x08, 0x00, 0x00, 0x00, 0x10,
   0x48, 0x92, 0x24, 0x49, 0x12, 0x08, 0x00, 0x00, 0x00, 0x10, 0x08, 0x00,
   0x00, 0x00, 0x10, 0x48, 0x92, 0x24, 0x49, 0x12, 0x08, 0x00, 0x00, 0x00,
   0x10, 0x08, 0x00, 0x00, 0x00, 0x10, 0x48, 0x92, 0x24, 0x49, 0x12, 0x08,
   0x00, 0x00, 0x00, 0x10, 0x08, 0x00, 0x00, 0x00, 0x10, 0x48, 0x92, 0x24,
   0x49, 0x12, 0x08, 0x00, 0x00, 0x00, 0x10, 0x08, 0x00, 0x00, 0x00, 0x10,
   0x48, 0x92, 0x24, 0x49, 0x12, 0x08, 0x00, 0x00, 0x00, 0x10, 0x08, 0x00,
   0x00, 0x00, 0x10, 0x48, 0x92, 0x24, 0x49, 0x12, 0x08, 0x00, 0x00, 0x00,
   0x10, 0x08, 0x00, 0x00, 0x00, 0x10, 0x48, 0x92, 0x24, 0x49, 0x12, 0x08,
   0x00, 0x00, 0x00, 0x10, 0x08, 0x00, 0x00, 0x00, 0x10, 0x48, 0x92, 0x24,
   0x49, 0x12, 0x08, 0x00, 0x00, 0x00, 0x10, 0x08, 0x00, 0x00, 0x00, 0x10,
   0x48, 0x92, 0x24, 0x49, 0x12, 0x08, 0x00, 0x00, 0x00, 0x10, 0x08, 0x00,
   0x00, 0x00, 0x10, 0xf8, 0xff, 0xff, 0xff, 0x1f};
```

```
!
! XWaste resource file
!
*directoryBox*width:          200
*filenameBox*width:           150

*menuShell*hSpace:  0
*menuShell*vSpace:  0
*menuShell*Command.width: 200
*menuShell*borderWidth: 1
*menuBox.Command.translations:  #replace\n\
    <Enter>:                highlight()\n\
    <Leave>:                reset()\n\
    <BtnDown>,<BtnUp>:        set() notify() unset()
*wasteBasket.translations:  #replace\n\
    <Btn1Down>,<Btn1Up>:      selectFile()\n\
    <Btn2Down>,<Btn2Up>:      menuDown()\n\
    <Btn3Down>,<Btn3Up>:      menuUp()\n\
    <Expose>:               fillBasket()
*fileSpecForm*translations: #override\n\
    Ctrl<Key>J:             beep()\n\
    Ctrl<Key>O:             beep()\n\
    Ctrl<Key>M:             beep()\n\
    <Key>Linefeed:          beep()\n\
    <Key>Return:        beep()
!*iconic:   yes
```

L

Miscellaneous Library Functions

```
/****    Ximisc.h    ****    declarations for libXimisc.a   ****/


XFontStruct *load_font();
void query_set_pos();



/****    load.font.c    ****/

#include <stdio.h>
#include <X11/Intrinsic.h>
#include <X11/StringDefs.h>

#include "Ximisc.h"


/*
load_font() loads the specified font and returns a pointer
to the font structure.
*/

XFontStruct *load_font(w, app_name, font_name)
Widget w;
char *app_name, *font_name;
{
    static XFontStruct *font;

    if ((font = XLoadQueryFont(XtDisplay(w), font_name)) == NULL) {
        fprintf(stderr,
```

```
            "%s: unable to load font %s!\n",
            app_name, font_name);
        font = XLoadQueryFont(XtDisplay(w), "fixed");
    }
    return font;
}   /* load_font */



/****    query.pos.c    ****/

#include <stdio.h>
#include <X11/Xlib.h>
#include <X11/Xos.h>
#include <X11/IntrinsicP.h>
#include <X11/StringDefs.h>

#include "Ximisc.h"


/*
query_set_pos() tests the current pointer position
and sets the coordinates for the popup shell.
*/

void query_set_pos(w)
Widget w;
{
    Window dummy_win;
    int root_x, root_y, dummy_xy;
    unsigned int dummy_keys;
    XtWidgetGeometry new_pos;
    Arg args[3];
    int i;

    XQueryPointer(XtDisplay(w->core.parent),
        XtWindow(XtParent(w->core.parent)),
        &dummy_win, &dummy_win, &root_x,
        &root_y, &dummy_xy, &dummy_xy, &dummy_keys);
/*  new_pos.request_mode = CWX | CWY;
    new_pos.x = root_x - 40;
    new_pos.y = root_y - 10;
    XtMakeGeometryRequest(w->core.parent, &new_pos,
        (XtWidgetGeometry *) NULL); ** won't work with Motif **/
    i = 0;
    XtSetArg(args[i], XtNx, (XtArgVal) (root_x - 40)); i++;
    XtSetArg(args[i], XtNy, (XtArgVal) (root_y - 10)); i++;
    XtSetValues(w->core.parent, args, i);
}   /* query_set_pos*/
```

M

XiStrSelect: An Abstract String Selection Widget

```
/****    StrSelect.h    ****/

/****    public declarations/definitions for StrSelect.c    ****/

#ifndef _XiStrSelect_h
#define _XiStrSelect_h  1

/*******************************************************************
*  Copyright (c) 1990 Iris Computing Laboratories.
*
*  This software is provided for demonstration purposes only.  As
*  freely-distributed, modifiable source code, this software carries
*  absolutely no warranty.
*******************************************************************/


/*******************************************************************
This widget implements a string selection box.  The basic idea is
that a string/buffer can be displayed in a window (a simple
pixmap-based widget) with client-specified line/row delimiters.
One possible usage for this widget would be the display of
filenames in a window.
   The string selection box allows the user to select an entry from
the window; by default, a click-left operation makes a selection.
The selected entry is highlighted in reverse video.  The public
function XiStrSelectGetSelection() retrieves the currently selected
entry.
   The application programmer can specify the reference string in
one of two ways:  (1) the resource XiNreferenceString can be set to
```

```
point to the client string, or (2) the public function
XiStrSelectSetString() can be used change the reference string
dynamically.  The reference string must exist external to the
string selection box widget.  The string selection box makes a
private copy of the reference string, because it uses strtok() to
break the string into rows.
   A convenience function, XiStrSelectPopup() is available for
popping up the string selection box, IF it resides in a top-level
shell.  (This function simply invokes XtPopup() on the parent of
the string selection widget.  This function would not be useful,
if, for example, the string selection widget is a child of, say,
a viewport.
   Note that the pixmap cannot be resized.  Typically, the client
would create the pixmap inside a viewport and, possibly, allow the
viewport to be resized.  There are no limits on the size of the
reference string and the selected string--they are maintained in
dynamically allocated primary storage.
   An application may need to make preparations for a StrSelect
widget's handing of font dimensions.  Specifically, a StrSelect
widget adds spacing to the height of the specified font in
determining the height of a row within the pixmap; see the
XiNrowSpacing resource below.  Thus, in some cases, a higher level
widget that uses a StrSelect widget may need to make its own
row/column size determinations in order to coordinate its own
dimensions with those of the pixmap.  Note that you can set the
row spacing to 0, if you don't want the spacing to be added.
   The client program can use resources to set the font, the size
of the box in row/column metrics, the delimiters that break the
string into rows, the pixmap cursor, etc.  Most of the resources
are used only during widget creation.
   Several of the calls to fprintf() are "optional."

Resources:

Name            Class           Data Type       Default      Modify?
----            -----           ---------       -------      -------
XiNreference-   XiCReference-   String          "Nothing to OK
String          String                          display!"
XiNdelimiters   XiCDelimiters   String          "\n\r\t"     OK
XiNpixmapRows   XiCPixmapRows   int             50
XiNpixmapColumnsXiCPixmapColumnsint             100
XiNrowSpacing   XiCRowSpacing   int             2 (pixels)
XiNfont         XiCFont         XFontStruct *   XtDefaultFont

   Public interfaces are described below.
******************************************************************/

#ifdef X11R3
#include <X11/Simple.h>
#else
#include <X11/Xaw/Simple.h>
#endif


/*
Resource definitions:
*/
```

```
#define XiNreferenceString  "referenceString"    /* OK to modify */
#define XiNdelimiters       "delimiters"         /* OK to modify */
#define XiNfont             "font"
#define XiNpixmapRows       "pixmapRows"
#define XiNpixmapColumns    "pixmapColumns"
#define XiNrowSpacing       "rowSpacing"
#define XiCReferenceString  "ReferenceString"
#define XiCDelimiters       "Delimiters"
#define XiCFont             "Font"
#define XiCPixmapRows       "PixmapRows"
#define XiCPixmapColumns    "PixmapColumns"
#define XiCRowSpacing       "RowSpacing"


typedef struct _XiStrSelectClassRec *XiStrSelectWidgetClass;
typedef struct _XiStrSelectRec *XiStrSelectWidget;

extern WidgetClass xiStrSelectWidgetClass;


/*
Public functions:
*/

extern void XiStrSelectPopup();
/*  XiStrSelectWidget str_select_widget;
*/

extern char *XiStrSelectGetSelection();
/*  XiStrSelectWidget str_select_widget;
*/

extern void XiStrSelectSetString();
/*  XiStrSelectWidget str_select_widget;
    char *string;
*/

extern void XiStrSelectRedisplay();
/*  XiStrSelectWidget str_select_widget;
*/

extern void XiStrSelectReset();
/*  XiStrSelectWidget str_select_widget;
*/


#endif /* _XiStrSelect_h  */



/****    StrSelectP.h    ****/

/****    private declarations/definitions for StrSelect.c    ****/


#ifndef _XiStrSelectP_h
```

```
#define _XiStrSelectP_h


#include "StrSelect.h"
#ifdef X11R3
#include <X11/SimpleP.h>
#else
#include <X11/Xaw/SimpleP.h>
#endif


#define STR_NOTHING                  "Nothing to display!"

#define STR_DEFAULT_WIDTH            300
#define STR_DEFAULT_HEIGHT           150

#define STR_DEFAULT_PIXMAP_ROWS      50
#define STR_DEFAULT_PIXMAP_COLUMNS   100
#define STR_DEFAULT_ROW_SPACING      2
#define STR_MIN_ROWS                 2
#define STR_MIN_COLUMNS              5


#define STR_MAX_STR                  500
#define STR_MAX_SELECTION            1000


#define STR_NO_HIGHLIGHT     -1  /* ignore mouse, just     */
                                 /* redisplay strings      */
#define STR_NO_STR           -2  /* no currently selected str */

#define STR_DELIMITERS    "\n\r\t"        /* used with strtok() */
#define EOS               '\0'


typedef struct _XiStrSelectClassPart {        /* class definition */
    int dummy;
} XiStrSelectClassPart;

typedef struct _XiStrSelectClassRec {
    CoreClassPart core_class;
    SimpleClassPart simple_class;
    XiStrSelectClassPart str_select_class;
} XiStrSelectClassRec;

extern XiStrSelectClassRec xiStrSelectClassRec;


typedef struct _XiStrSelectPart {        /* instance definition */
    char *str;                           /* the string/buffer */
    char *buffer;                        /* internal copy of str,    */
                                         /* strtok() modifies arg.   */
    char *delimiters;                    /* what separates each line */
    char *selection;                     /* holds current selection */
    XFontStruct *font;
    int pixmap_rows, pixmap_columns;     /* row/column metrics */
    int pixmap_width, pixmap_height;     /* pixel metrics */
```

```
    int row_spacing;                    /* space between rows */
    int row_increment;                  /* height of a row */
    Pixmap pixmap;
    GC gc;                              /* regular text display GC */
    GC cgc;                             /* clear text GC */
    GC hgc;                             /* highlight text GC */
    int current_str;
    int current_num_strs;
} XiStrSelectPart;


typedef struct _XiStrSelectRec {
    CorePart core;
    SimplePart simple;
    XiStrSelectPart str_select;
} XiStrSelectRec;


#endif  /* _XiStrSelectP_h */



/**  StrSelect.c  ** simple string selection box implementation  **/


#include <stdio.h>

#include <X11/Xlib.h>
#include <X11/Xos.h>
#include <X11/IntrinsicP.h>
#include <X11/StringDefs.h>
#include <X11/Shell.h>

#ifdef X11R3
#include <X11/Simple.h>
#else
#include <X11/Xaw/XawInit.h>
#include <X11/Xaw/Simple.h>
#endif

#include "StrSelectP.h"


/*
Class Methods:
*/

static void Initialize();
static void Destroy();
static Boolean SetValues();
static void Redisplay();


/*
Private support functions:
*/
```

```
static void create_offscreen_pixmap();
static void fill_pixmap_and_redisplay();
static void fill_pixmap();
static void redisplay_pixmap();
static void select_str();


/*
Translations and actions:
*/

static void SelectStr();

static char pixmap_translations[] =
    "<Btn1Down>:  select()";

static XtActionsRec pixmap_actions[] = {
    {"select", (XtActionProc) SelectStr},
};


/*
Resource table:
*/

#define res_offset(field) XtOffset(XiStrSelectWidget, field)

static XtResource resources[] = {
    {XiNreferenceString, XiCReferenceString, XtRString,
        sizeof(char *), res_offset(str_select.str),
        XtRString, STR_NOTHING},
    {XiNdelimiters, XiCDelimiters, XtRString, sizeof(char *),
        res_offset(str_select.delimiters),
        XtRString, STR_DELIMITERS},
    {XiNfont, XiCFont, XtRFontStruct, sizeof(XFontStruct *),
        res_offset(str_select.font),
        XtRString, "XtDefaultFont"},
    {XiNpixmapRows, XiCPixmapRows, XtRInt, sizeof(int),
        res_offset(str_select.pixmap_rows),
        XtRImmediate, (caddr_t) STR_DEFAULT_PIXMAP_ROWS},
    {XiNpixmapColumns, XiCPixmapColumns, XtRInt, sizeof(int),
        res_offset(str_select.pixmap_columns),
        XtRImmediate, (caddr_t) STR_DEFAULT_PIXMAP_COLUMNS},
    {XiNrowSpacing, XiCRowSpacing, XtRInt, sizeof(int),
        res_offset(str_select.row_spacing),
        XtRImmediate, (caddr_t) STR_DEFAULT_ROW_SPACING},
};


/*
Define storage for the class here:
*/

XiStrSelectClassRec XistrSelectClassRec = {
    { /* core_class variables */
        (WidgetClass) &simpleClassRec,  /* ancestor */
        "StrSelect",                    /* class name */
```

```
        sizeof(XiStrSelectRec),           /* widget size */
#ifdef X11R3
        NULL,                             /* class initialize */
#else
        XawInitializeWidgetSet,           /* class initialize */
#endif
        NULL,                             /* class part init. */
        FALSE,                            /* class inited */
        Initialize,                       /* initialize */
        NULL,                             /* initialize hook */
        XtInheritRealize,                 /* realize */
        pixmap_actions,                   /* actions */
        XtNumber(pixmap_actions),         /* number of actions */
        resources,                        /* resources */
        XtNumber(resources),              /* number of resources */
        NULLQUARK,                        /* xrm class */
        TRUE,                             /* compress motions */
        TRUE,                             /* compress exposures */
        TRUE,                             /* compress enter/leave */
        FALSE,                            /* visibility interest */
        Destroy,                          /* destroy */
        NULL,                             /* resize */
        Redisplay,                        /* expose */
        SetValues,                        /* set values */
        NULL,                             /* set values hook */
        XtInheritSetValuesAlmost,         /* set values almost */
        NULL,                             /* get values hook */
        NULL,                             /* accept focus */
        XtVersion,                        /* version */
        NULL,                             /* callback private */
        pixmap_translations,              /* translation table */
        XtInheritQueryGeometry,           /* query geometry */
        XtInheritDisplayAccelerator,      /* display accelerator */
        NULL,                             /* extension */
    },
    { /* simple_class variables */
        XtInheritChangeSensitive,
    },
    { /* str_select_class variables */
        0,
    },
}; /* XistrSelectClassRec */


WidgetClass xiStrSelectWidgetClass =
    (WidgetClass) &XistrSelectClassRec;


/*
XiStrSelectWidget methods:
*/

/*
Initialize() initializes each instance of a string selection box.
A string selection box implements a pixmap in a SimpleWidget.
*/
/*ARGSUSED*/
```

```
static void Initialize(request, new)
XiStrSelectWidget request, new;
{
    if (new->str_select.pixmap_rows < STR_MIN_ROWS)
        new->str_select.pixmap_rows = STR_DEFAULT_PIXMAP_ROWS;
    if (new->str_select.pixmap_columns < STR_MIN_COLUMNS)
        new->str_select.pixmap_columns = STR_DEFAULT_PIXMAP_COLUMNS;
    if (!new->str_select.str)
        new->str_select.str = STR_NOTHING;
    if (!new->str_select.delimiters)
        new->str_select.delimiters = STR_DELIMITERS;
    if (!strlen(new->str_select.delimiters))
        new->str_select.delimiters = STR_DELIMITERS;

    create_offscreen_pixmap(new);

    new->str_select.selection = NULL;
    new->str_select.buffer = NULL;
    new->core.width = new->str_select.pixmap_width;
    new->core.height = new->str_select.pixmap_height;

    fill_pixmap(new, STR_NO_HIGHLIGHT);
}   /* Initialize */


/*
Destroy() cleans up dynamic data structures.
*/

static void Destroy(w)
XiStrSelectWidget w;
{
    if (w->str_select.buffer != NULL)
        XtFree(w->str_select.buffer);
    if (w->str_select.selection != NULL)
        XtFree(w->str_select.selection);
    if (w->str_select.gc != NULL)
        XFreeGC(XtDisplay(w), w->str_select.gc);
    if (w->str_select.cgc != NULL)
        XFreeGC(XtDisplay(w), w->str_select.cgc);
    if (w->str_select.hgc != NULL)
        XFreeGC(XtDisplay(w), w->str_select.hgc);
    if (w->str_select.pixmap != NULL)
        XFreePixmap(XtDisplay(w), w->str_select.pixmap);
}   /* Destroy */


/*
SetValues() handles modifications to resource-related
instance variables.  Since all pixmap-related processing is
based on 'pixmap_width' and 'pixmap_height', and these fields
are modified only during widget creation, it really isn't
necessary to check for modified row and column metrics; this
applies to several other resources as well.
*/
/*ARGSUSED*/
static Boolean SetValues(current, request, new)
```

```
Widget current, request, new;
{
    XiStrSelectWidget sw = (XiStrSelectWidget) new;
    XiStrSelectWidget old_sw = (XiStrSelectWidget) current;

    if (!sw->str_select.str)
        sw->str_select.str = STR_NOTHING;
    if (!sw->str_select.delimiters)
        sw->str_select.delimiters = STR_DELIMITERS;
    if (!strlen(sw->str_select.delimiters))
        sw->str_select.delimiters = STR_DELIMITERS;
    if (strcmp(sw->str_select.str, old_sw->str_select.str))
        fill_pixmap(sw, STR_NO_HIGHLIGHT);
    if (strcmp(sw->str_select.delimiters,
            old_sw->str_select.delimiters))
        fill_pixmap(sw, STR_NO_HIGHLIGHT);
    return FALSE;
}   /* SetValues */


/*
Redisplay() calls redisplay_pixmap() to update the pixmap
window upon an exposure.  Note that the pixmap is not updated--
just the pixmap window.
*/
/*ARGSUSED*/
static void Redisplay(w, event)
Widget w;
XEvent *event;
{
    redisplay_pixmap(w);
}   /* Redisplay */


/*
Actions functions:
*/

/*
SelectStr() simply calls the private function select_str().
*/

static void SelectStr(w, event)
Widget w;
XEvent *event;
{
    select_str(w, event);
}   /* SelectStr */


/*
Public functions:
*/

/*
XiStrSelectPopup() invokes (pops up) the string selection box.
This convenience is useful ONLY if the string selection box's
```

```
parent is a pop-up shell.
*/

void XiStrSelectPopup(ssw)
XiStrSelectWidget ssw;
{
/*  if (XtIsShell(ssw->core.parent)) **** won't work with X11R4 ****/
    if (XtIsSubclass(ssw->core.parent, (WidgetClass) shellWidgetClass))
        XtPopup(ssw->core.parent, XtGrabNone);
}   /* XiStrSelectPopup */


/*
XiStrSelectGetSelection() retrieves the value stored in the private
field 'selection'; this is the currently selected string.
*/

char *XiStrSelectGetSelection(ssw)
XiStrSelectWidget ssw;
{
    return ssw->str_select.selection;
}   /* XiStrSelectGetSelection */


/*
XiStrSelectSetString() establishes a pointer to the string
(buffer) that the widget displays.  It assumes that a zero-
length string is OK.
*/

void XiStrSelectSetString(ssw, str)
XiStrSelectWidget ssw;
char *str;
{
    if (!str)           /* check for null pointer */
        fprintf(stderr,
        "string selection box: the reference string is null!\n");
    ssw->str_select.str = str;
    fill_pixmap(ssw, STR_NO_HIGHLIGHT);
}   /* XiStrSelectSetString */


/*
XiStrSelectRedisplay() allows an application to force a
redisplay of the pixmap.
*/

void XiStrSelectRedisplay(ssw)
XiStrSelectWidget ssw;
{
    redisplay_pixmap(ssw);
}   /* XiStrSelectRedisplay */


/*
XiStrSelectReset() allows an application to force the
clearing of the pixmap and related variables.
```

```
redisplay of the pixmap.
*/

void XiStrSelectReset(ssw)
XiStrSelectWidget ssw;
{
    ssw->str_select.current_str = STR_NO_STR;
    ssw->str_select.str = NULL;
    if (ssw->str_select.selection != NULL) {
        XtFree(ssw->str_select.selection);
        ssw->str_select.selection = NULL;
    }
    if (ssw->str_select.buffer != NULL)
        XtFree(ssw->str_select.buffer);
    XFillRectangle(XtDisplay(ssw), ssw->str_select.pixmap,
        ssw->str_select.cgc, 0, 0, ssw->core.width, ssw->core.height);
    if (XtIsRealized(ssw))
        XClearWindow(XtDisplay(ssw), XtWindow(ssw));
}   /* XiStrSelectReset */


/*
Support functions:
*/

/*
create_offscreen_pixmap() creates and sets the dimensions
of the string selection box pixmap.  It also creates three GCs:
    gc  -- for standard text display,
    hgc -- for highlighted/selected text, and
    cgc -- for clearing the pixmap.
There are numerous data type inconsistencies in the various X
data structures for fonts, pixmaps, etc., so just use 'int';
expressions will be converted to 'unsigned int'.
*/

static void create_offscreen_pixmap(w)
XiStrSelectWidget w;
{
    XGCValues values;
    Display *display = XtDisplay(w);
    int screen = XDefaultScreen(display);
    int depth = XDisplayPlanes(display, screen);

    values.foreground = XBlackPixel(display, screen);
    values.background = XWhitePixel(display, screen);
    values.font = w->str_select.font->fid;
    w->str_select.gc = XCreateGC(XtDisplay(w),
        RootWindowOfScreen(XtScreen(w)),
        GCForeground | GCBackground | GCFont, &values);
    w->str_select.cgc = XCreateGC(XtDisplay(w),
        RootWindowOfScreen(XtScreen(w)),
        GCForeground | GCBackground | GCFont, &values);
    XSetFunction(XtDisplay(w), w->str_select.cgc, GXclear);
    values.foreground = XWhitePixel(display, screen);
    values.background = XBlackPixel(display, screen);
    w->str_select.hgc = XCreateGC(XtDisplay(w),
```

```
        RootWindowOfScreen(XtScreen(w)),
        GCForeground | GCBackground | GCFont, &values);
    w->str_select.row_increment =
        w->str_select.font->max_bounds.ascent +
        w->str_select.font->max_bounds.descent +
        w->str_select.row_spacing;
    w->str_select.pixmap_width = w->str_select.pixmap_columns *
        w->str_select.font->max_bounds.width;
    w->str_select.pixmap_height = w->str_select.pixmap_rows *
        w->str_select.row_increment;
    w->str_select.pixmap = XCreatePixmap(XtDisplay(w),
        RootWindowOfScreen(XtScreen(w)), w->str_select.pixmap_width,
        w->str_select.pixmap_height, depth);
}   /* create_offscreen_pixmap */


/*
fill_pixmap_and_redisplay() builds the pixmap and refreshes
the window.
*/

static void fill_pixmap_and_redisplay(w, highlight_position)
XiStrSelectWidget w;
int highlight_position;
{
    fill_pixmap(w, highlight_position);
    redisplay_pixmap(w);
}   /* fill_pixmap_and_redisplay */


/*
fill_pixmap() tests for errors and then displays the string
on the pixmap.  NOTE: This function sets the current selection.
*/

static void fill_pixmap(w, highlight_position)
XiStrSelectWidget w;
int highlight_position;
{
    int len, offset;
    char *next;

    if (!w->str_select.str)
        return;
    if (!strlen(w->str_select.str)) {
        fprintf(stderr,         /** !!! remove? **/
        "string selection box: reference string is empty!\n");
        return;
    }
    w->str_select.current_str = STR_NO_STR;
    if (w->str_select.selection != NULL) {
        XtFree(w->str_select.selection);
        w->str_select.selection = NULL;
    }
    if (w->str_select.buffer != NULL)
        XtFree(w->str_select.buffer);
    /*
```

```
    copy the user's string -- strtok() modifies its string argument
    */
    if ((len = strlen(w->str_select.str)) > -1) {
        w->str_select.buffer = XtMalloc((unsigned) (len + 1));
        strcpy(w->str_select.buffer, w->str_select.str);
    }
    else
        w->str_select.buffer = "";
    /*
    clear pixmap before it filling with a new string:
    */
    XFillRectangle(XtDisplay(w), w->str_select.pixmap,
        w->str_select.cgc, 0, 0, w->core.width, w->core.height);
    next = (char *)
        strtok(w->str_select.buffer, w->str_select.delimiters);
    for (offset = w->str_select.row_increment,
            w->str_select.current_num_strs = 0;
            next != NULL && offset < w->str_select.pixmap_height;
            offset += w->str_select.row_increment,
            w->str_select.current_num_strs++) {
        len = strlen(next);
        XDrawImageString(XtDisplay(w), w->str_select.pixmap,
            w->str_select.gc, 0, offset, next, len);
        if (highlight_position != STR_NO_HIGHLIGHT)
            if (highlight_position ==
                    w->str_select.current_num_strs) {
                /* this is it */
                XDrawImageString(XtDisplay(w), w->str_select.pixmap,
                    w->str_select.hgc, 0, offset, next, len);
                w->str_select.current_str =
                    w->str_select.current_num_strs;
                w->str_select.selection =
                    XtMalloc((unsigned) (len + 1));
                strcpy(w->str_select.selection, next);
            }
        next = (char *) strtok(NULL, w->str_select.delimiters);
    }
}   /* fill_pixmap */


/*
redisplay_pixmap() copies the pixmap to the window.
*/

static void redisplay_pixmap(w)
XiStrSelectWidget w;
{
    if (!XtIsRealized(w))
        return;
    XCopyArea(XtDisplay(w), w->str_select.pixmap,
        XtWindow(w),
        w->str_select.gc, 0, 0, w->str_select.pixmap_width,
        w->str_select.pixmap_height, 0, 0);
}   /* redisplay_pixmap */


/*
```

```
select_str() calculates the "row" offset for a string/item and then
calls fill_pixmap_and_redisplay() to either clear the current
highlighted string or highlight another string, depending on the
legitimacy of the position.  The vertical button position is
"adjusted" by 1/2 the height of a row.  NOTE: This function
indirectly sets/modifies the current selection.
*/

static void select_str(w, event)
XiStrSelectWidget w;
XEvent *event;
{
    int highlight_position;

    highlight_position =
        (event->xbutton.y - (w->str_select.row_increment / 2)) /
            w->str_select.row_increment;
    if (highlight_position > w->str_select.current_num_strs)
        fill_pixmap_and_redisplay(w, STR_NO_HIGHLIGHT);
    else
        fill_pixmap_and_redisplay(w, highlight_position);
}   /* select_str */


/****  teststrsel.c  ****  tests the string selection box widget ****/


#include <stdio.h>
#include <X11/Intrinsic.h>
#include <X11/StringDefs.h>
#include <X11/Shell.h>
#include <X11/cursorfont.h>

#ifdef X11R3
#include <X11/Box.h>
#include <X11/Command.h>
#else
#include <X11/Xaw/Box.h>
#include <X11/Xaw/Command.h>
#endif

#include <Ximisc.h>
#include "StrSelect.h"


/*
Functions:
*/

void Done(), Quit(), PrintSelection1(), PrintSelection2(),
    TestSelectBox1(), TestSelectBox2();


/*
Private globals:
*/
```

```
static Widget strSelectShell1, strSelectShell2,
    testSelectBox1, testSelectBox2,
    doneButton1, doneButton2;

static XFontStruct *font;

static char *test_str1 = "This is string selection box 1:\n\
Line 2\nLine 3\nLine 4";
static char *test_str2 = "This is string selection box 2:\n\
Line 2\nLine 3\nLine 4";


/*
main() sets up a button-activated string selection box.  A simple
callback is used to test the retrieval facilities for the
currently selected string.  NOTE:  It's important to test for
proper handling of multiple widgets, and to test both methods for
specifying a reference string.
*/

void main(argc, argv)
int argc;
char **argv;
{
    Widget topLevel, testBox, strSelectButton1, strSelectButton2,
        printButton1, printButton2, quitButton;
    Arg args[5];
    int i;
    char *delimiters = "\n";
    Cursor pixmap_cursor;

    topLevel = XtInitialize(argv[0], "TestStrSel",
        NULL, 0, &argc, argv);
    font = load_font(topLevel, "teststrsel", "8x13");
    i = 0;
    XtSetArg(args[i], XtNallowShellResize, (XtArgVal) TRUE); i++;
    strSelectShell1 = XtCreatePopupShell("strSelectShell1",
        transientShellWidgetClass, topLevel, args, i);
    i = 0;
    XtSetArg(args[i], XtNallowShellResize, (XtArgVal) TRUE); i++;
    strSelectShell2 = XtCreatePopupShell("strSelectShell2",
        transientShellWidgetClass, topLevel, args, i);
    i = 0;
    XtSetArg(args[i], XiNdelimiters, (XtArgVal) delimiters); i++;
    XtSetArg(args[i], XiNreferenceString, (XtArgVal) test_str1); i++;
    XtSetArg(args[i], XiNpixmapRows, (XtArgVal) 15); i++;
    XtSetArg(args[i], XiNpixmapColumns, (XtArgVal) 35); i++;
    testSelectBox1 = XtCreateManagedWidget("testSelectBox1",
        xiStrSelectWidgetClass, strSelectShell1, args, i);
    i = 0;
    XtSetArg(args[i], XiNfont, (XtArgVal) font); i++;
    XtSetArg(args[i], XiNpixmapRows, (XtArgVal) 5); i++;
    XtSetArg(args[i], XiNpixmapColumns, (XtArgVal) 31); i++;
/*  pixmap_cursor = XCreateFontCursor(XtDisplay(topLevel), XC_right_ptr);
    XtSetArg(args[i], XtNcursor, (XtArgVal) pixmap_cursor); i++;*/
    testSelectBox2 = XtCreateManagedWidget("testSelectBox2",
```

```
        xiStrSelectWidgetClass, strSelectShell2, args, i);
    XiStrSelectSetString(testSelectBox2, test_str2);
    testBox = XtCreateManagedWidget("box", boxWidgetClass,
        topLevel, NULL, 0);
    i = 0;
    XtSetArg(args[i], XtNlabel, (XtArgVal) "Str Selection Box 1"); i++;
    strSelectButton1 = XtCreateManagedWidget("strSelectButton1",
        commandWidgetClass, testBox, args, i);
    XtAddCallback(strSelectButton1, XtNcallback, TestSelectBox1, NULL);
    i = 0;
    XtSetArg(args[i], XtNlabel, (XtArgVal) "Str Selection Box 2"); i++;
    strSelectButton2 = XtCreateManagedWidget("strSelectButton2",
        commandWidgetClass, testBox, args, i);
    XtAddCallback(strSelectButton2, XtNcallback, TestSelectBox2, NULL);
    i = 0;
    XtSetArg(args[i], XtNlabel, (XtArgVal) "Print Selection 1"); i++;
    printButton1 = XtCreateManagedWidget("printButton1",
        commandWidgetClass, testBox, args, i);
    XtAddCallback(printButton1, XtNcallback, PrintSelection1, NULL);
    i = 0;
    XtSetArg(args[i], XtNlabel, (XtArgVal) "Print Selection 2"); i++;
    printButton2 = XtCreateManagedWidget("printButton2",
        commandWidgetClass, testBox, args, i);
    XtAddCallback(printButton2, XtNcallback, PrintSelection2, NULL);
    i = 0;
    XtSetArg(args[i], XtNlabel, (XtArgVal) "Dismiss:  Box 1"); i++;
    doneButton1 = XtCreateManagedWidget("doneButton1",
        commandWidgetClass, testBox, args, i);
    XtAddCallback(doneButton1, XtNcallback, Done, NULL);
    i = 0;
    XtSetArg(args[i], XtNlabel, (XtArgVal) "Dismiss:  Box 2"); i++;
    doneButton2 = XtCreateManagedWidget("doneButton2",
        commandWidgetClass, testBox, args, i);
    XtAddCallback(doneButton2, XtNcallback, Done, NULL);
    i = 0;
    XtSetArg(args[i], XtNlabel, (XtArgVal) "Quit"); i++;
    quitButton = XtCreateManagedWidget("quitButton",
        commandWidgetClass, testBox, args, i);
    XtAddCallback(quitButton, XtNcallback, Quit, NULL);
    XtRealizeWidget(topLevel);
    XtMainLoop();
}   /* main */


/*ARGSUSED*/
void TestSelectBox1(w, client_data, call_data)
Widget w;
caddr_t client_data, call_data;
{
    XiStrSelectPopup(testSelectBox1);
}   /* TestSelectBox1 */


/*ARGSUSED*/
void TestSelectBox2(w, client_data, call_data)
Widget w;
caddr_t client_data, call_data;
```

```
{
    XiStrSelectPopup(testSelectBox2);
}   /* TestSelectBox2 */


/*ARGSUSED*/
void PrintSelection1(w, client_data, call_data)
Widget w;
caddr_t client_data, call_data;
{
    char *selection = XiStrSelectGetSelection(testSelectBox1);

    printf("The current selection is: %s\n",
        (selection) ? selection : "");
}   /* PrintSelection1 */


/*ARGSUSED*/
void PrintSelection2(w, client_data, call_data)
Widget w;
caddr_t client_data, call_data;
{
    char *selection = XiStrSelectGetSelection(testSelectBox2);

    printf("The current selection is: %s\n",
        (selection) ? selection : "");
}   /* PrintSelection2 */


/*ARGSUSED*/
void Done(w, client_data, call_data)
Widget w;
caddr_t client_data, call_data;
{
    if (w == doneButton1)
        XtPopdown(strSelectShell1);
    else if (w == doneButton2)
        XtPopdown(strSelectShell2);
}   /* Done */


/*ARGSUSED*/
void Quit(w, client_data, call_data)
Widget w;
caddr_t client_data, call_data;
{
    XFreeFont(XtDisplay(w), font);
    exit(0);
}   /* Quit */
```

XiAlert: A General-purpose Alert Widget

```
/****    Alert.h    ****/

/****    public declarations/definitions for Alert.c    ****/

#ifndef _XiAlert_h
#define _XiAlert_h  1

/*******************************************************************
*  Copyright (c) 1990 Iris Computing Laboratories.
*
*  This software is provided for demonstration purposes only.  As
*  freely-distributed, modifiable source code, this software carries
*  absolutely no warranty.
*******************************************************************/

/*******************************************************************
An Alert widget implements a pop-up, blocking, message window that
supports buttons.  It can be used to query the user with yes-no-
cancel type messages, or for simple warning and informatory mes-
sages that require a one-button, "continue" type response.  The
client can create multiple alert boxes.
   An Alert widget is shell-less; the client must provide the
enclosing shell.  A convenience function, XiAlertPopup(), is
provided for popping up the alert box.  It returns the button
values associated with the selected button.  The second argument
provides the alert box message and the third argument is either
XiBEEP or XiNOBEEP.  The duration of the beep is controlled by a
resource, XiNbeepDuration.  A separate convenience function,
```

```
XiAlertBeep(), is available for sounding the terminal bell with the
duration specified by XiNbeepDuration.
   A client can add buttons to an alert box with XiAlertAddButton().
A button label, a button value (integer), a callback function,
and callback data can be associated with each button.
   A convenience function, XiAlertResetProperKeyboardFocus(), can
be used to associate a client-supplied function for resetting the
keyboard focus after each invocation of the pop-up alert box.  By
default, no keyboard focus-setting function is executed after a
pop-down operation.  The keyboard focus issue sometimes arises with
certain combinations of widgets and window managers.

Resources:

Name             Class            Data Type       Default       Modify?
----             -----            ---------       -------       -------
XiNmessage       XiCMessage       String          ""            OK
XiNbeepDuration  XiCBeepDuration  int             1             OK
XiNfont          XiCFont          XFontStruct *   XtDefaultFont

   Public interfaces are described below.
*********************************************************************/

#ifdef X11R3
#include <X11/Form.h>
#else
#include <X11/Xaw/Form.h>
#endif


/*
Used with XiAlertPopup():
*/

#define XiNOBEEP    0
#define XiBEEP      1


/*
Resource definitions:
*/

#define XiNmessage        "message"           /* OK to modify */
#define XiNbeepDuration   "beepDuration"      /* OK to modify */
#define XiNfont           "font"
#define XiCMessage        "Message"
#define XiCBeepDuration   "BeepDuration"
#define XiCFont           "Font"


typedef struct _XiAlertClassRec *XiAlertWidgetClass;
typedef struct _XiAlertRec *XiAlertWidget;

extern WidgetClass xiAlertWidgetClass;


/*
```

```
Public functions:
*/

extern void XiAlertAddButton();
/*  XiAlertWidget alert_widget;
    char *button_name;
    int button_value;
    void (*callback_proc)();
    caddr_t callback_arg;
*/

extern int XiAlertPopup();
/*  XiAlertWidget alert_widget;
    char *message;
    Boolean ring_bell;
*/

extern int XiAlertMap();
/*  XiAlertWidget alert_widget;
*/

extern void XiAlertBeep();
/*  XiAlertwidget alert_widget;
    int num_beeps;
*/

extern void XiAlertResetProperKeyboardFocus();
/*  void (*reset_keyboard_focus_proc)();
*/

#endif /* _XiAlert_h  */



/****    AlertP.h    ****/

/****    private declarations/definitions for Alert.c    ****/


#ifndef _XiAlertP_h
#define _XiAlertP_h


#include "Alert.h"
#ifdef X11R3
#include <X11/FormP.h>
#else
#include <X11/Xaw/FormP.h>
#endif


#define ALERT_MAX_BUTTONS           5

#define ALERT_STD_BEEP_DURATION     1
#define ALERT_MAX_BEEP_DURATION     25
#define ALERT_DEFAULT_WIDTH         400
#define ALERT_DEFAULT_HEIGHT        175
```

```
#define ALERT_DEFAULT_MSG        "A message goes here!"


typedef struct _XiAlertClassPart {       /* class definition */
    int dummy;
} XiAlertClassPart;

typedef struct _XiAlertClassRec {
    CoreClassPart core_class;
    CompositeClassPart composite_class;
    ConstraintClassPart constraint_class;
    FormClassPart form_class;
    XiAlertClassPart alert_class;
} XiAlertClassRec;

extern XiAlertClassRec xiAlertClassRec;

typedef struct _XiAlertButtonPart {
    Widget wid;
    int value;
} XiAlertButtonPart;

typedef struct _XiAlertPart {            /* instance definition */
    char *msg;
    int std_beep_duration;
    XFontStruct *font;
    Widget msgW;
    XiAlertButtonPart buttonW[ALERT_MAX_BUTTONS];
    int num_buttons;
    int query_result;
    int query_wait;
} XiAlertPart;


typedef struct _XiAlertRec {
    CorePart core;
    CompositePart composite;
    ConstraintPart constraint;
    FormPart form;
    XiAlertPart alert;
} XiAlertRec;


typedef struct {
    int dummy;
} XiAlertConstraintsPart;


typedef struct _XiAlertConstraintsRec {
    FormConstraintsPart form;
    XiAlertConstraintsPart alert;
} XiAlertConstraintsRec, *XiAlertConstraints;

#endif  /* _XiAlertP_h */
```

```
/****  Alert.c  ****  simple alert box implementation  ****/


#include <stdio.h>

#include <X11/Xlib.h>
#include <X11/Xos.h>
#include <X11/IntrinsicP.h>
#include <X11/StringDefs.h>

#ifdef X11R3
#include <X11/Command.h>
#include <X11/Form.h>
#include <X11/Label.h>
#else
#include <X11/Xaw/XawInit.h>
#include <X11/Xaw/Command.h>
#include <X11/Xaw/Form.h>
#include <X11/Xaw/Label.h>
#endif

#include "AlertP.h"


static XtResource resources[] = {
    {XiNmessage, XiCMessage, XtRString, sizeof(char *),
        XtOffset(XiAlertWidget, alert.msg), XtRString, ""},
    {XiNbeepDuration, XiCBeepDuration, XtRInt, sizeof(int),
        XtOffset(XiAlertWidget, alert.std_beep_duration),
        XtRImmediate, (caddr_t) ALERT_STD_BEEP_DURATION},
    {XiNfont, XiCFont, XtRFontStruct, sizeof(XFontStruct *),
        XtOffset(XiAlertWidget, alert.font),
        XtRString, "XtDefaultFont"},
};


/*
Class Methods:
*/

static void Initialize();
static void ConstraintInitialize();
static Boolean SetValues();
static void Destroy();


/*
Private support functions:
*/

static void internal_callback_proc();
static int get_query_result();
static void alert_beep();
static void alert_reset_proper_keyboard_focus();
```

```
/*
This is a pointer to a function to execute if the keyboard focus
needs resetting after pop-up operations.  See the functions
XiAlertSetResetProperKeyboardFocus() and
alert_reset_proper_keyboard_focus() in this module.
*/

static void (*reset_keyboard_focus_proc)();


/*
Define storage for the class here:
*/

XiAlertClassRec XialertClassRec = {
    { /* core_class variables */
        (WidgetClass) &formClassRec,      /* ancestor */
        "Alert",                          /* class name */
        sizeof(XiAlertRec),               /* widget size */
#ifdef X11R3
        NULL,                             /* class initialize */
#else
        XawInitializeWidgetSet,           /* class initialize */
#endif
        NULL,                             /* class part init. */
        FALSE,                            /* class inited */
        Initialize,                       /* initialize */
        NULL,                             /* initialize hook */
        XtInheritRealize,                 /* realize */
        NULL,                             /* actions */
        0,                                /* number of actions */
        resources,                        /* resources */
        XtNumber(resources),              /* number of resources */
        NULLQUARK,                        /* xrm class */
        TRUE,                             /* compress motions */
        TRUE,                             /* compress exposures */
        TRUE,                             /* compress enter/leave */
        FALSE,                            /* visibility interest */
        Destroy,                          /* destroy */
        XtInheritResize,                  /* resize */
        XtInheritExpose,                  /* expose */
        SetValues,                        /* set values */
        NULL,                             /* set values hook */
        XtInheritSetValuesAlmost,         /* set values almost */
        NULL,                             /* get values hook */
        NULL,                             /* accept focus */
        XtVersion,                        /* version */
        NULL,                             /* callback private */
        NULL,                             /* translation table */
        XtInheritQueryGeometry,           /* query geometry */
        XtInheritDisplayAccelerator,      /* display accelerator */
        NULL,                             /* extension */
    },
    { /* composite_class variables */
        XtInheritGeometryManager,         /* geometry manager */
        XtInheritChangeManaged,           /* change managed */
        XtInheritInsertChild,             /* insert child */
```

```
        XtInheritDeleteChild,           /* delete child */
        NULL,                           /* extension */
    },
    { /* constraint_class fields */
        NULL,                           /* subresources */
        0,                              /* number of subresources */
        sizeof(XiAlertConstraintsRec),  /* record size */
        ConstraintInitialize,           /* initialize */
        NULL,                           /* destroy */
        NULL,                           /* set values */
        NULL,                           /* extension */
    },
    { /* form_class fields */
#ifdef X11R3
        0,
#else
        XtInheritLayout,
#endif
    },
    { /* alert_class variables */
        0,
    },
}; /* XialertClassRec */


WidgetClass xiAlertWidgetClass = (WidgetClass) &XialertClassRec;


/*
XiAlertWidget methods:
*/

/*
Initialize() creates the label widget for the alert box
message; it has a zero-width border.  Other variables are
initialized as well.
*/
/*ARGSUSED*/
static void Initialize(request, new)
XiAlertWidget request, new;
{
    Arg args[5];
    int i;

    if (new->core.width == 0)
        new->core.width = ALERT_DEFAULT_WIDTH;
    if (new->core.height == 0)
        new->core.height = ALERT_DEFAULT_HEIGHT;
    if (new->alert.std_beep_duration < 0 ||
            new->alert.std_beep_duration > ALERT_MAX_BEEP_DURATION)
        new->alert.std_beep_duration = ALERT_STD_BEEP_DURATION;
    i = 0;
    XtSetArg(args[i], XtNlabel,
        (XtArgVal) ALERT_DEFAULT_MSG); i++;
    XtSetArg(args[i], XtNborderWidth, (XtArgVal) 0); i++;
    XtSetArg(args[i], XtNresizable, (XtArgVal) TRUE); i++;
    XtSetArg(args[i], XtNfont, (XtArgVal) new->alert.font); i++;
```

```
    new->alert.msgW = XtCreateManagedWidget("message",
        labelWidgetClass, new, args, i);
    new->alert.num_buttons = 0;
}   /* Initialize */


/*
ConstraintInitialize() sets up the form widget that
houses the alert message and buttons.
*/
/*ARGSUSED*/
static void ConstraintInitialize(request, new)
Widget request, new;
{
    XiAlertWidget aw = (XiAlertWidget) new->core.parent;
    Widget *child, *children = aw->composite.children;
    XiAlertConstraints constraint =
        (XiAlertConstraints) new->core.constraints;

    if (!XtIsSubclass(new, commandWidgetClass))
        return;
    constraint->form.left = constraint->form.right = XtChainLeft;
    constraint->form.vert_base = aw->alert.msgW;
    if (aw->composite.num_children > 1) {
        for (child = children + aw->composite.num_children - 1;
                child > children; child--) {
            if (XtIsManaged(*child) &&
                    XtIsSubclass(*child, commandWidgetClass)) {
                constraint->form.horiz_base = *child;
                break;
            }
        }
    }
}   /* ConstraintInitialize */


/*
SetValues() updates the stored message or the beep duration.
*/
/*ARGSUSED*/
static Boolean SetValues(current, request, new)
Widget current, request, new;
{
    XiAlertWidget aw = (XiAlertWidget) new;
    XiAlertWidget old_aw = (XiAlertWidget) current;
    Arg args[2];
    int i;

    if (aw->alert.msg != NULL) {
        i = 0;
        XtSetArg(args[i], XtNlabel, (XtArgVal) aw->alert.msg); i++;
        XtSetValues(aw->alert.msgW, args, i);
    }
    if (aw->alert.std_beep_duration < 0 ||
            aw->alert.std_beep_duration > ALERT_MAX_BEEP_DURATION)
        aw->alert.std_beep_duration = ALERT_STD_BEEP_DURATION;
    return FALSE;
```

```
}   /* SetValues */


/*
Destroy() frees encapsulated widgets.
*/

static void Destroy(aw)
XiAlertWidget aw;
{
    int i;

    XtDestroyWidget(aw->alert.msgW);
    for (i = 0; i < aw->alert.num_buttons; i++)
        XtDestroyWidget(aw->alert.buttonW[i].wid);
}   /* Destroy */


/*
Public functions:
*/

/*
XiAlertAddButton() adds buttons to an alert box, one at a time.
A value is associated with each button; this value is returned
by XiAlertPopup(), the function that invokes the alert box.  A
callback function may be registered with the button as well.
A hidden/internal callback function is used to pop down the
alert box after a button selection; see internal_callback_proc().
*/

void XiAlertAddButton(aw, button_name, button_value,
    callback_proc, client_data)
XiAlertWidget aw;
char *button_name;
int button_value;
void (*callback_proc)();    /* or, XtCallbackProc callback_proc; */
caddr_t client_data;
{
    Arg args[7];
    int i;

    if (aw->alert.num_buttons >= ALERT_MAX_BUTTONS) {
        fprintf(stderr,
            "alert box: too many buttons for the alert box\n");
        fprintf(stderr,
            "alert box: the maximum number of buttons is: %d.\n",
            ALERT_MAX_BUTTONS);
        return;
    }
    i = 0;
    XtSetArg(args[i], XtNlabel, (XtArgVal) button_name); i++;
    XtSetArg(args[i], XtNfont, (XtArgVal) aw->alert.font); i++;
    aw->alert.buttonW[aw->alert.num_buttons].wid =
        XtCreateManagedWidget(button_name, commandWidgetClass,
            aw, args, i);
    aw->alert.buttonW[aw->alert.num_buttons].value = button_value;
```

```
    XtAddCallback(aw->alert.buttonW[aw->alert.num_buttons].wid,
        XtNcallback, internal_callback_proc, button_value);
    if (callback_proc != NULL)
        XtAddCallback(aw->alert.buttonW[aw->alert.num_buttons].wid,
            XtNcallback, callback_proc, client_data);
    aw->alert.num_buttons++;
}   /* XiAlertAddButton */


/*
XiAlertPopup() pops up a message window.  It is the working
interface to the alert box that's used by the application.
*/

int XiAlertPopup(aw, msg, ring_bell)
XiAlertWidget aw;
char *msg;
Boolean ring_bell;
{
    Arg args[3];
    int i;

    query_set_pos(aw);
    if (ring_bell)
        XiAlertBeep(aw, aw->alert.std_beep_duration);
    i = 0;
    XtSetArg(args[i], XiNmessage, (XtArgVal) msg); i++;
    XtSetValues(aw, args, i);
    XtPopup(aw->core.parent, XtGrabExclusive);
    return get_query_result(aw);
}   /* XiAlertPopup */


/*
XiAlertMap() is like XiAlertPopup(), except it uses the message
previously set with XtSetValues().  You can turn off the (automatic)
beep by setting the beep-duration resource to 0.
*/

int XiAlertMap(aw)
XiAlertWidget aw;
{
    query_set_pos(aw);
    XiAlertBeep(aw, aw->alert.std_beep_duration);
    XtPopup(aw->core.parent, XtGrabExclusive);
    return get_query_result(aw);
}   /* XiAlertMap */


/*
XiAlertBeep() is provided for consistency to allow independent
beeps by the application programmer.
*/

void XiAlertBeep(w, num_beeps)
Widget w;
int num_beeps;
```

```
{
    alert_beep(w, num_beeps);
}   /* XiAlertBeep */


/*
XiAlertResetProperKeyboardFocus() establishes a pointer to
the client's procedure that handles keyboard focus operations.
See the procedure alert_reset_proper_keyboard_focus().
*/

void XiAlertResetProperKeyboardFocus(rkfp)
void (*rkfp)();
{
    reset_keyboard_focus_proc = rkfp;
}   /* XiAlertResetProperKeyboardFocus */


/*
Support functions:
*/

/*
internal_callback_proc() is installed as the first callback
function for each button; see XiAlertAddButton().  Primarily,
it handles removal of the alert box.
*/
/*ARGSUSED*/
static void internal_callback_proc(w, button_value, call_data)
Widget w;    /* the button */
int button_value;
caddr_t call_data;
{
    XiAlertWidget aw = (XiAlertWidget) w->core.parent;

    aw->alert.query_result = button_value;
    aw->alert.query_wait = FALSE;
    XtPopdown(aw->core.parent);
    alert_reset_proper_keyboard_focus();
}   /* internal_callback_proc */


/*
get_query_result() blocks until a button is pressed.
*/

static int get_query_result(aw)
XiAlertWidget aw;
{
    XEvent event;

    aw->alert.query_wait = TRUE;
    while (aw->alert.query_wait) {
        XtNextEvent(&event);
        XtDispatchEvent(&event);
    }
    return aw->alert.query_result;
```

```
}   /* get_alert_result */


/*
alert_beep() rings the system bell n times.
*/

static void alert_beep(aw, num_beeps)
XiAlertWidget aw;
int num_beeps;
{
    while (num_beeps-- > 0)
        XBell(XtDisplay(aw->core.parent), 50);
}   /* alert_beep */


/*
alert_reset_proper_keyboard_focus() allows the keyboard focus to be
reestablished after after a transient shell is popped up and down.
Calling this routine is necessary with (old) twm, but not with uwm.
*/

static void alert_reset_proper_keyboard_focus()
{
    if (reset_keyboard_focus_proc == NULL)
        return;
    reset_keyboard_focus_proc();
}   /* alert_reset_proper_keyboard_focus */



/****   testalert.c   ****   tests the alert box widget ****/


#include <stdio.h>
#include <X11/Intrinsic.h>
#include <X11/StringDefs.h>
#include <X11/Shell.h>

#ifdef X11R3
#include <X11/Box.h>
#include <X11/Command.h>
#else
#include <X11/Xaw/Box.h>
#include <X11/Xaw/Command.h>
#endif
#include <Ximisc.h>
#include "Alert.h"


/*
Functions:
*/

void TestAlertBox1(), TestAlertBox2(), Quit(), AlertCB();
```

```
/*
Private globals:
*/

static Widget testAlert1, testAlert2;
static XFontStruct *font;


void main(argc, argv)
int argc;
char **argv;
{
    Widget topLevel, testBox, alertShell1, alertShell2,
        testButton1, testButton2, quitButton;
    Arg args[7];
    int i;

    topLevel = XtInitialize(argv[0], "TestAlert",
        NULL, 0, &argc, argv);
    font = load_font(topLevel, "testalert", "8x13");
    i = 0;
    XtSetArg(args[i], XtNallowShellResize, (XtArgVal) TRUE); i++;
    alertShell1 = XtCreatePopupShell("alertShell1",
        transientShellWidgetClass, topLevel, args, i);
    i = 0;
    XtSetArg(args[i], XtNfont,      /* test this one with   */
        (XtArgVal) font); i++;      /* an alternate font    */
    testAlert1 = XtCreateManagedWidget("testAlert1",
        xiAlertWidgetClass, alertShell1, args, i);
    i = 0;
    XtSetArg(args[i], XtNallowShellResize, (XtArgVal) TRUE); i++;
    alertShell2 = XtCreatePopupShell("alertShell2",
        transientShellWidgetClass, topLevel, args, i);
    testAlert2 = XtCreateManagedWidget("testAlert2",
        xiAlertWidgetClass, alertShell2, NULL, 0);

    testBox = XtCreateManagedWidget("box", boxWidgetClass,
        topLevel, NULL, 0);
    i = 0;
    XtSetArg(args[i], XtNlabel, (XtArgVal) "Button Set 1..."); i++;
    testButton1 = XtCreateManagedWidget("testButton1",
        commandWidgetClass, testBox, args, i);
    i = 0;
    XtSetArg(args[i], XtNlabel, (XtArgVal) "Button Set 2..."); i++;
    testButton2 = XtCreateManagedWidget("testButton2",
        commandWidgetClass, testBox, args, i);
    i = 0;
    XtSetArg(args[i], XtNlabel, (XtArgVal) "Quit"); i++;
    quitButton = XtCreateManagedWidget("quitButton",
        commandWidgetClass, testBox, args, i);
    XtAddCallback(testButton1, XtNcallback, TestAlertBox1, NULL);
    XtAddCallback(testButton2, XtNcallback, TestAlertBox2, NULL);
    XtAddCallback(quitButton, XtNcallback, Quit, NULL);
    XiAlertAddButton(testAlert1, "Button 1", 3, AlertCB, "three");
    XiAlertAddButton(testAlert1, "Button 2", 6, AlertCB, "six");
    XiAlertAddButton(testAlert1, "Button 3", 9, AlertCB, "nine");
    XiAlertAddButton(testAlert2, "Button 1", 2, AlertCB, "two");
```

```
    XiAlertAddButton(testAlert2, "Button 2", 4, AlertCB, "four");
    XtRealizeWidget(topLevel);
    XtMainLoop();
}   /* main */


/*ARGSUSED*/
void TestAlertBox1(w, client_data, call_data)
Widget w;
caddr_t client_data, call_data;
{
    int result;

    result = XiAlertPopup(testAlert1,
        "This is a test!  Press any button...", XiBEEP);
    /*
    Normally, you would do something useful with the value attached
    to the pressed button; for now, just print the value.
    */
    printf("You chose the button with value: %d\n", result);
}   /* TestAlertBox1 */


/*ARGSUSED*/
void TestAlertBox2(w, client_data, call_data)
Widget w;
caddr_t client_data, call_data;
{
    Arg args[3];
    int i, result;

    i = 0;
    XtSetArg(args[i], XiNmessage,
        (XtArgVal) "Testing alert box #2!  Press any button..."); i++;
    XtSetArg(args[i], XiNbeepDuration, (XtArgVal) 4); i++;
    XtSetValues(testAlert2, args, i);
    result = XiAlertMap(testAlert2);
    /*
    Normally, you would do something useful with the value attached
    to the pressed button; for now, just print the value.
    */
    printf("You chose the button with value: %d\n", result);
}   /* TestAlertBox2 */


/*ARGSUSED*/
void AlertCB(w, client_data, call_data)
Widget w;
caddr_t client_data, call_data;
{
    printf("A button was pressed...\n");
    printf("Its callback data was: %s\n", client_data);
}   /* AlertCB */


/*ARGSUSED*/
void Quit(w, client_data, call_data)
```

```
Widget w;
caddr_t client_data, call_data;
{
    XFreeFont(XtDisplay(w), font);
    printf("Program terminated...\n");
    exit(0);
}   /* Quit */
```

Modifying *xwaste*'s *alert.c* Module to Incorporate XiAlert

```
/****     alert.h     ****/

/****     external declarations for alert.c     ****/


#ifndef ALERT_H
#define ALERT_H 1

#include <X11/Intrinsic.h>
#include <X11/StringDefs.h>
#include <X11/Shell.h>


#include "Alert.h"


#include <stdio.h>


#define ALERT_YES        -1
#define ALERT_NO         -2
#define ALERT_CANCEL     -3



/*
Function declarations:
*/
```

```
extern void alert_create_ync(), alert_create_continue();
extern void alert(), alert_beep();
extern int alert_query();
extern void set_alert_reset_proper_keyboard_focus();


#endif



/****    alert.c    ****    simple alert box implementation    ****/


#include "alert.h"


/*
Private globals:
*/

static Widget alertShellYesNoCancel, alertShellContinue;
static Widget alertYesNoCancel, alertContinue;


/*
alert_create_ync() creates a yes-no-cancel, three-button alert box.
*/

void alert_create_ync(parent)
Widget parent;
{
    Arg args[3];
    int i;

    i = 0;
    XtSetArg(args[i], XtNallowShellResize, (XtArgVal) TRUE); i++;
    alertShellYesNoCancel = XtCreatePopupShell("alertShellYesNoCancel",
        transientShellWidgetClass, parent, args, i);
    alertYesNoCancel = XtCreateManagedWidget("alertYesNoCancel",
        xiAlertWidgetClass, alertShellYesNoCancel, NULL, 0);
    XiAlertAddButton(alertYesNoCancel, "Yes", ALERT_YES, NULL, NULL);
    XiAlertAddButton(alertYesNoCancel, "No", ALERT_NO, NULL, NULL);
    XiAlertAddButton(alertYesNoCancel, "Cancel", ALERT_CANCEL, NULL, NULL);
}   /* alert_create_ync */


/*
alert_create_continue() creates a one-button alert box.
*/

void alert_create_continue(parent)
Widget parent;
{
    Arg args[3];
    int i;
```

```
    i = 0;
    XtSetArg(args[i], XtNallowShellResize, (XtArgVal) TRUE); i++;
    alertShellContinue = XtCreatePopupShell("alertShellContinue",
        transientShellWidgetClass, parent, args, i);
    alertContinue = XtCreateManagedWidget("alertContinue",
        xiAlertWidgetClass, alertShellContinue, NULL, 0);
    XiAlertAddButton(alertContinue, "Continue", NULL, NULL, NULL);
}   /* alert_create_continue */


/*
alert() pops up a message window.
*/

void alert(msg)
char *msg;
{
    XiAlertPopup(alertContinue, msg, XiNOBEEP);
}   /* alert */


/*
alert_query() pops up a dialog window.
*/

int alert_query(msg)
char *msg;
{
    return XiAlertPopup(alertYesNoCancel, msg, XiNOBEEP);
}   /* alert_query */


/*
alert_beep() rings the system bell n times.
*/

void alert_beep(num_beeps)
int num_beeps;
{
    XiAlertBeep(alertContinue, num_beeps);
}   /* alert_beep */


/*
set_alert_reset_proper_keyboard_focus() establishes a pointer to
the client's procedure that handles keyboard focus operations.
See the procedure alert_reset_proper_keyboard_focus().
*/

void set_alert_reset_proper_keyboard_focus(rkfp)
void (*rkfp)();
{
    XiAlertResetProperKeyboardFocus(rkfp);
}   /* set_alert_reset_proper_keyboard_focus */
```

P

XiFileSelect: A General-purpose File Selection Widget

```
/****     FileSelect.h     ****/

/****     public declarations/definitions for FileSelect.c     ****/

#ifndef _XiFileSelect_h
#define _XiFileSelect_h 1

/*******************************************************************
*  Copyright (c) 1990 Iris Computing Laboratories.
*
*  This software is provided for demonstration purposes only.  As
*  freely-distributed, modifiable source code, this software carries
*  absolutely no warranty.
*******************************************************************/

/*******************************************************************
This module implements a file selection box that can be used by
an application to allow the user to choose/specify a file.  The user
can (1) pop up the file selection box, (2) specify a file filter,
(3) click-left on the 'Filter' button to display matching files, and
then (4) click-left on a file to select it.  The application program
can determine the selected file by calling the public function
XiFileSelectGetSelection(), which returns a pointer to the selected
filename.  Using XiFileSelectAddApplyProc() the application can
supply a callback function that's executed each time the user
presses the 'Apply' button.
  The file selection box is housed in a vertical pane widget.
The primary components of the pane are the text entry area for the
```

```
file filter, the scrollable display area (viewport) for listing
filenames, and the command buttons.  By default, the string selection
widget inherits its cursor from its parent.
   Typically, the file selection box would be created as a child of
a popup shell.  It's possible for the file selection box to reside
somewhere other than in a popup shell, for example, as a component of
a top-level window, or some subordinate window.  If the parent of the
the file selection box is not a popup shell, the 'Dismiss' button
is inappropriate, and it will not be included.  In the latter case,
note that it is the application's responsibility to put the file
selection box where it won't be overlaid by another widget.  Note
that Xt may resize the file selection box, if it is not a child of
a popup shell; hence, the row/column dimensions for the viewport
are approximate.
   This implementation takes a conservative approach with respect to
maintaining the list of filenames that are displayed in the viewport.
Specifically, each time the user presses the 'Filter' button, or
selects a file, the widget rebuilds the list of filenames.  Thus, if
the user enters a new filter, but fails to press the 'Filter' button
to update the display, pressing the 'Select' button will update the
viewport before making the selection.
   Although various features of the file selection box are fixed
(hard-coded), a number of features can be modified by the resources
given below.  For example, the pixmap dimensions can be specified
at creation via resource, but once it is initialized, the pixmap
cannot be resized.  Typically, the application programmer would
create the viewport to be smaller than the underlying pixmap.  Both
viewport and pixmap dimensions use row/column metrics.
   Exposures are handled by the respective internal widgets.
   Several of the calls to fprintf() are "optional."

Resources:

Name             Class            Data Type       Default      Modify?
----             -----            ---------       -------      -------
XiNfilter        XiCfilter        String          "*"
XiNfilterWidth   XiCFilterWidth   Dimension       150 (pixels)
XiNrows          XiCRows          int             10
XiNcolumns       XiCColumns       int             30
XiNpixmapRows    XiCPixmapRows    int             50
XiNpixmapColumnsXiCPixmapColumnsint               100
XiNrowSpacing    XiCRowSpacing    int             2 (pixels)
XiNpixmapCursor XiCPixmapCursor Cursor            None
XiNpixmapFont    XiCPixmapFont    XFontStruct *   XtDefaultFont

   Public interfaces are described below.
*********************************************************************/

#ifdef X11R3
#include <X11/VPaned.h>
#else
#include <X11/Xaw/Paned.h>
#endif


/*
Resource definitions:
```

```
*/

#define XiNfilter               "filter"
#define XiNfilterWidth          "filterWidth"
#define XiNrows                 "rows"
#define XiNcolumns              "columns"
#define XiNpixmapRows           "pixmapRows"
#define XiNpixmapColumns        "pixmapColumns"
#define XiNrowSpacing           "rowSpacing"
#define XiNpixmapCursor         "pixmapCursor"
#define XiNpixmapFont           "pixmapFont"
#define XiCFilter               "Filter"
#define XiCFilterWidth          "FilterWidth"
#define XiCRows                 "Rows"
#define XiCColumns              "Columns"
#define XiCPixmapRows           "PixmapRows"
#define XiCPixmapColumns        "PixmapColumns"
#define XiCRowSpacing           "RowSpacing"
#define XiCPixmapCursor         "PixmapCursor"
#define XiCPixmapFont           "PixmapFont"


typedef struct _XiFileSelectClassRec *XiFileSelectWidgetClass;
typedef struct _XiFileSelectRec *XiFileSelectWidget;

extern WidgetClass xiFileSelectWidgetClass;


/*
Public functions:
*/

extern void XiFileSelectPopup();
/*  XiFileSelectWidget file_select_widget;
*/

extern char *XiFileSelectGetSelection();
/*  XiFileSelectWidget file_select_widget;
*/

extern void XiFileSelectAddApplyProc();
/*  XiFileSelectWidget file_select_widget;
*/

extern void XiFileSelectRefresh();
/*  XiFileSelectWidget file_select_widget;
*/


#endif /* _XiFileSelect_h  */



/****    FileSelecP.h    ****/

/****    private declarations/definitions for FileSelect.c    ****/
```

```
#ifndef _XiFileSelectP_h
#define _XiFileSelectP_h


#include "FileSelect.h"
#ifdef X11R3
#include <X11/VPanedP.h>
#else
#include <X11/Xaw/PanedP.h>
#endif

#define FILE_DEFAULT_FILTER         "*"

#define FILE_DEFAULT_WIDTH          300
#define FILE_DEFAULT_HEIGHT         150
#define FILE_DEFAULT_FILTER_WIDTH   150

#define FILE_DEFAULT_ROWS           10
#define FILE_DEFAULT_COLUMNS        30
#define FILE_DEFAULT_PIXMAP_ROWS    50
#define FILE_DEFAULT_PIXMAP_COLUMNS 100
#define FILE_DEFAULT_ROW_SPACING    2

#define FILE_MIN_FILTER_WIDTH       20
#define FILE_MIN_ROWS               1
#define FILE_MIN_COLUMNS            10

#define FILE_MAX_FILTER             100
#define FILE_MAX_FILE_SPEC          1280    /* 1024 + 255 + 1 */

#define FILE_DELIMITERS         "\n\r\t "   /* used with strtok() */
#define EOS                     '\0'

#define FILE_NO_HIGHLIGHT       -1  /* ignore mouse, just    */
                                    /* redisplay files        */
#define FILE_NO_FILE            -2  /* no currently selected file */


typedef struct _XiFileSelectClassPart {     /* class definition */
    int dummy;
} XiFileSelectClassPart;

typedef struct _XiFileSelectClassRec {
    CoreClassPart core_class;
    CompositeClassPart composite_class;
    ConstraintClassPart constraint_class;
#ifdef X11R3
    VPanedClassPart vpaned_class;
#else
    PanedClassPart vpaned_class;
#endif
    XiFileSelectClassPart file_select_class;
} XiFileSelectClassRec;

extern XiFileSelectClassRec xiFileSelectClassRec;
```

```
typedef struct _XiFileSelectPart {          /* instance definition */
    char *filenames;                        /* the list of files */
    char *filter;                           /* text entry area */
    char *default_filter;                   /* start-up filter */
    XFontStruct *font;
    Dimension filter_width;                 /* ftr. window size--pixels */
    int rows, columns;                      /* for the viewport */
    int row_spacing;                        /* space between rows */
    int pixmap_rows, pixmap_columns;        /* row/column metrics */
    Cursor pixmap_cursor;
    Widget viewportW, strSelectW;
    Widget filterBoxW, labelW, filterW;
    Widget buttonBoxW, dismissButtonW,
        filterButtonW, applyButtonW;
} XiFileSelectPart;


typedef struct _XiFileSelectRec {
    CorePart core;
    CompositePart composite;
    ConstraintPart constraint;
#ifdef X11R3
    VPanedPart vpaned;
#else
    PanedPart vpaned;
#endif
    XiFileSelectPart file_select;
} XiFileSelectRec;


typedef struct {
    int dummy;
} XiFileSelectConstraintsPart;

typedef struct _XiFileSelectConstraintsRec {
#ifdef X11R3
    VPanedConstraintsPart vpaned;
#else
    PanedConstraintsPart vpaned;
#endif
    XiFileSelectConstraintsPart file_select;
} XiFileSelectConstraintsRec, *XiFileSelectConstraints;

#endif  /* _XiFileSelectP_h */



/**  FileSelect.c  ** simple file selection box implementation  **/


#include <stdio.h>
#include <sys/types.h>
#include <sys/stat.h> /* stat() is used to verify file existence */

#include <X11/Xlib.h>
#include <X11/Xos.h>
```

```
#include <X11/cursorfont.h>
#include <X11/IntrinsicP.h>
#include <X11/StringDefs.h>
#include <X11/Shell.h>

#ifdef X11R3
#include <X11/AsciiText.h>
#include <X11/Box.h>
#include <X11/Command.h>
#include <X11/Viewport.h>
#else
#include <X11/Xaw/XawInit.h>
#include <X11/Xaw/AsciiText.h>
#include <X11/Xaw/Box.h>
#include <X11/Xaw/Command.h>
#include <X11/Xaw/Viewport.h>
#endif

#include "StrSelect.h"
#include "FileSelecP.h"


/*
Cursor place-holder:
*/

static Cursor default_pixmap_cursor = None;


/*
Resource table:
*/

#define res_offset(field) XtOffset(XiFileSelectWidget, field)

static XtResource resources[] = {
    {XiNfilter, XiCFilter, XtRString, sizeof(char *),
        res_offset(file_select.default_filter),
        XtRString, FILE_DEFAULT_FILTER},
    {XiNfilterWidth, XiCFilterWidth, XtRDimension, sizeof(Dimension),
        res_offset(file_select.filter_width),
        XtRImmediate, (caddr_t) FILE_DEFAULT_FILTER_WIDTH},
    {XiNrows, XiCRows, XtRInt, sizeof(int),
        res_offset(file_select.rows),
        XtRImmediate, (caddr_t) FILE_DEFAULT_ROWS},
    {XiNcolumns, XiCColumns, XtRInt, sizeof(int),
        res_offset(file_select.columns),
        XtRImmediate, (caddr_t) FILE_DEFAULT_COLUMNS},
    {XiNpixmapRows, XiCPixmapRows, XtRInt, sizeof(int),
        res_offset(file_select.pixmap_rows),
        XtRImmediate, (caddr_t) FILE_DEFAULT_PIXMAP_ROWS},
    {XiNpixmapColumns, XiCPixmapColumns, XtRInt, sizeof(int),
        res_offset(file_select.pixmap_columns),
        XtRImmediate, (caddr_t) FILE_DEFAULT_PIXMAP_COLUMNS},
    {XiNrowSpacing, XiCRowSpacing, XtRInt, sizeof(int),
        res_offset(file_select.row_spacing),
        XtRImmediate, (caddr_t) FILE_DEFAULT_ROW_SPACING},
```

```
    {XiNpixmapCursor, XiCPixmapCursor, XtRCursor, sizeof(Cursor),
        res_offset(file_select.pixmap_cursor),
        XtRCursor, (caddr_t) &default_pixmap_cursor},
    {XiNpixmapFont, XiCPixmapFont, XtRFontStruct,
        sizeof(XFontStruct *), res_offset(file_select.font),
        XtRString, "XtDefaultFont"},
};


/*
Class Methods:
*/

static void Initialize();
static void Destroy();
static Boolean SetValues();

/*
Action functions:
*/

static void Beep();

/*
Private support functions:
*/

static void FileSelectBoxDismiss();
static void FileSelectBoxFilter();
static void get_font_width_height();
static void set_filename_reference_buffer();
static char *expand_file_spec();
static int load_buffer();
static int file_size();
static int get_home_directory();


/*
Define storage for the class here:
*/

XiFileSelectClassRec XifileSelectClassRec = {
    { /* core_class variables */
#ifdef X11R3
        (WidgetClass) &vPanedClassRec,  /* ancestor */
#else
        (WidgetClass) &panedClassRec,   /* ancestor */
#endif
        "FileSelect",                   /* class name */
        sizeof(XiFileSelectRec),        /* widget size */
#ifdef X11R3
        NULL,                           /* class initialize */
#else
        XawInitializeWidgetSet,         /* class initialize */
#endif
        NULL,                           /* class part init. */
        FALSE,                          /* class inited */
```

```
        Initialize,                        /* initialize */
        NULL,                              /* initialize hook */
        XtInheritRealize,                  /* realize */
        NULL,                              /* actions */
        0,                                 /* number of actions */
        resources,                         /* resources */
        XtNumber(resources),               /* number of resources */
        NULLQUARK,                         /* xrm class */
        TRUE,                              /* compress motions */
        TRUE,                              /* compress exposures */
        TRUE,                              /* compress enter/leave */
        FALSE,                             /* visibility interest */
        Destroy,                           /* destroy */
        XtInheritResize,                   /* resize */
        XtInheritExpose,                   /* expose */
        SetValues,                         /* set values */
        NULL,                              /* set values hook */
        XtInheritSetValuesAlmost,          /* set values almost */
        NULL,                              /* get values hook */
        NULL,                              /* accept focus */
        XtVersion,                         /* version */
        NULL,                              /* callback private */
        NULL,                              /* translation table */
        XtInheritQueryGeometry,            /* query geometry */
        XtInheritDisplayAccelerator,       /* display accelerator */
        NULL,                              /* extension */
    },
    { /* composite_class variables */
        XtInheritGeometryManager,          /* geometry manager */
        XtInheritChangeManaged,            /* change managed */
        XtInheritInsertChild,              /* insert child */
        XtInheritDeleteChild,              /* delete child */
        NULL,                              /* extension */
    },
    { /* constraint_class fields */
        NULL,                              /* subresources */
        0,                                 /* number of subresources */
        sizeof(XiFileSelectConstraintsRec),    /* record size */
        NULL,                              /* initialize */
        NULL,                              /* destroy */
        NULL,                              /* set values */
        NULL,                              /* extension */
    },
    { /* vpaned_class variables */
#ifdef X11R3
        XtInheritSetMinMax,
        XtInheritRefigureMode,
#else
        0,
#endif
    },
    { /* file_select_class variables */
        0,
    },
}; /* XifileSelectClassRec */
```

```
WidgetClass xiFileSelectWidgetClass =
    (WidgetClass) &XifileSelectClassRec;


/*
XiFileSelectWidget methods:
*/

/*
Initialize() initializes each instance of a file selection box.
A file selection box is a compound widget containing several
subordinate widgets.  NOTE:  Viewport width/height are approx.
due to the presence of scrollbars; Initialize() could provide
more complex calculations, but it's probably not necessary.  Note
that the file selection box may be resized (automatically) in an
application.
   As currently designed, a number of features can't be modified by
the user, e.g., the border width of the file filter text entry box.
However, it is straightforward to provide resources for the
hard-coded features, as has been done with, for example, the file
filter box width.  For simplicity, the client program CANNOT add
additional buttons, etc.
*/
/*ARGSUSED*/
static void Initialize(request, new)
XiFileSelectWidget request, new;
{
     static char filter_translations[] =
         "#override\n\
         Ctrl<Key>J:        beep()\n\
         Ctrl<Key>M:        beep()\n\
         Ctrl<Key>O:        beep()\n\
         <Key>Linefeed:     beep()\n\
         <Key>Return:  beep()";
     static XtActionsRec filter_actions[] = {
         {"beep", (XtActionProc) Beep},
     };
     XtTranslations filter_trans_table;

     Arg args[15];
     int i, col_width, row_height;

     new->file_select.filenames = NULL;
     if (new->file_select.rows < FILE_MIN_ROWS)
         new->file_select.rows = FILE_DEFAULT_ROWS;
     if (new->file_select.columns < FILE_MIN_COLUMNS)
         new->file_select.columns = FILE_DEFAULT_COLUMNS;
     if (new->file_select.pixmap_rows < FILE_MIN_ROWS)
         new->file_select.pixmap_rows = FILE_DEFAULT_PIXMAP_ROWS;
     if (new->file_select.pixmap_columns < FILE_MIN_COLUMNS)
         new->file_select.pixmap_columns = FILE_DEFAULT_PIXMAP_COLUMNS;
     if (!strlen(new->file_select.default_filter))
         new->file_select.default_filter = FILE_DEFAULT_FILTER;

     get_font_width_height(new, &col_width, &row_height);
     row_height += new->file_select.row_spacing;
```

```
    /*
    A VPaned widget doesn't allow a (normal) width change.
    Here, we force the width of the pane to be that of the
    viewport (at least before resizing)--the area for
    displaying files is more important that the text area
    for displaying the file filter.
    */
    new->core.width = (new->file_select.columns + 2) * col_width;
    new->core.height = (new->file_select.rows + 2) * row_height;

    /*
    add/create actions/translations:
    */
    XtAddActions(filter_actions, XtNumber(filter_actions));
    filter_trans_table =
        XtParseTranslationTable(filter_translations);

    /*
    create a box to house the filter label and text entry area:
    */
    new->file_select.filterBoxW = XtCreateManagedWidget("filterBox",
        boxWidgetClass, new, NULL, 0);

    /*
    create the filter label:
    */
    i = 0;
    XtSetArg(args[i], XtNborderWidth, (XtArgVal) 0); i++;
    XtSetArg(args[i], XtNlabel, (XtArgVal) "Filter:"); i++;
    new->file_select.labelW = XtCreateManagedWidget("filterLabel",
        labelWidgetClass, new->file_select.filterBoxW, args, i);

    /*
    create the text entry area for the file filter:
    */
    i = 0;
#ifdef X11R3
    new->file_select.filter = XtMalloc(FILE_MAX_FILTER + 1);
    strncpy(new->file_select.filter, new->file_select.default_filter,
        FILE_MAX_FILTER);
    if (strlen(new->file_select.default_filter) >= FILE_MAX_FILTER)
        new->file_select.filter[FILE_MAX_FILTER] = EOS;
    XtSetArg(args[i], XtNtextOptions,
        (XtArgVal) (resizeWidth | resizeHeight)); i++;
    XtSetArg(args[i], XtNeditType, (XtArgVal) XttextEdit); i++;
#else
    new->file_select.filter = new->file_select.default_filter;
    XtSetArg(args[i], XtNresize, (XtArgVal) XawtextResizeBoth); i++;
    XtSetArg(args[i], XtNeditType, (XtArgVal) XawtextEdit); i++;
#endif
    XtSetArg(args[i], XtNstring,
        (XtArgVal) new->file_select.filter); i++;
    XtSetArg(args[i], XtNborderWidth, (XtArgVal) 1); i++;
    XtSetArg(args[i], XtNlength, (XtArgVal) FILE_MAX_FILTER); i++;
    XtSetArg(args[i], XtNwidth,
        (XtArgVal) new->file_select.filter_width); i++;
    XtSetArg(args[i], XtNresizable, TRUE); i++;
```

```
    new->file_select.filterW = XtCreateManagedWidget("filterText",
#ifdef X11R3
        asciiStringWidgetClass,
#else
        asciiTextWidgetClass,
#endif
        new->file_select.filterBoxW, args, i);
    XtOverrideTranslations(new->file_select.filterW,
        filter_trans_table);

    /*
    create the button box:
    */
    new->file_select.buttonBoxW =
        XtCreateManagedWidget("fileButtonBox",
            boxWidgetClass, new, NULL, 0);

    /*
    create the viewport to house the StrSelect widget:
    */
    i = 0;
    XtSetArg(args[i], XtNallowHoriz, (XtArgVal) TRUE); i++;
    XtSetArg(args[i], XtNallowVert, (XtArgVal) TRUE); i++;
    XtSetArg(args[i], XtNforceBars, (XtArgVal) TRUE); i++;
    XtSetArg(args[i], XtNheight,
        (XtArgVal) new->file_select.rows * row_height); i++;
    XtSetArg(args[i], XtNwidth,
        (XtArgVal) new->file_select.columns * col_width); i++;
    new->file_select.viewportW = XtCreateManagedWidget("fileViewport",
        viewportWidgetClass, new, args, i);

    /*
    create the StrSelect widget:
    */
    i = 0;
    XtSetArg(args[i], XiNdelimiters, (XtArgVal) FILE_DELIMITERS); i++;
    XtSetArg(args[i], XiNfont,
        (XtArgVal) new->file_select.font); i++;
    XtSetArg(args[i], XiNpixmapColumns,
        (XtArgVal) new->file_select.pixmap_columns); i++;
    XtSetArg(args[i], XiNpixmapRows,
        (XtArgVal) new->file_select.pixmap_rows); i++;
    if (new->file_select.pixmap_cursor != None) {
        XtSetArg(args[i], XtNcursor,
            (XtArgVal) new->file_select.pixmap_cursor); i++;
    }
    new->file_select.strSelectW = XtCreateManagedWidget("fileListBox",
        xiStrSelectWidgetClass, new->file_select.viewportW, args, i);
    set_filename_reference_buffer(new);

    /*
    create the individual buttons:
    */
    i = 0;
    XtSetArg(args[i], XtNlabel, (XtArgVal) "Filter"); i++;
    new->file_select.filterButtonW =
        XtCreateManagedWidget("fileButtonFilter",
```

```
            commandWidgetClass, new->file_select.buttonBoxW, args, i);
    XtAddCallback(new->file_select.filterButtonW, XtNcallback,
        FileSelectBoxFilter, NULL);

    i = 0;
    XtSetArg(args[i], XtNlabel, (XtArgVal) "Apply"); i++;
    new->file_select.applyButtonW =
        XtCreateManagedWidget("fileButtonApply",
            commandWidgetClass, new->file_select.buttonBoxW, args, i);
    /*
    Note:  The client should use XiFileSelectAddApplyProc() to
    add the callback for the previous button.
    */

    if (XtIsSubclass(XtParent(new), shellWidgetClass)) {
        i = 0;
        XtSetArg(args[i], XtNlabel, (XtArgVal) "Dismiss"); i++;
        new->file_select.dismissButtonW =
            XtCreateManagedWidget("fileButtonDismiss",
                commandWidgetClass, new->file_select.buttonBoxW,
                args, i);
        XtAddCallback(new->file_select.dismissButtonW, XtNcallback,
            FileSelectBoxDismiss, NULL);
    }
}   /* Initialize */


/*
Destroy() cleans up dynamic data structures.
*/

static void Destroy(w)
XiFileSelectWidget w;
{
    XtDestroyWidget(w->file_select.labelW);
    XtDestroyWidget(w->file_select.filterW);
    XtDestroyWidget(w->file_select.filterBoxW);
    XtDestroyWidget(w->file_select.viewportW);
    XtDestroyWidget(w->file_select.strSelectW);
    XtDestroyWidget(w->file_select.applyButtonW);
    XtDestroyWidget(w->file_select.dismissButtonW);
    XtDestroyWidget(w->file_select.filterButtonW);
    XtDestroyWidget(w->file_select.buttonBoxW);
    if (w->file_select.filenames != NULL)
        free(w->file_select.filenames);
}   /* Destroy */


/*
SetValues() handles modifications to resource-related instance
variables.  Typically, these don't need to be checked--most
resources are used during widget initialization only; others
simply assume the new values.
*/
/*ARGSUSED*/
static Boolean SetValues(current, request, new)
Widget current, request, new;
```

```
{
    /*
    at present, nothing to update...
    */
    return FALSE;
}   /* SetValues */


/*
Actions functions:
*/

/*
Beep() is a general-purpose function; one use is to beep the
user if they try to enter a character that results in a line
feed operation; see Initialize().
*/
/*ARGSUSED*/
static void Beep(w, event)
Widget w;
XEvent *event;
{
    XBell(XtDisplay(w), 50);
}   /* Beep */


/*
Public functions:
*/

/*
XiFileSelectPopup() invokes (pops up) the file selection box.  This
convenience function is useful ONLY if the the file selection box's
parent is a popup shell.
*/

void XiFileSelectPopup(fsw)
XiFileSelectWidget fsw;
{
    /*
    shell -> file selection box -> ...
    */
    if (XtIsSubclass(XtParent(fsw), shellWidgetClass))
        XtPopup(fsw->core.parent, XtGrabNone);
}   /* XiFileSelectPopup */


/*
XiFileSelectGetSelection() retrieves the value stored in the
private field 'selection'; this is the currently selected
file.  Unlike XiStrSelectGetSelection(), this (higher level)
function doesn't allow the return value to be null.
*/

char *XiFileSelectGetSelection(fsw)
XiFileSelectWidget fsw;
{
```

```
    char *select;

    if ((select = XiStrSelectGetSelection(fsw->file_select.strSelectW))
            != NULL)
        return select;
    else
        return "";
}   /* XiFileSelectGetSelection */


/*
XiFileSelectAddApplyProc() allows the user to register a function
(procedure) to be executed when the apply button is pressed.  Note
that no data is returned; an application should retrieve the
current selection with XiFileSelectGetSelection().
*/

void XiFileSelectAddApplyProc(fsw, callback_proc)
XiFileSelectWidget fsw;
void (*callback_proc)();
{
    if (callback_proc != NULL)
        XtAddCallback(fsw->file_select.applyButtonW, XtNcallback,
            callback_proc, NULL);
}   /* XiFileSelectAddApplyProc */


/*
XiFileSelectRefresh() allows the application programmer to update
the file selection box window manually.  This function does NOT
check for changes to the filter.
*/

void XiFileSelectRefresh(fsw)
XiFileSelectWidget fsw;
{
    set_filename_reference_buffer(fsw);
    XiStrSelectRedisplay(fsw->file_select.strSelectW);
}   /* XiFileSelectRefresh */


/*
Internal Callback functions:
*/

/*ARGSUSED*/
static void FileSelectBoxDismiss(w, client_data, call_data)
Widget w;
caddr_t client_data, call_data;
{
    /*
    shell -> file selection box -> button box -> button
    */
    XiFileSelectWidget fsw =
        (XiFileSelectWidget) XtParent(w->core.parent);
    if (XtIsSubclass(XtParent(fsw), shellWidgetClass))
        XtPopdown(XtParent(fsw));
```

```
}   /* FileSelectBoxDismiss */


/*ARGSUSED*/
static void FileSelectBoxFilter(w, client_data, call_data)
Widget w;
caddr_t client_data, call_data;
{
    /*
    shell -> file selection box -> button box -> button
    */
    XiFileSelectWidget fsw =
        (XiFileSelectWidget) XtParent(w->core.parent);

#ifdef X11R3
#else
    Arg args[1];
    char *filter_text;

    XtSetArg(args[0], XtNstring, &filter_text);
    XtGetValues(fsw->file_select.filterW, args, 1);
    fsw->file_select.filter = filter_text;
#endif
    set_filename_reference_buffer(fsw);
    XiStrSelectRedisplay(fsw->file_select.strSelectW);
}   /* FileSelectBoxFilter */


/*
Support functions:
*/

/*
get_font_width_height() determines the font width and height so
that the row and column resources will be in sync with the pixmap
created by the StrSelect widget.
*/

static void get_font_width_height(w, font_width, font_height)
XiFileSelectWidget w;
int *font_width, *font_height;
{
    *font_width = w->file_select.font->max_bounds.width;
    *font_height = w->file_select.font->max_bounds.ascent +
        w->file_select.font->max_bounds.descent;
}   /* get_font_width_height */


/*
set_filename_reference_buffer() expands the file specification
given by the filter, and then updates the StrSelect widget's
reference string.
*/

static void set_filename_reference_buffer(w)
XiFileSelectWidget w;
{
```

```
    char *filename_buffer, *filter;
    int match;

    if (!*w->file_select.filter) {
        fprintf(stderr,                       /** !!! remove? **/
            "file selection box: no value for filter!\n");
        XiStrSelectReset(w->file_select.strSelectW);
        return;
    }

    filename_buffer = expand_file_spec(w->file_select.filter);

    if (filename_buffer == NULL) {
        fprintf(stderr,
        "file selection box: error attempting to expand filter!\n");
        XiStrSelectReset(w->file_select.strSelectW);
        return;
    }

    if (w->file_select.filenames != NULL)
        free(w->file_select.filenames);
    w->file_select.filenames = filename_buffer;

    /*
    Check to see if the expansion is nothing more than the filter,
    and if so, make sure that there is no matching file.  Note
    that the expanded filename will have a linefeed appended.
    */
    if (strlen(w->file_select.filter) + 1 ==
            strlen(filename_buffer)) {
        match = TRUE;
        filter = w->file_select.filter;
        while (*filename_buffer && *filter)
            if (*filename_buffer++ != *filter++)
                match = FALSE;
        if (match && file_size(w->file_select.filter) == -1) {
            fprintf(stderr,                   /** !!! remove? **/
                "file selection box: no match for filter!\n");
            free(w->file_select.filenames);
            w->file_select.filenames = NULL;
            XiStrSelectReset(w->file_select.strSelectW);
        }
        else
            XiStrSelectSetString(w->file_select.strSelectW,
                w->file_select.filenames);
    }
    else
        XiStrSelectSetString(w->file_select.strSelectW,
            w->file_select.filenames);
}   /* set_filename_reference_buffer */


/*
expand_file_spec() takes a file spec. as an argument and
returns a pointer to a dynamically allocated list of filenames
that are produced by expanding the file spec.  The calling
function is responsible for freeing the dynamic storage when
```

```
it is no longer needed.
*/

static char *expand_file_spec(file_spec)
char *file_spec;
{
    static char *file_spec_buffer;
    char temp_file[40], alt_file_spec[FILE_MAX_FILTER + 1];
    char cmdstring[FILE_MAX_FILTER + 9 + 40];

    if (!*file_spec)
        return NULL;
    if (strlen(file_spec) >= FILE_MAX_FILTER) {
        fprintf(stderr,
        "file selection box: filter has too many characters!\n");
        return NULL;
    }
    while (*file_spec && *file_spec == ' ')
        file_spec++;
    if (*file_spec == '') {
        if (get_home_directory(alt_file_spec)) {
            file_spec++;    /* skip the '' */
            strncat(alt_file_spec, file_spec,
                FILE_MAX_FILTER - strlen(alt_file_spec));
            file_spec = alt_file_spec;
        }
    }
    sprintf(temp_file, "%s.%d", "Xi.temp.filenames", getpid());
    unlink(temp_file);       /* if it exists */
    sprintf(cmdstring, "echo %s > %s", file_spec, temp_file);
    system(cmdstring);
    if (file_size(temp_file) == -1) {
        fprintf(stderr,
        "file selection box: unknown error while expanding filter!\n");
        return NULL;
    }
    if ((file_spec_buffer =
            (char *) malloc((unsigned) (file_size(temp_file) + 1)))
            == NULL) {
        fprintf(stderr,
        "file selection box: memory allocation error\n\
 while expanding filter!\n");
        unlink(temp_file);
        return NULL;
    }
    if (!load_buffer(temp_file, file_spec_buffer)) {
        fprintf(stderr,
        "file selection box: unknown temp file error\n\
 while expanding filter!\n");
        free(file_spec_buffer);
        unlink(temp_file);
        return NULL;
    }
    unlink(temp_file);
    return file_spec_buffer;
}   /* expand_file_spec */
```

```
/*
load_buffer() loads a buffer with text from a file.
*/

static int load_buffer(file_spec, buffer)
char *file_spec, *buffer;
{
    FILE *file_ptr;

    if ((file_ptr = fopen(file_spec, "r")) == NULL)
        return FALSE;
    while ((*buffer = fgetc(file_ptr)) != EOF)
        buffer++;
    *buffer = EOS;
    fclose(file_ptr);
    return TRUE;
}   /* load_buffer */


/*
file_size() checks for the existence of a file using stat(),
returning -1 for a nonexistent file and the file size otherwise.
*/

static int file_size(file_spec)
char *file_spec;
{
    struct stat statbuf;

    if (stat(file_spec, &statbuf) < 0)
        return -1;
    else
        return (int)statbuf.st_size;
}   /* file_size */


/*
get_home_directory() examines the environment for the value of HOME.
*/

static int get_home_directory(directory)
char *directory;
{
    char *home;

    if ((home = (char *) getenv("HOME")) == NULL) {
        fprintf(stderr,
    "file selection box: unable to determine your home directory!\n");
        return FALSE;
    }
    strcpy(directory, home);
    return TRUE;
}   /* get_home_directory */
```

```
/****  testfilesel.c  ****  tests the file selection box widget ****/


#include <stdio.h>
#include <X11/Intrinsic.h>
#include <X11/StringDefs.h>
#include <X11/Shell.h>

#ifdef X11R3
#include <X11/Box.h>
#include <X11/Command.h>
#else
#include <X11/Xaw/Box.h>
#include <X11/Xaw/Command.h>
#endif

#include <Ximisc.h>
#include "FileSelect.h"


/*
Functions:
*/

void Quit(), PrintSelection(), TestFileSelectBox();


/*
Private globals:
*/

static Widget testFileSelectBox;
static XFontStruct *font;


/*
main() sets up a button-activated file selection box inside a
popup shell.  A simple callback is used to test the retrieval
facilities for the currently selected file.
*/

void main(argc, argv)
int argc;
char **argv;
{
    Widget topLevel, fileSelectShell, testBox,
        testButton, quitButton;
    Arg args[5];
    int i;

    topLevel = XtInitialize(argv[0], "TestFileSel", NULL, 0, &argc, argv);
    font = load_font(topLevel, "testfilesel", "8x13");
    i = 0;
    XtSetArg(args[i], XtNallowShellResize, (XtArgVal) TRUE); i++;
    fileSelectShell = XtCreatePopupShell("fileSelectShell",
        transientShellWidgetClass, topLevel, args, i);
    i = 0;
```

```
    XtSetArg(args[i], XiNpixmapFont, (XtArgVal) font); i++;
    testFileSelectBox = XtCreateManagedWidget("testFileSelectBox",
        xiFileSelectWidgetClass, fileSelectShell, args, i);
    XiFileSelectAddApplyProc(testFileSelectBox, PrintSelection);
    testBox = XtCreateManagedWidget("box", boxWidgetClass,
        topLevel, NULL, 0);
    i = 0;
    XtSetArg(args[i], XtNlabel, (XtArgVal) "File Selection Box"); i++;
    testButton = XtCreateManagedWidget("testButton",
        commandWidgetClass, testBox, args, i);
    XtAddCallback(testButton, XtNcallback, TestFileSelectBox, NULL);
    i = 0;
    XtSetArg(args[i], XtNlabel, (XtArgVal) "Quit"); i++;
    quitButton = XtCreateManagedWidget("quitButton",
        commandWidgetClass, testBox, args, i);
    XtAddCallback(quitButton, XtNcallback, Quit, NULL);
    XtRealizeWidget(topLevel);
    XtMainLoop();
}   /* main */


/*ARGSUSED*/
void TestFileSelectBox(w, client_data, call_data)
Widget w;
caddr_t client_data, call_data;
{
    XiFileSelectPopup(testFileSelectBox);
}   /* TestFileSelectBox */


/*ARGSUSED*/
void PrintSelection(w, client_data, call_data)
Widget w;
caddr_t client_data, call_data;
{
    /*
    Alternate approach:
    */
    printf("The current selection is: %s\n",
        XiFileSelectGetSelection(testFileSelectBox));
}   /* PrintSelection */


/*ARGSUSED*/
void Quit(w, client_data, call_data)
Widget w;
caddr_t client_data, call_data;
{
    XFreeFont(XtDisplay(w), font);
    exit(0);
}   /* Quit */


/****  testfilesel2.c  ****  tests the file selection box widget ****/
```

```
#include <stdio.h>
#include <X11/Intrinsic.h>
#include <X11/StringDefs.h>
#include <X11/Shell.h>
#include <X11/cursorfont.h>


#ifdef X11R3
#include <X11/Box.h>
#include <X11/Command.h>
#include <X11/Form.h>
#else
#include <X11/Xaw/Box.h>
#include <X11/Xaw/Command.h>
#include <X11/Xaw/Form.h>
#endif

#include <Ximisc.h>
#include "FileSelect.h"


/*
Functions:
*/

void Quit(), PrintSelection();

/*
Private globals:
*/

static Widget testFileSelectBox;
static XFontStruct *font;


/*
main() sets up a button-activated file selection box inside a
box widget in the main window.  A simple callback is used to
test the retrieval facilities for the currently selected file.
*/

void main(argc, argv)
int argc;
char **argv;
{
    Widget topLevel, testBox, quitButton;
    Arg args[5];
    int i;
    Cursor pixmap_cursor;

    topLevel = XtInitialize(argv[0], "TestFileSel2",
        NULL, 0, &argc, argv);
    font = load_font(topLevel, "testfilesel2", "8x13");
    testBox = XtCreateManagedWidget("testBox", formWidgetClass,
        topLevel, NULL, 0);
    i = 0;
    XtSetArg(args[i], XiNrows,          /* just testing */
```

```
        (XtArgVal) 20); i++;
    XtSetArg(args[i], XiNcolumns,        /* just testing */
        (XtArgVal) 40); i++;
/*  pixmap_cursor = XCreateFontCursor(XtDisplay(topLevel), XC_dot);
    XtSetArg(args[i], XiNpixmapCursor, (XtArgVal) pixmap_cursor); i++;*/
    XtSetArg(args[i], XiNrowSpacing,     /* just testing */
        (XtArgVal) 5); i++;
    XtSetArg(args[i], XiNpixmapFont,     /* just testing */
        (XtArgVal) font); i++;
    testFileSelectBox = XtCreateManagedWidget("testFileSelectBox",
        xiFileSelectWidgetClass, testBox, args, i);
    XiFileSelectAddApplyProc(testFileSelectBox, PrintSelection);
    i = 0;
    XtSetArg(args[i], XtNlabel, (XtArgVal) "Quit"); i++;
    XtSetArg(args[i], XtNfromVert, (XtArgVal) testFileSelectBox); i++;
    quitButton = XtCreateManagedWidget("quitButton",
        commandWidgetClass, testBox, args, i);
    XtAddCallback(quitButton, XtNcallback, Quit, NULL);
    XtRealizeWidget(topLevel);
    XtMainLoop();
}   /* main */


/*ARGSUSED*/
void PrintSelection(w, client_data, call_data)
Widget w;
caddr_t client_data, call_data;
{
    printf("The current selection is: %s\n",
        XiFileSelectGetSelection(testFileSelectBox));
}   /* PrintSelection */


/*ARGSUSED*/
void Quit(w, client_data, call_data)
Widget w;
caddr_t client_data, call_data;
{
    XFreeFont(XtDisplay(w), font);
    exit(0);
}   /* Quit */
```

XiButton: A Non-command, Button Widget

```
/****    Button.h    ****/

/****    public declarations/definitions for Button.c    ****/

#ifndef _XiButton_h
#define _XiButton_h 1

/*******************************************************************
*  Copyright (c) 1990 Iris Computing Laboratories.
*
*  This software is provided for demonstration purposes only.  As
*  freely-distributed, modifiable source code, this software carries
*  absolutely no warranty.
*******************************************************************/

/*******************************************************************
A Button widget is a simple, non-command, button.  Although a button
widget could be created for stand-alone use, it is designed to serve
as a foundation widget for building higher level widgets, such as
choice boxes and menus.
   A Button widget supports a selection callback list.  A button also
allows an integer value to be associated with it.  This feature is
provided so that the client program can associate an application-
specific value with each button in, say, a choice box, and then
determine which button is currently selected by manipulating button
values.  Note, however, that the client is responsible for imposing
this logic on a SET of buttons; a button widget can only get and set
button values.  The public function XiButtonGetValue() returns the
```

```
integer value associated with a button.  A value can be provided or
modified dynamically with a resource value or by calling the function
XiButtonSetValue().
   A Button widget can be selected and deselected.  By default, this
action operates as a toggle via a <ClickLeft>; however, a higher
level widget can override the default behavior.  Two public
functions, XiButtonSelect() and XiButtonDeselect(), can be used for
programmatic selection and deselection, respectively.  A selected
button is "highlighted" with a one-pixel wide rectangle inside the
button's border.  When a button is selected, its callback list, if
any, is traversed--after all other selection operations are complete.
A third function, XiButtonSelectNoCB(), can be use to programmati-
cally select a button without executing any associated callbacks.
   A Button widget's label can be modified dynamically; however, the
pixmap and window are not resized in this case.  If the new label is
longer, there may be clipping in the Button window.  Note that by
default the width of a button is based on the number of characters in
(length of) the label.  Thus, by default a collection of buttons will
having varying width.  The client can override this behavior with the
XiNlength resource, which specifies the number of characters to use
in determining a button's length/width.  For example, when adding
several buttons to a higher-level widget, or application, you can
determine the maximum number of characters in the longest label, and
then use this value for the XiNlength resource for each button in
order to produce buttons of uniform length/width.  This resource is
used only during the creation of buttons; you can not "expand" a
button dynamically.

Resources (see Button.h also):

Name          Class          Data Type        Default       Modify?
----          -----          ---------        -------       -------
XiNlabel      XiCLabel       String           ""            OK
XiNlength     XiCLength      int              strlen(
                                              label)
XiNvalue      XiCValue       int              -1            OK
XiNselect-    XiCSelect-     XtCallbackList   NULL          OK
Callback      Callback
XiNfont       XiCFont        XFontStruct *    XtDefaultFont

   Public interfaces are described below.
*********************************************************************/

#ifdef X11R3
#include <X11/Simple.h>
#else
#include <X11/Xaw/Simple.h>
#endif


#define XiBUTTON_NOVALUE        -1


/*
Resource definitions:
*/
```

```
#define XiNlabel                    "label"         /* OK to modify */
#define XiNlength                   "length"
#define XiNvalue                    "value"         /* OK to modify */
#define XiNselectCallback           "selectCallback"/* OK to modify */
#define XiNwidth                    "width"
#define XiNheight                   "height"
#define XiNborderWidth              "borderWidth"
#define XiNfont                     "font"
#define XiCLabel                    "Label"
#define XiCLength                   "Length"
#define XiCValue                    "Value"
#define XiCSelectCallback           "SelectCallback"
#define XiCCallback                 "Callback"
#define XiCWidth                    "Width"
#define XiCHeight                   "Height"
#define XiCBorderWidth              "BorderWidth"
#define XiCFont                     "Font"


typedef struct _XiButtonClassRec *XiButtonWidgetClass;
typedef struct _XiButtonRec *XiButtonWidget;

extern WidgetClass xiButtonWidgetClass;


/*
Public functions:
*/

extern int XiButtonGetValue();
/*  XiButtonWidget button_widget;
*/

extern void XiButtonSetValue();
/*  XiButtonWidget button_widget;
    int value;
*/

extern int XiButtonIsSelected();
/*  XiButtonWidget button_widget;
*/

extern void XiButtonSelect();
/*  XiButtonWidget button_widget;
*/

extern void XiButtonSelectNoCB();
/*  XiButtonWidget button_widget;
*/

extern void XiButtonDeselect();
/*  XiButtonWidget button_widget;
*/

#endif /* _XiButton_h  */
```

```
/****    ButtonP.h    ****/

/****    private declarations/definitions for Button.c    ****/


#ifndef _XiButtonP_h
#define _XiButtonP_h


#include "Button.h"
#ifdef X11R3
#include <X11/SimpleP.h>
#else
#include <X11/Xaw/SimpleP.h>
#endif


#define BTN_NOTHING                     ""
#define BTN_DEFAULT_VALUE               XiBUTTON_NOVALUE
#define BTN_DEFAULT_LENGTH              -1

#define BTN_DEFAULT_WIDTH               75
#define BTN_DEFAULT_HEIGHT              30

#define BTN_INTERNAL_HORIZ_PAD          5
#define BTN_INTERNAL_VERT_PAD           5

#define BTN_WITH_CB                     -1
#define BTN_WITHOUT_CB                  -2


#define EOS                             '\0'


typedef struct _XiButtonClassPart {     /* class definition */
    int dummy;
} XiButtonClassPart;

typedef struct _XiButtonClassRec {
    CoreClassPart core_class;
    SimpleClassPart simple_class;
    XiButtonClassPart button_class;
} XiButtonClassRec;

extern XiButtonClassRec xiButtonClassRec;


typedef struct _XiButtonPart {          /* instance definition */
    char *label;                /* resource-supplied label */
    char *private_label;        /* private copy of label */
    XFontStruct *font;
    Pixmap pixmap;
    GC gc;                      /* for text and rectangle */
    GC cgc;                     /* clears the rectangle */
    Dimension width, height;    /* does not include padding */
    Boolean selected;           /* is button currently selected? */
```

```
    int value;                  /* optional */
    int length;                 /* length in chars. of button text */
    XtCallbackList cb_list;     /* see select_button() */
} XiButtonPart;


typedef struct _XiButtonRec {
    CorePart core;
    SimplePart simple;
    XiButtonPart button;
} XiButtonRec;


#endif  /* _XiButtonP_h */



/**  Button.c  ** a simple button implementation  **/


#include <stdio.h>

#include <X11/Xlib.h>
#include <X11/Xos.h>
#include <X11/IntrinsicP.h>
#include <X11/StringDefs.h>

#ifdef X11R3
#include <X11/Simple.h>
#else
#include <X11/Xaw/XawInit.h>
#include <X11/Xaw/Simple.h>
#endif

#include "ButtonP.h"


/*
Class Methods:
*/

static void Initialize();
static void Destroy();
static Boolean SetValues();
static void Redisplay();


/*
Private support functions:
*/

static int create_button_pixmap();
static int allocate_and_center_button_text();
static void fill_pixmap_and_redisplay();
static void fill_pixmap();
static void redisplay_pixmap();
static void select_button();
```

```
static void deselect_button();


/*
Translations and actions:
*/

static void SelectButton();

static char button_translations[] =
    "<Btn1Down>:  select()";

static XtActionsRec button_actions[] = {
    {"select", (XtActionProc) SelectButton},
};


/*
Resource table:
*/

#define res_offset(field) XtOffset(XiButtonWidget, field)

static XtResource resources[] = {
    {XiNlabel, XiCLabel, XtRString, sizeof(char *),
        res_offset(button.label),
        XtRString, BTN_NOTHING},
    {XiNlength, XiCLength, XtRInt, sizeof(int),
        res_offset(button.length),
        XtRImmediate, (caddr_t) BTN_DEFAULT_LENGTH},
    {XiNvalue, XiCValue, XtRInt, sizeof(int),
        res_offset(button.value),
        XtRImmediate, (caddr_t) BTN_DEFAULT_VALUE},
    {XiNfont, XiCFont, XtRFontStruct, sizeof(XFontStruct *),
        res_offset(button.font),
        XtRString, "XtDefaultFont"},
    {XiNselectCallback, XiCSelectCallback, XtRCallback,
        sizeof(caddr_t), res_offset(button.cb_list),
        XtRCallback, (caddr_t) NULL},
};


/*
Define storage for the class here:
*/

XiButtonClassRec XibuttonClassRec = {
    { /* core_class variables */
        (WidgetClass) &simpleClassRec,  /* ancestor */
        "Button",                       /* class name */
        sizeof(XiButtonRec),            /* widget size */
#ifdef X11R3
        NULL,                           /* class initialize */
#else
        XawInitializeWidgetSet,         /* class initialize */
#endif
        NULL,                           /* class part init. */
```

```
        FALSE,                          /* class inited */
        Initialize,                     /* initialize */
        NULL,                           /* initialize hook */
        XtInheritRealize,               /* realize */
        button_actions,                 /* actions */
        XtNumber(button_actions),       /* number of actions */
        resources,                      /* resources */
        XtNumber(resources),            /* number of resources */
        NULLQUARK,                      /* xrm class */
        TRUE,                           /* compress motions */
        TRUE,                           /* compress exposures */
        TRUE,                           /* compress enter/leave */
        FALSE,                          /* visibility interest */
        Destroy,                        /* destroy */
        NULL,                           /* resize */
        Redisplay,                      /* expose */
        SetValues,                      /* set values */
        NULL,                           /* set values hook */
        XtInheritSetValuesAlmost,       /* set values almost */
        NULL,                           /* get values hook */
        NULL,                           /* accept focus */
        XtVersion,                      /* version */
        NULL,                           /* callback private */
        button_translations,            /* translation table */
        XtInheritQueryGeometry,         /* query geometry */
        XtInheritDisplayAccelerator,    /* display accelerator */
        NULL,                           /* extension */
    },
    { /* simple_class variables */
        XtInheritChangeSensitive,
    },
    { /* button_class variables */
        0,
    },
}; /* XibuttonClassRec */


WidgetClass xiButtonWidgetClass = (WidgetClass) &XibuttonClassRec;


/*
XiButtonWidget methods:
*/

/*
Initialize() initializes each instance of a button.
A button implements a pixmap in a Simple widget.
*/
/*ARGSUSED*/
static void Initialize(request, new)
XiButtonWidget request, new;
{
    if (!new->button.label)
        new->button.label = BTN_NOTHING;
    create_button_pixmap(new);
    new->button.selected = FALSE;
    fill_pixmap(new);
```

```
}   /* Initialize */


/*
Destroy() cleans up dynamic data structures.
*/

static void Destroy(w)
XiButtonWidget w;
{
    if (w->button.private_label != NULL)
        XtFree(w->button.private_label);
    if (w->button.gc != NULL)
        XFreeGC(XtDisplay(w), w->button.gc);
    if (w->button.cgc != NULL)
        XFreeGC(XtDisplay(w), w->button.cgc);
    if (w->button.pixmap != NULL)
        XFreePixmap(XtDisplay(w), w->button.pixmap);
}   /* Destroy */


/*
SetValues() handles dynamic modifications to resource-related
instance variables, where necessary.  Most resources are used
only during widget creation.  The 'value' field can be set by
a resource either during creation or dynamically; however, its
value doesn't need to be checked here.  If a button's 'label'
field is changed dynamically via a resource setting, it's
necessary to free and then reallocate space for the label.
This implementation does NOT dynamically resize the pixmap, if
the label text changes.
*/
/*ARGSUSED*/
static Boolean SetValues(current, request, new)
Widget current, request, new;
{
    XiButtonWidget bw = (XiButtonWidget) new;
    XiButtonWidget old_bw = (XiButtonWidget) current;

    if (!bw->button.label)
        bw->button.label = BTN_NOTHING;
    if (strcmp(bw->button.label, old_bw->button.label)) {
        if (old_bw->button.private_label != NULL)
            XtFree(old_bw->button.private_label);
        /*
        does NOT resize pixmap:
        */
        allocate_and_center_button_text(bw, strlen(bw->button.label));
        fill_pixmap(bw);
    }
    return TRUE;
}   /* SetValues */


/*
Redisplay() calls redisplay_pixmap() to update the pixmap
window upon an exposure.
```

```
*/
/*ARGSUSED*/
static void Redisplay(w, event)
Widget w;
XEvent *event;
{
    redisplay_pixmap(w);
}   /* Redisplay */


/*
Actions functions:
*/
/*ARGSUSED*/
static void SelectButton(w, event)
XiButtonWidget w;
XEvent *event;
{
    if (w->button.selected)
        deselect_button(w);
    else
        select_button(w, BTN_WITH_CB);
}   /* SelectButton */


/*
Public functions:
*/

/*
XiButtonGetValue() returns the button's value.
This is an optional field.
*/

int XiButtonGetValue(w)
XiButtonWidget w;
{
    return w->button.value;
}   /* XiButtonGetValue */


/*
XiButtonSetValue() sets the button's value.
This is an optional field.
*/

void XiButtonSetValue(w, value)
XiButtonWidget w;
int value;
{
    w->button.value = value;
}   /* XiButtonSetValue */


/*
XiButtonIsSelected() determines whether or not
the button is currently selected.
```

```
*/

int XiButtonIsSelected(w)
XiButtonWidget w;
{
    return (int) w->button.selected;
}   /* XiButtonIsSelected */


/*
XiButtonSelect() programmatically selects a button.
*/

void XiButtonSelect(w)
XiButtonWidget w;
{
    if (!w->button.selected)
        select_button(w, BTN_WITH_CB);
}   /* XiButtonSelect */


/*
XiButtonSelectNoCB() programmatically selects a button,
but doesn't attempt to execute any associated callbacks.
*/

void XiButtonSelectNoCB(w)
XiButtonWidget w;
{
    if (!w->button.selected)
        select_button(w, BTN_WITHOUT_CB);
}   /* XiButtonSelect */


/*
XiButtonDeselect() programmatically deselects a button.
*/

void XiButtonDeselect(w)
XiButtonWidget w;
{
    if (w->button.selected)
        deselect_button(w);
}   /* XiButtonDeselect */


/*
Support functions:
*/

/*
create_button_pixmap() creates the GCs, allocates the button's
text, and builds the button's pixmap.
*/

static int create_button_pixmap(w)
XiButtonWidget w;
```

```
{
    XGCValues values;
    Display *display = XtDisplay(w);
    int num_btn_chars, screen = XDefaultScreen(display);
    int depth = XDisplayPlanes(display, screen);

    values.foreground = XBlackPixel(display, screen);
    values.background = XWhitePixel(display, screen);
    values.font = w->button.font->fid;
    w->button.gc = XCreateGC(XtDisplay(w),
        RootWindowOfScreen(XtScreen(w)),
        GCForeground | GCBackground | GCFont, &values);
    w->button.cgc = XCreateGC(XtDisplay(w),
        RootWindowOfScreen(XtScreen(w)),
        GCForeground | GCBackground | GCFont, &values);
    XSetFunction(XtDisplay(w), w->button.cgc, GXclear);

    num_btn_chars = (w->button.length == BTN_DEFAULT_LENGTH) ?
        strlen(w->button.label) : w->button.length;
    if (!allocate_and_center_button_text(w, num_btn_chars))
        fprintf(stderr,
        "button: unable to allocate space for the button's text!\n");

    if (w->core.width == 0) {
        if (*w->button.private_label)
            w->core.width = strlen(w->button.private_label) *
                w->button.font->max_bounds.width;
        else
            w->core.width = BTN_DEFAULT_WIDTH;
    }
    if (w->core.height == 0) {
        if (*w->button.private_label)
            w->core.height = w->button.font->max_bounds.ascent +
                w->button.font->max_bounds.descent;
        else
            w->core.height = BTN_DEFAULT_HEIGHT;
    }
    w->core.width = w->button.width =
        w->core.width + (2 * BTN_INTERNAL_HORIZ_PAD);
    w->core.height = w->button.height =
        w->core.height + (2 * BTN_INTERNAL_VERT_PAD);
    w->button.pixmap = XCreatePixmap(XtDisplay(w),
        RootWindowOfScreen(XtScreen(w)),
        w->button.width, w->button.height, depth);
}   /* create_button_pixmap */


/*
allocate_and_center_button_text() creates a private (safe)
copy of the client's button text string.
*/


static int allocate_and_center_button_text(w, total_len)
XiButtonWidget w;
int total_len;
{
    int j, odd_num, pad_len;
```

```
    j = strlen(w->button.label);         /* center each item */
    if ((pad_len = (total_len - j) / 2) < 0)
        return FALSE;
    odd_num = ((((total_len - j) / 2) * 2) != (total_len - j)) ?
        TRUE : FALSE;
    w->button.private_label =
        (char *) XtMalloc((unsigned) (j + (2 * pad_len) + 2));
    if (w->button.private_label == NULL)
        return FALSE;
    for ( ; j > -1; j--)
        w->button.private_label[j + pad_len] = w->button.label[j];
    for (j = 0; j < pad_len; j++)
        w->button.private_label[j] = ' ';
    while (pad_len--)
        strcat(w->button.private_label, " ");
    if (odd_num)
        strcat(w->button.private_label, " ");
    return TRUE;
}   /* allocate_and_center_button_text */


/*
fill_pixmap_and_redisplay() builds the pixmap and refreshes
the window.
*/

static void fill_pixmap_and_redisplay(w)
XiButtonWidget w;
{
    fill_pixmap(w);
    redisplay_pixmap(w);
}   /* fill_pixmap_and_redisplay */


/*
fill_pixmap() tests for errors and then displays the label
on the pixmap.
*/

static void fill_pixmap(w)
XiButtonWidget w;
{
    if (!w->button.label || !*w->button.label)
        return;
    deselect_button(w);
    /*
    clear pixmap before it filling with a new label:
    */
    XFillRectangle(XtDisplay(w), w->button.pixmap,
        w->button.cgc, 0, 0, w->button.width, w->button.height);
    XDrawImageString(XtDisplay(w), w->button.pixmap,
        w->button.gc, BTN_INTERNAL_HORIZ_PAD,
        w->button.font->max_bounds.ascent + BTN_INTERNAL_VERT_PAD,
        w->button.private_label, strlen(w->button.private_label));
}   /* fill_pixmap */
```

```
/*
redisplay_pixmap() copies the pixmap to the window.
*/

static void redisplay_pixmap(w)
XiButtonWidget w;
{
    if (!XtIsRealized(w))
        return;
    XCopyArea(XtDisplay(w), w->button.pixmap,
        XtWindow(w),
        w->button.gc, 0, 0, w->button.width,
        w->button.height, 0, 0);
}   /* redisplay_pixmap */


/*
select_button() draws a one pixel wide rectangle
on the inside of the pixmap, and then, if requested,
calls functions on the client-specified callback list.
*/

static void select_button(w, call_CB)
XiButtonWidget w;
int call_CB;
{
    w->button.selected = TRUE;
    XDrawRectangle(XtDisplay(w), w->button.pixmap, w->button.gc,
        1, 1, w->button.width - 3, w->button.height - 3);
    redisplay_pixmap(w);
    if (call_CB == BTN_WITH_CB)
        XtCallCallbacks(w, XiNselectCallback,
            (caddr_t) &w->button.value);
}   /* select_button */


/*
deselect_button() erases the one pixel wide rectangle
on the inside of the pixmap.
*/

static void deselect_button(w)
XiButtonWidget w;
{
    w->button.selected = FALSE;
    XDrawRectangle(XtDisplay(w), w->button.pixmap, w->button.cgc,
        1, 1, w->button.width - 3, w->button.height - 3);
    redisplay_pixmap(w);
}   /* deselect_button */


/****  testbutton.c  ****  tests the button widget  ****/


#include <stdio.h>
```

```
#include <X11/Intrinsic.h>
#include <X11/StringDefs.h>
#include <X11/Shell.h>

#ifdef X11R3
#include <X11/Command.h>
#include <X11/Form.h>
#else
#include <X11/Xaw/Command.h>
#include <X11/Xaw/Form.h>
#endif

#include <Ximisc.h>
#include "Button.h"


/*
Functions:
*/

void ChangeLabel(), PrintSelection(), Quit();


/*
Private globals:
*/

static Widget testButton;
static XFontStruct *font;


/*
main() sets up a button inside a box with command buttons for
quitting the application and dynamically changing the button's
label.  Several resource values are tested.
*/

void main(argc, argv)
int argc;
char **argv;
{
    Widget topLevel, testBox, changeButton, quit;
    Arg args[10];
    int i;

    topLevel = XtInitialize(argv[0], "TestButton",
        NULL, 0, &argc, argv);
    font = load_font(topLevel, "testbutton", "8x13");
    i = 0;
    testBox = XtCreateManagedWidget("testBox", formWidgetClass,
        topLevel, args, i);
    i = 0;
    XtSetArg(args[i], XiNlabel, (XtArgVal) "Test Button"); i++;
    XtSetArg(args[i], XiNborderWidth, (XtArgVal) 2); i++;
    XtSetArg(args[i], XiNfont, (XtArgVal) font); i++;
/*  XtSetArg(args[i], XiNvalue, (XtArgVal) 10); i++;         */
/*  XtSetArg(args[i], XiNlength, (XtArgVal) 15); i++;        */
```

```
/*  XtSetArg(args[i], XiNwidth, (XtArgVal) 150); i++;            */
/*  XtSetArg(args[i], XiNheight, (XtArgVal) 100); i++;           */
    testButton = XtCreateManagedWidget("testButton",
        xiButtonWidgetClass, testBox, args, i);
    XtAddCallback(testButton, XiNselectCallback,
        PrintSelection, NULL);
/*  XiButtonSetValue(testButton, 15);                             */
    i = 0;
    XtSetArg(args[i], XtNlabel, (XtArgVal) "Quit"); i++;
    XtSetArg(args[i], XtNfromVert, (XtArgVal) testButton); i++;
    quit = XtCreateManagedWidget("quit",
        commandWidgetClass, testBox, args, i);
    XtAddCallback(quit, XtNcallback, Quit, NULL);
    i = 0;
    XtSetArg(args[i], XtNlabel, (XtArgVal) "Change Label"); i++;
    XtSetArg(args[i], XtNfromVert, (XtArgVal) quit); i++;
    changeButton = XtCreateManagedWidget("changeButton",
        commandWidgetClass, testBox, args, i);
    XtAddCallback(changeButton, XtNcallback, ChangeLabel, NULL);
    XtRealizeWidget(topLevel);
    XtMainLoop();
}   /* main */


/*ARGSUSED*/
void PrintSelection(w, client_data, call_data)
Widget w;
caddr_t client_data, call_data;
{
    if (XiButtonGetValue(w) == XiBUTTON_NOVALUE)
        printf("The current button has NO value.\n");
    else
        printf("The current button has value: %d\n",
            XiButtonGetValue(w));
}   /* PrintSelection */


/*ARGSUSED*/
void ChangeLabel(w, client_data, call_data)
Widget w;
caddr_t client_data, call_data;
{
    Arg args[2];
    int i;

    i = 0;
    XtSetArg(args[i], XiNlabel, (XtArgVal) "New Label"); i++;
    XtSetValues(testButton, args, i);
}   /* ChangeLabel */


/*ARGSUSED*/
void Quit(w, client_data, call_data)
Widget w;
caddr_t client_data, call_data;
{
    printf("Button value: %d\n", XiButtonGetValue(testButton));
```

```
    XFreeFont(XtDisplay(w), font);
    exit(0);
}   /* Quit */
```

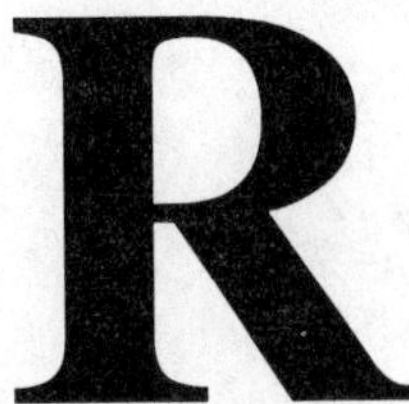

XiChoice: A Configurable, Item Selection Widget

```
/****    Choice.h    ****/

/****    public declarations/definitions for Choice.c    ****/

#ifndef _XiChoice_h
#define _XiChoice_h 1

/*******************************************************************
*  Copyright (c) 1990 Iris Computing Laboratories.
*
*  This software is provided for demonstration purposes only.  As
*  freely-distributed, modifiable source code, this software carries
*  absolutely no warranty.
*******************************************************************/

/*******************************************************************
A Choice widget is a simple, multiple-choice selection box for speci-
fying, or choosing from, several application options.  For example,
a calculator might employ a choice box for allowing the user to
select one of several numeric bases.  A Choice widget collects
Button widgets within a box, allowing the client to select one, or
more, buttons (items), depending on the value of the resource
XiNexclusive.
   The label, if any, appears, by default, in the top of the choice
box; this can be altered with the resource XiNlabelOnLeft.  Items,
by default, are arranged from left to right below the label/title;
this can be altered with the resource XiNvertical.
   The choice box inherits its cursor from its parent; however, you
```

```
can specify a different cursor for the ITEMS/BUTTONS using the
resource XiNitemCursor.
   Items are added subsequent to choice box creation using either
XiChoiceAddItem() for adding items one at a time or
XiChoiceAddItems() for adding items via an array specification.  The
latter approach is strongly recommended, since this widget supports
two different forms, namely, standard choice boxes and simple menus.
XiChoiceAddItem() is a low-level function that requires FOUR argu-
ments, even if, in the case of menus, only three arguments are
appropriate.  XiChoiceAddItems() accommodates two different data
types for its second argument, either XiChoiceItem or
XiChoiceMenuItem.  Examples of how to set up both forms are given
below.
   For exclusive-mode choice boxes that are NOT in menu form, a
default item can be specified using the resource XiNdefaultItem.
Note that it is possible for the user to de-select the default item,
leaving no items selected.  It is the responsibility of the client
to monitor this condition, if it isn't acceptable, and reset the
default using one of the public functions listed below.
   For choice boxes, the border width of the buttons defaults to that
for the choice box itself.  You can override the default with the
resource XiNitemBorderWidth.  Note that for horizontal choice boxes
where each item label is a single word, try setting the border width
for BOTH the box and the items to 0, using the common resource
XtNborderWidth in the standard way.  Also, locate the choice box la-
bel on the left with XiNlabelOnLeft.  For many applications, these
settings provide a one-line, "clean and uncluttered" appearance.  If
any item label is more than one word, try setting the choice box
border to 0 and the item border to 1.

Resources (see Button.h also):

Name            Class           Data Type       Default        Modify?
----            -----           ---------       -------        -------
XiNlabel        XiCLabel        String          ""             OK
XiNexclusive    XiCExclusive    Boolean         FALSE
XiNvertical     XiCVertical     Boolean         FALSE
XiNmenuForm     XiCMenuForm     Boolean         FALSE
XiNdefaultItem  XiCDefaultItem  int             1
XiNlabelOnLeft  XiCLabelOnLeft  Boolean         FALSE
XiNitemCursor   XiCItemCursor   Cursor          None
XiNitemBorder-  XiCItemBorder-  int             same as
Width           Width                           choice box
XiNfont         XiCFont         XFontStruct *   XtDefaultFont

   Public interfaces are described below.
******************************************************************/

#include "Button.h"


/*
Resource definitions (see Button.h also):
*/

#define XiNlabel                        "label"
#define XiNexclusive                    "exclusive"
```

```
#define XiNdefaultItem                  "defaultItem"
#define XiNlabelOnLeft                  "labelOnLeft"
#define XiNvertical                     "vertical"
#define XiNmenuForm                     "menuForm"
#define XiNitemBorderWidth              "itemBorderWidth"
#define XiNitemCursor                   "itemCursor"
#define XiCLabel                        "Label"
#define XiCExclusive                    "Exclusive"
#define XiCDefaultItem                  "DefaultItem"
#define XiCLabelOnLeft                  "LabelOnLeft"
#define XiCVertical                     "Vertical"
#define XiCMenuForm                     "MenuForm"
#define XiCItemBorderWidth              "ItemBorderWidth"
#define XiCItemCursor                   "ItemCursor"


typedef struct _XiChoiceClassRec *XiChoiceWidgetClass;
typedef struct _XiChoiceRec *XiChoiceWidget;

extern WidgetClass xiChoiceWidgetClass;


/****
XiChoiceItem is used with XiChoiceAddItems() (note the plural) to
define a null-terminated list of items of type XiChoiceItem, allowing
choice items to be defined with an array specification and added to
the box with one function call, instead of individually with
XiChoiceAddItem().  Example:

static XiChoiceItem item_list[] = {
    {"Bin", 2, ChoiceCB, "Binary Data"},
    {"Dec", 10, ChoiceCB, "Decimal Data"},
    {NULL, NULL, NULL, NULL},
};
    ...
    example = XtCreateManagedWidget("example",
        xiChoiceWidgetClass, exampleParent, args, i);
    XiChoiceAddItems(example, item_list);
    ...

****/


typedef struct {
    char *label;
    int value;
    void (*callback_proc)();        /* or, ...           */
/*  XtCallbackProc callback_proc; **** client's view?   */
    caddr_t client_data;
} XiChoiceItem;


/****
XiChoiceMenuItem is used with XiChoiceAddItems() to define a
null-terminated list of items of type XiChoiceMenuItem, allowing
menu items to be defined with an array specification and added
to the menu with one function call, instead of individually with
```

```
XiChoiceAdditem().  Example:

static XiChoiceMenuItem item_list[] = {
    {"Menu Label 1", MenuCB, "Menu Data 1"},
    {"Menu Label 2", MenuCB, "Menu Data 2"},
    {NULL, NULL, NULL},
};
    ...
    example = XtCreateManagedWidget("example",
        xiChoiceWidgetClass, exampleParent, args, i);
    XiChoiceAddItems(example, item_list);
    ...

****/

typedef struct {
    char *label;
    void (*callback_proc)();        /* or, ...          */
/*  XtCallbackProc callback_proc; **** client's view?   */
    caddr_t client_data;
} XiChoiceMenuItem;


/*
Public functions:
*/

extern void XiChoiceMenuPopup();
/*  XiChoiceWidget choice_widget;
*/

extern int XiChoiceIsExclusive();
/*  XiChoiceWidget choice_widget;
*/

extern void XiChoiceAddItems();                /* plural */
/*  XiChoiceWidget choice_widget;
    caddr_t item_addr;
*/

extern void XiChoiceAddItem();                 /* singular */
/*  XiChoiceWidget choice_widget;
    char *item_label;
    int item_value;
    void (*callback_proc)();    or, XtCallbackProc callback_proc;
    caddr_t client_data;
*/

extern int *XiChoiceGetItems();
/*  XiChoiceWidget choice_widget;
*/

extern int XiChoiceGetSelectedItem();          /* exclusive mode only */
/*  XiChoiceWidget choice_widget;
*/

extern int XiChoiceGetDefaultItem();           /* exclusive mode only */
```

```
/*  XiChoiceWidget choice_widget;
*/

extern int XiChoiceSelectedItemIsDefault(); /* exclusive mode only */
/*  XiChoiceWidget choice_widget;
*/

extern int XiChoiceGetNumItems();
/*  XiChoiceWidget choice_widget;
*/

extern int XiChoiceGetValue();                /* NOT zero-based */
/*  XiChoiceWidget choice_widget;
    int item_number;
*/

extern void XiChoiceSelectItem();             /* NOT zero-based */
/*  XiChoiceWidget choice_widget;
    int item_number;
*/

extern void XiChoiceDeselectItem();           /* NOT zero-based */
/*  XiChoiceWidget choice_widget;
    int item_number;
*/

extern int XiChoiceItemIsSelected();          /* NOT zero-based */
/*  XiChoiceWidget choice_widget;
    int item_number;
*/

#endif /* _XiChoice_h  */


/****    ChoiceP.h    ****/

/****    private declarations/definitions for Choice.c    ****/

#ifndef _XiChoiceP_h
#define _XiChoiceP_h

#include "Choice.h"
#ifdef X11R3
#include <X11/FormP.h>
#else
#include <X11/Xaw/FormP.h>
#endif
#include "ButtonP.h"


#define CHOICE_DEFAULT_LABEL             ""

#define CHOICE_DEFAULT_ITEM              1

#define CHOICE_DEFAULT_WIDTH             100
#define CHOICE_DEFAULT_HEIGHT            65
```

```
#define CHOICE_DEFAULT_BTN_BORDER_WIDTH -1

#define CHOICE_MAX_ITEMS                10

#define CHOICE_IGNORE_ITEM_LEN          -1

#define EOS                     '\0'


typedef struct _XiChoiceClassPart {     /* class definition */
    int dummy;
} XiChoiceClassPart;

typedef struct _XiChoiceClassRec {
    CoreClassPart core_class;
    CompositeClassPart composite_class;
    ConstraintClassPart constraint_class;
    FormClassPart form_class;
    XiChoiceClassPart choice_class;
} XiChoiceClassRec;

extern XiChoiceClassRec xiChoiceClassRec;


typedef struct _XiChoiceItemPart {
    XiButtonWidget wid;
    int value;
} XiChoiceItemPart;


typedef struct _XiChoicePart {          /* instance definition */
    char *label;
    XFontStruct *font;          /* used during dimension calc.s */
    Cursor item_cursor;         /* used for buttons */
    Dimension width, height;    /* dimensions of the frame */
    int btn_border_width;       /* negative used to set default */
    Widget labelW;
    XiChoiceItemPart itemW[CHOICE_MAX_ITEMS];
    int num_items;
    int default_item;
    int items_selected[CHOICE_MAX_ITEMS];/* public list; see    */
                                        /* XiChoiceGetItems()   */
    Boolean exclusive;          /* allow exclusive choices only? */
    Boolean label_on_left;      /* label place on left or on top */
    Boolean vertical;           /* vertical or horiz. orientation? */
    int max_item_len;           /* used for uniform length items */
    Boolean menu_form;          /* impose menu policy? */
} XiChoicePart;


typedef struct _XiChoiceRec {
    CorePart core;
    CompositePart composite;
    ConstraintPart constraint;
    FormPart form;
    XiChoicePart choice;
```

```
} XiChoiceRec;


typedef struct {
    int dummy;
} XiChoiceConstraintsPart;


typedef struct _XiChoiceConstraintsRec {
    FormConstraintsPart form;
    XiChoiceConstraintsPart choice;
} XiChoiceConstraintsRec, *XiChoiceConstraints;

#endif  /* _XiChoiceP_h */


/**  Choice.c  ** a simple choice box implementation  **/


#include <stdio.h>

#include <X11/Xlib.h>
#include <X11/Xos.h>
#include <X11/IntrinsicP.h>
#include <X11/StringDefs.h>

#ifdef X11R3
#include <X11/Form.h>
#include <X11/Label.h>
#else
#include <X11/Xaw/XawInit.h>
#include <X11/Xaw/Form.h>
#include <X11/Xaw/Label.h>
#endif

#include <Ximisc.h>
#include "ChoiceP.h"


/*
Class Methods:
*/

static void Initialize();
static void ConstraintInitialize();
static void Destroy();


/*
Private support functions:
*/

static void internal_callback_proc();
static void remove_menu();
```

```
/*
Cursor place-holder:
*/

static Cursor default_item_cursor = None;


/*
Resource table:
*/

#define res_offset(field) XtOffset(XiChoiceWidget, field)

static XtResource resources[] = {
    {XiNlabel, XiCLabel, XtRString,
        sizeof(char *), res_offset(choice.label),
        XtRString, CHOICE_DEFAULT_LABEL},
    {XiNexclusive, XiCExclusive, XtRBoolean, sizeof(Boolean),
        res_offset(choice.exclusive),
        XtRImmediate, (caddr_t) FALSE},
    {XiNitemBorderWidth, XiCItemBorderWidth, XtRInt,
        sizeof(int), res_offset(choice.btn_border_width),
        XtRImmediate, (caddr_t) CHOICE_DEFAULT_BTN_BORDER_WIDTH},
    {XiNdefaultItem, XiCDefaultItem, XtRInt, sizeof(int),
        res_offset(choice.default_item),
        XtRImmediate, (caddr_t) CHOICE_DEFAULT_ITEM},
    {XiNlabelOnLeft, XiCLabelOnLeft, XtRBoolean, sizeof(Boolean),
        res_offset(choice.label_on_left),
        XtRImmediate, (caddr_t) FALSE},
    {XiNvertical, XiCVertical, XtRBoolean, sizeof(Boolean),
        res_offset(choice.vertical),
        XtRImmediate, (caddr_t) FALSE},
    {XiNmenuForm, XiCMenuForm, XtRBoolean, sizeof(Boolean),
        res_offset(choice.menu_form),
        XtRImmediate, (caddr_t) FALSE},
    {XiNitemCursor, XiCItemCursor, XtRCursor, sizeof(Cursor),
        res_offset(choice.item_cursor),
        XtRCursor, (caddr_t) &default_item_cursor},
    {XiNfont, XiCFont, XtRFontStruct, sizeof(XFontStruct *),
        res_offset(choice.font),
        XtRString, "XtDefaultFont"},
};


/*
Define storage for the class here:
*/

XiChoiceClassRec XichoiceClassRec = {
    { /* core_class variables */
        (WidgetClass) &formClassRec,      /* ancestor */
        "Choice",                         /* class name */
        sizeof(XiChoiceRec),              /* widget size */
#ifdef X11R3
        NULL,                             /* class initialize */
#else
        XawInitializeWidgetSet,           /* class initialize */
```

```
#endif
        NULL,                           /* class part init. */
        FALSE,                          /* class inited */
        Initialize,                     /* initialize */
        NULL,                           /* initialize hook */
        XtInheritRealize,               /* realize */
        NULL,                           /* actions */
        0,                              /* number of actions */
        resources,                      /* resources */
        XtNumber(resources),            /* number of resources */
        NULLQUARK,                      /* xrm class */
        TRUE,                           /* compress motions */
        TRUE,                           /* compress exposures */
        TRUE,                           /* compress enter/leave */
        FALSE,                          /* visibility interest */
        Destroy,                        /* destroy */
        XtInheritResize,                /* resize */
        XtInheritExpose,                /* expose */
        NULL,                           /* set values */
        NULL,                           /* set values hook */
        XtInheritSetValuesAlmost,       /* set values almost */
        NULL,                           /* get values hook */
        NULL,                           /* accept focus */
        XtVersion,                      /* version */
        NULL,                           /* callback private */
        NULL,                           /* translation table */
        XtInheritQueryGeometry,         /* query geometry */
        XtInheritDisplayAccelerator,    /* display accelerator */
        NULL,                           /* extension */
    },
    { /* composite_class variables */
        XtInheritGeometryManager,       /* geometry manager */
        XtInheritChangeManaged,         /* change managed */
        XtInheritInsertChild,           /* insert child */
        XtInheritDeleteChild,           /* delete child */
        NULL,                           /* extension */
    },
    { /* constraint_class fields */
        NULL,                           /* subresources */
        0,                              /* number of subresources */
        sizeof(XiChoiceConstraintsRec), /* record size */
        ConstraintInitialize,           /* initialize */
        NULL,                           /* destroy */
        NULL,                           /* set values */
        NULL,                           /* extension */
    },
    { /* form_class fields */
#ifdef X11R3
        0,
#else
        XtInheritLayout,
#endif
    },
    { /* choice_class variables */
        0,
    },
}; /* XichoiceClassRec */
```

```
WidgetClass xiChoiceWidgetClass = (WidgetClass) &XichoiceClassRec;


/*
XiChoiceWidget methods:
*/

/*
Initialize() initializes each instance of a choice box.
*/
/*ARGSUSED*/
static void Initialize(request, new)
XiChoiceWidget request, new;
{
    Arg args[5];
    int i;

    if (new->core.width == 0)
        new->core.width = CHOICE_DEFAULT_WIDTH;
    if (new->core.height == 0)
        new->core.height = CHOICE_DEFAULT_HEIGHT;

    if (*new->choice.label) {
        i = 0;
        XtSetArg(args[i], XtNlabel,
            (XtArgVal) new->choice.label); i++;
        XtSetArg(args[i], XtNborderWidth, (XtArgVal) 0); i++;
        XtSetArg(args[i], XtNresizable, (XtArgVal) TRUE); i++;
        XtSetArg(args[i], XtNfont, (XtArgVal) new->choice.font); i++;
        new->choice.labelW = XtCreateManagedWidget("label",
            labelWidgetClass, new, args, i);
    }
    else
        new->choice.labelW = NULL;
    new->choice.num_items = 0;
    new->choice.items_selected[0] = 0;

    if (new->choice.menu_form) {            /* force these values */
        new->choice.vertical = TRUE;
        new->choice.exclusive = TRUE;
        new->choice.default_item = FALSE;
        new->choice.max_item_len = CHOICE_IGNORE_ITEM_LEN;
        XtAddEventHandler(new, ButtonPressMask, FALSE, remove_menu,
            NULL);
    }
    else if (new->choice.exclusive) {
        if (new->choice.default_item < 1)
            new->choice.default_item = CHOICE_DEFAULT_ITEM;
    }
}   /* Initialize */


/*
ConstraintInitialize() organizes the form widget that
houses the choice label and items.  Note that the label
```

```
is optional; its presence or absence must be considered
when traversing the list of children.
*/
/*ARGSUSED*/
static void ConstraintInitialize(request, new)
Widget request, new;
{
    XiChoiceWidget cw = (XiChoiceWidget) new->core.parent;
    Widget *child, *children = cw->composite.children;
    XiChoiceConstraints constraint =
        (XiChoiceConstraints) new->core.constraints;
    int label;

    if (cw->choice.label_on_left &&
            XtIsSubclass(new, labelWidgetClass) &&
            cw->choice.btn_border_width !=
                CHOICE_DEFAULT_BTN_BORDER_WIDTH)
        constraint->form.dy +=
            constraint->form.dy + cw->choice.btn_border_width - 1;
    if (!XtIsSubclass(new, xiButtonWidgetClass))
        return;
    if (cw->choice.vertical)
        constraint->form.top = constraint->form.bottom = XtChainTop;
    else
        constraint->form.left = constraint->form.right = XtChainLeft;
    if (!cw->choice.label_on_left &&
            (!cw->choice.vertical || cw->choice.menu_form))
        constraint->form.vert_base = cw->choice.labelW;
    if (cw->choice.label_on_left && cw->choice.vertical)
        constraint->form.horiz_base = cw->choice.labelW;
    if (cw->composite.num_children == 0)
        return;
    label = (cw->choice.labelW != NULL && !cw->choice.label_on_left) ?
        1 : 0;
    if (cw->composite.num_children == 1 && label == 1)
        return;
    for (child = children + cw->composite.num_children - 1;
            child >= (children + label); child--) {
        if (XtIsManaged(*child)) {
            if (cw->choice.menu_form)
                constraint->form.vert_base = *child;
            else if (cw->choice.vertical &&
                    XtIsSubclass(*child, xiButtonWidgetClass))
                constraint->form.vert_base = *child;
            else
                constraint->form.horiz_base = *child;
            break;
        }
    }
}   /* ConstraintInitialize */


/*
Destroy() cleans up data structures, if any, and removes the
event handler.
*/
```

```
static void Destroy(w)
XiChoiceWidget w;
{
    int i;

    XtDestroyWidget(w->choice.labelW);
    for (i = 0; i < w->choice.num_items; i++)
        XtDestroyWidget(w->choice.itemW[i].wid);
    XtRemoveEventHandler(w, ButtonPressMask, FALSE, remove_menu,
        NULL);
}   /* Destroy */


/*
Public functions:
*/

/*
XiChoiceMenuPopup() uses query_set_pos() to pop up a
choice widget under the cursor.
*/

void XiChoiceMenuPopup(w)
XiChoiceWidget w;
{
    if (!w->choice.menu_form)
        return;
    query_set_pos(w);
    XtPopup(w->core.parent, XtGrabNone);
}   /* XiChoiceMenuPopup */


/*
XiChoiceIsExclusive() tests whether or not the choice box
is operating in exclusive mode.
*/

int XiChoiceIsExclusive(w)
XiChoiceWidget w;
{
    return (int) w->choice.exclusive;
}   /* XiChoiceIsExclusive */


/*
XiChoiceAddItems() is a convenience function for adding multiple items
to a choice box after the box has been created; see XiChoiceAddItem()
and Choice.h.  Note that the second argument varies in structure,
depending on the type of choice box.  For a menu, its type is
XiChoiceMenuItem, and for a standard choice box, its type is
XiChoiceItem.  Example #1 (standard choice box):

    static XiChoiceItem item_list[] = {
        {"Bin", 2, ChoiceCB, "Binary Data"},
        {"Dec", 10, ChoiceCB, "Decimal Data"},
        {NULL, NULL, NULL, NULL},
    };
```

```
    ...
    i = 0;
    ...
    example = XtCreateManagedWidget("example",
        xiChoiceWidgetClass, exampleParent, args, i);
    XiChoiceAddItems(example, item_list);
    ...

Example #2 (menu):

static XiChoiceMenuItem item_list[] = {
    {"Menu Label 1", MenuCB, "Menu Data 1"},
    {"Menu Label 2", MenuCB, "Menu Data 2"},
    {NULL, NULL, NULL},
};
    ...
    i = 0;
    ...
    example = XtCreateManagedWidget("example",
        xiChoiceWidgetClass, exampleParent, args, i);
    XiChoiceAddItems(example, item_list);
    ...

*/

void XiChoiceAddItems(cw, item_addr)
XiChoiceWidget cw;
caddr_t item_addr;
{
    int i, len, more_items = FALSE;

    if (item_addr == NULL) {
        fprintf(stderr, "choice box: item list is null!\n");
        return;
    }
    if (cw->choice.menu_form) {
        XiChoiceMenuItem *item = (XiChoiceMenuItem *) item_addr;
        cw->choice.max_item_len = 0;
        for (i = 0; item[i].label && i < CHOICE_MAX_ITEMS; i++)
            if ((len = strlen(item[i].label)) > cw->choice.max_item_len)
                cw->choice.max_item_len = len;
        for (i = 0; item[i].label && i < CHOICE_MAX_ITEMS; i++)
            XiChoiceAddItem(cw, item[i].label, FALSE,
                item[i].callback_proc, item[i].client_data);
        if (item[i].label != NULL)
            more_items = TRUE;
    }
    else {
        XiChoiceItem *item = (XiChoiceItem *) item_addr;
        for (i = 0; item[i].label && i < CHOICE_MAX_ITEMS; i++)
            XiChoiceAddItem(cw, item[i].label, item[i].value,
                item[i].callback_proc, item[i].client_data);
        if (item[i].label != NULL)
            more_items = TRUE;
    }
    if (i == CHOICE_MAX_ITEMS && more_items) {
        fprintf(stderr,
```

```
            "choice box: too many items for the choice box!\n");
        fprintf(stderr,
            "choice box: the maximum number of items is: %d.\n",
            CHOICE_MAX_ITEMS);
    }
}   /* XiChoiceAddItems */


/*
XiChoiceAddItem() is used to add items to a choice box after
the box has been created.  Buttons/items are added in left-
to-right order.  This form of item entry probably shouldn't be
publically accessible; use XiChoiceAddItems() below.
*/

void XiChoiceAddItem(cw, item_name, item_value,
    callback_proc, client_data)
XiChoiceWidget cw;
char *item_name;
int item_value;
void (*callback_proc)();    /* or, XtCallbackProc callback_proc; */
caddr_t client_data;
{
    Arg args[10];
    int i;

    if (cw->choice.num_items >= CHOICE_MAX_ITEMS) {
        fprintf(stderr,
            "choice box: too many items for the choice box!\n");
        fprintf(stderr,
            "choice box: the maximum number of items is: %d.\n",
            CHOICE_MAX_ITEMS);
        return;
    }
    i = 0;
    XtSetArg(args[i], XiNlabel, (XtArgVal) item_name); i++;
    /*
    item 1 ==> itemW[0]:
    */  XtSetArg(args[i], XiNvalue,
        (XtArgVal) (cw->choice.num_items + 1)); i++;
    if (cw->choice.btn_border_width !=
            CHOICE_DEFAULT_BTN_BORDER_WIDTH) {
        XtSetArg(args[i], XiNborderWidth,
            (XtArgVal) cw->choice.btn_border_width); i++;
    }
    if (cw->choice.item_cursor != None) {
        XtSetArg(args[i], XtNcursor,
            (XtArgVal) cw->choice.item_cursor); i++;
    }
    XtSetArg(args[i], XiNfont, (XtArgVal) cw->choice.font); i++;
    if (cw->choice.menu_form &&
            cw->choice.max_item_len != CHOICE_IGNORE_ITEM_LEN) {
        XtSetArg(args[i], XiNlength,
            (XtArgVal) cw->choice.max_item_len); i++;
    }
    cw->choice.itemW[cw->choice.num_items].wid = (XiButtonWidget)
        XtCreateManagedWidget(item_name, xiButtonWidgetClass,
```

```
            cw, args, i);
    XtAddCallback(cw->choice.itemW[cw->choice.num_items].wid,
        XiNselectCallback, internal_callback_proc, NULL);
    if (callback_proc != NULL)
        XtAddCallback(cw->choice.itemW[cw->choice.num_items].wid,
            XiNselectCallback, callback_proc, client_data);
    cw->choice.itemW[cw->choice.num_items].value = item_value;
    cw->choice.num_items++;
    if (cw->choice.exclusive &&
            (cw->choice.num_items == cw->choice.default_item))
        XiButtonSelect(cw->choice.itemW[cw->choice.num_items - 1].wid);
}   /* XiChoiceAddItem */


/*
XiChoiceGetItems() returns a (pointer to a) zero-terminated list
of the currently selected items.  Item numbers are NOT zero-
based, that is: item 1 ==> itemW[0].  The list is an array of
integers.
*/

int *XiChoiceGetItems(w)
XiChoiceWidget w;
{
    int i, j;

    for (i = j = 0; i < w->choice.num_items; i++)
        if (XiButtonIsSelected(w->choice.itemW[i].wid))
            w->choice.items_selected[j++] = i + 1;
    w->choice.items_selected[j] = 0;
    return w->choice.items_selected;
}   /* XiChoiceGetItems */


/*
XiChoiceGetSelectedItem() returns the currently
selected item for an exclusive choice box.
Note:  item 1 ==> itemW[0].
*/

int XiChoiceGetSelectedItem(w)
XiChoiceWidget w;
{
    int i;

    if (!w->choice.exclusive)
        return FALSE;
    for (i = 0; i < w->choice.num_items; i++)
        if (XiButtonIsSelected(w->choice.itemW[i].wid))
            return i + 1;
    return FALSE;
}   /* XiChoiceGetSelectedItem */


/*
XiChoiceGetDefaultItem() returns the default
item number.  Note:  item 1 ==> itemW[0].
```

```
*/

int XiChoiceGetDefaultItem(w)
XiChoiceWidget w;
{
    if (!w->choice.exclusive)
        return FALSE;
    return w->choice.default_item;
}   /* XiChoiceGetDefaultItem */


/*
XiChoiceSelectedItemIsDefault() tests whether or not
the selected item is the default item.
*/

int XiChoiceSelectedItemIsDefault(w)
XiChoiceWidget w;
{
    if (!w->choice.exclusive)
        return FALSE;
    if (XiChoiceGetNumItems(w) != 1)
        return FALSE;
    return (XiChoiceGetSelectedItem(w) == w->choice.default_item);
}   /* XiChoiceSelectedItemIsDefault */


/*
XiChoiceGetNumItems() returns the number (quantity)
of currently selected items.
*/

int XiChoiceGetNumItems(w)
XiChoiceWidget w;
{
    int i, num_items_selected;

    for (i = num_items_selected = 0; i < w->choice.num_items; i++)
        if (XiButtonIsSelected(w->choice.itemW[i].wid))
            num_items_selected++;
    return num_items_selected;
}   /* XiChoiceGetNumItems */


/*
XiChoiceGetValue() retrieves the user-specified value of
the i'th item.  The returned value is the value
associated with the item using XiChoiceAddItem().
Note:  item 1 ==> itemW[0].
*/

int XiChoiceGetValue(w, item)
XiChoiceWidget w;
int item;
{
    return w->choice.itemW[item - 1].value;
}   /* XiChoiceGetValue */
```

```
/*
XiChoiceSelectItem() allows programmatic selection
of an item.
*/

void XiChoiceSelectItem(w, item)
XiChoiceWidget w;
int item;
{
    int i;

    if (item < 1 || item > w->choice.num_items)
        return;
    XiButtonSelectNoCB(w->choice.itemW[item - 1].wid);
    if (!w->choice.exclusive)
        return;
    for (i = 1; i <= w->choice.num_items; i++)
        if (i != item)
            XiButtonDeselect(w->choice.itemW[i - 1].wid);
}   /* XiChoiceSelectItem */


/*
XiChoiceDeselectItem() allows programmatic de-selection
of an item.
*/

void XiChoiceDeselectItem(w, item)
XiChoiceWidget w;
int item;
{
    if (item < 1 || item > w->choice.num_items)
        return;
    XiButtonDeselect(w->choice.itemW[item - 1].wid);
}   /* XiChoiceDeselectItem */


/*
XiChoiceItemIsSelected() allows programmatic testing of
of an item's status.
*/

int XiChoiceItemIsSelected(w, item)
XiChoiceWidget w;
int item;
{
    if (item < 1 || item > w->choice.num_items)
        return FALSE;
    return XiButtonIsSelected(w->choice.itemW[item - 1].wid);
}   /* XiChoiceItemIsSelected */


/*
Support functions:
*/
```

```
/*
internal_callback_proc() is installed as a private callback
function for each (internal) button; see XiChoiceAddItem().
The "exclusive" policy is enforced here -- if other items are
already selected, they must be de-selected.
*/
/*ARGSUSED*/
static void internal_callback_proc(w, client_data, call_data)
Widget w;
caddr_t client_data;
caddr_t call_data;
{
    XiButtonWidget bw = (XiButtonWidget) w;
    XiChoiceWidget cw = (XiChoiceWidget) bw->core.parent;
    int i;

    if (!cw->choice.exclusive)
        return;
    for (i = 0; i < cw->choice.num_items; i++)
        if (cw->choice.itemW[i].wid != bw)
            XiButtonDeselect(cw->choice.itemW[i].wid);
    if (!cw->choice.menu_form)
        return;
    XtPopdown(cw->core.parent);
    XiButtonDeselect(bw);
}   /* internal_callback_proc */


/*
For choice boxes in menu form, remove_menu() pops down the menu
if the user clicks the left mouse button in anywhere inside the
widget other than on a button.
*/
/*ARGSUSED*/
static void remove_menu(w, client_data, event)
XiChoiceWidget w;
caddr_t client_data;
XEvent *event;
{
    if (event->xbutton.button == Button1)
        XtPopdown(w->core.parent);
}   /* remove_menu */



/****  testchoice.c  ****  tests the choice box widget ****/


#include <stdio.h>
#include <X11/Intrinsic.h>
#include <X11/StringDefs.h>
#include <X11/Shell.h>
#include <X11/cursorfont.h>

#ifdef X11R3
#include <X11/Command.h>
```

```
#include <X11/Form.h>
#else
#include <X11/Xaw/Command.h>
#include <X11/Xaw/Form.h>
#endif

#include <Ximisc.h>
#include "Choice.h"


/*
Functions:
*/

void PrintItemInfo(), Quit();


/*
Private globals:
*/

static Widget testChoice;
static XFontStruct *font;


/*
main() sets up a choice box with command buttons for quitting
the application and for testing several of the Choice widget
functions.  Several resource values are tested as well.
*/

void main(argc, argv)
int argc;
char **argv;
{
    Widget topLevel, testBox, printItemInfo, quit;
    Arg args[10];
    int i;
    Cursor dot_cursor;

    topLevel = XtInitialize(argv[0], "TestChoice",
        NULL, 0, &argc, argv);
    font = load_font(topLevel, "testchoice", "6x13");
    i = 0;
    testBox = XtCreateManagedWidget("testBox", formWidgetClass,
        topLevel, args, i);
    i = 0;
    XtSetArg(args[i], XiNlabel, (XtArgVal) "Demo Choice Box"); i++;
/*  XtSetArg(args[i], XtNborderWidth, (XtArgVal) 2); i++;         */
/*  XtSetArg(args[i], XiNfont, (XtArgVal) font); i++;             */
/*  XtSetArg(args[i], XiNdefaultItem, (XtArgVal) 3); i++;         */
/*  XtSetArg(args[i], XiNexclusive, (XtArgVal) TRUE); i++;        */
/*  dot_cursor = XCreateFontCursor(XtDisplay(topLevel), XC_dot);
    XtSetArg(args[i], XiNitemCursor, (XtArgVal) dot_cursor); i++;*/
    testChoice = XtCreateManagedWidget("testChoice",
        xiChoiceWidgetClass, testBox, args, i);
    XiChoiceAddItem(testChoice, "Item 1", 10, NULL, NULL);
```

```
    XiChoiceAddItem(testChoice, "Item 2", 20, NULL, NULL);
    XiChoiceAddItem(testChoice, "Item 3", 30, NULL, NULL);
    i = 0;
    XtSetArg(args[i], XtNlabel, (XtArgVal) "Quit"); i++;
    XtSetArg(args[i], XtNfromVert, (XtArgVal) testChoice); i++;
    quit = XtCreateManagedWidget("quit",
        commandWidgetClass, testBox, args, i);
    XtAddCallback(quit, XtNcallback, Quit, NULL);
    i = 0;
    XtSetArg(args[i], XtNlabel, (XtArgVal) "Print Item Info"); i++;
    XtSetArg(args[i], XtNfromVert, (XtArgVal) quit); i++;
    printItemInfo = XtCreateManagedWidget("printItemInfo",
        commandWidgetClass, testBox, args, i);
    XtAddCallback(printItemInfo, XtNcallback, PrintItemInfo, NULL);
    XtRealizeWidget(topLevel);
    XtMainLoop();
}   /* main */


/*ARGSUSED*/
void PrintItemInfo(w, client_data, call_data)
Widget w;
caddr_t client_data, call_data;
{
    int *item = XiChoiceGetItems(testChoice);

    printf("\nCurrently selected item(s) are:\n");
    if (XiChoiceGetNumItems(testChoice) == 0)
        printf("-- none --\n");
    else
        while (*item) {
            printf("Choice item: %d; ", *item);
            printf("Choice value: %d\n",
                XiChoiceGetValue(testChoice, *item++));
        }
    printf("Number of items currently selected: %d\n",
        XiChoiceGetNumItems(testChoice));
    printf("Choice mode: %s\n", (XiChoiceIsExclusive(testChoice)) ?
        "Exclusive" : "Non-exclusive");
    if (XiChoiceIsExclusive(testChoice))    /* test these function */
        printf("Current item is item #: %d\n",
            XiChoiceGetSelectedItem(testChoice));
    if (XiChoiceSelectedItemIsDefault(testChoice))
        printf("(The current item is the default.)\n");
}   /* PrintItemInfo */


/*ARGSUSED*/
void Quit(w, client_data, call_data)
Widget w;
caddr_t client_data, call_data;
{
    XFreeFont(XtDisplay(w), font);
    exit(0);
}   /* Quit */
```

```
/****  testchoice2.c  ****  tests the choice box widget ****/


#include <stdio.h>
#include <X11/Intrinsic.h>
#include <X11/StringDefs.h>
#include <X11/Shell.h>

#ifdef X11R3
#include <X11/Command.h>
#include <X11/Form.h>
#else
#include <X11/Xaw/Command.h>
#include <X11/Xaw/Form.h>
#endif

#include <Ximisc.h>
#include "Choice.h"


/*
Functions:
*/

void PrintItemInfo(), Quit(), SelectDefault();


/*
Private globals:
*/

static Widget testChoice;
static XFontStruct *font;
static XiChoiceItem item_list[] = { /* alphabetical ordering */
    {"Bin", 2, NULL, NULL},
    {"Dec", 10, NULL, NULL},
    {"Hex", 16, NULL, NULL},
    {"Oct", 8, NULL, NULL},
    {NULL, NULL, NULL, NULL},
};


/*
main() sets up a choice box with command buttons for quitting
the application and for testing several of the Choice widget
functions.  Several resource values are tested as well.
*/

void main(argc, argv)
int argc;
char **argv;
{
    Widget topLevel, testBox, printItemInfo, selectDefault, quit;
    Arg args[10];
    int i;
```

```
    topLevel = XtInitialize(argv[0], "TestChoice2",
        NULL, 0, &argc, argv);
    font = load_font(topLevel, "testchoice2", "8x13");
    i = 0;
    testBox = XtCreateManagedWidget("testBox", formWidgetClass,
        topLevel, args, i);
    i = 0;
    XtSetArg(args[i], XiNlabel, (XtArgVal) "Base:"); i++;
    XtSetArg(args[i], XtNborderWidth, (XtArgVal) 0); i++;
    XtSetArg(args[i], XiNitemBorderWidth, (XtArgVal) 0); i++;
/*  XtSetArg(args[i], XiNvertical, (XtArgVal) TRUE); i++;       */
    XtSetArg(args[i], XiNfont, (XtArgVal) font); i++;
    XtSetArg(args[i], XiNdefaultItem, (XtArgVal) 2); i++;
    XtSetArg(args[i], XiNexclusive, (XtArgVal) TRUE); i++;
    XtSetArg(args[i], XiNlabelOnLeft, (XtArgVal) TRUE); i++;
    testChoice = XtCreateManagedWidget("testChoice",
        xiChoiceWidgetClass, testBox, args, i);
    XiChoiceAddItems(testChoice, item_list);
    i = 0;
    XtSetArg(args[i], XtNlabel, (XtArgVal) "Quit"); i++;
    XtSetArg(args[i], XtNfromVert, (XtArgVal) testChoice); i++;
    quit = XtCreateManagedWidget("quit",
        commandWidgetClass, testBox, args, i);
    XtAddCallback(quit, XtNcallback, Quit, NULL);
    i = 0;
    XtSetArg(args[i], XtNlabel, (XtArgVal) "Print Item Info"); i++;
    XtSetArg(args[i], XtNfromVert, (XtArgVal) quit); i++;
    printItemInfo = XtCreateManagedWidget("printItemInfo",
        commandWidgetClass, testBox, args, i);
    XtAddCallback(printItemInfo, XtNcallback, PrintItemInfo, NULL);
    i = 0;
    XtSetArg(args[i], XtNlabel, (XtArgVal) "Select Default Item"); i++;
    XtSetArg(args[i], XtNfromVert, (XtArgVal) printItemInfo); i++;
    selectDefault = XtCreateManagedWidget("selectDefault",
        commandWidgetClass, testBox, args, i);
    XtAddCallback(selectDefault, XtNcallback, SelectDefault, NULL);
    XtRealizeWidget(topLevel);
    XtMainLoop();
}   /* main */


/*ARGSUSED*/
void PrintItemInfo(w, client_data, call_data)
Widget w;
caddr_t client_data, call_data;
{
    int i, *item = XiChoiceGetItems(testChoice);

    printf("\nCurrently selected item(s) are:\n");
    if (XiChoiceGetNumItems(testChoice) == 0)
        printf("-- none --\n");
    else
        while (*item) {
            printf("Choice item: %d; ", *item);
            printf("Choice value: %d\n",
                XiChoiceGetValue(testChoice, *item++));
        }
```

```
    if (XiChoiceItemIsSelected(testChoice, 3)) {
        printf("Note: the third item was selected,\n");
        printf("but it's just been deselected.\n");
        XiChoiceDeselectItem(testChoice, 3);
    }
    printf("Number of items currently selected: %d\n",
        XiChoiceGetNumItems(testChoice));
    printf("Choice mode: %s\n", (XiChoiceIsExclusive(testChoice)) ?
        "Exclusive" : "Non-exclusive");
    if (i = XiChoiceGetDefaultItem(testChoice))
        printf("The default item is item #: %d\n", i);
    if (XiChoiceIsExclusive(testChoice))
        printf("Current item is item #: %d\n",
            XiChoiceGetSelectedItem(testChoice));
    if (XiChoiceSelectedItemIsDefault(testChoice))
        printf("(The current item is the default.)\n");
}   /* PrintItemInfo */


/*ARGSUSED*/
void SelectDefault(w, client_data, call_data)
Widget w;
caddr_t client_data, call_data;
{
    XiChoiceSelectItem(testChoice,
        XiChoiceGetDefaultItem(testChoice));
}   /* SelectDefault */


/*ARGSUSED*/
void Quit(w, client_data, call_data)
Widget w;
caddr_t client_data, call_data;
{
    XFreeFont(XtDisplay(w), font);
    exit(0);
}   /* Quit */



/**  testmenu.c  **  tests the menu version of the choice widget **/


#include <stdio.h>
#include <X11/Intrinsic.h>
#include <X11/StringDefs.h>
#include <X11/Shell.h>

#ifdef  X11R3
#include <X11/Command.h>
#include <X11/Form.h>
#else
#include <X11/Xaw/Command.h>
#include <X11/Xaw/Form.h>
#endif

#include <Ximisc.h>
```

```
#include "Choice.h"


/*
Functions:
*/

void Quit(), DoMenu(), MenuCB();


/*
Private globals:
*/

static Widget menuShell, autoChoice;

static XiChoiceMenuItem auto_list[] = {
/*  {<manufacturer>,  <action>, <action data>},    */
    {"BMW 2002",        MenuCB,      "Enough said."},
    {"Mazda 626",       MenuCB,      "4-door performance!"},
    {"Saab 9000",       MenuCB,      "Wow!"},
    {"Volvo 242",       MenuCB,      "A durable classic."},
    {NULL,              NULL,        NULL},
};


/*
main() sets up a choice box with command buttons for quitting
the application and for testing several of the Choice widget
functions.  Several resource values are tested as well.
*/

void main(argc, argv)
int argc;
char **argv;
{
    Widget topLevel, testBox, doMenu, quit;
    Arg args[10];
    int i;

    topLevel = XtInitialize(argv[0], "TestMenu",
        NULL, 0, &argc, argv);
    i = 0;
    testBox = XtCreateManagedWidget("testBox", formWidgetClass,
        topLevel, args, i);
    i = 0;
    menuShell = XtCreatePopupShell("menuShell",
        transientShellWidgetClass, topLevel, args, i);
/*  XtSetArg(args[i], XiNlabelOnLeft, (XtArgVal) TRUE); i++;*/
    XtSetArg(args[i], XiNlabel, (XtArgVal) "Great Cars"); i++;
    XtSetArg(args[i], XiNitemBorderWidth, (XtArgVal) 1); i++;
    XtSetArg(args[i], XiNmenuForm, (XtArgVal) TRUE); i++;
    autoChoice = XtCreateManagedWidget("autoChoice",
        xiChoiceWidgetClass, menuShell, args, i);
    XiChoiceAddItems(autoChoice, auto_list);
    i = 0;
    XtSetArg(args[i], XtNlabel, (XtArgVal) "Quit"); i++;
```

```
    quit = XtCreateManagedWidget("quit",
        commandWidgetClass, testBox, args, i);
    XtAddCallback(quit, XtNcallback, Quit, NULL);
    i = 0;
    XtSetArg(args[i], XtNlabel, (XtArgVal) "Great Cars"); i++;
    XtSetArg(args[i], XtNfromHoriz, (XtArgVal) quit); i++;
    doMenu = XtCreateManagedWidget("doMenu",
        commandWidgetClass, testBox, args, i);
    XtAddCallback(doMenu, XtNcallback, DoMenu, NULL);
    XtRealizeWidget(topLevel);
    XtMainLoop();
}   /* main */


/*ARGSUSED*/
void DoMenu(w, client_data, call_data)
Widget w;
caddr_t client_data, call_data;
{
    XiChoiceMenuPopup(autoChoice);
}   /* DoMenu */


/*ARGSUSED*/
void MenuCB(w, client_data, call_data)
Widget w;
caddr_t client_data, call_data;
{
    printf("\n%s\n", client_data);
}   /* MenuCB */


/*ARGSUSED*/
void Quit(w, client_data, call_data)
Widget w;
caddr_t client_data, call_data;
{
    exit(0);
}   /* Quit */
```

S

xdelete: A File Deletion Utility

```
/****  xdelete.c  ****  tests the file selection box widget ****/

/*******************************************************************
 *  Copyright (c) 1990 Iris Computing Laboratories.
 *
 *  This software is provided for demonstration purposes only.  As
 *  freely-distributed, modifiable source code, this software carries
 *  absolutely no warranty.
 *******************************************************************/


#include <stdio.h>
#include <X11/Intrinsic.h>
#include <X11/StringDefs.h>
#include <X11/Shell.h>


#ifdef X11R3
#include <X11/Box.h>
#include <X11/Command.h>
#include <X11/Form.h>
#else
#include <X11/Xaw/Box.h>
#include <X11/Xaw/Command.h>
#include <X11/Xaw/Form.h>
#endif

#include "Ximisc.h"
#include "Alert.h"
#include "FileSelect.h"
```

```
/*
Functions:
*/

void Quit(), RemoveFile();

/*
Private globals:
*/

static Widget alertBox, deleteFileBox;


/*
main() sets up a button-activated file selection box inside a
box widget in the main window.  A simple callback is used to
perform the file deletion.
*/

void main(argc, argv)
int argc;
char **argv;
{
    Widget topLevel, alertShell, deleteBox, quitButton;
    Arg args[3];
    int i;

    topLevel = XtInitialize(argv[0], "XDelete",
        NULL, 0, &argc, argv);
    i = 0;
    XtSetArg(args[i], XtNallowShellResize, (XtArgVal) TRUE); i++;
    alertShell = XtCreatePopupShell("alertShell",
        transientShellWidgetClass, topLevel, args, i);
    i = 0;
    alertBox = XtCreateManagedWidget("alertBox",
        xiAlertWidgetClass, alertShell, args, i);
    XiAlertAddButton(alertBox, "Continue", 0, NULL, NULL);
    deleteBox = XtCreateManagedWidget("deleteBox", formWidgetClass,
        topLevel, NULL, 0);
    i = 0;
    XtSetArg(args[i], XiNrows, (XtArgVal) 15); i++;
    XtSetArg(args[i], XiNcolumns, (XtArgVal) 30); i++;
    deleteFileBox = XtCreateManagedWidget("deleteFileBox",
        xiFileSelectWidgetClass, deleteBox, args, i);
    XiFileSelectAddApplyProc(deleteFileBox, RemoveFile);
    i = 0;
    XtSetArg(args[i], XtNlabel, (XtArgVal) "Quit"); i++;
    XtSetArg(args[i], XtNfromVert, (XtArgVal) deleteFileBox); i++;
    quitButton = XtCreateManagedWidget("quitButton",
        commandWidgetClass, deleteBox, args, i);
    XtAddCallback(quitButton, XtNcallback, Quit, NULL);
    XtRealizeWidget(topLevel);
    XtMainLoop();
}   /* main */
```

```
/*
RemoveFile() unlinks the file specified by the current selection.
*/
/*ARGSUSED*/
void RemoveFile(w, client_data, call_data)
Widget w;
caddr_t client_data, call_data;
{
    char *filename = XiFileSelectGetSelection(deleteFileBox);

    if (!*filename) {
        XiAlertPopup(alertBox,
            "You must select a file first.",
            XiNOBEEP);
        return;
    }
    unlink(filename);
    XiFileSelectRefresh(deleteFileBox);
}   /* RemoveFile */


/*ARGSUSED*/
void Quit(w, client_data, call_data)
Widget w;
caddr_t client_data, call_data;
{
    exit(0);
}   /* Quit */
```

T

xconvert: A Base Conversion Utility

```
/****  xconvert.c  ****/

/*******************************************************************
*  Copyright (c) 1990 Iris Computing Laboratories.
*
*  This software is provided for demonstration purposes only.  As
*  freely-distributed, modifiable source code, this software carries
*  absolutely no warranty.
*******************************************************************/

/*
xconvert is a demo program that tests the choice box and
text entry widgets.  It allows the user to enter an integer
and convert it to a different numeric base.
   The previous numeric base, that is, the base to use in
converting the displayed text to a new base, is stored in
the variable old_base.  At start-up, old_base == DEC.
*/


#include <stdio.h>
#include <string.h>
#include <ctype.h>

#include <X11/Intrinsic.h>
#include <X11/StringDefs.h>
#include <X11/Shell.h>
```

```
#ifdef X11R3
#include <X11/Box.h>
#include <X11/Command.h>
#include <X11/Form.h>
#else
#include <X11/Xaw/Box.h>
#include <X11/Xaw/Command.h>
#include <X11/Xaw/Form.h>
#endif
#include <Ximisc.h>
#include "Alert.h"
#include "Choice.h"
#include "SimpleText.h"


#define EOS '\0'

#define MAX_STR 100

#define BIN 2
#define OCT 8
#define DEC 10
#define HEX 16


/*
Functions:
*/

void Clear(), Convert(), Quit(), UpdateBase();

char *integer_to_bin_str();
int bin_str_to_integer();



/*
Private globals:
*/

static Widget alertBox, baseSelection, textEntry;

static XiChoiceItem item_list[] = { /* alphabetical ordering */
    {"Bin", BIN, UpdateBase, NULL},
    {"Dec", DEC, UpdateBase, NULL},
    {"Hex", HEX, UpdateBase, NULL},
    {"Oct", OCT, UpdateBase, NULL},
    {NULL, NULL, NULL, NULL},
};

static int old_base = DEC, base = DEC;


/*
main() builds the converter within a form widget.
*/
```

```
void main(argc, argv)
int argc;
char **argv;
{
    Widget topLevel, alertShell, convertBox, clearBtn, convertBtn,
        quitBtn;
    Arg args[10];
    int i;

    topLevel = XtInitialize(argv[0], "XConvert",
        NULL, 0, &argc, argv);
    i = 0;
    XtSetArg(args[i], XtNallowShellResize, (XtArgVal) TRUE); i++;
    alertShell = XtCreatePopupShell("alertShell",
        transientShellWidgetClass, topLevel, args, i);
    i = 0;
    alertBox = XtCreateManagedWidget("alertBox",
        xiAlertWidgetClass, alertShell, args, i);
    XiAlertAddButton(alertBox, "Continue", 0, NULL, NULL);
    convertBox = XtCreateManagedWidget("convertBox", formWidgetClass,
        topLevel, NULL, 0);
    i = 0;
    XtSetArg(args[i], XtNborderWidth, (XtArgVal) 0); i++;
    XtSetArg(args[i], XiNlabel, (XtArgVal) "Integer:"); i++;
    XtSetArg(args[i], XiNtextWidth, (XtArgVal) 130); i++;
    XtSetArg(args[i], XiNtext, (XtArgVal) ""); i++;
    textEntry = XtCreateManagedWidget("textEntry",
        xiSimpleTextWidgetClass, convertBox, args, i);
    i = 0;
    XtSetArg(args[i], XtNfromVert, (XtArgVal) textEntry); i++;
    XtSetArg(args[i], XiNlabel, (XtArgVal) "    Base:"); i++;
    XtSetArg(args[i], XiNborderWidth, (XtArgVal) 0); i++;
    XtSetArg(args[i], XiNitemBorderWidth, (XtArgVal) 0); i++;
    XtSetArg(args[i], XiNexclusive, (XtArgVal) TRUE); i++;
    XtSetArg(args[i], XiNdefaultItem, (XtArgVal) 2); i++;    /* DEC */
    XtSetArg(args[i], XiNlabelOnLeft, (XtArgVal) TRUE); i++;
    baseSelection = XtCreateManagedWidget("baseSelection",
        xiChoiceWidgetClass, convertBox, args, i);
    XiChoiceAddItems(baseSelection, item_list);
    i = 0;
    XtSetArg(args[i], XtNfromVert, (XtArgVal) baseSelection); i++;
    XtSetArg(args[i], XtNlabel, (XtArgVal) "Clear"); i++;
    clearBtn = XtCreateManagedWidget("clearBtn",
        commandWidgetClass, convertBox, args, i);
    XtAddCallback(clearBtn, XtNcallback, Clear, NULL);
    i = 0;
    XtSetArg(args[i], XtNfromVert, (XtArgVal) baseSelection); i++;
    XtSetArg(args[i], XtNfromHoriz, (XtArgVal) clearBtn); i++;
    XtSetArg(args[i], XtNlabel, (XtArgVal) "Convert"); i++;
    convertBtn = XtCreateManagedWidget("convertBtn",
        commandWidgetClass, convertBox, args, i);
    XtAddCallback(convertBtn, XtNcallback, Convert, NULL);
    i = 0;
    XtSetArg(args[i], XtNfromVert, (XtArgVal) baseSelection); i++;
    XtSetArg(args[i], XtNfromHoriz, (XtArgVal) convertBtn); i++;
    XtSetArg(args[i], XtNlabel, (XtArgVal) "Quit"); i++;
    quitBtn = XtCreateManagedWidget("quitBtn",
```

```
        commandWidgetClass, convertBox, args, i);
    XtAddCallback(quitBtn, XtNcallback, Quit, NULL);
    XtRealizeWidget(topLevel);
    XtMainLoop();
}   /* main */


/*
Clear() clears out the display.
*/
/*ARGSUSED*/
void Clear(w, client_data, call_data)
Widget w;
caddr_t client_data, call_data;
{
    XiSimpleTextSetString(textEntry, "");
}   /* Clear */


/*
Convert() interprets the value in the display based on the
value of old_base, replacing the displayed value with the
converted value.
*/
/*ARGSUSED*/
void Convert(w, client_data, call_data)
Widget w;
caddr_t client_data, call_data;
{
    static char output[MAX_STR];
    char *text;
    int number, result;

    text = XiSimpleTextGetString(textEntry);
    if (!strlen(text))
        return;
    if (old_base == HEX)
        result = sscanf(text, "%x", &number);
    else if (old_base == OCT)
        result = sscanf(text, "%o", &number);
    else if (old_base == BIN)
         number = bin_str_to_integer(text, &result);
    else
        result = sscanf(text, "%d", &number);
    if (result == 0) {
        XiAlertPopup(alertBox,
            "Invalid data for the specified numeric base.",
            XiNOBEEP);
        return;
    }
    if (base == HEX)
        sprintf(output, "%x", number);
    else if (base == OCT)
        sprintf(output, "%o", number);
    else if (base == BIN)
        sprintf(output, "%s", integer_to_bin_str(number));
    else
```

```
        sprintf(output, "%d", number);
    XiSimpleTextSetString(textEntry, output);
}   /* Convert */


/*
UpdateBase() maintains the current and previous bases.
*/
/*ARGSUSED*/
void UpdateBase(w, client_data, call_data)
Widget w;
caddr_t client_data, call_data;
{
    old_base = base;
    base = XiChoiceGetValue(baseSelection,
        XiChoiceGetSelectedItem(baseSelection));
}   /* UpdateBase */


/*ARGSUSED*/
void Quit(w, client_data, call_data)
Widget w;
caddr_t client_data, call_data;
{
    exit(0);
}   /* Quit */


/*
integer_to_bin_str() converts an integer to a binary string.
*/

char *integer_to_bin_str(n)
int n;
{
    static char bin_str[MAX_STR];
    int i, j = 0;

    if (n) {
        for (i = 31; i > -1; i--) {
            bin_str[i] = (n & 1) ? '1' : '0';
            n >>= 1;
        }
        for (i = 0; i < 32 && bin_str[i] == '0'; i++)
            ;
        for ( ; bin_str[i]; i++, j++)
            bin_str[j] = bin_str[i];
    }
    else
        bin_str[j++] = '0';
    bin_str[j] = EOS;
    return bin_str;
}   /* integer_to_bin_str */


/*
bin_str_to_integer() converts a binary string to an integer.
```

```
*/

int bin_str_to_integer(bin_str, convert_ok)
char *bin_str;
int *convert_ok;
{
    *convert_ok = TRUE;      /* not relevant at present */
    return (int)strtol(bin_str, (char **)NULL, 2);
}   /* bin_str_to_integer */
```

U

XiSimpleText: A One-line Text Entry Widget

```
/****     SimpleText.h     ****/

/****     public declarations/definitions for SimpleText.c     ****/

#ifndef _XiSimpleText_h
#define _XiSimpleText_h 1

/*********************************************************************
*  Copyright (c) 1990 Iris Computing Laboratories.
*
*  This software is provided for demonstration purposes only.  As
*  freely-distributed, modifiable source code, this software carries
*  absolutely no warranty.
*********************************************************************/

/*********************************************************************
A SimpleText widget implements a one-line text entry widget, based
on the Athena text widget.  Unlike the Athena dialog widget, it does
not support buttons.
   A convenience function, XiSimpleTextGetString(), can be used to
retrieve the current text string.  Likewise, XiSimpleTextSetString()
can be used to replace the current text string.

Resources:

Name             Class            Data Type        Default      Modify?
----             -----            ---------        -------      -------
XiNlabel         XiCLabel         String           ""
```

```
XiNtext          XiCText          String          ""
XiNtextWidth     XiCTextWidth     int             200
XiNfont          XiCFont          XFontStruct *   XtDefaultFont

   Public interfaces are described below.
*****************************************************************/

#ifdef X11R3
#include <X11/Form.h>
#else
#include <X11/Xaw/Form.h>
#endif



/*
Resource definitions:
*/

#define XiNlabel         "label"
#define XiNtext          "text"
#define XiNtextWidth     "textWidth"
#define XiNfont          "font"
#define XiCLabel         "Label"
#define XiCText          "Text"
#define XiCTextWidth     "TextWidth"
#define XiCFont          "Font"


typedef struct _XiSimpleTextClassRec *XiSimpleTextWidgetClass;
typedef struct _XiSimpleTextRec *XiSimpleTextWidget;

extern WidgetClass xiSimpleTextWidgetClass;


/*
Public functions:
*/

extern char *XiSimpleTextGetString();
/*  XiSimpleTextwidget simple_text_widget;
*/

extern void XiSimpleTextSetString();
/*  XiSimpleTextwidget simple_text_widget;
    char *string;
*/

#endif /* _XiSimpleText_h  */



/****    SimpleTexP.h    ****/

/****    private declarations/definitions for SimpleText.c    ****/
```

```
#ifndef _XiSimpleTextP_h
#define _XiSimpleTextP_h


#include "SimpleText.h"
#ifdef X11R3
#include <X11/FormP.h>
#else
#include <X11/Xaw/FormP.h>
#endif


#define TEXT_DEFAULT_WIDTH      400
#define TEXT_DEFAULT_HEIGHT     175
#define TEXT_DEFAULT_TEXT_WIDTH 300

#define TEXT_DEFAULT_LABEL      ""
#define TEXT_DEFAULT_TEXT       ""

#define TEXT_MAX_TEXT_LEN       256


typedef struct _XiSimpleTextClassPart {      /* class definition */
    int dummy;
} XiSimpleTextClassPart;

typedef struct _XiSimpleTextClassRec {
    CoreClassPart core_class;
    CompositeClassPart composite_class;
    ConstraintClassPart constraint_class;
    FormClassPart form_class;
    XiSimpleTextClassPart simple_text_class;
} XiSimpleTextClassRec;

extern XiSimpleTextClassRec xiSimpleTextClassRec;

typedef struct _XiSimpleTextPart {           /* instance definition */
    char *label;
    char *text;
    char *default_text;
    Dimension text_width;
    XFontStruct *font;
    Widget labelW;
    Widget textW;
} XiSimpleTextPart;


typedef struct _XiSimpleTextRec {
    CorePart core;
    CompositePart composite;
    ConstraintPart constraint;
    FormPart form;
    XiSimpleTextPart simple_text;
} XiSimpleTextRec;


typedef struct {
```

```
    int dummy;
} XiSimpleTextConstraintsPart;


typedef struct _XiSimpleTextConstraintsRec {
    FormConstraintsPart form;
    XiSimpleTextConstraintsPart simple_text;
} XiSimpleTextConstraintsRec, *XiSimpleTextConstraints;

#endif  /* _XiSimpleTextP_h */



/****  SimpleText.c  ****  simple text entry box implementation  ****/


#include <stdio.h>

#include <X11/Xlib.h>
#include <X11/Xos.h>
#include <X11/IntrinsicP.h>
#include <X11/StringDefs.h>

#ifdef X11R3
#include <X11/AsciiText.h>
#include <X11/Form.h>
#include <X11/Label.h>
#else
#include <X11/Xaw/XawInit.h>
#include <X11/Xaw/AsciiText.h>
#include <X11/Xaw/Form.h>
#include <X11/Xaw/Label.h>
#endif

#include <Ximisc.h>
#include "SimpleTexP.h"


static XtResource resources[] = {
    {XiNlabel, XiCLabel, XtRString, sizeof(char *),
        XtOffset(XiSimpleTextWidget, simple_text.label),
        XtRString, TEXT_DEFAULT_LABEL},
    {XiNtext, XiCText, XtRString, sizeof(char *),
        XtOffset(XiSimpleTextWidget, simple_text.default_text),
        XtRString, TEXT_DEFAULT_TEXT},
    {XiNtextWidth, XiCTextWidth, XtRDimension, sizeof(Dimension),
        XtOffset(XiSimpleTextWidget, simple_text.text_width),
        XtRImmediate, (caddr_t) TEXT_DEFAULT_TEXT_WIDTH},
    {XiNfont, XiCFont, XtRFontStruct, sizeof(XFontStruct *),
        XtOffset(XiSimpleTextWidget, simple_text.font),
        XtRString, "XtDefaultFont"},
};


/*
Class Methods:
*/
```

```
static void Initialize();
static void ConstraintInitialize();
static Boolean SetValues();
static void Destroy();


/*
Action functions:
*/

static void Beep();


/*
Define storage for the class here:
*/

XiSimpleTextClassRec XisimpleTextClassRec = {
    { /* core_class variables */
        (WidgetClass) &formClassRec,        /* ancestor */
        "SimpleText",                       /* class name */
        sizeof(XiSimpleTextRec),            /* widget size */
#ifdef X11R3
        NULL,                               /* class initialize */
#else
        XawInitializeWidgetSet,             /* class initialize */
#endif
        NULL,                               /* class part init. */
        FALSE,                              /* class inited */
        Initialize,                         /* initialize */
        NULL,                               /* initialize hook */
        XtInheritRealize,                   /* realize */
        NULL,                               /* actions */
        0,                                  /* number of actions */
        resources,                          /* resources */
        XtNumber(resources),                /* number of resources */
        NULLQUARK,                          /* xrm class */
        TRUE,                               /* compress motions */
        TRUE,                               /* compress exposures */
        TRUE,                               /* compress enter/leave */
        FALSE,                              /* visibility interest */
        Destroy,                            /* destroy */
        XtInheritResize,                    /* resize */
        XtInheritExpose,                    /* expose */
        SetValues,                          /* set values */
        NULL,                               /* set values hook */
        XtInheritSetValuesAlmost,           /* set values almost */
        NULL,                               /* get values hook */
        NULL,                               /* accept focus */
        XtVersion,                          /* version */
        NULL,                               /* callback private */
        NULL,                               /* translation table */
        XtInheritQueryGeometry,             /* query geometry */
        XtInheritDisplayAccelerator,        /* display accelerator */
        NULL,                               /* extension */
    },
```

```
    { /* composite_class variables */
        XtInheritGeometryManager,           /* geometry manager */
        XtInheritChangeManaged,             /* change managed */
        XtInheritInsertChild,               /* insert child */
        XtInheritDeleteChild,               /* delete child */
        NULL,                               /* extension */
    },
    { /* constraint_class fields */
        NULL,                               /* subresources */
        0,                                  /* number of subresources */
        sizeof(XiSimpleTextConstraintsRec), /* record size */
        ConstraintInitialize,               /* initialize */
        NULL,                               /* destroy */
        NULL,                               /* set values */
        NULL,                               /* extension */
    },
    { /* form_class fields */
#ifdef X11R3
        0,
#else
        XtInheritLayout,
#endif
    },
    { /* simple_text_class variables */
        0,
    },
}; /* XisimpleTextClassRec */


WidgetClass xiSimpleTextWidgetClass =
    (WidgetClass) &XisimpleTextClassRec;


/*
XiSimpleTextWidget methods:
*/

/*
Initialize() creates the label and text widget for the text
entry box; it has a zero-width border.  Other variables are
initialized as well.
*/
/*ARGSUSED*/
static void Initialize(request, new)
XiSimpleTextWidget request, new;
{
    static char text_translations[] =
        "#override\n\
        Ctrl<Key>J:       beep()\n\
        Ctrl<Key>M:       beep()\n\
        Ctrl<Key>O:       beep()\n\
        <Key>Linefeed:    beep()\n\
        <Key>Return:  beep()";
    static XtActionsRec text_actions[] = {
        {"beep", (XtActionProc) Beep},
    };
    XtTranslations text_trans_table;
```

```
    Arg args[10];
    int i;

    /*
    add/create actions/translations:
    */
    XtAddActions(text_actions, XtNumber(text_actions));
    text_trans_table = XtParseTranslationTable(text_translations);

    if (new->core.width == 0)
        new->core.width = TEXT_DEFAULT_WIDTH;
    if (new->core.height == 0)
        new->core.height = TEXT_DEFAULT_HEIGHT;

    /*
    create the text entry label:
    */
    new->simple_text.labelW = NULL;
    if (*new->simple_text.label) {
        i = 0;
        XtSetArg(args[i], XtNlabel,
            (XtArgVal) new->simple_text.label); i++;
        XtSetArg(args[i], XtNborderWidth, (XtArgVal) 0); i++;
        XtSetArg(args[i], XtNfont,
            (XtArgVal) new->simple_text.font); i++;
        new->simple_text.labelW = XtCreateManagedWidget("label",
            labelWidgetClass, new, args, i);
    }

    /*
    create the text entry area:
    */
    i = 0;
#ifdef X11R3
    new->simple_text.text = XtMalloc(TEXT_MAX_TEXT_LEN + 1);
    strncpy(new->simple_text.text, new->simple_text.default_text,
        TEXT_MAX_TEXT_LEN);
    if (strlen(new->simple_text.default_text) >= TEXT_MAX_TEXT_LEN)
        new->simple_text.text[TEXT_MAX_TEXT_LEN] = '\0';
    XtSetArg(args[i], XtNeditType, (XtArgVal) XttextEdit); i++;
#else
    new->simple_text.text = new->simple_text.default_text;
    XtSetArg(args[i], XtNeditType, (XtArgVal) XawtextEdit); i++;
#endif
    XtSetArg(args[i], XtNstring,
        (XtArgVal) new->simple_text.text); i++;
    /*
    Philosophy?  This will override resource database requests:
    */
/*  XtSetArg(args[i], XtNborderWidth, (XtArgVal) 1); i++;*/
    XtSetArg(args[i], XtNlength, (XtArgVal) TEXT_MAX_TEXT_LEN); i++;
    XtSetArg(args[i], XtNwidth,
        (XtArgVal) new->simple_text.text_width); i++;
    XtSetArg(args[i], XtNfont,
        (XtArgVal) new->simple_text.font); i++;
    new->simple_text.textW = XtCreateManagedWidget("text",
#ifdef X11R3
```

```
        asciiStringWidgetClass,
#else
        asciiTextWidgetClass,
#endif
        new, args, i);
    XtOverrideTranslations(new->simple_text.textW, text_trans_table);
}   /* Initialize */


/*
ConstraintInitialize() sets up the form widget for the
label, if it exists, and the text entry field.
*/
/*ARGSUSED*/
static void ConstraintInitialize(request, new)
Widget request, new;
{
    XiSimpleTextWidget stw = (XiSimpleTextWidget) new->core.parent;
    XiSimpleTextConstraints constraints =
        (XiSimpleTextConstraints) new->core.constraints;

    if (stw->simple_text.labelW == NULL)
        return;
#ifdef X11R3
    if (!XtIsSubclass(new, asciiStringWidgetClass))
#else
    if (!XtIsSubclass(new, asciiTextWidgetClass))
#endif
        return;
    constraints->form.left = constraints->form.right = XtChainLeft;
    constraints->form.horiz_base = stw->simple_text.labelW;
}   /* ConstraintInitialize */


/*
SetValues() updates resource-related widget values.
*/
/*ARGSUSED*/
static Boolean SetValues(current, request, new)
Widget current, request, new;
{
    /*
    at present, nothing to update...
    */
    return FALSE;
}   /* SetValues */


/*
Destroy() frees dynamic data structures.
*/

static void Destroy(stw)
XiSimpleTextWidget stw;
{
    XtDestroyWidget(stw->simple_text.labelW);
    XtDestroyWidget(stw->simple_text.textW);
```

```
}   /* Destroy */


/*
Public functions:
*/

char *XiSimpleTextGetString(stw)
XiSimpleTextWidget stw;
{
#ifdef X11R3
    return stw->simple_text.text;
#else
    Arg args[1];
    char *text;

    XtSetArg(args[0], XtNstring, (XtArgVal) &text);
    XtGetValues(stw->simple_text.textW, args, 1);
    return text;
#endif
}   /* XiSimpleTextGetString */


void XiSimpleTextSetString(stw, str)
XiSimpleTextWidget stw;
char *str;
{
    Arg args[1];
    int str_len = strlen(str);

#ifdef X11R3
    strncpy(stw->simple_text.text, str, TEXT_MAX_TEXT_LEN);
    if (str_len >= TEXT_MAX_TEXT_LEN) {
        str_len = TEXT_MAX_TEXT_LEN;
        stw->simple_text.text[str_len] = '\0';
    }
    XtTextSetInsertionPoint(stw->simple_text.textW, 0);
    XtTextSetLastPos(stw->simple_text.textW, strlen(str));
    XtTextDisplay(stw->simple_text.textW);
#else
    XtSetArg(args[0], XtNstring, (XtArgVal) str);
    XtSetValues(stw->simple_text.textW, args, 1);
#endif
}   /* XiSimpleTextSetString */


/*
Beep() is a general-purpose function; one use is to beep the
user if they try to enter a character that results in a line
feed operation; see Initialize().
*/
/*ARGSUSED*/
static void Beep(w, event)
Widget w;
XEvent *event;
{
    XBell(XtDisplay(w), 50);
```

```
}   /* Beep */


/****  testtext.c  ****  tests the simple text entry widget ****/


#include <stdio.h>
#include <X11/Intrinsic.h>
#include <X11/StringDefs.h>
#include <X11/Shell.h>

#ifdef X11R3
#include <X11/Box.h>
#include <X11/Command.h>
#include <X11/Form.h>
#else
#include <X11/Xaw/Box.h>
#include <X11/Xaw/Command.h>
#include <X11/Xaw/Form.h>
#endif
#include <Ximisc.h>
#include "SimpleText.h"


/*
Functions:
*/

void TestGetText(), TestSetText(), Quit();


/*
Private globals:
*/

static Widget testText;
static XFontStruct *font;


void main(argc, argv)
int argc;
char **argv;
{
    Widget topLevel, testBox, getButton, setButton, quitButton;
    Arg args[7];
    int i;

    topLevel = XtInitialize(argv[0], "TestText",
        NULL, 0, &argc, argv);
    font = load_font(topLevel, "testtext", "8x13");
    testBox = XtCreateManagedWidget("testBox", formWidgetClass,
        topLevel, NULL, 0);
    i = 0;
    XtSetArg(args[i], XtNborderWidth, (XtArgVal) 0); i++;
    XtSetArg(args[i], XiNtextWidth, (XtArgVal) 200); i++;
    XtSetArg(args[i], XiNlabel, (XtArgVal) "Any Label:"); i++;
```

```
    XtSetArg(args[i], XiNtext, (XtArgVal) "Start-up Text"); i++;
    XtSetArg(args[i], XtNfont,        /* test with an     */
        (XtArgVal) font); i++;        /* alternate font   */
    testText = XtCreateManagedWidget("testText",
        xiSimpleTextWidgetClass, testBox, args, i);
    i = 0;
    XtSetArg(args[i], XtNfromVert, (XtArgVal) testText); i++;
    XtSetArg(args[i], XtNlabel, (XtArgVal) "Get Text"); i++;
    getButton = XtCreateManagedWidget("getButton",
        commandWidgetClass, testBox, args, i);
    i = 0;
    XtSetArg(args[i], XtNfromVert, (XtArgVal) testText); i++;
    XtSetArg(args[i], XtNfromHoriz, (XtArgVal) getButton); i++;
    XtSetArg(args[i], XtNlabel, (XtArgVal) "Set Text"); i++;
    setButton = XtCreateManagedWidget("setButton",
        commandWidgetClass, testBox, args, i);
    i = 0;
    XtSetArg(args[i], XtNfromVert, (XtArgVal) testText); i++;
    XtSetArg(args[i], XtNfromHoriz, (XtArgVal) setButton); i++;
    XtSetArg(args[i], XtNlabel, (XtArgVal) "Quit"); i++;
    quitButton = XtCreateManagedWidget("quitButton",
        commandWidgetClass, testBox, args, i);
    XtAddCallback(getButton, XtNcallback, TestGetText, NULL);
    XtAddCallback(setButton, XtNcallback, TestSetText, NULL);
    XtAddCallback(quitButton, XtNcallback, Quit, NULL);
    XtRealizeWidget(topLevel);
    XtMainLoop();
}   /* main */


/*ARGSUSED*/
void TestGetText(w, client_data, call_data)
Widget w;
caddr_t client_data, call_data;
{
    char *text;

    text = XiSimpleTextGetString(testText);
    printf("Text entry box text is: %s\n", text);
}   /* TestGetText */


/*ARGSUSED*/
void TestSetText(w, client_data, call_data)
Widget w;
caddr_t client_data, call_data;
{
    XiSimpleTextSetString(testText, "abcdef");
}   /* TestSetText */


/*ARGSUSED*/
void Quit(w, client_data, call_data)
Widget w;
caddr_t client_data, call_data;
{
    XFreeFont(XtDisplay(w), font);
```

```
    exit(0);
}   /* Quit */
```

References

Goldberg, A. and Robson, D. *Smalltalk-80: The language and its implementation*. Reading, MA: Addison-Wesley, 1983.

Goldstein, T. The object-oriented programmer, Part two: composition. *The C++ Report*, *1*, No. 5, 4–6.

Johnson, R. E. The importance of being abstract. *The C++ Report*, *1*, No. 3, 1–5, 1989.

Johnson, R. E. and Foote B. Designing reusable classes. *Journal of Object-oriented Programming*, *1*, No. 2, 22–35, 1988.

Jones, O. *Introduction to the X Window System*. Englewood Cliffs, NJ: Prentice Hall, 1989.

Lippman, S. *C++ primer*. Reading, MA: Addison-Wesley, 1989.

Meyer, B. Harnessing multiple inheritance. *Journal of Object-oriented Programming*, *1*, No. 4, 48–51, 1988a.

Meyer, B. *Object-oriented software construction*. Englewood Cliffs, NJ: Prentice Hall, 1988b.

Nye, A. *Xlib™ programming manual*. Sebastopol, CA: O'Reilly & Associates, Inc., 1988.

Nye, A. *Xlib™ reference manual*. Sebastopol, CA: O'Reilly & Associates, Inc., 1988.

Nye, A. and O'Reilly, T. *X™ Toolkit Intrinsics programming manual.* Sebastopol, CA: O'Reilly & Associates, Inc., 1990.

O'Reilly, T. *X™ Toolkit Intrinsics reference manual.* Sebastopol, CA: O'Reilly & Associates, Inc., 1990.

OSF. *Open Software Foundation/Motif™ programmer's reference.* Englewood Cliffs, NJ: Prentice Hall, 1990.

Quercia, V. and O'Reilly, T. *X Window System™ user's guide.* Sebastopol, CA: O'Reilly & Associates, Inc., 1989.

Smith, J. D. *Reusability and software construction: C and C++.* New York: John Wiley & Sons, Inc., 1990.

Sun Microsystems®. *OpenWindows™ Version 2 user's guide.* Part Number: 800-4930-10. Mountain View, CA: Sun Microsystems, Inc., 1990.

Stroustrup, B. *The C++ programming language.* Reading, MA: Addison-Wesley, 1986.

The Whitewater Group. *Actor 2.0 reference manual.* Evanston, IL: The Whitewater Group, 1990.

Young, D. A. *The X Window System™, programming and applications with Xt™, OSF/Motif™ edition.* Englewood Cliffs, NJ: Prentice Hall, 1990.

Index

A

B

K

L

M

N

O

P

Q

R

U

V

W

X

Y